The Great Trek

The Great Trek UNCUT

Escape from British Rule: The Boer Exodus from the Cape Colony, 1836

Robin Binckes

30° South Publishers (Pty) Ltd.

Helion & Company Ltd.

Also by Robin Binckes:
Canvas under the Sky (2011)

Co-published in 2013 by:

30° South Publishers (Pty) Ltd.
16 Ivy Road
Pinetown 3610
South Africa
email: info@30degreessouth.co.za
website: www.30degreessouth.co.za

and

Helion & Company Limited
26 Willow Road
Solihull
West Midlands
B91 1UE
England
Tel. 0121 705 3393
Fax 0121 711 4075
email: info@helion.co.uk
website: www.helion.co.uk

Designed & typeset by SA Publishing Services, South Africa (kerrincocks@gmail.com)
Cover design by Kerrin Cocks
Printed in the UK by Lightning Source, Milton Keynes, Buckinghamshire
and in South Africa by Pinetown Printers (Pty) Ltd, Pinetown, KwaZulu-Natal

ISBN 978-1-920143-68-8 (South Africa)
ISBN 978-1-908916-28-0 (UK)

British Library Cataloguing-in-Publication Data
A catalogue record for this book is available from the British Library

"A man is always a teller of tales, he lives surrounded by his stories and the stories of others, he sees everything that happens to him through them; and he tries to live his own life as if he were telling a story"
—Jean-Paul Sartre

★★★

To my wife Margie, my children, Michael, Lexi, Samantha, Jacques, Gregory, Patrick, Christopher and Roberta; my grandson Jordan; my family, Mike and Ann, Helen, Bridgid and Scotty, Jane and Don, Sharon, Tony and Di, Christopher and Katie;
all my wonderful friends here and abroad who enrich my life through their friendship, as well as Chris and Kerrin.

This book is in memory of Mom, Dad, Joan and Jack.

Contents

List of maps

List of illustrations

Acknowledgements

I am grateful to my wife Margie, who read every word and supported me every inch of the way. My children also encouraged me on this long journey with their comments. Bearnárd O'Riain, knowing how I love to be praised, said all the right things to ensure that when I flagged, I would push on instead of giving up. Similarly, Tony O'Hagan took the time to read my manuscript and provided commentary that encouraged me to continue. Frank van der Tas read and commented on the manuscript and patiently pointed out errors that I had made.

I look to Peter Harris for inspiration, as he is an exemplary South African writer. I am thankful to the staff at the Cape Town Archives and the library at the Voortrekker Monument as well as to Chris and Kerrin Cocks, who gave me a break and published my historical novel *Canvas under the Sky*, giving me the wonderful opportunity to write the *The Great Trek*. I appreciate that many of my friends stood by me and encouraged me when *Canvas under the Sky* created controversy. Thank you all for having faith in me. I hope that this book lives up to your expectations and justifies your belief in me.

To Kate O'Connor who painstakingly edited the manuscript, thank you.

To Chris Gibbons, Jackie Grobler, Jacques Pauw, Mongane Serote, Jeremy Maggs and Nick Binedell who took the time and trouble not only to read the manuscript but also to comment and make suggestions. Thank you.

To the Voortrekkers, those men women and children who inspired *Canvas under the Sky* and the subsequent *The Great Trek*, I thank you and salute your memory. I hope that as you look down, you feel I have done justice to your story and are as proud of me as I am of you.

Robin Binckes
Johannesburg
January 2013

Author's note

"Until the lions are taught to write, history will always be written by the hunters"
—anonymous

The idea for this book is from Chris and Kerrin Cocks of 30° South, my publishers. When I first met them with my manuscript *Canvas under the Sky*, a historical novel on the Great Trek, they proposed that I expand certain concepts. The book thus evolved into a journey through our country's history.

Although the focus is on the Great Trek, it is impossible to divorce this incredible journey from earlier events in southern Africa. It is also impossible to divorce the effects of the Great Trek from the events of today. While this story concludes in 1852, it is in reality still unfolding today. The Great Trek was the epicentre of a cultural, economic, military and social explosion that spanned the length of this country, leaving behind a legacy that should be treasured forever. The story of the Voortrekkers is often associated with the Afrikaners. However, the journey of the Voortrekkers belongs to all South Africans—Black, White, Coloured and Indian. For too long, the story had been sanitized, with the characters presented as cardboard cut-outs and the events resembling scenes from a play with poor actors. The story is anything but bland. It entails passion, pride, violence and compassion as well as courage and is arguably the most exciting story in our history.

Storytelling is one of the traditions of our people. In *The Great Trek*, I have endeavoured to present a narrative that will be enjoyable to readers as well as document our history for future generations. The story and facts speak for themselves. However, in writing this book, I travelled from Cape Town to the banks of the Zambezi, from the White Umfolozi River to Blood River and Maputo. I have been a conduit for some of the greatest recorders of our history, such as Gustav S. Preller, G.E. Cory, George McCall Theal, G.B.A. Gerdener, E.J.G. Norval, Richard Elphick, J.M. Soga, John Bird, Noel Mostert, J.B. Peires and, of course, for some of the characters' own writings and diaries, such as those of William Wood, Jan Bantjies, Reverend Smit, Allen Gardiner, Louis Trichardt, Sarel Cilliers, Dutch explorer Robert Gordon and French explorer and adventurer Adolphe Delegorgue, as well as many more.

I have attempted to channel their thoughts and feelings and have included many facts in an attempt to entertain and inform. I have been guided in my efforts by the styles and techniques used in Philip Caputo's *A Rumor of War*, Antony Beevor's *D-Day: The Battle for Normandy*, Martin Windrow's *The Last Valley*, Justin Cartwright's *To Heaven by Water* and Peter Harris's *In a Different*

Time. I hope that their influence is evident in my work and, if it is not, then I have done them a disservice. For the past three years, these authors' books have been my constant companions and friends and, like spiritual guides, they have revealed to me historical gems of interest.

I have endeavoured to pull the threads together of the works of far greater historians and writers than me. These rich and brightly coloured threads of our past combine into the colourful tapestry of the present day. This tapestry expresses the emotions and actions of many groups in our society and will hopefully contribute in some small way to South Africa's ongoing and sometimes painful process of reconciliation and understanding.

As I wrote this book, I sometimes felt that the ghosts of great men such as Andries Pretorius, the colourful Gert Maritz, passionate Piet Retief, devout Sarel Cilliers, cheerful Piet Uys and even dour Andries Potgieter and Louis Trichardt guided my thoughts. My intention is that they will come alive for the reader and share their incredible journey and experiences and, most importantly, feelings.

There are mistakes in the book; of that, I have no doubt. Despite every effort to ensure complete factual accuracy, there are different interpretations of events and people from which I have drawn. Where two or more versions of the same event have been described differently by different authors or sources, I have made a call on what I believe is the correct interpretation. You, the reader, may call it differently. Although many dates are included, this book is not meant to be purely chronological. Rather, it records a series of events and stories; the dates act as milestones and are unimportant. However, the people, their fears, feelings and dreams are.

Some aspects of the book may be controversial and promote debate, which would make me happy. That said, I have not deliberately set out to be controversial. I also did not set out to glorify or denigrate any group. The facts speak for themselves and I wrote this book out of a deep love for this country and its people. The facts will assist you in forming your own opinions on the people and events that have shaped our country.

What do I hope for this book? Firstly, I hope that it helps South Africans of all colours to understand our collective history and to be proud of our heritage. Secondly, I hope that people visiting South Africa or who are interested in the country will gain an understanding of our past and of who we are today because of it. Above all, I hope people will laugh, and cry, as they immerse themselves in this story about an incredible era in our history. Naturally, I also hope that the critics enjoy the book, that bookshop managers and owners give it exposure in their stores and that it becomes a bestseller!

CHAPTER 1

The Portuguese search for the land of milk and honey

San—Prester John—Batholomeu Dias—voyages of exploration—
Khoikhoi—death of de Almeida

A small man with yellowish-brown skin and a leathery face that looked as though it had been scorched by 35 summers sat on his haunches, hunched over two sticks that he was vigorously rubbing together. He was no more than 137 centimetres tall and his brown, wrinkled skin hung in folds around his protruding stomach, which glistened in the late afternoon sun because he had smeared it with animal fat.

Eventually, a thin worm of smoke rose from the wood. He stopped rubbing the sticks together to adjust the quiver on his shoulders as it was chafing him. It contained 12 arrows with poisoned bone tips[1] and he had made it from the bark of a euphorbia tree. He had dipped his arrowheads into poison extracted from snakes and caterpillars and any animal he shot would die in minutes, even if only slightly wounded.

When he started rubbing the twigs again, his small but well-proportioned body moved from side to side with the effort and his penis swung out from under his kudu-skin loincloth. Occasionally, he shifted position to achieve better friction, shuffling his bare feet.

When a tiny flame finally flickered, he swiftly covered the burning sticks with dry leaves. The blue smoke puffed into his face and made his eyes water. He blew gently on the small flame until the fire flared and flames cheerily danced. He had made fire.

!Xue !Xue the San, or Bushman, squinted at the setting sun, his small, deep-set eyes narrowing as he studied several shapes and clouds of dust emerging over a ridge about ten kilometres away. He eventually could make out the herders urging their cattle on, red dust hanging over them like a protective cloud.

!Xue !Xue watched the distant specks grow larger. He assumed the herders were his pastoralist cousins, the Khoikhoi[2] (translated as men of men). Nevertheless, he hid behind some dry shrubs. When they were closer, !Xue !Xue could see that these people were foreigners. He had never seen such tall people. He gazed in astonishment at the large black figures. They were completely unlike the Khoikhoi, with their small frames and light complexions. The pastoralist

Khoikhoi had travelled from what is now known as Botswana and lived relatively peaceably alongside the hunter-gatherer San, although the men sometimes stole their cattle and provisions and seduced their women. The San were looked down upon by the Khoikhoi because of their nomadic existence and lack of cattle.

The year was 250 AD and !Xue !Xue had seen the first Bantu people. Over the next few hundred years, many more Bantu would travel to southern Africa from West Africa in search of grazing.[3]

Many believe that the Bantu (meaning the people or humans) are descendents of the biblical 12 Tribes of Israel and genetic testing has revealed that men from the Bantu-speaking Lemba tribe found in Zimbabwe and South Africa as well as Mozambique and Malawi have Y-chromosomes that are Semitic in origin. One sub-clan, the Buba, even shares genetic traits with the Jewish priest class, the Kohanim.

With a shake of his head, !Xue !Xue rushed out from behind the bushes and hurriedly stamped out the flames of his fire, gathered his bow and spear and jogged effortlessly away from the approaching herders and cattle, heading for his people on the western side of the Fish River.

!Xue !Xue was well used to running long distances at a rapid pace, which he maintained for two days, stopping only to drink and find food. Like all San people, !Xue !Xue was one with the wilderness in which he lived. He was adept at finding subterranean water reservoirs and he quenched his thirst by sucking the cool water up with a reed. Along the route, !Xue !Xue gathered berries, nuts, roots and ant larvae. When he was exceptionally hungry, he speared a rabbit, which he ate raw so that he would not need to slow down. He was also lucky enough to find a honeycomb and he ate half of it, saving the other half so it could crystallize and be eaten later.[4]

Finally, !Xue !Xue joined his family and the small group of Khoisan known as the Gonaqua in their settlement east of the Fish River. Each of the 73 small huts made of mud, grass, leaves and twigs was 1.2 metres in diameter and 0.9 metres tall and slept one or two people. The earth had been scooped out and filled with grass to provide soft bedding and a fireplace marked the entrance to each hut.

Like the approximately 10,000 Khoikhoi in that region, the Gonaqua were descendents of the Hamcumqua. Clustered in groups or tribes from the Highveld down to the coast, the majority of the Khoikhoi lived on the southeastern side of the peninsula around Table Bay.

Thirsty and tired after his journey, !Xue !Xue refreshed himself by drinking soured milk. He watched the women nearby shaking cowhide sacks filled with cream that would eventually become butter, which could be smeared onto their bodies. They spoke animatedly in their strange click language of |Xam, their voices sometimes resembling the cracking of dry sticks or the sucking sound of a cow lifting its hooves from sticky mud. !Xue !Xue then picked a stalk of dagga (marijuana) and chewed it.[5] He described the Bantu he had observed on the other side of the Fish River with clicks and hand signs to the San who had gathered round him. Stimulated by the dagga, !Xue !Xue probably exaggerated the size and power of the Bantu. His fellow Gonaqua were concerned and afraid and broke out into a chorus of anxious clicks as they discussed this potential threat.

Over time, the Nguni-speaking Bantu moved down the eastern coast of southern Africa and, simultaneously, the Sotho-speaking Bantu moved inland, settling on the vast open grazing lands east of what became known as the Fish River.

Summers retreated into winters and winters gave way to rainy seasons, with little changing over the next thousand years. The rolling grassland plains that extended to the ocean provided lush grazing for many herds of elephant, buffalo, springbok, eland, zebra and kudu and were also home to giraffe, rhino and cats such as lion, leopard and cheetah, which slunk through the long grasses stalking their prey. Similarly, the San tracked and killed smaller animals for their meat and hides or skins.

The Khoikhoi and the San populations gradually grew, despite occasional wars against one another. These were usually about stolen cattle, or women, rather than land ownership.[6] The San were loyal to the Khoikhoi and served as soldiers when they fought other San, Khoikhoi and the Nguni-speaking Bantu, in return for food and meat. While the San revered the earth, the Khoikhoi revered their cattle, even riding them into battle.

Not only did the Khoikhoi use oxen as a mode of transport, they also used them in battle as battering rams or a living wall behind which they could hide. These cattle were trained to respond to the commands and instructions of the Khoikhoi, who called each head of cattle by name using gentle tones and clicks. Later, these Khoikhoi became known as Hottentots due to the many clicks and sounds making up their vernacular.

The name Hottentot was given to the Khoikhoi by the Dutch and means 'stammerer'.

Early callers at the Cape claimed that "when they are merry they leap up and down and continually sing the word Hottentot and nothing else and keep this up for long, from this they are generally called Hottentots by the Dutch".[7]

Gradually, the Nguni-speaking Bantu to the north and along the east coast evolved into the Zulu (which means people of the heavens). To the south and abutting the Khoi's territory bordered by the Fish River were the Xhosa (derived from a Khoi word meaning the angry men). The Xhosa and Khoikhoi existed quite comfortably alongside one another and there were only occasional skirmishes over cattle and women. While the Khoikhoi introduced the Xhosa to dagga,[8] which grew prolifically in the area, the Xhosa allowed the Khoikhoi to cohort with their women.

The close proximity and intermarriage of the Xhosa and the Khoikhoi led the Xhosa to assimilate many aspects of Khoi culture and language. To this day, the Xhosa have lighter complexions than their Zulu neighbours and the Xhosa language contains many Khoi words and phrases. However, there were distinct differences between the Xhosa and Khoikhoi in terms of physical traits and practices. The Khoikhoi were smaller, wirier and lighter skinned than the Xhosa and had wizened faces and large buttocks. The Xhosa, on the other hand, were tall, darker skinned and had fleshy lips and flattened noses. With the Khoikhoi, individuals owned cattle, whereas the Nguni-speaking Bantu (Xhosa and Zulu) saw cattle as belonging to the tribe or community.

It was into this peaceful scene that the Portuguese dropped, muddying the future, like earth being dropped into crystal-clear water. The Portuguese were the dominant sea power at that time and, spurred on by the legend of Prester John and his fortune, they began to explore the coast of Africa. They were certainly not the first explorers from outside Africa. The existence of pottery, copper and metal in southern Africa dating back to the tenth and eleventh centuries suggests trade with the outside world was no new phenomenon in Africa. In fact, Phoenician, Arab and Chinese traders had been bartering with the people of Africa long before the Portuguese arrived.

In the 15th and 16th centuries, European countries were preoccupied with the legendary Prester John.[9] It was believed that this mysterious king controlled immense wealth and ruled over a gigantic empire somewhere in Africa. The legend had been based upon a letter that was circulated around Europe in the 12th century. It described a vast Christian empire controlled by Prester John that was in danger of being taken over by heathens and infidels. The kingdom was said to be a land "where honey flows and milk everywhere abounds". The rivers were rumoured to be "running with gold" and Prester John allegedly owned the elusive Fountain of Youth. Initially, Prester John's lands were known as the Three Indias. It was believed they were to be found in Asia and Christians from several European countries carried out exhaustive and unsuccessful searches for these lands during the 14th century, allegedly in a bid to save Prester John

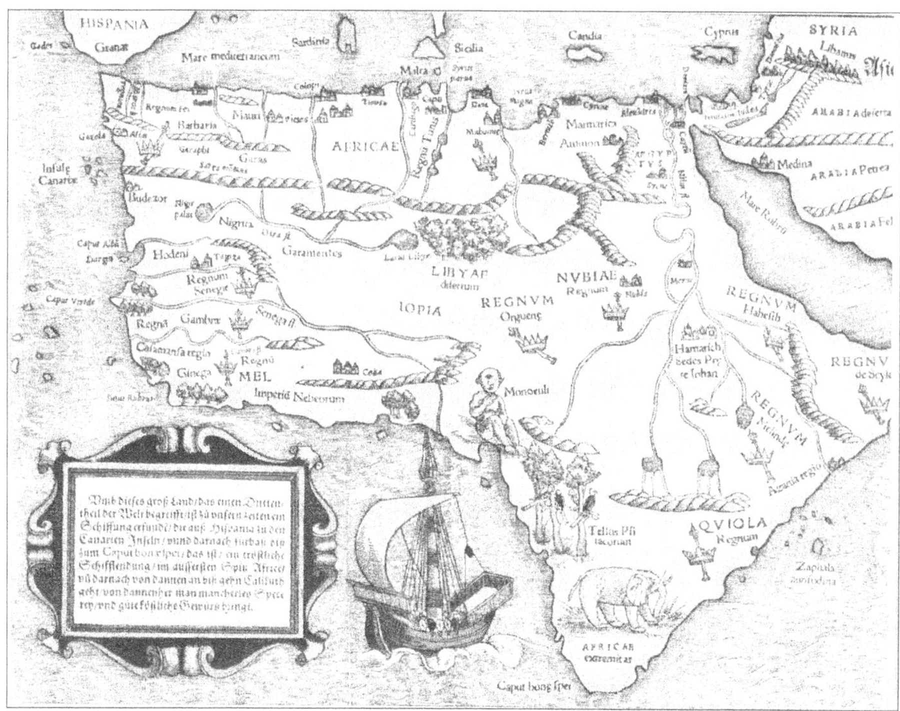

from barbarians and infidels and, no doubt, to appropriate his riches and control the Fountain of Youth. The legend surrounding Prester John's empire was so strongly ingrained in people's minds that it did not die easily. As late as the 17th century, cartographers were drawing up maps outlining his kingdom as being in Ethiopia. Subsequently, several European powers set out to explore Africa in the hope of finding Prester John's lands. In the 15th century, the Portuguese, under Prince Henrique (Henry the Navigator) and, after his death, King João II, sent explorers south to find Prester John's empire and the sea route to the rich spice fields of India.

Over a 20-year period, the goal of rounding the Cape came closer and closer. In 1461 the coast of present-day Liberia was reached and, in 1471, the equator was crossed. Then, in 1484, a small fleet under Portuguese explorer Diogo Cão crossed the equator and reached the mouth of the Congo.[10]

Then, in August 1486, King João II gave nobleman and knight of the Royal Court Bartholomeu Dias command of an expedition of two fifty-ton caravels (small, highly manoeuvrable sailing ships) and a smaller store ship to explore the coastline of Africa further and to find the elusive Prester John.[11]

Previous expeditions had run out of food. However, this time, a supply ship would accompany the explorers and there would be no turning back.[12] The caravels hugged the coastline as they slowly made their way down the west coast of Africa. The store ship was left near the equator with nine crew members[13] while the rest of the fleet continued its slow and perilous journey. Records show that confusion arose as to the exact position at their next stop on the present-day Namibian coastline. Their ignorance of compass deviation and imperfections in the making of the compasses[14] led Dias to think that he was at latitude 24° south when he was actually 2.5° farther south.[15] Here, at *Angra Pequena*, which Dias renamed *Angra dos Ilhéus* (Bay of Islets), Dias and his crew set foot on the rich earth of southern Africa for the first time and became the first Europeans to do so.[16] They could find no sign of human life in the area.

They stocked up on fresh water, caught fish and gathered eggs from seafowl, briefly enjoying the security of solid land under their feet. Before leaving, Dias dropped off one of four negress prisoners that he had aboard, abandoning her to an unknown fate. Dias had left Portugal via the Tagus River with four negress convicts who had been taken from the coast of Guinea and had almost certainly been sentenced to death.[17] (Distributing criminals in foreign lands under orders to explore was a common practice at the time and many of these convicts were willing to brave the unknown in exchange for their freedom.) They were to be dropped off at four different points along the coast of Africa and were to seek Prester John and sing his praises to all those they encountered. In addition, they were to explore their new locale and report to the first white person they met.

After leaving the Bay of Islets, Dias attempted to keep in sight of the land. However, unfavourable winds forced him to tack and he reached an inlet that he named *Angra das Voltas* (Bay of Turnings). He remained there for five days due to bad weather and left one of the negresses behind when the ship departed.

Sadly, several weeks later, one of the negress prisoners died. Another was dropped off near the mouth of the Orange River, leaving only one still to deposit somewhere.[18]

He had planned to hug the coastline but a turbulent sea and a raging storm forced him to head deeper out to sea, where the crew lost sight of the land. The two tiny caravels were tossed about in the angry sea as though they were as light as corks. Fearing the worst, Dias had his crew reef (draw in) the sails.[19] He and the terrified crew then sat out the storm, which raged for 14 days without letting up. Lightning lit the skies and thunder rolled furiously, while the rain lashed down on the crew, who were huddled together on deck praying.

As soon as the storm ended, the shaken crew rigged the sails. "Helmsman! Steer due east," Dias commanded. He hoped that they would soon see land. However, Dias quickly realized that they must have passed the southernmost tip of Africa. "Helmsman! Turn due north!" he redirected them. The two ships heeled in unison, the winds filling their sails so that they looked like graceful swans with full, contented bellies. They reversed course, sailing toward Africa on the placid, deep-blue waters of the Indian Ocean.[20]

There was great delight among the crew when they heard a shout from the crow's nest: "Land ahoy! Land in sight!" Some of the men cheered and others wept with relief.

Dias took up his telescope and made out a small inlet in a bay, which he would later name *Angra dos Vaquerio* (Bay of the Herdsmen).[21]

As the two caravels neared the bay, the crew crowded the rails and gazed in delight at herds of cattle grazing on the rich grasslands near the shore. The Khoikhoi herders watched the ships in amazement and terror. They had never seen such vessels before and marvelled at the giant wooden structures with billowing white sails. They quickly rounded up their cattle and fled into the interior to escape the approaching ships and imminent danger.

This was an opportunity for Dias's crew to get fresh water and, after refitting the ships,[22] which had taken a battering during the storm, Dias set sail again. This time, he skirted around the coastline in good weather and finally put ashore a few days later at Mossel Bay.[23] There, the Khoikhoi watched the intruders from a distance.

When Dias and crew threw tiny bells and trinkets on the beach for them, the Khoikhoi ignored them, perhaps sensing that the arrival of these Europeans signalled the start of encroachment and conflict.

One of the Khoikhoi then hurled a stone at the sailors. Dias angrily picked up a crossbow and shot at one of the Khoikhoi, fatally wounding him in the chest. This was the first time an indigenous person had been killed by a white man in southern Africa.[24]

Probably disturbed by the incident, Dias quickly set sail again. The caravels then anchored at *Bahia de Lagoa* (Bay of the Lagoon), now known as Algoa Bay. Dias ordered that the last of the negress prisoners be put ashore here.[25]

The small rowing boat with the unhappy prisoner in it left the caravel, rocking in the heavy swell. The frightened negress pleaded with Dias to take her back, sobbing hysterically. Unmoved, Dias cupped his hands to his mouth and shouted, "Do not fear! We will be back to hear your news of Prester John and his land."[26] She was never seen again.

Dias was determined to continue up the east coast of southern Africa but, after the long and difficult voyage thus far, his crew had had enough. A delegation approached Dias and begged that they be allowed to return to the supply ship waiting at the equator and then sail on to Portugal. The persuasive Dias pleaded that the men remain loyal to him and continue up the coast for another three days.[27] The men agreed to stick it out.

When Dias eventually returned to Portugal and reported on his journey to King João II, he explained that "All began to complain and to demand with one voice that they should go no further, saying ... that they had explored a sufficient length of coast for one voyage, and had now discovered the greatest novelty of the whole exploration, which was that the coast ran generally east, whence it would appear that they had passed some great Cape which it would be better to turn back and discover".[28]

The three-day grace period that Dias's men had granted him enabled the two caravels to reach the mouth of a river that they named *João Infante*. This could have been the Fish, Kowie or Keiskamma rivers.[29] The captain of the *São Pantaleão* supply caravel was the first man to step ashore here.

True to his word, Dias then set sail for the store ship, where he picked up the nine men he had left there, set fire to the store ship and headed on to Portugal.[30] The crew arrived home in December 1488, after having journeyed for 16 months and 17 days.[31] It was nearly ten years before the next expedition set off to round what the Portuguese aptly called the Cape of Storms.

King João II died in 1495 and was succeeded by his cousin, Don Manuel.[32] The new king ordered the construction of two ships that were more than double the size of the caravels Dias had previously sailed, after Dias advised him that the caravels from the previous trip had been totally unsuited to the stormy seas off the coast of southern Africa. In addition, Dias recommended that the new ships be built with rounded bows, broad square sterns, high poop decks and forecastles, low waists and long beams, which would assist the crew to better cope with the rough seas around the Cape.[33]

The *São Gabriel* weighed 120 tons while the *São Rafael* was 100 tons. In contrast, the caravels used in Dias's previous expedition had been only 50 tons.[34] When the ships were ready and all preparations were complete, the fleet made its way down the Tagus River to Rastello and anchored in front of Belém, the port area of Lisbon.[35] Dias accompanied the two ships in another caravel. He was to act as a guide and to accompany the expedition to the Cape Verde Islands, before sending them on their way.

It seems strange that he should have been entrusted with this task, as he had not sailed the route to the Cape Verde Islands and neither had Vasco da Gama, the commander of the expedition. It is speculated that between the time of Dias's previous voyage and the commencement of da Gama's, secret exploratory expeditions had been sent from Portugal to discover the best route to sail around the Cape. It was rumoured that Portuguese explorers had already successfully navigated the Cape via the Cape Verde Islands but wanted to keep the route secret, particularly from the Spanish.

The formidable, cold[36] da Gama was appointed commander of this exploration after his younger brother Paulo da Gama had declined the position.[37] He could not have known that his exploits and achievements on this trip would earn him the title of Viceroy of India in 1524, some 27 years later. Da Gama was not well liked by his crew. The men considered their unmarried 37-year-old commander to be extremely stern when it came to maintaining discipline. Nevertheless, da Gama was an experienced sailor and had the attributes necessary to command complete obedience from his crew and the respect of those he met.[38]

Word of the expedition had spread and a crowd had already gathered in the harbour at Lisbon to watch the historic departure of the fleet, which comprised the two new ships, the *São Gabriel*[39] and the *São Rafael*, Bartholomeu Dias's caravel, an additional caravel called the *Berrio* and a store ship. Before da Gama and his senior officers climbed aboard the ships on 8 July 1497,[40] they spent the afternoon in prayer. They then solemnly made their way toward the docks, accompanied by several friars and priests and a large procession of locals who were carrying candles, singing hymns and chanting prayers. The air was heavy with the scent of incense. Just before boarding, the crew knelt with heads bowed and the vicar pronounced absolution.[41] Da Gama concluded the prayers, saying, "May God, our Lord, let us complete our journey in His service. Amen."[42]

Their sins forgiven, da Gama and his men were ready to set sail. An early evening breeze made for an easy exit from the harbour and into the open ocean. The ships carried 170 men, including a priest as well as several convicts who would be put ashore in remote and dangerous places to gather information for the benefit of later explorers. Little did they know that their voyage to India via the Cape would be hazardous and would take over six months and leave more than half of the crew dead.

The Cape Verde Islands was designated a rendezvous point, in case the fleet became separated.[43] Two weeks after leaving Lisbon, a raging storm drove the ships apart. Although they had lost sight of each other, they continued toward the Cape Verde Islands, where they met up eight days later. After anchoring off the island of Santiago, the crew repaired the damaged ships and took on fresh water. Soon after leaving the Cape Verde Islands, Dias's caravel left the fleet and headed back to Portugal, stopping first at *São Jorge da Mina* (on the Gold Coast of Ghana).[44]

During the next four months at sea, the fleet encountered heavy storms and winds. Da Gama was confident that he would bisect the coast of southern Africa and ordered that the ships turn east.[45] At this point, water supplies must have been low and food sparse, with all fresh produce and meat having been finished earlier. The crew would have been immensely relieved when da Gama's navigation proved successful and they saw the coast of southern Africa for the first time on Saturday 4 November 1497.[46] After studying the coastline, da Gama decided there was nowhere suitable to drop anchor. The fleet then hugged the coast for a further three days before finally anchoring in a large protected bay, which da Gama named Saint Helena.[47]

Da Gama went ashore but found no signs of life or fresh water. So, he commanded Captain Nicolau Coelho to continue sailing up the coast in the *Berrio* to search for fresh water.[48] Only 27 kilometres from Saint Helena, Coelho found the mouth of the Berg River. There, the crew replenished their water barrels and killed a number of seals. After months at sea with dwindling food rations, the crew must have thought the cooked flesh of the seals to be delicious.[49]

When the rest of the fleet rejoined the *Berrio*, da Gama went ashore. He was so preoccupied with trying to establish the longitude and latitude of their position that he scarcely heard the warning shout from his men about two Khoikhoi who were gathering honey and herbs near the shore.

Da Gama quickly ordered his men to capture the natives. A few of his men stealthily crept up to the unsuspecting Khoikhoi before grabbing them. The Khoikhoi were startled by the arrival of the Europeans and one of them managed to escape his would-be captors. Sadly, his terrified companion was taken prisoner.[50] The prisoner was brought before da Gama, who ordered the men to feed him.[51] After the initial shock and terror had worn off and the Khoikhoi realized that he was not going to be harmed by these strange people, the like of which he had never seen before, he began to relax and seemed to enjoy the attention and food that was being lavished on him. The following day, he was given some clothing and trinkets before being set free. Delighted with the treatment he had received at the hands of his newfound friends, his report to his fellow tribesmen was extremely positive. As such, a group of some 20 Khoikhoi soon arrived on the beach to see the Europeans for themselves.

The Portuguese showered the Khoikhoi with pewter rings, tiny bells, beads and other inexpensive gifts.[52] Although communication was difficult, the atmosphere was friendly and there was a mutual sense of camaraderie. One of the crew, Fernão Veloso, asked da Gama whether he could go with the Khoikhoi to their home, some 13 or 14 kilometres away. Naturally, da Gama gave Veloso permission, as he was anxious to learn more about this strange land and its people.[53] Veloso appears to have become paranoid while walking with the Khoikhoi. He started to suspect that they would attack him, so he doubled back. His hosts were no doubt confused by his behaviour, especially when he started sprinting away from them toward the boats, shouting for help. His puzzled hosts trotted behind him, unsure what he was doing. Da Gama glanced up from his evening meal and saw Veloso being pursued by the Khoikhoi on the beach. He leaped up from the table and ordered that some of the crew row him ashore so he could find out what the problem was. A few boats from the other ships followed. When the first rowboat beached, some of the Khoikhoi rushed toward it enthusiastically. The crew mistook the Khoikhoi's excitement for aggression and lashed out at them with their fists. Two of the Khoikhoi staggered backwards, their faces bloody from repeated blows.[54] The Khoikhoi were incensed by the crew's seemingly unprovoked attack and started pelting them with stones, throwing assegais and firing their bows. The Portuguese then retaliated by firing their crossbows at the Khoikhoi. They succeeded in driving the Khoikhoi away, but not before da Gama and Gonçalo Álvares had been wounded. The Khoikhoi ran inland, away from the sophisticated weaponry of the Portuguese, and Veloso scrambled to the safety of a boat. The crew quickly rowed back to the ships, with the wounded da Gama and Álvares in tow.[55]

Da Gama set sail again on 16 November and doubled around the Cape four days later.[56] Then, on 26 November, the fleet anchored at Mossel Bay, where Dias had already killed one of the Khoikhoi.

The fleet had only been moored in the bay for a few days when a group of Khoikhoi men and women riding pack oxen approached. Da Gama thought they were not threatening, so he went ashore in one of the small boats, hoping to meet with them.[57]

The Khoikhoi were delighted with the inexpensive baubles and trinkets doled out by the Portuguese and da Gama and crew were richly rewarded with gifts from the Khoikhoi, such as valuable ivory arm bracelets.[58] A festive atmosphere soon prevailed, despite the language barrier and there was much backslapping and laughter. To the delight of the Portuguese seamen, the Khoikhoi brought a few sheep to slaughter. While the sheep sizzled on the fire, the Khoikhoi played reed flutes to entertain the Portuguese, who tapped their feet and clapped along to the rhythmic melodies. Other Khoikhoi danced to the music, much to the amusement of the visitors,[59] who soon joined in. The occasion was so celebratory that da Gama ordered the Portuguese musicians to improvise on their trumpets. The sounds of trumpets and reed flutes and the rhythmical clapping and shouting must surely have come together in a strangely pleasant Afro-Latin arrangement.

At some stage, the Portuguese may have again mistaken the Khoikhoi's exuberance for aggression, as arguments broke out between the crew and the Khoikhoi.[60] Da Gama immediately ordered his men back to the ships, pulled up anchor and set sail. He wanted to get away from the Khoikhoi as fast as possible, as he thought they were becoming a nuisance. The Khoikhoi ran along the beach, waving and shouting at the ships moving farther along the bay.[61] Da Gama then ordered that a cannon be fired to chase them away. The thunderous cannon fire terrified the Khoikhoi and, on seeing the damage the cannon ball caused, they fled inland with their cattle.[62]

The fleet remained in the bay for 13 days and after the crew had taken on fresh water, da Gama ordered that all provisions be moved from the store ship to the other three ships. When the men had completed this, the store ship was set alight on 8 December and the *São Gabriel*, *São Rafael* and *Berrio* departed to continue their voyage.[63] While anchored in the bay, the Portuguese erected one of their marker beacons (*padrãos*) and a wooden cross to commemorate their arrival.

As the three ships heeled into the wind and moved out of the bay, leaving the blazing store ship behind, the crew saw the Khoikhoi knocking down the *padrãos* and wooden cross, thereby removing all traces of the Europeans' visit.[64] A violent storm ensued as the fleet slowly moved up the east coast of southern Africa. The dwindling crew was terrified.[65] The fact that so many men had already fallen sick and died made sailing the ships more and more difficult, especially in poor weather. The landscape gradually changed, to the delight of the crew. The barren landscape at Saint Helena was replaced with lush vegetation that rolled down to the beaches. As the fleet hugged the shore, the crew could see abundant trees, thick grass and herds of cattle lazily grazing on the plentiful greenery.[66]

On 25 December, when the fleet was just north of the Umzimkulu River,[67] da Gama named the area Natal, or 'Birth', to commemorate the day that Christians first saw this land. The fleet then headed out to sea, only setting course for the coast some 12 days later and anchoring at the mouth of the Limpopo River, which da Gama named *Rio dos Reis* (River of Kings).[68]

Da Gama and his men were struck by how different the people on the shore were to the Khoikhoi. They had much larger builds and their skins were much darker. The first Bantu encountered by Europeans appeared to be friendly. Da Gama was encouraged by the warm reception they received and sent two men ashore with gifts for the chief, namely red cloth and a copper bracelet. The two emissaries stayed with the Bantu for the night and were treated well. The friendliness of the people was demonstrated again the following day, when the chief sent a number of hens to da Gama as a reciprocal gift. Confident that the Bantu were unlikely to present a threat to the safety of the ships and men, da Gama encouraged the men to barter with them. So, the Portuguese traded linen, which the Bantu appeared to favour above other offered items, in return for millet.[69]

On 15 January, da Gama left two convicts behind with instructions to collect information on the people and terrain, which they would convey to him on his return. While the convicts had attained a sense of freedom, they were no doubt terrified about being ejected into a strange and foreign world filled with dangerous 'savages' and must have questioned their safety.

Having replenished their water and fresh food supplies, courtesy of the Bantu, the three ships departed for India. They stopped at various ports up the east coast of Africa, including Melinde (now Malindi in Kenya), before finally anchoring in India on 16 May 1498 at a point just below Calcutta (at the Calicut port).[70] During the nine months and eight days of the voyage, more than half of the 170 men had died. While the cost of the voyage had been high, the gateway to the riches of the east had finally been opened.

For the next hundred years, the Portuguese fleets sailed around the Cape en route to India, but deliberately avoided anchoring at the Cape because of its treacherous coastline and because they did not trust the local people. Both Dias and da Gama had experienced violence at the hands of the Khoikhoi, which would become a pattern for future explorers.

Next to incur the wrath of the Khoikhoi was Portuguese explorer António de Saldanha. In 1503, his fleet of three ships sailed into Table Bay due to navigational error (a frequently experienced problem at that time). Historian Noël Mostert records that "he climbed a mountain, very flat and level on the top, which we now call 'The Table of the Cape of Good Hope', from whence he saw the end of the Cape, and the sea that lies beyond it to the east … and from these landmarks he knew that it was indeed the Cape of Good Hope …"[71] De Saldanha named the bay Saldanha Bay. However, Dutch navigator Joris van Spilbergen renamed it Table Bay in 1601 and transferred the name Saldanha Bay to a bay on the West Coast.[72] While de Saldanha and crew filled their water casks from mountain streams, a small group of Khoikhoi approached. Using sign language, the Khoikhoi conveyed that they would like to trade two cows and a sheep for various trinkets.[93]

As the crew headed back to their ships, about 200 Khoikhoi attacked them with sticks and spears and de Saldanha was superficially wounded in the short skirmish that followed. The crew hastened back to the safety of the ships and sailed out the bay.[73] This incident confirmed the fear that the Cape was a dangerous and inhospitable place, something that another navigator, Duarte Pacheco Pereira, confirmed on his return to Portugal. "No profit is to be obtained from this land, so I will not waste time by describing it further," he reported.[74]

Pereira's condemnation of the Cape, coupled with the bad experiences of all those who had gone ashore there, prompted King Manuel to issue a royal decree in 1507 stating that no ships were to call on the South African coast, unless it was an emergency, and that fleets should anchor off Mozambique, which was considered to be less dangerous.[75]

Despite this royal edict, Portuguese navigator and Viceroy to India Dom Francisco de Almeida decided to anchor in Table Bay in 1510 because his crew needed fresh water after having been at sea for three months. This decision had disastrous consequences. The Khoikhoi resented their intrusion and turned their anger on the crew, killing de Almeida and a number of his men. These were the first Europeans to be killed by the local people of southern Africa. The 60-year-old de Almeida's fleet of three ships (the *Garcia*, *Santa Cruz* and *Belém*) had been returning to Portugal from India. Several high officials who had served under de Almeida in India and who had completed their three-year contracts were with him on this perilous return voyage, which departed India on 19 November 1509.[76] After anchoring in the bay, a group of men went ashore to fill their barrels with fresh water. The Khoikhoi, who had seen the ships entering the bay, went to the beach to wait for the men to disembark. There, they traded cattle for linen, calico and iron.[77] The Khoikhoi appeared to be so friendly that a group of 12 crew got permission from de Almeida to walk with them to their kraal five or six kilometres away, where they traded more goods for cattle. However, tension between the Portuguese and Khoikhoi soon reared its head.

While the crew were herding their new cattle back to the ships, a fight broke out. Perhaps the difference in cultures and the language barrier fuelled the Khoikhoi's animosity. It is quite possible that the Portuguese were belittling the Khoikhoi, as they considered themselves to be superior to the semi-naked, fat-smeared and therefore smelly 'savages' who carried primitive bow and arrows, sticks and spears. The incensed Khoikhoi hit the Portuguese across their faces with sticks, drawing blood and hurting both their pride and bodies. Somewhat downcast and humiliated by their treatment, the sailors returned to the ships.[78] The majority of the crew felt that the savages should be taught a lesson and learn respect for the Europeans.

So, early the following morning, before the sun peeped over the blue horizon and sparkled and danced on the sea, 150 soldiers rowed quietly to the beach, armed with crossbows, swords and lances. A reluctant and tired de Almeida led the attack. Having spent years away from Portugal, he was desperate to return to his homeland, where he would spend his remaining years basking in the glory of his achievements as Viceroy to India. He sighed loudly as the boats edged toward the shore, saying, "Ah, wither, do they carry my sixty years?"[79]

Once ashore, the Portuguese stealthily made their way to the kraal, leaving the master of the *Garcia* to protect the beached boats. The Portuguese swooped on the unsuspecting Khoikhoi, rounding up and taking their cattle. Some soldiers grabbed a few of the Khoikhoi children as hostages. About 170 Khoikhoi reacted to their children's screams by violently attacking the Portuguese with stones and assegais. The sophisticated weapons of the Portuguese proved no match against those of the angry Khoikhoi and de Almeida ordered a retreat. The Portuguese sailors dragged the protesting children with them toward the beach, fleeing in twos and threes. The irate Khoikhoi naturally pursued them, running over the sand "so lightly that they moved like birds".[80]

The fleeing Portuguese soldiers were bogged down by their heavy armour and the Khoikhoi rapidly caught up to them. Just before reaching the beach, the Khoikhoi started whistling shrilly and, to the amazement of the Portuguese, the Khoikhoi cattle responded to the whistles, forming a barrier in front of the Khoikhoi. Intent on saving themselves, the Portuguese lost interest in the children, who were able to make good their escape.

The Khoikhoi hurled their assegais at the Portuguese with unerring accuracy, killing many of the men scrambling toward the boats. As one of the survivors later explained, the Khoikhoi "came into the body of our men, taking back the oxen; and by whistling to these and making other signs (since they are trained to this warlike device), they made them surround our men ... like a defensive wall, from behind which came so many fire-hardened sticks that some of us began to fall wounded or trodden by the cattle".[81]

The Portuguese survivors, including an exhausted, sad and frightened de Almeida, finally reached the beach. They shouted in alarm upon seeing that the boats had returned to the ships. A strong breeze had sprung up and the master of the *Garcia*, Diogo d'Unhos, had decided it would be safest to row the boats back to the ships.

Some of the soldiers panicked and ran along the beach to a spot from which it would be easier for the boats to rescue them when they returned. De Almeida, however, was out of breath and wounded, having already been hit by several stones and sticks. He awaited his fate on the beach, along with many of his men and some of his senior officials, most of whom had enjoyed a sedentary lifestyle and creature comforts as government officials in India. They stood with their backs to the sea, facing the approaching Khoikhoi.

De Almeida must have realized that the end was near. He handed the royal standard he'd been entrusted with to one of the Portuguese soldiers, hoping that it could be saved when he died. Moments later, a spear pierced de Almeida's throat. He fell to the ground, clutching his throat as his blood stained the golden sand and his life drained away. The Khoikhoi then killed nine of the senior Portuguese captains and 12 senior government officials[82] with ruthless efficiency. The royal standard was trampled into the sand during the massacre. De Almeida's former tutor, Diogo Pires, heard the shouts that De Almeida was dead and pushed his way through the crowd. "Let me die with him!" he cried, upon seeing de Almeida's lifeless body. His wish was granted: an assegai slammed into him and he died next to his pupil.

The men on the ships had seen the horror unfolding on the beach and had dispatched boats to rescue their compatriots. By the time the boats reached shallow waters, the Portuguese had lost many men and the fierce Khoikhoi had driven the survivors into the sea. Some were already knee-deep in the water while others were hopelessly trying to defend themselves with just their heads above water. The carnage continued, with the Khoikhoi throwing stones and assegais at the sailors and the crew, who pulled their injured comrades onto the boats, where they collapsed, bleeding and exhausted. Back at the ships, the relieved crew counted 65 corpses[83] lying on the beach. They were stunned into silence, which was broken only by muffled sobs and cries of pain from the wounded.

Later that day, as the sun was sliding into the depths of the darkening sea, a sad and tense party was sent ashore to bury their dead. A gruesome scene awaited them: all of the corpses had been stripped naked. Even more horrifying was that de Almeida's body had been mutilated. His stomach had been cut open and his intestines were hanging out. One can only assume that his body was covered with flies and other small predatory creatures.

The corpses were hurriedly buried by the designated gravediggers, who were terrified that the Khoikhoi would attack them as they dug the shallow graves and constantly scanned the nearby thickets for potential movement. Those who had died before reaching the beach were left where they had fallen, as it was getting dark and the risk of going inland seemed too high.

Early the following morning, the three ships raised anchor and set sail for Portugal, watched by the Khoikhoi, who had defeated some of the most sophisticated and highly trained soldiers of the time. This incident would mark the last intrusion in southern Africa by Portuguese navigators.

CHAPTER 2

British flirtation with the Cape

Secret route—English East India Company—trade with the Khoikhoi—Core—the Cape as a penal colony—Britain claims the Cape—Harry—the Haarlem

The Portuguese were the dominant nautical power for another century and a half and their sailing routes to India remained a national secret. The long voyages to the East gradually eroded Portugal's pool of capable seamen and by the end of the 15th century, men with little or no seafaring experience were being recruited. Urban legend at the time claimed that on one occasion when a master of a ship discovered that his crew were totally incapable of distinguishing port from starboard, he tied a bundle of garlic to one side of the ship and a bundle of onions to the other and advised his officer to instruct his helmsmen by "tell[ing] them to onion the helm or garlic their helm. They will understand quickly enough".[84]

During the 16th century, Portuguese ships skirted around the Cape and many never returned to Portugal, either having sunk during violent storms or been dashed on the rocks of the southern African coast. The *Soares* sank west of Mossel Bay in 1503, the *São João do Biscoitinho* off Ponta do Ouro in 1551, the *São Jerónimo* north of Richards Bay in 1552, the *São João* near Port Edward in 1552, the *São Bento* off the Msikaba River mouth in 1554, the *Santo Alberto* near East London in 1593, the *Espíritu Santo* off Haga Haga in 1608, the *Nossa Senhora da Atalaia do Pinheiro* near Cefane River in 1647 and the *Sacramento* off Schoenmakerskop the same year.[85] It is possible that many more Portuguese ships sank along the route but were not recorded as lost at sea. It is estimated that of all the ships that left Portugal for the East, only half returned safely. Allied to the hazards of the lengthy sea journey was the loss of life through sickness and disease.

Portuguese dominance of the route around the Cape during the 16th century is self-evident: there are no records of shipwrecks of other nations other than that of the Danish *Jaeger* in 1619, which sank off Woodstock Beach.

In 1595, a Dutchman called Jan Huyghen van Linschoten gave up the secret of the sea route to India. He had spent six years in Goa and on his return to Holland, he published sailing instructions to the East.[86]

Opening up the route to the East led to the formation of the English East India Company in 1600 and the Dutch East India Company in 1602. These companies were so powerful that they had their own armies as well as tremendous political influence. The Dutch East India Company dominated the East in the early 17th century, gaining control of the Spice Islands in the Indonesian archipelago. There, they established their capital at Djakarta and called it Batavia. Later, it became one of the biggest suppliers of slaves to southern Africa.

The English East India Company was set up in Surat in India. Elizabethan merchant and entrepreneur Sir Thomas Smythe was head of the company and was based in London. He soon realized that the Cape would offer the ships an opportunity to break up the journey from England to India, and vice versa, and to obtain meat and produce from the Khoikhoi as well as to stock up on fresh water.

Smythe and the top brass at the East India Company received many glowing reports about the Cape from the ships that stopped there and thought it would be an ideal place to erect a settlement. Smythe received a letter from a senior merchant called Thomas Aldworth that stated, "I have never seen a better land in my life. Although it was mid-winter the grass came up to our knees; it is full of woods and lovely rivers of fresh water, with much deer, fish and birds, and the abundance of cows and ewes is astonishing ... The climate is very healthy ... arriving their with our people sick, they all regained their health and strength within twenty-one days".[87]

Many others endorsed Aldworth's views. For instance, missionary Reverend Patrick Copeland reported to Smythe that, "The people are loving, afraid at first, by reason of the unkindness of the Dutch who came here and who killed and stole their cattle".[88] Aldworth, with the support of other merchants, proposed to Smythe that 100 convicts should be taken to the Cape each year and that a colony be established.

The increased maritime traffic at the Cape had not gone unnoticed by the Khoikhoi. As the frequency of ships calling at the Cape increased, so too did the fear and alarm of the Khoikhoi. They were concerned that either the English or Dutch would settle permanently in the Cape.[89] How right they were to be worried.

Trade between the Khoikhoi and the visitors took place under clouds of suspicion and mistrust from both parties. The Khoikhoi must have infuriated the Europeans when they performed their favourite trick: after a deal had been struck, they would start whistling and the Europeans' new cattle would run after them.

The crewmembers that traded with the Khoikhoi in the 1500s were delighted with the meagre payment demanded by the Khoikhoi, who especially prized junk such as iron scraps and spike nails. In 1591, an ox could be purchased for two knives and a sheep for one. The Khoikhoi used their bartered iron to make arrowheads and assegai blades that would give them an edge when battling their enemies.[90] In fact, frequent fights occurred within the tribe over the much sought-after iron.

From 1609 onward, the Khoikhoi's demand for iron suddenly ceased. The approximately 1,200 Khoikhoi near the peninsula evidently had abundant iron arrow and assegai heads and it was naturally not in their interests to trade iron with their cousins in the interior, thereby strengthening their armies. For a time, the Khoikhoi obstinately demanded copper as trading currency. Then, copper became less fashionable with the Khoikhoi and they insisted on being remunerated with brass. Naturally, the Europeans were irritated when the Khoikhoi's love for cheap iron (usually scrap) was replaced with the desire for more valuable copper and brass. Most Europeans blamed a Khoikhoi named Coree for forcing up the price of sheep and oxen.

Swayed by recommendations from English East India Company explorers and missionaries, Smythe felt that the first step toward establishing a settlement at the Cape would be to appoint a local representative to act in the best interests of the English while they traded with the Khoikhoi. He decided that at least one Khoikhoi should be taken to England and taught about English customs. On Smythe's orders, a Khoikhoi chieftain called Coree and his companion were tricked into boarding a ship bound for England in May 1613.

Seeing their beloved cloud-topped Table Mountain disappearing as the ships sailed out of Table Bay must have been extremely traumatic for the two abducted Khoikhoi. After days at sea, they must have realized that they would probably never see their homes and loved ones again. Coree's companion soon died and it is presumed that he was overwhelmed by his fear and sadness.

Upon disembarking in a grey and wet England, Coree was taken to Smythe's home in London. Here, Smythe tried to "civilize" and "make a gentleman" out of his prisoner. Coree was made to wear armour and taught English, which he soon mastered. He demonstrated his proficiency in the language by sobbing, "Coree home go. Home go!" while lying prostrate on the floor.

Coree did not take kindly to being paraded around as though he was a circus attraction and his observers sometimes arrogantly remarked that he was ungrateful for the opportunities he'd been offered. They casually overlooked that he had been kidnapped, taken to a land with a freezing climate, looked down on by all he met and treated like a dress-up doll.

In June 1614, Coree was taken home to the Cape on the *Hector*,[91] as it was felt that he had been suitably 'civilized' to carry out his task as trade liaison between the English and Khoikhoi. His delight at seeing Table Mountain again and feeling the warm African sun on his skin knew no bounds. As soon as he stepped off the ship, he threw off his European clothes, wrapped himself in sheepskins and sprinted inland.

The following year, on 6 June 1615, the British fleet arrived carrying Sir Thomas Rowe, whom King James I had appointed as special envoy to the Great Mogul of India, the fourth ruler of the Mogul Empire. Coree waited on the shore to welcome the fleet and to trade with the sailors. As one English sailor commented wryly when the Khoikhoi demanded brass instead of pig iron, "It would have been much better for us, and those who come after us, if Coree had never ever seen England".[92]

Coree welcomed his former captors warmly and invited a few of the crew to visit his kraal with him so that they could see how he lived. Coree's people also greeted the visitors enthusiastically. In fact, several of them indicated that they wanted to go back to England with the ships. "Sir Thomas Smythe English Shipps," they chorused, repeating the English phrase Coree had taught them.[93] They had no doubt been impressed with Coree's exaggerated stories of life in England.

The ships housed ten convicts who had been given the choice of either coming to the Cape or being hung. The prisoners included renowned highwayman Captain James Crosse, who had once been a yeoman of the Royal Guard. The captain gathered the convicts together to give them parting instructions. "Be thankful to the King for his mercy and behave as befitting Christians. You are to journey into the interior and see what information can be found which will benefit our country and the English East India Company," the captain advised them.[94] The frightened convicts were then loaded into boats that took them ashore. No doubt, many of them wished that they had opted for the gallows at Tyburn and a swift death over the uncertainty of being left in the Cape.

These men were to establish an English 'plantation' (colony) and had each been given a knapsack containing a spade, a small tent, turnip seed to plant as well as bread and dried fish. They had also been given a short pike, a sword and two knives with which to protect themselves.

Coree and his people had realized by now that these men were being left behind. They attacked the Englishmen, killing one and wounding several others. Coree returned to the beach and demanded that the captain tell him why these men were being left behind. When he was told that these men were convicts that Smythe had sent, he saw how he could turn this situation to his advantage: he promised that he would not attack the Englishmen if he were given an English-style house. He also insisted that the convicts be given muskets with which they would protect his people against possible attacks by other Khoikhoi.

Crosse, unofficial leader of the convicts, had watched Coree negotiating. He concluded that Coree should not be trusted. He implored the captain to give him and the men a small boat in which they could row to the safety of Robben Island, about 12 kilometres offshore. The captain agreed to his request and the convicts set off for Robben Island, where they were sure the Khoikhoi could not follow. What Crosse could never have known was that the island was infested with giant rats and snakes and had no fresh water. As such, the men had to row to the mainland to fetch water during their eight-month stay on Robben Island. It was not long before they wrecked their boat and were effectively marooned.

The captain of the *Gift* later reported: "Coree told us that Captain Crosse had attempted to reach the shore on a wooden raft he built, after their boat had been wrecked. He and two others had completed half the journey when two whales came out of the water next to the raft. One of the whales was so close that Crosse and the men touched it with a wooden pole. The whales sank down below the surface. Crosse was terrified of the whales and was numb with cold from the sea. He returned to the island and after washing and putting on dry clothes attempted once more to reach the mainland on the raft. Before he left he instructed one of the men on the island to watch his progress. This was done. Coree said that he watched Crosse for a long way and then he suddenly lost sight of him."[95]

An English ship rescued three of the convicts, while a Portuguese ship rescued the other seven. The three that were taken back to England must have been overjoyed that their ordeal was over. However, their joy was short-lived: they were hanged within hours of returning to the green fields of England, with the Chief Justice explaining that they had been "executed upon their former condemnation, for which they were banished".[96]

In June 1616, Smythe sent three more condemned men to the Cape on the *Swan*. When they learned what had befallen their predecessors, they fell to their knees and begged Captain Joseph to hang them instead of leaving them at the Cape. Captain Joseph responded coldly to their tearful pleas. "I have no commission to execute you," he said. "My orders are to leave you here, and that I must do." The men were taken ashore two days later.[97]

Coree again tried to form an alliance with the Europeans against his enemies. In 1617, he offered to 'assist' the English by leading them inland to find cattle. However, they soon arrived at a place where over 5,000 warriors from an opposing tribe were assembled with their 10,000 cattle. The English realized that Coree and his men expected them to lend armed support in exchange for cattle and, in the face of such unbalanced odds, they declined his offer.[98] By all accounts, Coree had become an unpopular figure. All those who called at the Cape blamed him for dramatically pushing up the asking price of cattle. His unpopularity was reflected in the way he died: Dutch sailors hanged him in 1627 when he refused to provide them with fresh produce.

On 24 June 1620, a fleet of six English ships under the joint command of Commodore Shillinge and Commodore Humphrey Fitzherbert put into Table Bay, where nine Dutch ships were already anchored. As a friendly relationship existed between the Dutch and the English at the Cape (even though the respective navies sometimes clashed on the high seas), Fitzherbert lost no time in going across to the Dutch command ship to pay his respects and no doubt to enjoy some genever (a juniper-flavoured spirit). There, one of the sailors casually informed Fitzherbert that the Dutch had been inspecting the country around the Cape with a view to establishing a settlement in Table Valley the following year. Fitzherbert was alarmed by this news and reported what he had heard to Shillinge, who agreed that if the Dutch were to succeed with their proposed settlement, it would limit English rights in the Cape.[99] They were particularly concerned that the Dutch would limit access to fresh water by issuing licences, for which they would have to pay, to calling ships to obtain water.[100]

Shillinge swiftly called a meeting with the senior officers of the fleet. At this meeting, all agreed that Shillinge should quickly proclaim the sovereignty of King James I over the whole country, as only a few men would be needed to retain possession of Table Bay. They reasoned that farmed produce would be of great value to calling English ships and that the Hottentots were not a threat, as they had no real structures or leadership. They also believed that the natives could be converted to Christianity easily. Above all, they wanted to gain control of the Cape before the Dutch did.

On 3 July 1620, the crew from the six English ships rowed ashore for a ceremony on Lion's Rump, which Shillinge later renamed King James's Mountain. Shillinge loudly read out the proclamation of sovereignty to the few hundred assembled men, who were dressed in their finest navy clothing. The men then proudly hoisted the flag of Saint George, its red cross signalling to all as it fluttered in the breeze that the English had claimed the Cape. The officers and crew solemnly saluted the flag before it was carefully lowered, folded and handed over to the wide-eyed Khoikhoi, who had silently watched the Europeans claiming their land. The English rather naïvely believed that the Khoikhoi would cheerfully show the flag to future visitors. After the ceremony, the men returned to their waiting ships, no doubt pleased that they had further extended the English sphere of influence. Interestingly, these unauthorized proceedings were never ratified by the directors of the English East India Company or by the government of England.

Captain Jan Cornelius Kunst of the Dutch ship *Schiedam* watched the ceremony taking place but raised no objection to it.[101] However, when the flag-raising ceremony was over, some of his officers erected a cairn of stones to mark the place of occupation and buried a packet of dispatches recording the event next to a stone slab marked with the Dutch East India Company's symbol, VOC, or *Vereenigde Oost-Indische Compagnie*. The engraving denoted that the Dutch had taken possession of the Cape before the English did.[102]

Although one would expect that the hurried declaration of occupation by the English would have caused friction with the Dutch, representatives of the Dutch and English East India companies had an unspoken alliance. These rivals in naval and trade spheres needed to protect themselves from French and Danish designs on the East. So, when the Dutch proposed that a jointly controlled refreshment station with the English be established in the Cape, the English accepted it.

In 1619, the Hereen XVII, a body of 17 shareholders that was also referred to as the Lords Seventeen, from the Dutch East India Company instructed the commodore of its fleet to search the Cape coastline for a suitable place to set up the refreshment station. On his return several months later, he reported that Table Bay boasted the most suitable harbour and site.

The English also sent a scout to look for the ideal spot for the proposed refreshment station. In 1622, Captain Johnson of the *Rose* was chosen for this purpose. However, it would appear that he was already biased against the Cape as he had had a bad experience on his previous voyage there. When his ship had arrived on 28 January 1620, eight of his crew went ashore with fishing nets to catch fish near the mouth of the Salt River. They never returned and only four of their bodies were found. Johnson believed that the Khoikhoi had murdered all those who had gone ashore.[103] As such, he did not recommend any area in the Cape as an ideal refreshment station site. Faced with conflicting reports, the Dutch and English East India companies abandoned the idea of a joint refreshment station at the Cape and went their separate but parallel ways.

As the number of English ships calling at the Cape increased, the English established an informal postal system in which they left letters on the outward-bound journey with Chief Autshumato of the Khoikhoi (otherwise known as Harry or Hadah). He would then pass them on to ships returning to England.[104] Unlike his predecessor, Coree, Harry was a likeable, confident and cheerful man whom the English trusted. They decided that he should learn English so that he could act as an interpreter for them in negotiations with the Khoikhoi. So, in 1632, Harry was taken to the English trading post at the port of Bantam in Java to learn English.

When he returned to the Cape several months later, he requested that he be left on Robben Island, where he established a small settlement with about 20 other 'Strandlopers' (lit. 'beach walkers). Harry's band of Khoikhoi had earned this name because they lived off the sea and on the beaches, keeping no cattle. On Robben Island, they felt safe from attack by other Khoikhoi groups such as the Cochoqua and Peninsular Khoikhoi and Harry could still make himself useful to ships putting into Table Bay. As soon as a ship was sighted nearing the bay, the Strandlopers would gain its attention by lighting fires. In time, Harry also carried out assignments for the Dutch, translating for them, bartering on their behalf and acting as their 'postman'.[105]

It was only in 1647 that the first permanent structure was erected at the Cape, out of necessity. After Dutch ships the *Haarlem*, *Oliphant* and *Schiedam* became separated from the fleet commanded by Jeremias van Vliet on 25 March 1647, they continued toward Table Bay, with the *Haarlem* arriving there first. However, another ship was already in the bay and as senior crewmember Leendert Janszen explained, "Our captain, Vice-Commander Reijnier van't Zum sent our Chief Mate, Claes Winckels in a skiff to find out what ship lay at anchor."[106]

Shortly after Winckels had been dispatched, a stiff breeze came up and the *Haarlem* ran aground in the pounding surf. The crew screamed in terror as the waves crashed into the side of the ship, believing that the ship would be smashed to splinters. Fortunately, it did not shatter, but it was firmly wedged into the sand. Van't Zum ordered four cannon shots to be fired to attract the attention of the other ship, which ignored their request for assistance. The strong waves drove the *Haarlem* even harder into the sand and the captain soon realized that the ship would probably break up. So, Van't Zum ordered a skiff to row to shore with some of the crew, which included two carpenters who would begin making a shelter for the crew. The skiff met with disaster and was swamped by the heavy seas. The men swam for their lives and although they reached the safety of the shore, they were without the means to return to the ship as the skiff had sunk. One of the carpenters had drowned, as he could not swim.

By the following morning, the *Oliphant* and *Schiedam* had put into the bay and they requested assistance from two English ships to salvage the *Haarlem*'s cargo. The English sent two longboats to transfer some of the goods, including cinnamon, camphor, mace and Japanese coats, to the *Oliphant*. While the crew from the *Haarlem* walked along the beach toward the English ships, the Khoikhoi attacked them. When they eventually reached the ships, 40 men were allowed to board. The English ships subsequently set sail for Europe the next day, leaving 60 of the crew stranded at the Cape. Having no skiff in which to row to shore, Van't Zum fashioned a makeshift boat out of two barrels and went to join his men on shore.

The crew from the *Schiedam* assisted Van't Zum's men with constructing a fort, which was erected on a tall, steep sand dune. The men built a palisade and set up four cannon that had been salvaged from the doomed *Haarlem*, with one on each corner of the fort. They then dug a well so that the men would have access to fresh water.

Once the fort had been completed, the men headed to the beach to salvage whatever cargo and gear they could from the *Haarlem*, such as cables, cannon and masts.[107] The majority of the cargo was pepper though, which had fermented below deck after seawater poured into the cargo hold. The gas given off by the fermenting pepper was so toxic that all of the rats below deck had died and one of the sailors was almost overcome by the poisonous gas. The men under Leendert Janszen fired a cannonball at the deck to smash it open and then widened the hole with axes and allowed the gas to escape.

No sooner had the 60 men taken up accommodation in the 42-square-metre fort[108] than the Khoikhoi approached them to barter. When the Khoikhoi first visited the fort, the marooned sailors did not trust them and warned them to stay away. However, they threw them biscuits and tobacco when the Khoikhoi promised to bring cattle.

The following day, the Khoikhoi arrived with crayfish instead of cattle. After months at sea, the men craved red meat and they explained this to the Khoikhoi, who brought five sheep two weeks later. The Khoikhoi were fascinated with the fort and tried to persuade the men to allow them into it. However, the Dutch sailors repeatedly denied their request, which angered the Khoikhoi.

In April 1648, a fleet of 12 ships arrived. It was bound for Holland and picked up the salvaged cargo, goods and equipment as well as the men from the fort 18 days after dropping anchor at Table Bay.[109]

Jan van Riebeeck, who would become a pivotal figure in early South African history, was onboard one of the ships, the *Coninck van Polen*. He was being taken back to Holland in disgrace, to be dismissed from the company for illicit private trading.

Back in Holland, Janszen presented a document to the Lords Seventeen motivating a case for setting up a permanent settlement at the Cape. He painted a glowing picture of the Cape, suggesting that fruit and vegetable gardens could be established due to the temperate climate. His report also described the Khoikhoi in favourable terms and when he was challenged on the Khoikhoi attacks that had occurred, he argued that Dutch farmers would have behaved in the same way if they had been attacked or had their cattle taken. Janszen proved to be extremely persuasive, especially as he claimed that the Khoikhoi could be made to learn Dutch and converted to Christianity.

The Lords Seventeen accepted Janszen's recommendations and plans began in 1651 to found a refreshment station in the Cape. So ended the era of exploration. Many would say that from here on, the era of exploitation began.

The Portuguese and the Dutch had lost many ships and men in the process of discovering the Cape. The outbound voyages to the Cape typically took over four months and ships sometimes had to wait for up to a month before a strong wind picked up so that they could set sail, by which time the fresh food and provisions had already been depleted. Conditions onboard the ships were appalling. People were crammed into the ships in unthinkable conditions together with various types of cargo and disease and sickness spread like wildfire. Typically, between a third and half of the people onboard died before returning home. For instance, on one trip from Lisbon to Goa, approximately 1,630 of the original 5,228 soldiers died before reaching India.[110] Similarly, when the *Hector* was found drifting 19 kilometres off the coast of the Cape in 1606, only ten of its original crew of 350 were still alive but were so few that they were unable to sail the ship.[111]

Some ships simply disappeared at sea. As recorded by a Dutch East India Company soldier who was recuperating at the Cape in 1674, "Some ships never get here ... A ship had been seen from the top of the hill lying near the shore, which steered directly for the Cape, but which suddenly disappeared when the wind turned against her and we all believe that she was lost because all her crew lay sick and could no longer sail her".

It was common for men on the shore to have to board a ship to assist with anchoring in Table Bay, as the ship's crew were often too weak to complete the task after a long voyage.[112] Even with a fit and healthy crew, anchoring could be difficult. Adverse winds could delay a ship from anchoring in the bay, sometimes by as much as eight days from the first sighting of the ship from Table Mountain.

The fresh produce and meat on the ships inevitably ran out, with the only edible remnants being salted meat, hard biscuits and 'long life' vegetables such as onions and potatoes.[113] As such, scurvy was the biggest killer on these long voyages. However, dysentery, typhoid and other diseases associated with unhygienic conditions were rampant. In the overcrowded and poorly ventilated ships, lice, cockroaches, giant rats and fleas flourished. In addition, condensation

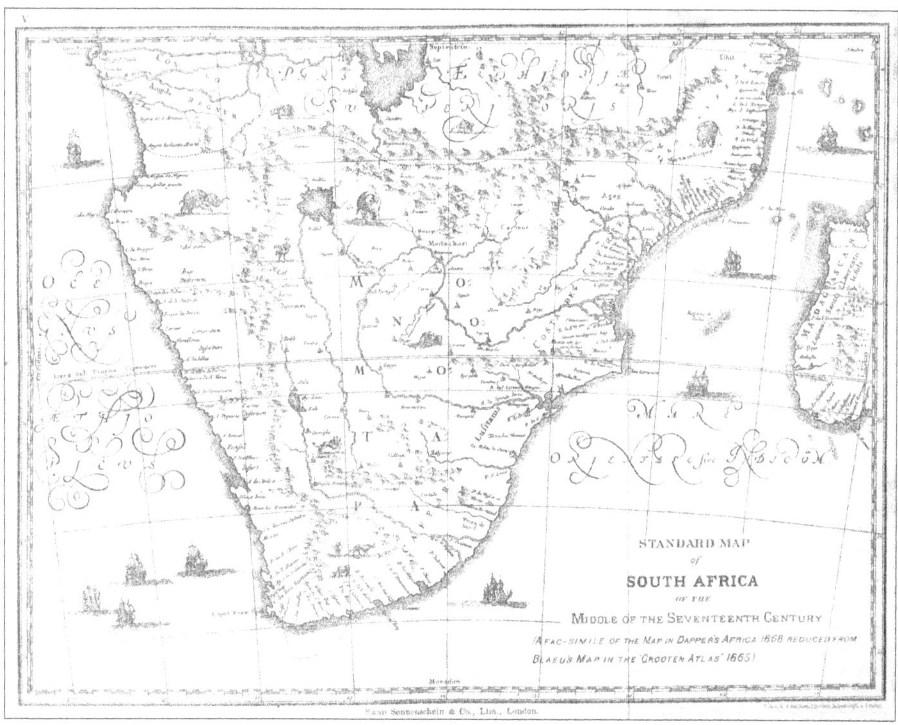

dripped from the bulkheads, causing a permanent stench of damp, which was mixed with that of urine and faeces. The lavatories were known as the heads. They were small platforms located on the outside of the ship, toward the bow. Anybody who was grievously ill was unable to get to them and bad weather prevented those who were still healthy from doing so. As such, the crew urinated and defecated inside the ship. The stink of urine and faeces also permeated the crew's clothes, which were never changed during the four- or five-month voyage and reeked due to their unwashed bodies. Those that succumbed to illness lay below deck, water drops from condensation on the bulkheads dripping on them and mixing with seawater, urine, faeces and vomit sloshing over them. The malodorous grey water moved back and forth with the rolling of the ship, washing clothes, boots and goods from one side of the ship to the other. The stench in these cramped and disgusting quarters due to sweat, filth, urine, faeces and smoke from stoves and pipes must have been enough to induce vomiting. As sexually transmitted diseases were rife among the sailors, the already disgusting odour must have been augmented by the rank smell emitted by those with gonorrhoea and syphilis. Considering how rife homosexuality was onboard, there must have been many crew afflicted with these diseases. However, men caught engaging in homosexuality were put to death.

Below deck, the men slept on wide benches with 20 or 30 men to a bench. While they slept, lice crawled over them and giant rats and cockroaches scurried around this vermin's paradise. When a sailor died, his corpse was sewn up in his bedding, a cannonball was attached to his feet and his body was dumped unceremoniously overboard.

Fights frequently broke out among the men and robbery and murder could be conducted almost with impunity; unless one was caught in the act. Soldiers and sailors were lashed mercilessly, even for minor offences. For more serious acts such as stabbing, the punishment would start with three rounds of keelhauling. This involved tying the offending sailor to a line that was looped under the ship, then throwing him overboard and dragging him under the keel to the other side. As the hull was often covered in barnacles and other marine life with sharp edges, the offender would be covered in cuts, sometimes losing limbs when pulled too quickly. If the offender was pulled too slowly, there was a very real possibility of drowning. The keelhauling over, the sailor would receive 300 blows with a wooden club and then have his knife-wielding hand nailed to the mast.[114] After witnessing punishments like these, it is a wonder that any crime occurred on board.

Imagine how the sailors must have felt seeing land after five months at sea living under these conditions. Seeing seaweed floating on the sea's surface and birds circling overhead, followed by the hazy outline of the shore and Table Mountain as they approached the Cape must surely have delighted the men and filled them with relief.

The Cape was indeed a paradise and the sailors must have thought that the abundant wild fruit and fresh meat was like manna from heaven. The clear rivers and streams that tumbled down to the sea also teemed with fish. As recorded by sailor John Jourdain of the *Ascension*, "We caught many fish with our seine net, in a river [Salt River]. In one haul of the net we caught more than 300 fish larger than 46 centimetres in length. In two hours we managed to net enough fish to feed the crews of two ships for a day, and then on the way back to the ships in the mouth of the river we netted over 3,500 mullets which were dried, salted and taken on the voyage home".[115]

After being at sea for so long, the sailors were astonished by what they saw: inland lakes with wallowing hippo; giant herds of buffalo and lumbering elephants thundering over the plains; herds of skittish zebra and kudu grazing and jackal, leopard and hyena stalking through the long grass in pursuit of prey. Having arrived at the Cape, the sailors were finally liberated from the confinement and dismal conditions of the ship and were free to explore the picturesque landscape before them.

CHAPTER 3

Second chance for Van Riebeeck

Van Riebeeck arrives—starvation—Eva—slavery—Doman—free burghers—first Khoikhoi-Dutch war—Van Meerhof—Trekboers—the Castle—Van Qaelberg—French annexation and European wars—second Khoikhoi war

The first Dutch settlers arrived at Table Bay on 6 April 1652 in the *Drommedaris, Reijger* and *De Goede Hoop*. The fleet had originally comprised five ships when it left Holland but two, the *Oliphant* and the *Walvisch*, had turned back because they were overloaded. These ships arrived in the Cape the following month, having lost 130 crew.[116]

Aboard the *Drommedaris* was Jan van Riebeeck, who had been brought back from Tongking (now Tonkin in Vietnam) to Holland in disgrace and suspended from duty when he had been caught profiteering by his employer, the Dutch East India Company. Fortunately, he was soon given a second chance to prove himself to the company and was sent to the Cape as commander of the tiny settlement that had been established.

As the *Drommedaris*, *Reijger* and *De Goede Hoop* anchored in the bay, 33-year-old Van Riebeeck must have drawn a sigh of relief. The journey had not been as bad as it could have been. After all, only two men had died and his 23-year-old wife, Maria, had survived the journey.

Van Riebeeck was not a large man. However, his small stature belied a strong voice and a commanding presence. He was outspoken and unhesitating when it came to giving orders.[117] Long curly black hair complemented his swarthy features and his well-groomed moustache made him appear to be of Italian rather than Dutch descent. He was also known to be a snappy dresser.

The Dutch East India Company had awarded Van Riebeeck a five-year contract in the role of "merchant and head of the Company in the Cape of Good Hope". Although many of his contemporaries may have envied his title, Van Riebeeck saw this position as a stepping stone to his true desires: becoming a merchant in India by the age of 40 and redeeming himself for his previous misdemeanours.

About 90 men and women disembarked from the three ships. They had come to the Cape to establish themselves as *boeren* (farmers) and would grow fruit and vegetables to supply the Dutch East India Company's ships that stopped there en route to India.[118]

Right from the outset, the settlers met with hardships. They were worried about their safety from the Khoikhoi and although the newcomers forged a relationship with the locals, they did not trust them. Van Riebeeck had been instructed by the Hereen XVII to treat the Khoikhoi fairly and to establish good relationships with them. As such, Van Riebeeck welcomed the arrival of Harry, the Khoikhoi who had been taken to England to learn English.[119]

On landing, Van Riebeeck immediately set about building a fort, using mud to build the walls.[120] During the year it took to complete the fort, the settlers lived in tents and mud huts.

The first winter they faced was one of the harshest the Cape had experienced in many years. There was even snow on Table Mountain. Strong winds and lashing rain destroyed their gardens, diminishing their access to fresh produce. The settlers also discovered that their inexperience with hunting made shooting the abundant game far more difficult than they had anticipated. Resorting to using traps and snares also proved unfruitful and, worst of all, the Khoikhoi did not come to barter the plentiful cattle they could see grazing nearby. This lack of fresh produce led to sickness and malnutrition and many complained that living in the Cape was worse than being on the ships. Van Riebeeck wrote in his diary of his concerns about dwindling supplies: "We shall soon have to stop work … as a result of the weakness of our people from lack of food. Our stock of barley and peas as well as beef and pork is nearly exhausted. We now have only three cows and four sheep from the natives whose fires we see on the far side of the bay."[121]

On 11 November 1652, it was recorded in official documents in the archives that "The food is getting so scarce that in future it will be impossible to give the men what they need, much less their fill".[122] In desperation, a small group of settlers eventually sailed to Robben Island to collect birds' eggs and kill penguins for food.

The conditions deteriorated to such an extent that many of the settlers felt mutinous. For instance, Jan Danielssen was seen wandering around the settlement in rags and carrying two knives. When asked what he was doing, he angrily replied, "If it happens again like last year that we get so little to eat, yet have to work all the same, I shall finish the commander with the knives". Despite pleading that he had uttered the words out of "pure dejection", Danielssen was sentenced to be keelhauled and was put in chains for six months.[123]

At night, Van Riebeeck anxiously watched the fires of the Khoikhoi as they got closer to the settlement. He could not have known that these Khoikhoi moved their cattle into the peninsula area to graze once a year.

Van Riebeeck turned to Harry for advice about the Khoikhoi's intentions, even though he was suspicious of Harry and worried about the power he enjoyed with both the Dutch settlers and the Khoikhoi. He noted how Harry was extremely manipulative, holding the upper hand in all negotiations between the Khoikhoi and the Dutch because he could communicate with both parties. He had a hunch that Harry was advising the Khoikhoi to push up the asking price for cattle brought to the fort.

The Khoikhoi's evident reluctance to trade cattle coupled with the daily sight of thousands of cattle nearby must have tempted the Dutch to attack the Khoikhoi herders and to seize some of the cattle.[124] However, the thought of incurring the wrath of Van Riebeeck was sufficient deterrent. His punishments were known to be harsh and just one rude word uttered to Van Riebeeck or his officers could result in the offender receiving 100 blows with the butt of a musket.

The conditions at the settlement eventually started to improve. Eight months after landing, the settlers were churning their first butter using cream obtained from the few cows they had and they started salting penguin and seal meat, as they were not able to source fresh meat from the Khoikhoi. When they moved into the fort a few months later, one can only imagine their relief to be away from the Khoikhoi and carnivorous wild animals. Conditions were so tough that many of the men deserted, fleeing to the Portuguese territory of Mozambique.

Van Riebeeck and Maria took Harry's niece into their home. She was about 12 years old and they called her Eva. They dressed her in European clothes and taught her about Christianity and to speak Dutch. Eva learned quickly and, much to everyone's satisfaction, she soon was acting as translator between the Dutch and the Khoikhoi. All translation had previously been carried out almost exclusively by her uncle, Harry.

Van Riebeeck's frustration with the Khoikhoi's reluctance to trade with the settlers grew day by day. He wrote to Holland, "The Hottentots [Khoikhoi] … came grazing their cattle within our sight, only half a mile from the fort, but they refused to barter even one. It is a hard task for me to keep our people from attacking them and taking their cattle and so alleviate their hunger. I managed to restrain them."[125] After eighteen months at the Cape, the settlers only had 42 cattle and 100 sheep. They did not keep these for long though.

In early 1654, Van Riebeeck begged the Hereen XVII to allow him to retaliate against the Khoikhoi. Their reply arrived nine months later at the end of 1654. It stressed the need to be lenient toward the Khoikhoi and denied him the right to punish them.

Van Riebeeck's hands were effectively tied and he must have found this response incredibly frustrating. The 110 men at the settlement had to work day and night, guarding against the Khoikhoi at night and working the land during the day.

Van Riebeeck had already written to the Dutch East India Company six weeks after his arrival to request that slaves be sent to the Cape to supplement his meagre labour force.[126] However, this request had been denied. Nevertheless, the Van Riebeeck household employed two Madagascan slave girls: Eva and 'Cleijn' Eva, gifts from the King of Antongil to Van Riebeeck's wife Maria. French Admiral de la Roche St André later gave the Van Riebeecks two young Arab slave girls from Abyssinia when he visited the Cape.

It was only when a visiting commissioner expressed his unhappiness that the Van Riebeecks had accepted the slaves as gifts that these girls were 'hired out' to other company officials.[127] No longer having exclusive use of the four slaves, Van Riebeeck commissioned Jacob Reijniers, who was married to Van Riebeeck's niece, to purchase a slave woman from Batavia for him in 1653. He also bought a small family of slaves from Commander Pieter Kemp. The family comprised Domingo and Angela from Bengal and their three children.[128]

The first marriage between a white settler and slave at the Cape was between Jan Woutersz van Middelburg and Catharina Anthonis of Bengal in 1656. When a fleet called in at the Cape on its return voyage to Holland from the East, Catharina Anthonis had been onboard as slave to the fleet commander Caspaer van der Boogaerden. Jan Woutersz stayed behind at the Cape and was given the role of caretaker of Robben Island. He lived there with his wife and they had their first child on the island.[129] Five years after the first slaves, on 28 March 1658, the Indiaman *Amersfoort* anchored in Table Bay. Onboard were 174 Angolan slaves who had been taken from a Portuguese ship bound for Brazil. A further 28 slaves from Guinea were dropped off at the Cape a few weeks later by the *Hasselt* yacht.[130] No doubt, these slaves were relieved to walk about unchained after having been shackled with leg irons below deck for the duration of their voyage.

The floodgates had opened and slaves poured into the colony at almost the same rate as the settlers from Holland. The slaves were sourced from many West African countries such as Angola and Guinea and from stinking prisons in Malaya and Madagascar. During the Dutch East India Company's tenure at the Cape, about 65,000 slaves were imported.[131]

One Sunday morning, a young Dutch herd boy was murdered by the Khoikhoi, who seized the livestock he had been tending. The crime seemed opportunistic: the Dutch had been attending a church service at Van Riebeeck's home when the boy was attacked.[132] Moreover, Harry and the Khoikhoi under his leadership disappeared during the service. Shortly after this incident, Van Riebeeck met a Khoikhoi whom he thought looked like a *dominee* (minister) due to his "honest face". He called him Doman and described him as being "a very simple person who is entirely devoted to us". He resolved to send him to Batavia to learn Dutch so that he could be of assistance to the settlers.

When Doman returned to the Cape in 1658, one of the officials from Batavia remarked to Van Riebeeck that "He has learned so much about Christianity to which he has become attached, that his studies of Christianity should continue on a daily basis. We hope that through him many of the other Khoikhoi will become positively influenced".[133]

Shortly after Doman returned to the settlement, Van Riebeeck appointed him as a translator. Now able to communicate in Dutch, Doman lost no time in confirming Van Riebeeck's suspicion that Harry and the Strandlopers had killed the herd boy and taken the cattle and sheep. He also related that Harry had hidden the livestock from the Dutch as well as the Goringhaiqua, an enemy of the Strandlopers, and that the Goringhaiqua had seized the animals for themselves when they discovered them.

The Khoikhoi became more resentful of the small Dutch community when it became apparent that the Dutch were there to stay. As their resentment grew, so did their reluctance to trade cattle. Tensions between the two groups grew, until the Khoikhoi finally made their move: about 50 tribesmen climbed up to the defensive ditch surrounding the fort and began constructing mud and thatch huts next to it.

Van Riebeeck described the incident such: "We wanted them to be farther away from us and indicated that to them, but they responded aggressively saying that this land was theirs and not ours, and that they would build their huts wherever they wished to. Furthermore, if we would not agree to them being there they would attack us and kill us with the aid of many people from the interior. They pointed out to us that they could easily surmount the walls of our fort as the walls sloped and were made of mud, which made climbing them easy."[134]

Fortunately, Harry arrived at this point in the confrontation. He requested that the Dutch protect him from neighbouring tribes, which he feared were trying to kill him. To curry favour, he informed Van Riebeeck that the Goringhaiqua had stolen the cattle and sheep and killed the herd boy. Van Riebeeck had no choice but to accept this story as being true as the Goringhaiqua had the livestock. He promptly restored Harry to his former position as translator and intermediary for trade negotiations with the Khoikhoi.

Although the Dutch did not entirely trust Harry and Harry suspected they would double-cross him, they needed each other. It was a marriage of convenience in which the two parties were like scorpions circling one another, each anticipating a fatal sting.

Harry then engaged with the Khoikhoi on behalf of the Dutch to restore trade relations. In no time, Harry amassed immense wealth in the form of cattle. By 1658, he had at least 260 sheep and 227 cattle, which comprised more than ten percent of the total cattle on the peninsula. The wealthier he became, the more the hostility from other tribes declined and Harry ultimately became the spokesperson for the Peninsular Khoikhoi, who referred to themselves as 'Harry's people'.[135]

Four years after settling at the Cape, the Dutch had spread farther inland and were even farming wheat in the inland areas. Naturally, they selected land that was protected from the strong Cape winds to farm. However, they considered the whole of the peninsula to be theirs.

Van Riebeeck was anxious to preserve the rich grasslands for grazing by Dutch-owned cattle, prevent livestock theft by the Khoikhoi and to increase the productivity of the refreshment station at the Cape. He proposed cutting a 32-kilometre canal across the Cape Flats for irrigation based on the advice of a senior Dutch official who was visiting the Cape, Rijkloff van Goens.[136] He suggested that a series of small forts and watch houses be built along the canal and, desperate to deter the Peninsular Khoikhoi from stealing their livestock, both Van Riebeeck and Van Goens advocated capturing some of the indigenous people and holding them hostage at the forts. Their thinking was to lure them into Hout Bay area and to provide the detained Khoikhoi with grazing for their cattle, thereby enabling the Dutch to barter with them for cattle whenever they needed to. Their idea was rejected by higher authorities in Amsterdam, but not before work had already started on the canal. Perhaps fortunately for Van Riebeeck and Van Goens, heavy rains washed away the diggings.[137]

Van Riebeeck then instructed that watchtowers and small forts be erected on the borders of the peninsula. From these, the Dutch could watch over their small herds and they certainly discouraged the Khoikhoi's constant thievery of livestock. However, such measures could not prevent other types of theft. For instance, the Khoikhoi stole some buttons that they cut from several young children's clothes while they were playing outside the fort. They would steal whatever they could lay their hands on!

To increase productivity at the Cape, Van Riebeeck proposed that the Dutch East India Company allow 'free men' to settle at the Cape, irrespective of whether they were employees of the company. Moreover, he suggested that these new settlers be granted as much freehold land as they required to farm. They would then be mandated to sell a portion of their produce and meat to the company at fixed prices, which would then supply the ships calling at the Cape.

Van Riebeeck recognized that the best-suited candidates to become 'free farmers' were the soldiers, sailors or Dutch East India Company employees already at the Cape. He was eager to implement this plan and did not want to wait for new settlers. So, in 1657, Van Riebeeck released nine men from their contracts and allocated each a farm that was about 11.4 hectares, or 28 acres,[138] on the eastern side of Table Mountain in Liesbeek Valley.

Being a 'free burgher' certainly sounded like an attractive option to settlers, especially considering that each farmer would receive a loan from the Dutch East India Company to enable him to purchase seed and implements. However, they were obliged to sell much of their produce and meat to the company at fixed prices and were prohibited from trading with the Khoikhoi directly and with calling ships. They also faced arbitrary restrictions such as not being allowed to walk or ride across Dutch East India Company properties without permission from a company official.[139]

Harry and several other Khoikhoi chiefs complained to Van Riebeeck about the farming operations, which had resulted in them losing their land and being cut off from water sources.[140] However, the foundation for expansion had already been laid down and their unhappiness was ignored.

The Hereen XVII then granted Van Riebeeck permission to explore the interior in 1658. Parties from the small colony journeying into the interior soon met with previously unknown Khoikhoi groups such as the Guriqua and Namaqua and began to trade with them. Significantly, the Dutch were no longer totally reliant on the Peninsular Khoikhoi to supply meat.[141]

In the Cape, tension simmered between the Khoikhoi and the small contingent of Dutch who had started work on a fort that would eventually be known as the Castle. Seeing the Dutch strengthening the earthen ramparts and wooden walls of the existing structure alarmed the Khoikhoi, as it was becoming more and more apparent that the Dutch would be staying. They demonstrated their resentment in any way they could. For instance, when their cattle had finished grazing, they would burn the cow dung so that the Dutch could not collect it to use as manure back at the fort.

Around the same time, Van Riebeeck started to receive reports that the free burghers in Liesbeeck Valley were stealing cattle from the Khoikhoi. Then, some of the slaves that had been brought from Guinea fled to the interior and Van Riebeeck suspected that the Khoikhoi were hiding them. He promptly sent for

Harry and asked him to assist in getting the slaves back. Harry refused. Van Riebeeck then turned to Doman for help.

"Surely you know who is hiding the slaves and where they are," Van Riebeeck said to Doman, who replied coolly, "I know nothing."

Eva had watched this exchange and warned Van Riebeeck that Doman was not to be trusted. She told Van Riebeeck that he was secretly working against the Dutch. "He has even criticized me for helping you. He told me that he was a Khoikhoi and not a Dutchman and claimed that I ingratiate myself with you," she explained.[142]

Urged on by Eva and some of the free burghers, Van Riebeeck hit on the idea to take several Khoikhoi hostage. He ordered the soldiers to arrest several leaders from the Goringhaiqua tribe as he suspected they were harbouring the slaves. Schacher and Otegno, sons of Chief Gogosoa of the Goringhaiqua were abducted. When Gogosoa learned what the Dutch had done, he expressed his outrage, claiming his tribe was being victimized unfairly.[143] To even the score, the Dutch soldiers then arrested a few Gorachouqua men.

Soon after this, Harry was arrested. Doman, who no doubt saw the Strandlopers leader as his rival, informed Van Riebeeck that Harry had been defrauding the Dutch East India Company. Harry's niece, Eva, also confirmed Doman's accusation when Harry was brought before the Council of Policy,[144] which banished him to Robben Island. (The wily Harry managed to escape the island in 1659 in a leaky boat that he must have stolen from the Dutch. As an elderly Khoikhoi who had never rowed or sailed before, his successful crossing to the mainland was just short of miraculous. Once ashore, Harry had to put aside his ambitions of pastoral wealth as he had lost his leadership of the Strandlopers. He became a translator and spokesman for the Goringhaiqua and Gorachouqua, until he died in 1663.)

When leaders from the Goringhaiqua, Gorachouqua and Strandlopers were taken captive, the Khoikhoi resistance folded. To Van Riebeeck's delight, the slaves promptly returned to the Castle. Hostage-taking had proved to be an effective tactic to keep the Khoikhoi in line.

By this stage, Van Riebeeck realized that Doman was becoming something of a liability. He had been incensed when the Dutch took hostages and his subsequent hostility toward Van Riebeeck prompted the commander to write to higher authorities in Amsterdam: "We shall have some evil turn to look for at his hand; it were much to be desired that he had never been to Batavia ... because he has learned the perfect use of firearms, and we have enough to do to keep such out of his hands."[145]

Doman had also learned what a threat the Dutch were to the Khoikhoi culture and people while in Batavia.

The third interpreter, Eva, had become extremely powerful because of her position in the Van Riebeeck household and her ability to speak Dutch and Portuguese. However, it was her strong relationship with her own people that made her such a valuable source of information to Van Riebeeck.

Both the Khoikhoi and the Dutch saw her as trustworthy and her excellent diplomatic skills ensured she was an integral figure in initiating trade between the parties. One reason she seemed to be able to move seamlessly between the two groups was that she made an effort to respect the cultural norms of whichever party she was with. For instance, when with the Dutch she wore Dutch dresses and clothes, ate Dutch food and confided to those close to her that she had a "Dutch heart" and, most importantly, that she embraced Christianity.[146] When with the Khoikhoi, she wore the traditional animal skins and would ride an ox, which was considered a privilege and denoted a position of high station among the Khoikhoi.

Doman and Eva disliked each other intensely and constant sniping and sarcasm characterized their exchanges. "Look out! There comes the advocate of the Dutch; she will tell her people some stories and lies, and will finally betray them all," Doman taunted on one occasion.[147]

Doman turned out not to be the 'simple' man Van Riebeeck had initially thought him to be. He was underhanded and determined to bring about the downfall of the Dutch. When he left the fort to join the Khoikhoi, he managed to persuade the reluctant Chief Gogosoa of the Goringhaiqua as well as several young leaders from the Goringhaiqua, Gorachouqua and Ankaiso to form a coalition that would declare war on the Dutch. Doman advised the chiefs that the best time to attack would be in winter and ideally when it was raining, as rain would wet the Dutch cannon' match cords and prevent the gunpowder from igniting.

Eva heard of Doman's plan and immediately reported it to Van Riebeeck. However, the Dutch could do nothing but wait for the attack–and pray that God would be on their side. "Prayers were offered … for God's help and blessing in these perilous and distracted times … this wet weather is very favourable to them, as no one can keep his gun dry, which from Doman's instructions they know well, and therefore choose such opportunities," Van Riebeeck commented.[148]

Under Doman's command and the cover of darkness, the Khoikhoi attacked at the beginning of May 1659. They targeted the farmers' cattle and sheep. The colonists were already frustrated by the Khoikhoi's constant niggling and incensed by this attack. They pleaded with Van Riebeeck to allow them to retaliate. After meeting with the Council of Policy on 19 May 1659 and, with the support of one of the friendly Khoikhoi chiefs, Oedasoa, who no doubt wanted to strengthen his position with the Dutch, Van Riebeeck gave the order: "Punish Doman and his bandits–seize them and shoot them on sight!"[149]

The first Khoikhoi–Dutch war had begun.

The Khoikhoi attacks had escalated and the devastating speed with which hundreds of Khoikhoi swarmed onto farms frightened the Dutch free farmers. The Khoikhoi were difficult to shoot as they were extremely agile and knew the landscape very well. Even though the Khoikhoi had no guns, they were tactically efficient warriors: their nighttime raids often took place when it was raining, which resulted in the Dutch being unable to see them and clumsy and slow attempts to shoot or catch the lightning-quick Khoikhoi as they made off with cattle, burned crops and destroyed the humble dwellings of the free farmers. Many settlers fled to the protection of the fort with whatever possessions they could bundle together.[150]

Fortunately, very few lives were lost during the raids as Doman preferred to disrupt the lives of the colonists rather than to kill them and thereby incur their full anger and retribution.

Doman was a master strategist. He cultivated the settlers' fear of being attacked by successfully spreading rumours and misinformation among the Dutch. For instance, he ensured that Eva heard of an impending attack on the fort. "They will soon take all the cattle that are left with the free farmers and murder the men as well as their wives and children They are also going to attack the fort by climbing over the earth walls and once inside they are going to attack the people in their houses,"[151] Eva warned Van Riebeeck when she learned of the plan. She was terrified that the attack was imminent and worried about what would happen to her should she be captured by the raiding Khoikhoi. "Mynheer van Riebeeck, take good care. I am leaving the fort and shall not return for a long time, your land will now be fully at war,"[152] she told Van Riebeeck before leaving to join her tribe.

Van Riebeeck immediately ordered that the slaves be unshackled in readiness for the attack. They were given muskets and turnpikes to help defend the fort.[153] He then instructed his men to position the cannon and to move the remaining cattle into a central kraal that would be guarded.

The attack never happened. Doman was reluctant to attack the fort because he knew that his men would be easy to shoot in a frontal attack. However, he continued to instigate opportunistic raids. During one farm attack on 19 July

1659, Doman took a bullet in his shoulder that paralyzed his arm. One of the Khoikhoi prisoners captured in a skirmish explained the Khoikhoi's sentiments about the Dutch and why they were attacking the farms. "We saw you taking the best land and grazing, where our cattle used to graze ... You moved into our lands and started to build houses and farms, taking more and more of our land which has belonged to us for many, many years, before we can even remember. We decided to dishearten you, and hoped that you would leave us and go away. Doman also told us that if we attacked the fort, you, the Dutch, would leave the country," he elaborated.[154]

During the year that the Khoikhoi waged war on the Dutch, five farms were destroyed, two were partially damaged and over 100 cattle and sheep were taken. The biggest injury was to the pride of the Dutch, who had effectively been outsmarted and outmanoeuvred by the Khoikhoi.[155] The war finally ended in April 1660 when Doman and other Khoikhoi leaders met with Van Riebeeck at the fort. Van Riebeeck later reported that "They informed me that they were unhappy about us, every day taking more of their land, and asked me how I would feel, and whether it would have been permitted, if they had come to Holland and acted in the same way! I told them clearly that we won this land from them, justly, in a defensive war and that we intended keeping it."[156]

Once again, Eva demonstrated her diplomatic skills. She played a pivotal role in negotiating the agreement that Van Riebeeck made with the Khoikhoi, which permitted the Khoikhoi to graze their cattle on land unoccupied by the Dutch. Van Riebeeck demonstrated great generosity during the negotiations: he allowed Doman to keep most of the cattle and goods that the Khoikhoi had seized.

Shortly after this meeting had concluded, Van Riebeeck ordered that almond hedges be planted around the farm perimeters to prevent would-be cattle thievery. He also facilitated the delivery of horses from Batavia, which would greatly improve the mobility of the Dutch when chasing cattle raiders.

When Van Riebeeck's term ended in 1662, he and his family sailed to India, where Van Riebeeck took up his new post with the Dutch East India Company. Gerrit van Harn had been appointed as Van Riebeeck's successor. However, sickness had broken out on the *Wapen van Holland* carrying the new commander and many died, including Van Harn.[157] As such, Van Riebeeck had had to spend an extra year as commander of the colony.

Van Riebeeck had every reason to be pleased with himself: he had established trading relationships with new groups of Khoikhoi in the interior and the colony seemed to be secure. However, the settlers at the Cape comprised an unhappy society prone to violence, hate and corruption.

Many of the approximately 150 burghers living in the Cape in 1662[158] hated the Dutch East India Company and tried to flee the Cape, either stowing away on calling ships or deserting to the interior. Those who travelled inland were often eaten by wild animals or captured by the Khoikhoi, who brought them back to the Dutch East India Company for a reward. Similarly, the Khoikhoi were remunerated with brandy and tobacco for returning runaway slaves. This led the black slaves to hate the Khoikhoi, who hated them in equal measure because they stole their goods while on the run.

The whites fought one another in drunken brawls, stole from each other and threatened their superiors with violence whenever they disagreed with them. The colonists also cheated, deserted, lied to and schemed against their employer and although the Council of Policy and various governors imposed severe and brutal penalties for such behaviour, these had little to no effect on the settlers' conduct.

Offenders were either flogged, keelhauled, drawn and quartered, chained for months (and sometimes years), burned, staked though their hands or tongues, shot, drowned or hanged. A punishment was typically symbolic of the crime. For instance, four sheep thieves were sentenced to hard labour for between five and 15 years and were stripped naked. However, they were provided with sheepskins to cover their heads and shoulders.[159]

Not only did Van Riebeeck leave this unhappy society behind, he also left Eva. Having lived in the Van Riebeeck household for ten years, with only occasional visits to her own people, Eva must have been devastated. She had been abandoned by the family she had come to love and lost her high status in the settler community.

After Van Riebeeck left, Eva spent more and more time sharing her charms and bed with sailors from visiting ships and by November 1663, she had two illegitimate 'coloured children' fathered by Europeans.[160] It is possible that Eva, a highly intelligent woman with a loving nature and who was evidently sexually attractive,[161] had played a far greater role in Van Riebeeck's life than that of translator. Allowing 19 months for two terms of pregnancy would mean that Eva's first child was conceived before Van Riebeeck left on 7 May 1662.[162]

When Eva was 21, she met Danish surgeon and adventurer Pieter Van Meerhof. He was a leader in the colony and his proposal offered Eva safety and security. Soon after they married in 1664, Van Meerhof was transferred to Robben Island, where Eva began to drink heavily.[163]

He was then appointed to command an expedition to Madagascar, where he was killed, leaving Eva a widow with three children. Fortunately, the Dutch

East India Company allocated Eva a home in an old pottery workshop when she returned to the Cape.

Although Eva was sometimes included in social events, she soon lost favour with the settlers due to her alcoholism and prostitution. At a dinner in 1669 at the Castle, she got drunk and hurled abuse at the commander and other guests. The shocked commander summoned her to appear before him the following day and threatened her with banishment to Robben Island should her behaviour not improve.

Terrified by the prospect of being sent back to Robben Island, Eva grabbed her belongings and fled the colony, leaving her children behind, destitute and naked. She hid behind some sand dunes by the sea, where she met a group of Khoikhoi and sold her bedding to them for tobacco. The authorities found and arrested her shortly after this.[164]

The Council of Policy banished her to Robben Island, where she spent the remaining five years of her life. She was allowed to visit the mainland occasionally, but was never considered to have shown sufficient moral improvement to be allowed back permanently.[165] As one settler observed, "She returned to her own vomit and to the dogs. It took her death to extinguish the fires of her lust, showing quite clearly how, no matter what pretences she showed of civilization, she reverted to her natural instincts."[166] Eva died a lonely and sad death in 1674. She was 31 years old.

Meanwhile, the settlement was growing. By 1657, there were four taverns near the fort, vegetables were growing in the company gardens, burghers had set up small businesses as tailors, carpenters, bakers and the like and when the Dutch East India Company lessened the restrictions placed on the settlers, they started trading with calling ships.[167] Soon, many of the burghers depended on trade with ships anchoring at the Cape.

Of the ships that called at Table Bay each year, 25 belonged to the Dutch East India Company, 17 were English and six were French and they collectively brought over 5,000 visitors to the Cape.[168] In contrast, the combined total of all the Khoikhoi clans was estimated to be 50,000 people.[169]

As mentioned, Gerrit van Harn was appointed as Van Riebeeck's successor when Van Riebeeck was offered a new posting by the Dutch East India Company in India. Van Harn took ill on the journey out and died at sea. Van Riebeeck had to wait for Zacharius Wagenaar a full year before he was able to leave.[170]

By the time Zacharias Wagenaar became governor of the Cape in 1662, the refreshment station had evolved into a small colony with expanding frontiers.

The Cape was like an expanding balloon. The first war against the Khoikhoi had resulted in the Dutch taking occupation of the whole of the Cape Peninsula.[171] They also occupied Saldanha Bay in 1670 to pre-empt occupation by a hostile power, particularly by France, and established farms in the Hottentots Holland region in 1672. Moreover, many of the colony's imported slaves fled to the interior, as did soldiers and sailors from calling Dutch East India Company ships as well as free farmers who resented the stringent rules imposed on them and disliked paying taxes.[172] Most of these fugitives from the colony were desperate and violent. They attacked Khoikhoi villages, killing and plundering as they eked out a miserable existence.

As early as 1658, the problem of runaway slaves had been identified as a real source of danger. One of the officials had reported to Van Riebeeck, "The number of male and female slaves who are now fugitives amounts to twenty-eight and they are becoming a formidable group. Moreover, it is feared that they will gather at a certain place known to all the slaves, to which they all flee and there attempt to form a strong group, and because they are much bolder and braver than the Hottentots and will multiply in the course of time, the Hon. Company will have good cause to fear them more than the natives unless steps are taken in time."[173]

As predicted, the number of runaway slaves grew to such an extent that they banded together to roam the fringes of the colony, where they terrorized the Khoikhoi and anyone else they encountered.

Hunting expeditions also contributed to expanding the colony boundaries. Many of the emigrant farmers enjoyed hunting and their hunting expeditions contributed to the formation of a new society, that of the 'Trekboer'. These game hunts enabled the hunters to explore the interior and they met various Khoikhoi tribes, thereby expanding their opportunities to either buy or steal cattle. Gradually, they accumulated sufficient capital, in the form of stock, to start a cattle post.[174] Soon, each man wanted his own farm and by 1730, all land within 190 kilometres of the fort with water on it was occupied by these new farmers.

The Trekboers had been born.[175]

Tension between England and Holland was escalating. England had already attacked Dutch factories on the coast of Guinea and seized a number of Dutch ships in the Channel, although war had not been officially declared. As such, Commander Wagenaar thought it would be prudent to upscale the aging and crumbling clay fort that had been built some 12 years earlier. The Hereen XVII endorsed his desire to rebuild it with stone, as the stone fort would be able to sustain heavy gunfire and accommodate more soldiers. An engineer, Peter Dombaer, was then appointed to draw up the plans and oversee the work. He chose a construction site on the eastern side of the settlement as this position would best equip the settlers to defend the fort from any attack from the sea and inland. Faced with a shortage of labour, Wagenaar detained 300 Dutch East India Company soldiers from passing ships to assist with quarrying the stone required for the fort and hired wagons and oxen from farmers at a rate of six shillings and three pence per day.

On Saturday 2 June 1666, the cornerstones would be laid down. The colony celebrated this momentous occasion with a gala day that commenced with the rising sun. Wagons trundled into the peninsula carrying the farmers, their wives and children from places as far afield as Rondebosch and Wynberg. Sailors wearing their best 'blues' rowed ashore to join the festivities and officials and company servants dressed in their Sunday bests.[176]

The crowd applauded loudly as four giant slabs of hewn stone were lowered into the trench that would serve as the foundation of the thick walls of the fort. Three leading citizens and Wagenaar oversaw the operation.

When the applause died down, Wagenaar stepped forward, cleared his throat and delivered a speech that moved many to tears: "Our victories are extending further and further and all the black and yellow people are being suppressed. We are building a stone wall out of the earth that thundering cannon cannot destroy. Before, against our Hottentots [Khoikhoi], our walls were built of earth. Now we can boast of stone against other enemies. In this way, we frighten off the Europeans, as well as the Asians, the Americans and the wild Africans. In this way, holy Christendom is made known and finds a place in wild, heathen lands. We praise the almighty reign of God and say in unison: Augustus's empire, victorious Alexander and Caesar's great kingdom, none of these had the honour of laying a stone at the end of the earth!"[177]

Two of the commander's best oxen and six of his finest sheep were then slaughtered and 100 loaves of freshly baked bread were put onto the otherwise bare tables. The smell of roasting meat and plentiful beer flowing from eight casks of Cape ale ensured high spirits and united the people in a common cause.[178]

Sadly, Wagenaar was replaced after only four and a half years due to ill health. The new commander of the Cape, Cornelis van Qaelberg, was a tyrant who settlers described as being selfish, cruel toward his subordinates and fawning toward his superiors. He certainly did not endear himself with the settlers by making snobbish statements such as, "Prosperous subjects are insolent. Therefore keep them all poor. That way we will have fewer difficulties". He also earned the animosity of the free farmers when he prohibited them from trading for cattle with the Khoikhoi.

A few months after his appointment, Van Qaelberg made a colossal error in judgment that would see him removed as commander of the Cape. When a French fleet headed by Marquis de Montdevergue sailed into Table Bay, it fired a five-cannon-shot salute and Van Qaelberg ordered that his men return suit. He then visited de Montdevergue on the *St Jean* and offered to supply the French fleet with whatever they required. Considering that the French had ambitions of taking over trade with the East from the Dutch and were attempting to establish a French equivalent of the Dutch East India Company, de Montdevergue was surprised but delighted by Van Qaelberg's reception and accepted the offer speedily, lest Van Qaelberg changed his mind.

By the time the French set sail, Van Qaelberg had replenished their supplies and repaired all of the damage incurred by the ships in the wild storms they had passed through coming to the Cape. One would have thought these ships belonged to the Dutch East India Company going on Van Qaelberg's enthusiastic assistance of and expenditure on a foreign power that, unbeknown to Van Qaelberg, had designs on seizing control of the Cape. The naïve Van Qaelberg was unaware that Louis XIV of France had ordered his men to occupy Saldanha Bay and establish a residency there.

Having supplied the French ships with vast quantities of fresh produce, Van Qaelberg had to send three expeditions to the interior to trade with the Khoikhoi in order to replenish the Dutch East India Company's own meat requirements.[179]

Unsurprisingly, the Hereen XVII was most displeased to learn of Van Qaelberg's kindness (at the expense of the colony) toward the French, which was discovered a full year after the incident.[180] They immediately dispatched Jacob Borghorst to the Cape to replace Van Qaelberg.

Shortly after arriving and despite being in poor health, Borghorst marched into a meeting of the Council of Policy on the morning of Monday 18 June and proceeded to read the letter of dismissal for Van Qaelberg to the assembled group. Although shocked by the news, Van Qaelberg had no choice but to hand over command of the colony to Borghorst,[181] whose health steadily declined. He spent less than two years in office before being replaced by Pieter Hackius on 25 March 1670. However, much expansion occurred during Borghorst's tenure and the Hereen XVII began to see that the Cape could become a viable permanent settlement.

While Borghorst temporarily halted construction on the stone fort, it was nevertheless a symbol of permanency. Borghorst allowed hunting trips into the interior. These hunting trips allowed the farmers to explore more of the land. Under his command, the expansion of the settlers continued unabated and many new farms were established inland from the Cape. Borghorst also made land available to the burghers in the Hottentots Holland district.[182] More and more of the cattle farmers began pushing their way beyond the loose boundaries of the Cape. These Trekboers also began to move away from authority and control of the colony and showed signs of wanderlust, which would continue for centuries. As Borghorst commented resignedly, "The whole of Africa would not be sufficient to accommodate and satisfy the Trekboers."[183]

They moved where they wished and seldom erected permanent homes. Rather, they lived in their wagons near whichever water source they could find and then registered the land with the Dutch East India Company. Their farms were known as 'loan farms' and were typically about 6,000 acres, with the boundaries being determined by trotting a horse along the four cardinal points of the compass for half an hour in each direction.

Back at the colony, a French ship carrying Admiral de la Haye sailed into Table Bay in September 1670. While he asked for provisions and stores, the remaining six ships in the fleet anchored at Saldanha Bay, where the crew attacked and overpowered the handful of Dutch East India Company soldiers stationed there under the command of Sergeant Hieronymus Cruse. After overpowering them, they imprisoned the soldiers and tore down the company flag, replacing it with the French tricolour flag. Cruse could do nothing but protest bitterly against their actions because Hackius had no available soldiers to send to Saldanha Bay to assist them.

Fortunately for the settlers, Admiral de la Haye had made his point: that the French could occupy Saldanha Bay at any stage. He released the prisoners and commanded his fleet to depart Saldanha Bay, leaving the French flag erected.

This incident prompted the authorities to reinforce the garrison at the Cape with 300 men, who promptly reoccupied Saldanha Bay, lowered the French flag (and surely trampled on it) and then raised the Dutch East India flag. So ended the French annexation of the Cape.[184]

By August 1671, Hackius was bedridden and incapable of running the settlement. For the three months leading up to his death on 30 November 1671, he had to rely on his officers to maintain order in the colony.[185]

The Hereen XVII decided to increase their stronghold at the Cape due to mounting tension between the Dutch, French and English. Efforts to finish building the Castle were renewed, assisted by the delivery of bricks, tiles, wood as well as engineers from Holland.

After Hackius's death, the Council of Policy ran the Cape until Isbrand Goske was appointed to the new position of governor on 2 October 1672. His salary was 83 rix-dollars per month.

During the preceding ten years, 370 Dutch East India Company ships had put into Table Bay as well as 26 French, nine English and two Danish ships. No less than 81,000 souls were fed and refreshed, watered, bedded and had their spirits and bodies renewed in the Cape during this period.[186] By 1672, the Cape had a European population of 64 burghers, of which 39 were married. There were 65 children, 53 Dutch manservants and about 370 Dutch East India Company servants and soldiers. In total, there were no more than 600 settlers.[187]

When the Franco-Dutch War finally erupted on 31 July 1672, with England allied to France,[188] Governor Goske was extremely worried as to what the fallout would be for the Cape. He frantically tried to prepare the Cape for an attack by Holland's enemies by prioritizing work on the Castle. However, sea traffic had fallen off substantially due to the war in Europe and visiting labour had dropped. As such, Goske focused on repairing the crumbling clay fort that had been built 22 years earlier. If the Cape were to be attacked, Goske would send all the cattle away from the fort to ensure they did not fall into enemy hands. He also sent Sergeant Cruythof and 12 men to erect buildings in the Hottentots Holland district.[189]

Fortunately, the appointment of William of Orange as the supreme commander of Holland, *stadtholder* of Holland and Zeeland and captain and admiral-general of all the provinces in Holland signalled a turning point in the war.

In a dramatic ploy, William of Orange had all the French-occupied lowlands of Holland flooded. A patriotic and strong army of Dutchmen were also readied to evacuate and ship 200,000 Dutch citizens to islands in the East, where a new republic called Batavia would be established.

Then the balance of power changed: a combination of European powers, including Spanish and German troops, came to the aid of the Dutch.[190] After the Dutch had been joined by German and Spanish soldiers as well as thousands of Dutch civilians who took up arms, England was obliged to make peace in 1674.[191]

Since the arrival of the Dutch in the Cape, some of the major Khoikhoi clans had split and formed sub-groups. For instance, the Chainouqua had evolved into two clans under captains Klaas and Koopman, respectively. The Cape government recognized each of these men as legitimate leaders of their people and presented each with a staff with the Dutch East India Company monogram engraved on the brass head.

Klaas became a firm friend of the Dutch and cooperated fully by supplying them with cattle and other goods when needed or requested. This close friendship between the Dutch and Klaas served to alienate other Khoikhoi groups such as the largest group of Cochoquas headed by Chief Gonnema. Intensely jealous of the favouritism bestowed on Klaas by the Dutch, Gonnema ordered 40 of the Cochoqua to attack a Dutch hunting party in 1672. During this assault, the Cochoqua stole all of their cattle and wagons, but let the men escape with their lives.

Seven months later, Gonnema's people attacked and murdered eight burghers who had taken their slaves and two wagons on a hunting expedition. Shortly thereafter, Kees, one of the Cochoqua captains, ordered his men to attack the post at Saldanha, where they killed four Europeans.[192]

When Gonnema's Cochoqua murdered a second hippopotamus hunting party in 1673, a force of settlers set out to teach Gonnema and his people a lesson. A 72-man expedition led by Ensign Cruse set off to attack the Cochoqua.

When they arrived at Gonnema's kraal, they found that all of the Khoikhoi had fled only moments earlier, leaving the cooking fires still burning. They stormed into the huts to search for conclusive evidence that these people had murdered the burghers and found some of the burghers' clothes.[193] Incensed, they started tracking the Khoikhoi, who had to abandon their cattle to escape their pursuers. The settlers quickly rounded this booty up, unaware that they were being tracked by the stealthy Khoikhoi.

No sooner had the burghers halted their homeward march to rest than the Khoikhoi attacked them with silent fury, hurling assegais and shooting arrows at the weary men. While they hurried to organize themselves, one of the burghers was wounded and two horses fell dying as poisoned arrows thudded into their sides. The Dutch unleashed a volley of gunfire to drive the Khoikhoi back and capitalized on their retreat to make for home, minus at least ten of their party and with 800 head of cattle and 900 sheep in tow.[194]

This incident spurred other Khoikhoi tribes to ally with the Dutch against Gonnema to show that they were peaceful. These newfound Dutch supporters included the Little Namaqua and Little Guriqua tribes and the Peninsular Khoikhoi captains Kuiper and Schacher as well as Chainouqua captains Koopman and Klaas.[195]

Encouraged by the support shown by some of the Khoikhoi groups and determined to put an end to the fighting, Goske ordered that "Any Khoikhoi seen carrying an assegai is to be shot on sight, as is any Khoikhoi seen travelling at night". Thus started the second Khoikhoi-Dutch war, which was to continue for four years until 1677.

When Khoikhoi captains Klaas, Schacher and Kuiper brought Goske four of Gonnema's men who had attacked Cruse and his burghers five days earlier, a committee was hastily formed to judge the men. The makeshift court found the four unfortunates guilty of murder and sentenced them to death—at the hands of those who had captured them.

Delighted with this decision, the captains assembled their Goringhaiqua and Gorachouqua warriors in front of the fort, positioning the prostrate prisoners in front of them with their hands and feet tightly bound. The sentenced men watched, eyes wide with terror, as the warriors danced around them in a frenzy, stamping their feet and waving their clubbed sticks in the air. On and on the dance went and the burghers watched in amusement, which changed to shock when one of the warriors leaped forward without warning and smashed his stick down on one of the convicted men's heads, accompanied by a roar of delight from the frenzied dancers. One after the other the warriors leaped forward and each delivered a cruel blow to the prisoners until their bodies lay bleeding and battered and very dead. The bloodthirsty warriors then dragged what remained of the four battered unfortunates to the sea, into which they were thrown amid shouts of jubilation.

A scene of great revelry followed as the Khoikhoi warriors celebrated the occasion, enjoying the arrack (a spirit distilled from coconut or rice) and tobacco the governor distributed to reward them for their loyalty.[196]

The burghers continued to feel that the Dutch East India Company was exploiting them. So, in 1676, they presented a number of demands tabled in a petition to a visiting official, Nicolaas Verberg, who was returning to Holland from India. When Verberg presented these requests to the Hereen XVII, they were met with a mixed reaction.

The emigrant farmers had asked that ownership of cattle they had taken from Gonnema be vested to them. This request was granted. They also asked that they be allowed to sell wine, grain and fruit to anyone at the best possible price and not at a price set by the Dutch East India Company as well as requested the same trading rights as free men in Batavia. Finally, they appealed to the Hereen XVII to allocate those who had no land freehold farms in the Hottentots Holland district and to supply these people with cattle they could lease. It would be some time before these demands would be met, in one form or another.[197]

In subsequent years, the pattern of violence between certain Khoikhoi groups and the burghers continued, with murders, cattle robbery and fighting being perpetrated by both parties. The emigrant farmers had started the commando system as a means to retaliate against the Khoikhoi. In addition, guards were permanently placed in redoubts (small and enclosed defensive structures) to watch for potential Khoikhoi cattle thieves.

By 1679, the Franco–Dutch War had ended and Governor Bax was commanding the colony. It had grown to encompass 87 free men, 55 women, 117 children, 30 European manservants, 133 male slaves, 38 female slaves and 20 slave children.[198]

Several significant milestones characterize 1679 at the Cape: Governor Bax granted two burghers permission to graze their sheep along the Eerste River and gave two others land east of the Tygerberg Mountains.[199] In addition, the fort was finally completed. Its five points were then named after the titles of William of Orange: Buren, Nassau, Catzenellenbogen, Oranje and Leerdam.[200]

Sadly, Governor Bax caught a very bad cold in the winter of 1678 and died on 29 June 1678. It would be 16 months before his successor was sworn in and during this time, the Hereen XVII decided that the role of commander was more appropriate to the Cape context than that of governor.

CHAPTER 4

Reaching the land of the Xhosa

Simon van der Stel—establishment of law and order—exploring the interior—Stavenisse—land of the Xhosa—Rolihlahla

Nearly three decades had passed since the arrival of the first Dutch settlers and the Khoikhoi were reluctantly beginning to accept the inevitable: these foreigners would not be leaving the Cape. Consequently, some Khoikhoi moved into the interior, away from the Europeans and the lands upon which they were encroaching.

These first Khoikhoi 'trekkers' were members of the Gorachouqua and the Goringhaiqua tribes and the new band looked to a man called Kora for leadership. Chief Kora directed them east, until they finally settled on a high plateau above the Orange River. There, his people were joined by band after band of Khoikhoi refugees from the peninsula, until the Koraqua, or Korana, group grew to such an extent that it presented a real threat to any who crossed its path—and to the many whose paths it crossed deliberately.[201]

The *Vrije Zee* carrying the Cape's new commander, Simon van der Stel, and his four sons cast anchor in Table Bay on 12 October 1679.[202] As he stepped ashore, a sergeant ordered the militia to present arms, which they did, smartly smacking the butts of their rifles with a resounding crack. Several of the men then fired a volley of salute and the cannon was also discharged.

Disembarking two days before his fortieth birthday, Van der Stel immediately made a good impression on the citizens of the Cape. He was witty, intelligent, good-natured and polite and although a small man, he had a big personality that was complemented by a cheerful face, a twinkle in his eye and a wonderful knack for storytelling. In fact, his entertaining storytelling held his audiences spellbound and was enjoyed by many. He was an absolute gentleman and he loved the finer things in life, when he could afford them. He was also generous, the consummate host and patriotic to a fault. In addition, He treasured and admired all things Dutch.

His only known Achilles' heel was one shared by many others: he was greedy and wished to amass great personal wealth. Consequently, his arrival ushered in a new era of growth for the Cape and altered the character of the area.[203]

Upon arrival, Van Der Stel found a colony comprising 289 Europeans and 191 slaves. It consisted of settlements around the foot of Table Mountain that were clustered around the massive walls of the Castle. Within the Castle, there were residences for government officers, barracks for soldiers and storehouses for food and wine.[204]

Outposts had also been established at Saldanha Bay and Hottentots Holland, a cattle station existed at Tygerberg and the seven free burghers were farming on leasehold farms on the neck of the land. The East Coast had been explored as far as the present-day town of George and northward about 80 kilometres beyond the Elephant River.[205]

For the first few months of his stay, Van der Stel set about learning all he could about the colony and threw himself into ensuring its profitability and sustainability with great energy and determination. His initial activities focused on developing a beautiful area of the Cape, which he called Stellenbosch, into an agricultural hub. He oversaw the eight families that settled in the area to farm and was delighted with their progress. In the space of a few years, some 15 or 16 other farmers had moved into the area and were growing wheat so successfully that bread was being sold to burghers and visiting sailors.

Van der Stel recognized the value of the Chainouqua leader Klaas and allowed him to buy cattle and sheep from other Khoikhoi for the Dutch East India Company's use. Klaas earned a 20 per cent commission fee on the purchased livestock. Employing Klaas in this way proved to be a successful tactic that resulted in tremendous growth of the Dutch East India Company's stockholding.[206]

Van der Stel also saw to the enlargement and improvement of the gardens near the Castle, which are much admired to this day. Farther afield, he fostered relationships with the Khoikhoi, as he believed that there must be some form of mineral wealth in the interior.

This landscape of growth and relative peace was marred when a visiting company official from Holland, Rijkloff van Goens, exercised his senior rank to Van der Stel by taking control of the colony for seven months.

During this time, Van Goens granted Van der Stel's son, Adrian, special hunting and fishing privileges not enjoyed by other emigrant farmers. For instance, he was allowed to catch fish in False Bay without paying taxes on them and to shoot an unlimited amount of game and birdlife. Many burghers felt great bitterness and resentment toward the young Van der Stel due to the relaxing of the usually strict hunting protocols.

In April 1685, another official arrived from Holland with the authority to rectify anything that he found wrong at the Cape. Hendrik Adriaan van Rheede, the Lord of Mydrecht, remained for only three months but made many changes to the society at the colony during his tenure. For instance, Van Rheede granted the burghers permission to build a school. The first teacher appointed was Sybrand Mankadan, whose responsibilities as a teacher included visiting the sick and being district secretary. Van Rheede also established a 'petty' civil court that would hear minor civil matters in which the disputed amount was less than 70 rix-dollars.[207]

To augment the civil court, Van der Stel reconstituted the High Court of Justice and appointed a landdrost in Stellenbosch who would look after the Dutch East India Company's interests in that area and head up the Court of the Landdrost, which heard minor civil matters, imposed taxes and acted as a district council.[208]

During Van der Stel's term as commander, a policy was introduced that entitled male mixed-race slaves to freedom at the age of 25 and females at 22, provided the slave professed to be a Christian, had been christened and spoke Dutch. All mixed-race slave children were sent to school, where they were taught Christianity and Dutch, and all slave owners were obliged to christen mixed-race babies born to slaves.[209]

While marriage between black slaves and Europeans was prohibited, marriage between Europeans and mixed-descent slaves was permitted[210] and the Dutch East India Company strove to treat all slaves fairly.

All attempts to curtail relationships between the white burghers and the slaves and Hottentots were unsuccessful and the frequency of mixed relationships continued to grow due to the absence of female burghers. So much so that Van Rheede reported to the Hereen XVII in 1685 that he had been shocked to learn that a large number of the children, 32 boys and 26 girls, in the slave lodge had white fathers.

Like many officers of the Dutch East India Company, Van der Stel wasted no time in selecting a piece of land for himself when officers were finally permitted to own and farm land and sell their produce to the company for the same prices as those paid to emigrant farmers.

Van der Stel was determined to find out more about the interior of the country and as soon as Van Rheede sailed out of Table Bay, he organized the largest expedition yet mounted to explore the northern area of the interior. Van der Stel's party of explorers that departed on 25 August 1685 comprised 56 Europeans and 46 wagon drivers, several Khoikhoi translators and three slaves to attend to the explorers. The group was split between 15 wagons, which necessitated 120 oxen (plus 200 spare), and took five carts, 13 horses, eight mules, a small boat for river crossings as well as two small cannon that would be used to demonstrate their military prowess to any Khoikhoi they encountered.[211]

Van der Stel and his party returned on 26 January 1686, having travelled 483 kilometres north of the Castle to the Copper Mountains, where they found vast deposits of copper ore. During the journey, Van der Stel had met several tribal chiefs without incident and had improved his knowledge of the land and the people considerably. Although he believed his group had made a favourable impression with the Khoikhoi they encountered, the Namaqua almost certainly perceived the Europeans to be arrogant and patronizing. This view was reinforced when Van der Stel haughtily asserted the Dutch East India Company's sovereignty over them. Other tribes also experienced Van der Stel's imperialist attitude when, for example, he interfered in the affairs of one tribe by forcing them to appoint a chief of his choice. He had also forced chiefs on two occasions to punish Namaqua people who had offended him in some way.[212] Naturally, these actions left a bitter taste in the mouths of the Namaqua.

After leaving the Copper Mountains, the explorers travelled toward the sea and camped at the mouth of a great river known as Vigiti Magna, which was later named the Groot River and then the Orange River. For the remainder of their homeward journey, fresh water was scarce and the cattle became dehydrated and ill. They were constantly on the lookout for fresh water as well as bays that could make suitable harbours and ports. Fortunately, they suffered few losses.

Van der Stel knew that life in the Cape would be more tolerable for the burghers if they had Dutch wives and he persuaded the Hereen XVII to send 48 marriageable girls to the colony. Nevertheless, only a handful of orphaned girls were dropped off at the Cape, with three arriving in 1685 and seven or eight the following year. Within weeks, these girls were married off to the most prosperous burghers, some of whom were growing grapes in the Stellenbosch area.

The commander of the Cape had recognized winemaking as a business of the future and had imported various cuttings from different European sources. He also encouraged the farmers to experiment with growing crops such as rice, hops, olives and millet, which he sourced from Natal.

On a dull, overcast night on 16 February 1686, the Dutch East India Company's ship the *Stavenisse* ran aground 112 kilometres south of the Bay of Natal. Skipper Willem Knyf had miscalculated the ship's latitude.[213] When the lookout shouted "Land ahoy! Land ahoy!", he had been dismissed as foolish by the chief mate, who informed him that he was seeing a mist belt, not land. Believing that he was far from land, Knyf ignored his lookout's warning and returned to his charts.

Minutes later, the terrified lookout could see the white foam of the breakers and shouted, "Land on the port bow!" The crew responded rapidly, lowering the two bow anchors into a sea that was surprisingly calm. All eyes strained to make out the danger ahead on this very dark night which magnified the sounds of the bow anchors cables as they snapped, and the grinding of the ship on the rocks and breaking up of the hull.[214] Water then cascaded through the hole in the ship's side and the crew scrambled off the ship. Eleven men drowned in the surf and 60 made it to shore. The wet and cold men huddled together for warmth on the beach and as the sun peeped over the horizon, they saw that one side of the wreck had disappeared, as had the masts. Their cargo of pepper from the East had spilled from the ship and looked like scum on the sea's surface.

The crewmembers salvaged the sails that had been washed up on the beach and stretched them over a frame to make a rough shelter. During the next few days, they scrambled aboard the ship to retrieve compasses, charts, altitude-measuring instruments, some casks of pork and biscuits and some clothing.

The 60 survivors held a meeting three days after the ship had run aground. There, they decided that the 57 men capable of walking would set out overland to the Cape. The three severely injured officers were to be left behind in the makeshift tent. However, two days after the group left, the skipper and nine others who had found the country too rough to continue rejoined them.

For the next ten days, those who remained behind repaired a rowing boat that had been washed up off the *Stavenisse*. They intended to sail to the Cape with all the goods they could carry. However, as they manhandled the small boat through the surf, trying to keep the bow pointed seawards, a large wave tipped the boat over and tumbled everything into the sea. Everything was lost and they were lucky to escape with their lives.[215]

The bedraggled, wet and disappointed men staggered onto the beach, where another surprise awaited them. They were surrounded by as many as 1,000 tall black warriors carrying assegais and shields and wearing skins with hide wrist and ankle bracelets and cattails. These were not the Khoikhoi or Khoisan, but the Bantu.[216]

It was soon apparent that they meant the shipwrecked men no harm. They indicated that they wanted to trade bread and millet for nails and bolts from the shipwreck. However, as soon as the Bantu realized where the Europeans' currency for barter came from, they ceased bartering for iron and instead hacked and burned the wreck to gain access to it. There was little the survivors could do other than watch their ship being further destroyed.

Depressed, hungry and forlorn, the crew could not believe their eyes when two Englishmen arrived at their camp a few days later. These strangers informed them that they had also been shipwrecked off the Bay of Natal about eight months earlier, from a vessel that was ironically named the *Good Hope*. They had been living with the black people in an area near where they had been wrecked and had learned to speak their language. Most significantly, they had plenty of beads and copper rings to trade and were willing to help the Dutchmen. "We have enough merchandise to buy bread and meat from the black people for all of you and the five of us, for fifty years," one of the Englishmen boasted.[217]

The three injured officers from the *Stavenisse* stayed behind with one of the Englishmen while the rest of the Dutchmen followed the other Englishman toward the Bay of Natal, where they would join up with the other English shipwreck survivors. Shortly after the group left, one of the injured men died. By then, the other two had recovered sufficiently to make the journey to reunite with their countrymen. When the latecomers arrived at the camp, they learned that one of the Dutchmen had been attacked and trampled by an elephant. So, the party now comprised ten Dutchmen and five Englishmen.

After four months of idleness, they decided to build a boat from the remains of the *Good Hope*, which was marooned on the rocks nearby. Timber from the *Good Hope* was plentiful and easy to gather, but they had to employ several Bantu to porter iron from the wreck of the *Stavenisse*.[218]

Just before they finished building their boat, the 20-ton *Bona Ventura* was wrecked in St Lucia Bay on Christmas Day. The sole survivors, eight men and a boy started walking to the Cape and were delighted to join the party already at the Bay of Natal.[219]

The 15-metre-long and four-metre-wide ship was ready one year and one day after the *Stavenisse* had run aground. The men named her *Centaurus* and, once they had stocked her with food and water, the group of 19 men set sail on 17 February 1687. At the last moment, five of the men found it too difficult to swap the nubile bodies of the Bantu for the dangers of the sea and so remained behind.[220]

The *Centaurus* arrived safely in Table Bay eleven days later. To the men's surprise, no word had been heard of the 48 survivors from the *Stavenisse* who had set off to walk to the Cape.[221] Greatly troubled by this, they decided to refurbish the *Centaurus*, which would be sent to search for the survivors nine months later.

Two months into the voyage, the crew of the *Centaurus* spotted people off Cove Rock (East London) waving to them. Naturally, they assumed these were Khoikhoi and sailed on. However, the captain had time to think the matter over that night and he ordered the boat to return to Cove Rock.

On nearing their destination, they saw a raft in the water with three naked white men on it. They immediately took the three survivors from the *Stavenisse* onboard, where they learned that there were 18 more men on the shore as well as a young French boy, Guillaume Chenut, from another wrecked ship. For some reason, he had been spared when the Bantu murdered his shipmates. Since the massacre, he had been living among the Bantu people known as the Xhosa under the protection of one of their chiefs, Sotopa.[222]

When the crew from the *Centaurus* went to fetch the others, it was discovered that three of the survivors were missing, presumably having chosen to live among the Xhosa rather than go to the Cape.

Van der Stel stepped in to assist with finding the 30 *Stavenisse* survivors still unaccounted for. He sent a galiot, a single-masted ship, the *Noord,* on 19 October 1688 to search the coast for them but without much hope of success, as it had been two and a half years since the *Stavenisse* had been wrecked.

Nearly three weeks into the voyage, the ship anchored off the Bluff of Natal, where, against all odds, two white men were seen waving frantically from the beach. A boat was promptly sent ashore to pick up the overwhelmed and grateful men.

A few days later, an old man was spotted near the mouth of the Buffalo River. Despite the rough surf, he braved swimming out to the *Noord* and climbed aboard.

At this stage, it was decided that there was little point in continuing the search for other survivors. Thus, the *Noord* set sail for home, with the skipper noting all possible bays and inlets that could be used in future. On 6 February 1688, the *Noord* arrived in the Cape, where the survivors explained what had happened to the 48 men who had set off overland.

On the journey overland, they had encountered friendly Bantu who assisted them by giving them food and shelter after they had been attacked by Bushmen (San). These San had murdered one of the party, stripped the survivors naked and then stolen everything they had. In this state, they finally reached the land of the Xhosa, having lost four of their party. Two men drowned attempting to cross a flooded river and two more had to be left behind, too exhausted to continue.[223]

The Xhosa took them in and warned them not to continue with their journey, explaining that any Bushmen they met would murder them. However, 12 of the bravest, or stupidest, men ignored the warning and set off. They were never heard of again.

The information on the Xhosa culture, traditions and language brought back by the survivors was extremely valuable to Van der Stel and the Hereen XVII. They enthusiastically described the land of the Xhosa as a beautiful countryside full of cattle, with rolling hills and valleys covered in lush grass and plentiful streams and rivers that eventually emptied into the Indian Ocean after cutting across the golden beaches. They also described how hospitable and friendly the Xhosa were—every village or kraal had a place set aside for entertaining visitors—although cautioned that they were also thieves and liars.[224] The survivors joked that it was best to arrive naked unless one wanted the metal on one's person and the clothes on one's back to be stolen.

The survivors told Van der Stel that there would be no point in making slaves of the Xhosa, because their strong family ties would ensure that they fled the colony to return home.

It is uncertain where the Xhosa originated from but they most certainly were a branch of the Bantu people that migrated down Africa from the third century onwards and which eventually formed four distinct streams: the Venda, the Sotho–Tswana, the Tsonga and the Nguni people.[225]

The Xhosa appear to be a cross between nomadic herders and settled farmers. While some scholars believe they descend from the Hamites that occupied the western seaboard of the Red Sea and from the Negroid race,[226] others argue that their language is similar to that of Malayan and Polynesian people. Still others highlight the similarity between the Jewish religion and that of the Xhosa people and connect the Arabs from the East Coast of Africa with the East Coast Bantu.[227]

The Xhosa (and Zulu) are part of the Nguni group that was found south of the Zambezi River by the 14th century and possibly much earlier. When they got to the Kalahari Desert, they skirted to the west, driving the Khoikhoi toward the coast and eventually, broke up into subgroups or clans, some of which moved southeast in search of better grazing before settling north of the Vaal River. The Nguni then drifted down into the coastal strip between the Drakensberg and the sea, where they encountered the San.[228]

Three of these Nguni groups, the Mtetwa, the Lala and the Debe remained in the area that is today known as KwaZulu-Natal while the Tonga moved north and the Xhosa and Ntungwa clans moved south. The Xhosa moved furthest south, stopping when they reached the Great Fish River in the 17th or 18th century, where they found excellent grazing.[229]

Each of these Nguni groups consisted of clans that were made up of five to 50 or more families descended from a common ancestor. In KwaZulu-Natal, there were approximately 800 clans, all of which were ruled by hereditary chieftains. Lesser chieftains ruled over just a few hundred people whereas more powerful chieftains ruled over thousands and many clans.[230]

All Xhosa claim a bond through Chief Xhosa, who lived prior to 1535.[231] While each branch of the Xhosa tribe was and is totally independent, with its own ruling structure, it is unified through Chief Xhosa. As the Xhosa are polygamists, Chief Xhosa took a number of wives and had many sons. Presumably, his firstborn son succeeded him as ruler, took wives and had sons of his own. Within a few generations, Chief Xhosa had thousands of descendents and as each family grew, new clans were formed. These clans constituted the Xhosa tribe.[232]

The core tribe also adopted outside clans of separate origin during times of war, drought or other natural disasters, as these forced other tribes to move into the lands of the Xhosa.

Intermarriage with the Xhosa resulted in the outsider being declared Xhosa by blood, but he or she would retain his or her original clan and tribal name. There are eleven clans of pure Xhosa stock: the Cira, Jwara, Tshawe, Kwemnta, Qwambi, Kwayi, Dange, Ntinde, Hleke, Gwali and the Mbalu.

After 1720, two of the sons of the great chief Phalo, Gcaleka and Rarabe, split the tribe into two sections, adding four tribes under Gcaleka, which were known by his name. Ten tribes were added under Rarabe, initially known as the Ama-Rarabe but later as the Ama-Ngqika, named after Rarabe's grandson.[233]

In one of the first descriptions of the Xhosa men, a Portuguese castaway noted that "The men of this country are very lean and upright, tall of stature and handsome". The men were, and are, well proportioned, have superb posture, large eyes, sparkling white teeth, high cheekbones, an aquiline nose and dark, tightly curled hair.

Men wore nothing more than a sheath covering the penis. In cold weather, or on special occasions, a man would wear a cloak of animal skin that had been softened by being beaten with a club. He would then accessorize with copper armbands, ivory bangles and a necklace made from animal teeth. In contrast, the women usually wore a skirt made of skin and sometimes sported an apron bound around the upper body to cover her breasts. It was common practice to leave one's breasts exposed though.[234] Both the men and women had skin that glowed with health due to their practice of rubbing their bodies with red ochre mixed with grease and herbs.

Every adult male was a warrior and when the Xhosa went to war with other tribes, its warriors each carried fighting sticks, or *ibunguza*, that were usually made from olive wood, were over a metre long and ended in a knob or burl that was just smaller than a man's clenched fist; ten or more assegais; short, broad-bladed stabbing spears for close combat as well as throwing spears over two metres long and with narrow, double-edged blades. A warrior complemented these weapons with a tough, ox-hide shield that was nearly two metres long.[235]

The Xhosa exercised a strict code of conduct during war. For instance, if victorious, they would return some of the captured cattle to the vanquished party, as they considered it immoral to cause people to starve, and would release captives without demanding a ransom. In addition, they ensured that women and children were never deliberately hurt or killed in battle.[236]

They lived in scattered homesteads consisting of beehive-shaped huts arranged in a semi-circle and that were made from thatch woven into a framework. The interior of the huts was smoky and dim and were cool in summer and warm in winter. In the colder months, a wood fire smouldered constantly in each hut, warming the floor, which had been smeared with dried cow dung. Dry wood was piled against the inner wall, ready to be hauled onto the fire when it burned down.

Each kraal boasted a cattle pen, in keeping with the Xhosa idea that wealth and status were reflected by the number of cattle one owned. Three forces ruled the Xhosa: their ancestral spirits, loyalty and tradition.

Their loyalty to the family, the clan, the tribe and to the Bantu nation[237] stems from the *ubuntu* philosophy that is part of their everyday lives. Archbishop Emeritus Desmond Tutu not only practised *ubuntu* but also defined it in 1990 when he said, "A person is only a person through other people. It is about the essence of being human, it is part of the gift that Africa will give to the world. It embraces hospitality, caring about others, being able to go the extra mile for the sake of others. We believe that a person is a person through another person, that my humanity is caught up, bound up, inextricably, with yours. When I dehumanize you, I inexorably dehumanize myself."[238]

The Xhosa have proudly preserved their traditions for hundreds upon hundreds of years and many customs are still practised today, such as that described in the following story that took place in 1934.

Rolihlahla Mphakanyiswa was the son of a Xhosa sub-chief. His father's high status meant that his family owned more cattle than others living in the small village of Mvusu in the Transkei did.

By the age of five, Rolihlahla was entrusted with caring for his father's cattle as they grazed in the nearby rolling hills and knew how to find edible berries. He could milk a cow, catch fish using a piece of string and a bent piece of metal as a hook and could shoot a flying bird out of the sky with his catapult.

Tall for his age, he had great skill with stick fighting and would arm himself with two sticks, using one to defend himself from blows and the other to attack his opponent. He usually acquitted himself very well against boys twice his age. When Rolihlahla was six years old, his father was summoned to a meeting by the local white magistrate. At this meeting, the magistrate removed his powers as sub-chief due to insubordination because he had ignored a summons to another meeting. When Rolihlahla's father lost his standing in Mnezo, the family became impoverished and was forced to move to the village of Qunu. A year after arriving in Qunu, one of the new neighbours approached Rolihlaha's father and advised him to send his bright son to school.

Rolihlahla convinced his father that he could walk the many kilometres to the mission school. However, there was no money to buy Rolihlahla clothes. So, his father cut a pair of his long trousers just above the knee to make a pair of long pants for the seven-year-old. As Rolihlahla later remembered, "I tied them around my waist with a blue cord and they hung on me like a sack of mealies, but never in my life had I been prouder of a pair of trousers than that pair my father made for me."

Rolihlahla's father died a year after his son started school and Jongintaba Dalindyebo, acting chief of the Thembu people, took him in. Dalindyebo saw that Rolihlahla had a strong character and hoped that the boy would be a positive influence on his own son, Justice, who was being groomed for the position of chief.

As custom dictated, Rolihlahla and Justice were set to participate in a ritual of manhood, *abaquetha*, when they were sixteen. During this three-month process, boys would be isolated from the tribe, taught the traditions of their people and, ultimately, become men after completing the initiation or circumcision ceremony. Up until this point, Xhosa tradition considered these boys to have no standing in the community. In contrast, young girls were valued as they would be able to earn *lobola* for their families when they reached a marriageable age. The bride dowry would be based on the attributes of the bride-to-be and parents therefore sought to develop their daughters' skills and talents so they could demand more cattle from the suitor's family.

Rolihlahla and Justice joined 22 other boys of similar age one Friday night to start their initiation process, which commenced with the group dancing naked with the girls from their village. The following morning, their initiation leaders took them to the river, where they washed them symbolically, once over their fronts and once over their backs. They then shaved their heads, painted their faces with white ochre (which the boys would not be permitted to wash off for the full three months) and gave them a knotted ox tail to wear as a necklace as well as a white blanket to wrap around themselves and a fighting stick.

For the next three months, they would have no contact with their families and friends back in the village while they learned the customs and traditions of the

Xhosa nation. Finally, the time for the circumcision ceremony had arrived. The group was instructed to sit next to the river huddled under their blankets. The *incibi*, the man who had been appointed by the tribe to carry out the circumcision ceremony, would arrive soon.

As Rolihlahla later recalled, "My heart was pounding with fear. I knew that I was about to experience pain and I was scared that I would show my fear or pain. It is acceptable for a young boy to show fear or pain, but not a man. I was about to become a man."

As the boys waited, they calmed themselves by looking at their surroundings. As usual, the rolling green hills of the Transkei were dotted with small mud huts with thatched roofs and smoke curling lazily from the fires inside them. They listened to birds chattering in the trees lining the river and to cows lowing and sheep bleating from the distant hills. They then heard the sound they had all been dreading: the approaching footsteps of the *incibi*.

The *incibi* entered into the spirit of the occasion and, carrying a fighting stick in his hand and waving an assegai, he shouted in mock anger, "*Zipi ezi zhinja? Zipi ezi zintoamande-yezi amadoda?*" (Where are these dogs? Where are these things that I must turn into men?)

The shouts wafted down to the waiting boys on the early morning breeze and Rolihlahla's heart hammered against his chest bone as he thought of what lay ahead. The shrieks of the boys who were being circumcised pierced the quiet of the morning. Then Rolihlahla heard Justice yell. It would be his turn soon. Finally, the *incibi* knelt in front of Rolihlahla and looked him in the eyes, his face only a few centimetres away from that of the terrified teen. Sweat rolled down the *incibi*'s face in spite of the cold weather. Rolihlahla was also sweating—from terror.

The *incibi* pulled Rolihlahla's foreskin forward and swiftly brought down the blade. The searing pain Rolihlahla felt made him momentarily forget what he was meant to do. However, he recovered quickly and shouted, "*Ndiyindoda*!" (I am a man!) It was done. It was over. Rolihlahla was given the tribal name of Dalibhunga to mark the day that he became a man. He was also given the clan name of Madiba.

In time, he would become the most prominent Xhosa in history and would be known by the Christian name his teacher at the little mission school had given him when she could not pronounce or spell Rolihlahla. She had arbitrarily decided to call him Nelson, after the British naval officer Admiral Nelson Horatio.

Rolihlahla would become known as Nelson Mandela.

CHAPTER 5

The birth of the Trekboers

French Huguenots—Khoikhoi wars—Klaas—Willem van der Stel—trade restrictions lifted—Trekboers—clash of the Xhosa and Trekboers—corruption and privilige—Adam Tas—rebellion—smallpox—commando system—660 men drown in Table Bay—death of Noordt—Chief Phalo—Barbier's execution—loan farms—Tulbagh—Meermin—Van Plettenberg

Around the same time that the Dutch survivors from the *Stavenisse* met the Xhosa for the first time, French Protestants were fleeing to Holland to escape religious persecution. When the refugees flooded into Holland between 1685 and 1687, the Hereen XVII recognized that this was a golden opportunity to entice new settlers to sail to the Cape. They promptly dispatched eight young women from an orphanage in Rotterdam as well as a group of French Huguenots.

The first of five ships carrying the Huguenots, the *Voorschoten*, arrived in April 1688, after a four-month voyage. The others followed over the next year. One of the ships, the *China*, took seven months to arrive and all of its crew and passengers were ill. Overall, twelve of the Huguenots died on the journey.

When the *Zuid Beveland* arrived carrying more Huguenots and a Protestant pastor, a small crowd of the Huguenots and burghers gathered on the wooden jetty to welcome them. A little boat left the anchored ship to carry people ashore and capsized when a squall came up suddenly. To the horror of those watching, three officers and five of the crew drowned.[239]

These French settlers were assisted by donations from the burghers. The Hereen XVII also supplied them with 12 wagons and transported them to their allotted farms in the Stellenbosch, Franschoek and Drakenstein areas.

A further 40 Huguenots arrived in January 1689 on the *Wapen van Alkmaar* and in May 1689 on the *Zion*. By this stage, 176 Huguenots had arrived in the Cape, including many widows, widowers with children and families.[240] In subsequent years, the Huguenots continued to arrive in groups of two or three families at a time.

The emigrant farmers had welcomed the Huguenots, even providing them with material aid. In this context, it was not surprising that Van der Stel was horrified when a delegation of Huguenots approached him in 1689 to request permission to build their own church and thereby break away from the Dutch

Reformed Church in Stellenbosch. This challenged Van der Stel's ambition of building a Little Holland in the colony. As such, he was furious and accused the delegates of being ungrateful. "You shall have nothing of the kind," Van der Stel shouted. "This is rank sedition. We have treated you better than we do our own Hollanders. First it will be a church, then your own magistrate and then your own prince. You are the most impertinent and ungrateful people on the face of the earth. After all we have done for you, this is the way you turn on us?"[241]

This exchange caused bad blood between the Huguenots and Van der Stel and his burghers. Some Huguenots even declared at an open meeting that they would not marry the Dutch, meaning that they would not marry at all. Similarly, some burghers refused to speak to the French and one burgher was overheard saying, "I would rather share my bread with a Hottentot or a dog rather than a Frenchman."

The Huguenots sent a request for their own church to the Hereen XVII, which resolved in 1690 to permit the Huguenots to build their own church at Drakenstein. The Hereen XVII simultaneously instructed Van der Stel to encourage the Huguenots to mix with the Dutch to speed up the integration of the two groups. As a result, in the course of two generations of intermarrying, the two groups became one.

The new Huguenot church opened its doors in December 1692.

The Huguenot settlers were joined by a few German and Dutch settlers, who dribbled into the little settlement in the following years. As more settlers arrived, more land was granted to them, namely that of the Hottentots, the Goringhaiqua and Cochoqua. In the few years since the new settlers had arrived, these Hottentots had become poorer. Apart from losing the land they considered theirs, they had developed a fondness for brandy and tobacco and were happy to trade cattle for these two highly valued items. Some of the less scrupulous settlers exploited their penchant for drinking and smoking, despite the penalties they faced from the Dutch East India Company for trading with the Hottentots.

Constant fighting with neighbouring tribes as well as the loss of the cattle to Bushmen robbers contributed to the lack of cattle owned by the Hottentots. The Bushmen had been driven off the land they occupied into the Drakenstein Mountains, but frequently raided the cattle of the burghers and the Hottentots. They were regarded as bandits and outlaws and, being fleet of foot and as wary as timid buck, they were seldom caught.

In March 1689, the Namaqua and the Grigriqua crossed the Elephant River en masse and attacked the Cochoqua near Saldanha Bay. The Dutch frequently had to intervene, using force to restore order between the warring tribes of

Hottentots. The Hottentots had also bowed to the inevitable: acceptance of Dutch rule. Van der Stel and his committee always settled any dispute. Moreover, new chiefs were always given a *palangbanger*, a staff with a copper head with the VOC symbol engraved upon it.[242]

The two Hottentot captains of the Chainouqua, Klaas and Koopman, were constantly vying for Van der Stel's favour. Van der Stel preferred Klaas and therefore always sided with him against Koopman. Klaas acted as an agent for the burghers and set about to amass his cattle. However, this necessitated a great deal of travel. Klaas gradually tired of the travelling, which forced the burghers to journey into the interior to trade. Once the burghers had familiarized themselves with the interior, Klaas recognized that they would soon realize he was dispensable. Despite his newfound reluctance to travel and to act as an agent for the burghers, Klaas resented the burghers carrying on trade without him. Matters finally reached a head when Klaas verbally abused Sergeant Izaak Schryver, who had led a bartering party to the interior.

Koopman recognized that Klaas had blotted his copybook and that the time was right for him to improve his standing with Van der Stel. He approached the commander of the Cape and accused Klaas of being involved in illicit trade directly with the burghers. Klaas instantly fell from grace and Van der Stel sided with Klaas's rival, which meant Koopman was now Van der Stel's favourite Chainouqua.

Klaas had married the daughter of Goukou, chief of the Hessequa, and in 1693, Koopman called on Van der Stel for assistance as he had heard that Klaas and the Hessequa were going to attack the Chainouqua. Aided by a burgher captain, Willem Padt, Koopman and some of his Chainouqua followers attacked Klaas and took him prisoner. He was then sent to Robben Island. Public sympathy for Klaas was high, as he had dealt with and, in many cases, assisted many burghers over the years. As such, Van der Stel released him.

He returned to the mainland to find that Koopman had not only seized his cattle and possessions, but his wife as well. When Van der Stel called on the wife to choose between Koopman and Klaas, she chose Koopman. The bitter Klaas immediately resumed bickering with Koopman and things exploded when his wife decided to leave Koopman to return to him. Determined to prevent his rival from taking his prize possession, Koopman killed her. An enraged Klaas then attacked Koopman with the help of the Hessequa and took his cattle. Unfortunately, he also took cattle belonging to the Dutch East India Company that Koopman had been looking after.

When asked to return the cattle, Klaas was unable to do so as he and the

Hessequa had killed and eaten them. Klaas once again became public enemy number one. He would remain so until he was killed in a skirmish with Koopman and his followers in June 1702.

Hostilities broke out between France and Holland on 26 November 1687. However, this news only reached the Cape the following year. In April 1689, a French ship, the *Normande*, put into Table Bay carrying valuable cargo. De Courcelles, her captain, was unaware of events taking place in Europe and had no idea of the hostile reception his crew would receive. When de Courcelles sent a small boat ashore to greet the Dutch authorities, his men were taken prisoner. The Dutch then commandeered the French men's clothes and rowed toward the *Normande* flying the French flag. Seeing the men returning, de Courcelles assumed that all had gone well and instructed his crew to fire a salute. Thereafter, Dutch sailors from ships in the harbour boarded the *Normande* and attacked his men. They quickly wounded eight French soldiers and de Courcelles surrendered in order to avoid more bloodshed.

Van der Stel and the five Dutch ships in the bay then used the *Normande* as a decoy and enticed a second French ship, the *Coche*, to come closer. The Dutch warship, the *Nederland*, fired at her from less than a ship's length away and her captain had no choice but to surrender. The Dutch seamen plundered the cargo of the two ships, which was valued at over £50,000. The captured *Normande* and *Coche* were later renamed *Goede Hoop* and *Afrika*, respectively.

By 1691, there were about a thousand permanent white settlers and 50 Asians, who enjoyed the same privileges as the white settlers but were considered socially inferior to them. The colonists owned 285 male slaves and 44 slave children. The growing band of runaway slaves that lived in the mountains, sometimes among the Bushmen, continued to rob and attack the burghers and the Hottentots.

Despite these difficulties, the stockholding of the burghers had increased dramatically and now included 261 horses, 4,198 head of horned cattle, a massive flock of 48,700 sheep and 220 goats. The burghers were also exporting wheat to Europe and barley, rye and grapes were being grown in large quantities. Vegetables flourished in private gardens as well as in those of the Dutch East India Company.

Each burgher was contributing taxes of about 45 shillings per annum to the economy of the Cape, the law was enforced through courts in De Kaap and Stellenbosch and the Lord was devoutly worshipped in churches in De Kaap, Stellenbosch and Drakenstein.

In the small settlement known as De Kaap, licenses to own the rights to sell wine, spirits, bread and meat as well as other items were auctioned annually. The highest bidders had the rights to sell to the settlers and the crews and passengers of the approximately 44 ships that were calling at the Cape each year.[243]

Since the 1650s, ships had been fitted with more modern and larger sails. This ensured that voyages from Holland to the Cape were quicker. However, they were not any easier. Scurvy and sickness among the crews and passengers still killed many of those that left Europe with the hope of a better life in the Cape. Moreover, conditions onboard the ships were so bad that vessels frequently arrived with insufficient crew left alive to sail the ship into Table Bay. For instance, the *Schoondyke* arrived at the Cape in 1693 with every one of the 120 voyagers sick. She had left Holland with a crew of 254 and 134 had died on the journey.

The mortality rate aboard ships travelling to the Cape did not improve with time. In 1695, a fleet of eleven ships arrived at the Cape with 678 men so ill that they were unable to walk and several died while being transported to the hospital. The death count during the trip was 228. Sometimes ships arrived with as few as four men still able to work onboard, out of a crew of 150.[244]

Van der Stel had been promoted to governor on 1 June 1691 and his successors would also enjoy this title. His son, Willem Adriaan van der Stel, arrived from Holland on 23 January 1699 and became governor of the Cape shortly after arriving.

With Willem ruling over the Cape, his father was able to spend his remaining 13 years living on the land he had been granted by the Dutch East India Company and he became wealthier through his wine and lucrative government and monopolistic contracts in the fishing industry that he managed to secure because of his contacts.

Life for the settlers, the Bushmen and the Hottentots was not easy at the turn of the century. The settlers faced the constant threat of losing their cattle to raiding Khoikhoi as well as other hardships, including restrictions imposed by the Dutch East India Company as well as occasional droughts and floods. Nevertheless, the colony continued to flourish and its expansion resulted in the Khoikhoi being pushed off their grazing lands. The Bushmen had already been displaced and had sought refuge in the mountains and isolated areas.

In February 1700, Willem Van der Stel removed the restrictions limiting trade between the Hottentots and the burghers. This opened up new avenues for the burghers and spawned a new breed of burgher. They now could trade cattle directly with the Hottentots and, consequently, cattle farming became an attractive and popular occupation.

More and more of the burghers changed from crop farming to cattle farming.

When grazing was poor, it was a simple matter for a burgher to move onto the next piece of unoccupied land, thereby displacing the Bushmen and Hottentots, who were forced farther and farther away from De Kaap. A new type of settler was being moulded: the Trekboer.

Hardy, tough, ambitious and independent, the Trekboer was typically someone who loved the outdoors, paid little respect to the authorities, rules and restrictions of the Cape and only visited its rigid society out of necessity. The Trekboers lived in tented wagons and taught their children the Word of God using their most prized book, the Holy Bible. At night, families would huddle together under the tarpaulin canvas roof of their wagon to listen to their father read from the Bible. The Trekboers hunted for the pot and lived off the land, eating berries and roots, and eventually became almost as knowledgeable as the Bushmen about the earth. They could ride horses and shoot skilfully. Tough and hard as dried biltong, the Trekboers let nothing stand in their way. In March 1702, a group of 45 of these men crossed the Hottentots Holland Mountains to explore what lay beyond.

Near the Great Fish River early one morning, they met up with a group of Xhosa who were living with Hottentots. To their surprise, the Xhosa attacked the Europeans. Fortunately, the men were able to speedily organize their defences and a three-hour battle raged as they fought off their attackers. The firepower of the burghers proved to be too much for the Xhosa and they retreated to the hills. The Dutch chased them until that evening, when the Xhosa turned to fight them. Only one of the Europeans was killed while many Xhosa were mown down by the Dutchmen's guns. The burghers took several Xhosa prisoners and later beat them to death.

On their way back to the Cape, the burghers were angry about the attack by the Xhosa and, hell-bent on revenge and unable or unwilling to differentiate between the Xhosa and the Hottentots, they attacked Gonaqua and other Hottentot kraals, shooting and murdering innocent people and stealing their livestock, before returning to the Cape with several thousand sheep and cattle.

Knowing full well that they were guilty of serious crimes, the 44 men entered into a pact of silence and denial and a covenant not to betray each other. They signed this promise in a document that they titled 'The Christian Voyage'. They were never punished for what they had done.[245]

To encourage the successful rearing of the Trekboers' sheep and cattle, the Dutch East India Company allowed these burghers to move to tracts of land far from where they lived to graze their livestock in the winter months. In the early 18th century, they were not charged rent for the land on which they grazed their cattle.

A severe drought between 1698 and 1705 caused great difficulties for the burghers, particularly those farming crops such as wheat, barley and grapes. Their struggle to survive and thrive during this period made them acutely aware of the behaviour of Willem van der Stel and his officials, who steadily enriched themselves despite the drought.

A visiting commissioner from the Hereen XVII, Wouter Valckenier, had granted Willem van der Stel 400 morgen (about 850 acres) of freehold land to farm for himself. He then allocated a piece of land next to his 400 morgen at Hottentots Holland to one of his officials and bought it from him at a nominal rate. He named this farm Vergelegen, which translates as 'situated far away'.[246]

Without the Hereen XVII's knowledge, Willem Van der Stel spent much of his time that should have been devoted to the settlement's business to pursuing his own interests on the farm. He had planted over half a million vines, which represented one quarter of all the vines in the settlement at that time, as well as orchards and mealie fields. In addition, he kept his over 600 cattle and 8,000 sheep at a variety of grazing places on land that did not belong to him, on the other side of the Hottentots Holland Mountains. Willem van der Stel ensured that his favoured senior officials and family were also allocated land to farm.

When it came to selling produce in the small and limited market of the settlement, these privileged few had the first option to do so, which meant that the rest of the burghers sometimes struggled to find buyers for their produce. Resentment against the Van der Stel family and in particular, against Governor Willem van der Stel grew. The burghers drew up a secret petition and sent it to the governor-general and council of India in Batavia, but no action was taken.

Not content with waiting for action, one of the burghers, Adam Tas, wrote a letter to the directors of the Dutch East India Company in Amsterdam. In the 38-paragraph letter, he outlined the nepotism and cronyism of Willem Van der Stel and accused him and his officials of corruption, extortion and oppression. This letter was signed by 63 disgruntled burghers. Some of the charges were as a result of 'sour grapes' on the part of the burghers, but many of the serious charges were valid.[247] The letter was given to one of the burghers for safekeeping with the intention being to send the letter to the Hereen XVII with the next homeward-bound fleet. One of Willem van der Stel's officials had warned him that a document had been sent to Batavia and he guessed correctly that the unhappy burghers would send a follow-up letter to Holland. Despite his best efforts and spying officials, he was unable to establish who the ringleaders of the protest were and soon became so agitated that he was on the verge of panic. As a result, he began to act irrationally.

He had a document drawn up that extolled his virtues as governor. On his orders, this document was taken from house to house by the landdrost of Stellenbosch, who was accompanied by armed guards and intimidated and threatened 240 burghers into signing it. Some refused to sign it, despite the fact that they were warned that they would be watched closely marked in future for any possible misdemeanours.

Willem van der Stel suspected that Tas was behind the protests and ordered armed guards to seize him. Early on the morning of Sunday 28 February 1706, under cover of darkness, the militia quietly surrounded the home of Adam Tas. On a given command, the officers demanded entry into the house and grabbed a surprised Adam Tas, searched his home and carried his writing desk away for the governor to search for evidence of his treason. The protesting Tas was dragged away and thrown into the cells at the Castle, where he remained for 14 months.[248]

When Willem van der Stel examined the writing desk, he found the document he was looking for: a draft copy of the letter being secretly held for the fleet to carry to Holland. The document listed all of the names of the unhappy burghers and detailed the charges against him. With the consent of his council in the Cape, Willem Van der Stel then issued a *plakkaat* (edict) stating that all persons were forbidden to take part in any conspiracy or to sign any document that was slanderous or malicious toward the authorities. The sentence for the ringleaders who drafted any such document was severe corporal punishment and possibly execution and anyone suspected of inciting discontent against the Cape governor and his officials could be arrested.

Van der Stel was hell-bent on intimidating the burghers into submission and persuading them to sign his letter of commendation. He ordered the arrest of several of Tas's supporters, had two men, Wessel Pretorius and Jacob van der Heiden, thrown into the cells and Jan Rotterdam sent to Batavia. He also ordered that Pieter van der Bijl, Henning Huisen, Ferdinand Appel and Jan van Meerland be sent to Holland to stand trial for sedition and conspiracy. This group was confined onboard the ships in the harbour while their wives and families pleaded desperately with the governor for a fair trial. This was denied them. In an attempt to blackmail the men into submission, the governor agreed to grant them a trial … if the men would sign the document extolling his virtues. They refused to do so.[249]

Before the ships left for Holland on 4 April 1706, Willem Van der Stel arrested a further four burghers and had them locked in the cells. A physician, Abraham Bogaert, was on the same ship as the condemned men and was sympathetic to the burghers' cause. Most importantly, he had in his possession the document Willem Van der Stel had sought to prevent from reaching the Hereen XVII. Once the ship was safely at sea, Bogaert handed the damning document to Henning.[250]

As the ships prepared to sail out of Table Bay, it would appear that Willem van der Stel was suddenly struck by doubt as to whether he was doing the right thing by sending the men to Amsterdam. He questioned whether doing so would merely strengthen their case. He ran down to the jetty and ordered a galiot to take him out to the ships, from which, it would appear, he intended to take the prisoners back to shore. He was too late though. The ship's sails had already unfurled and the wind was pushing the vessels on their way. He commanded the galiot to follow them and only gave up chase when it reached Robben Island. Cursing angrily, Willem Van der Stel had to return empty-handed to De Kaap.[251] The letter was on its way.

More arrests were made and a further group of men was summoned to appear in court by the governor. They refused to appear and, consequently, were sentenced to be banished to Mauritius for five years and were heavily fined. When this sentence was made public at the end of August, the resentment and anger of the burghers bubbled over.

The burghers decided to act. Messages were sent to the farmers in Waveren, Riebeek Kasteel and Drakenstein and in the early hours of the morning of 18 September, farmers from these areas banded together. Accompanied by a Frenchman with a drum, they rode into Stellenbosch and to the offices of Landdrost Starrenburg carrying muskets and ammunition. The magistrate came outside to see what the disturbance was about and tried to talk to the burghers, but his voice was drowned by the incessant drumbeat. He then turned his attention to the drummer and ordered him to be silent. The French drummer ignored the command, feigning complete ignorance of Dutch. A humiliated and frustrated Starrenburg was not sure what to do next and when a crowd gathered to watch his humiliation, he became enraged. Some of the onlookers began to dance to the beat of the drum and one woman boldly shouted at Starrenburg that the women did not intend to submit to the tyranny of corrupt officials, claiming that they would be as formidable to deal with as the men would. Unsure how to deal with the protest, a mortified Starrenburg turned on his heel and headed into his house.[252]

Soon after this protest, two of the men who had been banished to Mauritius appeared in court and openly jeered at the presiding Starrenburg. Evidently, all respect for the governor and his officials had disappeared. An attempt was made to capture some of the burgher ringleaders, but the armed men attempting to seize them failed. Those who had been sentenced to be banished to Mauritius fled across Twenty-four Rivers and hid in a forest below the Elsenbosch mountain range. However, Starrenburg's men caught and arrested two of them and sent them to the *Mauritius Packet* to await its departure for Mauritius.

Willem Van der Stel attempted to shore up his rickety position by firing elected members of the council and replacing them with his cronies. However, his efforts were in vain. Jan Rotterdam arrived back from Batavia with the news that the governor-general and council of India had paid no attention to Willem van der Stel's charges against him. In addition, some of the burghers had received letters from Europe informing them that the Hereen XVII had decided in their favour against Willem Van der Stel and they gleefully relayed this news to him.

It was all over for Willem Van der Stel and his peers.

On 16 April 1707, before the ship carrying the five men bound for Mauritius left, the *Kattendijk* arrived with a letter for Willem van der Stel from the Hereen XVII. The skipper of the *Kattendijk* duly handed him his letter of dismissal in front of his nervous officials.[253] The burghers had been exonerated, Willem Van der Stel and his senior henchmen were dismissed and summoned to return to Holland, those burghers imprisoned in the Castle were released and a new governor, Louis van Assenburgh, was appointed.

The Hereen XVII generously allowed Willem van der Stel's father to keep his farm until the time of his death, whereupon all property that he owned would revert to the Dutch East India Company. However, the company took back Willem van der Stel's farm and allocated the land to be auctioned off as four farms. Thereafter, instructions were issued that no company employee at whatever level could own or lease land, or trade in corn, wine or cattle and the burghers were given the right to trade in cattle with whomever they pleased.[254]

During the five years that Van Assenburgh was governor, little changed at the Cape. He sought to entertain the people at the colony by organizing a fight between bulls and dogs at the Castle, but this held little appeal for them. Of greater appeal was that brewer Willem Mensk was granted a monopoly to set up a brewery to supply the thirsty sailors, soldiers and company employees with a variety of beers.

In 1713, a major calamity struck the small settlement. Clothing belonging to people on the ships, who had been ill at sea and recovered, was sent to be washed at the slave lodge. The women who washed the clothes were struck down with smallpox and within six months, nearly 200 of the 500 slaves in the colony had died. Like a juggernaut of death, the disease then rolled over the Europeans and then on to the Hottentots.[255] Fear of the dreaded sickness swept the colony and as the people withdrew into the fragile protection of their homes, a great silence descended on the streets and the children's playgrounds in the settlement. Everyone remained indoors and practically every family was affected. There were so many sick that it was impossible to obtain a nurse.

Slave women were paid to help nurse the sick and so many coffins were made that the settlement stores ran out of wooden planks. While the poor could not afford a coffin, those servants who managed to scrape together enough money for one lost out to the middle and upper classes. An air of gloom and fear hung over the Cape.

Significantly, on 10 May 1713, two doves fell to the ground from the parapet of the governor's house. They fluttered briefly on the ground, their wings twitching in a flurry of feathers, and then died, with no obvious signs of illness or injury. The settlers took this to be an ominous omen. And it was. By the end of the cruel winter, more than a quarter of the 1,900 burgher men, women and children in the settlement had died.[256]

The disease relentlessly moved on, creating havoc among the Hottentots, who had little to no immunity to the virus. Most of those infected died. As the number of Hottentot mortalities soared, many attempted to outrun the disease by crossing the mountains in the East.[257] As soon as the fleeing Hottentots crossed the mountains, other tribes massacred them in a vain attempt to stop the tsunami of death from reaching them.

Those that survived the massacres returned to their villages and waited for the Grim Reaper to appear to them. The dead were left to rot where they died, which caused the stench of rotting meat and death to blanket the Cape. Whole villages and tribes disappeared as all those in the path of the smallpox tsunami died.

Because the Bushmen were isolated and lived in remote parts, they fared better than the Hottentots. In fact, the Hottentot people were almost totally wiped out. A population of over 30,000 people were decimated. The threat that the Hottentots had represented to the settlers was replaced by the threat of attacks and robberies by the Bushmen, who would come down from the mountains where they lived to steal farmers' cattle. They had a knack for vanishing like the mist when pursued.

In August 1715, Bushmen murdered a shepherd at Drakenstein and drove off over 700 sheep belonging to one of the burghers. In response, the governor authorized the aggrieved farmer's neighbours to retaliate, pursue the Bushmen and recover the cattle. (This type of commando unit would become an extremely effective tactical fighting force and would be employed right up until 2002/03, when such militant groups were disbanded by the ANC government after the arrest of members of a right-wing group known as *Die Boeremag.*) Gangs of fugitive slaves had also not slacked in their efforts to plunder the farmers' cattle and sheep.

Between 1715 and 1724, the ships calling at the Cape increased significantly. By 1724, approximately seven ships anchored at the Cape each month and many of these vessels carried over 300 men.[258]

On Sunday 14 June 1722, Table Bay was as pretty as a picture. The harbour was dotted with ten ships, some of which were on their outward-bound journey to India while others were returning to Holland. However, a stiff breeze from the northwest was blowing and it soon grew into a strong wind and then matured into a gale. The following day, the gale died down, but this was to be the calm before the real storm. That night, the wind veered north-northwest and on Tuesday morning, the grey sea was being whipped into a frenzy, with white seahorses charging across the watery seascape. When darkness fell, the gale reached speeds the likes of which the experienced seafarers had spent their lives dreading. As the winter sun weakly lit the sky at dawn, the angry waves roared in the empty bay. Every ship had either sunk or been smashed on the rocks and in Table Bay 660 men had perished.[259]

Five years later, Pieter Gysbert Noordt was installed as governor of the Cape on 25 June 1727. He had only visited the settlement once before, several years earlier, as director of fortifications. Noordt was an unpleasant and coarse man who made enemies easily. He was only governor for two years and two months before he died. Thirteen soldiers had deserted from the colony as a result of Noordt's treatment of them and his theft of monies due to them. Noordt sent a party of burghers to capture them and, during a prolonged battle, one of the defectors was shot, eight were captured and thrown into the dungeon at the Castle known as *Donkergat* (black hole) and three returned of their own accord and surrendered. The latter were tried and found guilty by the Council of Policy, which sentenced them to run the gauntlet ten times before being sent to Batavia as sailors.[260] When the sentence was read out, Noordt jumped up and shouted, "They shall hang! The brutes! They shall hang!" Despite protests from the Council of Policy, Noordt changed their ruling, saying dismissively, "*Ik neem dit aan mij.*" (I am taking it upon myself!). He then signed a warrant of execution.[261]

On the day of scheduled execution, the approximately 99 soldiers not on guard assembled in the marketplace and divided into three companies. Two of the companies were armed with muskets while the third, which comprised the best soldiers, was armed with long pikes about six and a half metres long. The pikemen took up position between two lines of infantry and the battalion then marched in formation to the governor's house. The members of the Council of Policy accompanied them, escorted by a sergeant, a corporal and 12 grenadiers. Also in this procession were the convicted men, who were guarded by a corporal and six soldiers armed with short pikes, as well as the executioner and his helpers. When all were assembled before the governor's residence, the secretary to the Council of Policy mounted the stairs outside it and read out the sentences of the condemned. The prisoners were aghast as the full realization of their punishment struck home.

The troops then marched to the place of execution to the macabre music a band was playing and formed a ring with their pikes, with each soldier grasping one end of his own pike and that of the soldier next to him. The musketeers then took up position within and outside the ring. They had been ordered to keep the area free of encroaching onlookers. The prisoners were brought toward the gallows by the heavily guarded executioner and his assistants and the bareheaded court messenger followed them with a retinue of soldiers, solemnly walking forward while carrying his silver-tipped staff that denoted his office. All of the dignitaries of the Cape had gathered in full ceremonial dress to watch the executions and many spectators hovered near Noordt's home to watch the spectacle unfold. The white-faced prisoners knelt to listen to a clergyman intone his pleas to the Lord to save their souls. Then it was their turn to pray in quavering voices. Having done so, they turned to each other and bade one another an emotional farewell.

One by one, they were led to the gallows. So moving was the scene that many of the onlookers, including members of the Council of Policy, were moved to tears. As the rope was being put around the neck of the last man, he shouted desperately, "Wait a moment! I have something to say". The hangman paused and there was silence from the expectant crowd. The man turned his face toward Noordt's residence and yelled, "I summon thee at this very moment before the judgement seat of the Omniscient God, that thou mayest there answer for my soul and the souls of my companions." Then he exclaimed, "Now! In God's name!" as he mounted the ladder. On reaching the top, the hangman tied another rope around his neck and secured the ropes to the nail on the gallows before pushing him off the ladder. He died without even a quiver.[262]

When the executions were over, the members of the Council of Policy went to the governor's home to record the executions formally. They marched up to the house in a procession and through the heavy wooden doors into the great hall where meetings of the Council of Policy were held. The governor sat at the far end of the room in an armchair in his office and ignored them when they bowed to him. One of the magistrates approached the governor to report on the proceedings. He stopped in his tracks. "The Governor is dead!" he screamed. "The Governor is dead!"

The council members rushed toward the motionless man and shrank back in horror as they saw his face, which in death was full of despair. His appearance was so dreadful that the council members were terrified, as they remembered the last words of the final prisoner being executed.[263] So ended the rule of Noordt on 27 April 1729.

Disaster again struck in Table Bay on 27 May 1737. This time, nine ships caught up in a gale drifted helplessly on the white and angry waves after their anchor cables had parted, before being pounded to pieces or thrown onto the rocks by the frothing surf. Out of 739 crew, 208 drowned.[264]

After the storm had subsided, four looters were seen pilfering the cargo that lay scattered on the beach. The men were caught and hanged on the hastily erected gallows at the water's edge and their bodies were left to dangle for days, as a warning to other would-be looters.[265]

The second confrontation with the Xhosa occurred in 1736, 34 years after the first.

Over the years, much of the interior had been explored, mainly by parties of elephant hunters who had discovered much about the land above the Cape on their travels in search of ivory. It was one of these parties that clashed with the Xhosa while travelling east from the Cape in May 1736 under their leader, Hermanus Hübner.[266] The group passed through the land occupied by the Hottentot Gonaqua, through the territory under Xhosa ruler Chief Phalo and into that of the Thembu.

On the return journey, they stopped to rest at Chief Phalo's kraal. From there, nine men decided to continue homewards with seven wagons heavily loaded with ivory, while six remained behind with four laden wagons and intended to follow them a few days later. Those returning home were delayed for a number of days on the banks of a flooded river.

On the eighth day after leaving Phalo's kraal, two Hottentots who had been with their companions burst out of the bushes and breathlessly blurted out the news to the men on the riverbank that the Xhosa had murdered those who had remained at the kraal, including Hermanus Hübner.[267] According to these Hottentots, Hübner had suddenly been fatally stabbed while he talked with several Xhosa. The tribe members then murdered and mutilated the bodies of the other white men before removing everything from the wagons, including three barrels with over 60 kilograms of gunpowder. They had then smashed open the barrels, piled the gunpowder into a heap and set the wagons on fire so they could get at the iron parts. A spark flew onto the stockpiled gunpowder and ignited it, causing a massive explosion to shake the earth. When the smoke cleared, the ground was littered with the bodies of dead and injured Xhosa.

The party of men by the river were terrified by the news and feared for their lives. Fortunately, the level of the river had dropped and they were able to cross the river with their wagons. However, a short distance from the river, the fleeing men realized that the Xhosa were following them. Unsure what to do, they halted the wagons to wait for the horde of Xhosa to approach them. When the Xhosa were in range, the burghers opened fire on them and killed a good number of them, which they were particularly pleased about as they were running out of ammunition. The burghers abandoned their wagons soon after this skirmish and fled on foot to the Cape, where they safely arrived on 10 July 1737. It had been over a year since they had departed.[268]

The burghers once again levelled accusations of corruption against the authorities in the Cape. This time, they complained about the conduct of Acting Governor Daniël van den Henghel, and, in particular, about the law that had been reintroduced that forbade the burghers from trading cattle with the Hottentots.

Led by firebrand Etienne Barbier, a group of armed dissidents rode to the church in Paarl and addressed the congregation as they came out after the service. The congregation listened avidly to Barbier read a document that accused the acting governor of favouring the Chinese and Hottentots over the Europeans. He called on the burghers not to pay taxes and circulated several seditious papers to burghers who appeared to be sympathetic to their cause.[269]

Barbier was declared an outlaw shortly after this incident and an order for his arrest was issued stating that he should be shot on sight should he resist arrest. After Barbier was declared an outlaw, Bushmen raided several farms in the Piketberg and Bokkeveld areas. They murdered two farmers and a number of slaves during this latest attack on the burghers.

The farmers had grown increasingly frightened by the frequent Bushmen raids and this incident prompted many of them to abandon their farms and move into the relative safety of the settlement near the Castle.[270] The government ordered that a commando unit be raised and encouraged the burgher men to join it, going so far as to grant amnesty to all those who had sided with Barbier, who was in hiding. At this point, a farmer betrayed Barbier's whereabouts to the authorities. He was caught, thrown into the Donkergat, tried and sentenced to death.[271]

Just two days after he had been captured, he was taken from his cell and dragged in front of a double wooden cross.[272] There, the assistant executioner, a Hottentot, stripped him naked and bound him tightly to the wheel. The executioner then raised his hatchet and swung down with all his strength at Barbier's right wrist. Blood spurted from the stump at the end of Barbier's right arm as his severed hand fell to the ground. Next, the executioner severed his head from his neck with one almighty blow. Barbier's body was then cut into quarters and his entrails were buried underneath the gallows. The four body parts were readied to be sent to the four outlying districts, where each section would be mounted onto a stake as a warning to all the burghers of what happened to rebels. Similarly, the grisly hand and blood-spattered head were nailed to a stake set up in Herr Street to remind people in the village of the dangers of opposing the government.[273]

Hendrik Swellengrebel succeeded Governor van den Henghel in April 1739. Swellengrebel abolished the system of 'loan places' that had been implemented to encourage the settlers to farm cattle. These loan places had an area of 6,000 acres and were used as grazing areas by the burghers. Each one had to be at least an hour's walk from the centre of the loan place of one's neighbour. The farmers were not allowed to subdivide the land and when a farmer's sons married, they travelled farther afield to stake out their own loan farm.[274] As such, more and more land was being occupied as loan farms. Swellengrebel sold the loan places to the occupiers for a reasonable sum and they were converted into freehold titles.[275]

As the burghers pushed farther and farther away from the Cape and encroached on the hunting grounds of the Bushmen, the Bushmen retaliated by attacking outlying farms. More often than not, the commandos sent to recover stolen cattle and retaliate against the Bushmen met with heavy opposition. In one confrontation with the Bushmen in October 1740, the burghers killed more than 60 Bushmen and wounded many. They killed a further 40 in subsequent months, at which point the Bushmen leaders, Waterboer, Anthonie Dragonder and Klein Jantje, approached the commander for peace.[276] The peace was short-lived though.

When Swellengrebel requested retirement in 1750, the Council of Policy asked that the Dutch East India Company directors appoint Ryk Tulbagh as his successor. They granted the request and handed over the administration of the Cape to Tulbagh on 27 February 1751.[277]

Tulbagh was concerned with all aspects of life at the Cape and soon made it clear that he would not tolerate the corruption and bribery that had become part of everyday life for company employees because of the poor salaries they received. He even made a point of staying abreast of developments in the work of Nicolas Louis de Lacaille, a member of the Royal Academy of Sciences at Paris who had come to the Cape to carry out astronomical studies.

Saturday 8 April 1752 was observed as a day of thanksgiving for the 100 years of occupation of the colony and special church services were held at Cape Town, Stellenbosch, Drakenstein, Roodezand and Zwarland.

During 1756, the drama of the *Meermin* unfolded. The *Meermin* was a slave ship that had been sent to Madagascar to purchase 140 slaves for the Dutch East India Company, after it had been decided that too many slaves had been brought in from India. On the return voyage to the Cape, the Captain, Gerrit Mulder, instructed that the prisoners be unchained and, somewhat stupidly, a few days later, tasked them with cleaning and polishing assegais. The slaves seized the opportunity to kill 24 of the crew. The remaining 29 crew were imprisoned below deck for the next 24 hours. One of the women slaves then negotiated the terms of prisoners' release: they would not be harmed if they sailed the slaves back to Madagascar.

The prisoners reluctantly accepted this ultimatum. However, the crew steered the ship toward Cape Agulhas. The slaves were unaware that anything was amiss until four days later, when 'Madagascar' was sighted. When they were several kilometres from the coast, the slaves demanded that the sailors drop anchor. Fifty slaves then climbed into two boats and rowed for the shore, where they would light fires to signal that it was safe for the others to join them.

After the group landed on the beach, they saw the farmhouse of Matthys Rostock and grew suspicious that they had been tricked. However, Rostock quickly spread the word about the slaves on the beach to neighbouring farmers, who attacked them before they could escape inland. The slaves would not surrender, despite being called upon to do so. Consequently, the farmers opened fire and killed 14 of them before taking the other 36 prisoner.

The sailors trapped on the *Meermin* saw the farmers running toward the shore and hastily wrote a message outlining what had happened. They put the message in a bottle and dropped it in the surf, hoping the bottle would drift toward the shore. They had requested that three fires be lit on the beach if the note was found. When the farmers found the note, they duly lit the fires, which the slaves on the ship took to mean that it was safe for them to make for the shore. Unaware that their fellow slaves were either dead or being held captive, several slaves cut the anchor cable of the *Meermin*, which then drifted shoreward and onto a sandbank. A group of six slaves then rowed ashore in a small boat. When they landed, the farmers shot one of the slaves and took the other five prisoner.

Meanwhile, the remaining slaves on the *Meermin* had realized that they had been tricked and attacked the crew in a battle that raged for three hours. Fortunately, the crew was able to fend them off. The slaves soon recognized that they had no choice but to surrender. They agreed to be shackled and were then ferried by the Dutch safely to shore. The 112 slaves that had survived the mutiny were then transported to the Cape in three wagons.[278]

Smallpox reappeared in the colony in 1755 and, once again, the outbreak could be attributed to calling ships. In the month of July, 489 Europeans, 33 free blacks and 580 slaves died. The exceptionally cold weather in July had also caused many to die of respiratory ailments. Fortunately, when the weather got warmer, the high mortality rate in the colony dropped. Should the death rate of July have prevailed until the end of the year, the settlement would have had no people left alive.

During this smallpox epidemic, two hospitals were established—one for poor whites and the other for blacks. Despite this, 963 whites and 1,109 blacks died between May and October 1755, which lowered the population to 5,510 whites and 6, 279 black and Malay slaves.[279] To compound the ill health of the colony, leprosy was also experienced at this time. The disease paid little attention to colour.

In 1760, Jacobus Coetsee left his farm to travel north to hunt elephants. Accompanied by 12 Hottentots, he crossed the Orange River and became the first white man to have done so. When he returned, he reported to the authorities that he had encountered a black tribe called the Damrocqua and described that they wore linen clothes and had long hair.

Coetsee's alleged dealings with the Damrocqua prompted the authorities to mount an expedition headed by Captain Hop. The party departed on 16 August 1761 in 15 wagons and included a botanist, Jan Andries Auge, a surgeon and mineralogist, Carel Christoffel Rykvoet, and a surveyor, Carel Frederik Brink as well as 13 burghers. They returned on 27 April 1762 with the verdict that the longhaired people in linen clothing did not exist.

The Cape became known as Cape Town while Tulbagh was governor. One of his great accomplishments was that he had managed to stabilize the relationship between the colony and the Hottentots. However, the Bushmen were still carrying out frequent cattle raids. In the spring of 1754, a retaliatory raid was carried out by a commando that butchered 64 of the Bushmen in their stronghold in the mountains. Similarly, when Bushmen raided farms in May 1758, a commando led by David van der Merwe killed 56 Bushmen. They pursued the robbers for 14 days and recovered practically all of their cattle. These raids by the Bushmen and retaliations by the burghers continued along the Nieuwveld Mountains and on both sides of the Roggeveld Mountains. Only occasionally did Bushmen kill burghers and their Hottentot herders.

The expanding frontiers of the colony led Tulbagh to establish a commission to investigate the state of affairs on the farms farthest from Cape Town. The commission found that many farms with large herds had been established between the Gamtoos and the Fish rivers and that the farmers on these lands were not paying rent to the Dutch East India Company. The commission also found evidence of large-scale cattle trading with the Xhosa, despite this having been forbidden in 1739.

On 13 February 1770, the Council of Policy resolved that the borders of the colonial boundary would be on the northern side of the Stellenbosch side of the Zwartberg, the corresponding range farther eastward, the hills known as Bruintjieshoogte, and on the southern side (Swellendam side) of the Gamtoos River. Instructions were issued that all persons living on farms beyond those limits were to return to the colony.[280]

Tulbagh suffered from ill health and died on 11 August 1771. His successor was Joachim van Plettenberg. He was appointed governor of the Cape by the Prince of Orange after Baron van Oudtshoorn died at sea on the *Asia*, 19 days after leaving Holland. His body was placed in a leaden coffin and he was buried at the Cape some months later.

Despite the boundaries set by Tulbagh, white farmers had settled as far as the Little Fish River. However, Van Plettenberg would only extend the colony boundaries to the Fish River and the Bushman's River in 1775.

In 1772, the first exports of wheat, rye, barley, wine and tallow were sent to Holland and, soon after this, the settlers started exporting to India. As such, the sea route around the Cape was becoming busier. Between 1751 and 1771, approximately 70 ships put into Table Bay and Simon's Town each year. However, from 1772 until 1780, the average number of calling ships leaped to 117.[281]

Van Plettenberg received a petition in January 1778 requesting that the settlers be allowed to establish a church and landdrost court on the eastern border, where there had been numerous attacks by Bushmen.Van Plettenberg, together with his secretary, Olof Gottlieb de Wet, surgeon Johan Michael Seyd, Lieutenant Christiaan Philip van Heiden and Captain Robert Jacob Gordon set off toward the eastern frontier. They stopped to meet with the farmers in the Sneeuberg Mountains, who requested a minister and a landdrost. Van Plettenberg promised to direct their request to the Council of Policy on his return, which he did. The group then continued on their journey, hugging the right bank of the Great Fish River.

On 6 November 1778, the governor's party arrived at a bay that had been called *Bahia Formosa* (the beautiful bay) by Portuguese explorer Manuel da Perestrello. There, they erected a stone pillar engraved with the arms of the United Provinces (the emblem of the Dutch East India Company) and the arms of the governor

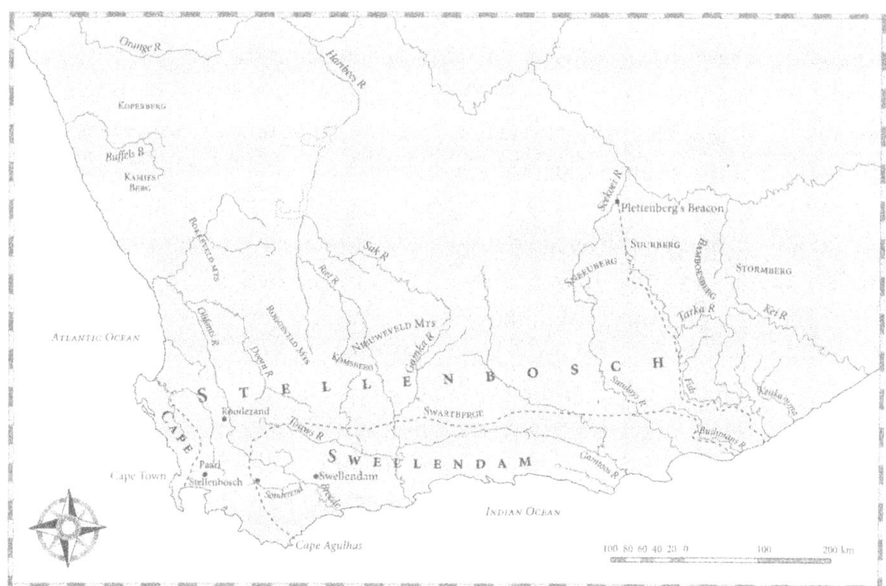

before renaming the bay Plettenberg Bay. Captain Gordon and Van Plettenberg split up at this point. Gordon turned northwest while Van Plettenberg explored the areas south and west of the bay. Shortly after leaving the bay, Van Plettenberg met with some minor Xhosa chiefs and was able to negotiate that the boundary between the Europeans and the Xhosa be designated as the Fish River. The Council of Policy subsequently ratified this in 1780. By extending the boundary to the Fish River, the area known as the Zuurveld—Albany and Bathurst—was included in the colony.

During Van Plettenberg's tenure, dissatisfaction among the burghers increased. The corruption and bribery that had been stopped by Tulbagh flourished. Much to the dismay of the burghers, government officials did what they pleased. Eighteen 'offenders' were banished by the governor from the colony in an eight-year period. (Tulbagh had only banished ten settlers in 20 years.) However, word of the American Revolution began to arrive and burghers discussed issues of civil rights and liberties at length. Matters came to a head when the governor instructed black 'scavengers', who were usually employed to pick up drunks, to drag a burgher from his home and place him aboard the *Honkop* to be deported to Batavia due to his involvement in a domestic quarrel. On his arrival in Batavia, the man complained about how he had been treated and was given permission to return to the Cape. Sadly, he died on the return journey.

At a Council of Policy meeting on 30 March 1779, a letter was read in which 300 to 400 burghers requested that a delegation be elected to go to Holland to inform the directors of the Dutch East India Company of the conditions in the colony. The council refused this request. Undeterred by this decision, the burghers elected Jacobus van Reenen, Barend Jacob Artois, Tieleman Roos and Nicolaas Godfried Heyns to proceed to Holland carrying a document signed by 404 burghers that outlined the burghers' complaints in 37 clauses. The document accused the company officials of corruption and requested that certain changes be made. For instance, the burghers asked that they be allowed to dispose of farm produce in markets other than that of the Dutch East India Company; that they be permitted to punish slaves without seeking permission from authorities; that the laws of the colony be defined clearly and communicated to them; that seven burghers be allowed seats on the Council of Policy; that the high court should comprise equal numbers of officials and burghers; that any right of appeal should be heard in Holland and not Batavia; that they be allowed to export goods to Holland and India and to deal in slaves from Madagascar and the East Coast of Africa; that more churches should be built; that wine should be purchased by the Dutch East India Company for 26 rix-dollars a legger; that foreigners should not be allowed to travel around the country and that farms of an inferior quality should be rented at a lower rate than 16 rix-dollars. The directors sent a copy of the petition to Van Plettenberg, who replied on 21 March 1781 and defended his officials and himself in a lengthy response, concluding by requesting to be relieved of his duties.

CHAPTER 6

Corruption and discontent

Trekboers move on—shoot to kill—Van Jaarsveld—tobacco massacre—First Frontier War—boundaries pushed—Xhosa resistance—Maynier—abandonement of farms—Coenraad de Buys—Second Frontier War—Nationals—Graaff-Reinet revolt

The Bushmen's hunting grounds were becoming more and more crowded and farmers setting up operations were displacing the Hottentots. The expansion of the settlers' agricultural activities also drove many burghers to explore the interior. These Trekboers moved eastward on two courses: the first path was along the northern borders of the Great Karoo and the second was parallel to the coast. The Trekboers were restless people who moved at the pace of their oxen and lived in their wagons, visiting the Cape only when they needed to.

Even the Trekboers' clothing reflected that they were different to the settlers at the colony: they frequently wore animal skins and furs, in the fashion of the Hottentots and Bushmen. As they moved farther from the Cape, so their visits and attachment to the Cape lessened. However, they remained dependent upon the Cape for their lifeblood—gunpowder and ammunition. Their language also began to change and was influenced by French, then a little German and then Hottentot. The biggest influencing factor, however, was the language of the slaves from Malaya. So, very slowly and bit by bit, the Afrikaans language started to evolve. (It would only replace its parent language, Dutch, as an official language of South Africa in 1925.) These pioneers of the veld were nomadic, living mainly in their wagons. They seldom put roots down for long and when they did, they built homes made of reeds or mud huts with floors of compacted dung, incorporating few or no luxuries or refinements.

They moved constantly with their herds of sheep and cattle in search of fresh grazing or they moved simply because they wanted to. They travelled mainly at night, with each family unit journeying independently of others. After all, most Trekboers enjoyed being independent and it was common practice for a family to move if the smoke from a neighbour's home was visible.[282] As such, each family became a strong, independent and self-contained unit.

Although fractious, quarrelsome and jealous of others, the Trekboers developed a rich tradition of hospitality that was unequalled anywhere else in the world and travellers knew that they would be well treated when overnighting with these people of the veld. They were a law unto themselves, owing their allegiance to neither king nor country, and were ruled only by God's Word. Austere and devout, the father figure would read to his family from the Bible each day and lead them in prayer and worship. He was the unchallenged head and leader of the family. Despite their dour and Calvinistic attitudes, the Trekboers remained free from the conventions and restrictions of the Cape.

The men were usually large, strong and had a vigorous sexual appetite[283] that they, in many cases, satisfied with not only a wife but also Hottentot women[284] They frequently had more than one mistress and sometimes raised large illegitimate families, creating a mixed-blood generation of children who were referred to as 'bastaards'.[285] Their hygiene also left a great deal to be desired. They and their servants relieved themselves in the open, near their dwellings, which created an unhealthy and unsanitary surround to the home.

When Governor Swellengrebel visited these nomads, he described the typical Trekboer home as "a one-room house of clay, roofed with reeds, and no chimney even, with the smoke curling upward through a hole in the roof, a reed door with a rope to tie it closed, and a four-sided hole for a window. Sleeping arrangements are in Hottentot fashion, that is lying together on the floor of clay and dung".[286] As Swellengrebel observed, the Trekboer husband slept next to his wife, but also alongside his Hottentot women servants and mistresses. In fact, many Trekboer men took "a Hottentot woman or two" as wives and considered themselves 'married' to these women.[287]

Visitors to Trekboer homes were always impressed by the hospitality displayed to them, but shocked by their hosts' quality of life. Fleas, lice and flies invaded their lives to such an extent that the Trekboers covered their skins in grease or lard to keep these vermin away, just as the Hottentots did. Visitors also perceived them to be lazy and indolent they slept or gratified themselves in every sensual delight each day while the Hottentots cared for their sheep and cattle.[288]

Dagga, or marijuana, was traded between the Bushmen, Hottentots and Xhosa and the dried plant was traditionally smoked with a pipe made from an ox horn by the Hottentots, Xhosa and Zulu, but was also enjoyed as snuff on social occasions.[289] As dagga grew wild, it is highly probable that the Trekboers also used it. Known for their love of tobacco and living cheek to jowl with the Hottentots and the Xhosa, the Trekboers would surely have enjoyed the drug. Dagga was smoked through a special pipe made from the horn of an ox. The smoke was drawn through the pipe over water to cool it. However, dagga was preferred as snuff and was used on social occasions. A small quantity was placed in the palm of the hand, usually an ivory spoon was used, and then the contents would be sniffed from the palm of the hand. Perhaps dagga consumption is what led to them being described as "indolent" by many of the early travellers and explorers.

When the Europeans started moving up the East Coast, they trampled the hunting grounds of the Bushmen, shot their game and stole their water. The Bushmen naturally struck back but it is not known whether a single incident sparked their retaliation or whether they had simply had enough of the foreigners. The frequent attacks by the Bushmen followed the Trekboers along an extended battle line that was over 200 kilometres long and all the way down the Great Escarpment, from areas north of the Cape to the Sneeuberg Mountains.[290]

The Dutch East India Company retaliated in turn, assembling commando units comprised of burghers who were given temporary military status. The authorities also enlisted the aid of the burghers' half-caste sons and coloured Hottentot servants. This signalled the start of a longstanding system that involved conscripting the Hottentots into the army as mercenaries to assist the frontiersmen to battle their enemies—first the Bushmen and later, the Xhosa. The company instructed the commandos to engage in friendly negotiations only when they had succeeded in driving the Bushmen out of their hiding places. This was a best-case scenario. In the worst case, the commandos could totally destroy the Bushmen with impunity from the authorities. In effect, the frontiersmen were given a blank cheque to commit genocide if they so wished.[291] Normally, the commandos applied the worst-case scenario option or took prisoners that would either be freed or allocated as slaves among the poorest of the burghers when the hostilities ended. For example, one commando unit sent out to deal with the Bushmen along the Great Escarpment in 1774 killed more than 500 Bushmen and took more than 200 prisoners.

The commandos had little effect in curtailing the Bushmen's harassment and terrorism in the following years and the Bushmen became the common enemy of the Hottentots, the Xhosa and the Trekboers, all of whom were graziers. The Bushmen enraged their enemies by not only stealing and killing their cattle, but also by behaving in a vindictive and wasteful way. They killed for killing's sake. Naturalist Henry Lichtenstein described the Bushmen's evident contempt for life during a farm attack: "One of the farmers … when he went out in the morning, found near his house, his whole herd, consisting of 40 oxen, together with 200 sheep, several dogs and horses, slaughtered and some Hottentots who were employed to guard them, all murdered, not a single one having escaped." However, the Bushmen seldom attacked and killed the frontiersmen and their families. The burghers' staff were less fortunate. It seems that the Bushmen's objective was to rob and steal and that the frequently-murdered Hottentot herdsmen were casualties rather than targets. Nevertheless, this did not diminish the terror the frontiersmen felt regarding the mostly nighttime attacks.

The Bushmen frequently carried lion skins as an aid to their banditry as the scent from the lion skin would cause the cattle and sheep to stampede and thereby distract the herdsmen. Barricaded behind doors, the frontiersmen would shoot at the will-o'-the-wisp figures as they herded off their cattle and showered their homes with arrows and spears.

The relentless attacks made the frontiersmen more and more ruthless in their retaliation. Eventually, the Bushmen were being shot on sight,[292] with ammunition provided by the government for large-scale elimination. Wounded prisoners were sometimes shot rather than kept alive and defenceless women and children did not receive better treatment than their male counterparts did.

Over a six-year period, it was reported that one small commando unit had been responsible for killing more than 3,200 Bushmen, while another claimed over 2,700 Bushmen fatalities.[293] Today, these killings are not referred to as being a result of warfare but, correctly, as genocide,[294] which were carried out over many years by Xhosa, Khoikhoi and other Bantu-speaking people, as well as by the Boers. Unfortunately, this phenomenon of newcomers wiping out the inhabitants of the conquered land is common and took place in all continents.

When a quarrel broke out among different clans of the Xhosa in 1779, some of them entered the colony territory and sheltered near the Bushman's River while others crossed the Fish River and spread over the districts of present-day Somerset East and Albany. The Xhosa that had crossed the Fish River stated that they did not wish to quarrel with the burghers. However, soon after they had arrived, they began to steal the burghers' cattle and the farmers in the Zuurveld and along the Bushman's River were forced to abandon their farms and to seek safety elsewhere. The Xhosa chief, Rarabe, sent a message to the burghers informing them that those stealing their cattle were rebels and he asked for their assistance to stop them.

During 1779 and 1880, two commando units attacked the Xhosa, one under Josua Joubert from Bruintjieshoogte and the other under Pieter Hendrik Ferreira from the Zuurveld and farmers west of Bushman's River. Although cattle were recovered, not all of the Xhosa were driven back over the Fish River. When Governor Van Plettenberg appointed Adriaan van Jaarsveld as military commander of the eastern frontier, one of his first instructions was to remove the Xhosa across the Fish River by force. He was requested to first endeavour to come to a peaceful agreement with them, if they would retire across the Fish

River. Van Plettenberg realized that he would be fighting on two fronts: the Xhosa along the proclaimed colony boundary and the Bushman at the edge of the Great Escarpment. He wanted a peaceful settlement with the Xhosa and hoped that they would return across the Fish River without a fight. However, he was less inclined toward peace with the Bushmen and readily accepted the instruction that, "unless they surrendered, they were to be killed".

Van Jaarsveld made his base at the burned-out farm of Willem Prinsloo and went to talk to the Xhosa. When they refused to return over the Fish River, he gave them an ultimatum of four days. Four days later, he returned to the Dange tribe and a hostile reception. As Van Jaarsveld and his men approached the Xhosa, the warriors began to move toward and among the burghers. Van Jaarsveld shouted at the Xhosa to back off. However, this was to no avail. He ordered his men to remain in their saddles and to retreat in formation. The Xhosa followed them closely and Van Jaarsveld realized that if the Xhosa attacked first, his men would be overrun. He asked his men to hand over all of their tobacco and cut it into small bits, which he then used as a decoy. He walked about 12 paces in front of his men and threw the tobacco toward the Xhosa, calling their attention to it. The Xhosa left the burghers and scrambled to pick up the pieces of tobacco. As they did so, Van Jaarsveld shouted for his men to open fire. The burghers killed these Xhosa in cold blood. This incident in 1781 marked the start of the First Frontier War.[295] There would be nine wars in the next 100 years.

The colonists called for stronger action from the authorities to rid them of the Bushmen's terrorism. However, apart from the commando units comprising the burghers, no major military force was raised to clear the Bushmen from the area, once and for all. At the same time, the Dutch East India Company was not happy about the reported cruelty shown toward the Bushmen by the burgher commandos.

On 14 February 1785, Lieutenant Colonel Cornelis Jacob van de Graaff took over from Van Plettenberg as governor of the colony.

In the Nieuwveld area, the burghers had no cattle to sell to the Dutch East India Company for meat, as the Bushmen had stolen most of their herds. Added to this, there was a shortage of ammunition.

By 1786, these factors were compounded by a severe drought that drove all of the colonists out of Nieuwveld and into the area adjacent to it known as Koup.

In nearby Roggeveld, the situation was no better. When Bushmen attacked 'Poortegal', the farm owned by Roggeveld resident Veldwachtmeester Gerrit Maritz, he attempted to pursue them as they made off with nearly all of his sheep. The commando that he led was reluctant to chase after the Bushmen and

Maritz was horrified at the attitude of these Boers, whom he described as "surly" and as "shirking their responsibility". In fact, many of the Boers from the area sent Hottentots in their place, as they were so tired of the relentless battle with the Bushmen.[296]

As the boundaries of the colony continued to be stretched by the movement of the Trekboers to the north and east, Governor Van de Graaff established a new district named Graaff-Reinet, in honour of his wife, Reinet, in 1785.[297]

As the Trekboers moved farther up the East Coast, the Dutch East India Company became alarmed at the possibility of an eventual clash between the frontiersmen and the Xhosa. From now on, the people at the frontier not only had to contend with attacks and stock theft by Bushmen and Hottentots, but also with the Xhosa resistance to the encroachment of the settlers.

After the Trekboers had suffered heavy cattle losses at the hands of the Xhosa, they put together a petition and sent it to the landdrost at Graaff-Reinet. They requested support and the right to retrieve the cattle that had been stolen from three of the Trekboers, Isaac Meyer, Andres du Pree and Coenraad de Buys. The petition ended with the words, "We cannot sensibly endure it any longer".[298]

For the first time, limits and boundaries to the colony were defined formally. These boundaries were at Bruintjieshoogte in the north and at the Gamtoos River, near Algoa Bay, on the West Coast. However, some of the Trekboers had already settled beyond these areas.[299] Fortunately, there appeared to be a tacit understanding between the Xhosa and these burghers that the Fish River would form the boundary.

There was a great deal of rivalry and jousting for power among the Xhosa chiefs at this time and the burghers met frequently with one of the most powerful Xhosa chiefs, Ndlambe, to exchange gifts and arrive at an agreement to commit to peaceful coexistence. Despite the amicability of the exchanges, which were led by Mr Woeke, who had been landdrost of Graaff-Reinet since December 1785, the loss of burghers' livestock continued.

Matters came to a head in March 1789 when thousands of Xhosa, headed by chiefs Langa, Chungwa and others, cast down the gauntlet by crossing the Fish River. They then spread out over the Zuurveld, causing the resident farmers to abandon their farms and flee from the approaching hordes. The landdrost at the Zuurveld ordered the burgher captain Daniel Willem Kuhne to prepare to defend the area and sent a message to the Cape calling for 100 soldiers to assist the frontiersmen.

The reaction from the Cape authorities was anything but supportive. In fact, the landdrost was criticized for his approach to the crisis and a new district secretary,

Honoratus Christiaan Maynier, was appointed for Graaff-Reinet. Maynier was duly instructed to 'buy off' the Xhosa and to 'persuade' them to return over the Fish River, using various goods he was provided with for this purpose.[300]

In the meantime, Captain Kuhne had raised a commando unit, which headed toward the Fish River to engage the Xhosa in battle. However, the group fell back without firing a shot as Kuhne received instructions not to attack the Xhosa. In effect, he had been ordered to 'turn the other cheek'. The burghers under his command were furious, believing that the Dutch East India Company had gone soft by not punishing the Xhosa for the damage they had caused.

In subsequent meetings between the burghers and the Xhosa, the Xhosa insisted that land between the Fish River and the Kowie River belonged to them. In an effort to settle the matter without conflict, Maynier and a delegation of men known to be friendly toward the Xhosa arranged to meet with several chiefs. At this meeting, they were informed that Chungwa and Tshaka were unable to make it as they had sick family members. Nevertheless, the two minor chiefs who represented them made it clear to the delegation that they did not consider their actions to be hostile, as they owned the land between the Fish and Kowie rivers, having purchased it from a Hottentot called Ruiter many years before.

After the meeting, the Xhosa heard that the burghers were preparing to attack them and they abandoned the land in a panic, fleeing over the Fish River and hiding in the dense bush near the Amatola Mountains. The burghers in the Graaff-Reinet district demonstrated their fury at the lack of support shown to them by the Dutch East India Company in their desire to retaliate against the Xhosa. They were openly disrespectful toward the local authorities and their contempt for them, combined with infighting between the officials, namely Maynier and Woeke, almost led to the collapse of control of the Graaff-Reinet district.

Maynier's conciliatory approach to dealing with the Xhosa did not extend to the Bushmen. He ordered a commando of over 200 men under Jan Pieter van der Walt to search for and destroy the Bushmen. However, the council at Graaff-Reinet offered an incentive of 15 guilders for every prisoner taken and delivered to the Cape in an effort to reduce the slaughter of the Bushmen. These prisoners would be sent to Robben Island.[301] Before the commando was mobilized, two hordes of Bushmen attacked a farm near the Leeuw River, where they killed a burgher and stole 11,000 sheep and 250 oxen. In response, Lieutenant Nicolaas Smit organized a group of 33 burghers from Swellendam to avenge this attack and to recover the stolen animals. They encountered one group of Bushmen under their leader Flamink on 24 July 1789 and slaughtered 300 Bushmen, including Flamink and women and children. They took 15 children prisoner and recovered some of the cattle and sheep as well as muskets.[302] Van der Walt led another burgher force, which killed a further 200 Bushmen in November 1789 and recovered more cattle and sheep. A few months later, these commando units were disbanded, having achieved their objective of crushing the Bushmen.

By 1792, more than 100 farms in the Graaff-Reinet district had been abandoned due to attacks by the Bushmen. The government called a meeting to develop a strategy to secure the frontier. (Woeke never attended this meeting. It was widely believed that he had a severe drinking problem and was incapacitated at the time.)

At this meeting, the Dutch East India Company appointed Johannes van der Walt as commandant of Nieuwveld and gave him the power to organize commandos and call up the burghers to attack the Bushmen. They also gave him two rent-free farms in this dangerous, arid and drought-stricken area.

In August and September 1793, a commando of 23 men under the command of Maritz set out to teach the Bushmen in the Kareeberg a lesson.

In a dawn attack near the Great Brak River in September, they attacked a Bushman kraal and killed 20 Bushmen and captured 16 of their children. Twelve days later, they attacked another kraal. This time, they killed 29 Bushmen and captured seven children. This meant there was one child for each Boer.

On 2 October, Maritz divided the children among the Boers in an unusual ceremony. Before handing over the children, each member of the commando had to sign a document stating that he would not harm or maltreat the child that had been allocated to him. They also had to witness that Maritz had led the commando in an irreproachable fashion. Since 1776, San children who had been captured by commandos were supposed to be registered with the local landdrost and their owners were to provide them with clothing, food and shelter. It is believed that most Boers ignored these regulations.

On 11 June 1793, two groups of Bushmen attacked the drovers in charge of cattle that belonged to a contractor who supplied meat to the Dutch East India Company. They killed a burgher, wounded a slave and drove off 11,000 sheep and 256 oxen during the attack at Leeuw River. Subsequently, Lieutenant Smit led 33 burghers from Swellendam in a chase of the Bushmen. They shot about 300 Bushmen and took 15 children prisoner. They managed to recover 860 sheep, 53 oxen, four horses and eight muskets.

In October 1793, Maritz reported to the authorities at the Cape that the country around him was in a state of uproar and that the Hottentots were to be feared by all, whether 'tame' or 'wild'. Indeed, the animosity between the Bushmen and Hottentots on the one side and the Boers and Hottentots on the other was escalating. The cruelty shown toward servants worsened, which fuelled their resentment toward and hatred of the burghers.[303] When Maynier replaced Woeke as landdrost of Graaff-Reinet in April 1789 due to Woeke's heavy drinking, the burghers made no bones about their disappointment. Maynier had little or no sympathy for their cause to retaliate against those who caused them problems. On the contrary, he was a humanitarian who saw the Xhosa and Bushmen as people who, if treated with respect and dignity, would learn to live alongside the burghers harmoniously. He preferred negotiation and compromise to the sword and the gun.

The polar opposite of Maynier was the Trekboer Coenraad de Buys. While he may have surpassed the average Trekboer male, he certainly illustrated the qualities they possessed. He was tough, an impressive physical specimen, virile, ruthless and domineering. Born in 1761, De Buys was a giant of a man. Over two metres tall, he had well-proportioned limbs and a purposeful stride. His movements displayed a certain grace and delicacy, despite his muscular build and size,[304] and his piercing blue eyes shone with intelligence and cunning. The sun had bleached his thick mop of brown hair and his height and bold features probably attracted a second look from men and women alike. His grandfather was one of the French Huguenots and he was the second son of Johannes de Buys, who died in 1769. De Buys farmed near the Bushman's River in the Zuurveld area and adopted many of the Xhosa ways of life, as the other Trekboers did. He was happy wearing clothing made of animal skins and sleeping on a dung-covered floor in his home of clay and thatch, where he was undisturbed by the masses of fleas, cockroaches and rats that crawled over everything and the thick blue wood smoke that filled his hut.

The life of sunshine and adventure contributed to the high libidos and active sex lives of the Trekboers. Coenraad de Buys was no exception. However, he was not interested in sleeping with white women. It was rumoured that his first concubine had been his nursemaid when he was a teenager. As he grew up, many Hottentot, coloured or 'Bastaard' and Xhosa women came to his bed willingly, attracted by his imposing physique, good looks, sharp and enquiring mind or eloquence. Those who resisted his charms, he forced himself upon. Like his contemporaries, De Buys viewed these Hottentot, coloured and Xhosa women as good enough to be invited or pulled into bed, but worthy of the Trekboers' contempt and ill-treatment.

Compounding De Buys's arrogance was his lack of compassion. He and other Trekboers frequently stole the Xhosa's cattle and in one instance when some Xhosa complained after he had taken their cattle, he made them lie on the ground and beat them, almost to death. He also ordered his Hottentot servants to shoot the Xhosa and frequently abducted Xhosa women to use as sexual partners.[305]

One of the Xhosa women he seized was the wife of the powerful Chief Langa, brother of Rarabe and Gcaleka, and chief of the Mbalu. Abducting the queen bee from a hive would have had far less dire consequences.

The Trekboers' did not understand the culture and heritage of the Xhosa and their disrespect for them extended to Xhosa royalty and chiefs, which shocked, offended and angered the Xhosa people. For instance, one of de Buys's friends and neighbours locked Chungwa, the son of the chief of the Gqunukhwebe, Tshaka, in his mill. After threatening him with violence, he ordered that he turn the mill himself.[306] The Trekboers were already under pressure from the Hottentots attacking their farms and were now foolishly antagonizing the Xhosa. In April 1793, Maynier learned that the Boers in Graaff-Reinet were considering aligning themselves with one of the Xhosa chiefs, Ndlambe, against Langa's Mbalu and Tshaka's Gqunukhwebe. A frontier officer, Barend Lindeque, had arranged a rendezvous with Ndlambe at which he and his Boer commando would join with Ndlambe's warriors to attack the Mbalu and Gqunukhwebe.

Lindeque and approximately 200 men approached the rendezvous point on horseback. As they topped the rise, they saw row after row of Ndlambe's warriors with glistening ebony bodies covered in red ochre. The warriors were in battle formation and carried assegais, fighting sticks and hide shields, while the leaders sported headdresses with feathers from the Blue Crane. The dust swirled as the chanting warriors stamped their bare feet in preparation for the fighting ahead.

The Boers watched in astonishment as the warriors readied themselves for war. They had never seen the massed ranks of Xhosa warriors before and despite the fact that these men were their allies, what they saw and heard terrified them. The ground shook during the war dance, the warriors' voices thundered up to the Boers on the rise and Ndlambe's warriors danced themselves into a frenzy. As one unit, the Boers turned their horses and galloped homeward.[307]

When news of the Boers' rapid retreat reached the settlers, rumour after rumour swept the frontier and panic set in. Many of the Trekboers hastily threw their meagre possessions onto their wagons and abandoned their farms and homes. Seizing the moment, the Mbalu and the Gqunukhwebe attacked in May 1793. This signalled the start of the second frontier war. The Xhosa hit back at the settlers for the humiliation and cruelty they had suffered at the hands of people such as De Buys and the Bezuidenhouts, who were cast in a similar mould to De Buys. They viciously burned and looted farms in the Zuurveld, forcing the peaceable Maynier to retaliate. He ordered a commando to drive the Xhosa back over the Fish River, but not before De Buys's farm and all of his possessions had been destroyed. When chiefs Langa and Tshaka retreated across the Fish River with their warriors, they met with the ally of the Boers, Chief Ndlambe and his soldiers. In the ensuing battle, Tshaka was killed and Langa was taken prisoner.[308] After several more skirmishes on both sides of the Fish River, Maynier negotiated an uneasy truce with the Mbalu and Gqunukhwebe in November 1793, against the wishes of De Buys's faction.

After Maynier met with Chungwa, who had taken over from his father, Tshaka, as chief of the Gqunukhwebe and with Nqeno, who had taken over from his father, Langa, as chief of the Mbalu, the Xhosa retreated over the Fish River.

Maynier abhorred unnecessary violence. As such, he recognized and was vocal about the fact that the harsh and frequently unjust treatment of the Hottentots in Graaff-Reinet could drive them to align themselves with the Xhosa. His apparent sympathy for the black and coloured population greatly angered the burghers. This was not their only grievance, however. The burghers were unhappy about the high taxes that were being levied against them, that a toll had been implemented for using a pontoon to cross the Breede River and that anyone who wished to marry had to appear in front of the matrimonial court in Cape Town, some 600 kilometres from Graaff-Reinet[309] Their main complaints though were about Maynier's compassion for the Xhosa, Bushmen and Hottentots and the Dutch East India Company's reluctance to provide support for their ongoing battle with the Bushmen and Xhosa, who harassed them constantly.

Eventually, a delegation of burghers went to Cape Town to request that Maynier be recalled and that their complaints be redressed. The commissioner general, Abraham Josias Sluysken, told them that he would not even investigate their complaints, despite the fact that they had provided him with concrete evidence that contradicted Maynier's reports of peace and contentment in the Zuurveld. Sluysken dismissed the burghers' claims that they were frequently attacked and robbed by the Xhosa and Bushmen.[310] Having been rebuffed by the authorities, the disappointed burghers became rebellious and returned to Graaff-Reinet determined to take matters into their own hands.

Graaff-Reinet was at this time as basic as the people who lived there. A visitor described the capital of the frontier district as "a small collection of mud huts placed some distance from each other. The line of huts roughly forms a street. At the top of the street stands the house of the landdrost, also constructed of mud, together with a few hovels that are used for local government. There are no businesses such as butchers or bakers, no beer and no wine".[311] Led by Van Jaarsveld, a group of 40 burghers that included tough men of the frontier such as

De Buys, Cornelius Bezuidenhout and Marthinus Prinsloo had a fiery meeting in Graaff-Reinet to discuss their next move. They decided that Maynier had to go.

During a meeting with the local council, the *heemraden*, of Graaff-Reinet two days later, on 6 February 1795, the burghers accused Maynier of sheltering runaway servants and criminals, claiming that he was employing more than 120 of these fugitives from justice on his own farms. Whenever they had complained to Maynier about these runaways, who were frequently guilty of housebreaking and robbery, Maynier had refused to act against them. Prinsloo, Jan Durand and Pieter Joubert led the argument for the burghers. Maynier initially protested vehemently against their verbal barrage of accusations but eventually realized that his enemies would not back down. He agreed to step down as landdrost and to leave the district. However, the burghers were not satisfied with this. They also demanded that he hand over his criminal protégés. In particular, they wanted Maynier to give up a man who had come to him to complain about "outrageous ill treatment" at the hands of Bezuidenhout. The named criminals were rounded up in front of the assembled burghers and Maynier and were severely thrashed.[312]

Shortly after this incident, Maynier left the district for Cape Town and the burghers removed the lieutenant of the militia, Cornelis Coetzee, and two more of Maynier's supporters from office. Sluysken made several feeble attempts to recover control of Graaff-Reinet from the burghers, who elected their own representatives to run the district. The burghers showed their disdain for the Dutch East India Company by displaying the red, white and blue tricolour flag of Holland instead of the orange cockades worn by officers of the Dutch East India Company to symbolise their allegiance to William of Orange. They called themselves 'Nationals' and, despite declaring that their opposition was not against the Dutch East India Company but against corrupt servants of the company, the rebellious burghers in Graaff-Reinet made an enemy of the group.

When the burghers then accused Maynier of sheltering runaway servants and criminals, which was borne out by the fact that more than 120 Hottentots were working for him, Sluysken sent a commission consisting of Olof Gottlieb de Wet, president of the High Court of Justice, Captain Von Hugel and Jan Andries Truter to try to calm them. The burghers demanded Maynier's dismissal and the commission complied with their wishes, appointing Lambert Philip van der Poel as provisional landdrost. The burghers also insisted that the members of the commission travel to the frontier, where they would be able to see that the Xhosa occupied the Zuurveld area.[313] The commission refused to do so but

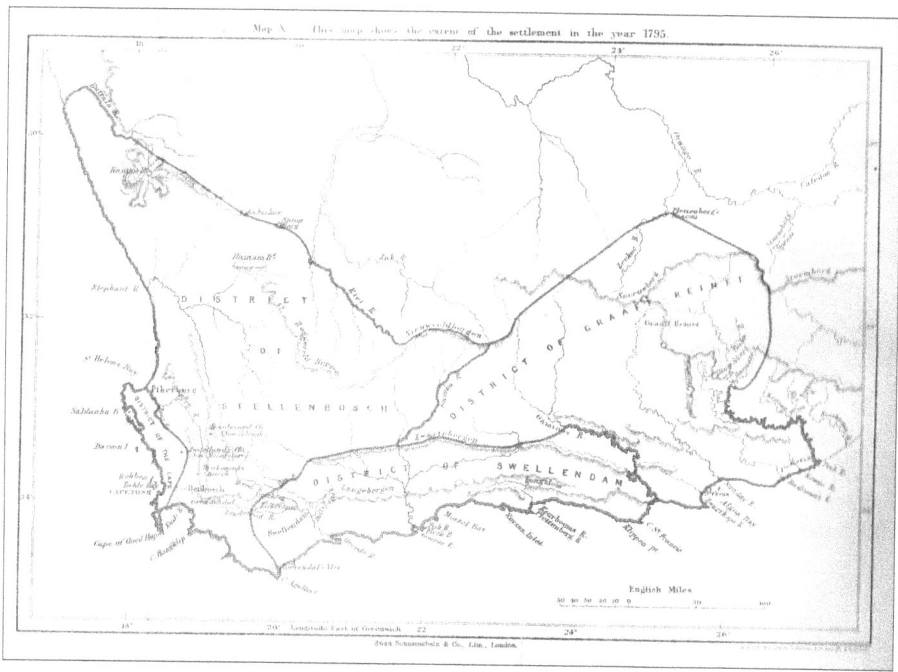

agreed to receive and evaluate any evidence the burghers provided to prove that this was the case. On 6 July 1795, six elected representatives of the burghers, Prinsloo, Barend Bester, Christiaan Botha, Christian Lotter, Hendrik Klopper and Andries Krugel, attended a meeting with the *heemraden*. At this meeting, each of the officials appointed by the Dutch East India Company was asked whether he would serve under the new burgher administration. Van der Poel agreed to do so and was appointed landdrost.

When Van der Poel set off to visit Cape Town shortly after this meeting, the burghers appointed Jan Booysen to act as landdrost until he returned. However, Sluysken prevented Van der Poel from returning to Graaff-Reinet. Consequently, the burghers appointed Carel David Gerotz as provisional landdrost. They also appointed Van Jaarsveld as president of the Council of War on 27 August 1795.

While the revolt raged in Graaff-Reinet, the burghers in the nearby district of Swellendam started to buck authority. They accused local landdrost, Anthony Alexander Faure, of corruption and gathered outside the *drostdy* (the offices of a landdrost) to insist that he step down as landdrost. Persuaded by the many weapons the burghers were carrying, he complied with their demand. They then appointed their own leader, Hermanus Steyn, as landdrost of Swellendam.

The Dutch East India Company had lost control of Graaff-Reinet and Swellendam.

CHAPTER 7

The return of the 'Bushmen of the Sea'

Little Paris—William of Orange—Patriots—British troops arrive—Gordon's death—Stockenström—Graaff-Reinet rebellion—Macartney—Lady Anne Barnard—De Buys outlawed—Ngqika—new boundaries—ill treatment of Hottentots—Vandeleur marches on Graaff-Reinet—Redcoats at the Sundays River—defiance of Chungwa—Lieutenant Chumney—attack on Boers—Boer unhappiness

By the last decade of the 1700s, Europeans were referring to Cape Town as 'Little Paris', as the people there lived in grace and style. High fashion and fine furnishings predominated and property prices soared. Balls, receptions and pomp and ceremony marked the day-to-day lives of those living in Little Paris. Alcohol played a large part in the lives of all at this time and liquor houses proliferated, particularly as around 14 ships called at the Cape each month. The expanding society and influx of visitors also encouraged the establishment of other businesses, such as bakeries and butcheries. Shooting competitions, dogfights, baboon baiting, gambling and cock fighting entertained the lower ranks of the approximately 3,000 Dutch East India Company employees, while the upper class amused themselves with garden parties, balls and parades.

Although Cape Town was a veritable showpiece of extravagance and peacockery, the Dutch East India Company was on its last legs. Despite rolling out desperate cost-cutting measures, it was a case of too little, too late.

While the drama was unfolding in Graaff-Reinet and Swellendam, back in Europe, the Dutch East India Company was experiencing great financial difficulty and was in its death throes. In addition, the major powers, Britain, France and Holland were gearing up for a showdown. France and Holland were already at war and Holland and England had already signed a mutual agreement to protect each other's African or Asian interests. French troops had invaded Holland and forced the Prince of Orange to seek refuge in England on 18 January 1795. There, he requested that the British government of William Pitt assist the Dutch. Subsequently, Britain's minister of war, Henry Dundas, dispatched an advance squadron of ships to the Cape to protect it from the French. He sent a letter with the squadron of ships ordering the Dutch to cooperate with the British.[314] However, the British fleet arrived at the Cape on 11 June 1795, before the people at the Cape had learned that the Prince of Orange had been deposed.

Admiral George Keith Elphinstone and Major General James Craig brought a letter with them from the exiled William of Orange requesting that the Cape government admit the British as allies and advised them that the British would help protect them from a French attack. Some of the burghers were loyal 'Orangists' and still supported the Prince of Orange, while others were 'patriots'. In addition, the authorities at the Cape were not of the same mind on how to respond to this letter.

Colonel Robert Gordon proposed to the Council of Policy at the Cape that the British be made welcome as allies but was overruled by his colleagues. Gordon stated that although he was prepared to accept the British as allies and protectors of the Prince of Orange, he would fight to the end if Britain attempted to take the Cape for itself.[315] A compromise was finally reached: the British ships were allowed to source fresh food and provisions, but the soldiers onboard were not allowed to come ashore.

The situation became more confused when an American ship arrived carrying news that Holland was now a satellite state of France and was to be known as the Batavian Republic. The burghers decided to resist the British occupation. The red flag of war, or the 'blood flag', was hoisted at the Castle and burghers from the country districts scurried into the town, while many panicky families fled to Stellenbosch to escape the looming conflict. A military camp was established at Wynberg and ditches were dug around the town in preparation for the British attack. The British forces proved to be too powerful. When between 4,000 and 5,000 British troops were attacked by the burgher cavalry's nearly 500 men near Muizenberg, only 17 British soldiers were wounded and only one sailor died. It was all over.[316]

Commissioner Sluysken and his Council of Policy surrendered on 16 September 1795. On this day, 1,200 British troops and 200 artillerymen marched to the Castle and assembled on the open ground in front of it. The Dutch troops marched out to beating drums, past the lines of triumphant British troops, and laid down their weapons and lowered their flags. Britain had taken the Cape.[317]

Some of the burghers were furious that the Council of Policy had decided to surrender and one of them even attempted to assault Gordon, commander of the burgher forces. Although the British agreed that the control of the Cape would be returned to the Dutch once hostilities abroad ended, Dundas had never intended to relinquish this and, with the formation of the Batavian Republic, was even less inclined to honour that part of the deal. Some members of the Council of Policy at the Cape rapidly allied with the British and happily accepted employment with their new masters. Moreover, 391 members of the national battalion, mostly German, accepted the change in leadership with alacrity when offered five guineas to shift allegiance.

Gordon was devastated that the government was to be recognized as being under the king of Great Britain, instead of under William of Orange. The British had effectively 'stolen' the Cape.

Disappointment and shame over his role in the surrender of the Cape to the British, coupled with ill health and matrimonial and financial problems, led Gordon to kill himself on the night of 25 October 1796.[318]

Aside from being a military man, he had also been an explorer and had participated in at least four expeditions north of the Cape, on which he had recorded his discoveries regarding the local fauna and flora. Significantly, he had named the Orange River on one of these expeditions in 1777 and had established the first herd of purebred Spanish merino sheep in the Cape.[319]

The powerful Dutch East India Company finally collapsed in 1799 and liquidated.

Although those at the Cape may have surrendered to British rule, the burghers in the interior never did. The British had to bend over backwards to be accepted by the burghers, or Nationals, in Graaff-Reinet and Swellendam. After many conciliatory moves by the British, the Nationals in Swellendam signed an oath of allegiance to the king.

In March 1796, Andries Stockenström was appointed as secretary of Swellendam. Stockenström had worked as clerk for the Dutch East India Company in Cape Town and had been responsible for purchasing negress slaves for a ship that transported slaves from Madagascar to the Cape.

Craig was appointed as commandant of the town and settlement of the Cape of Good Hope. One of his first tasks in office was to dispatch Frans Reinhard Bresler to Graff-Reinet with instructions to listen to the burghers' views and complaints. When Bresler arrived, he was given accommodation in the *drostdy* and treated civilly. He was, however, not allowed to enter the courtroom.

On 22 February 1796, all of the burgher leaders gathered and summoned Bresler to state what business he had in Graaff-Reinet. Bresler read out his commission to the gathering and announced that he was replacing Friedrich Carl Grotz as commander of the Graaff-Reinet commando as well as that he would convene a meeting of the *heemraden* at two o'clock. The burghers were furious, especially as Bresler informed them that their representatives could not attend the meeting as they would no longer be recognized as officials of the area.

At two o'clock, Bresler ordered the *drostdy* bell to be rung. He then handed the British flag to a servant and instructed him to raise it. As the red, white and blue flag of England fluttered in the afternoon breeze at the top of the flagpole, an angry crowd surrounded Bresler. "Lower that flag immediately," Jacobus Joubert shouted. Bresler refused. Assisted by Jan Groning, Joubert pushed Bresler aside, grabbed the flag guy-ropes and pulled the flag down, to the cheers of the burghers. Bresler shouted over the din and asked whether the burghers would recognize the king of England as ruler and representative of the government. They shouted that they had already appointed their own "protector of the voice of the people", Marthinus Prinsloo, and that he had instructed them not to sign the oath of allegiance to the king.[320]

On 22 March 1796, Bresler was summoned to appear before the burghers' elected representatives. On his way to the meeting, Bresler had to push his way through a hostile crowd and ignore their jeers and taunts. When he finally reached the front of the crowd and the burgher representatives, he attempted to read out a proclamation made by Craig. Despite Marthinus Prinsloo calling for silence, Bresler was interrupted by heckling and yells by the burghers and, in particular, by Carel Triegard.

Van Jaarsveld then announced to Bresler that the burghers intended to retain their own government and read out terms to which the burghers would agree. The humiliated Bresler quietly left Graaff-Reinet two days later to report to Craig in Cape Town.

Craig was furious when he heard the news about the rebellion of the burghers in Graaff-Reinet. He immediately ordered a force of 300 men to travel to Stellenbosch, where they would prepare to attack Graaff-Reinet at short notice. He also ordered a complete stoppage on the provision of all supplies to Graaff-Reinet and halted the supply of any gunpowder and ammunition to the rebels, effectively cutting off their lifeblood.

When word reached the rebels that a Dutch fleet of nine war ships carrying nearly 2,000 soldiers and more than 350 guns[321] surrendered to the British without a fight, their spirits were broken. The presence of a large number of British soldiers and warships totally diminished their enthusiasm for a clash with the British.[322]

In August 1796, a document containing the signatures of the residents of Graaff-Reinet and surrounding areas pledging allegiance to the king was sent to the Cape. This document was taken to Craig and arrived in the nick of time: Craig was able to recall the force he had dispatched to subdue the rebels a few days earlier. However, the inhabitants of certain areas such as Bruintjieshoogte, the Zuurveld and Zwartkops River had not signed the document and, led by Marthinus Prinsloo, they settled for signing a petition that was sent to the Cape.

(They had initially talked of attacking the British forces.) This petition was signed by 31 burghers and contained several demands, or 'requests'.

In their letter, the burghers asked that they be allowed to enter the territory of the Xhosa so that they could recover their cattle that had been stolen. They asked permission to occupy land between the Kat and the Koonap rivers and that Bresler not be instated as landdrost, but rather replaced by someone more sympathetic to the Boers' causes. They also requested that the *heemraden* members be voted for and not appointed by the British government.[323]

Craig, a hard but fair man, rejected all of their requests and stressed that they were to treat the Xhosa with kindness and were not to attack or provoke them under any circumstances. Facing this brick wall, the burghers backed down and licked their wounds. They decided to bide their time, as they were sure that a foreign power such as France would attack the Cape at some point and assist them in overthrowing the British.

Lord Macartney was installed as governor of the Cape on 5 May 1797 and Major General Francis Dundas was appointed as lieutenant governor and military commander. Sir John Barrow became Macartney's private secretary and Andrew Barnard became the new colonial secretary. As Macartney's wife had not come to the Cape, it was agreed that Lady Anne Barnard would act as Macartney's unofficial hostess. Whereas Macartney's attitude toward the burghers and their problems remained unsympathetic and he was extremely anti their cause of identifying with the revolutionaries in Europe, Lady Barnard did everything in her power to meet with and to understand the Boers. She was determined to break through what she described as "their sulky and ill-affected" demeanour toward the British. She invited all of the 'respectable' Dutch families to dinner parties at her home and entertained and charmed them.

Although cranky, short-tempered and suffering from various ailments, ranging from piles to gout, Macartney abolished some of the cruel punishments previously doled out in the colony, such as breaking a man on the wheel. Nevertheless, he disapproved and despised any burgher who talked about or demonstrated republican ideals.

Macartney called on all residents of the colony to restate their allegiance to King George III. Those who held back from taking the oath of allegiance were swiftly visited by mounted infantry, or dragoons, whereafter these reluctant loyalists tended to change their minds. In some cases, those that refused to sign the oath were banished from the country. The commandant of Swellendam was one such person. He managed to evade the authorities for a year before he was captured, put aboard a ship and sent into exile.

There was an air of decisiveness in the colony thanks to Macartney and his team. He soon announced that all Xhosa who worked for the colonists should be discharged and sent across the Fish River and that none of the burghers should cross the Fish River without special permission. As De Buys was living on the eastern side of the Fish River among the Xhosa, contrary to the officials' stipulations, Macartney declared De Buys an outlaw and put a price on his head.

Macartney recognized his ignorance of the geography and people of the Cape. "I neither know nor can I learn where this Graaff-Reinet lies, whether it is 500 or 5,000 miles from Cape Town," he stated on one occasion.[324]

Shortly after this, he sent Barrow and Bresler on a tour of inspection of the colony and had Bresler installed as landdrost of Graaff-Reinet. Bresler and Barrow were accompanied by a Hottentot called Willem Hasebek, who would serve as translator, as well as two Boer guides, Jan du Plessis and Hendrik van Rensburg. Along their journey, they met with various small Xhosa clans and requested that these Xhosa return across the Fish River to their own lands. Without exception, they were told that the Xhosa would oblige but that they were scared of the powerful Chief Ngqika, who had defeated his uncle, Ndlambe, in battle and was keeping him as a prisoner.

Referred to as "He who stamps the ground while fighting" by his peers, Ngqika cut a fine figure of a man.[325] He was just less than two metres tall and carried himself with elegance and grace, but was decidedly macho. His face was more bronze than black and he had animated dark eyes that shone with intelligence. He had bright, perfectly-shaped white teeth and a broad mouth that frequently broke into a smile. His skin was soft, smooth and shiny due to the animal fat he smeared on it and he wore a kaross of animal skins draped over his shoulders. He also wore a headdress comprising a beaded band and an assortment of feathers, including that of the blue crane.[326]

When Bresler and Barrow met with Ngqika, they conveyed to him the fears expressed by the minor chiefs. He denied that he meant the minor clans any harm and stated that he would welcome them back to 'his' side of the Fish River. He also agreed to send a message of peace to all of the tribes in the colony and promised that none of his people would trade with the colonists or cross the Fish River. In addition, he agreed that all Xhosa should remain east of the Fish River.

After meeting with Ngqika, Bresler and Barrow then met with Chungwa, who had succeeded his father, Tshaka, and asked him to leave the Zuurveld and cross to the eastern side of the Fish River. In contrast to the warm response they had received from Ngqika, Chungwa's reaction was cool and dismissive. He refused to move his people.

In July 1798, Macartney defined the limits of the colony, declaring the boundaries to be: the Fish River, from the sea to Esterhuis Port at the end of Kaga Mountain; Kaga Mountain to the Tarka Mountains, to the Bamboes Mountains, to the Zuur Mountains, to the beacon of Plettenberg on the Zeekoe River, to Table Mountain; the Nieuwveld Mountains, to the source of the Riet River; the Riet and Fish rivers behind the Roggeveld Mountains; the Spionberg Mountain; the Kabiskow Peak; the Long Mountain; the northern point of the Kamies Mountain and the Buffalo River to the Atlantic.

No person was allowed to graze their cattle or settle outside of these boundaries. The penalty for doing so was banishment and the confiscation of all of one's property.

Macartney was too late in declaring these boundaries: Trekboers had already established farms up to the Orange River[327] and colonists were already living beyond these borders. However, the government did not attempt to bring these people back. As for the outlawed De Buys, he evaded capture and continued to live among the Xhosa east of the Fish River, as did many other men with a similar character.[328]

The Englishmen's visit had left Ngqika with misgivings about them. Moreover, he had not been impressed with their gifts. In fact, he had felt insulted that they thought that his cooperation could be bought for cheap trinkets and 'worthless' items. He wondered who these strange people were and recognized that they were so different to the Boers with whom he had become accustomed.

When he asked De Buys to explain who these white men were, De Buys did not hesitate to answer, "They are the Bushmen of the sea", thereby firmly implanting the idea that the British were robbers and traitors in Ngqika's mind.

The Xhosa were not the only ones who were unhappy with the presence of the British. The burghers in Graaff-Reinet complained bitterly that the British did not provide them with protection against the Xhosa and Hottentots. They took out their frustration on their Hottentot servants, who they considered to be on a par with animals, and often beat them or withheld their earnings. As the burghers were not allowed to trade the Hottentots as slaves, they therefore perceived them not to have any value.

When Barrow visited Graaff-Reinet, he noted the animosity toward the burghers building up in the Khoikhoi servant population. He described the burghers' treatment of the Hottentot servants such: "They beat or whip the Hottentots with thongs made from the skin of a hippopotamus called a sjambok. The whip is tough, hard and heavy as lead. Many of the Boers shoot their servants with small shot in the arms and legs so as to hurt them but not to kill. These poor people have lost their lands to the Boers, lost their possessions and are now treated worse than dogs."[329]

The burghers in Graaff-Reinet were outraged when an aging Van Jaarsveld was charged with fraud in January 1799. When this hero of the *volk*, the people, famous for distracting the Xhosa by throwing tobacco pieces to them and then shooting them, was arrested and sent for trial in Cape Town, De Buys, Prinsloo, Bezuidenhout and other hardliners believed that the charges against him had been trumped up. They were certain that the real reason for his arrest was that he had clashed with the British.

When officials loaded Van Jaarsveld into a wagon outside the *drostdy*, about 40 men answered Marthinus Prinsloo's call to save Van Jaarsveld and set off after the wagon in hot pursuit. They caught up with it two days later and surrounded it. The sergeant and two dragoons accompanying Van Jaarsveld saw that they stood little chance of success against the burghers and handed over their prisoner.[330]

On 22 February, De Buys and Prinsloo led 30 burghers into Graaff-Reinet who were hell-bent on causing trouble. When they threatened Bresler and members of the *heemraden* with violence, eight British dragoons quickly lined up and the British flag was hoisted up the flagpole. Standing under the fluttering flag, Sergeant Maxwell Irwin called his men to attention and warned the burghers, "Hands off the landdrost. If you attack him you had better beware, as we will defend him to the last man."

In light of such bravery, the Boers backed off.

The new acting governor, Major General Dundas dispatched a strong detachment of dragoons and Hottentot troops under the command of Brigadier General Thomas Vandeleur. These men travelled to Graaff-Reinet on foot, while Vandeleur sent two companies of soldiers and more Hottentot troops aboard two brigs, the *Star* and the *Hope*. After the ships landed in Algoa Bay, these troops would then march approximately 300 kilometres to Graaff-Reinet. On the journey up the coast, Vandeleur learned of the burghers' dissension and unhappiness about the lack of support provided to them by the British. Fearing that more and more recruits would join the rebellious band of burghers in Graaff-Reinet, he instructed all burghers that he encountered to remain on their farms and warned them that the penalty of death would be applied if they did not. Of course, word spread like wildfire among the burghers about the Hottentot troops that Vandeleur was leading to attack their compatriots.

When the British and Hottentot soldiers reached Graaff-Reinet on 19 March, they found that more than 100 Hottentot servants (who were no doubt tired of the Boers' cruelty) had drifted into the town to enlist under Vandeleur. In addition, over 500 women and children called on the British to protect them from the Boers. The Boers were disheartened by the opposition shown by the townsfolk and servants and subsequently gave up all ideas of resistance, laying down their arms on 6 April 1799. Vandeleur offered most of the burghers in the resistance amnesty and a pardon, but sent 18 to Algoa Bay, where they were put aboard the British war ship called the *Rattlesnake*, which was bound for the Cape.

Upon arrival there, they were imprisoned in the Castle. However, the main leaders, De Buys, Bezuidenhout, Jan Botha, Christoffel Botha, Frans Kruger, Jan Knoetsen and Jan Steenberg, managed to escape from Graaff-Reinet and coaxed their horses to gallop to the Fish River, which they crossed in order to live among the Xhosa. Vandeleur offered a reward of £200 per fugitive, dead or alive.

No sooner had Vandeleur quelled the burgher uprising than the Xhosa struck. Ndlambe had escaped from his nephew, Ngqika, and his followers rapidly joined him on the settlers' side of the Fish River and spread into the Zuurveld. Vandeleur and Barrow had reached Algoa Bay with their troops by this stage and as soon as they heard of the Xhosa invasion, they decided that the time was ripe to clear the Xhosa from the Zuurveld, as they already had a strong force of British troops and Hottentot soldiers assembled and within range of the Zuurveld.[331]

Soon after leaving Algoa Bay, the marching troops saw a crowd of over 500 people[320] heading toward them. Vandeleur assumed the approaching people were burghers, as many of them were wearing breeches and three-cornered hats and carried muskets. As the crowd drew nearer, however, he realized that this was a motley group of Hottentots.

When the two parties reached each other, the Hottentot leader, Klaas Stuurman stepped forward to identify himself and state their cause. "We are servants of the Boers and are sick and tired of how we have been treated by them," he said. "They took our land from us and made us work for them so that we can live. They treat us cruelly and punish us most severely at the slightest provocation. We have had enough. It is impossible for us to bear the harsh and unfair treatment any longer. We call on the British to assist us to restore our independence before you too leave our country. We have taken these clothes and guns that you see as we have not been paid by the Boers, but so far we have not harmed anyone. However, we have yet a great deal of our blood to avenge."[332]

Vandeleur persuaded the Hottentots to hand over their muskets to the soldiers and agreed that the men, women and children could travel with his troops.

When the Hottentots learned that the British were planning to clear the Xhosa from the Zuurveld, over 100 of the men enlisted in the Hottentot corps. The remainder merely trudged along behind the troops, with many carrying large bundles of clothes that they had stolen from the Boers. Others wore their booty, adding layer after layer of clothing.

The British Redcoats and Hottentot civilians and soldiers finally reached Chief Chungwa and the Gqunukhwebe near the Sundays River. Here, Vandeleur demanded that Chungwa take his people back across the Fish River and insisted that they remain there. Chungwa agreed to do as Vandeleur asked, although his cooperation was surely borne from the recognition that his people were ill equipped to fight against the British and Hottentot troops at this stage. Vandeleur was pleased that bloodshed had been avoidable and he ordered his brigade to march through the frontier districts, as he wanted to check that the Boer uprising was well and truly over.

On the way back to Algoa Bay, the troops encountered Chief Chungwa. He had not moved his people from the area. When Vandeleur demanded that Chief Chungwa keep his promise to lead his people out of the Zuurveld, Chungwa defiantly refused to do so. The disobedience shown by the chief warranted some form of retribution and Vandeleur promptly commanded his men to fire a few rounds of grapeshot at the Gqunukhwebe. These were the first shots of the third frontier war.

The Xhosa scattered and many hid in the thick bush by the Sundays River. Protected by this bush, Chungwa's warriors hurled a shower of assegais at the Redcoats and Hottentot troops.[333] It was their turn to retreat.

Vandeleur worried that the Hottentot soldiers and civilians might join forces with Chungwa and the Gqunukhwebe, which would result in his men being outnumbered. He therefore ordered Barrow to proceed with the refugee Hottentots to Algoa Bay and then led his troops back to the Bushman's River, where they set up a temporary camp.

Earlier, Vandeleur had sent a patrol of 20 men under Lieutenant John Chumney of the 81st regiment east toward the Bushman's River on a reconnaissance mission. He had hoped to rejoin them at Bushman's River and was surprised not to find them there. Sadly, Chumney and most of his patrol were dead. A large body of Xhosa had surrounded them after leaping out of the dense bush and surprising them. They used their stabbing spears effectively at close range. Totally surprised by the attack, and at close quarters, the Redcoats were unable to use their muskets. The Xhosa made short work of 16 Redcoats with their stabbing spears and severely wounded Chumney. Realizing that he was perilously close to death with three assegais sticking into his body and that the Xhosa would relish finishing him off, Chumney lured the Xhosa away from the four remaining soldiers, who managed to escape the warriors and make their way back to Algoa Bay.[334] Back at the camp, Vandeleur readied his men for an attack he was sure would come. The men did not have to wait long for Chungwa and the Gqunukhwebe to attack. Fortunately, the Xhosa warriors had no cover as they charged toward the camp and Vandeleur's troops fired volley after volley of musket balls and grapeshot at them. At length, the Gqunukhwebe retreated, leaving behind many dead and wounded warriors.[335]

Meanwhile, rumours of the Hottentot uprising had spread along the frontier. Naturally, the Boers panicked and many fled their homes to make for the coast with their cattle and all their worldly belongings.

When Barrow and hundreds of Hottentot refugees arrived at Algoa Bay, where the warships were anchored, they found over 150 Boers camped on the beach. The Boers demanded that the British protect them from the Hottentots, whom they feared would attack them.

Both the Hottentots and Boers had sought protection from the British against each other and the animosity between the two camps was evident. Not wishing to demonstrate an alliance with either group, Barrow ordered his men to bring a light cannon off one of the warships and mounted it between the two camps so that it could be swivelled at either camp. No doubt, he also intended to communicate that fighting would not be tolerated.

Soon after this incident, Vandeleur sent word to Barrow requesting the assistance of the burghers and called up two commandos to reinforce the British troops. The Hottentots at Algoa Bay most likely deduced that the British would not align with their cause when they saw the burgher commandos set off to aid them. Led by Klaas Stuurman, Hans Trompetter and Boesak, they fled and eventually joined forces with the Xhosa in a killing and robbing spree in the Zuurveld.

The Xhosa and their Hottentot allies attacked and burned Boer homes and farms and plundered whatever they could. Although the Boers fought back desperately, their defence strategy was uncoordinated as they operated in small, independent groups.

By the end of July, the area had been totally ravaged and almost no houses were left standing east of the Gamtoos River. More than 29 Boers had been killed and great clouds of dust marked the mass movement of the Boers' stolen horses, cattle and sheep as they were driven over the Fish River.

Back in Cape Town, Dundas ordered a large burgher commando to be called up from Swellendam and Stellenbosch. He also instructed some 50 British dragoons and several companies from the 61st and 81st regiments to march to the war-ravaged area. Dundas himself set off for the frontier to take command of the situation, which was met with wry amusement by the people of the Cape.[336]

Much to the chagrin of the Boers, Dundas hoped to negotiate peace with the Xhosa and a settlement with the Hottentots. However, the Xhosa stole the cattle of the British troops outside Algoa Bay, well before the troops had arrived in Swellendam en route to the frontier. Consequently, the incensed Vandeleur ordered the execution of a Xhosa spy who had been captured.

Dundas chose Maynier to negotiate the peaceful return of the Gqunukhwebe over the Fish River and a settlement with the Hottentots.

Both tasks were relatively easy to conclude: the Xhosa were satisfied with having driven the Boers out of the area, burned down their homes and taken their livestock and readily agreed to return to the area between the Bushman's and Sundays rivers, while their allies were content to have struck back at the burghers for the mistreatment they had received from them. They were especially appeased by Maynier's promise that the British authorities would ensure that the Boers treated them fairly in future.

The Boers once again felt betrayed by the lack of action taken by the government—this time by the British. Even Dundas described his agreements as being more an "abandoning of war than concluding [of] a peace".

A permanent garrison of 300 soldiers was subsequently established at Algoa Bay and a stone fort, Fort Frederick, was built to supplement the prefabricated blockhouse in use.

Bitterness, stronger tasting than that of the aloe, took hold of the Boers at the frontier and the disgruntled burghers routinely spoke of how unfairly the British had acted toward them by taking a placatory stance on the violence perpetrated by the Xhosa and Hottentots against them. They questioned how the government could imprison, exile and outlaw Boers for expressing their dissatisfaction with the authorities, without spilling a drop of blood or destroying property, and yet not punish the Xhosa or Hottentots, who had plundered, robbed, burned homes and murdered innocent women and children. The burghers were also united in their hatred for Maynier, who they saw as protecting the Xhosa and Hottentots at their expense, and were flabbergasted when he was appointed a judge in the High Court of Justice and as resident commissioner of Graaff-Reinet … as a reward for outstanding service shown to the British.

CHAPTER 8

God's messengers arrive

Slaves—the slave lodge—sex and the slaves—Cupido—famous names—free blacks—Afrikaner—the first missionaries—Van der Kemp—De Buys and Ngqika—Ndlambe—Stuurman—Cape under Batavia—Third Frontier War

After the British negotiated peace with the Xhosa and their Hottentot allies, the Boers were a melting pot of various emotions. They were angry at the disregard shown to them by the government, saddened by the recent loss of their homes and loved ones and afraid of what the future would hold for them. And they had reason to be afraid. The Boers would soon be plagued by two more groups that would threaten these hardy people who were trying so hard to carve out a corner of Africa for themselves: the slaves, namely, the 'free blacks', and the missionaries. Slaves had formed an integral part of Cape society from as early as two months after the arrival of Van Riebeeck in April 1652, when he requested that slaves be sent to do the unpleasant work in the colony.

Six years later, the first major influx of slaves occurred with 228 from Dahomey (now Benin) and 174 from Angola. Some were kept by the Dutch East India Company and some were assigned or sold illegally to the free burghers. These slaves would be the only ones to come from West Africa during the tenure of the Dutch East India Company at the Cape.[337] Thereafter, slaves were brought in from three sources: Madagascar, Mozambique and the East Coast of Africa. They were either sourced by Dutch East India Company ships sent to conscript slaves from these regions, were brought by the company's ships when they returned to Holland from Batavia and Ceylon or were sold by foreign slave ships en route to America.[338]

Between 1654 and 1786, the Dutch East India Company made 33 slave-conscripting voyages to Madagascar and brought close to 3,000 slaves back to the Cape. This figure was much lower than that conscripted by Arab and French slave traders during this period, whom it is estimated took as many as 3,000 Madagascan slaves each per year.[339] Dutch East India Company slave buyers would trade brandy, firearms or the internationally accepted Spanish dollar coin for slaves. Slaves sold illegally to burghers fetched between 20 to 30 rix-dollars (derived from the Dutch *rijksdaalder* currency) per slave, which was a small sum considering that a slave could be sold at the Cape for three to four times as much.

While most slaves were purchased for the Dutch East India Company to use, a few of the officials purchased slaves for themselves or sold them to the burghers.

The crews and officials of many ships smuggled slaves onboard to sell to the burghers for a good profit and it would seem that the Dutch East India Company turned a blind eye to this illicit practice. Transient slavers, on the other hand, were required to seek permission from the company before selling their wares to individual burghers.

Before the British occupation of the Cape in 1795, approximately 100 slaves per year were imported for the burghers. After 1795, the number of slaves imported annually more than doubled to over 250. Naturally, these slaves introduced their native languages to the colony and, as the burghers were hard-pressed to communicate with their slaves, they incorporated elements of these foreign languages into their own developing language, Afrikaans.

The burghers typically assigned Dutch names to their slaves such as Katrina and Andries whereas the Company gave their slaves exotic names such as Cupido, Fortuyn and Coridon or named them after their place of origin or the month in which they had been bought.[340]

The majority of the Dutch East India Company's labour force comprised slaves. However, a small percentage of the workforce was made up of Asian and Indonesian convicts known as *bandieten*.

Also at the colony were several Asian political personalities who had been banished from the Indies by the Dutch East India Company. These included Indonesian princes and their retinues.[341]

The male slaves at the Cape far outnumbered the female slaves: in 1791, only a quarter of the over 14,000 slaves were female.

Dutch East India Company slaves lived in a slave lodge,[342] which housed over 800 slaves in the late 18th century and was divided into three sections. One section was allocated for the men, one for women and children and one for slave couples who had decided to live together. This lodge evolved into a house of prostitution that was frequented by many burghers, visiting sailors and officials. Many of the female slaves were extremely attractive, particularly those from the East Indies. Their exotic features and slender figures, coupled with the lack of white women at the Cape, made them irresistible to locals and foreigners.

Each evening, European sailors and soldiers entered the lodge to seek out female company. However, these men had to leave the premises at 9 o'clock, by which stage Dutch East India Company officials had already counted the slaves and locked the gates.[343]

The lodge was not the only area in the colony where men could solicit the sexual favours of the female slaves though. The men would often entertain the female slaves in taverns in return for sexual servitude and would sometimes host parties in rooms at a tavern or elsewhere, usually wild orgies, where the soldiers, sailors and women would feast and drink copious amounts of brandy and beer, smoke opium and marijuana and fornicate in full view of the others.

Prostitution was financially rewarding—to the extent that some male slaves encouraged their partners at the lodge to take a European lover.[344] In fact, many a slave woman dressed better than the wives of the Cape officials, having been rewarded with expensive and elegant clothes for a few hours of passion. This pattern of having a European lover extended to the female slaves of the burghers, who often consented to their slaves living with their lovers. Moreover, some burghers cohabited with a slave mistress for many years and had the option of selling the woman and sired children to another burgher upon tiring of them.[345]

The children of Dutch East India Company slaves fathered by European men fared a lot better than those of slaves in burgher households. Not only did they get to live in the slave lodge, they also received an education. From 1775, the offspring of slaves and Hottentot women were mandated by law to work for their mother's master until the age of 25.[346]

The Hottentot servants in the colony were also open to solicitation. It was commonly known that a Hottentot woman's husband would consent to his wife bestowing sexual pleasures on any man who offered him a good stick of tobacco.[347]

Although some of the early settlers under Van Riebeeck married slave women, relations between male slaves and white women was not accepted. In fact, any male slave who had sex with a white woman was automatically sentenced to death.

One slave, Cupido Bengal, admitted to having had sex with his master's daughter as well as with another European woman, before and after she married. He was sentenced to be hanged for seducing his master's daughter and to be burned at the gallows for the crime of adultery.[348]

It was self-evident that morals in the Cape were loose: during the 18th century, it was common for the teenage sons of wealthy and respectable parents to have affairs with and impregnate the slave girls in the household. Surprisingly, the white male's sexual escapades earned the admiration of his peers and family. Unsurprisingly, the slave girl was rebuked for her "wantonness".[349]

Between 1652 and 1800, more than 1,000 marriages or unions between white men and slave women occurred. Some of those recorded include illustrious Afrikaans names such as Pretorius, Potgieter, Retief, Smuts, Botha, Treurnicht,

Mulder and Hertzog.[350] When the Dutch East India Company sold slaves to the burghers, the auctioneer's assistant would advertise the auction by beating a metal disk with a drum stick. The auction attracted many prospective buyers, particularly as a festive atmosphere prevailed and those who attended it would be given tea, beer, wine, cakes, bread and cheese. The slave being auctioned was put on a table to allow for good viewing. However, he or she was not allowed to be touched until sold and could fetch between 50 and 1,000 rix-dollars or more, depending on his or her condition.[351]

One witness to a slave auction in the Cape described it as a fun occasion—except for the slaves. Many of the slaves "appeared to be deeply affected by their impending separation from friends with whom they had long shared servitude. Several were bathed in tears; others lamented loudly".[352]

Although slaves could be granted freedom by their owners, the Dutch East India Company eventually restricted the release of slaves, known as *vrijzwarten* or 'free blacks' after gaining their freedom. The authorities worried that the free blacks would become a drain on the economy of the Cape. As such, they mandated that slave owners furnish a deposit before freeing a slave, in case the freed slave became a drain on the 'poor fund', and approved all requests to release slaves from service. The free blacks—generally descendents of slaves but sometimes convicts from Asia who had served their term—were on a par socially with the slaves but were seen as inferior to Europeans and were seldom referred to as burghers. Moreover, they had to carry passes if they wished to leave the town.[353] Slaves that absconded from the colony were punished harshly if caught. The authorities maintained that any person accused of a serious crime could not be hanged or punished until he or she had confessed to the crime.[354] This naturally gave rise to a range of tortures designed to persuade the accused to admitting to his or her crime, whether guilty of it or not. These tortures included branding the offender's cheeks with a red-hot iron, chopping off his or her nose and ears; ripping out his or her tongue; tying him or her to a rack and stretching him or her until his or her joints became dislocated; whipping; and being lashed to a double cross and beaten severely with a heavy iron club. Of course, the accused could be thrown into a black hole and fed only bread and water for six weeks. The torturers were most effective at convincing suspected offenders to confess, which sealed their death warrants.

At the end of 1795, the population of 16,839 slaves exceeded that of the European population by nearly 2,000.[355]

Many slaves fled from the harsh treatment of their masters. Often, these runaways were criminals and convicts who sought their freedom and a return to a life of violence and crime. A number of these fugitive slaves moved north of the colony and joined forces with a Namaqua captain named Afrikaner. Together, they formed wild bands of brigands and attacked neighbouring burghers' farms as well as anyone they encountered. Afrikaner based himself and his motley army on an island in the Orange River. From here, his gang of murderers and robbers would sometimes travel over 400 kilometres to attack an isolated burgher homestead. It would appear that resisting Afrikaner was futile and usually led to a violent and unpleasant death.

In May 1799, Afrikaner and his gang embarked on a violent rampage that would finally prompt the burghers to action. First, they murdered a farmer, Jacobus Engelbrecht, and his coloured worker, Jan Tieltias, and stole their muskets, two wagons, 1,200 sheep and 300 cattle. Then, they killed a Hottentot servant of Gert du Toit and stole several of his wagons, before moving on to the farm of the widow of Pieter Theron, where they stole 2,500 sheep and goats and 146 cattle. Finally, they attacked the family of Johannes Botha and took everything that he owned except the clothes that he and his family were wearing. A reluctant commando was mounted under Johannes van Wyk to hunt down Afrikaner and his band. Afrikaner's reputation for violence and the huge number of supporters he had intimidated the commando, which gave up the chase when the horses tired. As such, Afrikaner managed to return to the Orange River with the booty.

Eyewitnesses claimed that Afrikaner's gang was over 100 men strong and was assisted by bitter and angry Bushmen who relished the idea of punishing the Trekboers for persecuting them. Van Wyk called for reinforcements and large quantities of powder and shot and set out after Afrikaner later that year with a commando of over 130 men. Once again, the commando was unsuccessful in its mission to bring down Afrikaner and his bandits. They had found it too difficult to cross Bushmanland due to a severe drought. However, they attacked several Bushmen kraals before disbanding. Encouraged by Afrikaner's successes against the burghers, the Hottentots began planning their own retaliation against them. Their plan to murder all the whites in the Bokkeveld area, steal their weapons and horses and to then join Afrikaner's gang was discovered by Field Cornet Louw of the Onder Bokkeveld. He duly informed the authorities of the plot ... then murdered the informant and those that had planned to join Afrikaner.

Afrikaner's aggression and crime was not only directed at the white Trekboers but also at other gangs in the vicinity of the Orange River, such as that led by a Xhosa man called Danster. Despite the fact that Danster and Afrikaner had once talked of merging their respective bands, Afrikaner betrayed Danster and slaughtered the majority of his followers.

In October 1799, a group of Hottentots from the Orange River visited Floris Visser of Roggeveld and begged for assistance against Afrikaner, who had attacked them twice already and promised more violence should they not join him in his quest to wipe out the Christians.

Visser attempted to put together a commando in December but was met with strong opposition from Gerrit Maritz, the field cornet of Middle Roggeveld.[356] Maritz argued that December was harvest time and pointed out the strength of Afrikaner's gang, which had by this time swelled with further disgruntled Bushmen. He also felt that sending a commando from Middle Roggeveld, which had not yet been attacked, would attract Afrikaner's wrath and retaliation.[357] Even though commandos from Stellenbosch were sent by Dundas to apprehend Afrikaner, he remained free and continued his attacks on Trekboers and Hottentots in the north. By this stage, Afrikaner and his followers controlled the Middle Orange River and their reign of terror extended over the whole of Middle Gariep for about 800 kilometres.

While the frontier bubbled and boiled with warfare as the Trekboers, Xhosa, Hottentots and Bushmen fought each other for cattle and land, new arrivals in the Cape fought for a different prize: the souls of man. In December 1798, the first of the missionaries from the London Missionary Society arrived in the colony to save the souls of the heathen and savages. The first missionaries to arrive were John Edmunds, Johannes Kicherer and William Edwards. They were led by Johannes Theodorus van der Kemp, a 50-year-old Dutchman who had been born to a Lutheran minister in Rotterdam in 1748.

Van der Kemp was tall and had a high forehead, which was accentuated by a receding hairline. The salt-and-pepper hair he did have was long and slightly wavy and he wore it swept back over his ears. His widely spaced brown eyes burned with religious zeal and his thin lips curled at the corners, which made him appear to be approachable. Although he could rub shoulders easily with aristocracy (he was a close friend of the Prince of Orange) and the upper class, he was just as comfortable mixing with the lowest of the low in any land. By nature, Van der Kemp was a scholar and had studied philosophy at Leiden University. He was a skilled linguist who was proficient in 16 languages, including Arabic and Hebrew. Nevertheless, he had swapped his books for the sword of a cavalry officer by joining the British army. For the next 16 years, he became a hell raiser. He drank, was promiscuous, swore and fought anyone he could—the last thing on his mind was the love of God and his fellow man during this period.

He fell in love with Christina Frank in 1777. A wool-spinner by trade, she was working at a mill when she first met Van der Kemp, who promptly asked her to move in to his house. The match was considered socially unacceptable given Van der Kemp's high station and their cohabitation greatly upset and embarrassed his friend William of Orange as well as his family and peers. Consequently, he resigned from the military and went to Edinburgh to study medicine. He then married Christina in 1780 and returned to Holland to practise medicine.

The death of his wife and daughter in a boating accident in 1791 would be the catalyst to his religious awakening. Devastated, Van der Kemp sought solace in theology and cosmology and was "born again in Christ".[358]

After being ordained in the Church of Scotland, Van der Kemp and fellow missionaries boarded the *Hillsborough*, a convict ship that was bound for Australia. When it called at the Cape to get fresh supplies, the four missionaries disembarked to start to "make the first serious and effectual inroads upon the territories of the Prince of Darkness, and to open the way for the deliverance of the wretched Caffres from the idolatry and barbarism which overwhelms their extensive country".[359]

The missionaries left Cape Town on 22 May 1799 to meet with one of the first missionaries in southern Africa, Reverend Michiel Christiaan Vos. Together, they then visited Baviaanskloof and the Moravian mission station there.[360]

After Vos had ordained Edwards and Edmunds,[361] the four new missionaries parted company, with Kicherer and Edwards heading north and Van der Kemp and Edmunds east.

On 6 August 1799, Edwards and Kicherer reached a spot one day's journey north of the Sak River. When they found two springs in the area, they decided that this was where they would establish a mission. They called it *Blijde Vooruitzicht* ('happy outlook') and intended to use it as a base from which to teach the Lord's Word to all.

While the Bushmen merely viewed the men from the London Missionary Society with curiosity, the Boers viewed them with hostility. One Boer, Martinus Coort, expressed the feelings of the majority of the Boers when he said, "I will do nothing for the peaceful Bushmen, nor the missionaries but wish that the missionaries are killed and the Bushmen dead."[362]

Van der Kemp and Edmunds fared no better with the Boers. When they arrived in Graaff-Reinet, they met with suspicion and enmity, despite having received Dundas's blessing to preach there. The two men could not have picked a worse time to try to impress the residents of Graaff-Reinet and outlying areas, as the third frontier war was raging and the area was virtually under siege by Chief Ndlambe and his Hottentot allies, who occupied the territories east and south of Graaff-Reinet. "Beautiful homesteads, still smoking from the fire that destroyed them, lay deserted by their owners, who were either killed or fled to safety, leaving no living creature in sight save perhaps a dog howling over a dead body, a wounded horse or a mutilated ox."[363]

The bruised and battered Boers were unsure what the missionaries hoped to achieve but had the feeling that whatever it was would be at their expense. When Van der Kemp and Edmunds asked for their assistance to travel from Graaff-Reinet to the 'Great Place' of Ngqika on the Tyumie River, their doubts and animosity mounted further. Moreover, the Boers were not allowed to cross the Fish River to the territory beyond it and should they do so, they would encounter rebel Boers such as Prinsloo and De Buys, who were in bed with their enemy, Ngqika.

De Buys in particular had become one of Ngqika's trusted counsellors and even lived with Ngqika's mother and was betrothed to Ngqika's 15-year-old daughter. Referred to by the Xhosa as Khula ('the big one'), De Buys also provided Ngqika with access to gunpowder. Both men were ambitious. De Buys had even tried to persuade Ngqika to join his rebel Boers in overthrowing the British. The Xhosa chief had refused to participate though. Presumably, he had been deterred by the proposal to install De Buys as king of the colony after the coup was completed.[364]

The Boers at Graaff-Reinet were amazed and amused by Van der Kemp's determination to travel to Ngqika's kraal through a virtual war zone to bring the Word of God to the heathen and to save the souls of the Xhosa. Simultaneously, they viewed his quest as a betrayal of Europeans, as they believed that Christianity belonged to the whites.

Faced with a lack of cooperation from the Boers and unable even to source a Boer guide for their expedition, Van der Kemp and Edmunds set off toward Ngqika's kraal with just a few Hottentot helpers. They left in the nick of time: rebel Boer leaders had hired four British army deserters to murder them.

They travelled north in an attempt to avoid the main area of fighting at Bruintjieshoogte and, after passing the Sneeuberg mountains, they encountered many Boer families fleeing from the onslaught of the Xhosa. These Boer refugees were astonished that Van der Kemp, Edmunds and their small band of Hottentots were unarmed and riding to meet the very army they were fleeing from.

Their comments and stares did not go unnoticed by the two missionaries and eventually had an impact: their resolve finally broke and they asked whether they could join a laager (a defensive formation of tented wagons, usually arranged in a circle or rectangle with minimal spaces between them) comprising some 40 Boer families encamped on a farm.

When the Boers discovered who they were and what their mission was about, they closed ranks on them and turned them away. Eventually, however, the leaders decided to let them join the laager.

The hostility toward Van der Kemp and Edmunds increased when Piet Prinsloo arrived at the laager. It was rumoured that this rather sullen Boer who lived at Ngqika's Great Place had instigated the plot to have the missionaries murdered, which would not have been surprising given how openly antagonistic he was toward them.

He had brought a letter with him from Vandeleur that pardoned the Boer rebels for their rebellion against the British. However, the Boers did not believe that this amnesty was genuine and thought that the British authorities were trying to trick the rebels into surrendering.

Piet Prinsloo also brought news that Ngqika had sent word to the Cape authorities that he and his people were remaining neutral in the fight between the bands of Ndlambe's followers and the colony. Ngqika had already established an image among the British that he was a man of peace and would not seek trouble with the British.[365]

That night, the missionaries must have felt very lonely and frightened as they huddled together in their tent for warmth. Far from the life and society they both knew so well and surrounded by burned-out farms and animosity and resentment from their reluctant hosts, they picked up on the Boers' fear of an imminent attack by Ndlambe and his supporters. The many scouts and Hottentots dashing in and out of the laager brought back reports on the enemy's movements and created an air of disquiet in the camp.

While waiting for the comfort of the early dawn light, Van der Kemp and Edmunds learned from Hottentot and Xhosa visitors that Ndlambe's warriors and his Hottentot supporters would soon attack the laager and that the rebel Boers had tried to turn Ngqika against them. The messengers also reassured them that they would not be harmed during the attack.

As guns and powder were being handed out and women and children took up positions alongside the menfolk in readiness for the attack, the burghers asked the missionaries to fight alongside them. However, they refused, explaining that they had no issue with the Xhosa. This must have been a final slap in the face of the Boers after the charity they had shown Van der Kemp and Edwards.

That night, a steady procession of Hottentot and Xhosa visitors arrived at the missionaries' wagon, which further fuelled the ill will the Boers felt toward them.

The following night, the Boers watched the Xhosa and Hottentots light their fires on the slopes below the wagons. Like many other Boers, Piet Prinsloo had witnessed the steady stream of visitors going in and out of the missionaries' tent the night before. He stormed into their tent and accused the men of stirring up the Xhosa to kill the Boers. Van der Kemp vehemently denied this accusation but Piet Prinsloo remained unconvinced of their innocence.

Ndlambe's army did not attack until the wagons were on the move the next morning. With the terrifying battle cry of "*Pakgati!*", they emerged from the bushes holding their assegais aloft and protecting themselves with cowhide skin shields. They swarmed toward the front and the left of the line of wagons and many were killed by the Boers' first volley of fire. However, Ndlambe's warriors and Hottentot allies were relentless. Van der Kemp and Edmunds were terrified spectators to the carnage around them and were impressed by the bravery shown by the Boers against such a formidable adversary. "Nothing surprised me more than the coolness and courage of the women and children," Van der Kemp commented after the battle.

An hour into the battle, the Xhosa and Hottentot contingent withdrew and the convoy of wagons hastily journeyed to open ground, where Piet Prinsloo ordered the Boers to form the circular laager that would protect the Trekboers from numerous attacks in the next 50 years. Afterwards, Van der Kemp led them in a prayer of thanksgiving.

To the Boers' great pleasure, the missionaries soon pressed on toward Ngqika's Great Place. When they neared the kraal on 20 September 1799, over 100 Rarabe surrounded them. They communicated as best they could that they wished to meet with Ngqika but the Rarabe barely acknowledged them. Fortunately, they soon saw the majestic figure of Ngqika heading toward them. He was wearing leopard skins and his cheeks and lips had been painted red with ochre.

He and his counsellors contemplated the Europeans in silence and the chief eventually shook hands with them, as he had learned to do from De Buys.

Van der Kemp seized the opportunity to present Ngqika with a tobacco box filled with buttons and brass, which the chief accepted without saying a word. When De Buys joined the party, the chief asked him to enquire as to the purpose of the missionaries' visit.

Van der Kemp explained matter-of-factly that he and Edmunds planned to settle in Ngqika's country and to instruct him and his people in matters that would ensure their happiness in this life and the next[366] He then addressed De Buys, saying "I suppose you are Mister Buys … the Lord has sent me to preach the Gospel to these people."

Unbeknown to the missionaries, Piet Prinsloo and De Buys had informed the chief that they were spies who intended to poison the wine they would present him. As such, Ngqika was wary of the strangers and advised them not to stay in the area, stating that it was a bad time to be in the vicinity due to the hostilities between the Xhosa and Boers. However, he gave them permission to pitch their tent and would relay his decision on whether they could stay on to preach after consulting with his mother, sister and Chief Ndlambe.

Over the next few days, De Buys attended the missionaries' daily prayer sessions and Van der Kemp and Edmunds soon warmed to him, especially when he offered to build them a house next to his, on the banks of the Keiskamma River. De Buys in turn appreciated the missionaries' brand of religion, which did not focus on dogma but on developing one's spirituality, faith and humanity.[367]

The friendship that developed between Van der Kemp and De Buys most likely stemmed from the fact that both men were eccentric, extremely strong personalities. However, Van der Kemp was in a league of his own with his quirky ways and the Xhosa marvelled at this strange white man who walked barefoot over rocky terrain covered with thorns, did not wear a hat in the scorching heat and seemed to care little for personal comforts.

When Ngqika asked him why he did not wear a hat and shoes as other white men did, he replied, "What does it signify to walk barefooted … if my feet may be shod with the gospel of peace? What if I had no hat to cover my head, if it may be protected with the helmet of salvation?"[368]

Edmunds did not embrace life among the Xhosa and was frightened of them. He longed for his creature comforts and must have felt as though he was in hell on earth.

The newfound friendship between De Buys and the missionaries confused Ngqika. De Buys and Piet Prinsloo had been adamant that the missionaries intended to kill him on behalf of the British, yet De Buys had befriended them. Consequently, Ngqika's confidence in De Buys waned and he began to distance himself from him.

Ngqika felt insecure and questioned whether his other counsellors were loyal to him. He became moody and was often surly or aggressive toward his counsellors, especially De Buys. The relationship between Chief Ngqika and De Buys became extremely volatile and the missionaries subsequently became increasingly nervous and unsettled. Eventually, De Buys decided to bring matters to a head: he saddled his horse, collected his oxen and made it clear that he was about to leave the kraal for good. As he had hoped, Ngqika demanded to know what he was doing and why. "You have declared that you would consider me as your father, but your conduct to me, in these last days, denies these feelings," De Buys replied coolly.

Ngqika hastily apologized for his ill treatment of De Buys and further placated him by promising to protect the missionaries. Moreover, he stated that he would allow them to set up a permanent mission station on the slopes of the Amatola Mountains across the Keiskamma River.

Shortly after this confrontation, De Buys and two British army deserters left the Great Place to select an appropriate site for the mission and to erect a rough home for Van der Kemp and Edmunds.

Soon after the missionaries had settled into their new home, a messenger arrived from Ngqika's kraal asking that they come to Great Place to meet with Landdrost Maynier. Van der Kemp returned to the kraal, where Maynier told him that Dundas insisted that the missionaries take up their ministry in Graaff-Reinet due to the dangers of living in Ngqika's territory.

In a spirit of reconciliation, Dundas would pardon De Buys if he returned to the colony across the Fish River. However, De Buys hated Dundas's envoy and blamed him for the Boers' many misfortunes. He refused to even see him.

Prompted by De Buys's negative reaction to Maynier, Ngqika decided to kill him. Fortunately for the landdrost, Ngqika's mother dissuaded him from doing so. When Ngqika heard that Van der Kemp intended leaving the mission, he refused to allow the poor man to leave. Consequently, only Edmunds left for the Cape. No doubt, he heaved a giant sigh of relief as he rode away and waved farewell to his fellow clergyman. After Edmunds left, Van der Kemp started to find his missionary work increasingly demanding and unrewarding. He had had little success converting the heathen to Christianity.

Only five Khoikhoi women and their children had accepted Christ and Ngqika had forbidden him from preaching to the Xhosa, who found the message of religion extremely confusing. They could not grasp or accept many concepts central to Christianity and their many questions illustrated their confusion. For instance, they asked: "How did these words get in the book you tell us about?", "How did the first man who wrote them know them?" and "If God is all-powerful and the devil the author of all sin, why doesn't God simply convert the devil and save everyone?"[369]

As one Xhosa commented, "I have gone once or twice to hear the missionaries but could not understand what they said, and so discontinued my visits, although I believe them to be good, kind people who do no harm."

Ndlambe managed to stir up opposition to Ngqika, who became more and more unpredictable. Accordingly, De Buys began to fear for his own safety.

At the end of 1800, De Buys told Ngqika that he and his rebels were going on an elephant hunt. Together with Van der Kemp and a party of some 58 people, including deserters from the British army and their Khoikhoi wives as well as the Boers' Xhosa mistresses and children, he departed from the Great Place. (It is assumed that only De Buys returned to Ngqika's kraal some time later.)

When they reached Graaff-Reinet five months later, Van der Kemp discovered that a young man named James Read had been sent to assist him with his ministry work in this new locale.

Van der Kemp finally found a ready audience in the Hottentots, who were flooding the village to seek protection from Ndlambe and his supporters. They responded eagerly to the preachings of Van der Kemp and Read.

Dissident and rebellious Hottentots, led by Klaas Stuurman, remained in the bush and attacked the Boers at every opportunity. When Maynier refused the Boers' request that he allow a commando to retaliate against the Hottentots, they were irate and laid charges against him for fictitious offences.

Maynier was called to the Cape to defend himself against these charges, which he successfully did. However, on his return to Graaff-Reinet, the Boers circulated a rumour that he intended to conscript Boers for the British army and navy. The Boers' fear of conscription soon gave way to intense anger: Van der Kemp and Read were teaching the Hottentots to read and write—which the majority of Boers could not do—in their church. They had had enough. They hauled Maynier to the church at the end of May 1801, forced him onto his hands and knees and made him scrub the floors and the seats of the church to remove any trace of the Hottentots. They then surrounded his office. Maynier retaliated by ordering a detachment of British and Hottentot soldiers to open fire on the Boers, who scattered and took cover. A day-long shootout between the troops and Boers ensued and whenever the Boer snipers spotted Van der Kemp in the street, they shot at him. Eventually, the Boers withdrew from the village.

Van der Kemp decided that as he was so disliked and resented in Graaff-Reinet, he would leave the village and set up a mission in a Hottentot community. He and Read departed with a retinue of approximately 300 Hottentot devotees.

Dundas finally gave the Boers permission to form a commando and in no time, 88 Boers rode out to battle Klaas Stuurman and his Hottentot followers. The Boers were defeated within 36 hours and lost all their cattle. The ultimate humiliation for the Boers though was that the Hottentots had even managed to seize the Boer commandant's own gun.[370]

Van der Kemp encountered the victorious Stuurman and his followers near Algoa Bay, where he lambasted the British to Van der Kemp and Read, claiming that when the British decided not to protect the Hottentots from the Boers, they had left them no choice but to defend themselves against their enemy using whatever means they could. Van der Kemp and Read had already found an abandoned farm near Algoa Bay that made an ideal site for the mission, which they would call Bethelsdorp. In the final leg of their journey there, only 77 of the 300 people remained with them. The others had joined Stuurman and his band of angry Hottentots.

In March 1802, Britain and France signed the Treaty of Amiens.

Part of the terms mandated that Britain return the Cape to the Dutch. Consequently, British troops left the frontier and returned to the Cape to prepare for their departure. The Cape was now the responsibility of the Dutch and controlled by the Batavian Republic.

The abruptness of the British troops' departure left those at the frontier burning with discontent and panic as the Boers were already coming off second best in the third frontier war. By the end of 1802, more than a third of the burghers' farms and homesteads had been razed to the ground and almost all of their cattle had been stolen. In addition, more than a quarter of the Boers had fled from the frontier to the safety of the Cape. Chaos and violence reined from the Great Fish River to the Gamtoos River and Van der Kemp and Read had to seek shelter in Fort Frederick along with a small force of Boers, whose homes were no more than smouldering ruins in blackened fields. Those fields that had not yet been burned were trampled by hordes of renegade Xhosa and Hottentots who plundered whatever goods, produce and livestock they could. The countryside was a picture of desolation, as epitomized in a letter by the Boer commander of Fort Frederick to authorities at the Cape: "We are stationed here, the last outpost of the Christian empire."[371]

CHAPTER 9

The wheel turns

Split of the Xhosa—France and Britain at war—return of the British—Britain takes the Cape—Caledon—Andries Stockenström—Xhosa cross the line—Ndlambe refuses to budge—Cradock—Fourth Frontier War—end of the Fourth Frontier War

When the Cape was handed over to the Batavian government in 1803,[372] the Batavians brought with them a commitment to human rights and a perception that the Boers were to blame for the ongoing hostilities in the colony. However, it wasn't long before they changed their tune and talked of "exterminating" the Hottentots.[373]

Both the new commissioner general, Jacob Abraham de Mist, and the governor, Lieutenant General Jan Willem Janssens were determined to bring peace to the Cape. De Mist promptly sent instructions to the Boers in Graaff-Reinet to immediately cease fighting with the Xhosa and the Hottentots. Subsequently, the Boer leaders met with the Xhosa and Hottentot leaders on 20 February 1803 and arrived at a truce.

Janssens then set off to the frontier to see for himself what was going on. He soon learned that the Xhosa loyalties had diversified. The Rarabe had split into two factions: those that supported Ngqika and those that supported Ndlambe. Ndlambe had moved into the Zuurveld across the boundary of the Great Fish River and was in effect on the colony's side west of the river whereas Ngqika was on the eastern side, which, as far as colony officials were concerned, was where he was supposed to be.

Janssen called a meeting with the chiefs that were in the Zuurveld. Ndlambe, Chungwa and Ndlambe's brother Jalousa were reluctant to attend this meeting and Janssen's attempts to persuade and bully them to take their people over the Fish River proved futile.

The chiefs explained that they were disinclined to cross to the eastern side of the Fish River because they were afraid of Ngqika, who was once again leaning on De Buys for counsel. Governor Janssen eventually withdrew from the meeting because "The odour of the Kaffirs made the General, who had already been feeling indisposed … feel sick".[374] Once recovered, Janssen set off to meet with Ngqika.

De Buys had arranged this meeting and although the colonists and authorities viewed him as an enemy to be feared and mistrusted, Janssen acknowledged that his assistance was needed. Janssen and his retinue approached the meeting next to the Fish River with some degree of awe. However, their begrudging admiration was reserved for and directed at the white enigma, Coenraad de Buys. Ngqika was nevertheless impressive in his regal red robe, as was his confident manner. He strode into Janssen's tent with his counsellors and shook his hand firmly. During the ensuing discussion, Ngqika impressed Janssen and his attendants with his insights and wisdom. Of course, De Buys was translating for Ngqika and no doubt tailored Ngqika's sentiments to suit the audience. As he was the only person at this meeting who could speak Xhosa and Dutch fluently, he held a unique and powerful position.

That night, Ngqika, his wives and mother dined with Janssen. The chief very quickly adapted to using a knife and fork and instructed his wives and mother to do the same. He enjoyed the strange food and wine of the Europeans, but did not drink much. Unlike his wives, who enjoyed the wine to excess.[375]

The Dutch were under the false impression that Ngqika could order the other chiefs back over the Great Fish River. Although he agreed that he would respect that the boundary for the colony would be the Great Fish River, he pointed out that he could not request the other chiefs to do likewise as he had no authority over them. He also reluctantly agreed that De Buys should leave his kraal and return to the colony.

War between England and France began in Europe on 18 May 1803. When the news finally reached the Cape and then Janssens at Great Place, he promptly returned to Cape Town to see to fortifying its defences in case of a sea attack.

De Mist realized that the key to long-lasting peace was to clear the western side of the Fish River of Xhosa. He also concluded that Graaff-Reinet was not an ideal town from which to control the activities in the Zuurveld. Consequently, he established a post that he called Uitenhage some 32 kilometres from Algoa Bay. He felt that this post would provide the ideal base from which to coordinate military and administrative functions for the Zuurveld and would give colonists the best chance of moving all of the Xhosa back over the Great Fish River. The Dutch played on the chiefs' fear of Ngqika by threatening a combined Ngqika–Dutch alliance in an attempt to persuade them to cease their cattle rustling and to return stolen cattle.

Van der Kemp and Read's mission station at Bethelsdorp had become a refuge for Hottentots fleeing from ill treatment by the Boers and conflict. Some 300 Hottentots lived around the mission station, under the watchful and protective eye of Van der Kemp, who sent a constant stream of critical reports about the

Boers' behaviour to authorities at the Cape. De Mist knew Van der Kemp from his earlier days at Leiden University and was shocked to hear how he now lived and about what he believed and the ideals to which he adhered.

Van der Kemp had purchased a 14-year-old slave girl from Madagascar and then married her.[376] He lived among the Hottentots, in the same rough manner, in a small hut made of mud and reeds. The only furniture he kept was two low rickety bedsteads with skins stretched over the frames, two stools and a shoddy looking table. His appearance had changed for the worse and he wore old clothes and was altogether unkempt, as he focused all his energies on his ministry rather than on material things.

The Dutch officials recognized that Van der Kemp and his ministry were a hindrance to ensuring peace on the frontier. They wanted the Hottentots back at work on the farms and gainfully employed by the Boers, not living by the mission station and receiving an education.

Gradually, tension between Van der Kemp and the Dutch authorities grew, to such an extent that Van der Kemp accused the Dutch of not caring for the wellbeing of the Hottentots and of forcing them to go back to work for the Boers. In 1805, Janssens ordered Read and Van der Kemp to cease teaching the Hottentots to write.[377]

In July, rumours reached Britain that the French intended seizing the Cape. A gigantic force of 61 ships under the command of Commodore Sir Home Popham and 7,000 troops under General Sir David Baird were rapidly assembled and dispatched to the Cape. The British were back.

The impressive fleet arrived off the Cape on 3 January 1806 and anchored in Table Bay the next day. The ships were supposed to moor at Bloubergstrand but rough seas made it impossible to do so. Early the next morning, three regiments attempted to row to shore. Sadly, the boat from the *Charlotte* capsized and 36 men from the 93rd regiment disappeared under the waves. Reports circulating at the time stated that they had cheered as they sank under the waters.[378]

The men of the other regiments who landed successfully met with only light resistance from a burgher commando, which attempted to repulse the invasion. The commando only lost one man and four were wounded. Janssen assembled as many men as possible to protect the Cape from the British invasion and marched toward Bloubergstrand to meet the British, leaving some burghers in Cape Town to guard the town and to ward off an attack from the foreign forces landing at Saldanha Bay. Janssen was at a severe disadvantage in that he only had 2,000 men whereas the British had 4,500 highly-trained and battle-hardened troops. Near Blouberg, Janssen's men formed into a thin line that covered the whole British front. Cheered on by his motley bunch of Dutch, Boers, French soldiers and sailors, Hottentot soldiers and the Waldeck Regiment of German mercenaries who had joined in, Janssen rode up and down his line of men, egging them forward.

The 16 cannon of the Dutch soon opened fire and the British returned an even more impressive volley. As cannon balls fell between the two forces, the nerves of the men in the Waldeck Regiment broke and they began to retreat, despite Janssens' shout to "Stand firm! Stand firm!"

Fear spread like the measles through Janssen's army, heightened by the terrifying sight of the determined faces of the men in the Highland Brigade as well as the sound of bagpipes wailing and the sight of swirling kilts as these soldiers prepared their bayonets for a charge. When Janssen ordered a retreat, the British had only lost one officer while only 14 of their rank and file were wounded and eight were missing. In contrast, 337 men from the Dutch side were thought to have died or fled, as they did not respond to their names being called at the muster later that day.

Janssen wanted to march the remnants of his army to the Hottentots Holland Mountains to regroup and set off in that direction. However, on 10 January 1806, Lieutenant Colonel von Prophalow, the commander of the troops at Cape Town, signed the articles of capitulation.[379] Baird was installed as acting governor. This time, the British intended staying.

Cape Town at that time had a total population of about 17,000 people: 7,000 were white, mainly of Dutch descent and about 8,000 were slaves, which included approximately 2,500 "prize negro" slaves and close to 1,000 Hottentot servants.[380]

When the Dutch surrendered to Baird, Van der Kemp and Read fell on their knees and cried out their thanks to God. Janssen had halted their work and they anticipated that Baird would look more kindly on their ministerial ambitions. In the short-term, they were right: Baird allowed them to return to Bethelsdorp and to continue with their work of saving souls. He also agreed that they could resume teaching the Hottentots to write. Delighted, the two men set off for Bethelsdorp, with Read travelling by sea to Algoa Bay and Van der Kemp by land. Their joy at being allowed to return to the mission station was short-lived. The Boers hated the two missionaries and resented the work they did with a passion, as they saw them as traitors to the white people. They also begrudged that Bethelsdorp attracted the unhappy Hottentots like bees to an open tin of Coca-Cola.

The centre comprised a sun-scorched and flyblown scattering of about 50 mud huts on an arid, bare piece of land. The church was a clay hut with a thatched roof and was surrounded by shabbily built huts that were so low that a person could not stand upright in them. There was hardly any water fit to drink and the people in the vicinity were naked or wore rags. In short, the place and people looked miserable and desolate. Nevertheless, it was probably the lifestyle of Van der Kemp and Read that caused the most animosity among the Boers. They believed they had sunk to the level of the Hottentots, whom they saw as lazy, indolent and untrustworthy.

The fact that both men lived like the Hottentots around them and had both taken wives who were not white—Van der Kemp had married a slave girl and Read a Hottentot girl of 14—did not endear them to the Boers, who held that the missionaries encouraged the Hottentots to make trouble with them. To compound Van der Kemp and Read's difficulties, Baird appointed an American, Jacob Cuyler, as landdrost of Uitenhage and commander of Fort Frederick at Algoa Bay. Cuyler was the polar opposite of the liberal and philanthropic Van der Kemp and soon reported to the authorities that Van der Kemp and Read were enticing the Hottentots away from the Boers' farms and so costing them their labour.

Van der Kemp retaliated by writing a series of letters to the governor in which he accused Cuyler of participating in and perpetuating the oppression of the Hottentots. Moreover, Read wrote a bitter letter to the London Missionary Society head office in England in which he charged the colonists with cruel crimes against the Hottentots. This letter was published in the London Missionary Society's magazine and caused an uproar among liberal-minded people in England. Van der Kemp demanded that the Hottentots be exempted from going on commando missions and that any service contract between a farmer and a Hottentot be witnessed by a missionary.

Cuyler wanted Van der Kemp removed from the frontier and when the 29-year-old Du Pré Alexander, Second Earl of Caledon, succeeded Baird as governor of the Cape, it seemed as though Cuyler would triumph over the missionaries.

On 1 November 1808, Lord Caledon offered the Hottentots full protection under law against harsh treatment by the Boers and proclaimed that all Hottentots employed on farms had to be given contracts and have stipulated wages. To minimize vagrancy, Caledon mandated that every Hottentot had to be registered and have a fixed abode. In addition, those Hottentots employed on farms were not allowed to leave without being issued with a pass by their employers. (Any colonist could stop a Hottentot at any time and demand to see his or her pass. If the Hottentot could not present a pass, he or she would be delivered to a field

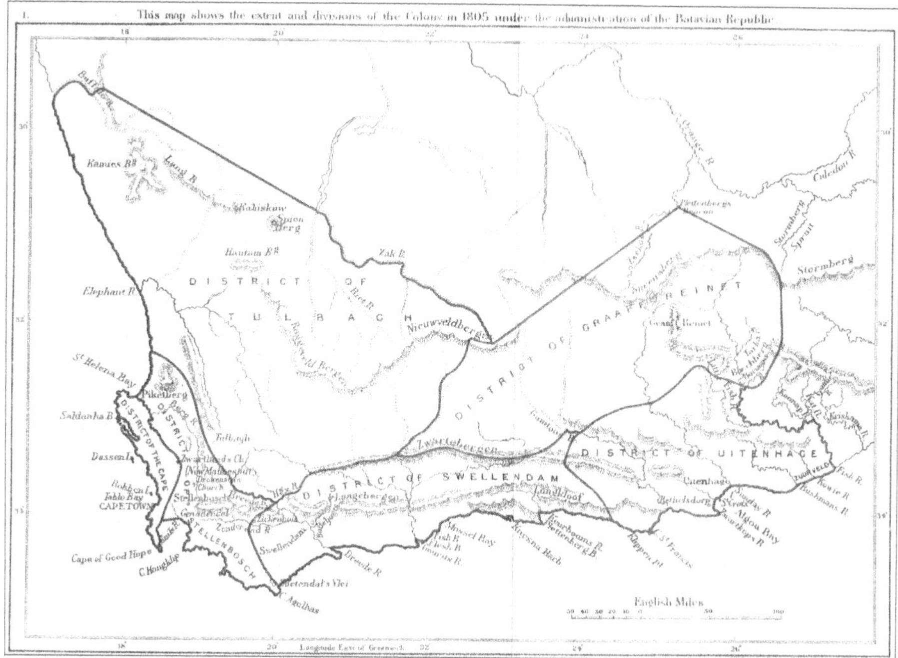

1. This map shows the extent and divisions of the Colony in 1805 under the administration of the Batavian Republic

cornet for punishment.) One of Caledon's first jobs was to relook the prevailing justice system. He determined that the centre of justice should remain in the Cape but introduced a system of circuit courts that took the judiciary on tour, to the main centres of the colony. When the Westminster government in London sent a copy of Read's letter to Caledon for investigation, he asked Cuyler to examine it and explore the validity of the missionaries' evidence. If the Boers on the frontier had disliked Van der Kemp and Read before, after they heard of this letter, they detested them.

Undeterred by the hornet's nest the missionaries were stirring up, Read wrote a further letter to London in which he accused Cuyler of being incapable of being objective in considering their evidence as he was married to the daughter of one of the farmers charged. He further claimed that there had been more than 100 murders of the Hottentots in their community. Read and an ailing Van der Kemp were summoned to the Cape to detail their charges against the Boers.

Van der Kemp was finally worn down by the continued lack of support shown for their ministry and decided that he would leave the Cape to go to Madagascar. Caledon resigned and was replaced as governor by a military man, Sir John Cradock, who handed Read's claims over to the circuit court. The charges included murder and assault and were levelled against 28 Boer men and women.

Van der Kemp's spirit was broken and his health deteriorated. He died on 9

December 1809, before the circuit court, called the "Black Circuit" by the Boers, had heard the case, which left Read to face the music on his own.

After hearing the evidence, the judges decided that none of the murders could be proved and only convicted on the charges of assault, illegal detention of children and withholding of wages. The judgements were a slap in the face for Read and undermined the missionaries' credibility for all time.

The way in which Read and Van der Kemp had been treated by the authorities and received by the Boers deterred the London Missionary Society from sending further representatives of the Lord to the Cape for another five years.

Turbulence on the frontier between the different groups of Xhosa continued under the British control. The two main protagonists were Ngqika and his uncle, Ndlambe, and both sporadically held and lost power over the Xhosa on the frontier due to the shifting loyalties of the minor chiefs such as Galata of the Gwali, Nqeno of the Mbalu and Xasa of the Dange. These minor chiefs switched allegiances as they saw fit.[381]

Matters reached a head in 1807 when one of Ndlambe's sons abducted one of Ngqika's wives. Ngqika retaliated by abducting Ndlambe's favourite wife, a beauty named Thuthula whom Ngqika had long fancied. Siko, another one of Ngqika's uncles, organized an uprising against Ngqika. He was supported by Ndlambe and King Hintsa of the Gcaleka. In the ensuing battle, an army led by two of Ndlambe's sons soundly defeated Ngqika's men. Subsequently, Ngqika fled with his few remaining followers into the Amatola Mountains. However, on the point of starvation, he was saved by some of the minor chiefs who had again shifted allegiance.

The balance of power tipped in Ngqika's favour due to the renewed support from the minor chiefs and he sent a message of peace to Ndlambe before returning east of the Fish River and being installed as the overall chief of the Rarabe.

Chief Chungwa of the Gqunukhwebe stayed aloof from the battle but was inadvertently drawn into the conflict when Ndlambe and his followers moved west of the Fish River into the Zuurveld, which Chungwa considered his, even though it was supposedly the terrain of the Boers.

While the Boers saw the Fish River as the boundary between all Xhosa and themselves, the Xhosa in the Zuurveld, namely Ndlambe and Chungwa and their respective factions, saw the Fish River as the border between themselves and Ngqika. Beyond Ngqika's territory, farther east and on the other side of the Kei River, was the country of King Hintsa, chief of the Gcaleka people and paramount chief of the Xhosa nation.

Keen to understand the problems, Caledon sent Lieutenant Colonel Richard Collins on a fact-finding mission to the frontier districts of the colony. While on this journey, Collins met a 16-year-old Boer called Andries Stockenström, the son of the landdrost of Graaff-Reinet, Andries Stockenström. Collins was not able to speak Dutch and, impressed with the boy, took him with on his exploratory journey as his interpreter. This chance meeting was the start of young Stockenström's career, which would span 21 years on the frontier and significantly influence the future of the colony and the events that transpired.

At a meeting with Ngqika, Collins learned that Ndlambe and Chungwa would never leave the Zuurveld and move east of the Fish River unless the British forced them to do so. He offered his own assistance to force them over the boundary. However, Ngqika's power had evidently diminished by this time and was declining daily. His mother, once all powerful in her own right, had returned to her people, the Thembu, as her lover, De Buys, was back in the colony. In addition, one of Ngqika's wives had fled Great Place after she was caught having sex with another man, whom Ngqika killed. (He soon found two new mistresses that had been introduced to him by the British: wine and brandy.)

Ngqika's rival, Ndlambe, controlled an army of some 3,000 warriors while Ngqika had less than half this number of men that he could call on.

When Ngqika told Collins that he was to shortly marry De Buys's daughter, as promised to him by De Buys, Collins expressed regret that she was already engaged to a man from the colony. Ngqika was furious at De Buys's latest betrayal. After this meeting, Collins met with Ndlambe. In contrast to Ngqika, he oozed confidence and power and even snubbed Collins by not slaughtering an ox for him. He also controlled the ensuing discussions. Collins then visited all of the minor chiefs before returning to the colony to submit his report to Caledon on the status of the frontier.

In the meantime, reports of increased cattle rustling and of brazen appearances of the Xhosa west of the Fish River in the Zuurveld emerged. Cuyler, a known Boer sympathizer, recommended that Chungwa and Ndlambe should be hanged if they refused to move their people across the Fish River onto the eastern side, as the government had instructed them to do. Much to the consternation of the Boers, the Xhosa moved deeper and deeper into the colonial territory on the western side of the river in search of fresh grazing. They appeared to be moving in a broad front past Bruintjieshoogte toward Graaff-Reinet in the north and past Algoa Bay on the coast. Moreover, Chungwa established several kraals about 250 kilometres west of Algoa Bay and one of the Dange chief's people were encamped halfway between the frontier and Cape Town.[382]

Rumours and stories swept the colony as the Boers realized their vulnerability to another Xhosa assault. Once again, the frontier was in a mess. Slave and Hottentot shepherds and cattle minders were being killed and herds of cattle and flocks of sheep were being raided. The Boers panicked and started abandoning their farms, which were promptly burned to the ground by the Xhosa. Boer neighbours congregated at central points and set up their wagons in laager formation.

Many Boers appealed for help to the Cape Town authorities. However, no help was forthcoming, despite what was observed by a British officer near Bruintjieshoogte: "Everywhere one looks, the countryside is overrun by the Xhosa. They have advanced farther into the Colony in every direction than ever before. Unless some decisive action is taken, I predict the most serious consequences."[383]

One family that was ruined by these attacks and that lost all of their cattle as well as their home was that of Salomon Maritz. He gave up farming and, on the point of destitution, moved to Graaff-Reinet with his seven children, including the seven-year-old Gerhardus Marthinus Maritz.

He was a highly devout man and became a missionary who worked among the slaves and the coloureds in Graaff-Reinet. He eked out a living by doing carpentry work.[384]

After Cuyler and Stockenström Sr had begged Caledon for assistance, the governor finally ordered that a commando be raised in June 1811. However, due to a row he had with Major General George Henry Grey as to who commanded the British forces, Caledon resigned before the commando was assembled.

Grey took over as acting governor and Caledon sailed for England in July. Subsequently, Cuyler and Stockenström Sr turned to Grey for assistance and presented him with a plan to rid the Zuurveld of the Xhosa. Grey sent a British officer, Captain Francis Evatt to meet with Ndlambe to establish when he intended taking his people back to the eastern side of the Fish River. Stockenström Jr accompanied him as translator. They met with a brick wall: not only did Ndlambe refuse to go, he also claimed that he had actually purchased the area on the western side of the Fish River from the Boers for 800 head of cattle and that he was therefore perfectly entitled to remain there. He made it clear that he did not intend to give up land that was actually his. When they met with Chungwa, he also claimed that the Zuurveld belonged to his people.

The arrival of Caledon's successor, a 49-year-old hardened career military man with 34 years' experience in the army relieved Grey of having to make any final decisions on the issue. Lieutenant General Sir John Cradock had joined the

British army at 15 and become a major by twenty-three. His previous posting had been as commander of British forces in Portugal, a post that he relinquished to no lesser personage than Sir Arthur Wellesley, Duke of Wellington, before being sent to the Cape.

Cradock immediately called for reports on the situation from the frontier. The outlook was grim: the Boers were fleeing the frontier—only one farm remained occupied east of Graaff-Reinet—and reports indicated that the Xhosa attacks were increasingly bold. He concluded that he had to launch a major military operation that would clear the Xhosa back over the Fish River once and for all and firmly establish the Fish River as the boundary that would be respected by both the Xhosa and the harassed Boers.

On 8 October 1811, Cradock called up burghers from Graaff-Reinet, Swellendam, George and Uitenhage to form commandos. Each unit would be commanded by its respective field cornet and be under the overall command of Lieutenant Colonel John Graham. Graham would also command the Cape Regiment, comprised of Hottentot soldiers who would soon garner for themselves a fiercesome reputation. The 19-year-old Stockenström Jr had joined the Cape Regiment and had become an ensign in the Cape Corps.

The 246 members of the Cape Corps left Cape Town for Algoa Bay with 214 British soldiers and officers on 10 October 1811 and joined the Boer commandos, which comprised several hundred Boers, and more than 1,000 Hottentot and British troops already in the frontier districts.

Graham had devised a three-prong attack: Stockenström Sr was to lead the Boer commando into the Zuurveld from the north, with his son acting as his aide-de-camp; Cuyler was to cross the Sundays River at the coast and march to Ndlambe's kraal; and a centre force led by Captain George Fraser and accompanied by Graham was to close in on the Xhosa, who would have been displaced by Stockenström and Cuyler's men.

The thick bush close to the coast gave the Xhosa an edge over the British soldiers and Boers. They were totally at home in the thick riverine bush and knew how to find and navigate the many narrow paths in it. Whenever danger threatened, they melted into the bush and avoided potential ambushes.

It must have been with some trepidation that the Boer commandos and British troops commenced their campaign on Christmas Day of 1811.

It was the start of the Fourth Frontier War.

They knew that the undergrowth that they had to pass through provided the perfect cover to the Xhosa warriors. While the Boers and British were being torn by thorns and getting lost, they waited for the terrifying war cry of the Xhosa as they emerged from the bush to kill them. Cuyler marched toward Chungwa's Great Place on 27 December 1811. As he and his troops passed through a thicket, a small band of Xhosa hurled a shower of assegais at his men and wounded one man. Cuyler then left his troops and rode ahead to Chungwa's kraal, where he found the Xhosa warriors already dressed for war. He issued an ultimatum to the ailing Chungwa: "You have [until] tomorrow to move your people back across the Fish River."

Graham instructed his men to be level-headed and fair in dealing with the Xhosa and to allow them time to collect their cattle before they dispersed. If they were not prepared to move, the Boers would drive their cattle over the Fish River and if they resisted, the troops would open fire. The Xhosa prepared for war, as they believed that the British and Boers were hell bent on battle and would attack them, no matter what they did.

The next day, Cuyler returned to Chungwa's kraal on horseback with 25 Boers and a Hottentot interpreter. As his party approached the kraal, they were surrounded by a party of Xhosa with shields and assegais whose faces and bodies were smeared with red ochre and who wore headdresses with feathers of the Blue Crane. The two parties looked at each other in silence. The Xhosa then parted to reveal the regal figure of Chief Ndlambe, the commander of all the Xhosa warriors.

He stood tall and erect as he scrutinized Cuyler and his men, who gazed at him with unveiled admiration. He advanced a few paces toward the British and cried out, "Here is no honey; I will eat honey, and to procure it I will cross the Sundays, Koega and Zwartkops rivers!" He stamped his foot in anger before continuing. "This country is mine! I won it in war and shall maintain it!"

He shook his assegai in the air menacingly and then blew a loud, shrill blast with a cow's horn. Immediately, 200 warriors emerged from the bushes and charged toward Cuyler's men. Cuyler shouted to his men to open fire on the Xhosa, who melted into the bush. He realized that not one shot had found its mark and promptly urged his horse to gallop out of reach of the assegais. His men followed, still shooting at targets that were impossible to hit in the failing light.[385]

Graham believed that if he could get Ndlambe to cross the Fish River, the other chiefs would follow suit and so decided to call for reinforcements from Cuyler so that he would have sufficient men to surround the thick scrub in which he believed Ndlambe and the main body of Xhosa warriors were hiding. He also sent for Stockenström Sr and his commando.

When Stockenström Sr received Graham's instructions, he told his son that he thought Graham was making a tactical mistake: if he withdrew his Boers from their position, the way would be clear for the Xhosa to attack Bruintjieshoogte and Graaff-Reinet. He departed with 40 Boers and left Stockenström Jr behind to defend Graaff-Reinet.

While travelling through beautiful countryside of rolling hills and valleys, the track Stockenström Sr had chosen ran through a narrow pass. As they approached it, Xhosa warriors began to emerge from the bush alongside it and stealthily assembled on both sides of the path. When Stockenström Sr saw the warriors, he held up his hand to stop his men. He then rode up to the warriors with only 12 of his men riding behind him. The others watched their progress tensely, guns ready.

He dismounted and calmly asked the Xhosa commanders to take their men across the Fish River to avoid bloodshed on both sides. While he was talking with them, however, a messenger arrived and whispered to the Xhosa leader what had taken place between Cuyler and Ndlambe the day before. The Xhosa warriors started whispering among themselves and grew more and more agitated. Although Stockenström Sr sensed trouble, he acted as though nothing was amiss and continued to talk with the leader.

When a Hottentot servant from the Xhosa retinue walked toward Stockenström Sr carrying a basket of milk, Stockenström Sr stopped talking and reached out to receive the gift with a grin of appreciation. As he did so, the Hottentot withdrew an assegai and stabbed Stockenström Sr with all the force he could muster. No sooner had Stockenström Sr fallen to the ground than the Xhosa hurled a hail of assegais at the Boers, killing eight more of them. The four remaining Boers fired at the warriors while retreating and joined the rest of their commando, who had watched the massacre in horror.

The Boers jumped on their horses and galloped away to spread the news of the attack. Unfortunately, they chose a circuitous route and before they arrived at Graham's camp, a Bushman bearer who had been with them and had slipped away staggered into the camp shouting that the Boers had been massacred and that he was being chased by the Xhosa army.

When Stockenström Jr heard the news of his father's death, he and a group of 18 Boers set out to track the Xhosa without delay. As they topped a ridge, they encountered the Xhosa coming up the hill and opened fire. They felled 16 Xhosa before retreating to the camp. There, he quickly ordered that the wagons be assembled into laager formation with the ammunition wagon in the centre, in case of a full-scale Xhosa attack. It did not materialize.

The Xhosa had finally avenged the murder of their warriors some 30 years before when Adriaan van Jaarsveld had scattered tobacco on the ground and then shot them in cold blood as they scrambled to pick it up. The Xhosa who had killed Stockenström Sr and his men were all members of the Dange tribe—and had lost many friends and relatives to Van Jaarsveld's men that day.

The wheel had come full circle.

Graham had received a message from Ndlambe requesting a meeting and was already on his way to the meeting when the news arrived regarding the massacre of Stockenström Sr and his men. Unaware of what had taken place, he arrived at the appointed rendezvous point with his small party of escorts. There was no sign of any Xhosa. Graham and his interpreter called out that they had arrived and were gratified when someone in the nearby bushes shouted back that Ndlambe would be there shortly. Soon, the bushes stirred and a Xhosa man emerged. Then another and another, until they were surrounded by warriors dressed for war. Then Ndlambe appeared.

He addressed Graham in a loud and threatening voice and his manner was aggressive. He demanded that Graham explain what right his people had to march into the Zuurveld, onto land that belonged to him and his people. While Graham was being shouted at, he saw two Boers galloping toward them. The Xhosa parted for the two riders, whose horses were panting and sweating due to the hard ride they had had, to enable them to deliver Graham a note. When he read the news about Stockenström Sr, he immediately realized the enormous danger he and he men were in. Without a flicker of emotion on his face, he looked straight at Ndlambe and informed him that the note was from the governor. Then, with a wry smile, he told Ndlambe that the governor had sent word acknowledging Ndlambe's right to be in the Zuurveld and that he had been ordered to withdraw his troops. He quickly ordered his men to mount their horses, saluted Ndlambe and told him to "cultivate the art of peace", before riding away with his escorts.

Once a safe distance from the Xhosa, Graham stopped to read the message to his men and then led them in heartfelt prayer to thank God for having delivered them from what they were sure was an ambush.

On 1 January 1812, Graham led a force of approximately 480 Boers and 120 Hottentots into the thick bush for a final assault on the Xhosa. Graham was determined to crush the Xhosa. He intended attacking them where they had never been attacked before—in the thick bush on the banks of the rivers.[386] He said, "My intention is to attack the savages in a way which I confidently hope will leave a lasting impression on their memories."

The Boers searched the thick bush for the elusive Xhosa, shooting at every shadow that moved. Despite their nervousness in the bush, the Boers were heartened by the determination shown by Graham to drive the Xhosa over the Fish River and approached their task with cheerfulness and enthusiasm.

Unseen by the Boers, the Gqunukhwebe people slipped through the bushes and over the Fish River.

After five days, the Boers had killed only 12 Xhosa warriors but managed to herd about 2,500 head of cattle out of the thick bush. The Boers were ecstatic that Chungwa, chief of the Gqunukhwebe, was among the 12 dead.

While the Boers were attempting to clear the forests of Xhosa, Ndlambe and his people made their escape east and crossed over the Fish River. For the next few weeks, Graham led his troops and the Boer forces in cleaning-out operations through kloofs, ravines and thick bush country. They killed about 30 Xhosa, took over 100 women and children prisoner and seized 600 head of cattle. Wherever they came across a kraal, they immediately set fire to it. Subsequently, the eastern side of the river was marked by the blackened ruins of hundreds of burned-out shells of mud-and-thatch huts.

Soon, there were no Xhosa left on the western side of the Fish River.[387] To deter any Xhosa from returning, Graham ordered that any Xhosa found in the colony should be shot on sight. Trade between the Boers and the Xhosa was also banned and the Fish River effectively became the boundary between the colonists and the Xhosa nation. The cattle taken from the Xhosa were shared among the Boers as compensation to those who had lost property because of them. Moreover, the Xhosa were told that 600 head would be returned to them once they had shown that they would remain on the other side of the Fish River and were behaving themselves. This time the settlers had proved successful in defeating the Xhosa. Some 2,000 troops, burghers and Hottentots had successfully driven 20,000 Xhosa warriors back over the Fish River. By March 1812, the Fourth Frontier War was officially over.

CHAPTER 10

Execution at Slagtersnek

Chain of forts—words rather than deeds—quitrent system—Booy and Bezuidenhout—anger mounts—Slagtersnek—the role of the prophets—Somerset—Spoor Law—Battle of Amalinde—Fifth Frontier War—attack on Grahamstown

After the Fourth Frontier War, Governor Cradock set about fortifying the colony's defences and sanctioned the construction of a row of forts between the sea and the second mountain chain. These forts were manned by British troops and burghers from Graaff-Reinet and Uitenhage to ensure that there were no more incursions by the Xhosa.

On 10 July 1812, 21-year-old Stockenström Jr was appointed deputy landdrost of Graaff-Reinet. Graham needed a new military headquarters and, together with Stockenström Jr, he decided that a farm set in a bowl of hills 30 kilometres from the Great Fish River and 135 kilometres from Uitenhage would make the ideal location for it. The post was named Grahamstown in honour of Colonel Graham and Cradock then named the overall area Albany, after the American town in which Cuyler had been born.

An exchange of letters between Lord Liverpool, secretary of state for the colonies in London, and Cradock made it very clear that although Cradock and Graham were determined to deal with the Xhosa by force and warfare, the government in London was not inclined to support this.

Well-intentioned Cradock may have been but his years of seeking military solutions were influencing his decisions. There was at this time a growth in awareness of human rights throughout the world and even Cradock could not ignore this increasing humanitarianism. Consequently, he asked Stockenström Jr what his views were on the treatment of coloured people.

Stockenström Jr responded that "strict and equal justice at all costs was the only safe course". Impressed by the young Boer's response, Cradock looked him in the eye and said, "Thar is the secret; you have it."[388]

In 1812, however, Cradock gave the farmers the right to the free labour of any Hottentot child born on their farms, from the age of eight to 18. So much for getting behind the human rights movement.

Despite the withdrawal of the Xhosa across the Fish River to the eastern side, the Boers still encountered difficulties—this time with the weather gods.

Drought in 1813 ravaged the land occupied by the Boers and, to compound matters, the number of cattle raids by the Xhosa was rapidly increasing.

Once more, Cradock acted firmly. He appointed Captain George Fraser to head up a powerful commando to clear the Xhosa back across the Fish River. He instated Stockenström Jr as Fraser's deputy and ordered them to show no mercy to the Xhosa other than to the women and children. As before, the Xhosa melted into the brush and the commando battled to find them.

The Boers' anxiety knew no bounds. On the one hand, they were frustrated with the seemingly seesawing attitude of the governors of the Cape and, on the other, were unsure whether they could truly trust the British to support them.

One night while on commando, Stockenström Jr woke to find his army of 500 Boers sitting on their haunches with their guns on their knees, prepared for battle and staring out into the darkness. When he asked them what they were doing and why, he learned that they believed they were to be marched to Algoa Bay, where they would be forced into the service of the British army or navy.

While on patrol one day, Stockenström Jr passed through some thick vegetation and was attacked by Xhosa. While assegais whizzed past him out of the bushes, one of his men shouted in warning, "The kaffir throws!" Stockenström Jr turned and shot his assailant. This one fatality would later come back to haunt him.

Cradock introduced a new form of farm ownership among the Boers. Previously, any man who wanted new pasture would select a site, put up a beacon and pace out half an hour's walk in each direction of the beacon to mark the boundaries. After one had filed a loan farm lease application, the authorities would come to inspect the property and finally approve the loan farm application. Thereafter, the farmer would rent the land for 26 rix-dollars per year and have to renew the lease annually. Although the occupant could dispose of his farm and assets at any time, he did not own the land.

Cradock introduced a system of 'quitrent' in an attempt to stop the Boers from moving farther and farther away from the Cape and to ensure that the Boers were not spread too thinly over a large area. With this system, farm boundaries were to be marked out and recorded and the amount of rent payable would depend on the size of the farm. In addition, ownership of the farm would pass from father to son or to the farmer's nearest descendent and farmers could now sell the land of the farms as well as the '*opstal*'.

Despite that the Boers had now attained ownership of the farms, many in isolated areas saw the changes in land ownership policy as yet another blow against them perpetrated by the British. Many Boers who had lost their farms worked on others' farms or squatted on rough, unwanted land while others were behind in their payments for their loan farms. In effect, Cradock's changes meant that many had to pay a higher rental than before. The feeling of discontent in the frontier districts grew at an alarming pace and the Boers began to view the British as an enemy hell bent on persecuting them.

In 1813, a Hottentot called Booy who was employed by Frederick Cornelius Bezuidenhout ran away. He claimed that Bezuidenhout had ill-treated him. Nevertheless, Stockenström Jr persuaded him to return to Bezuidenhout on the undertaking that he would investigate the matter. Soon after this incident, Cradock sailed away into the sunset of retirement. He was succeeded by Major General Lord Charles Somerset, who arrived in early 1814.

Booy persistently ran away from Bezuidenhout and kept claiming cruelty at the hands of his employer. When the authorities summoned Bezuidenhout to face these charges, he refused to appear before the court. Eventually, the judges of the circuit court sentenced him to one month in jail for contempt of court due to his repeated refusals to appear before them.

Landdrost Stockenström Jr, now with the rank of lieutenant, sent the deputy sheriff to seek assistance from commando field cornet Cornelis Johannes Olivier. When he was told that he was to arrest Bezuidenhout, he refused because he knew that Bezuidenhout would resist arrest and that his own life would be in danger. The deputy sheriff then sought assistance from Captain Andrews, the commander of the nearest military post. Andrews ordered Lieutenant Frans Rosseau and 12 Hottentot soldiers to accompany the deputy sheriff and his one constable to arrest Bezuidenhout on his farm, where he lived, much to Stockenström Jr's disgust, with a Hottentot women and his coloured son. On the morning of 16 October 1815, the Hottentot soldiers, Rosseau and Ensign McKay approached Bezuidenhout's farm. Bezuidenhout had been expecting a visit from the law and was prepared for it. When he saw them coming, he grabbed his elephant gun and passed a gun to his coloured servant Hans and to a young man who was staying with him called Jacob Erasmus. They then ran outside and took up their positions behind some large rocks.

Rosseau's men marched toward the homestead, unaware that they were being watched. Bezuidenhout and his two companions fired high and wide, as they hoped to scare away the soldiers, who immediately broke rank and took cover from the bullets whizzing above their heads.

When they returned fire, Bezuidenhout dashed to some caves near the river with his two companions hot on his heels. Bezuidenhout, Hans and Jacob were soon found by the Hottentot soldiers, who had followed them to their hiding place. They shouted to Bezuidenhout that he should give himself up. "I would rather die than surrender to a bunch of Hottentots," Bezuidenhout shouted back.

The stalemate continued for four hours. Rosseau then instructed his soldiers to enter the cave and seize them. They could only enter through the narrow opening to the cave one at a time and Bezuidenhout fired as soon as he saw the first intruder. He missed. He then picked up his spare gun and aimed a second time. However, the soldier shot Bezuidenhout before he could squeeze the trigger and he slumped to the ground with a bullet through his heart. It was all over. Hans and Erasmus lifted up their hands in surrender while looking at Bezuidenhout's corpse.[389]

At the funeral the next day, Bezuidenhout's family and friends stood solemnly around the grave. When the wooden coffin was lowered, Bezuidenhout's brother, Johannes, swore he would avenge the death of his sibling. "I will never rest until all the Hottentot soldiers have been driven from the colony and the officials who ordered them to kill my brother have been punished, and here I name Landdrost Stockenström, Field Cornet Philippus Opperman and Lieutenant Rosseau. This I swear," he said.[390]

The seeds for insurrection had been sown.

Other hotheads, particularly Hendrik Prinsloo, Marthinus Prinsloo's son, egged Johannes on and several meetings were held where revolution against the British was discussed. The Boers argued that the British tyrants and villains had made land rentals so high that they could not afford to live and that the British preferred the Hottentots to the Boers. Subsequently, a delegation of the revolutionaries was sent to meet with Ngqika to solicit his support in driving the British into the sea.

When the Boers met with Ngqika, they lied to him by claiming that all of the Boers between the frontier and Cape Town were ready to take on the British and that 600 Dutch soldiers had arrived to help them. Ngqika was no fool, however, and smelled a rat. To buy some time, he offered to discuss the matter with other Xhosa chiefs.

Prinsloo and Johannes then embarked on a recruitment campaign with the other farmers. They made promises, threatened, cajoled and used every trick in the book to get other Boers to join their revolution. However, the two men were not well liked by other Boers in the area. Unsurprisingly, when any farmer hesitated to support them, they were threatened physically and informed that their homes would be burned to the ground when the Xhosa joined them and invaded the colony again.

Rumours swept the frontier once more and Stockenström Jr and Cuyler heard about the proposed revolution. They immediately had Prinsloo arrested and

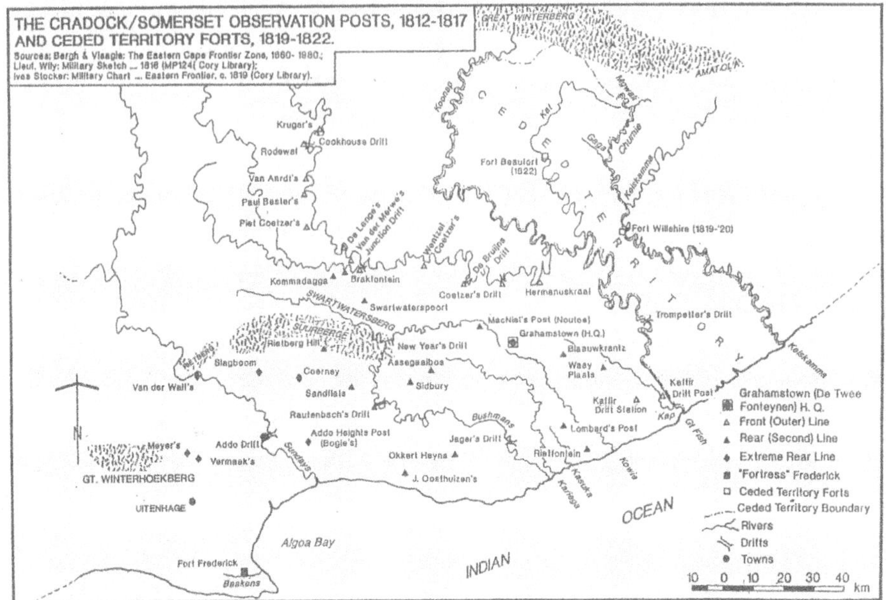

locked up on Willem Adriaan van Aardt's farm. Cuyler then marched against the rebels, who, on seeing that he and his men meant business, lost their eagerness to fight. Sixty surrendered without firing a shot and the others fled. Johannes and his family as well as three of the ringleaders of the uprising made for the Fish River, which they intended to cross over as they assumed they would receive Ngqika's protection. However, 130 Xhosa surrounded them before they reached the Fish River. The fugitive Boers sheltered behind their wagons and fired at their pursuers. Johannes's wife, Martha Faber, repeatedly loaded her husband's guns and passed them to him, urging him to keep shooting and not to surrender. Johannes's young son, Gerrit Pieter, stood next to his father and fired at the soldiers relentlessly. During the standoff, one Hottentot soldier was killed. Then, a hail of bullets fatally struck down Johannes and wounded Martha and the 12-year-old Gerrit.

The revolution was over. The troops rounded up the 39 remaining rebels, who were sent to Uitenhage to await trial. Of those arrested, only ten were landowners. The others were Boers who worked for landowners. Five of the main conspirators, including Hendrik Prinsloo, were sentenced to be hanged, while the others were sentenced to punishments ranging from monetary fines to banishment from the frontier. However, all had to watch the executions of their leaders at Captain Andrews' post on Van Aardt's farm, known as Slagtersnek.

On 9 March 1816, Reverend Herold read the five men their last rites. The men then requested that they be allowed to sing a hymn with their friends before they were executed. One of those present that day said that "they sang in the most clear voices" and that their singing was "extremely impressive".

As the last 'amen' was dying away, Stephanus Bothma, one of the five condemned men and, ironically, a descendent of the first burgher of the Cape colony, addressed the crowd. He warned them to behave themselves in future if they wanted to avoid meeting the same fate as he was about to. All five of the condemned men then climbed the scaffold from which five noosed ropes hung, and looked down at the five distinctly shaped graves below. Watched by a horrified crowd which included Bezuidenhout's wounded wife, the platform fell away from under the feet of the condemned men. The crowd screamed in horror as one man kicked and twitched as he died and the ropes on the remaining four snapped. The four Boers fell heavily to the ground in a cloud of dust, the ropes still around their necks.

The four dazed and confused men dusted themselves off and rushed toward Stockenström Jr, who was watching the proceedings with Cuyler. They begged him for mercy, while friends and relatives crowded around him shouting that this was a sign from the Lord that the men should not hang. Cuyler was unmoved by the weeping and wailing of the families and sent for new rope, which only arrived several hours later. While waiting, the condemned men watched their friend slowly turning and turning as a grim reminder of what lay ahead for them. The wailed prayers from the highly agitated crowd could do nothing to save them: they were soon hanged from the scaffold with necks broken.[391] The events at Slagtersnek that day left an indelible impression on the minds of all Boers who had witnessed them.

In 1816, Somerset gave the nod to the establishment of a mission station on the other side of the Great Fish River, in the land of Ngqika and the Xhosa. A young missionary called Joseph Williams, who had only recently arrived from England with his wife and baby son, was appointed to establish and run the mission, in the heart of the Xhosa territory. A daunting task. Williams and James Read set off to see Ndlambe and Ngqika, to solicit their support for the project. Both Ngqika and Ndlambe had prophets—Ntsikana and Nxele, respectively—as counsellors and these influential advisers wielded enormous influence and power over the two chiefs. These men would make Williams's task harder. Eventually, Read and Williams were allowed to choose a site for the mission station in a valley of the Tyumie River and Williams and his wife started to build the mission station.

When Read returned to Bethelsdorp, he became embroiled in a scandal: he committed adultery with the daughter of a Hottentot elder from the church and sired a boy with her. He was forced to leave Bethelsdorp for a time and was suspended by his superiors.

The Boers at the frontier were simmering due to the continued cattle rustling and attacks by the Xhosa. In addition, the rivalry and jostling for power between Ngqika and Ndlambe had worsened and Hintsa began to consider expanding his sphere of influence westward due to the ongoing troubles and divisions of the Rarabe under Ngqika and Ndlambe. (Hintsa favoured Ndlambe over Ngqika.[392])

Like his predecessors, Somerset was determined to bring peace and stability to the frontier area. Therefore, on 2 April 1817, he set off to assess the situation on the frontier and to meet with the Xhosa chiefs. In a bid to demonstrate the strength of the authorities, he took a massive force, including 100 dragoons, British infantry regiments, field artillerymen, Hottentot soldiers from the Cape Corps and 350 Boer commandos.

He met with chiefs Ngqika and Ndlambe on the banks of the Kat River, where he told them that when cattle were stolen there would be penalties. The aggrieved party would have to report his loss of cattle to the nearest military post and a military patrol would then track the stolen cattle and demand compensation from whoever was found to be in possession of them. If compensation was not forthcoming, the men would seize cattle from this person to compensate the aggrieved party.

Somerset called this protocol the 'Spoor Law', 'Patrol System' or 'Reprisal System'.

He also informed Ngqika and Ndlambe that the Xhosa would be allowed to cross over into the colony twice a month to trade in Grahamstown. The Xhosa chiefs would have to issue permits to those who wished to enter the colony and permit-holders would have to report to the nearest military post, from which soldiers would then escort them to Grahamstown. Somerset warned the chiefs to be extremely careful as to whom they awarded passes, as they would be held responsible for any wrongdoing of these people while in the colony. Further, Somerset promised to provide the chiefs' people with military protection should they be attacked.

By 1818, Williams had only converted four Xhosa to Christianity. He was eventually worn down by his constant fear of an attack by either Ngqika's men or Ndlambe's and by his solitary lifestyle among the Xhosa. He finally collapsed with fever and died five days later.

In the second half of 1818, most of the chiefs east of the Fish River were allied to Ndlambe. The support of the minor chiefs spurred Ndlambe on to plan a final assault that would destroy Ngqika once and for all.

In October 1818, Ndlambe rolled out his plan. His prophet and counsellor, Nxele, sent a raiding party to seize cattle from one of the minor chiefs under Ngqika, with the intention of drawing Ngqika's forces to retaliate … and into a trap. Ngqika fell for the bait. He ignored Ntsikana when he told him about his vision, in which he had seen the heads of Ngqika's people being devoured by ants, and which he interpreted as being a warning not to follow or attempt to catch the cattle thieves. By sunrise, Ngqika's army were marching eastward and when they emerged from a mountain pass named Debe Nek, they saw Ndlambe's warriors in battle formation on the plain below them.

The plain was covered with saucer-like cavities that the Xhosa called Amalinde. "*Huku*, today we have them!" Ngqika's commander, Makoyi, shouted with delight. [393]

Unbeknown to Makoyi, the small army of young, inexperienced warriors (known as the 'round heads') on the plain was only a fraction of the warriors Ndlambe had at his disposal. His battle-hardened warriors (denoted by the blue crane feathers worn in their headdresses) were hiding in the bushes nearby. When Ngqika's army halted on the mountain pass at midday, Ndlambe ordered his inexperienced warriors to attack them. They were quickly driven back by Ngqika's warriors, who, smelling victory, charged after them onto the open plain, led by Maqoma, Ngqika's son. (Hintsa is alleged to have been leading Ndlambe's warriors.) Ndlambe's young men led them to the hidden mass of highly trained warriors, who surged from the thick brush to confront them. With a mighty roar and a clash of shields and clubs, the two sides collided in a furious battle that lasted the whole afternoon. Ndlambe's forces eventually gained the upper hand on this unseasonably cold day.

The bodies of Ngqika's warriors lay thick and deep on the plain by the time that the sun had dipped behind the hills while many more of his warriors had been slaughtered on the slopes after fleeing the battlefield. Ndlambe's warriors built giant pyres on the plain to burn the corpses of those slain and, in the eerie light cast by the flickering flames, they massacred their wounded enemies one by one. Those who managed to crawl to the bushes under cover of darkness died either from their wounds or from exposure.

Ngqika's army had been totally crushed. He fled toward the Winterberg Mountains and sent messengers to the Cape to ask for assistance from Somerset. Ndlambe and his victorious warriors pursued Ngqika and his followers in subsequent months, burned their crops, storage pits and kraals whenever they found them and killed any occupants found. In numerous families, not one male member survived.

When stories of the battle first reached the colony, the people did not believe them. However, more and more reports filtered through about the massacre of Ngqika's people, until there could be no doubt that he had been defeated.[394]

Somerset ordered Lieutenant Colonel Thomas Brereton to assemble his forces with the utmost secrecy. When ready, the military commander of Grahamstown would drive Ndlambe's people across the Fish River. The seasoned military man was still wet behind the ears as far as understanding the Xhosa. As such, he had no idea that every move he made was being reported to Ndlambe by his spies and that the chief knew about the Hottentot and British troops drifting into Grahamstown to join his commando. Then, Stockenström Jr soon arrived in the little settlement with a contingent of Boers.

Brereton's combined forces of Boers, Hottentots, British soldiers and the remnants of Ngqika's army departed Grahamstown on 1 December 1818 to attack Ndlambe. They arrived at Ndlambe's kraal six days later, only to find it deserted: Ndlambe's army and people had fled with their cattle and were hiding in the thick bush alongside the Keiskamma River. After burning their huts, Brereton ordered his artillerymen to open fire on the nearby bush. These first shots signalled the start of the Fifth Frontier War.

When the cannon shells smashed through the thick undergrowth, the Xhosa's cattle panicked and charged out of the bush toward Brereton's troops, which swiftly corralled 10,000 head of cattle. They also managed to round up a further 13,000 from the surrounding area. Brereton had successfully seized the primary meat resource of Ndlambe's people. He had also aroused their anger, which would be avenged in time.

After this incident, 9,000 head of cattle were given to Ngqika to compensate him for the loss of his people at the hands of Ndlambe and his men. Some were also allocated to the Boer and Hottentot soldiers.[395]

Although Brereton was inexperienced with dealing with the Xhosa, he realized that he had stirred up a hornet's nest and warned Stockenström Jr that he thought Ndlambe might invade the colony.

His fears proved right. On Christmas Day of 1818, the Xhosa moved into the colony and attacked farms, burning, looting and taking cattle. Again, the Xhosa had chosen Christmas Day to attack. Panic swept the frontier and the Boers abandoned their farms as Ndlambe's army swarmed into the colony. Families gathered to pray for their safety and deliverance. As one farmer wrote in a desperate note to Brereton, "God alone knows what will become of us. We are all gathered here at my place and don't know how we shall get away. One can have no idea but that the whole of Kaffirland is here. For God's sake, please come to our assistance. We shall try to make our escape tomorrow if we are still alive; our lives are not safe moment to moment."[396]

By the end of January 1819, the settlers had been driven out of the frontier and much of the area of Albany, the former Zuurveld, was in the possession of the Xhosa. An alarmed Brereton sent Fraser to Cape Town for help and then promptly, and probably with a huge sigh of relief, retired and left for England. Somerset hastily appointed his replacement, Lieutenant Colonel Thomas Wiltshire, who was determined to capture or destroy Ndlambe and drive his people back over the Fish River.

Stockenström Jr had the ear of the governor. He believed the damage caused by Brereton's heavy-handed retaliation for cattle stealing left them no option but to launch a massive attack on Ndlambe and his followers and to drive them over the Fish River and possibly over the next large river, the Keiskamma.

The newly-appointed Thomas Wiltshire amassed over 3,300 men, including Hottentot and British soldiers and Boer commandos. Simultaneously, Ndlambe's prophet and warlord, Nxele, prepared Ndlambe's warriors to capture Grahamstown, as the 10,000 men at his disposal—including Hottentot fugitives, the minor Xhosa chiefs and their followers and a few deserters of the British army—could overwhelm the 450 soldiers and armed civilians in Grahamstown. Although they would have far less firepower than Wiltshire's army would, their assegais could be thrown accurately over 45 to 50 metres and their stabbing spears were extremely effective in close combat situations.

Nxele quietly moved his army into the bushes 25 kilometres from Grahamstown before making his first strategic move. He sent a messenger, Nquka, into Grahamstown to tell Wiltshire that the Xhosa were assembling east of the settlement. Foolishly, Wiltshire believed Nquka and immediately ordered 100 men to patrol the area, which weakened the defences of Grahamstown.

Two days later, on 21 May 1819, Nxele sent another Xhosa messenger to Wiltshire to tell him that he would meet with him over breakfast in Grahamstown the following day.[397] As the sun pinkened the sky early on the morning of 22 April 1819, Nxele stood in front of his 10,000 warriors. "Your ancestors will rise from the grave to help you in driving these people into the sea from whence they came. Do not fear their guns. Their bullets will turn to water," he assured his men[398] before leading them to high ground east of Grahamstown.

Wiltshire fell for another ruse by Nxele: he ordered his Hottentot soldiers out of Grahamstown to pursue Xhosa cattle rustlers. The Xhosa were waiting for him and charged, shouting their war cries as they came. Wiltshire recognized that he had been duped and sent a messenger back to Grahamstown to warn his next-in-command, Captain Trappes, of an imminent attack. Hopelessly outnumbered, he rallied his men and galloped to the town, where Captain Trappes had assembled the Redcoats on the parade ground. The Redcoats were horrified to see that an ever-thickening black line had started to form on the hilltops. In the next hour and a half, the black mass of warriors would come to look like a giant centipede as the Xhosa army was silently arranged into four divisions.

Between the parade ground and the hilltop on which the Xhosa waited for the signal to attack was a stream that formed a line of defence for the village. Grahamstown had no fort and the most secure buildings were the barracks for the Hottentot soldiers. Wiltshire ordered the cannon to be aimed toward the slope below the Xhosa and that they be loaded with shrapnel shells. These were hollow iron balls that contained bullets, a charge and fuse and would spray the enemy with their lethal contents when they exploded. Wiltshire gave the alarm and the civilian population of old men, women and children scurried to the barracks, which were guarded by 60 Hottentot soldiers. He then sent a line of his infantry across the river to await the charge of the Xhosa.

It was very quiet—even the birds had stopped chirping—and a heavy silence blanketed the scene. Nxele signalled the Xhosa warriors to advance. As they moved forward, they thumped their assegais against their ox hide shields. Soon they were running downhill, screaming "*Phagati!*" while firing their muskets and fanning out until they covered a wide area.

The front line of Redcoats began an orderly retreat and then the air exploded with the roar of the cannon discharging. The Xhosa movement slowed. Confused and bewildered by the cannon flashes, the Xhosa hesitated, holding up their arms to protect their eyes. Some were instantly levelled by the deadly cannon fire. A Hottentot hunter who had been one of Van der Kemp's Christian converts soon arrived on the scene with 130 men to join the British troops. Heartened by the swelling of their ranks, Wiltshire's men renewed their efforts.

Nxele had led one of the divisions to attack the Hottentot barracks and had already penetrated the hospital section when he saw his men in the main attack start to falter. He shouted at them not to flee, but to no avail. As Wiltshire's buglers sounded the charge, the Xhosa broke ranks and fled, chased by the jubilant British troops and their allies.

When the light of day arrived, the British, Hottentots and Boers gazed wide-eyed at the hundreds upon hundreds of corpses strewn about. Some estimate that over 2,000 Xhosa had been killed during the battle while many others died later from their wounds or were attacked by opportunistic wild animals. Ndlambe's army had suffered a ghastly defeat.

Three months later, Wiltshire had built up the defences in Grahamstown and then moved out of the settlement with 2,300 British troops, 1,000 Boers led by Stockenström Jr and Hottentots from the Cape Corps to sweep the area west of the Fish River and clear it of all Xhosa.

The colonial forces searched for the elusive Xhosa, who attacked them on 13 August 1819. The Xhosa suffered heavy losses before surrendering and when Nxele handed himself over to Stockenström, he was immediately handcuffed and transported to Cuyler at Graaff-Reinet.

Shortly after this, some of Ndlambe and Nxele's senior counsellors visited Wiltshire at his camp to beg that Ndlambe be allowed to see Nxele. However, he informed them that Nxele was already aboard a ship bound for Cape Town, where he was to stand trial.

Having cleared the area between the Great Fish and the Keiskamma rivers, Wiltshire now wanted to take the battle to the paramount chief of the Xhosa, Hintsa, on the other side of the Keiskamma River, as he wanted to drive the Xhosa over the Kei River. He had heard a rumour that Ndlambe was hiding near the Kei River and, with his newly acquired rocket launchers that could ignite bushes in seconds, he knew that the Xhosa would not be able to evade his men by hiding, as they had done in the past.

Bad weather and swollen rivers slowed the advance of the British troops, which enabled most of the Xhosa to stay ahead of them. The stragglers, mainly the infirm, old and women and children, were shot.

Ngqika and his son, Maqoma, accompanied Wiltshire and soon developed a taste for brandy. For Maqoma, this was disastrous, as he became a heavy drinker and, arguably, an alcoholic. Ndlambe fled northeast beyond the Kei River and made for the country of the Thembu. News of Wiltshire's advance had been relayed to Hintsa, who became increasingly concerned that he would be the next target. Influenced by Stockenström Jr, Wiltshire met with Hintsa and warned him against being involved in any future acts of hostility against the British. Hintsa was cowed.

For the moment, the British were in control. Hintsa was subdued and compliant; Ndlambe had been broken and was on the run, as were many of the minor chiefs; and Nxele had been sentenced to life imprisonment on Robben Island.

CHAPTER 11

Lambs to the slaughter: 1820 Settlers

1820 Settlers—a long way from home—Somerset—Piet Retief—shoddy work—bankruptcy and financial ruin—newspapers—new boundaries—London Missionary Society—Anti-Slavery Society—Commissioner General of the Frontier—Ordinance 50—expulsion of Maqoma

In 1819, the population of the Cape comprised 42,200 white people, 31,700 slaves, 24,450 Hottentots and about 2,000 free blacks and negro apprentices who had been taken off slave ships.[399]

In Britain, high unemployment brought about by the end of the Napoleonic Wars and the Industrial Revolution had led to dissatisfaction with the government and the country. Consequently, many desired to seek their fortunes in other parts of the world.

Somerset wanted to strengthen the resistance to the Xhosa in the Zuurveld by increasing the population of settlers and to establish a buffer zone between the Xhosa and the Cape. He therefore strongly urged the British government to establish a colonization scheme. To that end, the chancellor of the exchequer persuaded parliament to allocate £50,000 for the purpose of subsidizing settlers in the Cape colony. A circular from Downing Street at that time stipulated the terms of settlement for British citizens in the Cape. Suitable candidates were invited to put together parties of individuals or families to travel to the Cape and farms of 100 acres would be allocated (a viable farm at that time in the Zuurveld was 1,200 acres). In addition, a £10 deposit was to be paid to each family and thee settlers would be transported to the Cape and fed on the journey.

Ninety thousand people applied and over 4,000 were selected. Those chosen came from all walks of life: rope-makers, silversmiths, glass-cutters, labourers, carpenters, bricklayers, millers, plumbers, bakers, grocers, gunsmiths, tanners, tile-makers, some farmers and even 'whale catchers' all perceived that they had a better opportunity in a far-off land they knew very little about than in Britain. Even certain gentry banded together, imagining they would establish fiefdoms in the Cape.

Twenty-six ships embarked from England for the Cape. The first two, the *Nautilus* and the *Chapman*, arrived at Table Bay on 17 March 1820 and reached their final destination of Algoa Bay on 9 April. The remaining ships arrived in Algoa Bay in dribs and drabs, with the last one, the *Waterloo*, arriving on 24 May.[400]

Although many of the British ships called in at Table Bay, the settlers were not allowed to disembark for fear that they might refuse to go back onboard once they heard from residents what conditions were like on the frontier.

Cuyler had established a tented camp for the parties at Algoa Bay. Piet Retief, who lived in Grahamstown at the time, arranged that 96 wagons would be brought to ferry the new arrivals to their allocated farms in the Zuurveld. As the ships arrived, the settlers crowded the rails to gaze upon the land in which they hoped for a better life before being taken ashore by sailors in flat-bottomed surfboats.

After the boats were hauled on to the beach, soldiers of the 72nd and the 21st Light Dragoons and several Hottentots carried the women and children ashore. These Hottentots were the first 'black' people the settlers had seen. "I was expecting the black from his skin to come off and ruin my white dress,"[401] one of the children later complained about the Hottentot who had helped her.

After a few days at the tented camp, a class system had already manifested itself: the wealthier settlers sat reading under parasols outside their spacious and comfortable tents while the poorer settlers were accommodated a small distance away from them in the shabbier tents.

Soon, the settlers started on the ten-day journey to the frontier, accompanied by Trekboers who had been hired to fetch them and take them to their new farms. The settlers were also provided with rations, which were paid for with the money they had deposited in England. Rations should only have been provided during their first month in the country. However, the authorities eventually decided to extend the support given to the settlers until such time that they were in a position to fend for themselves. The settlers should have got an inkling of what lay ahead when Cuyler welcomed them. He offered them some sage and chilling advice: "Whenever you go out to plough, never leave your guns at home."

As they journeyed eastward to their allotted pieces of land, their initial excitement at seeing lovely green fields, some of them freshly planted, must have been replaced by disappointment when they passed the abandoned homes of many Boers and finally given way to fear and hopelessness upon arriving at the frontier, where they saw the farmhouses in the Zuurveld that had been burned by the Xhosa. In the whole area, there were only 38 Boer farmers left; the rest had fled.[402]

The Boers who had driven the wagons dropped the settlers at their respective farms with some reluctance and concern. They were puzzled as to what had possessed these foreigners to come settle in a war zone. The settlers watched the wagons trundle away, with sinking stomachs. Their last link with 'civilization' had disappeared. One of the settler children remembered seeing his mother sitting on the sea chest that contained all their worldly goods, with tears trickling down her cheeks as she thought of the terrifying night that lay head, during which she was sure they would be attacked and eaten by "wolves and tigers".[403] For others, their first night merely served as a reminder of how far removed they were from England. As Scotsman Thomas Pringle recalled, "I gazed up at the stars in the enormous skies sparkling with the constellations of the southern hemisphere and realized that a world divided us from the homes we knew and this new land."[404]

Despite the fact that the majority of the settlers were tradesmen, they endeavoured to succeed as farmers. Each of the settlers built his own dwelling out of reeds and cut wooden poles. They used either grass for their roofs or rushes and reeds plastered with clay. The floors were typically made of clay and a mat or rug served as the main door. Those settlers who found limestone whitewashed their homes in an attempt to make them appear more cheerful. Soon, the settlers were making bricks and their temporary dwellings were replaced by more permanent and attractive brick homes. Others started making them with a mixture of clay and straw or out of stone.[405]

Many gave up their farming enterprise when drought struck and others quit when blight obliterated the wheat crop. Most of the failed farmers drifted toward the village of Grahamstown, where they found an outlet for their trades and skills. Those that continued farming adopted the practices of the Boers. They started wearing broad hats and going barefoot and ate mutton, biltong, game meat, milk, dried fruit and *pap* (maize meal).

For nine months, little disturbed the peace of the new farmers. Then, on 7 January 1821, they ran for their guns as thousands of Xhosa spread along the ridge of nearby hills. Unbeknown to the settlers, Wiltshire had given the Xhosa permission to collect red clay from the area. The clay pits were located on the farm owned by Thomas Mahoney, who soon lost cattle to Xhosa visiting the farm for clay. Not long after these raids, a young British boy herding the family cattle was cruelly murdered. His jacket showed evidence of over 100 stab wounds.

Somerset sent Lieutenant Colonel Maurice Scott to apprehend the murderer. When Scott insisted that Ngqika execute the killer, Ngqika refused. After a show of force by the troops, who paraded and presented arms, Ngqika had the man strangled.

Dr John Philip, a missionary who had been sent to the Cape to save the good name of the London Missionary Society after it had been tarnished by the likes of Read and Van der Kemp, managed to persuade the acting governor, Sir Rufane Shaw Donkin, to once again allow missionaries to operate east of the Fish River. (Somerset was on leave in England at the time.) Giving Philip permission to do ministry work outside of the colony borders contradicted Somerset's policies and opened the way for a great influx of missionaries into the lands of the Xhosa in subsequent years.

Read returned to Bethelsdorp in January 1821. His suspension had not yet been lifted. Nevertheless, he performed a public act of repentance in front of his congregation and begged their forgiveness for his adultery. Very soon, Read was once again documenting Landdrost Cuyler's and the Boers' acts of violence against and harsh treatment of the Hottentots. When these charges reached Donkin via Philip, he dismissed them on the grounds that there was no evidence to support Read's claims.[406] Philip was annoyed with Read and felt that he had been made to look a fool.

He desperately wanted to stay in favour with Donkin and commented to the acting governor that Read was as naïve as a child for believing whatever the Hottentots told him, without bothering to check if there was evidence to support their assertions.

However, when Philip visited Bethelsdorp a few months later and found concrete evidence of Cuyler's wrongdoings in Read's office, he was horrified. Read's charges had been accurate. He immediately took the matter up with Donkin, who promised to act firmly against the injustices perpetrated against the Hottentots.

While Somerset was away, his son, Henry, had been keeping an eye on the activities of Donkin and Philip. When the ship carrying his father arrived in Table Bay on 30 November 1821, he rushed aboard to update him on Donkin's activities. Somerset stormed into the Castle the next morning, having rudely ignored a dinner invitation from Donkin the day before. As Somerset marched in through the front door, Donkin slunk out the back door, leaving his breakfast on the table.

Bickering and personal politics ruled the day after Somerset returned.

Little concern was paid to the welfare of the burghers and those on the frontier at Graaff-Reinet; everyone detested Cuyler. Somerset reversed many of the decisions made by Donkin in his absence, but retained two of the most important and far-reaching agreements: that of allowing the free movement of missionaries into the lands of the Xhosa and allowing trade between the colonists and the Xhosa, provided such trading took place under military supervision.

The missionaries responded to their freedom to preach to the Xhosa with relish. Like predators, they stalked the souls of the Xhosa. The most active missionaries were those from the London Missionary Society, the Wesleyans, who were led by William Shaw, who had been in the country since 1819. Hot on the heels of the Wesleyans in the hunt for converts was the Glasgow Missionary Society.

At this time, Somerset dropped Dutch as the official language of the Cape and replaced it with English. Not that this changed a great deal. Dutch was still the predominant language spoken in the colony.

The new landdrost in Graaff-Reinet that had been appointed by Somerset was not interested in the burghers' issues and it would be a full three years before anyone from government visited the frontier to assess the situation there.

Somerset soon fell out with the colonial secretary, Colonel Christopher Bird, which worsened the already unhappy situation of the British settlers and the Boers. On the frontier, drought, locusts and hardship prevailed and the settlers were not allowed to utilize slaves for their labour. Moreover, Hottentot labour was scarce. Somerset was totally unsympathetic toward the plight of the settlers, who came to be known as the '1820 settlers'. A more apt title might have been the '1820 suckers'.

Most of them were disillusioned by what they had found at the Cape. They had arrived expecting to "pick fruit from trees lining the sides of the roads" but instead encountered destitution. As Bartholomew Gunning wrote in a letter he sent to England, "You told me true when you said I might just as well blow out my brains than come upon this expedition."[407] Many had been misled by the leaders of their groups about what to expect, while others had been robbed by sailors and other settlers on the voyage. The unhappiness of the settlers increased daily and the authorities evaded dealing with their complaints.

Somerset wrote to the colonial secretary in England and described the settlers as lazy and troublesome. He claimed that they exaggerated their difficulties and that he had been fortunate in stopping any public protests up until that point. He also admitted that they had presented him with a petition that called for a public meeting with him.[408]

The colony was like a ship drifting in stormy seas—an accident waiting to happen.

Ngqika's sons, Maqoma and Tyali, had moved back into the lands around the Kat River. The authorities made no efforts to remove them.

When Maqoma stole some horses from one of the farms, William Ritchie Thompson, a young Scottish missionary, seized the horses from Maqoma and returned them to their rightful owner. Maqoma then attacked the mission station in the Tyumie Valley and seized 300 head of cattle. His father, Ngqika, was called to account and he restored half of the cattle to the missionaries. Somerset was determined that Ngqika should be shown who was in charge and that neither he nor the government was to be trifled with. He promptly gave the order that Ngqika should be seized.

Early on the morning of 22 February 1822, Lieutenant Colonel Scott ordered Captain Stuart to ride to Ngqika's kraal with 100 mounted soldiers to apprehend the chief. However, Ngqika fled to the Keiskamma River after being alerted to their approach by the furious barking of the Xhosa's dogs and the clattering of hooves of the British soldiers' horses. There, he hid for several months from the white men—particularly the missionaries, whom he now viewed with great mistrust.

Raids by the Xhosa on the farms of the Boers and settlers again increased.

At this time, the commandant of the frontier, Colonel Scott, decided that the military barracks should be in the centre of the town of Grahamstown. Piet Retief, who had been awarded the contract to provision the wagons to transport the 1820 settlers to their farms two years earlier, was not a man to miss an opportunity and agreed enthusiastically with Scott. He even offered his own home as the site for the new barracks and to build the necessary extensions himself.

Piet Retief's great-grandfather, François Retif, was one of the French Huguenots who had arrived in the Cape in 1688. François's son (who was named after him) married the daughter of another French Huguenot, Anna Marais, when she was 19 and he was thirty-three.[409] By this time, the family had adopted the Dutch spelling of Retief and spoke Dutch as their home language.

Piet Retief was born to Jacobus 'Koos' Retief and Deborah Joubert in 1780,[410] probably on the farm Soetendal, which was outside Wagenmakersvallei (now Wellington). After receiving a good education, he became a clerk in a store and gained experience trading by taking goods out to the farms to sell to farmers. He was soon well known and respected in the community and was able to express himself well, verbally and in writing.[411] Although Retief was of medium height, he had a commanding presence. Solid and broad-shouldered, he was prematurely greying at the temples and usually wore a broad-brimmed brown hat, a waistcoat under a heavy jacket and thick corduroy trousers. He had long sideburns that merged with a clipped dark beard and a moustache that drooped over the corners of his upper lip. His dark brown eyes were often brooding and could change from interested to angry in an instant.[412]

Piet Retief married Magdalene Johanna Greyling, who had been widowed when her husband was killed by the Xhosa along with Stockenström Sr's party in 1812. Affectionately known as Lenie, she was two years younger than Piet. However, by the time Piet married her at the age of 32, she had already had nine children. Four had died and of the remaining five, one was blind. When Piet married at 34, he was considered quite old according to the standards of the time. Nevertheless, he and Lena would have four children of their own and Piet was much loved by their children and his stepchildren.

Retief bought a farm called Mooimeisiefontein about 50 kilometres from Grahamstown but moved to the town in 1820. His peers described him as "the richest man in the Albany district and also one of the most honourable".[413] Retief never seemed to miss an opportunity to make money. Apart from owning a number of properties, he milled and traded in wheat, had a butchery, bakery as well as a liquor licence before venturing into the building trade[414] when he was awarded the contract to build the barracks extensions for 40,000 rix-dollars (about £3,000).

As he did not have sufficient capital to complete the building, he persuaded three others, presumably friends, Robert Hart, Lourens Cloete and Frederick Korsten, to stand surety for him. However, before the governor signed the contract, Retief tried to wriggle out of it as he realized that he had underquoted for the work. The governor would not let him off the hook and Retief soon appointed one of the settlers, a carpenter named Mr Hanger, to do the work. This proved to be a costly mistake.

The same year, the landdrost of Grahamstown, Graham Rivers, obtained permission from the Cape to upgrade the prison and to build a *drostdy* at the end of the town. His intention was to establish Grahamstown as an administrative centre for the Eastern Cape. After plans had been submitted and approved, the enthusiastic merchant-turned-builder, Piet Retief, was awarded the contract to build the *drostdy*. He would have 14 months to complete the work and would earn 23,000 rix-dollars (about £1,875). Retief again hired Mr Hanger as project manager.

Building commenced on the two sites in June 1822. Two months later, Piet Retief was appointed as the field commandant of all the burghers in the Albany district and was called out on commando against Maqoma.

While he was away, Hanger and his workmen were caught using rotten wood and substandard material and Scott stopped the second instalment of the contract money. When Scott finally agreed to pay Retief, he was mistakenly paid twice. However, the money was not immediately claimed back, as it was felt that Retief would view this payment as the instalment on the *drostdy* that was due shortly.

Isolated incidents of violence on the frontier began to increase and in two incidents, the Xhosa murdered whites. The violence and unrest generally occurred near the clay pits. While many of the British settlers had replaced their crops with cattle as they felt a better living could be made out of livestock farming, they hadn't taken into account the losses they would incur to raiding Xhosa. The more cattle that came into the area now known as Albany, the greater the temptation was for the Xhosa to steal them.

The British troops were thinly spread on the frontier. In the main, they were positioned at a series of forts set up to control the Xhosa and to prevent their movement into the colony. The discontent of the settlers became greater and greater. Faced with Somerset's refusal to acknowledge their grievances, 171 settlers signed a petition in March 1823 that set out their complaints and sent it to Lord Bathurst (the secretary of state for war and the colonies) in London.

A few months after the petition had been sent to London, Scott consulted Ngqika about the possibility of allowing the Xhosa into the colony to attend and participate at trading fairs with the British settlers and Boers. Ngqika was enthusiastic about the opportunity.

These fairs took place three times a week at Fort Wiltshire and a military bugle would be sounded to signal that the Xhosa could come to the fairground. When the fair concluded, all Xhosa had to return across the Fish River and no settlers would be allowed to follow them into the neutral territory.

By this time, more than 1,000 of the settlers had abandoned their farms on the eastern frontier due to drought, theft, stem rust and crop failure and only 438 men, 298 women and 843 children remained on the farms.[415]

Those that remained suffered another major setback: in October 1823, it started to rain ... and rain ... and rain. The heavy rainfall created streams that transformed into angry brown rivers that swept tree trunks, cattle, sheep and anything in their path. Fields were flooded and the topsoil was washed away. The products of the settlers' endless sweat and toil were destroyed, as were their homes. The settlers had never seen rain like it.[416]

Retief had finished building the barracks in April 1823 but they were destroyed by the October flood. Any semblance of craftsmanship collapsed as the walls crumbled, the foundations sank and the roof sprung leaks. The building was uninhabitable. Consequently, alternative accommodation had to be found for the soldiers. He was responsible for rebuilding the damaged parts, as stipulated in his contract. However, he refused to do so and the authorities opened a case against him in the circuit court. He lost the case and was forced to auction off the land and buildings, as they were in such a poor state.

Retief continued with the building of the *drostdy* but only completed the walls and the flat roof by the end of the contract term. When one of the Royal Engineers inspected the work, he declared that the *drostdy* had been poorly built and reported that 20,000 rix-dollars would be required to complete it. The governor then cancelled Retief's contract and instituted legal proceedings against him for a breach of contract. Retief lost the case and was sentenced to pay 5,000 rix-dollars in compensation. Furious with the ruling, he immediately laid charges against Rivers, claiming that he had interfered with the work and that he had caused the delays in construction. Again, he lost the case and had to pay Rivers's legal costs. Retief was bankrupt and a liquidator had all of his assets seized, including his properties.[417]

At the end of 1823, Thomas Pringle gave up farming and moved to Cape Town, as many other settlers had done before him. Together with a Scottish friend, John Fairbairn, he applied to Earl Bathurst in England to grant him permission to publish a monthly newspaper. Although Somerset opposed the request, Bathurst gave Pringle the go-ahead to start the *South African Journal*, which joined the *South African Commercial Advertiser*, founded by George Greig, as one of the first publications by the free press in the colony.

Both publications were openly critical of Somerset and his administration. Consequently, Greig was hauled before the furious governor after he had published evidence about one of the libel trials against him. He was told he had to submit any proof to the government for vetting before publication. Naturally, he refused to comply with Somerset's demand and stopped publication in protest. He was then banished from the colony and returned to England, where he launched his attacks on Somerset and his government through official circles there. (Greig later returned to the colony with Bathurst's blessing, having been given permission to publish his newspaper.)

In one of Pringle's first editions, he published an article on the plight of the British settlers that implied ineptitude by the government. Somerset sent for Pringle to haul him over the coals and told him that he would not be allowed to publish such articles in future. Pringle stared at Somerset in anger and indignation and replied, "I may not be equal to you in rank, however I am a freeborn British subject and aware of my rights. No man alive has the right to talk to me in that style."[418] After blight decimated the wheat crop of the settlers, they suffered their third bout of crop failure and were in a sorry state. On the plus side, the government abolished the obnoxious pass system that had mandated that settlers could only leave their farms for a specified period, if they had a duly signed permit to do so.[419]

In 1823, settlers were enrolled in the Albany Levy, which consisted of two troops of cavalry and five companies of infantry. (Those in the Albany Levy were provided with arms and ammunition by the government and were commanded by men who had been in the regular army and had military experience.) Simultaneously, a conscription drive saw to the growth of the Hottentot Regiment.

When Somerset's commanding officer died in 1823, Somerset appointed his son, Major Henry Somerset, as commander of the Cape Regiment.

Somerset Jr was soon promoted to lieutenant colonel, after which he started to flex his military muscle to show the Xhosa that he was in charge. As the early morning birds' calls sounded on 5 December 1823, Somerset Jr and his men crept up to Maqoma's kraal and, without warning, opened fire. They shot indiscriminately at any Xhosa they saw and killed 19, including women and children. Somerset Jr and his men then rounded up 7,000 head of cattle and triumphantly herded them back to Fort Beaufort, which chiefs Maqoma, Tyali and Ngqika perceived to be an ever-present flaunting of colonial power over them due to its proximity to their kraals. After this raid by Somerset Jr, the Xhosa withdrew east over the Fish River.[420]

In 1824, the governor realized that Ngqika's star had faded. Accordingly, Somerset used the missionary, Shaw, to communicate that a meeting between Ndlambe and Somerset Jr might be in the best interests of both the Xhosa and the colony. The rendezvous point would be at Line Drift, a crossing point on the Keiskamma River.

Ndlambe used Shaw too—as a hostage at the meeting, which he attended with chiefs who had allied with him previously as well as an army of some 2,000 to 3,000 warriors. Somerset Jr was accompanied by a commando of Boers and between 300 and 400 Hottentot soldiers of the Cape Corps.

A Boer messenger was sent to inform the Xhosa that Somerset Jr and his party would arrive at the rendezvous site at noon. Highly suspicious that they were being led into a trap, the Xhosa lined a ridge, thereby ensuring that they could not be surrounded if there was an attack by the troops and had an escape route.

Somerset Jr soon arrived to begin the talk with Ndlambe, who was 90 at this time and almost blind. He was also tired due to the years of fighting and conflict and readily agreed to return cattle stolen by the Xhosa as well as deserters from the British army or colony and promised Somerset Jr that he and his fellow chiefs would keep the cattle rustling in check. He also agreed that Shaw could build a mission station near his kraal and appoint a missionary to live among the Xhosa people.

In return, and against his father's wishes, Somerset Jr assured Ndlambe that when the chiefs needed to communicate with the British, they would be able to communicate directly with him and not via Ngqika. Somerset Jr also agreed that the Gqunukhwebe under Chief Phato would be allowed to remain in the area beyond the Keiskamma River to which they had already moved.

Under Somerset's watch, the Cape colony had further succumbed to maladministration, corruption, nepotism and discontent and was close to financial bankruptcy. Court cases against government officials were commonplace, as citizens tried to redress their complaints through the courts. However, as Somerset controlled every facet of the colony, the results of court actions against him and his cronies were a foregone conclusion.

In 1824, Stockenström Jr completed a survey to investigate the northern border of the colony and recommended changes to the boundary, which were approved by the colonial office on 9 September 1824.

The amended boundary ran along the Orange River, down to the Pramberg Mountains, then northwest to the sea, ending slightly above the mouth of the Buffalo River.

Five years after the British settlers had arrived, Somerset finally deigned to visit his subjects on the frontier in 1825. He dressed in his finest blue coat, wore a regal sash and carried a parasol to protect his delicate skin from the harsh sun of the Eastern Cape. The residents of Grahamstown watched him in stony silence as his carriage passed them, no doubt unimpressed by this man who looked "like a Christmas turkey".

Later that year, Bathurst wrote to Somerset to suggest that he return to England to answer his critics, many of whom were calling for his head and impeachment. However, Somerset managed to stall his departure from the Cape.

Two men with similar names began to play a role in the affairs of the colony. The first was Dr John Philip of the London Missionary Society, who saw himself as the ever-vigilant watchdog of public morals and protector of the rights of the underdogs and the other was Thomas Phillips, a qualified barrister and a man of means and influence who had arrived with the 1820 settlers. At the end of 1825, Thomas Phillips travelled to the interior to explore. While attending a celebration at an officers' mess at Fort Wiltshire at which Ngqika and the beautiful Thuthula—the woman Ngqika had abducted from Ndlambe—were also present, a messenger arrived to say that Somerset Jr had mustered a commando at Grahamstown. Nobody could fathom why he had marched off with the Hottentot cavalry, Boers and artillerymen armed with rockets. Fearing an attack on the Xhosa, Phillips immediately returned to Grahamstown and found the place in turmoil as rumours and speculation swept the streets. Phillips was informed that Somerset Jr had left with his army on 20 December 1825 and had not even had the courtesy to inform the local landdrost, Major William Dundas, of his intentions.

The facts, when discovered, were horrifying: acting on information that some cattle had been stolen from the colony by one of Ngqika's relatives, Somerset Jr and his army had surrounded the thief's kraal early one morning and opened fire on the Xhosa as they emerged from their huts. This time, 20 Xhosa, mostly women and children, were murdered. Even worse, after seizing 500 head of cattle, Somerset Jr had discovered that they had attacked the wrong kraal. Moreover, this kraal belonged to Chief Bhotomane of the Dange, who was considered a friend of the colony.

Realizing his error, Somerset Jr quickly returned the cattle to their rightful owners and attacked the next village, where innocent women and children were again shot. Unbelievably, he had attacked the wrong village and by the time he found the correct kraal, the robbers had fled.[421]

Soon after Somerset Jr's reprehensible massacres, the zealous Philip started to make waves. A commission of inquiry had been set up to investigate claims of ill-treatment of the Xhosa and the Hottentots by the Boers and the settlers and Philip submitted to them that Stockenström Jr, landdrost of Graff-Reinet, interfered with and obstructed the work of the mission stations; turned a blind eye when the Boers mistreated Bushmen and Hottentots and stole the Bushmen's land; and had an incompetent administration.

When the commissioners arrived in Uitenhage, they found a hostile reception awaiting them. The angry Boers were tired of the repeated accusations levelled against them by Philip. In Graaff-Reinet, they soon discovered that all charges against Stockenström Jr were fictitious and, contrary to what they had been told, the finances and controls of his district were in an exemplary order. The excellence of Stockenström Jr's administration was apparent, as was his care and interest in all matters of the colony. Moreover, after seeing the herds of Merino sheep that Stockenström Jr had introduced in the area, with the help of the governor, they were convinced that his efforts were to be lauded.[422]

Stockenström Jr submitted a report to the commissioners on how problems with the Bushmen could be overcome. He maintained that Christianity should be secondary to teaching the Bushmen how to fend for themselves by farming or working for the colonists and that the mission stations should not become a haven for the idle and evil.

To this end, he proposed that the Bushmen should be brought under a central control point of the mission station at Philippolis to learn how to farm. He was sure that when the Bushmen broke away from their nomadic existence, they would be less vulnerable to attacks by the Griqua, who, he argued, were not criticized by the missionaries because a number of them had converted to Christianity.

In his report, Stockenström Jr called for the missionaries to stop ignoring the actions of the Griqua and pointed out that if the Bushmen were allowed to continue being idle and to steal sheep, they could well progress to acts of rape and murder.[423]

Before Philip left for England in January 1826 to lobby for a more liberal policy toward the Hottentots, slaves and Xhosa people in the colony, he visited Stockenström Jr in Graaff-Reinet, accompanied by Pringle.

These adversaries debated about slaves, freedom, the Bushmen and race relations in the colony for a week. While Philip felt that the white man had no business in the Cape at all, Stockenström Jr expounded on his theories of signing treaties with the Xhosa chiefs as being the only way forward.

Stockenström Jr advocated fairness in dealing with the Xhosa and the Hottentots and felt that if the Xhosa were ever absorbed into the colony, their freedom and identity would disappear forever. Conversely, Philip felt that the way to freedom for the Xhosa was through Christianity. Stockenström Jr believed that nothing should be done to undermine the high status of the chief in the eyes of the tribe and that the tribal structure of the Xhosa and all tribes should be maintained. He argued that leading by example would eventually erode the chiefs' tendency to abuse their power and the belief in witchcraft. By the end of the week, the two men parted with a sense of respect for one another, despite their opposing views.

While staying at Stockenström Jr's home, Philip had written to the directors of the London Missionary Society and described the landdrost's views as liberal and well meaning. Although he implied that Stockenström Jr had had a change of heart, this was not the case: he had always been years ahead of the colonists at that time in terms of his liberal way of thinking.[424]

In England, Philip became the secretary of the Anti-Slavery Society, a position he would hold for the rest of his life. He also wrote a book called *Researches in South Africa* that vilified the Boers' treatment of the Hottentots and Xhosa as well as that by the government of the colony. The book caused an uproar in England and was perceived to be an expose of the cruelty toward and ill-treatment of the Hottentots and Xhosa. In the Cape, it was read with horror and disgust as all the actions of the colonists were condemned while robberies, murders and rapes by Hottentots and Xhosa were overlooked.

Back in England, Philip soon had a powerful liberal ally in Thomas Foxwell Buxton, an independent member of parliament. Buxton advocated that parliament grant the Hottentots and free blacks in the colony the same rights as the white colonists.

On 5 March 1826, Somerset, his wife and eldest daughter left the colony on the *Atlas* after the commission of enquiry had completed its investigation into matters in the Cape and had sent its report and recommendations to the British parliament. Somerset realized that it was game over for him as governor of the Cape, even though his fate was still being debated in parliament, and resigned in early 1827.[425]

Major General Sir Richard Bourke had been sent from London to the colony to serve as lieutenant governor of the Eastern Province, which included the frontier area, and when Somerset left the colony, he became acting governor. He appointed Stockenström Jr as commissioner general of the Eastern Cape frontier district.

Stockenström Jr was a good-looking man of average height, with brown eyes, a pronounced nose and curly dark hair that he swept back above his ears. Although he was only in his mid-thirties, his hair was greying on the sides and had long white sideburns that made him appear older than he was. His full mouth drooped at the corners, which imparted the sense that he was a serious man and he was always dapper and well turned out. Even in a crowd of men, he stood out as a strong personality.[426]

Upon his appointment as commissioner general, Stockenström Jr immediately turned his attention to the plight of the Bushmen. He soon sent a report to Bourke in which he proposed that a law should be passed whereby all free inhabitants, without reference to colour, would have equal rights. He beat Philip to the punch—the reverend was working toward exactly the same result in England—and became the man who had ensured the full freedom and civil rights of all free blacks in the colony.[427]

Ordinance 50 was passed by the council governing the Cape on 17 July 1828. The white colonists were dismayed by the passing of Ordinance 50 and feared that a wave of crime and attacks would result as the Hottentots abandoned their 'masters'. In reality, very little changed. The Hottentots had already been displaced from their land and were as poor as church mice. As such, they continued to seek employment from the whites. They did, however, embrace the abolishment of the pass laws.[428]

The new laws increased the mistrust of the government already prevalent among the Boers and settlers. Their hatred of Philip increased daily and when he returned to the colony on 7 September 1829[429] to take up the plight of the Xhosa, he found that he was so hated that fellow missionaries feared for his safety.

The Boers especially hated Stockenström Jr, who they viewed as a traitor and a puppet of the British. Rumblings of anger, that age-old prelude to conflict, emerged on the frontier again. Somerset Jr was the root cause of the discontent. Despite his father's decree that the land between the Fish and the Keiskamma rivers should be ceded to the colony but maintained as a 'no man's land', Somerset Jr had allowed Maqoma to return to the upper reaches of the Kat River. Stockenström Jr argued that by allowing people who were frequently referred to as the enemy to occupy those lands and to gain a footing in the colony was to break the colony's best line of defence.[430] However, Somerset Jr ignored this opposition and allowed Maqoma and his people to remain in the area.

Maqoma finally overplayed his hand by attacking a neighbouring tribe and stealing several thousand head of cattle. In addition, the number of cattle stolen from the settlers prompted Stockenström Jr to travel to the frontier in 1828. After receiving a tongue-lashing from Stockenström Jr, Maqoma agreed that he would ensure that his people would not give the colony any cause for complaint in future. In return, he was allowed to remain in the area.

Stockenström Jr was the commissioner general of the whole frontier while Somerset Jr was technically his subordinate, being the military commander of the same area. Neither of the two men had time for one another and operated as they saw fit, without consulting or involving each other in day-to-day operations.

When Lieutenant General Sir Lowry Cole arrived to take up his appointment as the governor of the Cape, he received many complaints about vagrancy and crime by the Hottentots. Intent on solving the ongoing problems between the settlers and the Hottentots, he established permanent settlements for the Hottentots near the towns. He turned a deaf ear to Stockenström Jr's warning that the proximity to alcohol would lead to the downfall of the Hottentots and his recommendation that settlements be some distance away from towns.

At the end of January 1829, Maqoma attacked a neighbouring chief, defeated his army and took 3,000 head of cattle.

When Stockenström Jr's decision to allow Maqoma to remain in the 'neutral territory' was challenged by the council and Cole asked him what he thought of Maqoma's actions, he explained that he had allowed Maqoma to remain in the area because he did not wish to go against the word of the previous governor. He then pointed out that Maqoma had broken his word to give the colony no cause for complaint and that he therefore should be punished.[431]

Cole agreed and gave Stockenström Jr permission to use force to move Maqoma and his people. Stockenström Jr departed Cape Town for Algoa Bay by sea. During the voyage, he struck upon the idea of relocating the Hottentots into the land soon to be vacated by Maqoma.

Early on the morning of 2 May 1828, Stockenström Jr and a force of 300 men commanded by Somerset Jr marched to Maqoma's kraal, watched by Glaswegian missionaries and their families. Most of Maqoma's people fled with their cattle but Maqoma hid in nearby bushes. Stockenström Jr pushed his way into the bushes and, when he found the chief, greeted him in a friendly manner by shaking his hand. He then spoke sternly to Maqoma and instructed him to return the cattle his people had stolen to their rightful owners, the Thembu people, before telling him that he had to abandon the land his people were currently occupying and that, until he did so, he would be considered an enemy of the colony. Stockenström Jr then informed him that the kraal would be burned by his soldiers.

Maqoma turned to Somerset, whom he perceived as a friend who had betrayed him. He bitterly told him that the British had succeeded in driving him off his land only because of their sophisticated weaponry and that God would judge them harshly for what they were doing.[432] When the soldiers started burning the huts the next day, one of the missionaries ordered the troops to stop, as it was the Sabbath. They did, briefly, only to continue when the missionary walked away.

Smoke filled the sky as the huts crackled and the dry thatch roofs flared up like tinderboxes. Orange flames danced as they moved from hut to hut and angry black smoke billowed as far as the eye could see.

The Xhosa watched in horror and dismay and one shouted, "Why are you burning my house?" No reply came from the sheepish soldiers.

Maqoma left the colony peacefully with his people but would always remember and never forgive his expulsion from land he saw as his. With no people left to convert, the missionaries also left the area.

CHAPTER 12

Going … going … going

Feelings of uncertainty—Louis Trichardt—poverty and ruin—Slavery Abolishment Act—Retief plans to leave—Uys—Potgieter—exploratory treks

After banishing the Xhosa from the area between the Fish and the Keiskamma rivers, Stockenström Jr was set on the idea of establishing a separate and consolidated area for the Hottentots and coloured people who had been scattered by the settlers. He reasoned that this settlement would serve as a human barrier against the Xhosa. Within three weeks of Maqoma's departure from the area, he had persuaded Cole of the wisdom of his plan and relocated Hottentots and coloured settlers into the land by the Kat River. Stockenström Jr hoped the Kat River Settlement would attract people of means who possessed stock and many who moved there did. However, the area also attracted vagrants and brigands.

Despite this and other difficulties similar to those experienced by the 1820 settlers, many of the farmers prospered. Soon, European style homes had been built and churches, schools and irrigation canals had been established. Little villages sprang up, gardens flourished and an orderly society resulted that hungered for education and progress. The residents conducted the administration of the Kat River Settlement and set up the local government. No whites were allowed to live in the settlement and liquor-selling canteens were not allowed.

The success of the Kat River Settlement proved to be a dilemma for the missionaries, who were not welcomed in the settlement, and highlighted their failure in Bethelsdorp. As such, they looked on the project with some degree of jealousy.

Stockenström Jr created a rod for his own back when he asked the formally disgraced missionary James Read, who now had nine coloured children, to lead a party of his best people from Bethelsdorp to the Kat River Settlement, even though he had no intention of allowing Read to remain there. Read did as requested and then stayed on in the Kat River Settlement. This was the last thing that Stockenström Jr wanted. He had never intended that the missionaries would become permanently involved in his project.

Fearing Read's influence, he immediately appointed William Ritchie Thompson as government missionary in opposition to Read. However, Read won the contest hands down, as he enjoyed the support of the Hottentots. Consequently, Thompson concentrated on preaching to the coloureds in the Kat

River Settlement and even told them that they were superior to the Hottentots because of the "colonial blood that coursed through their veins". Read felt uncomfortable being in the territory that Maqoma had occupied until recently but convinced himself that the chief had accepted his expulsion. He was wrong.[433]

The settlers, Boers and British watched the Kat River Settlement from the sidelines with growing concern and unease. The people lived there in a thriving and prosperous community and had proved the inaccuracies of their dire predictions that they would be attacked after Ordinance 50 was passed and that crime would soar. Like a burr under the saddle, so the Kat River Settlement became another cause of irritation for them.

The growing discontent among the Boers toward their colonial masters gave rise to a new restlessness: they started to look north and to cultivate the desire to leave the colony. At night, under the limitless black expanse of the skies and the millions of twinkling stars, Boers puffed on their pipes as they gazed thoughtfully into the distance and spoke quietly to their neighbours and families about their growing unhappiness and dissatisfaction with the British. With the British in control, the Boers no longer felt at home in their own country. The British had introduced their language as the official language, had replaced the rix-dollar with the British pound and seemed to favour the Hottentots over the Boers and settlers. In addition, it was rumoured that slaves would soon be freed. Some Boers had already crossed the borders and men such as Coenraad de Buys and Johannes Bezuidenhout had established themselves well outside the boundaries of the colony, despite having been forbidden to do so by the government. Those who considered leaving the colony to follow the trekking example set by their forefathers relished the idea of having their own language and of establishing their own customs and laws. There were already well-worn wagon trails up to the Orange River and the country on the other side of it started to look more and more attractive.

One of these discontented Boers was Louis Trichardt, who had been a field cornet in Somerset East.

Born on 10 August 1783 to an official of the Dutch East India Company, Trichardt married 15-year-old Susanna Bouwer in 1810 and lived in the district of Uitenhage, Graaff-Reinet, before moving to Somerset East.[434]

Trichardt was a member of an extremely conservative division of the Dutch Reformed Church and was a man of few words. Nevertheless, he had a wry sense of humour. He was seldom seen without his distinctive broad-brimmed black hat and always dressed in a blue or brown moleskin jacket that appeared too short for him, wide trousers and *veldskoene* (which are similar to moccasins).

He had dark hair, a thick beard and glowering eyes. The passing of Ordinance 50 convinced Trichardt that there was no future for him and his family in the colony.

In 1829, he instructed his 18-year-old son, Karel (Carolus), to pack his wagons, round up his 1,300 cattle, 8,000 goats and sheep and 33 horses and prepare the family to move east across the border into the land of the Xhosa, where they would join a handful of other disgruntled Boers to live outside the colony.[435]

Troublemaker Wienand Bezuidenhout, one of the infamous Bezuidenhout clan, returned to the colony in August 1829 and reported to Somerset Jr that the Xhosa were massing their warriors in preparation for an attack on the colony. The military commander responded exactly as Bezuidenhout had hoped he would: he immediately mobilized all of his troops and sent a warning to the governor of the impending attack.

Cole responded by dispatching Stockenström Jr to the frontier to verify the reports. When he interviewed and interrogated Bezuidenhout, he established that the report was a pack of lies. Nevertheless, panic spread among the settlers and Boers on the frontier.

In turn, the heightened activity of the troops led the Xhosa to believe that the British would soon attack them. Rumour and counter-rumour continued to ripple across the frontier area for some time, making all inhabitants, black and white, feel insecure.

What appeared to have been a deliberate campaign to destabilize the frontier was fuelled by one of the Prinsloo family, who warned that the Hottentots and coloureds in the Kat River Settlement were going to join the Xhosa in their imminent attack on the colony.

Stockenström Jr set out for the Kat River Settlement to investigate this rumour and found it to be totally false. When he arrived, he found the residents praying peacefully in church. The anxiety felt at the frontier was also heightened by the animosity between the commissioner general and his military commander.

Somerset Jr endorsed and frequently authorized parties to recover stolen cattle as part of the Reprisal System or Spoor Law. Although the law stipulated that troops could follow the tracks of the stolen animals and recoup them or take the same number of cattle in compensation at the kraal where the trail ended, the troops would often seize cattle from the first kraal they came across.

This meant that cattle were frequently taken from innocent people.

Stockenström Jr saw these raids as contributing to the instability of the frontier. Somerset Jr also introduced the commando system of calling up the Boers to reinforce his British soldiers whenever trouble was anticipated. These were supposed to be used in times of major conflict but Somerset Jr used them constantly.

Drought, scorching hot days and a scarcity of fresh produce affected Boers, settlers and Xhosa. Stockenström Jr sent reports from the frontier to the governor. And so did his troublesome military commander. The problem was that these reports were contradictory. In May 1829, Stockenström Jr wrote to the governor that the Xhosa were suffering very badly because of the drought and were stealing cattle from each other. However, he quickly added that "Not near the number of cattle reported as stolen by Caffres are actually so stolen; and what is stolen, the greatest proportion is lost by neglect".

Stockenström Jr felt strongly that crimes committed by the Xhosa were not organized or sanctioned by the chiefs and were committed by paupers and starving unfortunates. In Somerset Jr's letter, which arrived four days after that of his commissioner general, he asked the governor for reinforcements due to the hostility being shown toward the colonists by the Xhosa. Maqoma eventually approached Stockenström and asked him to allow him and his family to settle in the colony. However, Stockenström Jr summarily dismissed his request, which greatly angered the Xhosa chief.[436]

As if things were not bad enough, Reverend Thomas Phillips wrote many letters to England that were highly critical of the Boers and the commandos used in the Reprisal System.[437] He claimed that "The commandos, nineteen times out of twenty, take thousands of cattle from innocent Xhosa, sometimes more than ten thousand at a time".

As with Phillips's earlier campaign against the ill-treatment of the Hottentots, his messages about unfair treatment of the Xhosa filtered through to the decision-makers in England. He embarked on a five-month tour of the frontier districts to better acquaint himself with the plight of the Xhosa people and met with many Xhosa chiefs.

When the governor learned that Phillips had told chiefs such as Maqoma and his brother, Tyali, to write to the British parliament or the king of England about their grievances, warning bells sounded for both the colonists and the military.

In June 1830, a large commando went out in search of stolen cattle after having received the consent of both Somerset Jr and Stockenström Jr. During the operation that followed, Chief Sigcawu, Ndlambe's younger brother was shot and killed as he emerged from his hut. He was unarmed. The commando also took another chief captive and imprisoned him at Fort Wiltshire. The Xhosa were enraged by this incident and colonists along the frontier picked up the signals of their anger, like the sound of bees disturbed in a hive.

A few weeks later, Stockenström Jr bumped into Somerset Jr at the Grahamstown races, where the military commander informed him that he planned to send out another commando. Stockenström Jr refused to sanction it, so Somerset Jr requested permission from the governor, who granted it. That was the last straw for Stockenström Jr: he felt his authority had been undermined and that if he did not have control over the military activities on the frontier, then his position was a 'sham'. He began planning his departure from the colony to England, where he intended to present his case to the colonial office.

In 1830, 19-year-old Karel Trichardt met with the paramount chief of the Xhosa at his kraal in the land between the Kei and Bashee rivers, which would become known as the Transkei in later years. He asked him for land and was awarded a 90-year lease for 101 square kilometres of land near the Kei River.

After ten years in the colony, many of the 1820 settlers were destitute. Piet Retief was a provisional field cornet at this time and one of his duties was to watch over some woods near his farm. In his first report, he recorded that he had found 15 whites and 143 blacks living in the bushes in utter poverty. The names of the white people suggested they were all settlers.

Most of Retief's enterprises were disastrous and he was plagued by summonses related to his mounting debts. A further frustration to him was the poor quality of the field commandants in the area. Consequently, he recommended that Duncan Campbell (the civil commissioner for Albany and Somerset and one of the British settlers) appoint Louis Trichardt as a field cornet. Campbell decided against this.[438] Campbell had been one of the 1820 British settlers and initially settled in Caledon, where he unsuccessfully attempted to breed Southdown sheep that he had brought from England. (Later, he became one of the pioneers of the sheep industry.[439])

He then moved to Albany and was appointed to act as a special *heemraden* in Grahamstown in cases concerning the 1820 settlers before being appointed as civil commissioner of Albany and Somerset.

The first indication that Retief was considering leaving the colony was contained in a letter he sent to Campbell on 25 October 1832 after Campbell had rejected the burghers' request to hold a protest meeting to discuss affairs on the frontier. To Retief's embarrassment, he had actually invited Campbell to attend the meeting. Retief's letter implored Campbell to address the complaints and unhappiness of the burghers but stressed their loyalty to the government. He wrote that the burghers would rather live "in some desert land" than fight with the authorities.[440]

On 21 August 1833, the king of England signed a bill that abolished slavery in all 19 British possessions. The Slavery Abolition Act 1833 stipulated, among other things, that all slaves over six years old were to be apprenticed to their former masters for four or six years; each British territory would appoint special magistrates with exclusive jurisdiction over cases between apprentices and employers; £20,000,000 would be allocated for the British territories to pay out slave owners and the respective committees would calculate the compensation to be paid to them. The news that slaves were being freed was received with reasonable calmness by the colonists, Boers and British alike.

In 1833, Louis Trichardt and his family were living alongside the families of De Lange, Lodewijk Botha, Jakobus Hamman, Jacobus and Reinier Grobler beyond the borders of the colony. The British authorities believed that these 'fugitives' who were living peacefully among the Xhosa were in fact selling arms and gunpowder to them and encouraging them to resist the British. Consequently, the government accused Louis Trichardt of several misdemeanours, including cattle theft, and Colonel Harry Smith offered a reward of 500 head of cattle for his apprehension.

That same year, Somerset Jr went to England on leave but, before he left, he allowed Maqoma to move back into the territory from which he had been expelled in 1829.

In August 1833, Cole set sail for England. He had finally grown tired of dealing with the complexities of the colony. His military secretary, Lieutenant Colonel Thomas Francis Wade, would take over as acting governor until his replacement arrived. Before departing, Cole left written instructions that Maqoma's brother Tyali was to be expelled from the area between the Fish and the Keiskamma rivers. However, Wade soon discovered that Maqoma had moved back into the territory. Fortunately, Captain Robert Scott Aitcheson of the Cape Mounted Rifles persuaded Maqoma and chiefs Bhotomane and Tyali to return across the border without a fight.

Later that August, Piet Retief wrote to Campbell to request permission to go hunting beyond the Orange River with two members of the Greyling family. Campbell refused to give them permission—probably because he believed the men were scouting out the north with a view to leaving the colony—citing that the Greylings had perpetrated acts of an illegal nature on previous journeys outside the colony.[441]

Somerset Jr arrived back from England in December 1833 and, despite being instructed by Wade not to reverse anything that had been done in his absence, immediately allowed Maqoma and his hundreds of followers back into the colony.

The new governor, Sir Benjamin d'Urban, arrived on 16 January 1834. No sooner had he landed than a letter from Somerset Jr arrived requesting that he approve Maqoma's occupation of the ceded territory. Unfamiliar with the history surrounding Maqoma and unaware of the deviousness of the military commander, d'Urban gave his permission. However, Campbell ordered Maqoma and his people out again as he was aware of the standing orders put in place by Wade.

When Aitcheson was supervising the eviction of the Xhosa, one of the Boer bystanders turned to Aitcheson and asked, "Why are you moving the chief and his people?"

"I am acting on orders," Aitcheson replied matter-of-factly. He implied that the Xhosa had been guilty of cattle rustling.

"I feel very sorry for them," the Boer responded. "I have never lost a single beast since they have been here." He added thoughtfully, "They have even recovered cattle for me."[442]

Early in 1834, the authorities in the Cape were alarmed to hear that many Boers were crossing the Orange River with their slaves to ensure that they could retain them after 1 December 1834, when all slaves would be freed. At every opportunity, the Boers discussed the possibility of leaving the colony and organized covert meetings. There was also much deliberation on which direction to take and they debated whether it was better to head to Natal, the land of the legendry King Dingane of the Zulu, or northward through the area populated by the Hottentots and bastaards.

Andries Hendrik Potgieter, a farmer from the Tarka district, and Petrus Lafras Uys, a farmer in the Kromme River area who was also known as Piet, decided to send three small exploratory expeditions into the interior to scout out the land. To avoid arousing the ire of the British authorities and the participants being branded as rebels, they approached authorities for permission for three hunting trips. Permission was granted and they were told that they were permitted to trade with the Xhosa and any other tribes they encountered.[443]

The two Boer leaders, Potgieter and Uys, were totally dissimilar in terms of appearance and personality. The 37-year-old Uys was fair-haired, upbeat, confident, outgoing and relaxed. He was popular and well liked in both Uitenhage and Grahamstown, which he visited frequently to attend the horse races. He was an excellent communicator and had made many friends in the Boer community and among the British officers. He kept himself physically fit and was a very good horseman.[444] In contrast, Potgieter was a man of action who said little but commanded others' respect. Fiercely independent, he was also decisive, egotistical, intelligent and obstinate and someone that one would not want as an enemy.[445] At just under two metres tall and with a muscular build, Potgieter made a superb horseman. His hair was black, he had a grizzled beard and he usually wore the characteristically short jacket and trousers of a sect of the Dutch Reformed Church that would become known as 'doppers'. His clothing was almost always dark blue, which earned him the nickname of *Ou Blouberg* (Old Blue Mountain). He was also easily recognized due to his straw hat with green lining, which he seldom took off. Although his blue eyes were fierce, they lit up in the presence of children and, despite being known as a tough man and leader, he loved and spoiled children. Uys and Potgieter had different characters but shared two characteristics: wanderlust and an autonomous nature.

The three 'hunting expeditions' would head off in different directions and investigate the farming potential of the land they found. Johannes Andries Pretorius and his brother, Willem, were sent northwest to Damaraland. They found the land there to be arid due to drought. Ene Scholz and his small party were sent northward and returned with favourable reports, which would later influence the direction taken by the first trekkers. Uys led a group of 21, including his younger brothers, Johannes Zacharias Uys and Jacobus Johannes Uys, community leaders such as De Lange, men from the Moolman family and Gerhardus Johannes Rudolph. Their destination was Natal.

CHAPTER 13

"The land is dead!"

Journey to Natal—Hintsa—Sixth Frontier War—Boers on the move—d'Urban; Maqoma's frustration—slave compensation—invasion of the Colony—panic and fear—Salem and Gush—Xhosa attack Bathurst—enter Colonel Harry Smith—attack on Tyali—Boers drafted into the army—bush war—Cape Mounted Rifles—soldiers or herders? —across the Kei—the Mfengu—demands on Hintsa—the Mfengu become British—Queen Adelaide—the murder of Hintsa

The Boer party of 20 men and one woman left for Natal on 8 September 1834 with 14 wagons and many coloured attendants.[446] On the way, they called in at Trichardt's farm outside the colony, near the Indwe River.[447] That first night, as they sat in the flickering shadows of the firelight, they must have discussed their feelings and emotions about living under British rule, the general state of discontent and fear that prevailed on the frontier and the lack of control that the British displayed toward the Hottentots, Bushmen and Xhosa. They most likely also discussed the many negative comments being made about the Boers in the British journals.

After leaving Trichardt's farm, they travelled on a well-worn route through the lands of chiefs Hintsa and Faku toward the lush, semi-tropical lands of Natal. When Hintsa asked Uys where the party was going, Uys replied that he and his people sought land and asked whether he would be prepared to make land available for them to live on. Hintsa proposed that Uys and his people could use the land between the Tsomo River and the Umzimvubu River.

When Uys and his party arrived in the designated area, the chief of the Pondo, Faku, met them. "Where are you going?" the chief asked Uys.

"We are looking for land on which to live," he replied.

"How was the land that you have passed through?" Faku pressed.

"It looked lovely," Uys admitted.

Faku then offered Uys the land on the other side of the Umzimvubu River, up to the Umkomanzi River (Waterrivier), and told him that he would be very pleased if he and his people settled there between himself and Dingane, whom he saw as a constant threat. Uys reassured Faku that he would look at the land and consider it and that if the area was large enough, he would return with many people to settle there.[448]

On they travelled up the East Coast, along the same route that explorer Dr Andrew Smith had travelled two years earlier. The experienced traveller and adventurer had returned with glowing reports of Natal. When Uys and his party first saw Natal, they were not disappointed: rich grasslands rolled toward the horizon and boasted abundant herds of wildlife. "Only heaven itself could be more beautiful than these lovely lands," Uys said, turning to his companions.

They finally arrived at the tiny British settlement of Port Natal in February 1835,[449] to much backslapping and hand-pumping as they renewed friendships with some of the British whom they had met on the frontier before they moved to Natal.

During a meeting with the British agent, Allen Gardiner, Uys explained that they hoped to colonize Natal. As Gardiner and all those living in the small settlement were in a permanent state of anxiety about the proximity of Dingane, the king of the Zulu, they welcomed the idea of increasing their numbers.

After hunting elephant and game, Uys's group set off to see Dingane to ask him for land. When Uys and his party reached the Umvoti River, Richard King rode ahead to ask Dingane to grant the Boers an audience. Subsequently, Dingane sent four of his *indunas* (counsellors) and about 100 warriors to fetch Uys and escort him to Umgungundlovu (place of the great elephant). Unfortunately, when Dingane's delegation arrived at the river, Uys had a high fever and the flu and was unable to travel. As such, he sent his 15-year-old brother Johannes with the *indunas* to speak with Dingane on his behalf. When the young boy and the *indunas* reached the Tugela River, it was a raging torrent of angry brown water due to recent rains and they were unable to cross it.

Dingane sent more *indunas* to the Tugela River to hear what the boy had to say and, after Johannes shouted that he was requesting land from Dingane, the *indunas* took the message to their king, who agreed to give the Boers the land between the Tugela River and the Umzimvubu River. After Dingane's message was relayed to Johannes, the four *indunas* accompanying him made it clear that he was a hostage. The terrified youngster begged to be allowed to return to his brother and, feeling sorry for him and not wishing to create enemies, the *indunas* finally released him. When the party arrived at the Boers' camp, Johannes's brother, Piet Uys, gave the *indunas* a horse as a gift for Dingane as a token of his appreciation. From that day on, Johannes was nicknamed 'Jannie Hostage'.[450]

The return journey was slow, as the Boers' wagons were laden with ivory and skins that they would sell in the colony. When Uys visited Hintsa, he learned that the Sixth Frontier War was raging. Luckily, Hintsa sent 100 of his warriors, under the command of his son Kreli, to escort the party during the four-day journey to the safety of the colony. Shocked by the news of the outbreak of war but full of praise and wonder of the lands of Natal, Uys reported to d'Urban in Grahamstown in the last week of March 1834. He informed the governor that, despite the attractiveness of Natal, he had no intention of leaving the colony.

Word of their journey spread rapidly and Natal sounded as though it was a paradise waiting to be discovered, particularly to those who had lost everything at the hands of the Xhosa. After visiting his family, Uys inspected the damage caused by the Xhosa during his absence and arranged for compensation to be paid to him for freeing his slaves. He then reported for commando duty. During this war, he attained the rank of field cornet and gained a reputation for being courageous.[451]

Not long after the return of Uys's 'hunting expedition', Trichardt escaped the colony with his ten slaves, being seven men and three women. Despite having heard the rave reviews about Natal from Uys, Trichardt set off north and trekked toward the Orange River and freedom. He was determined to move as far from the British as possible and planned never to return to the colony.

He crossed the Great Fish River near the junction with the Kraai River and waited near the Caledon River[452] for the rest of the party to arrive. He was soon joined by about 30 Boer families, including those of Klaas Prins, Jan Pretorius, Hendrik Botha and Gert Scheepers.[453] Like Trichardt, they had been disappointed and disillusioned by the British administration in the Cape and were filled with an inherent wanderlust. This first group of trekkers became known as the *voorste mense*, or 'the first people'.

On crossing the Orange River and leaving the colony, they believed that they were no longer British subjects and therefore did not owe their allegiance to the king of England. They considered themselves free.[454] The Orange River had been named after William of Orange by the soldier-explorer Robert Jacob Gordon, the same Gordon who had surrendered the Cape to the British in 1805.[455]

As stories of 'greener pastures' filtered back into the colony, Boers trickled across the Orange River. Then, toward the end of 1834, it was reported that more than 1,000 Boer families had left the colony with over 200 slaves.[456] Even if this figure was exaggerated, an exodus was clearly underway. Tellingly, the route to the north had clear wagon wheel tracks due to the hundreds of wagons that lumbered along it.

Concerned about the Boers' exile from the colony, the authorities made it known that anyone who took or sent a slave over the border would be considered a criminal and be subject to penal exile.

One of Trichardt's slaves had run away, back to the colony, where he reported to the authorities that Trichardt and others had left the colony, were living across the Kei River and intended to travel to Natal. He explained that Trichardt had said he wanted to get as far away from the British as possible so that he could keep his slaves. He complained that he had treated his slaves well while in the colony, but had started mistreating them on the trek.

Campbell, now civil commissioner of Grahamstown, immediately ordered Captain Armstrong to cross the Orange River with a detachment of soldiers from the Cape Mounted Rifles and to bring back Trichardt's slaves as well as any other slaves that had been taken out of the colony. As Armstrong and his troopers approached the trekkers' camp, the Boers ran for their muzzle-loaders and took cover. Armstrong ordered his men to prepare to engage the Boers. "We are here to take the slaves back. Do not resist; otherwise, we will be forced to open fire," he shouted.

Some of the Boers immediately shouted back that they intended keeping their slaves. However, they eventually backed down and handed 14 slaves over to Armstrong.

When these slaves arrived back at the colony, they were given the option of going back into service as slaves until 1 December 1834 or of working for the colony. They all chose the former option.[457]

One of d'Urban's first acts as governor was to stop the implementation of the Vagrancy Act, which Wade had initiated. The Vagrancy Act stated that any Hottentot declared a vagrant could be drafted into forced public labour or contracted to one of the farmers. Essentially, it set out to undermine the liberties afforded to the Hottentots with Ordinance 50. D'Urban's opposition to the act endeared him to the missionaries, particularly Thomas Phillips and James Read, but antagonized Wade and the people on the frontier.

In the Kat River area, the proposed act caused alarm among the Hottentots. So much so that they started moving to the mission stations to seek asylum. Unintentionally, the colonists had alienated the Hottentots and were encouraging future alliances with the Xhosa.

While preoccupied with planning the freeing of the slaves in 1834, d'Urban made a fatal mistake: he did not visit the frontier and relied on information fed to him by his military commander on the frontier. Somerset Jr naturally played a game of smoke and mirrors with the governor about its affairs.

He was as erratic as ever and his patrols to seize stolen cattle had become increasingly brutal. Not only did his men burn kraals to the ground, they humiliated and abused the Xhosa on the frontier. Subsequently, the Xhosa became sullen and resentful toward the British.

D'Urban had become friendly with the Reverend Phillips who had visited chiefs Maqoma, Bhotomane, Kama and Dyani Tshatshu on the frontier in September 1834 on d'Urban's instructions. He was to sound out their views on the government's proposed treaty arrangement, which stipulated that the chiefs would receive annual stipends and gifts from the government in exchange for ensuring the peaceful conduct of their followers. The chiefs complained bitterly to him about the Reprisal System, the hut burnings and the unfair treatment of the Xhosa people.

The following month, Wade and Somerset Jr rode out of Fort Wiltshire to meet with Maqoma, who took them to see the area from which his people were being expelled. (The area was at the foothills of the Amatola Mountains and had never been formally incorporated into the colony.)

Wade was aghast at what he saw: thick black smoke twisting and twirling above huts engulfed in hungry flames, blackened crop fields and Xhosa scurrying from the troops driving them out of the land, clutching their meagre belongings. Maqoma made it clear to Wade that he and his people wanted this land to be returned to them as well as that of the Kat River Settlement.

On his way back to the Cape, Phillips and his party encountered agitated groups of Maqoma's men. They angrily reported that one of Maqoma's men had been sentenced to imprisonment for two months for trying to stop the soldiers from burning down his huts. Even worse, he had been flogged and received 50 lashes on his bare back. They asked Phillips what right the British had to punish the subject of a Xhosa chief.[458]

This was the first reported lashing of a Xhosa by the authorities and the Xhosa were humiliated and furious.

The next day, Maqoma visited Reverend Phillips at Fort Wiltshire and informed him that Somerset Jr had once again threatened him with an attack from his commando. This time, Somerset Jr alleged that the Xhosa had stolen 480 cattle and he demanded that Maqoma return them.

As they spoke, Reverend Phillips noticed smoke rising in the distance. Somerset Jr had made good on his threat. "Look!" Maqoma cried, pointing at the thick smoke. "We have had promises for 15 years. How much longer must we endure this treatment? We cannot endure it any longer."

Toward the end of 1834, cattle rustling and robberies by the Xhosa all but ceased on the frontier but there was tension in the air.

While Maqoma was preparing his people for war, Paramount Chief Hintsa relocated his people to the other side of the Kei River, deep into the interior, without explanation.

Covertly, assegai-makers were hard at work making their missiles of death and Xhosa spies trickled into the Kat River Settlement to 'visit friends'. They reported to Maqoma on the strength and position of British troops and occasionally stole horses to use in the battle.

On 1 December 1834, all 39,021 slaves in the colony were freed.

Despite the misgivings and unease of the colonists, the day passed peacefully and the colonists heaved a huge sigh of relief. The committee of "assistant commissioners of compensation" calculated that an amount of £3,410,290 and six shillings would be required to compensate the slave owners for 35,745 of the fit and able slaves.[459] This equated to £95 per slave.

The next day, a Boer reported to Fort Wiltshire that he had been robbed of three horses by Chief Nqeno's people, the Mbalu. Ensign Sparks of the Cape Mounted Rifles, a 20-year-old, weedy and inexperienced officer was sent out with his patrol of eleven men and four farmers to demand compensation of 40 head of cattle.

While herding the cattle back to the fort, the soldiers noticed that they were being followed by a few hundred Mbalu warriors who were armed with assegais and shields. Sparks immediately sent a messenger back to Nqeno to inform him of the impending confrontation. In turn, Nqeno sent his son, Stokwe, to intervene.

As Stokwe drew closer, he saw that the Xhosa were attacking the patrol and had all but surrounded the troopers. Five of the soldiers fired a warning volley over the heads of the warriors, who nevertheless advanced on the patrol. Stokwe risked being shot by the nervous and trigger-happy troopers to ride through the ranks of Xhosa warriors. When he reached Sparks, he told him that his father did not desire a confrontation with the colonial government and would send him to deliver another 20 head of cattle.

The patrol then proceeded toward Fort Wiltshire. However, ten kilometres further, a group of Xhosa warriors leaped out of the brush and began to taunt the troopers by grabbing the bridles of their horses and gesticulating angrily with their assegais. Chaos reigned as the horses, whinnying from terror and almost as frightened as their riders, reared and stamped their hooves in the red dust.

Some of the Xhosa attempted to herd off several cows and the men begged Sparks to allow them to open fire on them.

"Move away. If you do not, I will give the order to fire," Sparks warned them.

"You dare not shoot us!" one of the Xhosa shouted defiantly.

Badly shaken but unharmed, the soldiers continued at a brisk pace toward Fort Wiltshire with most of the cattle in tow. As the fort came into sight, the relieved men drove the cattle ahead. Sparks followed behind, using the time to regain his composure and to still his trembling hands.

As he passed one of the last bushes before the fort, a Xhosa warrior leaped out from behind it and hurled an assegai at him before running away. The blade passed through his arm and bright blood gushed down it. Shocked by what had happened, Sparks urged his horse to gallop for the safety of the fort.[460]

Somerset Jr was at the fort at the time and immediately set out to find Chief Nqeno with a strong force of men. They struggled to find him as he and his people had deserted his kraal, but when they eventually met, Somerset Jr told him in no uncertain terms that because of the actions of his people, he had forfeited the right to live on the western side of the Keiskamma River. He assured him that he would personally drive out every Xhosa west of the river and demanded 150 head of cattle as compensation.

Intent on keeping the peace, Nqeno was extremely reconciliatory and handed over 237 oxen and 18 horses.[461]

Keeping the Xhosa out of the ceded territory between the Keiskamma and Fish rivers was like using one's bare hands to carry water. Impossible. The biggest offenders were Chief Tyali and his followers. After receiving reports that the Xhosa were on the western side of the Fish River, Lieutenant William Sutton of the 75th regiment, a party of 12 troopers and a sergeant from the Cape Mounted Rifles set out to expel Chief Tyali's people on 10 December 1834. They also sought compensation for horses that had been stolen from several officers at the fort.

When the Xhosa refused to move, Sutton ordered his men to burn their huts and round up some cattle from the nearby holding pen. The soldiers had unwittingly taken the prize cattle of Chief Tyali and as Sutton's men herded them away, Xhosa warriors surrounded the men. Their hostility and anger was palpable.

"Fire warning shots!" Sutton shouted.

The Xhosa fell back, but not before they had successfully driven the cattle away from the troops. They then pursued the fleeing troopers as they made for the fort. Every time the Xhosa caught up with the soldiers, Sutton ordered his men to open fire, causing the Xhosa to scatter and dive for cover. The crackle of rifle fire could be heard from the fort and a detachment of troopers galloped out to assist Sutton and his men. On seeing the reinforcements arrive, the Xhosa retreated, under cover of darkness. Once at the safety of the fort, Sutton assessed the damage: Xhosa assegais had wounded one soldier and killed two horses.

The Xhosa had lost two men and two of the warriors were badly wounded.

Significantly, one of the wounded men was Tyali's brother, Xoxo.[462] To have drawn blood from a member of the Xhosa chief's family was tantamount to spitting in the chief's face. The die had been cast. On the night of 11 December 1834, the Xhosa lit signal fires between the Keiskamma and Bashee rivers to summon all the tribes to a war council. The settlers and Boers were unaware of the impending invasion, despite that some of the traders in the area had been warned by the Xhosa to leave.

Piet Retief, who had by this stage lost his farm and was financially ruined, wrote to Campbell on 15 December 1834 to warn him of rumours of the Xhosa's planned attack on the colony. The provisional field cornet explained that these rumours were being spread by malicious Hottentots in the Kat River Settlement and undertook to send the rumourmongers to Armstrong to be punished.[463]

Nevertheless, the rumours were true: the colony was on the brink of the mother of all wars. Despite some chiefs' reluctance to enter into a major conflict with the colony, the will of the people prevailed.

On 21 December 1834, the hills along the frontier looked as though they were covered in oozing black treacle as 12,000 to 15,000 Xhosa massed to attack the colony.

The poignant cry of "*Ilizwe lifile!*" (the land is dead) floated from hilltop to hilltop across the hills and down the valleys. Massed together row after row the Xhosa warriors were a formidable sight in their battle regalia. Each warrior carried a cow skin shield, a bundle of assegais and a fighting stick. The rippling muscles of his bare torso were accentuated by the red ochre with which he was painted and his shaven head was topped with a beaded band with striking Blue Crane feathers. The sight of the unified Xhosa army was sufficient to put even brave men to flight.

On 21 December 1834, the burghers and settlers watched aghast as a black mass of warriors, each covered in red-ochre and whistling high-pitched whistles of war as they waved their assegais and fighting sticks like a sea of reeds flowed over the hills. The Xhosa army streamed into the colony, sweeping away all before them as they burned homes and crops and took cattle and sheep without breaking momentum. After killing at least ten of the settler traders who lived among them, they poured over the borders of the colony from the Winterberg above the Kat River and down toward the sea, burning and killing as they moved across the land like a black tsunami.

White messengers galloped from farm to farm to warn the inhabitants of their imminent destruction and instructed the farmers to race for the towns, where there would be some security in numbers. Churches, schools and halls in Grahamstown, Bathurst, Salem and even Port Elizabeth were readied to accommodate the massive influx of terrified refugees. In Grahamstown the St. George's church was turned into a powder magazine and a shelter for women and children.

Maqoma's warriors struck first and led the attack. He and his followers crossed the Kat River just below Fort Beaufort. Tyali's warriors formed the next wave and kept inland, while the clans under chiefs Mhalla, Siyolo, Bhotomane and Nqeno stayed close to the sea. The three armies covered the whole frontier, forming a black tide that spanned over 150 kilometres and swept everything in its path away as they burned crops and homesteads to the ground.

As the settlers and the Boers ran for safety, driving their cattle and sheep before them, Somerset Jr defended the frontier as best he could, with only 755 men[464] at his disposal and already low on ammunition. Realizing that he did not have the resources to stop the invasion, he ordered the three outer forts of the colony to be abandoned.

News of the invasion sent a ripple of fear across the colony. One of the Boer leaders, 36-year-old Andries Pretorius, raised a massive commando of 800 Boers from the Graaff-Reinet area to come to the aid of the Boers and settlers on the eastern frontier.[465] Grahamstown was bursting at the seams and a scene of panic: scores of destitute and frightened people were pouring into the town in such numbers that houses adjacent to the church had to be used to accommodate them. The streets were barricaded in anticipation of an attack that everyone felt sure was coming. People dashed around like headless chickens, grabbing anything that could possibly serve as a weapon, including pitchforks and spades.

Every man who had a weapon was called to military service and rode out of town to assist and escort the streams of wagons and fleeing farmers making for the safety of Grahamstown. The refugees looked back at the pyres of black smoke rising from burning farms and watched as vultures speckled the sky as they circled overhead in eager anticipation of feasting on bodies and carcasses. Their wagons groaned under the weight of their hastily-loaded possessions and many were forced to walk alongside them, including women, children and the elderly. Some carried bundles or babies while others herded geese and ducks ahead of their wagons. The men folk rode next to their wagons, carrying their flintlock tower muskets and with powder horns slung around their necks. All of the weary travellers glanced nervously over their shoulders to see whether they were being pursued by the Xhosa.

The distant spires of thick black smoke marked the route of the Xhosa, who methodically destroyed farms while operating in small groups. Thousands of

Xhosa crossed the Fish River at Trompetter's Drift and swiftly killed trader Albert Kirkmann and 21 farmers. In Bathurst, the men cut down trees and hastily built a cattle kraal to accommodate the livestock they had been able to save from the attacking Xhosa. In the absence of Field Cornet Hercules Malan, Retief was commanding the burghers in this area and was assisted by his son, Jan Greyling.[466]

Retief and his commando were involved in several skirmishes with the attacking Xhosa. On 24 December 1834 and on Christmas Day, they killed five Xhosa and recovered 800 cattle. However, on the evening of 25 December 1834, he and his seven men were surrounded by the Xhosa warriors.

While the Xhosa inexpertly shot at the burghers with guns they had either stolen or obtained illegally through trade, Retief ordered the women and children to flee on foot. The seven men made their escape into the night when their ammunition started to run out. As they rode up the hills, Retief looked back at the orange flames leaping hungrily into the sky as his own farm was torched.[467]

Christmas day dawned with a sky that signalled what was to come. A blood red sun bathed the landscape in a bloody glow as a warning of the carnage to come.

That night, people scurried to the unfinished Anglican Church. They huddled together, wrapped in blankets, praying by the flickering light of a few lanterns and candles, while the men outside guarded the church.

Suddenly, shouts of alarm pierced the hitherto silent night as the Xhosa warriors charged out of the blackness, throwing lit torches at the thatched roofs as they shouted and whistled while moving through the town.

About 50 metres away from the settlers' defences, the troops opened fire, aiming at those carrying torches. A wall of lead smashed into the warriors. The Xhosa paused briefly, then rushed forward. The settlers fired again. The *lopers*—a heavy shot for use in the dark or bush—they were using meant every shot brought down a few Xhosa warriors. The settlers' firepower again drove the Xhosa back.

The women in the church could hear the shouts, screams and gunfire outside and prayed fervently that the Xhosa would not burst through the doors. Their sobs soon gave way to the cries of George Hills's wife giving birth to her first child. Sadly, her husband was killed that evening at Trompetter's Drift.[468]

Ammunition and powder were running low in Bathurst by the time Lieutenant Edward Forbes and a troop of men arrived with more weapons and ammunition sent from Grahamstown.[469] In the nick of time.

In nearby Salem, the Xhosa attack was prevented by the actions of a Quaker, Richard Gush. Accompanied by three other unarmed young men, Gush rode out to meet the approaching Xhosa. When the Xhosa saw Gush approaching, they stopped in their tracks and watched in amazement as he dismounted, took off his jacket to show that he was unarmed and shouted for their leader to come forward. When he did, Gush begged him not to attack the village. The Xhosa chief demanded food and gifts in return for sparing Salem. Immediately, Gush rode into the village, loaded his horse with bread and gifts and, still unarmed, returned to the waiting Xhosa and handed them over. Gush's bravery had saved Salem and its people from the wrath of the Xhosa.

Still on Christmas Day as the Xhosa invasion continued, Retief and two detachments rounded up the 202 women and children who had escaped the earlier Xhosa attack and led them to a farmhouse that was still under construction. They formed a protective barrier around it with wagons. As they did not have sufficient wagons to close the circular laager, Retief placed guards around the perimeter of the farmhouse and around the cattle kraal.

The clouds obscured the moon and the Xhosa managed to creep toward the cattle kraal, undetected in the inky black darkness. They slipped into the cattle kraal and, hitting the cattle with sticks, and with shouts and whistles they herded the cattle directly at the Boers' defences. The Boers fired over the cattle at their attackers but the cattle driven by the Xhosa stampeded, forcing the Boers to abandon their positions and run to safety. They escaped with their lives but the Xhosa drove away 2,000 head of cattle. In a second attack later that night, the Xhosa managed to drive off a further 2,000 head of cattle.

Fearing another major attack Retief scribbled a note to the field cornet of Klaas Smit River, asking for help. However, the field cornet had already fled Klaas Smit River by the time Retief penned the letter. Moreover, Retief's own field cornet, H. Malan, had also run away and had joined up with Field Cornet Viljoen. Retief was in a dangerous predicament: he was under attack and unable to move his people and their wagons. Further, he needed at least 120 oxen to pull the wagons and all of the oxen had been taken by the Xhosa.

News of their plight filtered through to Tarka and nine burghers came to assist the party. Stories of disaster were rampant throughout the colony. A trader named Warren who had sought shelter with the missionary Gottlieb Kayser had been hacked to death in front of him, despite Kayser sobbing and begging for Warren's life, while Thomas Mahoney—on whose farm the clay pits were situated—had his throat cut in front of his family. The Xhosa spared his wife and son.[470]

When the Xhosa had attacked Fort Brown, a small fort outside Grahamstown, the young British officer in command ordered his soldiers to drive all the Boer oxen out in the belief that the Xhosa would cease their attack on the fort and be

happy with the cattle. As the men began to carry out his command, Boer women ran outside the fort and began to drive the cattle back in, desperate to prevent the loss of their most prized possessions. One of the Boer men shouted at the officer, "If you don't order your men to stop, we will open fire on you!" The officer ordered his men to return the Boers' cattle. The 12 Boers in the fort then broke the Xhosa attack with accurate rifle fire.

Hearing about these and other atrocities struck terror into the hearts of the Boers and settlers. On 28 December 1834, Retief was appointed as provisional commandant of the Boer forces. Retief was now in command of a few hundred people who had nothing more than the clothes on their backs and had to provide food for them. He bought meat and provisions out of his own pocket, in the hope that he would be reimbursed by the government when the fighting was over.[471]

In his subsequent report to the government, Retief chastised the authorities for not providing protection to the Boers and settlers and expressed his lack of understanding as to why, if the Boers in his neighbourhood could drive the Xhosa out, the government could not muster up military might to do the same. He also expressed his view that the British favoured the Xhosa over the Boers and that he hoped that the eyes of the authorities had been opened by the Xhosa attacks and that things would change for the better.[472]

During the frontier wars, Retief commanded the respect of his fellow burghers and proved to be a better leader and organizer than he was a businessman. He was disciplined, resourceful and good at solving problems. He understood the problems of the people under his command and showed compassion and concern to all, irrespective of their station in life.[473]

The Xhosa cleverly avoided attacking the manned forts, choosing instead to surge past them to attack farms, which isolated the forts and their occupants. On 27 December 1834, Lieutenant Edward Forbes received news that the Xhosa were moving west in six divisions and that the attacks on Bathurst would intensify. Orders were given to evacuate those in Bathurst. Under the protection of Lieutenant William Gilfillan and a patrol of 18 men, a convoy of 70 wagons carried 600 women and children from Bathurst while the men folk rode alongside them. As the long convoy threaded its way through the hills toward Grahamstown, the Xhosa attacked. Gilfillan and his men shot four Xhosa and, fortunately, the group arrived at Grahamstown later that day without having incurred any casualties.[474]

Somerset Jr spent his days galloping from fort to fort to assess the danger. When he received a message from Grahamstown requesting his assistance, he relayed that the citizens would have to manage on their own as he had too few men with him. Arriving in the town on 29 December 1834, he surveyed the makeshift barricades made from sandbags, wagons and whatever else could be used to block the streets and realized how poor the defences were. Sure that another Xhosa attack was perilously close at hand, he considered evacuating Grahamstown. However, he was determined not to allow the Xhosa free rein to destroy the town.

Forces from Cape Town had not yet arrived at the frontier, as authorities had only learned of the violence sweeping the frontier late the previous evening. As elegantly dressed couples swirled around the dance floor at a ball at Government House in Cape Town, blissfully unaware of the tragedy unfolding on the frontier, a breathless messenger burst into the ballroom with a note for d'Urban from Somerset Jr. It had been written six days earlier and reported the Xhosa invasion in gory detail. D'Urban gave no hint to his guests of the news but immediately sent for the second command of the military forces, Colonel Harry Smith, and ordered him to immediately to go to Grahamstown.[475]

He set off two days later, after arrangements had been made for fresh horses to be prepared for him at staging posts along his 900-kilometre route. Troop reinforcements, which included the 72nd Highlanders, and provisions and stores were sent by ship from Simon's Town that same night.

Smith was a military man through and through. He had joined the army at the age of 16 and rose rapidly through the ranks. He served in Spain and it was here that he met two sisters, young women of 'high birth' who had fled to the British camp for protection. Within two weeks, the impulsive Smith married the younger sister, Juana María de los Dolores de León. She was 14 years old at the time and ten years younger than Smith. However, she faithfully accompanied him as he moved from battlefield to battlefield. Smith had been at the Cape since 1828 and had become more and more frustrated by the inactive life he led in Cape Town. Consequently, he must have been both excited and afraid when ordered to ride to the turbulent frontier. Smith was always smartly turned out and had a thin face, aquiline nose, widely-spaced, deep-set brown eyes, thin eyebrows and dark, crinkly hair that he had cropped short. His mouth curled down at the corners and his chin protruded slightly, which gave him an air of superiority.[476]

When the governor issued a call to arms, burghers from Swellendam and Worcester responded with enthusiasm and in due course marched to the war zone to assist their fellow burghers.[477] By the time that Smith rode out of Cape Town, more than 700 farms had been attacked and 456 farms had been burned to the ground; the Boers and settlers had lost over 114,000 head of cattle, 16,000 sheep and goats and nearly 6,000 horses to the Xhosa, who drove the livestock back to their lands across the Fish River.[478]

On New Year's Day on the frontier, Maqoma and Tyali sent messages to Somerset Jr in Grahamstown via missionaries the Xhosa knew and respected. Somerset Jr immediately sent the messages to d'Urban, even though he suspected the chiefs were up to no good. (In the messages, the chiefs cited Somerset Jr's actions and strong-arm tactics as being the reason for the invasion and war.[479])

While Smith was riding up the coast, Grahamstown suffered another blow: the *South African Commercial Advertiser* newspaper contained reports of the invasion but totally downplayed the attacks by the Xhosa and highlighted that the settlers and Boers were to blame for the invasion due to their ill treatment of the Xhosa. The editor of the newspaper was John Fairbairn, the son-in-law of the Dr Philip, and was therefore used as a mouthpiece for the reverend.

When those in Grahamstown read the paper on 2 January 1835, they were infuriated by the exaggerated and embellished stories of their mistreatment of the Xhosa and more than 450 angry people signed a petition voicing their unhappiness with the editor.

Smith rode into Grahamstown as the sun was starting to slip below the horizon on Tuesday 6 January 1835, escorted by six men of the Cape Mounted Rifles that Somerset Jr had sent to meet him when he approached. He absorbed every detail as his head swept from side to side as if watching a game of tennis: the maze of barricades leading up to the church that would slow the enemy's progress through the town but which would equally prevent and hinder access for any of the settlers; the streets full of destitute refugees who walked about in a daze in their tattered and dirty clothing, in many cases the only clothes they had been able to salvage from their farms; the wagons that littered the streets; the wounded and dead being offloaded from wagons, corpses of the dead mixed with the wounded; small groups huddled together agitatedly discussing the latest rumours; women weeping over lost loved ones and that every man capable of carrying a weapon was armed with a rifle, pistol, sword or in some cases even pitchforks. The people in the streets, however, paid little attention to him as he rode past.

The scene was so chaotic that Smith felt inclined to laugh but checked the impulse in light of the tragedy surrounding him. The defences of Grahamstown were so disorganized that Smith was sure that the people would have fired at each other in panic if an alarm was sounded that night.[480]

At Somerset Jr's residence, Oatlands, Smith was welcomed heartily and he conferred with Somerset Jr, Campbell and Lieutenant Colonel England late into the night. Smith grew angrier as the three men filled him in on the events that had occurred. He was shocked at Somerset Jr's evident lack of military capabilities and the poor defences he had erected in Grahamstown and disgusted that the military commander had even considered abandoning the frontier forts. Smith viewed Somerset Jr and his officers as cowards for having surrendered Bathurst to the Xhosa.

Early the next morning, Smith swung into action. He declared martial law, unaware that the governor had already done so. He announced that all men between 16 and 60 were to report to their local field cornets for military service and, within two hours, had organized a volunteer corps from the Grahamstown occupants that comprised four companies of infantry and one of cavalry.[481]

Smith took the reins admirably and, although prepared to listen to others, he answered to nobody but himself. For example, when members of the

Grahamstown Committee of Safety visited him, they explained how effective they had been since the alarm had first been sounded. Smith listened patiently, thanked them for their sterling efforts and promised to acquaint the governor with all that they had done. Then, as they were basking like rabbits in the sun under his praise, he promptly informed them that the committee no longer existed as he would be taking full responsibility for the safety of the frontier.

Smith dispatched Lieutenant Forbes of the 75th regiment and a body of troopers to reoccupy Bathurst, ordered that other outposts be manned and that the vulnerable areas of the frontier be patrolled. He purchased 200 horses and saddles and ordered England to move 50 of the men guarding the barricades to the entrances to the town, where they would patrol.

Smith's arrival and decisiveness was like a fresh breeze. His evident ability lessened the people's panic in Grahamstown; cheerfulness and hope replaced their despondency and fear. Faced with a shortage of men, he ordered the formation of a Hottentot corps—of the 1,300 men who joined up, 800 were auxiliaries to the regular troops and the balance were attached to the Cape Mounted Rifles[482]—as he felt that the show of Hottentot support for the colony would swing any vacillating Hottentots away from the possibility of allying with the Xhosa.

The uniforms for the Hottentot corps were made of green baize, the only material Smith found in large enough quantities in the several stores he searched. He immediately set the seamstresses in the town to work and was soon able to parade his Hottentot soldiers in their resplendent new green uniforms.

Smith wrote a reply to a long rambling message Tyali had sent to Somerset Jr. His message was short and sweet: "Return beyond the boundaries we have agreed to and surrender all of the cattle, horses and sheep you have stolen to the colony."

Early on the morning of 10 January 1835, before the reinforcements from the Cape had arrived, the cobbled streets of Grahamstown echoed with the sound of horses' clattering hooves and the rumble of a cannon being transported as Major Cox led a force of 76 British settler volunteers from Grahamstown, 90 burghers from Uitenhage and 40 Cape Mounted Rifles out of the town on a secret mission to attack the kraal of Chief Eno. (Smith had been delighted to find Cox in Grahamstown, as he had served with him in Spain.)

By the time that the troops arrived at Eno's kraal, he and his people had fled into the surrounding bushes. Eno had slipped away, right from under their noses, wearing disguise dressed in a woman's kaross. The colonial forces pursued the Xhosa into the thicket and killed 35 Xhosa, including Eno's two brothers and his son. The small army then journeyed past the scorched shell of the empty

Fort Wiltshire and set up camp. At three o'clock on the third morning, the troops moved out again. This time, they would attack Tyali's kraal near the foot of the Amatola Mountains. When Cox and his men crept up on Tyali's kraal, they discovered that he had escaped. Cox immediately ordered the village to be torched and, within minutes, the sky was black, as the dry thatch flared. Orange flames danced and licked the rising clouds of thick black smoke.

While Cox pursued Eno and Tyali, crowds lined the streets in Grahamstown and cheered the arrival of the 72nd regiment and burgher reinforcements from Graaff-Reinet (under W. van Ryneveld), Port Elizabeth, Swellendam and George (under field commandant J.I. Rademeyer). The 72nd regiment had brought stores and ammunition from Cape Town. Smith sent Somerset Jr with 400 burghers to clear the Xhosa from the Zuurberg Mountains and area near the Bushman's River.

In the ensuing skirmishes, it appeared that the Xhosa were coming off second best. In one engagement, Somerset Jr's men killed 12 Xhosa and in another, the military commander and 100 of the Boers held off an attack by between 1,000 and 1,500 of the enemy and managed to kill at least 40 of them. Fortunately, only one of the burghers was wounded, in the thigh.

D'Urban arrived in Grahamstown after a brief stopover in Port Elizabeth. He wanted to see for himself the severity of the Xhosa invasion and was devastated by the immense damage and loss of life caused by the Xhosa. Thoroughly shaken, d'Urban turned his attention to the plight of the settlers and Boers and established a Board of Relief to help the destitute refugees. He launched an appeal to the citizens of the colony for assistance and more than 1,800 families received clothing and comfort and more than 9,000 individuals received assistance from the government.[483] D'Urban was delighted with what Smith had achieved since arriving on the frontier and promoted him to full colonel.

Smith wished to invade the Xhosa's land on the western side of the Keiskamma River using three columns of troops. [484]However, having received reports that the Xhosa were massed in the thick bush near the Fish River, he sent England with 300 troops to clear them before starting the major offensive. Colonel England had not exactly covered himself in glory in the defence of Grahamstown prior to Smith's arrival and was nervous to confront the Xhosa in the bush. Smith began to draft Boers into the army from whichever districts he could. In addition, he drafted as many Hottentots as possible.

While the Hottentots were put on the same pay scale as the British soldiers, the British settlers and Boers drafted into the army received only food and ammunition and provided their own horses.[485]

After a half-hearted attempt to clear the Xhosa, England realized that he could never get the job done with the limited troops at his disposal and left a junior officer in charge of the clearing operation while he returned to Grahamstown to get reinforcements.

When England arrived at Smith's quarters, Smith was flabbergasted. He had expected news of victory but England's presence indicated defeat. He ignored his request for more men and snapped, "How could you leave your men?"

"I thought I could explain matters best myself," England stammered.

Smith marched him off to see d'Urban, who was as shocked as Smith had been by England's actions and immediately ordered Smith to personally lead the additional men to the western banks of the Fish River and to finish the operation.

On 7 February 1835, Smith marched out of Grahamstown with his force of 1,200 men, which comprised three divisions of nearly 400 men each assembled from the 72nd and 75th regiments, troops of artillerymen, soldiers from the Cape Mounted Rifles, the Hottentot Levy as well as Boers and settlers. When the army arrived at the Fish River, it was in flood and they could not immediately cross it. However, they could see the enemy on the hills overlooking the river. Smith finally decided that the waters had fallen sufficiently for his forces to cross and by seven that evening they successfully transported a six-pounder cannon and howitzer over the river. Smith led the centre column while England and Somerset Jr flanked him on either side with their men. The troops entered the thick bush in which the Xhosa hid, their nerves stretched as tight as banjo strings. Many of the troops were young Scotsmen from the 72nd Highlanders, and had never been in the bush before. Those who had realized the immense danger that was being concealed by foliage so dense that even the bright moonlight could not penetrate it.

Major Maclean called a halt after midnight and the men and boys of the 72nd Highlanders slumped to the ground to rest. The sentries peered into the dark, on the alert for movement by the Xhosa, while the rest of the men dozed.

"Kaffirs!" a sentry suddenly screamed, firing into the blackness.

There were shouts of alarm as the men grabbed their rifles. A fusillade erupted. "Cease fire! Cease fire!" Maclean yelled, realizing that the men were shooting at each other from their various positions.

As the early morning sunlight illuminated the thick bush, they discovered three dead soldiers and four severely wounded, moaning in agony on the ground. There was no evidence the Xhosa had been anywhere near them the night before.

That morning, Smith began his attack by firing the cannon into the kloofs where the Xhosa had been seen driving their cattle. The troops started ascending the hills in the thick bush. Soon, stampeding cattle bellowing in terror burst from the bushes in every direction as the shells exploded around them. The Xhosa warriors ran for cover among the cattle. The jumble of colonial forces, masses of Xhosa warriors and distraught cattle made it impossible to fire a weapon and the two sides resorted to hand-to-hand fighting.

The troops swung their rifles by the barrels and used them as clubs while the Xhosa snapped the hasps of their assegais and used them as stabbing spears. The Xhosa's modified spears caused incredible damage. One of the men was pinned by a Xhosa assegai through both legs. Two settlers pulled the assegai out as he screamed in pain—the wooden handle had to be drawn through the wounds on both legs.[486] After a few hours, 75 Xhosa had been killed and over 2,500 head of cattle captured. The colonial forces had lost eight men.

Over the next three days, many brief encounters took place and when the troops drove the Xhosa out of the bush, the Xhosa merely found new hiding places. Finally, Smith reported to d'Urban that he had successfully driven the Xhosa out of the bush by the Fish River. He could now focus on preparing to drive the Xhosa eastward toward the Kei River. Smith established a base camp for the commando that would invade the land of the Xhosa while he waited for d'Urban to give him the go-ahead to start the operation. He was champing at the bit to mobilize the men and eventually rode into Grahamstown to persuade d'Urban to allow him to launch the offensive with the troops at his disposal rather than waiting for more reinforcements to join them. However, d'Urban insisted that he be patient. A disappointed Smith then returned to the camp near Fort Wiltshire.

D'Urban finally arrived with reinforcements on 22 March 1835.

Two days later, the full force set out from the camp in an eight-kilometre column comprised of over 3,000 men, scores of wagons and six field guns to begin the major offensive against the Xhosa.

In front of the long column was a detachment of Boers, which were led by a sprightly 80-year-old veteran of four frontier wars.

The 1,537 Boers rode as though they had been born in the saddle and each man had a *kruithoring* (gunpowder horn) slung over one shoulder and *Sannas* (muskets) over the other. Most of these burghers from Swellendam, Graaff-Reinet, Somerset and Albany[487] were large, had black beards and wore broad-brimmed hats. Together, they made a formidable sight. The Boers led the whole column of troops, led by an 80-year-old white-bearded patriarch, veteran of four frontier wars. Behind them came the Hottentots and coloureds of the Cape Mounted Rifles, led by white officers wearing dark green caps and jackets. Each rode with a short double-barrelled carbine across his thighs and many puffed at a small pipe as they scanned the terrain for the enemy with sharp and watchful eyes. Behind the Cape Mounted Rifles were the Hottentot conscripts in their ill-fitting green uniforms that had been hastily sewn in Grahamstown. Smith rode behind the Hottentot conscripts with 20 men: 12 Boers and eight settlers. The settlers had formed a Corps of Guides and wore hats decorated with a band of leopard skin or ostrich feather. Behind them marched the 72nd Highlanders with their drums and bagpipes. They had modified their uniforms to suit the terrain and climate. Broad brims had been fitted to their caps and the traditional cross-belts and large black cartridge boxes had been replaced with lighter skin pouches worn on their belts. Their red jackets still stood out like sore thumbs, particularly in the bush, but Smith felt that the sight of the 72nd Highlanders would intimidate the enemy rather than prejudice them. Last was the artillery and the more than three-kilometre train of wagons. Each wagon was pulled by 20 oxen.

Smith had broken his men up into four divisions and appointed Somerset Jr, the one-armed Colonel John Peddie of the 72nd Highlanders, Cox and field commandant Stephanus van Wyk, a Boer, to lead them. In disgrace, England had been left to guard Grahamstown.

As Smith's army moved farther onto the slopes of the Amatola Mountains, they found the Xhosa to be like will-o'-the-wisps. Time and again, the invading army would find deserted groups of huts, with cooking fires still smouldering. The troops burned the huts and herded up the cattle. Only occasionally did skirmishes take place between Xhosa stragglers and the army.

The frustration of fighting such an elusive enemy grew and tension between the different factions of the colonial forces increased. The Boers, settlers and British looked down on the Hottentots, who were by far the best and most adaptable soldiers in the bush. (The Boers probably also resented them as they were paid salaries while they were not.) In turn, the British troops and settlers looked down on the Boers.

In one incident on the night of 3 April 1835, the Boers marching with the governor toward camp kept firing at random into the dark, in the hope that their shots would dissuade the Xhosa from attacking. Many of the bullets whizzed over the heads of those in the Corps of Guides and one of the shots fired wounded Mr Lloyd, who had to be carried back to camp in a makeshift sling. After the Boers fired at the soldiers of the Second Battalion in a similar fashion, the perception that they were cowards grew. Many of the troops and settlers were more afraid of being shot by the Boers than of being shot or killed by the Xhosa.[488] More than 3000 rounds of ammunition were expended by the Boers.[489] D'Urban was furious at the carelessness of the Boers and threatened to hang those responsible for firing on colonial forces in this way. He also warned the Boers that he would disarm them if there were any more incidents. Being singled out for criticism by d'Urban and Smith must have increased the Boers' mistrust in and resentfulness of the British.[490]

Very soon, a pattern of battle emerged: the troops would engage with small bands of Xhosa, round up their cattle, burn their kraals and move on. The troops spent more time herding cattle than they did fighting the Xhosa and as Smith wrote to his wife, he had no ambition to be a "Smithfield Market drover". The Boers felt the same way. As much as they respected Smith's military prowess, they resented his moodiness, apparent arrogance and fiercely British disposition.

D'Urban had always believed that Paramount Chief Hintsa was behind the actions of the Xhosa. When he had sent Commandant van Wyk to meet with Hintsa, as he could speak Xhosa, to demand that all the cattle belonging to the colony on the western side of the Kei River be returned and to ask Hintsa to assist the British forces against Tyali and the other chiefs, Hintsa had been rather evasive on both issues. Consequently, d'Urban decided to move farther into the interior with Smith and to invade Hintsa's lands.

The evening before they were to set off on this mission, d'Urban told Smith that he had had second thoughts about pitting his forces against those of Hintsa. He was concerned that while they moved inland, the Xhosa could come from behind them and attack Grahamstown and even Cape Town. Smith was furious at this change of plan and d'Urban's overly cautious approach. However, d'Urban summoned him in the middle of the night to tell him that he had again changed his mind and that the operation was on again.

For the next three days, the troops prepared to attack Hintsa while d'Urban kept questioning whether they were making a mistake. Finally, they arrived at the Kei River. After setting up camp, Smith received a note from d'Urban that contained various reasons as to why they should delay crossing the Kei River and invading Hintsa's lands. He raced to d'Urban's tent, where he talked the governor into proceeding with the plan. The next day, d'Urban told Smith to go on without him. Before he could change his mind, Smith raced ahead with his troops to the banks of the Kei River, where they saw the Xhosa crowded on the opposite bank. Smith used Van Wyk as an interpreter and the two parties shouted at each other over the waters of the Kei River.

"This is the land of the great chief, Hintsa," the Xhosa shouted. "You have no right to drink from the waters of the Kei, as they belong to Hintsa."

Van Wyk shouted back that they required all the colonial cattle to be returned and that Hintsa should inform them of what assistance he intended providing against the other Xhosa chiefs who had attacked the frontier. He yelled that d'Urban would give Hintsa five days to respond.

D'Urban had caught up with Smith by this stage. Smith again urged d'Urban to cross the river. D'Urban was hesitant. Smith could not stand the waiting any longer. Tired of the indecision, he took control. Smith turned to his troops. "Mount!" and then to d'Urban he rebelliously said. "General, I will cross and you will see every fellow fly before me. Then pray send the whole army on."

Prior to agreeing, d'Urban issued general orders to the troops that they were not to attack the Xhosa unless they were first attacked, and that there would be no stealing of cattle nor burning of crops or kraals.

The British army crossed the Kei River and invaded the lands of the paramount Chief of the Xhosa, Hintsa on 15 April, 1835 .[491] The convoy crawled like a giant centipede across the rolling green hills and valleys of the Transkei to Hintsa's kraal at Butterworth, where it was discovered that he had fled toward the White Kei River.

As the army was setting up camp at Butterworth, buglers sounded the alarm. Men ran for their weapons as they watched 2,000 warriors approaching, in full war dress and waving assegais and shields. As they approached, the troops heard them chanting a stirring war song. They appeared to come in peace. It was quickly established that these warriors were not Xhosa but Mfengu, an offshoot of the Zulu people. Much to d'Urban and Smith's relief, they were offering to assist in the fight against the Xhosa. Within a few days, there were more than 16,000 Mfengu camped on the hills with their women, children and cattle.

On 22 April 1835, a settler enjoyed a bottle of rum to excess and wandered out of the camp. He was murdered by the Xhosa.

Two days later, Smith called out his troops and, with great pomp and ceremony, fired a cannon, announced that the Mfengu were now British subjects and declared war on Hintsa. As the army marched deeper into the Transkei, Smith and his men swept the countryside, seizing cattle and burning Xhosa huts, including that of the Hintsa. In one of the deserted kraals, Smith took ornaments belonging to Hintsa's 'Great Wife', Nomsa.

Hintsa's emissaries soon arrived to discuss peace but d'Urban and Smith sent them away with the message that they would only talk to Hintsa.

Finally, Hintsa broke. On 29 April 1835, a group of 40 black horsemen could be seen approaching the British camp. The leader held a bundle of assegais in one hand and a sjambok dangled from his wrist. He nudged his horse forward, held out his hand to the officers near him and introduced himself. "Hintsa," he said proudly.

Hintsa was thickset, in his mid-forties and had jet-black skin and a face that Smith later described as "looking in every way like a black King George IV". He also carried himself with dignity and regal bearing.

Three camp stools were set outside Smith's tent for Hintsa, d'Urban and Smith. Watched by Hintsa's retinue of advisers and guards, Smith read a detailed document to Hintsa of all the colony's grievances against him. Then, d'Urban presented the colony's conditions for peace, which included that Hintsa would provide the colony with 50,000 head of cattle and 1,000 horses, half of which had to be paid immediately and the remainder in a year's time, and had to instruct chiefs Tyali, Maqoma and Nqeno to cease hostilities. While d'Urban read his lengthy document, stopping frequently for the interpreters to translate for the chief, Hintsa sighed repeatedly and shook his head. He was given 48 hours to consider the terms.

That night, d'Urban dined with Hintsa in his tent to the accompaniment of trumpets and bagpipes. One of the soldiers nearby described how Hintsa commented, "I like the fruits of the grape much more than grapeshot," when he was given wine.[492] Late that evening, Hintsa agreed to all of the conditions d'Urban had read to him.

The next morning, all of the troops were assembled before d'Urban, Smith and Hintsa, who publicly accepted all the terms d'Urban had laid down. Subsequently, Smith cried out dramatically, "Now let it be proclaimed far and near that the great Chief Hintsa has concluded peace with the great king of England. Let the cannon fire!"

With that, three guns boomed in succession and peace was declared. However, Hintsa had sent messages to Maqoma and Tyali informing them that he was a prisoner of the British and instructing his minor chiefs to drive the cattle still in their possession eastward, away from the British.

Unaware of Hintsa's duplicity and thinking that peace was imminent, Smith decided to move the troops on 2 May 1835.

On the way to the Kei River, the troops met with Hintsa's brother, Bhuru. He had 20 cows with him and claimed that these were the only cattle that he could find that belonged to the colony. "We will camp here until the 25,000 cattle and 500 horses Hintsa has promised are brought to me," Smith shouted in fury. Naturally, the men were despondent that their return home was being delayed and they grumbled that it would be better to retrieve the cattle themselves than to wait for the Xhosa to bring them in exchange for Hintsa's release. They recognized that the Xhosa loved their cattle more than anything—even Hintsa—and that no agreement would make them part with their cattle.[493]

Many of the troops were tired of fighting the Xhosa on and off and of Hintsa's cunning and deviousness. They wanted the war to end with a full-scale battle so they could be sent home. One of them was heard to say, "We are to stay here until Hintsa gives up his cattle. Shan't we grow grey here?"[494]

D'Urban and Smith recognized the colony would soon have another problem to deal with: a shortage of fresh produce. The majority of the Boers were serving in the army, which meant that most farming in the colony had ceased. Consequently, they decided to release some of the Boers from military service to return to their farms.[495]

Still waiting for the chiefs to send the cattle and horses, Smith received a message that Hintsa's Gcaleka had killed some of the Mfengu people. The Mfengu had started taking the cattle of the Gcaleka and bringing them to the British and the Gcaleka had retaliated by attacking the Mfengu.

D'Urban met with Hintsa under a tree near the camp. Three nooses were hanging from one of the branches. The governor berated him for the fact that he had only received 20 head of cattle instead of the thousands promised and tongue lashed Hintsa for the Mfengu killings. Hintsa viewed the Mfengu as scum and responded angrily, "Are they not my dogs?"[496]

D'Urban threatened to retaliate by killing two of Hintsa's people for every one of the Mfengu that Hintsa's people killed and added that if the killings were not stopped in the next three hours, he would hang Hintsa, his brother Bhuru and son Kreli. (Bhuru and Kreli were also being kept prisoner at the camp.)

Hintsa immediately sent word to stop the killings. Nevertheless, d'Urban made the three Xhosa chiefs sit under the tree for three hours with the nooses hanging above their heads.[497] Worried by the treachery of Hintsa, Smith rounded up the Xhosa in the camp and ordered 30 of his soldiers to stand in front of the Xhosa and the Corps of Guides to stand behind them. He then disarmed the Xhosa.

D'Urban planned to send all the Mfengu people across the river into the colony, where they would be under British protection, and he intended granting them land between the Fish and the Keiskamma rivers. They would also act as a buffer between the colony and the Xhosa, in exactly the same way as the 1820 settlers had before them. Moreover, d'Urban planned to extend the frontier of the colony to the Kei River, which would deny the Xhosa the protection of the thick bush on the banks of the Fish River.

Meanwhile, Smith's mercurial personality was creating new problems among the Boers and the Corps of Guides. He had a mouth like a sewer when he lost his temper. He could change in a flash from being reasonable and caring to arrogant, brash and abusive.

In one incident, Smith would not provide the men with tents, despite that it had been raining for a few days. When Major Bagot approached him on behalf of the cold and miserable men, Smith said, "The men do not want tents, as the weather is now going to clear up."[498]

Smith also used to belittle his own officers in front of the men by shouting, swearing and screaming at them. However, he craved popularity and could abuse someone and then try to entertain or amuse him minutes later, sometimes by singing in what he described as "my beautiful voice".

Smith's relationship with Hintsa was equally volatile and Hintsa was as confused by his mood swings as his troops were.

When things were going Smith's way, he was charming and amusing; when they weren't, he would explode in fury, shouting obscenities. One minute, he would describe Hintsa as a "fine fellow" and the next, he would describe him as a "cunning rogue".

After a week of waiting for Hintsa's people to deliver the cattle, Hintsa volunteered to lead Smith to the cattle.

On the cold night of 8 May 1835, the Mfengu began to assemble on the east bank of the Kei River, starting in ones and twos, then in family groups and then clans. Somerset Jr would lead them into the colony the following morning.

As the early morning mist swirled along the banks of the Kei River the next day, the troops watched in silent amazement as a black column that was two and a half kilometres wide and 12 kilometres long heading down the hills toward the river. The strange-looking procession of Mfengu drove their herds of cattle hard, their heads bent against the pouring cold rain which lashed down on them. Out of the swirling mist, the Mfungu's ghostlike figures appeared and disappeared as they walked, singing '*Siya Emlungweni*' (we are going to the land of the white people).

Somerset Jr was at the head of the procession and was followed by missionary John Ayliff and his wagons. Behind them, were more than 17,000 Mfengu and 22,000 head of cattle, most of which had been stolen from Hintsa's people. Small boys shepherded thousands of sheep and goats, which bleated wildly, while the Mfengu women carried their blankets, karosses and pots or balanced them on their heads.

The first Mfengu entered the cold waters of the Kei River, feeling their way by prodding the rocks underfoot with long staffs. The long snake of humanity and beasts followed in a continuous flow for the rest of the day, with the last of the

Mfengu and their cattle walking onto the land of the colony as the watery sun began to set.[499]

On the eastern bank of the Kei River on 10 May 1835, the British troops were formed up into ceremonial formation. The men stood in two lines, facing inwards, and the artillery was positioned to their right. Hintsa, his son, Sarili, and his brother, Chief Bhuru, were marched into the middle of the formation and Smith and d'Urban marched to its western side. The three Xhosa were sweating profusely, unsure what was going to occur next, but were careful not to display any emotion.

The governor then stepped forward and, in a loud voice that echoed off the steep cliffs banking the Kei River, proclaimed that the borders of the colony were now extended to the Kei River and that the land between the Keiskamma and the Kei rivers was to be called Queen Adelaide. (D'Urban had not been sanctioned by the British government to declare this extension of the colony.)

As the sun rose higher, d'Urban's voice rang out as he announced that all Xhosa were forever expelled from the colony and that, with the exception of the friendly Gqunukhwebe under Phato, any who returned would be treated as an enemy of the colony.

Afterwards, a 21-gun salute was fired. Each shot sounded like a clap of thunder and reverberated off the rocky crags, where the audience of baboons and vultures watched curiously as the men threw up their hats in jubilation and gave three cheers for King William.

After the annexation ceremony, Hintsa was marched to his tent, where d'Urban again warned him that if the British did not get the cattle promised them, he could be sent to Robben Island.

D'Urban had tired of waiting for the cattle to be returned and instructed Smith to allow Hintsa to lead him to where the cattle were being kept.

While Smith set off with his soldiers and Hintsa in search of the promised cattle, d'Urban and the remainder of the 1st division crossed back over the Kei River into the new province of Queen Adelaide, with Sarili and Bhuru as hostages. The strong force of 500 men, comprising 72nd Highlanders, Hottentot cavalry and members of the Corps of Guides, moved into the interior of the land today known as the Transkei with one heavily-loaded wagon and many packhorses.

Smith rode at the head of the column and, most of the time, Hintsa rode alongside him, watched keenly by George Southey, his brother William Southey and Mr Shaw of the Corps of Guides, who had been tasked with keeping an eye on the Xhosa chief.

Smith became more and more irritated as he suspected Hintsa was leading him on a wild goose chase. Although they often came across the spoor of the cattle, they never found any. It was as though the Xhosa knew when Smith's men were approaching. Hintsa picked up on Smith's anger and asked him to clarify the nature of their relationship. Smith told Hintsa that they were friends but warned him that he and his men would still shoot him if he attempted to escape.

On the evening of 11 May 1835, Hintsa suggested that they march toward the Bashee River at midnight. In due course, the party set off and soon found the spoor of the cattle. They followed their trail until eight the next morning, when Smith ordered the men to fall out for a rest next to a small stream. While the smells of breakfast being cooked wafted through the camp, Smith noticed that Hintsa seemed nervous and agitated.

Finally, Hintsa burst out in an angry voice, "What have the cattle done that you want them? Why must I see my people deprived of them?"

"You know why, far better than I," Smith replied. "The atrocities of your nation have left 7,000 of my countrymen destitute."

After breakfast, the men mounted their horses and set off again. They rode hard for several hours but still did not sight the cattle. "You see how my subjects treat me now?" Hintsa shouted to Smith. "They drive their cattle from me, despite the fact that I am their chief."

"I do not want your subjects' cattle," Smith replied matter-of-factly. "I am only interested in the cattle stolen from the colony and am here for those cattle, which I *will* have."

Eventually, Hintsa asked Smith to allow one of his principle counsellors, Umtini, to ride ahead to tell his people not to drive the cattle away and to explain that the troops would only take the cattle stolen from the colony. Although Smith smelled a rat, he agreed to Hintsa's request.

"You had better make sure you come back tonight," the military commander shouted to Umtini as he rode off.

"Depend upon it," Umtini shouted back.

Near the Ngqabara River, Smith observed from the spoor that the herd of cattle had divided. One group had gone left, up a very high mountain, while the other had gone right, up a steep and wooded hill overlooking the bushy riverbank. Smith chose to follow the track to the right. Everyone, except Smith, dismounted and walked up the steep path, leading their horses by the reins.[500] George Southey noticed that Hintsa was walking very slowly, as though trying to conserve the energy of his horse, and suspected that he might attempt to escape. He shouted to one of the Corps of Guides members near Hintsa to draw his pistol.

Soon after this, Hintsa climbed on his horse and urged it to speed up, until it was trotting past Smith. "Hintsa is off!" one of the men shouted.

"Hintsa! Stop!" Smith yelled after the Xhosa chief, who had ridden into a thicket. He aimed his pistol at him and Hintsa immediately guided his horse back onto the path and fell in behind Smith. He smiled at Smith mischievously.

Smith was sure that there would be no more trouble from Hintsa and that he merely wanted to see whether he really would shoot him. However, Smith again heard the cry "Hintsa is off!" as Hintsa galloped at full tilt past the Corps of Guides across open country toward a village near the river.

Smith led the chase after Hintsa and would have shot the fleeing chief if his two pistols hadn't misfired.

Eventually, Smith drew level with Hintsa, whose features were contorted in hatred and anger as he tried to stab him with his assegai. Because Smith was so close to Hintsa, Hintsa was unable to create space to deliver a telling blow. Smith threw his useless pistol at Hintsa and grabbed his kaross, pulling him from his horse. Smith galloped past the fallen Hintsa and shouted back, "Shoot, George and be damned to you!"[501] Smith shouted to George, who managed to shoot Hintsa in the left leg. Hintsa fell, but immediately sprang up and ran limping toward the nearby bush. "Shoot again!" Smith yelled. This time, George shot Hintsa in the side, the bullet passing through his chest, mortally wounding the chief. Hintsa fell, clutching his chest, pouring blood. Again he staggered to his feet before staggering into the thick brush and disappearing from sight. Lieutenant Balfour and Southey dismounted and chased after Hintsa. After scrambling down a steep bank, the two soldiers split up: Balfour went downstream and Southey upstream.

When George Southey emerged from the bush, scratched and bleeding, he stood on a rock at the water's edge to look for Hintsa. Suddenly, he heard the clink of metal against rock and spun around.

Southey saw a black face and an assegai in throwing position about to be hurled.

Hintsa cried, "*Musa ukundidubula!*" (Don't shoot! Mercy!) However, seeing the assegai poised to be thrown, Southey fired at him.

Hintsa's body rolled out from behind the rock[502] and Southey clambered toward him. He saw that Hintsa was still gripping the assegai and that part of his head had been blown away. Hintsa's brain matter and bits of skull splattered the bank nearby.[503]

George removed Hintsa's brass belt while other soldiers, who had rushed to the spot when they heard the shot, grabbed his beads, bracelets and assegai. One of the Southeys cut off an ear of the chief and another trooper the other as souveiniers. Shortly after this, Mr Ford, the assistant surgeon of the 72nd

Highlanders, pushed his way to the front of the crowd and extracted some of the chief's teeth.

On being told that Hintsa had been killed, Smith ordered that the body be brought back up the hill. However, by the time the party escorting Hintsa's body were halfway up the hill, a messenger informed them that Smith no longer wished to see it. Consequently, one of the soldiers let Hintsa's corpse slide off the horse that was carrying it and left it on the grass, where it lay wrapped in his blood-stained kaross. Later, some of the soldiers gave Smith a few of Hintsa's possessions and he sent an assegai and several bracelets home to his wife.[504]

After the death of Paramount Chief Hintsa, Smith and his troops managed to recover over 3,000 head of cattle, which they returned to the governor's camp west of the Kei River.[505] The Boers who served with the colonial forces frequently recognized their own stolen cattle. However, the authorities would not allow them to take them. Instead, the British took the cattle to a common pound, where they were sold or auctioned. The Boers were incensed at this apparent slap in the face. They had assisted the British during the Xhosa invasion as unpaid soldiers and many had lost their own horses in the process. To add insult to injury, they had to buy back their stolen cattle.

CHAPTER 14

Bitter is the aloe and bitter are the Boers

*Sarili—illegal arms trade—missionary rivalry—Select Committee on Aboriginals—
South African Commercial Advertiser—troop reinforcements—peace signed—
land given to Mfengu—Lord Glenelg—Boer anger at Stockenström—
slave compensation error—Glenelg disenchanted with d'Urban—rumour sweeps the frontier—
the Voortrekkers; Trichardt and Van Rensberg—Cilliers—crossing the Orange—
Thaba 'Nchu —Glenelg rejects occupation of Queen Adelaide—Retief takes up the cudgels—
Matabele—Mfecane—Griqua—Archbell*

In the wake of Hintsa's death, Sarili succeeded his father as paramount chief of the Xhosa. D'Urban demanded that Sarili accept that the new border for the colony extended to the west bank of the Kei River and told him that he would be expected to accommodate the other Xhosa chiefs and their people on his lands east of the Kei River once they were expelled from the colonial territory. To ensure his compliance, d'Urban reminded him that his uncle, Chief Bhuru, would remain a hostage in Grahamstown until the Xhosa had moved across the Kei River.

On 23 May 1835, the last of the Boers still serving in the colonial army were allowed to go back to their farms, where they were to plant mealies for the good of the colony. They were instructed to leave their horses behind for the troops and were told that they would be paid for them later.[506]

The authorities released these Boers from military service to save them from bankruptcy, as they weren't paid a salary in the army. However, their discharge created resentment among the Hottentots, who were not released from service to return to their lands.

The following day, d'Urban named the new capital of the province of Queen Adelaide King Williamstown and placed the town under the command of Smith, who took up residence with his wife in the ruined home of the missionary John Brownlee.

D'Urban and Smith believed that the war between the Xhosa and the colony was over, even though the Xhosa still launched sporadic attacks on the British soldiers' camps and stole cattle and murdered Hottentots in Queen Adelaide. Subsequently, a number of new forts were built in the frontier region.

The attacks by the Xhosa continued, although on a smaller scale than before, and the British troops retaliated by burning their huts, grain storage facilities and crops. Finally, to settle the fighting once and for all, Smith took a force of 2,000 men comprised of Boers, Hottentots, British soldiers, the Mfengu and Gqunukhwebe into the Amatola Mountains to attack Chief Maqoma on 1 June 1835.

Although the troops did not find the Xhosa, they burned down over 1,200 huts and destroyed immense stores of dried maize.

On 25 June 1835, Lieutenant Bailie and 28 Hottentots were dispatched from the new military base of King Williamstown to search for Xhosa in a kloof in the nearby mountains. Two days into the patrol, he and his Hottentot soldiers were surrounded by an enormous band of Xhosa. They fought bravely and when their ammunition ran out, they used their rifles as clubs. They were no match for the Xhosa though and all of the men in the patrol were killed.

The following month, two sailors were murdered by the Xhosa when they put ashore for water near the mouth of the Chalumna River.

The forts dotting the frontier did not deter the Xhosa from stealing and killing the cattle of the burghers and settlers and from attacking their farms. Moreover, the Xhosa murdered many farmers, including Retief's stepson, Jan Greyling, and their families. Soon, it became too dangerous for the settlers, Boers or British to set foot outside the villages, towns or forts. For instance, when a British soldier left the safety of the fort without a weapon to gather firewood, he was killed by the Xhosa within five minutes of venturing outside.

It was becoming increasingly apparent that the already stretched army and colonial forces could not keep the Xhosa out of Queen Adelaide, or even out of the Grahamstown area. Consequently, d'Urban recalled the Boers to military service.[507]

While Somerset Jr and his officers rode through Grahamstown like well-clothed and well-fed fat cats, the men in the new forts wore tattered and dirty uniforms and barely had enough food to feed themselves, let alone their starving horses. They also had little equipment and even ammunition was hard to come by.

Morale was at rock bottom in the army and the men were dog-tired—of fighting, being treated badly, wearing rags and being hungry.[508] Although the Xhosa had lost many of their cattle, homes and crops, they refused to move from the areas they had occupied before war between the Xhosa and colonists first erupted. Essentially, the Sixth Frontier War had achieved very little other than to increase the unhappiness of both sides.

The evident failure of the military to firmly establish the new boundary of the colony as the west bank of the Kei River caused Smith to look for a scapegoat: he accused the liberal missionary, James Read, of supplying guns to the Hottentots in the Kat River Settlement and implied that he was enabling the Hottentots to join forces with the Xhosa.

At the time, trading in arms was a lucrative enterprise and, in many cases, people in Cape Town purchased inferior quality arms and supplied these to the Xhosa. Some Boers, renegade soldiers and British settlers also traded arms with the Xhosa and paid little attention to the morality of the transactions. Smith's accusations against Read fuelled the resentment of the Boers and settlers toward the missionaries because of their ongoing support of the Hottentots and Xhosa. To add to the growing divisions on the frontier, rivalry between the London Missionary Society missionaries and the Wesleyan missionaries verged on open hostility.

In June 1835, this rivalry broke into open dissension when the Wesleyans agreed with d'Urban that the Xhosa were the aggressors and had conducted the Sixth Frontier War with cruelty and callousness and that the colonists had acted with restraint and had always upheld the principles of justice and mercy.[509] Subsequently, Dr Philip of the London Missionary Society turned to Thomas Buxton, his powerful ally in England, to lobby in the House of Parliament for a special committee to be formed to consider the frontier system in the colony. His letters to Buxton contained vitriolic attacks on the colonists and d'Urban, who had referred to the Xhosa as "irreclaimable savages". This particular comment prompted Dr Philip to write, "Sir Benjamin d"Urban has committed an offence against all the principles of natural and revealed religion. Not satisfied with taking their country from them, he has used an expression drawn from all the evil passion of the human heart."[510]

In July 1835, the Select Committee on Aborigines began its work in the Cape and other colonies with Buxton as its chairman. Its primary purpose was to investigate the treatment of indigenous people in British colonies and to ensure the protection of indigenous people's rights. Shortly after the formation of the committee, Buxton started the arduous process of collecting testimony from many witnesses.

Dr Philip also wrote a column in the *South African Commercial Advertiser* (edited by his son-in-law, John Fairbairn) under the pseudonym of 'A colonist' to spread his criticism of the settlers and Boers on the frontier. Fortunately, the *Grahamstown Journal* owned by Robert Godlonton presented a more balanced view of the situation on the frontier. As more and more negative commentary appeared in the *South African Commercial Advertiser*, d'Urban became reluctant to continue fighting the Xhosa. He instructed Major William Cox to avoid attacking the Xhosa and to take every opportunity to discuss peace with them. He also told Cox to inform the Xhosa that he would not be expelling them across the Kei River and that he would grant them land within the colony boundaries.

On 15 August, Cox met with Maqoma and Tyali, who were accompanied by 600 warriors in full battle dress. About half of their retinue carried illegal muskets.[511] The two chiefs reluctantly agreed to a truce with d'Urban but, when Cox mentioned that the Boers might be recalled to the colonial army, Maqoma responded angrily, saying, "Don't talk to us of the Boers. The Boers are your enemies. We have been supplied with powder by some of them; and they have told us to continue the war; others have told us also not to submit."[512]

When d'Urban received word that the Xhosa chiefs desired peace, he sent them a message explaining that if they would agree to become British subjects and live peacefully in the colony, the peace would be permanent.

Perhaps wary of some sort of trickery by the British, the Xhosa chiefs brought over 4,000 warriors to the next rendezvous. At this meeting with Smith, Cox and Captain Warden, Maqoma and Tyali agreed to meet with the governor on 11 September 1835 to settle the details of the peace agreement.

While d'Urban travelled to the frontier to meet with the chiefs, 540 men of the 27th regiment arrived from England on the *Rodney* and immediately set off for Grahamstown and the Boers were recalled into military service. This strengthening of forces did not go unnoticed by the Xhosa chiefs.

On 17 September 1835, all of the chiefs—including Mhalla of the Ndlambe, Nqeno of the Mbalu, Bhotomane of the Dange and Maqoma and Tyali of the Rarabe—signed the peace agreement with d'Urban and became British subjects. The 70,000 Xhosa could now live on the land in Queen Adelaide but, as aliens, could not own property there. However, that same day, 200 Xhosa drove off 200 head of cattle from a group of British settlers and a contractor's horses were stolen; the next day, Tobias Tharrat was fatally shot in the back; and the following week, the mission stations at the Kat River Settlement and Theophilus were attacked.

All Xhosa west of the Kei River were to submit to the laws of the colony and, despite being declared British subjects, if they crossed the Keiskamma River, they would be shot. Special government agents were sent to live among the various tribes and act as intermediaries between the Cape authorities and the Xhosa, who were allowed to retain their own laws and customs under the rule of the respective chiefs. D'Urban also declared that the province of Queen Adelaide would remain under martial law and granted the Mfengu land between the Keiskamma and Fish Rivers.

The war had been costly on both sides and although the Xhosa had only lost between 2,000 and 3,000 men and the colonial forces only about 100 during the frontier war of 1835, the impact was significant. The frontier farms had been totally devastated: 756 homes[513] had been reduced to blackened ruins and 58 wagons had become charcoal husks. The Boers and settlers had also lost much of their livestock, as 5,715 horses, 114,930 head of cattle and 161,930 sheep and goats had been driven off by the Xhosa.[514] Similarly, thousands of Xhosa huts had been burned and fields of black stubble marked where their crops had once grown.

D'Urban had written a full report on the Sixth Frontier War for his superiors in England and had described his actions in detail. It included an account of Hintsa's death and of the extension of the colony's borders and formation of Queen Adelaide. Dr Philip had also written a thorough report that recorded events in a markedly different way to that written by d'Urban. The new colonial secretary, Lord Glenelg, received both letters in September 1835, some months after the conclusion of the frontier war. While it appeared that Glenelg sympathized with the situation d'Urban had faced, he nevertheless warned d'Urban that he should avoid granting land to people or building new forts or other major works in the colony, as his dismissal as governor of the Cape was being debated.[515] Glenelg would also consider the evidence that had been presented in London to the Select Committee on Aborigines. In particular, Stockenström Jr had blamed the British government, the government of the Cape, the military on the frontier and the frontier farmers (British settlers and Boers) for having caused the war and the continuous frontier troubles. He had also proposed that to ensure peace and the preservation of the rights of the Xhosa and those on the frontier, protection should be provided for all and policies should not vacillate, as they had done before the Sixth Frontier War started.

When the British settlers and Boers learned of Stockenström Jr's damning evidence, they were furious with him. They could not believe that he had turned his back on them after all they had suffered at the hands of the Xhosa and in light of the continuing robberies and harassment. Although a relief fund was established to pay compensation to those who had suffered severe losses in the war, insufficient funds meant that many settlers and Boers were not compensated adequately or at all.

A letter by Retief to Campbell, the civil commissioner and resident magistrate of Albany, reflected the hard feelings of those who had borne the brunt of the conflict with the Xhosa. After detailing how many cattle had been lost in the district, he described the great danger and hardships experienced by him and others in the region. He then highlighted that the sense of injustice they felt was mainly due to the fact that the government had not provided them with sufficient ammunition to defend themselves and had treated them as if they were vagabond Hottentots or Xhosa.[516]

In an attempt to curb the ongoing cattle thefts, d'Urban announced that all Xhosa who were found within the borders of the colony without the requisite pass would be arrested. Unfortunately, there was insufficient manpower to carry out this instruction and the cattle rustling continued unabated. The governor also requested the field cornets of each district to draw up a list of men between the ages of 16 and 55 to protect the cattle retrieved from the Xhosa, which would be rounded up and corralled at centralized cattle kraals, such as that on Retief's farm.

The Boers were extremely dissatisfied with d'Urban's plan and claimed that while they were being conscripted into an army, their own properties and families would be left unprotected. So unpopular was d'Urban's idea that at least one of the field cornets refused to provide the list to the authorities.

More salt was rubbed into the wounds of the Boers when the governor withdrew the general licenses to sell gunpowder in a bid to prevent the sale of gunpowder to the Hottentots and Xhosa. This meant that the government would be the only supplier of gunpowder, which was already in short supply, and it would be even more difficult for the Boers to purchase a commodity that was essential to their survival.

Moreover, the livestock that the Boers protected included their stolen cattle that they would have to buy at auctions and many of these cattle died of illness in the centralized kraals or were killed by the military for food. To compound matters, word from England started to filter through that the compensation to be paid to previous slave owners would be less than half of the £3,410,290 and 6 shillings previously announced and that the average value of a slave would be £73, 9 shillings and 11 pence.

In addition, the Boers learned that successfully claimed compensation money would be paid out in England and not in the colony. Consequently, a petition was sent to London requesting that the payments be made in the Cape. However, Glenelg and the British parliament ignored this appeal and maintained that each compensation claim would have to be approved by commissioners in London. Furthermore, whatever amount was determined payable to the applicant would be subject to a deduction to cover the government's costs in implementing the Slavery Abolition Act 1833 as well as a deduction of 30 shillings to cover a stamp for each set of documents mailed.

Many of the Boer slave owners had mortgaged their slaves for property or money and in 1836, a swarm of agents arrived in the Cape to purchase claims from disappointed and distressed Boers—sometimes for less than half the value expected. Further, many of the Boers who applied for compensation received as little as one fifth or one sixth of what they had hoped for. Consequently, many of the farmers around Cape Town were financially ruined and agriculture ground to a halt. Families that had previously been comfortably off were plunged into debt when the final calculations for compensation were made in 1836.[517]

Glenelg formally replied to d'Urban's report in December 1835 with a long and damning indictment that clearly blamed the government of the Cape for having encouraged the recent war with the Xhosa. He described the killing of Chief Hintsa as having had no valid justification, stopping just short of describing it as murder. He indicated that d'Urban would have to renounce possession of the province of Queen Adelaide and hand the land back to the Xhosa by the end of 1836. He also informed d'Urban that a lieutenant governor would be appointed for the eastern districts; treaties were to be made with the local chiefs, who would be responsible for the restitution of stolen cattle and punishment of thieves; only missionaries would be allowed east of the Fish River; fairs for the exchange of commodities between the burghers, settlers and the Xhosa were to be established; and that British subjects, including Boers and settlers, would be punished by the courts for offences committed outside the borders of the colony.[518]

Although Glenelg invited d'Urban to make a case for himself, the tone of his letter indicated strongly that d'Urban's days were numbered at the Cape. While Glenelg's letter was on its way to d'Urban, he summoned Stockenström Jr, a former landdrost of Graaff-Reinet, to meet with him in London. (Stockenström Jr was living in Sweden at the time and left his wife and family in Holland before journeying to London.)

During the course of several meetings, Glenelg assessed whether Stockenström Jr would be the right person to send to the colony to act as lieutenant governor of the Eastern Cape. He needed someone who shared his own liberal ideas and those of the missionaries and, after extensively questioning Stockenström Jr on his views and beliefs, offered him the post. Stockenström Jr accepted the position on 7 January 1836.[519]

Toward the end of 1835, the Boers were coming to the inevitable conclusion that they would soon have to leave the colony. Their ill treatment by the British and the constant criticism of their actions by the media and missionaries did not bode well for them. In addition, rumours that Catholicism was to become compulsory throughout the colony, that their permanent conscription into the army was inevitable and that the Hottentots were to be given land they perceived to be theirs prompted many Boers to sell their farms. Although nobody was certain who started these rumours, many felt that land speculators who wished to capitalize on the Boers' existing nervousness and agitation were to blame for fuelling their fears in an attempt to pick up land at bargain prices.

Such was their hurry to leave the colony that one man sold his farm for a bulldog and a wagon, while another sold his for a wagon-load of groceries. Many sold their farms for a ridiculously small sum or else abandoned them to join those leaving the colony in tented wagons, taking only their cattle, sheep and goats with them.[520]

The canvas-covered wagons were usually six metres long and two metres tall and served as a bedroom, lounge, church and fort. Many of the Boers could not sleep all members of the family or group in their wagon because it was loaded with all their worldly goods. Consequently, they added makeshift tents to the wagons at night using sailcloth attached to the wagon's sides.

Furniture, bedding, ploughs, clothes, seed and, of course, the one commodity that they could not survive without, gunpowder, occupied every vacant centimetre of the wagon. (Gunpowder was sometimes hidden under false bottoms of the wagons in case the British stopped them and confiscated it.) Chickens and poultry were housed in *hokke* (cages) under the wagons, where they kept up their merry squawks as they swung to and fro while the wagons trundled along. Tea, coffee and sugar were carried in lead-lined chests and milk from the herds of cows was churned into butter using cleverly constructed contraptions linked to the turning wagon wheels. The Voortrekkers constructed crude ovens by digging holes and lining them with coals and used these to bake bread. They also shot game, which was in plentiful supply on the plains.

From 1834 onwards, the Voortrekkers crossed the Orange River and settled in small groups outside the colony. One of these early trekker families was that of 56-year-old Johannes Jacobus Janse van Rensburg, who was also known as 'Lang Hans'. After having served in the Sixth Frontier War, he moved north to trade ivory with the Portuguese in Mozambique and established his farm, Sewefontein. (Later, it would be converted to a mission station called Beersheba).

Late in 1834, Louis Trichardt and his small party of family and friends traded tobacco and other goods with Lang Hans.[521] They had been living in the Bamboesberg area, not far from present-day Heilbron. However, in January 1835, they joined several families near the Caledon River, with the intention of moving farther north.

Trichardt had frequently communicated with his old friend Hendrik Potgieter (Van Rensburg's cousin[522]), who lived in the Tarka district, via De Lange[523] (another of Potgieter's relatives). Their communications debated the pros and cons of travelling north into the interior or going east, over the Drakensberg Mountains into Natal. Trichardt had given serious thought to journeying to Natal. However, it would appear that his intense dislike for the British government had persuaded him to steer clear of Natal and the British stronghold there.[524]

Potgieter and Trichardt agreed that Van Rensburg and Trichardt would carry out a reconnaissance mission of the lands to the north and report their findings to Potgieter, who would join these *voorste mense* if the reports were favourable. The preparations for their departure were made difficult by the martial law in place in the frontier areas and gunpowder and other supplies had to be purchased in small quantities over a long period so as not to attract too much attention from the authorities. As it was, the authorities suspected Trichardt was selling arms and gunpowder to the Xhosa (and later accused him of having encouraged Hintsa to go to war against the British) and he had to move cautiously to avoid being arrested by the British.[525] While Trichardt was surreptitiously making his preparations, the British questioned whether or not he had already left the colony and, as early as August 1835, letters were exchanged between d'Urban and the local authorities trying to establish whether he had crossed the Orange River.[526] D'Urban even asked the local authorities to compile lists with all the names of the people who had crossed the border so that he could see whether a 'Louis' was among those who had left the colony. Somewhat naïvely, d'Urban hoped that his enquiries would be kept secret.[527]

While Smith recognized the growing discontent among the Boers, he mistakenly thought it was due to the hardships they had suffered during the Sixth Frontier War. Nevertheless, he warned d'Urban that the seeds of dissatisfaction were germinating among the Boers and would soon sprout.

In the Tarka district, the influential Potgieter was secretly organizing his party's departure from the colony. Ploughs, farming implements, a variety of seed and materials to maintain and repair weapons and wagons were purchased and items to barter were procured. Dried fruit, clothes, linen and household items were prioritized according to their usefulness and value and gunpowder was bought and hidden—not one of the Voortrekkers' wagons left the colony with less than 120 kilos of gunpowder stashed away.[528]

Trichardt was to trek north to Zoutpansberg, where he would await the arrival of the main body of trekkers under Potgieter. While in Zoutpansberg, he would send patrols to survey the wagon trails to the Portuguese ports of Lourenço Marques at Delagoa Bay or Inhambane, farther up the coast, in an attempt to establish whether trading with the Portuguese would be feasible in future.

In January 1836, as Stockenström Jr prepared to return to the colony as lieutenant governor of the Eastern Cape, while Trichardt and Van Rensburg and Boer followers joined forces to trek north in what would become known as the Great Trek.

Trichardt's party of 49 people included seven Boers with their wives, 34 children as well as an 87-year-old schoolmaster called Daniel Pfeffer, who would teach the children en route to the area near the Brak River.[529] Trichardt's second-in-command was the self-opinionated, quarrelsome and ambitious Jan Pretorius.[530] With the exception of Trichardt and his sons, Carolus and Petrus, the other four men in the group—Hendrik Botha, Gert Scheepers, Hans Strydom and Isaac Albach—were rather poor and owned few cattle. Prior to joining Trichardt, they had been squatters and not landowners. Consequently, most of the 50 horses, nearly 1,000 head of cattle and over 6,000 sheep and goats that travelled with the party belonged to Trichardt.[531] Van Rensburg's party also comprised 49 people: ten men, nine of whom brought wives along, and 30 children.

The combined parties of 98 people set off northward with a convoy of 18 wagons. However, Van Rensburg's group was able to travel much faster than Trichardt's party, as they were herding far fewer animals. As such, Van Rensburg's group would sometimes travel ahead of the other party. After camping near the present-day town of Middleburg in the Eastern Cape, the trekkers travelled in a northeasterly direction, which took them past Thaba 'Nchu and then veered north to cross the Vaal River.

Although the wagons rumbled through the lands of the Matabele unchallenged, the trekkers could not help but be unnerved by the wagon wheels crunching over the skeletons of men and women who had been killed by Chief Mzilikazi's Matabele and the many burned huts they passed. Their pace was leisurely and they stopped frequently to allow the livestock to graze. Moreover, when a lamb or calf was born, the wagons would halt so that the trekkers could give thanks to the Lord and to allow the new arrival time to become steady on its feet. Despite this, they usually managed eight to 15 kilometres per day.

The women usually sat on the front of the wagon on the *wakist*, or wagon chest, which often contained their daily clothing, while the young boys and servants led the 16 or so oxen pulling the wagons with their 2,000 kilogram loads through the tall grass, which stretched on as far as the eye could see to the west and to the hazy blue mountains of the Drakensberg to the east. They urged the straining oxen to keep moving using long whips or *riempies*.

The men strolled alongside the wagon, armed with front end loaders—which most could load and fire three times in one minute with excellent accuracy, even while on horseback—and *kruithorings* of gunpowder while the mass of livestock following behind were herded by servants, who whistled, shouted and cracked their whips to marshal the weary livestock. These animals cut a swathe through the grass as they trampled it underfoot, sometimes leaving tracks that lasted months and which other trekkers would follow.[532]

They passed Suikerbosrand, which had been the scene of a bloody clash between the Zulu and the Matabele a short while earlier, and then travelled down the valley of the Olifants River and through a mountain range that they named Sekwati Poort, after a Bapedi chief who lived to the east and had befriended them.[533]

In April 1836, conflict flared between the two Boer leaders. Van Rensburg and his party had shot a great many elephants for their ivory and intended to trade it with the Portuguese. When Trichardt warned Van Rensburg that he should spare his ammunition and focus on keeping the wagons light and in good condition for the last phase of the journey, Van Rensburg snapped, "I am man enough to look after my own trek."[534]

After this disagreement, the two parties split up and never saw each other again. However, they did stay in contact for a few weeks. Van Rensburg waited at Strydpoort for Potgieter's group of some 200 people to arrive, as he had received a message that they were on their way north. However, after several weeks, it was clear that they weren't coming. Eventually, Van Rensburg's group continued north into the Zoutpansberg area, where one of the men fell off his horse while hunting elephant next to the Sand River and broke his neck.[535] Shortly after this incident, they set off for Lourenço Marques.

The journey for Van Rensburg and his party became slower and slower as more and more of their cattle fell prey to the tsetse fly and succumbed to *nagana* (meaning 'loss of spirit' in Zulu), or sleeping sickness. Consequently, Van Rensburg redirected his party toward Inhambane, which he hoped would not be infested with the tsetse fly. By this time, many of the oxen had died and those still alive were sick and thin. As such, the wagons had to be pulled by relays of cattle.

After crossing the Lebombo Mountains in June 1836, Van Rensburg's tired party reached the Limpopo River, where they set up camp. Here, Chief Shoshangana of the Magwamba—known as the 'knobnoses' due to the mutilation of their noses that resulted in knob-like protuberances[536]—ordered his lieutenant, Malitel, to attack them, as he wanted the iron on their wagons and, probably, their guns.[537] The nine men bravely fought off wave upon wave of Magwamba warriors, firing blindly into the night while the women reloaded their muskets for them.

However, in the early hours of the morning, their ammunition started to run out. Sensing victory, the Magwamba drove a herd of cattle into the laager and, during the ensuing chaos, used the cattle as shields and penetrated the Voortrekkers' defences. One after another, the Magwamba fatally stabbed the men, women and children with assegais or smashed their heads with knobkerries.

Trichardt knew nothing of the bloodbath by the Limpopo River and he and his followers set up camp near a salt pan on the northwestern side of the Zoutpansberg Mountains, despite having learned of the dangers of the tsetse fly from Gabriel de Buys (the coloured son of Coenraad de Buys, who had by this stage become the leader of a band of refugees, criminals and robbers in the area). There, they would wait for Potgieter's party to catch up with them.

Potgieter had left his farm in the Tarka district in late 1835 with his immediate family, including his 80-year-old father, and some 200 relatives and friends in 40 wagons. When Potgieter's party reached the district of present-day Colesberg, they were joined by 34-year-old Sarel Cilliers, his wife and six young children and Cilliers and seven other families, including that of Casper Jan Hendrik Kruger (father to Stephanus Johannes Paulus Kruger, who was better known as Paul Kruger).

Cilliers was short, a little on the stout side and usually wore light trousers and a short black jacket. Clean-shaven, with long sideburns and fair hair that he combed forward, he was 'a man of God', having grown up tending his father's sheep with a Bible in hand. (At the age of ten, after having experienced what he referred to as a personal encounter with God, he began to convert his friends and other children to Christianity.[538]) Although pious and gentle, he loved to preach to others and prayed constantly—so much so that he would become known as the "prophet of the Great Trek"—and believed that the Lord had ordered him to lead his people to a better land.[539] His family was of French Huguenot stock and he had farmed north of Graaff-Reinet and then in the Hantam district of Colesberg. Cilliers had been part of a group of men who went on an expedition north to the Vet, Valsch and Sand rivers. On finding the land between the rivers unoccupied, a petition signed by 72 people was sent to the governor to request that this land be granted to the signatories. The request was turned down. Cilliers had also lost money in the slave compensation debacle. Instead of being paid 2,888 rix-dollars for his slaves, he was offered goods to the value of 500 rix-dollars.

Together, Potgieter and Cilliers's parties had over 70 wagons, 200 people and thousands of livestock, which made for a cumbersome caravan. As they rolled north, they left a dusty trail behind them as their animals chewed the grass down to the roots, making it appear that a swarm of locusts had devoured the veld.

Cilliers's religious zeal had a huge impact on the trekkers, many of whom were devout Christians and would miss the regular services they had attended in the colony. The *predikants* (ministers in the Dutch Reformed Church) had tried to dissuade the Boers from leaving the colony, warning them of the solitary existence ahead of them as they would never hear the Word of God again and, worst of all, that their children would remain unbaptized. Further, there were reports that some *predikants* had refused to baptize the children of Boers who were to journey into the interior. What's more, superiors of the Cape Synod had allegedly forbidden the minister of Cradock from visiting the Voortrekkers and ministering to them prior to their departure. Naturally, these actions caused great pain among a people renowned for their unshakeable faith.

Two months after leaving Colesberg, Potgieter and Cilliers's parties reached the Orange River. Their hearts sank as they gazed at the raging waters. The river was in flood and looked impossible to cross. Potgieter divided the men into teams and allocated tasks to them: some would cut down willowtrees growing nearby while others would lash the chopped logs together to make sturdy rafts to transport the wagons, people and all of their goods across the swollen Orange River. While the rafts were being built, some of the men swam across the swirling brown waters of the Orange River to the opposite bank with the livestock. The wagons were then loaded onto the rafts and pulled across to the other shore some 300 metres away. Then, the furniture, stores and provisions were floated over and finally, it was the women and children's turn.

As the last load of Voortrekker women crossed the mighty river watched by their men on the waiting bank, clutching their Bibles, the sound of singing whispered on the slight breeze and carried to the men on the far bank. They were singing hymns. The raft ground against the far bank as willing and strong hands of the men held the raft steady. The women walked ashore. As their feet stepped onto the dry virgin land, there were joyful shouts: "NOW we are free! NOW we are free!"

After crossing the Orange River, both groups of trekkers were asked to vote for an overall leader who would be responsible for ensuring order and discipline among the trekkers and, after the votes were tallied, Potgieter was declared the commandant. The wagons were then re-assembled, the goods were repacked and the procession set off again in a northerly direction for Thaba 'Nchu, which was also known as Blesberg (Bare or Blaze Mountain). Its whitened peak could be seen from a great distance and was caused by tons of vulture and dassie droppings that had accumulated over many years.

Back in the colony, the settlers and burghers were dismayed to learn that

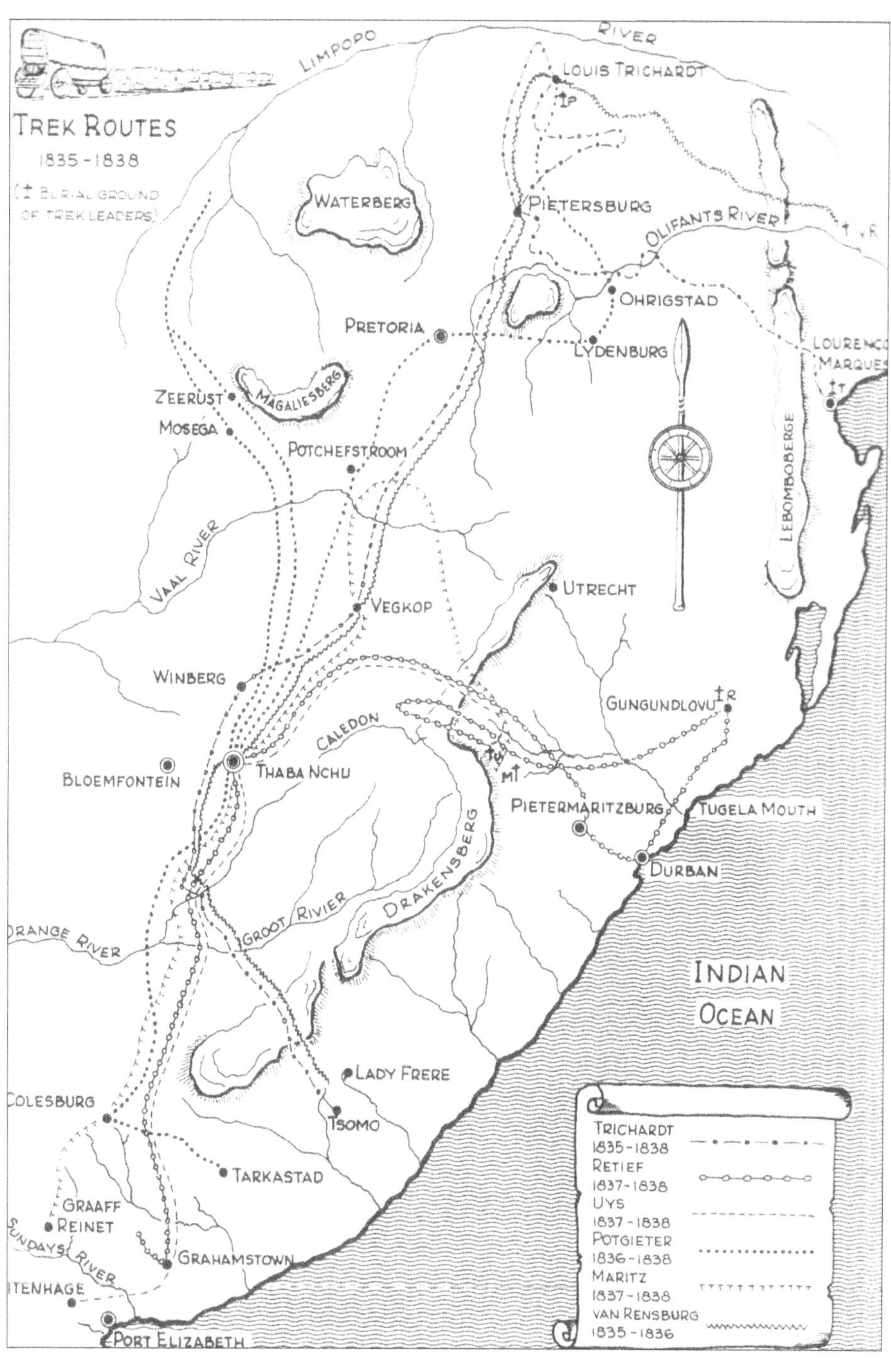
TREK ROUTES
1835-1838
(‡ BURIAL GROUND OF TREK LEADERS)
LIMPOPO
RIVER
LOUIS TRICHARDT
WATERBERG
PIETERSBURG
OLIFANTS RIVER
OHRIGSTAD
PRETORIA
LYDENBURG
ZEERUST
MAGALIESBERG
MOSEGA
POTCHEFSTROOM
LEBOMBOBERGE
VAAL RIVER
UTRECHT
VEGKOP
WINBERG
GUNGUNDLOVU
CALEDON
BLOEMFONTEIN
THABA NCHU
PIETERMARITZBURG
TUGELA MOUTH
DRAKENSBERG
DURBAN
GROOT RIVIER
RIVER
INDIAN
OCEAN
LADY FRERE
TSOMO
COLESBURG
TARKASTAD
GRAAFF
REINET
SUNDAYS RIVER
GRAHAMSTOWN
PORT ELIZABETH
TRICHARDT
1835-1838
RETIEF
1837-1838
UYS
1837-1838
POTGIETER
1836-1838
MARITZ
1837-1838
VAN RENSBURG
1835-1836

Stockenström Jr had been appointed as lieutenant governor of the Eastern Cape. They had by this stage already heard of some of the evidence he had presented to the Select Committee on Aborigines in London and were aghast at how his testimony portrayed them in such a bad light.

During a meeting in Grahamstown in February 1836, 41 burghers and settlers signed a letter to send to Retief that implored that he inform the governor of the "true conditions" on the frontier.[540] Although he was only a field commandant in the Winterberg district, he was recognized by all as the unofficial leader of the Boer community and as the intermediary between the Boers and authorities.[541] Retief then compiled a politely worded memorandum of the grievances of the majority of Boers and settlers in the Eastern Province for the civil commissioner in Grahamstown, who sent it to the government secretary.

He pointed out that only a year earlier, the burghers had been reduced to poverty when their farms were burned down in the Sixth Frontier War and that it seemed unlikely that they would receive any compensation from the government for their losses. In addition, his letter stated that many faced bankruptcy due to the government's tardiness in paying them for grain and other goods that they had sold to the authorities during the war. Moreover, he highlighted that they were distraught that many of their stolen cattle and horses were still in the hands of the Xhosa and that the Xhosa seemed to have not been punished for crimes committed against them.

Retief also emphasized that the farmers had not yet received compensation for the freeing of their slaves and that many of these freed slaves had become insolent and lazy once employed as servants. He stressed that farmers had to travel a great distance to the nearest town to appear before a magistrate to settle disputes with their servants, which not only endangered the farmer's family during his absence but was a time-consuming and costly exercise. Retief concluded the letter by stating that the farmers would have no alternative but to abandon their farms and move elsewhere if these grievances were not addressed.[542]

Rumour and speculation swept the frontier. One of the most terrifying of these rumours was that the Roman Catholic religion was to become compulsory throughout the colony; that all Boers were to be conscripted into the army to carry out compulsory military service; all the lands of the Boers was to be handed over to the Hottentots. Exactly who started the rumours, nobody is certain. Many believe that the source of the rumours was land speculators.[543]

One week after Retief wrote to Campbell, Stockenström Jr appeared for the eleventh time before the Select Committee on Aborigines in London. He was one of 39 witnesses that had been called to present their views on the ill treatment of the Xhosa, Bushmen and Hottentots in the Cape colony. (Dr Philip of the London Missionary Society had also been called to give testimony and he supported the evidence presented by Stockenström Jr. Considered a key witness, his evidence against the Boers and the settlers was damning and extremely biased.)

Stockenström Jr told the Select Committee on Aborigines that the loss of cattle experienced by the Boers and settlers was the sole cause of the turmoil on the frontier and he claimed that, despite the farmers' protestations, the cattle were usually seized by the Xhosa because of their neglect and carelessness. He then explained that the farmers punished the Xhosa unfairly for the loss of their cattle and that many unscrupulous farmers fabricated claims of cattle theft so as to have an excuse to raid cattle from the Xhosa. He condemned the commandos sent to recover cattle and claimed that these groups had systematically robbed the Xhosa and had, in some cases, murdered the Xhosa.

Stockenström also described the circumstances surrounding the death of Chief Hintsa and elaborated on the callous way in which his body had been treated by the troops. (The men had cut off his ears and stolen his bracelets and other possessions.)

Shortly after Stockenström Jr's final appearance before the Select Committee on Aborigines, d'Urban received a letter from Glenelg that rejected his occupation of the land between the Keiskamma and the Kei rivers and instructed that the province of Queen Adelaide should be allocated exclusively to the Xhosa. D'Urban's world collapsed and so did that of the many burghers and settlers who had viewed his policies in a positive light.

While Retief waited for a reply to his letter to the government, he was heckled by the impatient farmers. In turn, he peppered Campbell with queries about the government's silence. When Campbell eventually wrote to Retief in July 1836 (three months after Retief had written to him) to respond to Retief's complaints made on behalf of the burghers and settlers, his letter was dismissive and made it clear that the complaints would not be redressed by the government. He also indicated that Retief should stop pestering him. Retief then informed Campbell that his response had generated even greater dissatisfaction among the Boers and settlers and he expressed his hope that the next lieutenant governor would display a better understanding of the situation than that displayed by Campbell.

Having had no luck with Campbell, he then pleaded with Captain Armstrong to allow him and his men to arrest any Xhosa who did not have passes or had passes that had expired. However, Armstrong did not have the authority to grant this request. D'Urban, in contrast to Campbell, was becoming increasingly aware of the unhappiness of the Boers and wanted to stop their exodus across the frontier.

While Retief engaged in voluminous correspondence with his superiors in an attempt to get the authorities to assist the Boers and settlers on the frontier, Trichardt was establishing a settlement for his small party, which was putting down roots in Zoutpansberg with a view to remaining there permanently and Potgieter was leading the trekkers north toward Thaba 'Nchu. Their convoy of wagons and livestock moved at a snail's pace beyond the Orange River, through grasslands that appeared to be devoid of life and under a powder blue sky. Each day's trek was divided into *skofte* (shifts) that were usually between three and four hours long. After each *skof*, the convoy would halt so that the animals and children could rest and the children could be fed. Due to the lack of servants on the trek, all of the women and girls played a part in leading the wagons. When there were no young boys in the family to act as *voorlopers* (front-walkers), the young girls led the oxen and the women sitting on the *wakist* frequently whipped the straining oxen as forcefully as any of the men on the trek could do.[544]

Each morning, Potgieter sent three or four men ahead of the convoy on horseback to scout out the safest route and to select the site at which they would outspan that evening. As the convoy moved into the virgin territory north of the Vaal River, they encountered the Griqua, one of the four main groups that occupied the area known as the Highveld. (These four groups were the Matabele or Ndebele, led by Chief Mzilikazi; the Basotho, led by Chief Moshoeshoe; the Tlokwa, led by Sekonyela; and the mixed blood or coloured Griqua led by Adam Kok and Pieter Davids).

The most powerful of all these groups were the Matabele. During the several years it took for the Matabele to migrate to the Highveld from Natal, they left a wake of death and destruction spanning from the Drakensberg Mountains northward to the Highveld. Chief Mzilikazi moved his people due to conflict and warfare among the southern tribes in Natal and had split from the rest of the Zulu nation in 1813. Mzilikazi modelled his army on that of the 'Black Napoleon' (Shaka, king of the Zulu) and the Matabele killed thousands of warriors, women and children and decimated many tribes. Those tribes lucky enough to escape made for the Eastern Cape. (For instance, the Mfengu—sometimes referred to as the Fingoes by the colonists—arrived in the Eastern Cape during the Sixth Frontier War as a direct result of this historical event known as the *Mfecane* or *Difeqane*.) Having stolen vast numbers of cattle during their migration, the Matabele established their base in the Highveld on the edge of the area today known as Mpumalanga. From here, they were perfectly situated to carry out raids on the Basotho, Tlokwa and Griqua in the vicinity. The Basotho lived close to the Drakensberg Mountains (which they called *Quathlamba*) in the southeastern corner of the lands across the Orange River, as did the Tlokwa, and these tribes provided a safe haven for any strays or refugees from other tribes affected by the *Mfecane*. Maize and sorghum flourished in the lands around Thaba Bosiu, which served as Moshoeshoe's hilltop fortress, and he welcomed and protected the refugees fleeing from Mzilikazi and his warriors. And with good reason: Moshoeshoe was strengthening his own tribe by making them part of his kingdom. For instance, he allowed a group of Tswana under Chief Moroka II, a Barolong chief, to settle at Thaba 'Nchu, 80 kilometres from his stronghold.[545]

The Griqua comprised groups of coloured or mixed race people who were a constant source of harassment and danger to the Tlokwa (sometimes referred to as the 'wild cat people') and Basotho and, to a lesser extent, the Matabele. They possessed far more rifles and ammunition than these groups did and were recognized as excellent horsemen and marksmen. When Potgieter and his party of 200 trekkers approached Thaba 'Nchu, they encountered the Griqua and, to their great relief, the meeting was rather amicable.

Shortly after this, local Basotho approached them to barter maize, beans and other produce for cattle and sheep. Although the negotiations were friendly, the Basotho were evidently afraid of the Boers' sophisticated weaponry. However, they soon overcame their fear of the Boers' muskets and approached them to request that they hunt some wild animals for them to eat.[546]

When the procession of wagons weaved its way across the veld in the territory of Chief Moroka II, he welcomed the Voortrekkers with open arms, as he recognized that they could prove to be a valuable ally against the Matabele. (Earlier, Chief Moroka II had shown great hospitality to the Wesleyan missionaries led by Mr Archbell, who had set up a mission station at Thaba 'Nchu in 1833.[547] Subsequently, Archbell had established good relationships with the Griqua and the Basotho.)

The trekkers finally arrived at Thaba 'Nchu in May 1836. The elation they felt to finally outspan here must have been short-lived, however: the mountainside was not only covered in a thick layer of animal droppings, it was also strewn with the bleached human bones and skeletons of Barolong people who had been slaughtered by Mzilikazi's Matabele.[548] The white-topped mountain spelled out an ominous warning to the Voortrekkers of what lay ahead.

CHAPTER 15

The scattering of the people

Moving north—search for Van Rensberg party—return of Stockenström—Cape of Good Hope Punishment Act—murder on the Vaal—Battle of Vegkop

The Voortrekkers remained at Thaba 'Nchu for several weeks and used their time there to mend their wagons, hunt, make biltong and regroup for the journey farther north. Once rested and refreshed, Potgieter, Cilliers and their combined parties set off with their cattle, horses, goats and sheep, leaving huge clouds of dust swirling in their wake.

After crossing the Modder River, the patrols and hunting parties came across small settlements belonging to the Bushmen. When the Bushmen saw the white men approaching, they fled from their homes, which comprised three or four holes in the ground that were covered with branches and leaves to provide camouflage.

Near the next large river, the trekkers found abundant wildlife in the veld, including buffalo, eland, impala, zebra, giraffe and elephant and they relished the opportunity to hunt here. They were so impressed by the game to be had in the area that they named the river Vetrivier (Fat River). Here, they also encountered Chief Makwana and the remnants of his Bataung tribe. After experiencing the savagery of the Matabele, the Bataung (lion people) were on the verge of starvation: all of their crops had been burned and their stores had been taken by the Matabele, who had also made off with all their cattle, sheep and goats. Consequently, the Voortrekkers' arrival and their willingness to shoot game for them was met with great delight.[549] The Voortrekkers were shocked at the way the Bataung ate their meat raw and dripping in blood.[550]

Makwana had laid claim to the land between the Vet and the Vaal rivers but communicated to Potgieter that he would be willing to sell this land to the trekkers and allow them to settle there. He realized that the presence of the Boers would fortify his defences against the Matabele.

Subsequently, Potgieter exchanged cattle, sheep and goats for land between the Vet and the Vaal rivers and agreed to protect the Bataung from Chief Mzilikazi's marauding warriors and to live harmoniously alongside Makwana and his people, who would live in a small area on this land. Shortly after this, the Voortrekkers set off to explore their new lands.

After travelling through wide expanses of grasslands overlooked by the majestic Drakensberg Mountains, they approached the Sand River, where they found excellent grazing for their livestock.

The Voortrekkers thought that they had finally found a place where they could live in peace and prosper, despite their proximity to Mzilikazi and the Matabele.

They decided to settle for a few months at this site, which would later be known as Winburg,[551] and each family laid claim to a piece of land and began to plant crops.[552] Potgieter had already indicated that he wished to explore farther north and planned to meet up with the parties of Trichardt and Van Rensburg. (He was unaware that Van Rensburg's party were already dead.) On 25 May,[553] Potgieter called a meeting and told the trekkers that he and a scouting party would track down Trichardt and Van Rensburg. If their parties had discovered a better place at which to set up permanent residence, the scouting party would return to collect the other Voortrekkers. He also warned those who would remain behind not to venture north across the Vaal River in his absence, as they would in all likelihood draw the attention of the Matabele and risk being attacked. Potgieter's party, which included Cilliers and ten other men,[554] set off in two wagons and, just days after their departure, some of the trekkers near the Sand River crossed the Vaal River.

Months earlier, the heavy wagons of Trichardt and Van Rensburg's convoy and their thousands of livestock had flattened a path through the grass that resembled a firebreak and Potgieter's party was able to easily and quickly follow the route they had taken.

For the first 18 days of the journey, Potgieter and his men passed through an eerie landscape in shocked silence: hundreds of kraals ravaged by fire and with collapsed roofs dotted the grasslands and the two wagons frequently crunched over human bones from victims of the Matabele's savage attacks. Fortunately, the grasslands still boasted plentiful wildlife, which the Voortrekkers hunted and shared with the local tribesmen they encountered. This, coupled with the fact that they shot lion and leopard that preyed on the locals' cattle and sheep endeared them to these tribesmen. In particular, Cilliers was a superb marksman and, on one occasion, won the adulation of the locals when he killed a "wolf" (probably a leopard or lion) known to be a "child-eater".[555]

After passing through the area near which the town of Heidelberg stands today—and which Potgieter named Suikerbosrand (Sugarbush Ridge) after the Protea of the same name—the party crossed the Olifants River. From here on, they rapidly made for Zoutpansberg in an attempt to avoid meeting a Matabele patrol. As they approached the area, they encountered scores of friendly tribesmen and were particularly impressed by the many gold ornaments they wore as well as by the fertility of the land.

Finally, at the end of June 1836, they rode into Trichardt's camp on the western end of Zoutpansberg. The land that Trichardt had settled on had rich soil and abundant water and fruit trees, millet and mealies grew prolifically in the area. In addition, the gold and manufactured iron possessed by the friendly local tribesmen indicated that gold and iron ore were to be found in these lands. The scouting party appeared to have found the promised land.

After a few days, Potgieter and seven of his original party set off northward to find the route to the Portuguese coast and to see whether they could find Van Rensburg's group. Three of his party joined Trichardt on an expedition to look for the missing trekkers. They started riding eastward, past the Lebombo Mountains, and then headed south along the Limpopo River.

After several weeks, Potgieter's group decided to return to Zoutpansberg (presumably after having crossed the Limpopo River into present-day Zimbabwe) as their horses were becoming ill due to the tsetse fly prevalent in the region. While on the return leg of the journey, Potgieter's party met up with some members of the De Buys family, who had settled among the Magwamba after fleeing the colony.

By this stage, Coenraad de Buys had fathered many children, white and coloured, in areas spanning the Eastern Cape to Zoutpansberg. (After yet another brush with authorities, he had abandoned his large and spread-out family and was never heard from again.[556]) His sons, Doors and Gabriel Buys had dropped the 'de' of their surname and acted as guides for Potgieter's group, escorting them back to Trichardt's settlement near Zoutpansberg.

A despondent Trichardt returned on 16 August 1836 with the sad news that it appeared that every man, woman and child in Van Rensburg's trek had been killed. He added that they were lucky to have escaped with their lives.

While travelling along the Limpopo River toward its confluence with the Olifants River, they had called at a Magwamba kraal. There, they had seen some of the Magwamba carrying a telescope and mirror and Trichardt immediately recognized that these belonged to the Van Rensburg family.

When he asked the Magwamba from whom they had obtained these items, they told him that they had bartered with other tribes for them. He then questioned them on the whereabouts of the Van Rensburgs. Initially, they denied all knowledge of the trekkers but eventually conceded that they had heard that a party of white people had been murdered farther upriver.

Fearing the worst, Trichardt's group continued their search for the missing trekkers and soon came upon a second Magwamba kraal, where they learned that the Van Rensburg party had passed the kraal some months earlier.

Chief Sakana then invited the weary travellers to spend the night as it was nearly dark. Fortunately, Trichardt could understand Xhosa and heard the Magwamba whispering that they should kill these white men to prevent them from returning with others to avenge the deaths of those in Van Rensburg's party. Trichardt kept a cool head and a wary eye on the Magwamba that night and when Chief Sakana asked him whether he was going to keep looking for the Van Rensburgs, Trichardt told him that his men would return to their camp to fetch their wagons before picking up the trail from the kraal in two days' time. (Chief Sakana no doubt instructed his warriors to let the men be as he could then seize their wagons, weapons and goods when they returned.)

Trichardt's group sped back to their camp, where they found that Potgieter and several other men were preparing to travel south to the Sand River, where they would collect all those who wished to settle in the fertile lands around Zoutpansberg.[557]

Some of Trichardt's party, including the argumentative Jan Pretorius, Hendrik Botha, Gert Scheepers and his wife, Antjie, and Isaac Albach, did not believe that the Van Rensburgs were dead and set off to find them and make their own way to the coast of Mozambique.

After they left, the nearby Chief Ramabooya decided to attack Trichardt's camp, believing it to have been weakened by their departure and that of Potgieter's party. However, members of the Venda tribe warned Trichardt of the imminent attack and offered their assistance.

Chief Ramabooya and his men crept quietly up to the wagons, unaware that an army of Venda warriors as well as Trichardt's son, Carolus, were hiding in the bushes waiting for them. As soon as Chief Ramabooya's warriors were within range, the Venda burst from the bushes throwing their assegais while Carolus repeatedly fired at them, causing them to retreat.

A month into their journey, Pretorius's breakaway party called at a Magwamba kraal, where they saw a knapsack that belonged to one of the members of the Van Rensburg party. When Pretorius asked the Magwamba whether they knew what had become of the Van Rensburg group, they learned that the trekkers had been massacred but that two children had survived the attack and were being held hostage by Chief Sakana.

Jan Pretorius's party was tired and frightened and longed to return to Zoutpansberg. Further, many of their oxen had fallen ill with *nagana* (after being bitten by the tsetse fly). However, Jan Pretorius was too proud to send a message to Trichardt asking for help. Consequently, the newly widowed Antjie Scheepers secretly sent him a note with a young Bushman maid explaining their dire circumstances and Trichardt immediately dispatched his son Petrus with fresh oxen so the group could return to Zoutpansberg.

Back in the colony, the morale of the Boers and colonists had dipped to an all-time low as they contemplated what would be in store for them when the province of Queen Adelaide was returned to the Xhosa.

While many of the Boers planned to leave the colony for good, the British settlers compiled many letters of complaint about the British government's apparent ignorance of conditions on the frontier.

D'Urban was extremely frustrated and disappointed that he had not received clarification on questions he had posed to Glenelg about how he should deal with the increased military expenditure that would result from policing the borders when the colonists moved out of Queen Adelaide.[558] As it was, Smith was desperately short of troops to police the frontier and new province.

On 6 July 1836, the ship carrying the new lieutenant governor of the Eastern Cape dropped anchor in Table bay. However, a smallpox scare onboard meant that all the passengers, including Stockenström Jr, were quarantined onboard for three weeks and were only able to disembark on 25 July 1836. Although Stockenström Jr was of a lesser rank than d'Urban, both men knew that he was 'Glenelg's man' and would call the shots in governing the large population of Boers and British settlers on the frontier.

D'Urban discussed the colonial occupation of the lands between the Keiskamma and Kei rivers at length with Stockenström Jr and, although he believed that the colonial occupation of the area was for the good of the tribes on the frontier as well as the border colonists, [559]he had no choice but to follow Glenelg's instructions to move the colonists out.

Bitter and saddened by Glenelg's decision to return the region to the Xhosa, d'Urban ordered Smith to start withdrawing his troops from certain forts and to destroy any military equipment or premises that the Xhosa could use against the colony. He also reversed the state of martial law in the area, much to Smith's dismay. On receiving the news, Smith remarked, "The sooner we march out of the province the better, for how am I to 'eat up' a kaffir without it?"[560]

On 13 August 1836, the British parliament attempted to stop the Boers from emigrating from the colony by passing the Cape of Good Hope Punishment Act. This enabled the Cape government to punish all citizens of the colony, even if outside its borders, and declared that the authority of the colony extended south from the 25th degree of latitude.[561]

The Boers and settlers were determined to discredit Stockenström Jr and hoped to oust him as lieutenant governor of the Eastern Cape. On his journey to the frontier, Stockenström Jr stopped at George, where he learned that a Boer called Klopper had accused him of murdering a Xhosa man several years earlier.

Under oath, Klopper swore that while he had been on commando under Stockenström Jr (who had been the landdrost of Graaff-Reinet at the time), he had seen Stockenström Jr shoot an unarmed Xhosa in cold blood. He claimed that when the Xhosa had taken refuge under some nearby shrubbery, Stockenström Jr had fired at him from point blank range and that the wadding from his gun had ignited the leaves because he had been so close to the cowering Xhosa. He alleged that Stockenström Jr had then turned to Dolph Botha, whose brother had been killed by the Xhosa along with Stockenström Jr's father, and told him that by killing this Xhosa, he had avenged the death of his father and of Theunis Botha.[562]

Similarly, Smith was being investigated for his role in the killing of Chief Hintsa. By the time his trial started at Fort Wiltshire on 29 August 1836, Smith had begun to drink heavily. Twenty-one witnesses were called and after listening to their often contradictory testimony, the judges decided that no blame could be attached to a single person for the death of Chief Hintsa. Shortly after this, Smith stepped down as military commander in Queen Adelaide and Somerset Jr took overall control of the eastern districts.[563]

Although shocked by the vindictive claims Klopper had made, Stockenström Jr shrugged them off and continued to Grahamstown. When he rode into the town on 3 September 1836, his arrival was announced by a 17-gun salute. The public had been notified of his impending arrival and encouraged to turn out to welcome him. However, as he approached the inn at which he would be staying, he was greeted by a sullen crowd. The clatter of his horse's hooves on the cobbles was deafening compared to the unhappy murmur made by the many bystanders watching him stonily.

Shortly after his arrival, he received a petition signed by 412 inhabitants of the district of Albany that highlighted their view that the British government had an incorrect impression of the character and conduct of the colonists on the frontier and pointed out that they blamed the government for facilitating their ruin and suffering at the hands of the Xhosa. In addition, the letter stated clearly that they felt that Stockenström Jr's own version of events given to the Select Committee on Aborigines had been extremely damaging and had contributed to the negative perceptions about them that prevailed in England. Moreover, the letter added that his evidence had jeopardized their chances of receiving compensation for the losses they had incurred in the war. Stockenström Jr refused to officially accept the petition but replied to the letter stating that he would justify his actions and opinions in front of a competent and impartial authority.[564]

At a public meeting in Grahamstown on 5 September 1836, the speakers representing the settlers reiterated how angry the settlers were about Stockenström Jr's condemnation of them to the Select Committee on Aborigines, albeit in politely worded speeches. The settlers' resolutions were then tabled and sent to the *London Times* and other leading publications in England, in the vain hope that their views would be publicized. Shortly after this, Stockenström Jr headed for King Williamstown to relieve Smith of his command, leaving behind a seething Grahamstown population that was apprehensive about their future with him as their lieutenant governor.

By this time, Potgieter's small party were approaching the Vaal River. Potgieter sent R. Janse van Vuuren, A. De Lange, C. Liebenberg, D. Opperman and A. Swanepoel[565] ahead to collect fresh horses, while he and Cilliers followed them at a leisurely pace. When the five men neared the Vaal River, Opperman drew their attention to something in the water ... it was a Voortrekker wagon. Disturbed by what they had seen, they raced toward the riverbank, where they saw white, coloured and black bodies strewn about the area. It was clear that a desperate battle had taken place and that the trekkers had not heeded Potgieter's warning not to cross the Vaal River while they were away. In grim silence, the men discovered that Liebenberg's family were among the dead.

Later, they learned that Stephanus Erasmus had put together an elephant hunting party that included his three sons as well as Jan Claasen, Carel Kruger and Pieter Bekker and his son and that they had crossed the Vaal River with their coloured servants. One morning, the hunters split into three groups and, as usual, left their servants to look out for their five wagons, cattle and horses. Erasmus and one of his sons decided to return to the camp that evening, tired after a day in the saddle and frustrated at their failure to bag any elephant. However, as they approached it, they saw that it was surrounded by more than 500 Matabele warriors, who had already attacked the other two groups and killed two of his sons as well as Carel Kruger. (Fortunately, Claasen, Pieter Bekker and his son had managed to escape. However, Claasen was never seen alive again.) Terrified, Erasmus and his son wheeled their horses around and galloped away from the scene, heading for a Boer camp they had come across earlier.

After riding for five hours, they finally arrived at the camp, where they breathlessly warned the trekkers that the Matabele were on the warpath and begged the trek leaders, Piet Botha and Hermanus Steyn, to assemble a group to help them search for the rest of the hunters. Early the next morning, the search party set off and it was not long before they saw a 500-strong division of the Matabele army blocking their path. They fired at the Matabele, hoping to deter them from attacking them, then raced back toward the camp to warn the others that the Matabele were coming. Along the way, they scooped up a young boy called Diederik Frans Kruger who had been minding sheep and rode with him to the safety of the wagons. Botha and Steyn shouted to the trekkers to move the wagons into a laager while the frightened Boers scurried to prepare themselves for the battle ahead.

Within minutes of the laager being set up, the Matabele descended on them and Erasmus's son narrowly escaped being killed when he sped off on horseback to warn the Liebenberg camp some five kilometres away of an impending attack and to urge them to join the main party.

Time and again, the Matabele charged the wagons and each attack met with a wall of bullets from the 35 men defending the laager. During a lull in the fighting, the trekkers watched in astonishment as many horses belted past them as well as some panicked oxen still tied to a wagon's disselboom (pole to which the oxen were tethered). "Those are the Liebenberg's oxen!" one of the Boers shouted in horror.

By four o'clock that afternoon, it was all over: approximately a third of the Matabele warriors were dead and they reluctantly withdrew from the battle, taking over 1,000 head of cattle with them. While more than 150 bloody corpses of Matabele fighters lay around the wagons, inside the laager, there had been only one casualty, Adolf Bronkhorst. However, it was later discovered that a young boy called Christiaan Harmse had been murdered while looking after sheep and cattle near the camp[566]

Farther upriver, near the present-day town of Parys,[567] the Liebenbergs' camp had suffered heavy losses: six men two women and six children were killed. One of the fleeing coloured servants hid from the Matebele in the bushes with two children until help arrived. The 71-year-old Barend Liebenberg and his three sons, together with Johannes du Toit and a Scot, MacDonald, were all stabbed to death. The bodies of six children and two women, Anna Maria du Toit and the wife of Hendrik Liebenberg lay on the blood-stained grass alongside the wrecked wagons. Three children had been abducted by the Matabele as gifts for Mzilikazi. Twenty-six coloured servants were killed in the three camps. The trekkers had lost over 1,000 cattle and many thousands of sheep in addition to wagons burned and stolen.[568]

Six days after the attacks, Erasmus rode back to his camp to see whether he could find out what had happened to his two missing sons. There, he found the bodies of five of his coloured servants and hastily returned to join the other trekkers, who packed their wagons and headed south for the safety of the lands on the other side of the Vaal River. Sure that his sons had been killed by the Matabele, Erasmus decided to return to the relative safety of life in the colony.[569]

Potgieter's party were greatly saddened and worried by the massacre they had stumbled upon near the Vaal River and, after Sarel Cilliers led the men in prayer, they buried the victims, erecting wooden crosses on the mounds of piled earth. After this brief memorial, Potgieter's group crossed the Vaal River and followed the wagon tracks of the fleeing Voortrekkers south.

Some of those fleeing laagered near the Modder River, while others travelled all the way back to Thaba 'Nchu, where more and more wagons were arriving from the colony.[570] Finally, Potgieter's group joined the trekkers at a point near Heunings River (near the present-day town of Heilbron), where they were welcomed by a volley of gunfire.

Potgieter and Cilliers realized that Mzilikazi's generals would follow up their recent successes with further attacks and sent messages warning those in outlying areas of the imminent danger to them. They also ordered all settlers who had not already fled south and all trekkers who had crossed the Vaal River to return to the main body of Boers near Heunings River to consolidate their position.[571] Although many of the Voortrekkers at Thaba 'Nchu wanted to return to the colony, they were unsure how they would be received by the authorities.

They wrote to Campbell in early September 1836 to describe the horrific attacks on the trekkers who had crossed the Vaal River. The attack and the losses of the Liebenbergs and others were described and that some of those killed were infants "at the breast of their mothers". The letter stated that many of the trekkers wished to return to the colony but were unsure of how they would be treated if they returned. The letter concluded by stating that the Voortrekkers were like "lost sheep".[572]

Potgieter and Cilliers began to fortify the Voortrekkers' defences at their camp near Heunings River, ordering the men to chain the wagons together and to use thorny branches to fill every space between the 50 wagons as well as between the spokes of the wheels, with the exception of two openings that would be used as gateways. Zaribas, or the tactic of using thorn bushes to block up any and every crevice by which a warrior could ostensibly crawl through and gain access into the laager, was common throughout Africa, with zariba fences generally used to protect livestock from predators.

The 33 men and seven young boys who were old enough to handle a gun worked tirelessly on securing the laager, including 12-year-old Paul Kruger, who was destined to become the president of the South African Republic. On his first night at Heunings River, Cilliers repeatedly dreamed of the Matabele attack and, early the following morning, he called the trekkers together to pray to God to protect them from the Matabele.[573]

Potgieter and Cilliers had ordered the men to set up the laager immediately below a *koppie*, a small hill that would later be called Vegkop. It was about 1,000 metres long and dotted with mimosa bushes and, from its top, a scout could see for kilometres in all directions. The laager was in a square shape, to give the trekkers the best chance of sighting the enemy's approach from the open area to the south and was at the base of the hill, on the southern side, where the ground sloped gently down to a shallow stream.[574]

In the middle of the laager, four wagons were positioned together tightly[575] and were covered with planks and raw hides. The women and children would wait in these wagons during the battle and the injured would be brought there to receive medical attention. The Boers' horses were already saddled and were tethered to the wagons inside the laager, ready to be ridden at any time. In addition, at two opposite corners of the laager, they built wooden structures referred to as *schiet-hokken*, which would provide the men with cover while they fired on the Matabele. Two openings, each the size of a wagon, were left in the laager wall as gates. These could be swiftly closed by pushing a wagon into the open space. As a precaution Potgieter ordered men to grease the axels to ensure that they could be quickly moved into position if necessary. Even though the laager appeared to be impenetrable, Potgieter still felt that the trekkers were vulnerable. Consequently, he ordered the men to drive a small herd of cattle around and around the wagons in order to trample the grass surrounding them. They then dragged trees over the flattened grass to ensure that no hiding places remained for the Matabele. The more than 5,000 head of cattle and 50,000 sheep grazing the veld outside the laager would have to be sacrificed to the Matabele when the attack came.

Mzilikazi was disappointed that his regiments had not wiped out all of the Boers at the Vaal River and instructed his warriors at his stronghold of Mosega, some 300 kilometres from where the Voortrekkers were setting up their defensive laager, to ready themselves to attack.

The three American missionaries, Dr Alexander Wilson, Daniel Lindley and Henry Venables, who had been based near Mosega since January 1836[576] with Mzilikazi's permission, had been shocked when they saw the Matabele bringing back wagons and herds of cattle taken from Stephanus Erasmus's camp. Now, they watched in horror as the army of 6,000 Matabele warriors prepared for war. Mzilikazi was not at his military base of Mosega, but at his kraal at eGabeni (eKapain), and entrusted Mkalipi, one of his most respected generals, to prepare his regiments of 6,000 warriors.[577]

While the Boers waited anxiously for the attack to begin, they kept busy.

The laager was a hive of activity each day: women, boys and men made ammunition. They melted tin plates to make bullets and sewed small buckskin bags together, which they filled with a dozen or so slugs that had been nicked to make them even more lethal. When fired, these bags would burst, spreading the shot over a wide area. In addition, the men's *kruithorings* were carefully filled with gunpowder and their *Sannas* or *snaphane* were cleaned and oiled frequently.

Spare *snaphane* were piled inside the laager within easy reach of each man's designated position and each Boer would have at least three *snaphane* to use. These muskets were as tall as a man and almost as heavy. However, their advantage was that they could fire at least six times a minute from a stationary position. Moreover, each pile of *snaphane* was complemented by saucers containing a tidy heap of gunpowder as well as shot. (In the battle, the women and children would load the muskets, replenish the powder and shot and pass the weapons to the men to fire.[578])

Potgieter sent daily patrols, but they could see no sign of the Matabele approaching. Finally, on 15 October 1836, as the sun ducked slowly down for the night, the Voortrekkers' preparations were disturbed by the arrival of a group of terrified Bataung tribesmen running toward the laager. After Potgieter allowed them to enter the laager, the translators informed him that the Bataung had seen the approaching Matabele army a few kilometres' march from the wagons. Cilliers immediately called the trekkers together to lead them in prayer in the deepening gloom. Many of the women cried hysterically, [579]realizing that their small group did not have sufficient ammunition to shoot thousands of warriors, and Cilliers encouraged them to trust in God's mercy.

Shortly after the service, Potgieter ordered his brother Nicolaas, Jan Cilliers and Joachim Botha to ride out of the laager to establish exactly how far off the Matabele were. Following the directions given by the Bataung, they soon saw hundreds of fires flickering in the dark veld as the Matabele army prepared to settle for the night. When the scouts returned to the laager, they broke the news that the enemy forces numbered between 5,000 and 6,000 men and that it would take them only a few hours to reach the trekkers as they were about nine kilometres away.[580] That night, the Boer sentries peered into the dark in a state of nervousness. Every crack of a branch or sound of an animal moving in the dark sent butterflies fluttering in their stomachs.

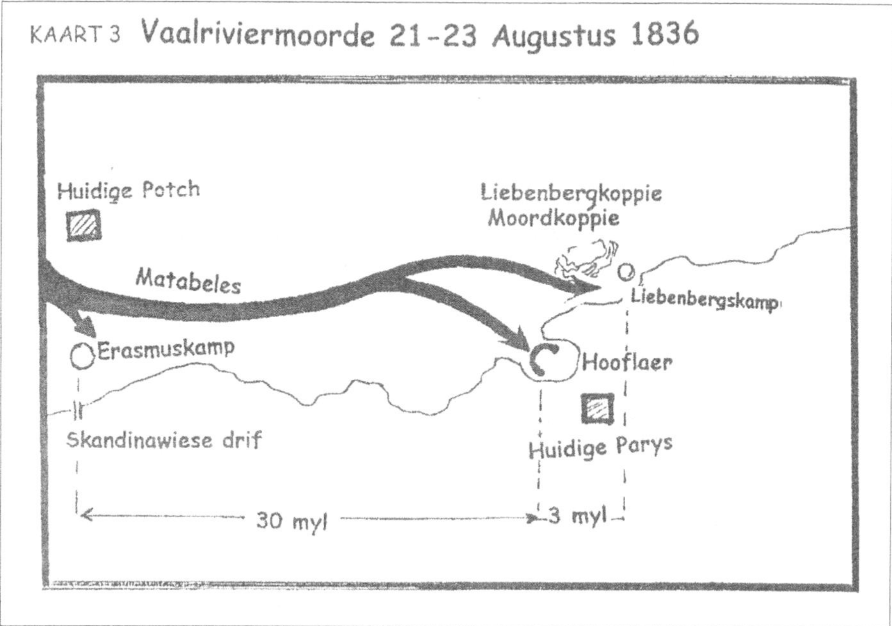

Early the next morning as the first rays of the sun warmed their cheeks, Potgieter and Cilliers led a party of 33 men out of the laager with a view to negotiating peace with the Matabele. After an hour's ride, they came upon a terrifying and daunting sight: row upon row of Matabele warriors sat in their respective regiments, demarcated by the colour of their ox-hide shields, waiting to be given the order to attack the Boers by their commander Nkalipi. Each warrior was equipped with a large, oval-shaped ox-hide shield topped with the tail of a wild cat. The hairy side of the shield faced outward and the shield was held by a stick on the inside. In his other hand the warrior carried an *induka*, or *knobkerrie*, a stout stick with a protuberance on the end used for smashing skulls, an *isika*, a stabbing spear with a razor-sharp 32-centimetre blade and a shaft of 100 centimetres for close combat, as well as an assegai with a 15-centimetre blade and longer shaft to be used as a throwing spear.

The muscular, fit and powerful warriors each wore a short cape made of jackal skin or ostrich feathers and cat-tail armbands. Their kilts were made from cats and monkeys' tails and they wore a garter of cow and cat tails as well as buffalo-hide sandals and a headdress with a plume of feathers. (The officers' headdresses boasted the distinctive tail feathers of the blue crane). [581]As the Boers tentatively approached the massed ranks of Matabele, they were watched with narrowed, suspicious eyes. "Not one shot is to be fired before we talk to the Matabele," Potgieter instructed his nervous men[582] while the warriors sank behind their tall shields, hissing loudly in a sound of derision. They made a sound like water being poured onto a boiling-hot rock: "Sssssssshhhhh!" Thereafter, Potgieter and Cilliers took off their hats and, holding their *Sannas* overhead with white cloths tied to the muzzles, they slowly approached, hoping that the Matabele would understand that they came in peace.

"What harm have we done to you? Why have you come to kill and murder us?" the Hottentot interpreter with them called out from some distance away.

The answer floated back on the morning breeze.: "We take orders from one man- Mzilikazi!"

With a roar that seemed to make the long swaying grass tremble, the 6,000 Matabele warriors leaped to their feet shouting their leader's name, "Mzilikazi! Mzilikazi!", before hurling their sticks and assegais at the three men, who, hunched forward in their saddles for protection, galloped back to their party.

As the Matabele surged forward like a black wave, the Boers dismounted and took aim. Their 35 *Sannas* thundered across the veld, spitting flames and lead from their muzzles, killing several Matabele. The Boers then leaped back onto their horses and galloped a further 50 metres back, before dismounting again to face the Matabele. The Matabele began to form their traditional battle formation, the 'horns of the beast', in an attempt to surround the Boers. (In this battle formation, the left and right 'horns' surround the enemy and the 'head' and 'chest' attack from the front.)

The accurate firing from the Boers from 100 paces away from the Matabele kept the warriors at bay and prevented them from throwing their assegais effectively, as they usually were not able to throw them more than 50 paces. The Boers repeated the process and fired again. When the smoke cleared, the Boers saw that many more Matabele had been killed or wounded and Potgieter and his men again retreated out of range of the Matabele's throwing spears, dismounted and fired. Each time their shooting was effective and the Matabele fell. They repeated this tactic 16 times,[583] killing over 200 Matabele. They then charged back to the safety of the laager.

Three of the riders, Floris 'Kort Floris' Visser, Marthinus van der Merwe Jr and Louw du Plessis, continued past the laager, urging their perspiring horses to give it all they had. Terrified out of their wits at what they had witnessed, they headed south, determined to put as much distance as possible between themselves and the Matabele. At the laager, the men ran to their designated positions between the wagons and peered out, *Sannas* at the ready. The Matabele had followed them and had split into three divisions of 2,000 men. They stopped before the Heunings River, approximately two kilometres[584] away from the wagons and beyond the range of the Boers' weapons. The trekkers watched as one group of warriors surrounded about 80 of their oxen and began to slaughter them. The shouts and laughter of the warriors could be heard above the bellows of the petrified oxen. The Boers could not tear their eyes away from the carnage and watched some of the Matabele sharpening their assegais on the rocks while others ate the meat from the oxen—raw and still dripping warm blood.

In horror, they realized that Barend du Plessis, a young shepherd, was somewhere outside the laager. The hysterics of his family were eventually replaced with overwhelming sadness as they realized that they could do nothing to save him.

The men cleaned their guns and made ready for the battle to come. Cilliers called the trekkers together and warned them that the women and children were not to cry or scream, no matter what the circumstances or how terrifying the battle was, lest their cries infuriate or goad the Matabele to further violence. He then instructed the men not to fire their *Sannas* until he had and called the trekkers to kneel in prayer. With his face turned heavenwards, he pleaded with the Lord to be merciful and to save them,[585] asking Him to help them in their hour of great need.[586]

Afterwards, Cilliers ordered a white sheet to be waved at the Matabele, in a last-minute and desperate attempt to convince them that the Boers wanted peace. However, this seemed to incense the Matabele, who hissed "Sssssssssshhhhhhh" like 10,000 angry snakes, and one of the lieutenants leaped to his feet and waved his red shield menacingly. The Matabele warriors charged the wagons from all sides, yelling "Mzilikazi!" and beating their ox-hide shields as they ran with their assegais poised like javelins.

Leading the charge was a giant Matabele of very distinctive colouring, more yellowish than the rest, who shouted encouragement to the warriors behind him. Cilliers was recognized as the best shooter among the Boers and squinted down the barrel of his *Sanna* while tracking the huge man's progress. Even though he had him clearly in his sights, he warned the men to hold their fire. "Hold your fire!" he shouted, keeping his aim on the leader as he charged. The Boers waited, squinting down their barrels at their selected targets as the Matabele drew closer. When the leader was only 20 metres from the wagons, Cilliers squeezed the trigger. The roar of his *Sanna* was audible even over the thunderous war cries of the Matabele and the men and boys in the laager immediately unleashed a mass volley at the Matabele. Smoke billowed from the barrels. The screams of pain and angry shouting of the Matabele floated through the thick acrid blue smoke as the lead struck home.[587] Assegais ripped into the canvas of the wagons and came whishing through the air, landing inside the laager like thrown javelins, where the trekkers remained calm and demonstrated a sense of grim determination.

The women reloaded the guns and held them ready for their men folk, thrusting them into their outstretched hands when they shouted "*Gee!*" (Give!). The Matabele tore at the thorn branches as they tried to penetrate the laager. Inside the laager the stench of gunpowder burned the nostrils, rising smoke and dust stung the eyes of the men and women as they fought wave after wave of warriors off. Some of the warriors started to climb up the wagons and over the canvas. When Mrs Abraham Swanepoel saw a black hand on the canvas near her, she promptly chopped it off and the screaming warrior fell writhing to the ground, his eyes fixed on his bloodied stump. Soon, many more Matabele were scrambling up the wagons and when the first warrior landed inside the laager, one of the women crushed his head with a big rock. The women splashed other would-be intruders with boiling water, scalding them and scarring them for life, and wielded axes with all the might they could muster. Consequently, many Matabele warriors' outstretched arms were severed as they clawed the canvas. Cilliers was stabbed in his leg, just above the knee. However, he merely gritted his teeth, pulled the assegai out and thrust it into the heart of the Matabele who had stabbed him. Realizing just how perilous climbing into the laager was, the warriors started throwing their assegais over the wagons. As hundreds of missiles fell like darts from the sky into the laager, the groans from the women who were hit turned to shrieks of anguish as Nicolaas Potgieter was killed, followed by Piet Botha a few minutes later. The terrified horses' eyes rolled back and they bucked and whinnied under the onslaught of the assegais, stirring up great clouds of red dust with their hooves.

Unable to dislodge the thorn bushes between the wagons, the Matabele grabbed the wheels of the wagons in an attempt to remove them. So hard did they try that several wagons were moved back several feet by the force of the attack but still not enough to slip into the laager. The Voortrekkers had fired their *Sannas* so often that the barrels were burning hot to the touch and the blue cordite smoke that resulted made it difficult to see outside the laager. Nevertheless, they easily identified Mkalipi and heard him shouting orders at his warriors.

Soon, the Matabele began to withdraw and the trekkers stopped firing to preserve their ammunition.

"Come on! Attack us again, you old women with blunt teeth!" Potgieter's brother, Jacobus, shouted after the retreating Matabele.

"Come out from behind your houses on wheels and fight us like men!" one of the Matabele yelled.

Through the smoke and dust, the Voortrekkers could see the bodies of the dead Matabele piled so high around the wagons they formed a wall of corpses and as the hot sun baked down, vultures were already circling overhead, ready to swoop down on the corpses below.

It looked as though the battle was over … until one of the Boers noticed that the corpses appeared to be sweating. "Dead men don't sweat!" he shouted.

The Boers shot at the corpses, many of which miraculously leaped up and ran off to safety.[588] Having failed to dupe the trekkers into letting their guard down, the Matabele dispersed, driving off the more than 100 horses, 5,000 head of cattle and 50,000 sheep outside the laager.

Potgieter's brother, Nicolaas, and his brother-in-law, Piet Botha, had been killed and the makeshift hospital in the laager reverberated with the moans of 14 men, women and children who had been seriously injured. Many more had sustained superficial injuries that required some form of treatment.

Seven of the trekkers' horses lay dead in the laager, with assegais sticking out of them, and they had lost all their livestock as well as the oxen that pulled their wagons. The canopies of the wagons had been shredded by the Matabele's assegais, with one wagon having been slashed 72 times, and 1,137 assegais had landed inside the laager.[589] Outside the laager, were the bodies of 430 Matabele.

Without their livestock, the trekkers would be stranded and ultimately vulnerable to further attacks. Consequently, Potgieter and several men chased after the herd of stolen animals, following the dust clouds they had made. When they reached the livestock, they tried to steer some of the animals at the rear of the herd away with them. However, the Matabele soon saw what they were doing and raced toward them with their assegais poised to throw as soon as they got a clear line of sight. The Boers had no choice but to beat a hasty retreat and returned to the laager empty-handed. From there, the trekkers watched helplessly as the Matabele made off with their cattle, until they disappeared from sight.

Bruised and battered but not cowed or defeated, the trekkers' children stood with their heads bowed as Cilliers read the stirring words of Psalm 118.[590] His voice broke with emotion when he read:

They surrounded me like bees;
They were quenched like a fire of thorns;
For in the name of the Lord I will destroy them.
You pushed me violently, that I might fall,
But the Lord helped me.
The Lord is my strength and my salvation.[591]

That evening, they wrapped the bodies of Nicolaas Potgieter and Piet Botha in canvas shrouds and, after Cilliers conducted a brief ceremony, lowered the bodies into shallow graves. They then lit tallow candles and posted sentries for the night, in case the Matabele returned.

The next morning, the full impact of their plight hit them: the swollen corpses of the Matabele lying around the wagons had already begun to rot and the smell was horrendous. Flies crawled over the burst flesh of their gunshot wounds and vultures perched on surrounding bushes and walked among the dead. In addition, during the night, hyenas and jackals had dragged some of the corpses into the Heunings River, which contaminated the water and made it undrinkable.[592]

As the people in the wagons began to stir, they heard the cries of thirst of the smaller children. Of great concern was that their fresh water would soon run out and the milking cows had been taken by the Matabele. Further, with no livestock to slaughter and as it was dangerous to go hunting, the trekkers were without meat. They had also run out of mealies. The marooned Voortrekkers had swapped one disaster for another: they now faced nature's weapons of vengeance—hunger and thirst.

Their anxiety was temporarily forgotten though when nine-year-old Barend du Plessis was seen walking through the veld, swinging his sjambok. Having given him up for dead, his family listened in amazement as he told them that he had hidden in some bushes during the battle and that he had waited until now to return, to make sure the Matabele were no longer in the area. Potgieter soon sent men out on horseback to see whether the Matabele had left any livestock behind. They discovered that the warriors had killed and skinned about 1,000 oxen.[593] The situation in the laager deteriorated daily. All of the trekkers were hungry and thirsty and the reek of decaying corpses became so nauseating that Potgieter burned animal skins and tar in a futile attempt to mask the stench.[594]

The cool nights were a welcome relief from the unrelenting heat of the Highveld sunshine, but sleep did not come easily to the exhausted trekkers, as they listened to lions, hyenas and jackals feeding on the corpses outside. Even more disturbing though was that the wild animals had torn off the limbs of the corpses and dragged them into the laager.[595] Some of the children and servants dragged some of the rotting corpses away from the wagons using ropes. However, there were simply too many bodies to make much progress in clearing the area around the wagons. Consequently, Potgieter ordered the men to harness the remaining horses to the wagons to pull the wagons to a point six kilometres away, upwind of the laager. This had to be done in relays as there were only a few horses left.

Eight days after the battle, some of the children went to play outside the laager armed with their bows and arrows. Next to the river, they came across a wounded Matabele. With shouts of excitement, from a safe distance away they shot a hail of arrows at him. When he successfully deflected the arrows using his shield, the boys divided into two groups and shot at him from opposite directions. The wounded man could not protect himself for long and eventually died at the hands of the children.[596]

Finally sure that the Matabele had cleared off, Potgieter sent his brother, Hermanus, and Nicholaas Smit with some Hottentot servants to ride the 250 kilometres to Thaba 'Nchu for help. The Voortrekkers in the laager could do little else but wait for help to return. With dwindling water, almost no food left and unable to move their wagons elsewhere, they were in a desperate situation.

CHAPTER 16

Revenge at Mosega

Maritz—Maritz treks—Reverend Smit—Retief's manifesto—
Maritz elected governor—attack on Mosega

While Potgieter's party waited for help near the Heunings River, the next group of trekkers arrived at Thaba 'Nchu from the colony, led by the flamboyant Gerhardus Marthinus Maritz. Affectionately known as 'Gert', he had grown up in the southeastern corner of the Graaff-Reinet district. (His grandfather had worked as a servant of the Dutch East India Company after leaving Germany in 1718). As a young boy, Maritz had lived through the attacks by the Xhosa and Hottentots in the Zuurveld. When his father lost all of his possessions during the conflict, his family had moved to Algoa Bay to live with his grandparents and then on to Graaff-Reinet. There, his father earned a living preaching and working as a missionary among the slaves and supplemented his meagre earnings by working as a carpenter. Maritz worked in his father's carpentry workshop and learned the trade.[597]

Maritz became a large man with a muscular physique. He was a smart dresser who would have been referred to as a "natty dresser" or a "dandy" by his peers and usually wore trousers under a long jacket and waistcoat and a distinctive grey woollen top hat. He kept his dark hair short and sported a small, neat beard. Warm and personable, his brown eyes often twinkled with humour. Nevertheless, he was not a man to be trifled with and could be impatient and inflexible. Some thought him overbearing but all acknowledged that he was a born leader. At the age of 23, he married 15-year-old Anghenita Maria Olivier, the daughter of a leading and respected Graaff-Reinet family.

Maritz was a fast learner and established a wagon-making business in Graaff-Reinet, at which he soon earned the reputation as being the best wagon-maker in the district. He was a devout Christian and the residents of Graaff-Reinet sought his advice frequently because he was considered an educated man with strong principles who was not afraid to speak his mind. For instance, he once cautioned Stockenström Jr when he was the landdrost of Graaff-Reinet that he was endangering the lives of children by allowing his horses to stray in the streets.[598] He took an active part in community affairs and became a warden in Graaff-Reinet and then acting field cornet there. Maritz was an avid reader, not only of his Bible but also of academic works and he owned several theological as well as legal books. Aside from being intelligent, he was also a man of action.

Having witnessed the devastation caused by the Xhosa on the frontier, Maritz had become more and more disillusioned with the colonial government and began to cast his eyes and thoughts northward, across the border. He had been infuriated by the way in which the slaves had been released in 1834. In particular, he was greatly angered by the fact that many of his friends and neighbours had suffered financial losses because of the slaves' emancipation and the lack of compensation they had received. He had had 12 slaves who worked in his wagon-making factory and he believed that the government demonstrated favouritism to non-white people in the colony. Moreover, he was wary of the encroaching Anglicization of the colony and the threat that this represented to his own language, Dutch.

In mid-September 1836, Maritz trundled out of Graaff-Reinet in his light-blue-painted wagons with his wife and six children. In the convoy of wagons were his 36-year-old sister, Susanna, and her husband, Erasmus Smit, an ordained minister that she had married at the age of 13;[599] his brothers, other family members and friends.[600]

Smit was a sickly 60-year-old who was squint-eyed and ugly but kind and zealous. He had been a missionary under James Read and had founded a mission station at Klipfontein before quitting the London Missionary Society. After working in Stellenbosch as a teacher at a government school for slaves, he returned to Graaff-Reinet. As he had no proof that he had been ordained by Read and because he had worked for the much-hated London Missionary Society, he had a great deal of trouble being accepted as a *predikant* by the Voortrekkers.[601] This, coupled with a domineering wife, possibly contributed to his heavy drinking.

Maritz's 'trek' comprised more than 100 wagons and vast flocks of sheep and herds of cattle. The departure of so many wagons, people and animals from Graaff-Reinet in a giant convoy no doubt would have prompted people to line the streets to watch the procession heading off for the unknown. As whips were cracked by the *voorlopers*, who shouted and tugged at the oxen pulling the wagons, the trekkers yelled their farewells above the bleating and bellowing of their animals to friends and neighbours.

The Trichardt party near Zoutpansberg had waited for Potgieter's group to return but, after losing many cattle to the tsetse fly, and concerned about the hot summer weather just around the corner, decided to move to a more protected site, along with those in Potgieter's original party.

They settled near the confluence of the Brakspruit and Dorp rivers and began to put down roots. At their tiny settlement that they called De Doorns,[602] they were reunited with a much deflated and subdued Pretorius in the latter part of February 1837, some six months after his group had left to find the Van Rensburg party.[603]

After crossing the Orange River at Sanddrif, Maritz and his party met some of the trekkers fleeing south from the wrath of Mzilikazi's army and learned of the slaughter of the Liebenbergs. Nevertheless, he decided to continue travelling north.

Hermanus Potgieter and Smit returned to the laager at Vegkop 15 days after having ridden off to seek help and told the listless and dehydrated Voortrekkers that food was on its way and that they would be taken back to Thaba 'Nchu shortly.

At Thaba 'Nchu, Reverend Archbell of the Wesleyan mission station had heard their story of the attack by the Matabele and persuaded Chief Moroka II of the Barolong to send cattle to pull the wagons back to Thaba 'Nchu and to provide the stranded trekkers with food, including mealies and dairy cows. He even dispatched some of his own oxen to Vegkop, as did a Griqua captain, Pieter Davids, and other trekkers in the vicinity.

By the time that Maritz's party crossed the Caledon River, it had grown substantially. De Lange and his family and friends had joined them and the trek now comprised over 100 wagons and 700 people, of which 200 were able to bear arms.[604] (De Lange already had a reputation as an outstanding scout and Maritz entrusted him to scout out the land ahead and to identify areas where the enemy might be located.)

Finally, Maritz's trek rode into the main camp of the Voortrekkers at Thaba 'Nchu on 19 November 1836, accompanied by the firing of *Sannas* and whoops of joy from onlookers. They were immediately surrounded by hundreds of jubilant Voortrekkers and Reverend Archbell and his wife came to welcome them.

The handful of Voortrekkers who had successfully beaten off the attack by the Matabele army at Vegkop were on their way to the main laager at Thaba 'Nchu and when they arrived the following day, every man, woman and child in the camp turned out to glimpse these heroes and to celebrate their bravery. Although Potgieter's party had lost thousands of cattle, goats and sheep to the Matabele, they were comforted by being surrounded by so many like-minded people. Wagons continued to stream into the camp and, by the beginning of December 1836, at least 1,800 trekkers were at Thaba 'Nchu.

For the next few weeks, the Voortrekkers repaired their wagons, made biltong and dried *wors* (sausage) and mended clothes. The men also hunted and bartered with Chief Moroka II's people. While the Dutch Reformed Church had condemned the Voortrekkers for leaving the colony and predicted their moral degeneration, their faith was stronger than ever. They read the Bible, prayed and sang psalms daily and constantly gave thanks to the Lord, irrespective of what cruel hand fate had dealt them.

On the first Sunday after Potgieter's party arrived at Thaba 'Nchu, many of the trekkers attended a service at the Wesleyan mission station, much to Reverend Smit's dismay.[605] Consequently, he preached to a small group of 20 faithful next to the wagons. Smit had hoped to be appointed the official trek minister, as he emphasized when Sybrand van Dyk asked him to baptize his child. He declined to do so, stating that he should not perform this duty until appointed minister by the trekkers.[606]

Back in the colony, things were hotting up. Stockenström Jr's field commandants informed him of the steady exodus of Boers from the colony and warned him that many more planned to follow suit. However, one of the British settlers, James Collett, wrote to Stockenström Jr to alert him to the fact that a large group of Boers wanted to meet with him to discuss their grievances and that they would shelve their plans to leave the colony if he would address their complaints.

When Retief had met with Stockenström Jr at the Kat River Settlement on 20 September 1835 to warn him of the Boers' unhappiness and about the vast number of Boer families who were leaving the colony, Stockenström Jr had been dismissive, believing that only a few more Boers would actually leave the Cape. Retief then wrote to d'Urban to reiterate his discussion with Stockenström Jr.

Subsequently, Stockenström Jr wrote to d'Urban and stressed that the Boers' unhappiness would continue until the government gave them some form of protection and could ensure their safety in the colony.[607] He also condemned the way in which the policies of the colonial government vacillated on the issue of allowing the Boers to retaliate against robbers and murderers and stated that he was not surprised that the Boers wished to leave the colony. He concluded his letter by requesting that the governor address their complaints.[608]

Despite the sympathy toward the Boers' situation expressed in his letter to d'Urban, Stockenström Jr's correspondence with Retief had been somewhat less compassionate. It would appear that the lieutenant governor of the Eastern Cape had been caught between a rock and a hard place: on the one hand, he understood the grievances of the Boers and settlers as he had grown up in the colony but, on the other, he was supportive of the growing movement to protect the human rights of all. Consequently, Stockenström Jr did little to address the grievances of those on the frontier.

Late in October 1835, Retief wrote to Stockenström Jr again. This time, he had written on behalf of the dissatisfied burghers in the Winterberg, who were greatly aggrieved that Stockenström Jr had not bothered to visit the area to hear their complaints. Retief also informed Stockenström Jr that ten families from the area planned to leave the colony because they felt unsafe and that they intended remaining beyond its borders until they heard from Retief that legislation had been passed that would guarantee their safety and protection.

Expecting that Stockenström Jr would visit the Winterberg, the people there had prepared a document outlining their complaints. It had been signed by 63 farmers as well as Retief. Soon, it became clear that Stockenström Jr would not come in person to hear their grievances and a frustrated Retief had sent the address to him.[609] Stockenström Jr's response had been scathing and highly critical of Retief. Nevertheless, Retief replied cordially and matter-of-factly repeated the burghers' objections.

Gradually, however, their correspondence had started to reflect their negative views of each other.

Retief had visited Stockenström Jr at the end of January 1836 with the intention of informing him that he would be leaving the colony. However, he had found Stockenström Jr to be so disagreeable at this meeting that he had kept silent on the matter.

In February 1836, Retief had written to Stockenström Jr to tell him that his fellow burghers had asked him to join them as they settled outside the borders of the colony. He stressed that he remained loyal to the colony and indicated that he envisaged taking on a leadership role among the trekkers, that he bore no animosity toward the colony and that he hoped that the feeling was mutual. He took a last swipe at missionaries such as Dr Philip and Read, explaining that he believed they had maligned the British settlers and Boers on the frontier and that he hoped that "our persecutors and slanderers shall not reach their goal". Finally, he had called on Stockenström Jr to protect the burghers who remained in the colony.[610]

Louis Meurant of the *Grahamstown Journal* had published Retief's *Manifesto of the Emigrant Farmers* on 2 February 1836. It had set out the main reasons for the migration of the Boers from the colony: firstly, they saw no end to the robbery and violence that they experienced at the hands of the Hottentots and Xhosa and believed that the future happiness and prosperity of their children was at stake; they were unhappy with the manner in which they had been compensated for the loss of their slaves and many had suffered severe financial loss; they were dissatisfied with the laws that protected the freed slaves; they feared further attacks from across the borders and were still reeling from the effects of the Sixth Frontier War; they were despondent about the lies, distortions and rumours about them that had been spread by the missionaries in England; they felt it was unjust to ban slavery but not to implement laws to control crime by servants and proper relations between a master and servant; they resented that they could not retaliate if attacked; they intended to draw up their own laws that they would provide to the colony and would severely punish any Boers who broke these laws; and they wished to govern themselves, without interference from the government.

The manifesto concluded by stating that the Boers knew they were swapping one set of difficulties for another but that they trusted that the Lord would guide them in their conduct.[611]

When Stockenström Jr had read the manifesto, he was livid and immediately ordered that Retief be struck off the roll of field commandants in the colony. However, d'Urban was annoyed by Stockenström Jr's petulant response and took him to task. He also named a fort on the frontier Post Retief, in Retief's honour.

Stockenström Jr had then written to d'Urban and accused Retief of having delusions of grandeur. He blamed him for having incited the Boers' dissatisfaction with the government and claimed that Retief hoped to be appointed governor of the Boers.[612]

In October 1836, the *Grahamstown Journal* had published an article relating to an occurrence on the lieutenant governor's farm, Kaga.

Ten oxen belonging to Stockenström Jr's Bailiff, Mr Theron, had disappeared from the farm and were believed to have been stolen by the Xhosa. When he reported the theft to Stockenström Jr, the lieutenant governor prevented him from pursuing the matter, telling him that the cattle must have strayed or been taken by "colonial thieves". The editorial claimed that Stockenström had attempted to conceal the theft, citing that the Xhosa had returned 18 oxen that had previously been stolen from Stockenström Jr, including one black ox that had been stolen from Theron.[613]

Stockenström Jr was furious about the report and sent it to his lawyer, who confirmed his view that the article was libellous[614] and possibly suggested to him that it would be in his interests to let sleeping dogs lie.

Retief was much admired by the community and enjoyed the support of the *Grahamstown Journal*. As such, he handed over the many letters he had written to and received from officials of the colony, including correspondence with Stockenström Jr, to the *Grahamstown Journal* for publication.

The letters were finally published on 17 November 1836 and the editorial expressed dismay that the government was forcing Retief, one of the colony's leading citizens, to "expatriate himself from the land of his birth". It also stated that the publication of such correspondence intended to show the "deplorable state of the country, and the intolerable difficulties which, under the present system, the border farmers have to contend with".[615]

Matters finally came to a head toward the end of November 1836, when Retief heard the news about the battle at Vegkop. He wrote to Stockenström Jr to inform him of his decision to leave the colony and that he would hand over his command as field cornet to another burgher. He apologized for the "hasty scratching" that characterized his agitation and the tone of his letter.[616]

Simultaneously, he wrote to Maritz and alerted him to the fact that many Boers from the Olifantshoek and Sundays River areas had already departed the colony and were on their way north while many other families would imminently leave from other districts and were constructing rafts with which to cross the Orange River to freedom.[617]

Stockenström Jr was hated by both the British settlers and Boers and d'Urban made no bones about the fact that he disagreed with Stockenström Jr's decision to build forts along the Fish River and resented the policies introduced by the lieutenant governor of the Eastern Cape.[618]

While Stockenström Jr and the British colonial secretary, Glenelg, viewed the Fish River as the boundary for the colony and desired that the forts beyond the Keiskamma River be abandoned, d'Urban felt that Glenelg's decision to give the land beyond the Keiskamma River back to the Xhosa necessitated maintaining the forts between the Fish and Keiskamma rivers.

On 2 December 1836, Potgieter summon those trekkers who had already crossed the Orange River and were camped in the lee of the Blesberg Mountains as well as others scattered over the area to a meeting at his laager at Thaba 'Nchu, which would also be attended by the various other groups camped there.

The trekkers were invited to select a civil governor and a commandant general and voted by secret ballot.[619] Subsequently, Maritz was elected governor and landdrost of the Voortrekker court while Potgieter was elected commandant general and would be in charge of the Voortrekkers' defences and serve as the chairman of any war council or *krygsraad* that was established. The members of the newly elected government, namely Johannes Gerhardus Bronkhorst, Christiaan Jacobus Liebenberg, Pieter Greyling, Daniel Kruger and Stephanus Jansen van Vuuren would assist Maritz with his duties.[620]

At this meeting, a simple constitution was drawn up and adopted and the trekkers would obey all of the laws and regulations passed at general meetings. In addition, the new government decided to attack Mzilikazi and the Matabele at Mosega, which is known today as the Marico area.[621] They hoped that this attack would teach Mzilikazi a lesson and prevent future attacks, as they realized it would not be safe to settle anywhere in his vicinity unless the threat of the Matabele was neutralized. Moreover, they intended to recover the cattle that had been stolen at Vegkop and to seize as much livestock as they could from the Matabele.

Early in December 1836 while the Voortrekkers were preparing for their campaign, reports from Chief Moroka II's people indicated that the Matabele were on their way to attack those at Thaba 'Nchu. Consequently, Maritz immediately positioned the wagons in laager formation.

Fortunately, it turned out that it was merely a small trek party of six wagons heading their way. Those already at the camp were delighted by the arrival of more Voortrekkers, as it had been assumed that these travellers had been killed by the Matabele.

The De Smit family confirmed that they had not seen any Matabele in the area but had seen thousands of head of cattle that had been taken at Vegkop wandering around on the banks of the Vaal River. They then told the Voortrekkers that they believed that Mzilikazi did not want the cattle and instead desired white girls and women and wished all the boys and men dead.[622]

On Saturday 10 December 1836, the Voortrekkers again heard a rumour that the Matabele were going to attack them. They were distraught as the heavy rainfall would render their flint guns useless and leave them defenceless. The men and boys hurriedly pushed the wagons together while Reverend Smit attempted to pacify the frightened women, encouraging them to place their trust in God.

Once again, it had been a false alarm: Reverend Archbell visited the camp to tell the Voortrekkers that his scouts had seen Mzilikazi retreating from the area. (Nevertheless, some of the wagons camped near the Modder River returned to join the main body of trekkers at Thaba 'Nchu.)

Later that day, the Voortrekkers entertained Chief Moroka II and three of his councillors and learned that more than a hundred wagons were assembled on the banks of the Orange River. As soon as the level of the water dropped, they planned to cross it and journey to Thaba 'Nchu.[623]

When the heavy rains finally let up, the Voortrekkers readied themselves to attack Mzilikazi and assembled a commando that comprised 107 trekkers, 40 Griqua under Pieter Davids (whose daughter and cousin had been kidnapped by Mzilikazi two years earlier), several Korana, about 60 of Chief Sekonyela's Tlokwa (or Mantatisi) and Barolong[624] and all had been offered a share in the anticipated booty.

Although the Voortrekkers had invited those Boers living south of the Orange River in the colony to join in the attack, the Cape authorities had learned of this invitation and had forbidden them from joining the expedition.[625]

Matlabe, a chief of the Barolong tribe, had volunteered to act as a guide for the commando, as he was familiar with the terrain and had served in the Matabele army under Mzilikazi some years earlier.

By the time the first group of the commando, led by Potgieter, departed Thaba 'Nchu on 2 January 1837, they had heard from scouts that Mzilikazi had moved from Mosega to eKapain, some 80 kilometres north of Mosega and about 480 kilometres from Thaba 'Nchu. The progress of the commando through scorched and deserted lands was slowed by the Barolong warriors, who marched on foot.

On the evening of 16 January 1837, the commando camped in the Kurrechaneberge, several kilometres from the Matabele settlement at Mosega. Fortunately, the commander-in-chief of the Matabele army was not in the area at the time and Mzilikazi was 120 kilometres farther north at eKapain.

The next day, the commando silently assembled in the hills southeast of Mosega and waited for the first morning light. While the main army took cover behind the many rocks and hid in the hills, Potgieter's scouts sought to determine how heavily guarded the kraals were. They soon reported that they had seen no lookouts and that the Matabele were still asleep.

As the first flush of light appeared, Potgieter and his men crept quietly up the left-hand side of the main kraal while Maritz led his group past the small mission station on the right-hand side, with a view to ensnaring the enemy in a two-prong attack.[626] When Potgieter opened fire, the rest of the commando followed his lead, unleashing a volley of gunfire on the shocked Matabele, who hastily rubbed the sleep from their eyes and grabbed their assegais and shields. Total chaos ensued as the Matabele scurried for cover, pursued by the Voortrekkers on horseback. Within minutes, the Matabele warriors rallied but their assegais were no match for the Boers' immense firepower. The terrified missionaries who lived among the Matabele huddled together in the huts as the mounted Voortrekkers galloped after their prey, firing their long-barrelled *Sannas* at the fleeing Matabele.

One of the slugs narrowly missed missionary Henry Venables, who was still lying in bed with his wife, stiff with shock. The bullet whizzed over Venables's head and smacked into the wall before falling onto the bed.[627] Potgieter entered the mission station and assured the nervous missionaries that the commando meant them no harm. He advised them to accompany the commando back to Thaba 'Nchu after the battle, explaining that Mzilikazi would probably target them in retaliation for the attack. He also warned them that he intended attacking Mzilikazi at eKapain and would return with a larger force.[628]

The Matabele screamed in pain and fear while the commando members set their huts alight. Soon, thick blue smoke covered the whole area, blocking out the sunlight, and the bodies of hundreds of Matabele men, women and children lay scattered around the crackling huts.

The Barolong swept up many of the Matabele who managed to escape the mounted Boers in the settlement.

During the battle, one of the missionaries' wives, Mrs Wilson, made *vetkoek* (a deep-fried pastry) for the Voortrekkers and picked up any bullets she found, as she was sure that they would eventually run out of bullets and wanted to assist in any way she could.[629] Some of the Matabele warriors fled toward the nearby river, where they futilely attempted to take a stand against the commando and were cut down by the Boers' bullets. The small groups that hid in the sorghum and mealie fields also met a violent end at the hands of the Voortrekkers. Potgieter instructed the men to throw open the gates of the cattle kraal. Subsequently, the men herded thousands of cattle away from Mosega. By eleven o'clock, it was all over.[630]

While hundreds of Matabele had been killed, the Voortrekkers and their allies had lost only two men, both Barolong. One had accidentally been shot by one of the Voortrekkers and the other had been stabbed by a Matabele who had surprised him while he was searching a hut for booty.[631] After having searched the ransacked huts in the vain hope of finding the abducted Liebenberg children, the commando returned to the mission station to collect those missionaries who had decided to come with them. The American missionaries had been at Mosega for several months and had achieved very little in terms of souls saved. Moreover, malaria had taken its toll in the area and some had lost their families. These factors, coupled with Potgieter's warning that Mzilikazi might vengefully target them for this attack, made it impossible for them to stay and they hastily gathered their possessions and loaded them into two wagons. (Their packing was so rushed that Venables was forced to leave all of his treasured books behind.)

The main force set off toward Thaba 'Nchu with the cattle and missionaries in tow, leaving behind the stolen wagons of Erasmus and the Liebenbergs that they had found at the settlement, as the additional wagons would slow them down.

Meanwhile, a commando of 21 men under Hermanus Steyn stayed behind to burn any huts still standing, while Cilliers's group of 25 men pursued the tracks of the refugee Matabele. Cilliers's group soon encountered a regiment of Matabele on a bush-covered koppie and Cilliers ordered his men to dismount and form a 'laager' with their horses. The Voortrekkers watched in astonishment as the Matabele warriors threw their shields and assegais to the ground and started running away. Reminiscing about the episode later, the men could only conclude that a 'higher power' had intervened on their behalf and this fortified their spirits sufficiently to continue their mission to eradicate Matabele fleeing from Mosega. However, their ammunition soon started to run low and they were forced to start the homeward journey with the over 7,000 head of cattle and thousands of sheep and goats that they had recovered.

Fearing an ambush by the Matabele, the Voortrekkers rode as fast as they could and travelled through the first night, with nerves as taut as piano wire. Several times, they cocked their guns in the darkness upon hearing wild game running through the bush.

On Saturday 28 January 1837, the Voortrekkers at Thaba 'Nchu welcomed the men in the returning commando with cheers and shouts of joy. Later, the men breathlessly recounted the tale of their successful attack on the fleeing Matabele and all congratulated Potgieter for leading a brilliant military campaign, crediting him with their overwhelming defeat of the Matabele.[632]

Although the Voortrekkers in the camp celebrated their victory, it was impossible to ignore that there had been a rift between Potgieter and Maritz. Their perfunctory conversation was strained and they avoided one another. One can only assume that the colourful Maritz resented having had to play second fiddle to the military prowess of the dour Potgieter on the battlefield and feared that Potgieter's heroism had undermined his seniority among the Voortrekkers. Similarly, Potgieter resented that Maritz had been elected as governor and felt that he was a better man for the job. The animosity between Maritz and Potgieter would later have a profound impact upon those at Thaba 'Nchu and upon the fate of the Voortrekkers.

CHAPTER 17

The trickle turns into a flood

Potgieter and Maritz clash—arrival of Retief—Retief becomes governor of the United Laagers—Potgieter plans another attack—Trichardt's journey—over the mountains

The Boers in the colony received the news of the Voortrekkers' victory over Mzilikazi with great excitement and many families promptly left the colony to head north, following the well-worn trail of their predecessors.

The raft on the Orange River had by this stage become a permanent fixture and many Boers from the colony would set up camp on the riverbank and travel to Thaba 'Nchu to visit the trekkers, without their wagons. Once satisfied that it was indeed safe beyond the Orange River, they would return to collect their wagons and transport them across the river.

As refugees poured into eKapain from Mosega, Mzilikazi heard from his warriors that the Boers who had attacked them had been like "ostriches hurling lightning at them". They laboured the swiftness of the attack, the mobility and speed of the Boers on horseback and identified Potgieter as the leader. Subsequently, Mzilikazi named Potgieter *Ndaleke* (the attacker) and, although he was annoyed that his warriors had been defeated, he viewed this defeat as having given him insight into how to fight *Ndaleke* in future.

The rift between Potgieter and Maritz deepened. Maritz was keen to have his brother-in-law, Reverend Smit, appointed as the minister to the trekkers but Potgieter refused to support the appointment. He argued that Smit had not been ordained, or at least could not prove that he had been. (It is likely that he argued against Smit's appointment because he felt that it would augment Maritz's influence over the Voortrekkers.)

Smit had become increasingly jealous and resentful of Reverend Archbell and believed that the popularity of the British missionary undermined his position among the Voortrekkers and the possibility of being appointed their minister. He hankered after the role, as he craved the high status associated with the position and prized the stipend he would earn. In light of the latest disagreement with Maritz, Potgieter and his supporters planned to leave Thaba 'Nchu. He had already identified a suitable place at which to settle permanently, on the land between the Vet and Vaal rivers that he had been given by Chief Makwana.

In March 1837, Potgieter's party set off north toward two farms (Waaifontein and Doringpoort) that were next to a tributary of the Vet River called Laaispruit. Tired of living in ox wagons, they began to build houses and soon had planted crops at the new settlement, which Potgieter named Winburg.

On 28 March 1837, a coloured man called Jan Bantjies announced to the Boers at Thaba 'Nchu that Retief was on his way there with many others and that his party had already crossed the Orange River.

Retief had left Grahamstown with 26 men, 27 women and 55 children. However, word of Retief's departure had spread across the colony and the 31 wagons in his trek were joined by a further 100 wagons at the Orange River. By the time he had crossed the Orange River, the men under his command had grown to 120 men[633] and one can assume that a similar number of women and children accompanied them.

As Retief neared Thaba 'Nchu, Maritz's followers began to spread out, scattering over a wide area from Thaba 'Nchu to the Vet River. The main concentration of trekkers were south of the Blesberg Mountains, where there was good grazing and water. As Potgieter's party had done, many built small houses and planted crops.

On 8 April 1837, Maritz rode out of Thaba 'Nchu to meet Retief, accompanied by one other member of the *heemraden* and escorted him to Potgieter's camp at Winburg, where an excited crowd greeted him enthusiastically. On the ride to Potgieter's camp, Maritz brought Retief up to speed on the differences of opinion between himself and Potgieter, the ongoing debate as to where the Voortrekkers should finally settle—some of the trekkers wished to move to Natal and its coast, while others had set their sights on land to the north—and the issue of the appointment of the trek minister.

Maritz also explained that the majority of the trekkers wished to appoint Retief as head of their government and assured him that he was perfectly suited to the position and would enjoy his wholehearted support as the new governor. After listening patiently, Retief told Maritz that he did not seek such a high office and was reluctant to accept this post. However, he agreed that he would consider the matter at length before making a final decision.

When the Boers in Potgieter's camp saw Retief's party approaching, they rushed from the more than 1,000 wagons and several laagers and waved their hats and fired their rifles in welcome. The enthusiasm shown by those at Winburg was not reflected by Potgieter, at least not when he learned that Maritz wanted to appoint Retief as their leader. Although he did not openly disagree with the proposed appointment, he was aloof and quiet in discussions thereof.

Finally, Retief agreed to the appointment, stating that he did so to appease the

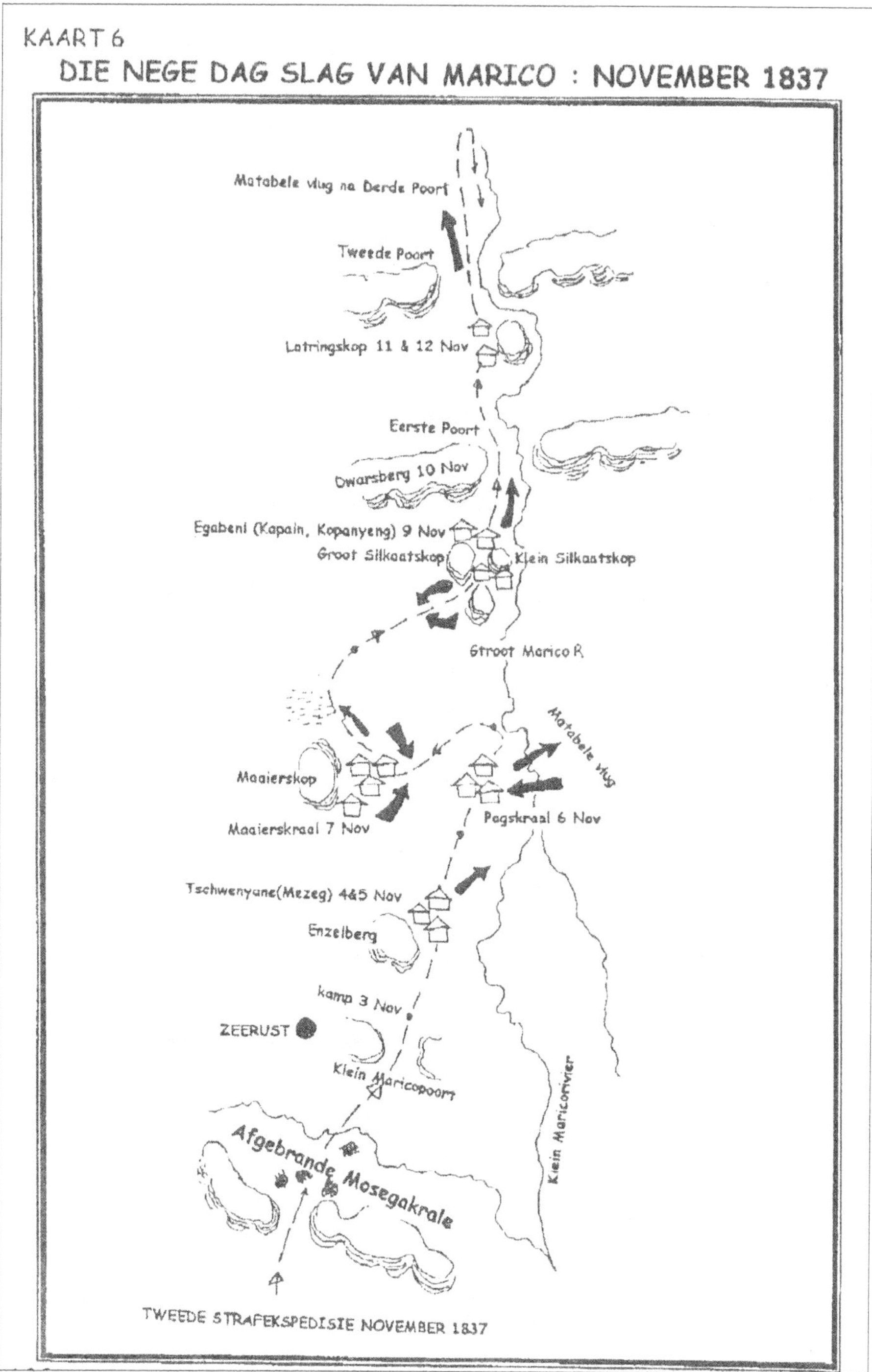
KAART 6
DIE NEGE DAG SLAG VAN MARICO : NOVEMBER 1837
Matabele vlug na Derde Poort
Tweede Poort
Latringskop 11 & 12 Nov
Eerste Poort
Dwarsberg 10 Nov
Egabeni (Kapain, Kopanyeng) 9 Nov
Groot Silkaatskop
Klein Silkaatskop
Groot Marico R
Matabele vlug
Maaierskop
Maaierskraal 7 Nov
Pagskraal 6 Nov
Tschwenyane(Mezeg) 4&5 Nov
Enzelberg
kamp 3 Nov
ZEERUST
Klein Maricopoort
Klein Maricorivier
Afgebrande Mosegakrale
TWEEDE STRAFEKSPEDISIE NOVEMBER 1837

trekkers. Maritz then called a meeting with all the Voortrekkers at his laager on Monday 17 April 1837, at which Retief was elected governor and commandant general of the new Volksraad while Maritz was elected president. He would have supreme legislative authority and would be assisted by five members of the *heemraden*.[634] Although Potgieter had been displaced by Retief, he had not the slightest intention of relinquishing his power.

Shortly after his appointment, Retief promised a relieved Reverend Smit that he would be the custodian of the Voortrekkers' spiritual needs and would be inducted as the minister that Sunday. However, when the news leaked of Smit's imminent appointment, at the church service where the announcement was to be made, many of the Voortrekkers voiced their disapproval.

After Reverend Smit delivered his sermon, he waited for the new commander to announce his appointment as minister. Instead, to Reverend Smit's horror, many members of the congregation started shouting their objections to his appointment. Seeing such dissatisfaction among the congregation, Retief had no choice but to cancel the reverend's inauguration. Shattered, disappointed and shamed, Reverend Smit returned to his camp, unable to believe what had happened. That evening, Retief visited him and assured him that he would be proposed as the Voortrekkers' spiritual leader and not Reverend Archbell.[635]

While Reverend Archbell enjoyed the support of Potgieter and Cilliers, Smit was backed by Maritz and Retief and, gradually, the chasm between the two camps widened. By this stage, Reverend Smit had become paranoid that Reverend Archbell was deliberately trying to undermine him and his chances of being the Voortrekkers' minister and thought of him as "a snake in the grass".[636]

Finally, on Sunday 21 May 1837, Reverend Smit's prayers were answered: the governor appointed him as the "first minister of the Reformed Church travelling to Port Natal, the Minister to the Voortrekkers".[637] Subsequently, Reverend Smit ordained himself during a ceremony.[638]

On 6 June 1837, a bell was sounded to summon the Voortrekkers to Retief's tent, where he would be sworn in as governor. (Potgieter and his followers did not attend the ceremony). After Retief addressed the 140 trekkers watching the proceedings, a proud Reverend Smit led them in prayer. Afterwards, the nine clauses of the *Constitution of Winburg* were framed and adopted and Reverend Smit swore Retief in as the new governor of the 'United Laagers'.

Subsequently, the Boers debated what they should name the new Voortrekker state to which they would travel. However, as some trekkers wanted to go north with Potgieter and others wanted to head to Natal, it was impossible to arrive at consensus on the name. Some suggestions included East Africa and New Eden[639] and Reverend Smit proposed "The Free Province of New Holland in South East Africa", which was received favourably and then immediately binned.

A few days after the swearing-in ceremony, Smit approached Retief and informed him that an important part of the oath had inadvertently been left out of the swearing-in ceremony of the governor, namely the words "the creed of the Dutch Reformed Church". Both men agreed that the oath should be repeated. As such, Retief was sworn in for the second time as governor of the United Laagers, on Sunday 11 June 1837.[640] He immediately contacted the local chiefs to negotiate that their people would live peacefully alongside the Voortrekkers.

Potgieter still had unfinished business with Mzilikazi and the Matabele and wanted to launch a final assault on eKapain. After he and his followers crossed the Vaal River, they set up their base camp, at which they prepared for the attack as well as for the trek north to join Louis Trichardt.[641] Potgieter was vehemently against moving to Natal as he believed that "where you have the sea, you have the English". However, unbeknown to Potgieter, Trichardt and his followers had endured great hardships in the settlement of De Doorns, despite having built wattle and daub huts, known as *hartbeeshusies*, and having established a school, workshop[642] and gardens.

Malaria had taken its toll: Anna Scheepers and Alida Strydom had died of the disease, while many other trekkers were gravely ill, as were their cattle. Moreover, their food had begun to run out. Trichardt believed that Potgieter and his people would not be joining them and decided to move with his followers to Delagoa Bay to escape the cursed mosquito and tsetse fly.

In March 1837, he had sent a letter with a black trader to the Portuguese at Delagoa Bay that outlined what had happened to the Van Rensburgs and asked for advice on how he could safely travel with his party to Delagoa Bay.[643] He dispatched another letter to Delagoa Bay with two Magwamba in April 1837 and requested that clothing, cotton, thread and needles be sent to them, followed by another letter in May 1837. He entrusted Doris Buys and a Magwamba called Waai Waai to take the letter, as both were familiar with the territory.

On 7 August 1837, Gabriel Buys arrived at Trichardt's camp with two Portuguese soldiers from Delagoa Bay. He told the trekkers that none of the Portuguese had been able translate Trichardt's letter but informed Trichardt that he and the soldiers would accompany him and his party to Delagoa Bay.

After loading their wagons, Trichardt and his party left De Doorns on 23 August 1837 and headed west before following the course of the Sand River.[644] As the crow flies, the distance from De Doorns to Delagoa Bay was about 450 kilometres and the route the Voortrekkers embarked upon would be challenging.

Not only were there no roads or tracks to follow, the travellers would also have to contend with lions, elephant, buffalo and snakes as well as the tsetse fly and malaria-carrying mosquitoes.

Trichardt had been told that the journey should take eleven days to complete. However, he soon realized that this estimate applied to journeying on foot and that it would take the cumbersome wagons several months to reach Delagoa Bay, especially as the Voortrekkers had vast herds of cattle and sheep to mind along the way.

Six days after leaving De Doorns, Trichardt's youngest daughter died. Nevertheless, the party wasted no time in pushing on after having buried her and travelled the usual eight to 10 kilometres per day.

The Boers never travelled on Sundays, as Trichardt insisted on observing the Sabbath, and on Sundays and other 'rest days', they attended to domestic affairs such as trading with locals, repairing wagons (particularly wheels), hunting for the pot, searching for missing cattle and scouting out the route ahead.

After passing Pietersburg (the present-day town of Polokwane), the procession crawled through the poort at Zebediela and criss-crossed the Olifants River 16 times as they battled their way east toward the coast.[645]

After finally leaving the Olifants River behind, they had to hack through dense bush to make a pathway for the wagons, cattle and sheep to climb the Drakensberg Mountains. The descent to the plains below was no less difficult though and they struggled down the perilously steep slopes.

With over 450 head of cattle, sheep and goats, they began their descent in the mist and rain on 9 December 1837 after taking off the rear wheels of the wagons and fastening tree branches below the axles to prevent the rivets from catching on the rough terrain. The men stood behind the back wheels and slowly released the *riems* (leather thongs) that had been tied to the wheels and managed the two oxen that were tethered to these wheels to serve as brakes. Slowing the momentum of the wagons was critical—they would have plummeted to the jagged rocks below if the trekkers had lost concentration for even a moment.

This arduous process had to be repeated with every wagon and the descent took six weeks and one day to complete.[646] It is little wonder that the weary trekkers outspanned for a fortnight once all the wagons had safely reached the eastern plain of the mountain on 28 January 1838.

After traversing the Drakensberg Mountains, the journey became easier. However, the rough and dangerous terrain they had conquered was soon replaced with other dangers: wild animals such as lion and leopard attacked and dragged off their livestock and marauding tribesmen raided their cattle and sheep at night.

As such, Trichardt and his people had to remain on guard constantly. Further, Chief Masipana (Ngotshipana) and his Sekororo harassed them continuously, stealing whatever livestock they could, whenever they could.

In February 1838, they were approached by a chieftainess named Mosali. She asked Trichardt to protect her people from a rival chief, Magoepie, who wished to kill her. Consequently, Trichardt arranged a meeting and acted as arbitrator for the two rivals. While he was able to successfully settle the dispute of Mosali and Magoepie, he had less luck in navigating the minefield of bickering and fighting among his own people.

By the time they lumbered over the Lebombo Mountains and then crossed numerous crocodile-infested rivers, their livestock had been plagued by the tsetse fly and their progress slowed even further. What's worse, when they drove their livestock through the deep Incomati River on 22 March 1838, at least 20 sheep were swept away, two sick oxen drowned and a third was pulled under by a crocodile.[647]

Four days later, the women and children were ferried over the river in the pouring rain by the Magwamba, who made dug-outs from tree trunks. The trekkers were running low on food and when a Portuguese man called Howie arrived on horseback on 6 April 1838, their spirits lifted. They learned that they were only a few kilometres from the coast and Howie would escort them to Delagoa Bay.

CHAPTER 18

Quo Vadis?

1820 Settlers saddened—north or Natal?—conflict between leaders starts—after effects of the Mfecane—Waterboer—treks divide; Pretorius—Battle of eKapain

While Trichardt and his people were on their epic journey to Delagoa Bay, a large number of trekkers were crossing the Orange River. By July 1837, more than 1,000 additional wagons had joined the trek. However, despite reports at that time that the Voortrekkers could "muster 1,600 armed men",[648] it is unlikely that there were more than 2,000 trekkers, of which more than half were children.[649]

There was still a clear divide between those who wished to journey north and those who wished to trek toward Natal. Nevertheless, the trekkers began to move. The new arrivals at Thaba 'Nchu included a large party under Pieter Jacobs that hailed from the Beaufort West district. Most of the people in this trek had some connection with the Slagtersnek insurrection that had happened 22 years earlier and bitterly resented the way in which the British had treated their family, friends and acquaintances.

Jacob de Klerk and 62 families travelled from near the Baviaans River in 30 wagons and the largest group, which comprised 100 trekkers, was under the leadership of 70-year-old patriarch Jacobus Johannes Uys and had left Uitenhage in April 1837. His son, the popular Petrus (or Piet) Lafras Uys, was however acknowledged as the real leader of these trekkers.

The dynamic, fair-haired Boer was a friend of Trichardt and, two years earlier, had been in contact with Dingane on his journey with the expedition that had scouted out whether Natal would be a suitable place at which the Boers could settle.

Near Grahamstown, the Uys trek had been approached by a deputation of British settlers and, in a moving ceremony, William Ritchie Thompson presented Jacobus with a massive Bible bound in Russian leather and inscribed with a message that God would guide them because they had always shown great faith. (The inscription also acknowledged that the trekkers had experienced great opposition from the Dutch Reformed Church.[650])

In Thompson's speech he expressed the settlers' sadness at their departure from the colony and pointed out that in the 17 years since the British settlers had arrived at the Cape, there had always been the greatest cordiality between these Englishmen and their Boer neighbours.[651]

Back at Thaba 'Nchu, Maritz and his followers prepared to leave. Although Maritz was unfriendly toward Potgieter, he agreed that it was in the Boers' best interests to move north and had made up his mind to join Potgieter north of the Vaal River. Conversely, Retief and those in his camp had their hearts set on travelling to Natal.

On 29 June 1837, Uys and several of his men rode into Maritz's camp, presumably to attempt to persuade him to join them in heading for Natal. However, after a heated argument broke out between Uys and Maritz, Uys's band of men hurriedly rode out of the camp.

Shortly after this incident, the Boers began their journey in July 1837, heading eastward along the Sand River, with Retief's party leading the convoy. Behind them, Maritz and then Potgieter's followers travelled at a leisurely pace.

Potgieter had not abandoned his plan to attack Mzilikazi and had intended to attack the Matabele on 1 June 1837. However, he had been hesitant to do so as he had heard persistent rumours that some of the Griqua captains would attack the Voortrekkers and didn't want to weaken the trekkers' defences with the absence of his fighting force. Retief was also aware of the rumours and responded by sending letters to all of the local chiefs and Griqua captains that warned them that there would be dire consequences for any party that attacked the trekkers.[652] Early in the trek, Retief's party, which included the Reverend Smit and his family, met a young man who informed them that it was rumoured in the colony that Retief had been dismissed from office and could be hanged for being a rebel. He also told them that the government intended bringing Reverend Smit back to the colony.

Although the Voortrekkers had yet to resolve the final destination of the trek, on 4 July 1837, Retief sent five men ahead on horseback to scout for a path over the Drakensberg into Natal[653] and his party set up camp near the Sand River (possibly in the area today known as Ventersburg), close to Maritz's convoy of wagons at the Doorn River.[654] Those in Retief's and Maritz's camps visited each other frequently and at night they chatted around the campfires, surrounded by the aroma of simmering *potjies*, about where they might end up. The two leaders also had lengthy discussions and arguments about the pros and cons of travelling to Natal or going north, to follow Trichardt's lead. There were some strange alliances at this time. Although Uys wished to travel to Natal, he aligned himself with Potgieter, who wanted to settle somewhere to the north, as both men resented that Retief had been chosen to be governor. Nevertheless, the parties of Uys and Potgieter travelled toward Natal, behind Retief's trek. Similarly, Maritz wished to take his people north, toward the Vaal River,[655] but travelled with Retief's trekkers toward Natal. As president of the Volksraad, Maritz probably felt that he owed his loyalty to Retief and therefore remained close to the governor's trek.

The tension between the 'pro northern trekkers' and 'pro Natal trekkers' escalated and many families were divided on the issue of where they wanted to settle and with whom they wanted to travel—including those of the leaders. For instance, Reverend Smit chose to travel with Retief as he felt he needed to support the governor, much to the annoyance of his brother-in-law, Maritz. Believing that Smit had betrayed him, Maritz demanded that he return an ox-wagon that he had lent him if he insisted on travelling with Retief and not him.

It can be assumed that the disagreements between the factions about where it would be best to settle threatened to become violent: on 14 July 1837, Retief visited Maritz's camp and, when he returned to his own, he announced that there was to be peace between the parties. The men in the camps then fired their guns in the air to mark the truce and, after the cannon in Maritz's camp was fired twice, Retief ordered that 12 shots be fired from the cannon in his camp. Over the booming of the cannon, the trekkers shouted, "Peace, everywhere peace!"[656]

This peace was short-lived, however. Two days later, the arguments resumed.

On 20 July 1837, Potgieter visited Retief to warn him that he had heard that the Griqua and Korana were waiting to attack Retief and his convoy. (It is quite possible that this rumour was started by those trekkers who did not wish to travel to Natal.) It was also rumoured that the colonial government was encouraging the Griqua to attack the Voortrekkers. When these rumours persisted, Retief visited Maritz. On returning to his camp, to his followers' great unhappiness, he relayed the news that Maritz had finally committed to travelling to Natal with them.[657]

The next day, Retief and Maritz composed and sent a letter to Stockenström Jr in the colony. In it, they reiterated their reasons for leaving the colony and stressed that although they had repeatedly and unsuccessfully beseeched the government to redress their problems, they felt no bitterness toward the colonists. They also pointed out that they believed that the local tribes and Griqua were being encouraged to attack them[658] and requested that the British authorities use their influence to prevent these assaults. Moreover, they emphasized that it was not the Voortrekkers' intention to mistreat the local tribesmen and that they wished to live in peace with them. They concluded by stating that they hoped that when compensation was paid for the freed slaves and losses incurred in the frontier wars, they would not be forgotten.[659]

The joy experienced by the approximately 3,000 Voortrekkers when the scouts finally returned on 28 July 1837 with the good news that they had found five routes over the Drakensberg Mountains that would be easy for the wagons to traverse was marred by the death of Reverend Smit's 21-year-old son, Salomon.[660]

After visiting Maritz, Uys and his trekkers at the Caledon River drew up a document that contained ten resolutions and detailed the intentions of the party. It totally disregarded the *Constitution of Winburg* that had been adopted by Retief's government three months earlier and in several paragraphs, it stated clearly that they rejected the new laws that had been established by a few individuals and which tended to enslave the trekkers.[661] The document also stressed that he and his party intended to settle in Natal and that they would use Port Natal as their harbour.

On 24 August 1837, it appeared that dissension between the different Voortrekker parties had flared up again. While Retief and his followers were camped by the Rietspruit River, he received Uys's letter and a copy of his party's new constitution, which had been signed by his father, Jacobus Uys and his brother, J.P. Moolman as well as Potgieter, J. Landman and 165 others.[662] Naturally, Retief was both hurt and concerned by this letter and he hastily rode to the various camps to talk with the trek leaders in an attempt to mend the growing discord between the different factions.

When Retief returned to his camp nine days later, he was jubilant, feeling that he had successfully smoothed things over. However, he had actually managed to pour oil on a smouldering fire and he soon heard of the growing dissension in the other camps. Once again, Retief set off to talk to the other trek leaders at their laagers and was determined to iron out their differences of opinion.[663]

During August 1837, the Zulu king, Dingane, decided to punish Mzilikazi for having broken away from the Zulu nation with his Matabele by sending an army to attack them. Dingane's warriors crossed the Pongola River and marched swiftly across the Highveld to the Zwartruggens Mountains, then attacked the unsuspecting Matabele, killing a whole regiment of them. They drove off huge herds of cattle and sheep, many of which had been stolen from the Voortrekkers.

The Matabele pursued the Zulu warriors and, after a bloody battle, managed to retrieve many of their livestock. Nevertheless, the Zulu returned to Dingane with sufficient stolen cattle to appease him that their attack on the Matabele had been a successful operation.[664]

As the trek continued along the Sand River, the Voortrekkers witnessed the utter devastation that had been wrought by the Matabele: whole villages had been burned to the ground and the scorched fields were littered with the carcasses of cattle and sheep and the bones of the Matabele's victims.[665]

On 1 September 1837, they camped for several days north of the present-day town of Senekal before travelling eastward past the present-day town of Paul Roux.

After journeying north of present-day Warden, Retief wrote to Stockenström Jr to bring him up to speed on their trek and experiences. In this letter, he referred to Uys's betrayal, namely his repudiation of Retief's appointment as governor of the Voortrekkers, and stressed that he would far rather not have been burdened with this appointment but that he accepted that it was the Lord's will that he should carry out his duties as best he could. He alerted Stockenström Jr to the rumour circulating that Andries Waterboer, the Griqua leader, was urging a number of Griqua captains to join him in attacking the trekkers and that his people would cross what he referred to as the Draakberg (Dragon mountain) into Natal, as this would shorten their journey by at least two months. He also expressed his intention to take a party of 50 men to visit Dingane and that the main body of trekkers would remain behind, as it would soon be lambing season and there would be no good grazing between their current position and the mountains because the grass had been burned by the Matabele during attacks on other tribes. He noted that he had heard many stories regarding Dingane that made him somewhat apprehensive about the planned visit. He sent a copy of this letter to the *Grahamstown Journal*, which published it in October 1837.[666]

As the trekkers' convoy inched closer to the Drakensberg Mountains, Retief frequently visited the other leaders' camps as part of his ongoing struggle to unite the parties. (Naturally, he had heard that some of the trekkers in the other camps were spreading lies and making slanderous comments about him[667] but realized that their unconstructive discourse would dissipate if he could make peace with the trek leaders.)

The day after the main body of trekkers outspanned near a spring on the south side of a mountain range on 12 September 1837, all of the trek leaders, including the recalcitrant Uys and Potgieter, arrived at the camp for a meeting with Retief.

During the heated discussions that ensued, some of the men brandished their *Sannas* threateningly[668] and the leaders stormed off. Despite this and although nothing had been resolved, Retief felt that relations between the leaders had improved somewhat.

As Uys was riding out of the main camp, someone shouted after him, "How will things go with the journey now? Will we all go to Natal together or will you be on your own?"

"Each party goes its own way. Some go forward in front, others go the same way but separate on the flank. Each is entitled to choose his own path and nobody brings up the rear," he shouted back, causing many in Retief's camp to mutter unhappily about the evident lack of consensus among the trek leaders.[669] That evening, after the other leaders had left, J. Rudolph read out verses from Psalm 109 to those in Retief's camp, who nodded their assent as they listened:

Do not keep silent,
O God of my praise!
For the mouth of the wicked and the mouth of the deceitful
Have opened against me;
They have spoken against me with a lying tongue.
They have surrounded me with words of hatred,
And fought against me without a cause.
In return for my love they are my accusers.
Let his days be few,
And let another take his office.
Let his children be fatherless,
And his wife a widow.
Let his children continually be vagabonds, and beg;
Let them seek their bread also from their desolate places.
Let the creditor seize all that he has
And let strangers plunder his labour.
Let this be the Lord's reward to my accusers,
And to those who speak evil against my person.

As Rudolph closed, the trekkers roared countless 'amens' as darkness fell over the veld.

On 16 September 1837, Potgieter and Maritz came to say farewell to Retief, who would continue east with his convoy of 50 wagons. Maritz promised Retief that after he and Potgieter had attacked and defeated Mzilikazi, he would lead his people to Natal to join him. Potgieter's and Maritz's parties trekked northeast over the Vaal River and, once they reached Suikerbosrand (near present-day Heidelberg), the two leaders set up separate laagers and began to prepare for the expedition to attack Mzilikazi. They were determined to drive him from the land, recover the cattle that had been taken and rescue the Liebenberg children he had kidnapped.[670]

The exodus of burghers from the colony continued and, in early October 1837, there was much excitement as a group of men approached Maritz's camp in horse-drawn wagons. The new arrivals included Maritz's good friend Andries

Pretorius and two of his brothers (Piet and Hercules Albertus) as well as friends Nicholaas Smit and Piet Loot and they wanted to assess how things were for the exiled trekkers before leaving the colony to join them.

Strong and confident,[671] the amicable Pretorius had shown his leadership qualities when commanding 800 Boers from Graaff-Reinet during the Sixth Frontier War and was considered charming by many, despite a tendency to be quite blunt. [672] The good-looking and slender Pretorius was over two metres tall and had slightly wavy black hair, a high forehead, aquiline nose and penetrating brown eyes that never missed a trick. His neat moustache drooped slightly around the corners of his full lips and his well-trimmed beard hugged the contours of his jaw line.

Seeing the Voortrekkers preparing for war, Pretorius requested that he and his men be allowed to accompany Potgieter's commando in the attack on Mzilikazi. While the trekkers made shot, cleaned their long *Sannas* and filled their *kruithorings* with gunpowder, Uys and his men arrived at the camp with two wagons, intent on helping them to prepare.

Uys and Maritz clashed on the issue of who would lead the commando to attack Mzilikazi. However, Maritz fell gravely ill and it was clear that he would be unable to accompany the commando. Consequently, it was decided that Potgieter and Uys would lead the men.

On 14 November 1837, the wives and children of 330 burghers waved tearful goodbyes to the men as they rode out of the laagers at Suikerbosrand with horse-drawn wagons, accompanied by about 50 coloured attendants and warriors from the Barolong tribe. The war party crossed the Vaal River at Commando Drift and then stopped near the present-day town of Klerksdorp, where they left the wagons under the care of 30 men and Andries Pretorius's party. Before journeying northwest, Potgieter agreed to cut them in on any booty they managed to take after the battle.

On 1 November 1837, the small army camped near the town of Malmani, south of Mosega. As they were unencumbered by livestock and wagons, they covered ground quickly and reached the abandoned ruins of Mosega the following day. After setting up camp at a site between Nooitgedacht and Rooisloot,[673] Potgieter and Uys called a war council meeting with their lieutenants and the Barolong chiefs Matlabe and Mongala. At this meeting, the Barolong chiefs explained the layout of Mezeg, where a large body of Matabele warriors were positioned.[674] Although their main target was eKapain, some two hours' ride from their current position, they considered it crucial to attack Mezeg before moving on to eKapain.

The men agreed that the tactics that the Voortrekkers had used so successfully against the Matabele at Vegkop were to be used again. Essentially, the mounted Voortrekkers would be strung out in a long line and each man would aim at a different warrior. They would ride up close to the enemy, deliver a volley of gunfire and then retreat. This would ensure that the warriors would not be given the opportunity to use their stabbing spears.[675]

Early on the morning of 4 November 1837, the Voortrekkers gathered and solemnly bowed their heads to pray before spreading out to surround Mezeg. Behind them, the Barolong warriors eagerly awaited the signal to attack.

"Fire!" Potgieter shouted at last, prompting a tremendous roar from the men's *Sannas* as they fired on the sleeping Matabele.

With the Matabele captains being at eKapain, the leaderless tribesmen dashed about as they tried to avoid being injured by the non-stop hail of lead bullets. Women and children screamed in terror as they fled the village, pursued by the Barolong, who set fire to their huts. Any Matabele who remained to fight were cut down.

One after the other, the kraals were ignited—it appeared as though a ribbon of fire stretched all the way from Mezeg to eKapain, like the lit fuse of an enormous firecracker.[676] The air thumped with the sound of drums as the Matabele beat out a warning to Mzilikazi of the attack and called for his aid.

Although one of Mzilikazi's generals, Kampu, rushed to Mezeg with his warriors, his men were forced to retreat under the heavy fire from the Voortrekkers' *Sannas*. That night, the Voortrekkers camped next to a spruit near the blazing village of Mezeg. [677]

The next day, the carnage continued as the Voortrekkers pursued the fleeing Matabele north. On hearing the news of the attack, Mzilikazi mobilized his warriors at eKapain and, accompanied by his general, Marap, launched a counter-attack on the Voortrekkers at Maaierskraal. There, the Matabele army formed the 'horns of the beast' in an attempt to surround the Voortrekkers. However, the commando assembled in a square formation, with their backs to each other and, in this way, successfully thwarted the Matabele warriors from hemming them in. They then charged and fired upon the isolated Matabele sections, having reloaded their *Sannas* while at full gallop. As the fighting moved north, the Voortrekkers were inspired by the courage shown by their leaders. Uys in particular earned their respect, as he was always in the thick of the battle, not at the fringes. Potgieter also had many close shaves: in one incident, a Matabele leaped from behind a clump of bushes and hurled an assegai that narrowly missed him. Potgieter instinctively galloped his horse straight at the man, grabbed him and threw him to the ground, where he lay senseless.

By 9 November 1837, the commando had fought and burned their way to eKapain, where the Matabele rallied for a final stand, attempting to halt the Voortrekkers' advance by riding 'fighting cattle' at them.

These beasts had sharpened horns and the warriors who rode them attempted to charge them into the Voortrekkers' horses at great speed. For a few minutes, the Voortrekkers were stunned by the novelty of the attack and then all hell broke loose as they opened fire. As the warrior jockeys urged the oxen on, the roar of the *Sannas* and the smell of blood terrified the oxen. They bellowed and snorted in panic before finally stampeding back into the Matabele ranks. Pandemonium broke out among the Matabele army and the warriors fled north, leaving behind more than 1,000 of their dead comrades at eKapain. After burning eKapain, the Voortrekkers chased after and killed many of the fleeing Matabele.

On 12 November 1837, a wave of Matabele refugees poured over a neck of the Dwarsberg and through the ridges of Tweedepoort, like black tar being poured from a pitcher. The Voortrekkers watched proudly as a nation fled from them with the cattle they had managed to save.

The Matabele for a time split into two sections and vanished into Bechuanaland in the north. Eventually, they reunited north of the Limpopo River and settled in an area which became known as Matabeleland (and later as Rhodesia and then Zimbabwe). Not one of the 330 Voortrekkers had been killed during the nine-day battle and subsequent skirmishes, whereas more than 3,000 of the 20,000 Matabele warriors had been killed. Moreover, Mzilikazi and his people were no longer a threat to the Voortrekkers, who now controlled the lands north of the Orange River, most of the old 'Transvaal' and from eastern Bechuanaland up to the Kalahari Desert and south to Kuruman.

On the journey back to Gatsrand, the Voortrekkers rounded up any stray cattle and sheep they found and shot any Matabele stragglers they discovered. The stench of death was so strong when they rode past the battlefield that many of the men pressed hankies to their faces to make it more bearable.

On 17 November 1837, General Marap and his remaining warriors attempted to salvage their pride and to attack the Voortrekkers while they were camped for the night. However, the Boer sentries spotted the Matabele sneaking up to their camp and sounded the alarm. Marap and his warriors promptly turned tail and fled, along with the hundreds of head of cattle they had rounded up.

The Voortrekkers met up with Pretorius at Gatsrand, where Potgieter distributed some of the cattle among those who had minded the wagons in their absence. He also gave 69 cattle to Chief Matlabe and his people in appreciation for their service in the battle against Mzilikazi. Pretorius and his men then

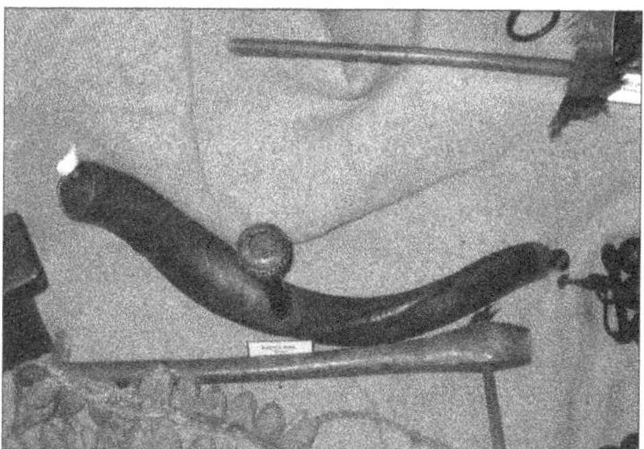

A Zulu dagga pipe fashioned from a kudu horn, likely used by the Trek Boers. *Ntonyanine Museum*

Xhosa Chief Ngqika. *Cape Archives*

Johannes Theodosius van der Kemp.

Above: Shaka, king of the Zulu. From a sketch by Lieutenant James King, a Port Natal merchant.

Left: Hintsa, Paramount Chief of the Xhosa. *Cape Archives*

Lord Charles Somerset. Governor of the Cape Colony, 1814–27. *South African Library, Cape Town*

Colonel Henry Somerset, Lord Charles's son. *South African Library, Cape Town*

Sir Andries Stockenström. *South African Library, Cape Town*

Colonel Harry Smith in 1835.

Colonel Sir Harry Smith, Governor of the Cape Colony 1847–52. *South African Library, Cape Town*

Left: Sarel Cilliers.

Far left: Xhosa Chief Maqoma. *South African Library, Cape Town*

Andries Wilhelmus Jacobus Pretorius.
G. Hauser / Voortrekker Monument

An engraving of outspanned Voortrekkers.

The field of battle at Vegkop as seen today. *Robin Binckes*

Sir Benjamin d'Urban, Governor of the Cape Colony, 1834-38.

The striking monument to the Battle of Vegkop. *Robin Binckes*

Dingane and his dog, Makwilana.

Umgungundlovu today. *Robin Binckes*

Dingane's killing fields at kwaMatiwane.
Robin Binckes

A stylized illustration of Dingane, done by R. Caton Woodville in 1847.

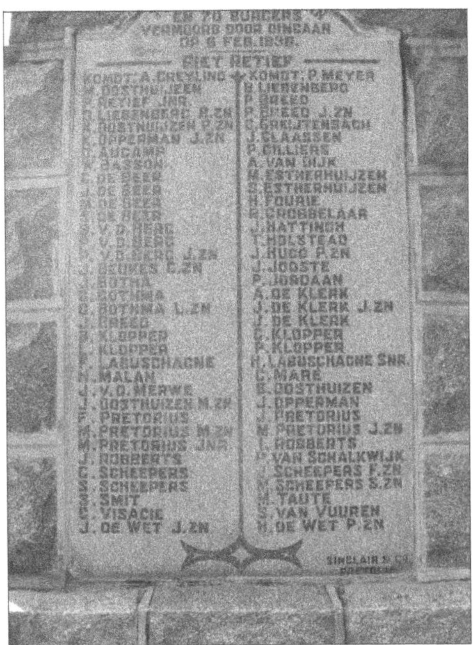

Above left & right & left: The Voortrekker memorial to Piet Retief and his men, kwaMatiwane.
Robin Binckes

Umkungunhlovu
4th Febry 1838.

Know all men by this that Whereas Pieter Retief Governor of the dutch Emigrant South Afrikans has retaken my Cattle which Sinkonyella had stolen which Cattle he the said Retief now deliver unto me — I Dingaan King of the Zoolas as hereby Certify and declare that I thought fit to resign unto him the said Retief and his Countrymen (on reward of the Case hereabove mentioned) the Place called Port Natal together with all the land annexed, that is to say from Dogela to the Omsoboebo River westward and from the Sea to the North as far as the land may be usefull and in my possession which I did by this and give unto them for their Everlasting property. —

Above: Dingane's spring where his maidens drew water, taken in 2011. *Robin Binckes*

Left: The treaty between Retief and Dingane, dated 4 February 1838. It was found ten months later, in a saddlebag near Retief's remains.

Above, centre right & right: The Battle of Blood River.

Blood River. *Robin Binckes*

The direction from which the Trekkers approached at Blood River. *Robin Binckes*

Left: Voortrekker leader Andries Hendrik Potgieter, with his second wife, the widow Van Emmenis.

The direction of the Zulu attack at Blood River. *Robin Binckes*

Boer cannon at Blood River. *Robin Binckes*

The Boer laager at Blood River. *Robin Binckes*

Above: Major T.C. Smith. *Durban Museum*

Above left: The British camp at Port Natal. *Jardine Collection*

Left: HMS *Southampton* covers the troop landings at Port Natal, 25 June 1842. *Jardine Collection*

Above: A Pietermaritzburg street scene, *c.* 1843–44. A pencil drawing by Colonel Coxon.

Middle right: Justice Cloete, 1861.

Right: Dick King.

The meeting of Pretorius and Potgieter at Rustenburg, 16 March 1852.

The Great Trek Centenary, 1936. This was a seminal event in Boer history and did much to stir Afrikaner nationalism.

Although the Great Trek Centenary was celebrated across the country, the primary event was held over several days at the Voortrekker Monument in Pretoria, with all the participants in period dress.

Left: Here 2,000 folk dancers perform at the Centenary in Pretoria.

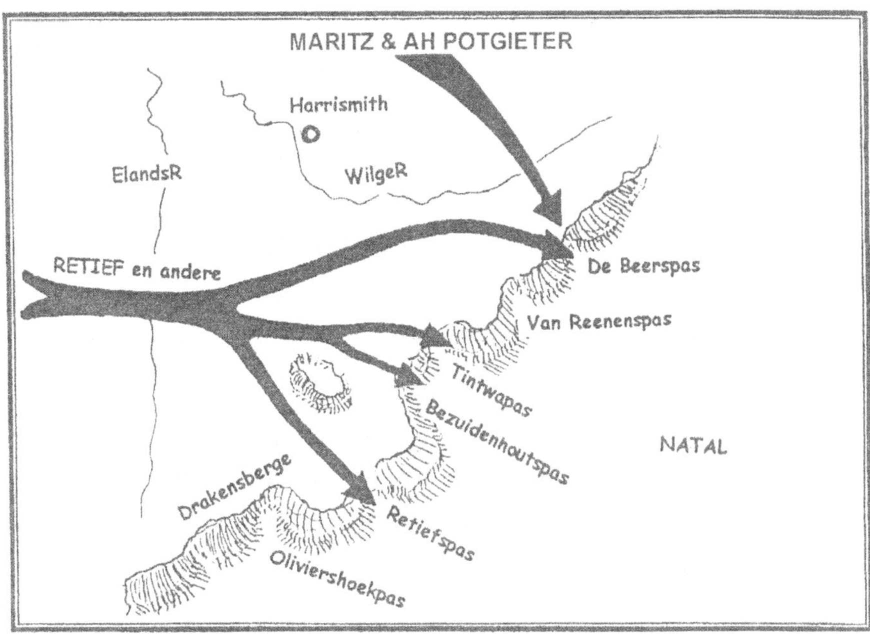

visited Retief's party near the Drakensberg Mountains before returning to the colony. (Pretorius returned to Letskraal, his farm near Graaff-Reinet, where he began to prepare to join the trek.) Maritz had recovered sufficiently to ride from Suikerbosrand to Gatsrand and greeted the victorious Potgieter and Uys warmly. However, he became furious when he learned that Potgieter had decided to first compensate those men who had not been compensated for the earlier raids on the Matabele before dividing up the remaining cattle among those who had taken part in the latest attack.

Maritz disagreed with Potgieter's logic and felt that the men who had fought in the previous battle had already been sufficiently compensated and that the cattle should be divided equally among all the men present. Unsurprisingly, Uys sided with Potgieter and the three leaders argued about the issue. The men looked on in concern as their red-faced leaders gesticulated and shouted at one another.

Potgieter ultimately won the day, as Maritz begrudgingly agreed to accept the majority decision that the booty would not be distributed equally. Maritz was now determined to follow Retief to Natal[678] while Potgieter wanted to journey north and to link up with his friend, Trichardt. Uys left Gatsrand and while his men returned to their main camp at Modder River, he joined Pretorius to visit Retief. Potgieter and Maritz returned to the main camp at Suikerbosrand and one can only assume that there was little conversation between the two men.

CHAPTER 19

British at Port Natal

Sekonyela—promised land—British welcome the Boers—Biggar and Gardiner—Gardiner and Dingane—Port Natal becomes Durban—Gardiner made chief—Owen—William Wood Jr—Gardiner returns

While camped in the foothills of the Drakensberg Mountains, Retief's party heard an alarming story: Barend Liebenberg had told Reverend Smit that he had seen Chief Sekonyela and some Tlokwa pass by with 50 men and 200 cattle and that these men had been riding horses and dressed in western style clothing. Of particular concern was that some of the Tlokwa had informed Liebenberg that they had recovered Chief Sekonyela's cattle from the Zulu and had taken these back to him. Naturally, Retief worried that the Zulu may have mistaken Sekonyela's raiders for Boers.[679]

Nevertheless, Retief continued to prepare to traverse the Drakensberg Mountains and to visit Dingane. After appointing Abraham Greyling as the acting commander of the trek, Retief and his son-in-law, Piet Meyer, left the camp in early October 1837 to catch up with the advance party of 14 men that had left two days before them with four baggage wagons. (Way to the north, Trichardt and his battered party were also making their way over the same mountain range on their journey to Delagoa Bay at this time.)

Shortly after Retief and Meyer left, Greyling called all of the trekkers together and instructed them to form a laager as he did not want them to be vulnerable to an attack. (Although there were 54 wagons available, only 30 were used in the laager while 24 were situated nearby, as some Boers refused to join the laager.)

While waiting for Retief to return, the trekkers set up camp on the escarpment, which they called Kerkenberg and they hunted for fresh meat. Although lion relentlessly attacked and killed their cattle, the group was optimistic, as they could sense that the end of their journey was near.[680]

On 5 October 1837, Retief and his men came to the edge of the plateau and gazed in wonder at the land below them. This was indeed the promised land. As it was early spring, the first rains had come, the grasslands below were lush and the trees were covered in fresh new leaves and blossoms. Acacia grew singly and in clumps and tall giant aloes with grey-green fleshy leaves dotted the land. The streams were muddy from the recent rains and were home to many hippo.

Grazing buffalo, elephant, gemsbuck, eland, giraffe and kudu occasionally startled as predators approached them. In the distance the light blue of the sky disappeared in a hazy blur. As the men stared in wonder at the beauty below, one of the men observed the shadow of the *berg* lying on the land ahead of them and remarked that a land so marked by shadow must itself lie under a curse. If Retief heard the remark, he made no comment.

The next day, the small party made their difficult descent down the mountain and followed animal tracks that they named the Steps Pass. At the bottom, they waited for a couple of days in the hope that Maritz and Erasmus would join them before continuing toward Port Natal. In the first leg of their journey, they experienced a strong sense of *déjà vu*: they passed many deserted and ravaged villages, as they had in Mzilikazi's lands.[681] As they rode through the Valley of a Thousand Hills, they were enamoured with the beauty of their surroundings, despite the humidity of this tropical paradise. Palm trees flourished here and they enjoyed fruit from banana trees and relished eating succulent pawpaws that they picked from branches sagging under the weight of the fruit. In the valleys, they passed through forests with stinkwood, tambuti and assegai trees as well as towering, majestic yellowwood trees that had trunks measuring up to eight metres.[682]

On 19 October 1837, they saw the settlement of Port Natal for the first time and as they rode into the settlement, the 53 Englishmen there fired their guns in welcome. The Englishmen and their leader, Alexander Biggar, greeted the Voortrekkers and took their tired horses to the stables. It was not long before the Voortrekkers realized that there were no white women among the settlers and that the Englishmen had taken black wives. They were also surprised to see that they lived in primitive, beehive-shaped mud and thatch huts similar to those of the Zulu.[683]

Biggar and his followers praised the Voortrekkers for their bravery in undertaking such a long journey across the country. However, a few Englishmen were evidently not pleased to see the Voortrekkers. At this time, there were two factions of British at Port Natal: those who followed Biggar and those who saw Captain Gardiner, a retired naval officer, as their leader. In light of the Voortrekkers' devoutness, it seems somehow ironic that Gardiner would be the one to sow the seeds of resentment against the new arrivals, as he had promised his wife on her deathbed that he would devote the rest of his life to bringing the Gospel to 'primitive' people.

Completely oblivious to the Sixth Frontier War that was raging between the colonists and Xhosa, Gardiner had arrived in the colony and plunged blindly into Xhosa territory with several wagons, accompanied by Mr Berken, a Polish gentleman that he had befriended on the sea voyage from England to the Cape.

After calling at Grahamstown, he departed the town with an interpreter, George Cyrus, and Berken on 12 December 1834.[684] He finally arrived at the little settlement of Port Natal in a state of hunger and exhaustion on 29 December, after having passed some of the mission stations in the area across the Kei River. Nevertheless, he wasted no time in setting off to see Dingane at the Zulu capital of Umgungundlovu: after purchasing a new wagon, he left Port Natal just two days later, despite having being warned of the imminent dangers of his trip by trader James Collis.

Most of the people at Port Natal were convinced that they would never see him again. However, Gardiner was amicably received by the Zulu, who showed him every hospitality they could as he journeyed to Umgungundlovu.

Having been alerted to Gardiner's approach, Dingane allotted him and his party two huts near those of Umhlela, one of his senior generals, and sent for him as soon as he arrived. While Dingane had dealt with many white traders, he was both surprised and bemused that Gardiner would want to come to his lands to preach God's Word.

Over the next few days, Dingane questioned Gardiner about the gifts that he had promised were on their way and made him describe them in minute detail. He then turned his attention to finding out more about Christianity and peppered Gardiner with questions such as: "Where is God?", "How did He give his Word?", "What nations will go to heaven and will mine be there?" and "Shall I live forever if I follow His Word?".

During these discussions with Dingane, generals Umhlela and Tambuza were present and they made no secret of their dislike and suspicion of Gardiner. In fact, their contempt for the British was so strong that Gardiner started to fear that they were plotting to have him killed.[685]

Gardiner frequently requested that Dingane grant him a house in which he could permanently live and that he allow him to set up a mission station nearby so that he could teach the Zulu people the Word of the Lord. However, Dingane was evasive on these issues, telling Gardiner that he needed to consult with Umhlela and Tambuza.

Gardiner had already selected what he thought was a suitable site for the mission station and amused himself by planning its design, in the hope that Dingane would relent and give him permission to build it.

Much to Dingane's joy, the long-awaited presents finally arrived. Although some of the gifts had been damaged on the journey, Dingane was especially pleased to be presented with a red baize cloak with a long silky nap and he draped the garment over his wide shoulders.

Umhlela and Tambuza blocked Gardiner from building his mission station. Evidently, they were more interested in being taught how to use firearms than the Lord's Word. When Gardiner tried to convince Dingane that all who had not yet discovered the Lord were damned, Dingane was unmoved and still would not give Gardiner permission to build the mission station.

After staying among the Zulu for a month, Gardiner decided to return to Port Natal and he told Dingane that he was going back there to fetch the balance of the gifts.[686] Upon his arrival at Port Natal on 14 March 1835, Gardiner was handed a letter that requested that he set up a mission station for the white people in Port Natal. It was signed by some of the leading residents of Port Natal, including John Cane, William Wood and James Collis.[687]

A delighted Gardiner realized that the mission station could not only serve the residents of the settlement but also the approximately 3,000 Zulu in the immediate vicinity of Port Natal and, by the end of March 1835, he had selected a site for the Berea Mission Station and had started preaching to the settlers as well as the Zulu. In addition, he had built a school for the Zulu children.

The residents of Port Natal lived in a permanent state of nervousness, as rumours frequently swept the settlement that the infamous Dingane would attack them—this was probably why the handful of settlers had at this stage done little to enhance the infrastructure of their settlement.

At a meeting called to discuss this threat, it was decided that the settlers would fortify their defences, despite the suggestion by some of the residents that they should rather "hide in the bushes" in the event of an assault by the Zulu.

In the next few days, a stockade was erected around a wattle house that was being built by Berken,[688] who soon decided to return to the colony on a trading ship called the *Circe*. Sadly, it is believed that the *Circe* sank somewhere between Port Natal and the Cape, as she was never heard of again and neither was Berken.[689]

A steady trickle of Zulu refugees had fled from the wrath of Dingane, for one reason or another, and, like drops of dew on a twig, had coalesced around Port Natal. When Gardiner heard that Dingane planned to come after these refugees with his army, a meeting was held at Cane's home on 25 April 1835 to discuss the dangers to the settlement posed by the refugees.

The settlers knew that if they protected the refugees, Dingane would retaliate against them and they agreed that Dingane should be approached to sign a treaty that guaranteed the safety of the settlement if the settlers did not shelter any of the refugees and notified him when refugees were spotted in the vicinity. They unanimously voted that Gardiner should negotiate the deal with Dingane.

Nine days later, Gardiner and his party arrived at Congella, one of Dingane's homes.[690] After settling into his designated hut, Gardiner was summoned to Dingane's kraal. The king was dressed in a blue cloak made of dungaree and displayed much interest in the bag of gifts that Gardiner's servant was carrying and duly instructed Gardiner to open it. Wide-eyed, Dingane smiled as Gardiner laid out a telescope; a pair of naval epaulettes; three pairs of gold bracelets; a silk sword belt; a small pair of binoculars; rolls of coloured cloth, red baize and printed calico; several coloured engravings portraying British costumes and sports as well as a view of Brighton's Pavilion and a full-length portrait of George IV.

When Dingane summoned Gardiner to another meeting with himself and generals Umhlela and Tambuza on 6 May 1835, Gardiner dressed for the occasion. He was resplendent in his full Scottish military uniform, complete with kilt and ceremonial sword, and Dingane examined the sword in fascination.

After Gardiner presented Dingane with the sword as a gift, he reported on the settlers' meeting about the refugees and proposed the terms of the treaty that they had agreed upon. Dingane listened thoughtfully as Gardiner talked, pulled bits of wood off the nearby fence as he considered the proposal. Finally, Dingane agreed to accept the terms that Gardiner had outlined.[691]

A few days later, Dingane requested that Gardiner send him a deserter called Mankanjana, who was hiding near Port Natal, as a sign of good faith. Gardiner agreed, on condition that Dingane would not punish Mankanjana.

When Gardiner went to say farewell to Dingane, the king instructed Gardiner to send back all of the deserters in Port Natal. However, Gardiner reminded Dingane tactfully that he had already concluded an agreement with him and that it was too late to change the terms of the agreement. He managed to persuade Dingane that going back on their agreement would make the settlers believe that he was not a man of his word.

On the way back to Port Natal, Gardiner learned that Dingane had sentenced a woman called Nonha to death for adultery and that she had fled to Port Natal with her manservant, Umbubu. He understood that he was obliged to send her back to Dingane to be punished, as per the agreement between Dingane and the settlers.

Upon arriving at Port Natal, Gardiner made enquiries about Nonha and Umbubu and instructed the settlers to capture Mankanjana. The three refugees were soon brought to him and he detained them at the mission station.

Determined to keep his word to Dingane but nervous that the king would treat the prisoners harshly, Gardiner decided to accompany them to Congella. The bound prisoners followed his wagon on foot and when they stopped to rest at the villages on their route, it soon became apparent that Dingane would execute his newly converted Zulu prisoners.

As Gardiner and the prisoners entered Congella, a large crowd gathered around them. Gardiner was perplexed that they were singing and chanting. However, Dingane explained that his subjects were paying tribute to Gardiner for bringing back the prisoners. Dingane interrogated the prisoners late into the night and Gardiner eventually retired to bed, convinced that they had no hope of escaping a death sentence.

The next morning, Dingane repeatedly told Gardiner that he had proved that the settlers would uphold their end of the agreement by returning these prisoners. He also stated that he had no intention of attacking the settlers. Gardiner realized that he had made a favourable impression on Dingane and his *indunas* and brazenly requested that the prisoners be pardoned. Although baffled by Gardiner's compassion for the prisoners, Dingane assured him that they would be imprisoned rather than executed. Gardiner did not want to push his luck by asking how long they would be imprisoned for and feared that they would never be freed. However, he consoled himself that life imprisonment was better than being executed.

Dingane then made Gardiner write to the settlers to demand that Nonha's children be sent to him. To Gardiner's horror, he learned that the prisoners had not been given any food during the two days that they had been in Congella. Consequently, he approached Dingane and requested that the prisoners be fed. However, Dingane coldly informed them that they were to be starved to death. Gardiner blamed himself for delivering them up to such a cruel and painful death and realized that he was helpless to save them. He counselled the prisoners to pray that God would save their souls. Despite being terribly hungry and dehydrated, the pitiful captives did not blame Gardiner for their desperate situation and even thanked him for trying to help them and wished him a pleasant journey back to Port Natal.[692])

Before leaving for the settlement, Gardiner met with Dingane and proposed that the king grant a full pardon to all refugees at Port Natal and that he escort them back to Dingane in future. The king accepted his suggestions and finally gave him permission to preach to the Zulu upon his return. When Gardiner arrived at Port Natal, he learned that there had been much resistance to handing over Nonha's children. In fact, a Zulu man had thrown himself on the ground and pleaded to be taken back to Dingane in place of the children. With a heavy heart, Gardiner sent the children back to the king with a note urging Dingane to execute the prisoners immediately if he planned to let them die, rather than starving them to death. A week later, news reached Gardiner that all of the prisoners in Dingane's custody had been executed.

At a meeting on 23 June 1835, the residents of Port Natal agreed to form a proper township that they named Durban, after the governor of the Cape colony. Soon after this, Thomas Halstead arrived in Durban after a trading trip into the Zulu territory. He informed Gardiner that Dingane had expelled him from Zululand and informed him that he would only allow Gardiner entry into Zululand from then on.[693] Gardiner was puzzled by this news and set off to see Dingane at Umgungundlovu to try to establish what had prompted Halstead's expulsion and why no other white people would be allowed to travel through Zululand.

He arrived at the kraal on 8 July 1835 and met with Dingane at his residence the following day, where Dingane lay on a mat, surrounded by about 50 women. Gardiner was much impressed by the choral recital the women staged for him. However, Dingane dismissed him almost immediately after the performance, thereby denying him the opportunity to discuss the reason for his visit.

Gardiner had to wait three days before Dingane sent *indunas* Umhlela and Tambuza to meet with him. The two generals conveyed that the Zulu believed that some of the settlers were helping and encouraging Dingane's subjects to desert and that he was considered accountable for the settlers' actions, as he had instigated the agreement between Dingane and the settlers. They requested that Gardiner meet with Dingane and them the following day. However, Gardiner persuaded them that they should meet on the Monday, as the following day was the Sabbath.

On the Sunday night, Gardiner was awakened by shouts and screams and when he sleepily staggered to the door of his hut to establish what was going on, he saw that many of the nearby huts were alight and people were rushing about trying to quell the flames.

With the assistance of many willing hands, the blazing fires were soon extinguished, but not before 32 huts had been burned down. (Dingane's subjects industriously rebuilt these houses by sunset the next day.)

With great trepidation, Gardiner met with Dingane and his generals on the Monday. Dingane made it clear that he no longer trusted the settlers in Port Natal and accused Halstead of being a liar and another settler, John Snelder, of actively encouraging some of Dingane's people to desert him. When Dingane told Gardiner that he viewed him as the chief of the white people in Port Natal, Gardiner politely pointed out that this was not so, that the settlers were not compelled to do as he said.

"You must have power. I give you all of the country called Isibubulungu—you must be chief over all the people there,"[694] Dingane said.

The area of *isiBubulungu* (the white people ford) was between the Tugela and Umzimkulu rivers to the north and south, respectively, and from the coast to Quathlamba, or Snowy Mountains. Umhlela and Tambuza told Gardiner later that the king had also granted him the district of Port Natal, from the Umgeni River to the Umzimkulu River.

The king solemnly informed Gardiner that he would hold him solely responsible for the affairs of the settlers and that all white people who wished to trade in or enter Zululand would have to first obtain permission from Gardiner. Subsequently, Dingane asked him to measure his feet and to have a pair of slippers made for him in Durban.

Before Gardiner returned to Durban, Dingane gave him a list of the names of 25 deserters suspected to be in the vicinity of the settlement and stressed that he expected Gardiner to track down, capture and return all of the fugitives to him. He emphasized that Durban was in his territory and that he needed an agent there to represent him in handling issues with the Europeans he had allowed to settle there. (He had previously made the same offer to trader Francis Flynn, but Flynn had turned him down.) Gardiner accepted the appointment and undertook to travel to Grahamstown to have the appointment ratified by the colonial government.[695] He met with Collis when he returned to Berea and explained what had taken place with Dingane and that he intended riding to Grahamstown to appraise d'Urban of developments and his new appointment as Dingane's liaison in Durban.

Gardiner then set off for Grahamstown on 20 July 1835 and, after witnessing much fighting and violence while travelling in the lands of the Xhosa, he realized that the overland trip was too dangerous. Consequently, he returned to Durban, where he planned to catch a ship heading for Algoa Bay, thereby skirting the bubbling cauldron of violence among the Xhosa.

However, when he arrived in Durban on 15 September 1835, he learned that no ship was expected to put into the port for some time. As such, he traversed the Drakensberg Mountains by wagon. After finally crossing the Kei River, he passed seven newly-constructed military posts between the Kei River and Grahamstown during this 185 kilometre leg of his journey. Fortunately, Colonel Smith provided him with a military escort from King Williamstown to

Grahamstown. When he rode into Grahamstown at two o'clock on the morning of Sunday 29 November 1835, he discovered that the governor was in Algoa Bay. His three-month journey[696] was to be extended by 160 kilometres.

When Gardiner arrived in Algoa Bay the next day, he met with d'Urban and appraised him of the situation in Natal and explained that Dingane had granted him land and had appointed him as his representative among the settlers. To the governor's pleasure, Gardiner informed him that they had renamed Port Natal in his honour and that he intended returning to England for a short period.

While d'Urban refused to formally annex Natal, he promised that he would soon appoint someone to govern the settlers in Gardiner's absence. He also sent a letter to Durban with the *Dove* with the instruction that it was to be delivered to Dingane. The letter expressed his delight that Dingane had concluded a treaty with the settlers at Durban and informed the king that he would dispatch an officer to Durban to represent him and take responsibility for all matters concerning the settlers there until Gardiner returned.

Satisfied that he had carried out his mission, Gardiner rode to Cape Town, where he left African shores behind onboard the *Liverpool* on 19 December 1835.[697] Gardiner arrived in England while the Select Committee on Aborigines was conducting its investigations into the treatment of the Xhosa, Bushmen and Hottentots in the Cape colony and proceeded to criticize the British settlers, citing that they were to blame for any difficulties experienced with the Xhosa and Zulu. He stayed in London for the rest of the year, during which time more settlers and other missionaries arrived in Durban.

When Gardiner returned to the Cape on 2 March 1837, Reverend Francis Owen accompanied him. Owen had trained as a barrister before entering the priesthood and the former vicar of Wadsley Parish Church in Sheffield had been assigned the unenviable task of converting Zulu souls to Christianity at Umgungundlovu. Encouraged by Gardiner, Owen decided to embark upon missionary work in the colony as a representative of the Church Missionary Society. After travelling overland to Durban, Owen met Dingane on 19 August 1837, eight kilometres from Umgungundlovu.

Dingane granted him permission to preach to the Zulu[698] in the *isigodlo* (king's residence) at Umgungundlovu. At the *isigodlo* the following Sunday, Dingane sat in an armchair surrounded by many women and no sooner had Owen begun preaching than Dingane interrupted him to ask where hell was. After offering the best explanation he could, Owen nervously proceeded with his sermon. However, it was not long before Dingane stopped him again. He was incredulous that anyone could "rise from the dead" and no doubt disturbed by the idea that his enemies and those he had killed in battle or executed could return to life. He asked Owen why the dead didn't rise immediately and whether they would be in bodily form or merely be spirits.

Needless to say, Owen's first attempt at converting the Zulu to Christianity was not a great success.

After choosing a site for his residence near Umgungundlovu, he returned to Durban to collect his wife and daughter as well as the 13-year-old son of William Wood, who was fluent in Zulu.

Wood Jr was wise beyond his years and knew a great deal about Dingane and the Zulu people, as he had lived among them. When his family moved to Port Natal when he was six, he started to learn Zulu with a passion and soon mastered the language. Naturally, Dingane's curiosity was piqued when he heard that a white boy could speak Zulu, particularly as he had never seen a white child before. He requested that Wood Jr come to Umgungundlovu to meet him and Wood Jr lived there among the Zulu for some time. When he was 12, he began school at the little mission station called Ginani. It was on the Msunduzi River (now known as the Dusi River) and was run by the American missionary George Champion. That same year, he became a trader and a hunter in partnership with Robert Russell. It is likely that Wood Jr first inspired Dingane's love of firearms as he had demonstrated to the king how to use them when he returned to Umgungundlovu in August 1836.[699]

With Dingane's permission, Owen's party took up permanent residence at Umgungundlovu on 10 October 1837. (In subsequent months, the white community in the area would comprise the Owen family, Wood Jr, a translator called Mr Hulley and a young Welsh woman called Jane Williams who had travelled to the Cape with the Owen family.[700])

The day after Owen arrived, Dingane sent for him. The king requested that Owen provide him with gunpowder. Aghast, Owen initially refused but then thought better of his actions and acquiesced.[701]

Before Gardiner returned to the colony with a new wife in tow, the settlers at Durban had offered their assistance to Dingane against the Swazi chief, Sobhuza. Under Cane, a force of about 40 settlers defeated Sobhuza and his warriors and recovered 15,000 head of cattle for Dingane. (Included in this small army was Wood Jr.)

Encouraged by the settlers' success against Sobhuza and having seen how effective their firearms had been, Dingane demanded that 100 settlers join him in attacking Mzilikazi. The reluctant settlers refused to participate but supplied him with firearms, for a price. Dingane was frustrated that the settlers were demanding what he perceived to be too high a price for the guns and ordered his warriors to attack a party of white hunters and to seize their muskets.

While Gardiner was on the high seas during his voyage to the Cape, two small groups of Zulu fled from Umgungundlovu and sought refuge in Durban. Dingane subsequently threatened to attack the settlement and the settlers promptly appointed Biggar as their commander and organized themselves and some Zulu men into troops.

When Dingane heard that the residents of Durban planned to defend themselves, he backed down and sent a conciliatory message to them. (In this message, he deviously claimed that Gardiner had orchestrated the policy to disallow any settlers into Zululand.)

To Gardiner's surprise, he found that the settlers had turned against him in his absence. When he learned that they had received word of his negative reports to the Select Committee on Aborigines in London and to the Cape government, he called a meeting with the settlers. At this gathering, he announced that authorities in England had appointed him a justice of the peace and that he had authority over the white people but not the Zulu. He also posted his first proclamation, which banned the sale of firearms to the Zulu. Angry shouts from the settlers ensued—Gardiner had succeeded in cementing himself as public enemy number one in Durban. In fact, he was so disliked by the residents there that he was forced to leave the settlement to live some 32 kilometres north of it[702] and, shortly after this meeting, some of the settlers compiled a letter protesting Gardiner's appointment as a magistrate and wrote to the editor of the *Grahamstown Journal* to complain about it.[703]

CHAPTER 20

When worlds collide

Retief travels to Dingane—Umgungundhlovu—festivities—
"Recover my cattle"—crossing the Drakensberg

Although Gardiner and his handful of supporters viewed Retief's arrival with mistrust and annoyance, fearing that they intended to take control of Durban,[704] Biggar and the majority of the settlers welcomed the arrival of the Boers, believing that the more white people in Durban, the better the residents would fare against any duplicity by Dingane. Moreover, Biggar wrote to the *Grahamstown Journal* that the arrival of the Boers would spur those in Natal to form their own government.[705]

Soon after arriving at Durban, Retief wrote to Dingane to request an audience with him. In his letter, he was at pains to point out that he and his people wished to live in peace with the Zulu. He wrote to Stockenström Jr to report on his journey across the Drakensberg Mountains and informed the lieutenant governor that he hoped to meet with Dingane. He also mentioned that Sekonyela's tribesmen had stolen cattle from the Zulu.[706]

Two days later, Biggar called a public meeting and formally welcomed Retief's party. He expressed the desire that British and Boers would live alongside one another harmoniously.

When Retief's letter reached Dingane on 26 October 1837, the king immediately called Owen to translate it for him and then dictated his response to Owen.

Dingane's letter stated that he wished to return 110 sheep that he had taken from Mzilikazi that he knew belonged to the Boers. Unfortunately, the 12 oxen had died but he wanted to give the Boers their skins as proof of his goodwill toward them. This must have pleased Retief and filled him with confidence that he would be well received by Dingane.

Retief and his party of 16 men, including Coenraad Meyer, Lucas Meyer, Barend Liebenberg, Daniel Bezuidenhout, Roelof Dreyer and Englishmen Halstead and Cane, soon left Durban in four wagons to commence the approximately 20-hour ride to Umgungundlovu.

While waiting for Retief to arrive, Dingane summoned Owen to his kraal and dictated a letter to Gardiner asking that he come to advise him about the Boers' inevitable request for land. He explained that he did not wish to share the land that he had already granted Gardiner with the Boers and that he would prefer them to settle in the area from which Mzilikazi had fled.

Retief's men travelled up the coast to the mouth of the Tugela River, where ten of the party remained behind to await the safe return of Retief and the others.[707] While descending a hill that overlooked the town of Umgungundlovu, the Boers were astonished by how huge Umgungundlovu was and marvelled at the between 1,400 and 1,700 beehive-shaped huts clustered around a kraal several acres in diameter and which was surrounded by a high bush fence that served as a protective wall.

The town was situated on a grassy slope that led down to a small tributary of the White Umfolozi River and, at its upper end, the Boers saw King Dingane's impressive *isigodlo*. It comprised several large huts on stilts that were up to six metres high and they would later learn that it included a council house and reception hall. The massive kraal was either used to house cattle or as a parade ground for Dingane's powerful army. As such, the huts surrounding it belonged to the warriors and each hut could accommodate 20 men. The four divisions of the army commanded by Umhlela stayed in the huts on the left-hand side while those commanded by Tambuza were on the other. Close to the warriors' huts were those of the members of Dingane's enormous harem. (Dingane reportedly had more than 500 women at his beck and call at this time.) Some huts served as store houses for the warriors' hide shields and other weapons and, as such, were on stilts so that the goods inside would be protected from damage by ants and other insects as well as rain.[708] The main entrance to the village was opposite the royal huts and there were several other smaller entrances in the thorn bush fence surrounding Umgungundlovu that could easily be closed in the event of an attack. The symbol of Zulu unity, the *inkatha yezwe yakwaZulu*, was kept at the *isigodlo*. This circular grass coil was about a metre in diameter and as thick as a man's calf and was wrapped in python skin. The *inkhata* incorporated many symbolic materials such as the body parts or items from vanquished chiefs, lions' fur or teeth and even grass upon which the *amabutho* (young warriors) had vomited during purification ceremonies before going into battle.

The *inkhata* reputedly had mystical spiritual powers and ensured strength and victory to the Zulu king and his army. It was handed down from king to king and grew larger each generation as it was added to. The sacred royal spear was kept next to the *inkhata* and was used by the king when he made sacrifices to his ancestors. The royal spear was an ancient throwing spear with a rusty blade and a shaft that had blackened with age and was also handed down from king to king. From the raised dais in the reception room at the *isigodlo*, Dingane could survey the whole of Umgungundlovu or admire his reflection cast by the dung floor, which was polished with animal fat and blood until it shone.[709710]

Opposite Umgungundlovu by a nearby stream was *kwaMatiwane*, a hill where Dingane would have his enemies (and sometimes friends) executed.[711] The smell of rotting human flesh sometimes wafted to those in the village and vultures permanently speckled the sky above it. The hill next to *kwaMatiwane* was called *Hlomo Amabutho* and this was where Dingane assembled his warriors before battle. The small collection of huts Dingane had allotted to Owen and his family and Wood Jr was near this. Executions were also carried out outside the royal homestead. While men were often bludgeoned with an *induka* (knobkerrie) or had their necks broken, women were throttled with a rope until their eyes popped out of their heads.[712]

Dingane had come to power shortly after attacking his brother Shaka on 22 September 1828. After being stabbed in his arm and back and through the torso with assegais, Shaka rolled onto his side and gasped a warning to his two murderers and brothers, Dingane and Mhlangana, that soon the country would be overrun by white men and locusts.[713]

At the time of Retief's visit, Dingane was 42 years old. He was very large, overweight and evidently strong. Nevertheless, he appeared to be in excellent health and took a pride in his appearance. He bathed every morning and routinely softened his skin with animal fat. His barber, Manokotsha kaPhangisa, had also tended to Shaka and would shave him each day and trim his beard, catching all of his hair and stubble in a small basket. Manokotsha would then burn this hair and pour the ash into a stream so that it didn't fall into the hands of a malevolent magician who could then use them to cast spells on the king. Similarly, a servant would rub Dingane's saliva and phlegm into the ground so that these could not fall into the wrong hands.[714] He had a very thick neck and a double chin and would often use a snuff spoon to wipe perspiration from his chin. He smiled often and had small, short teeth. Dingane was embarrassed that three of his front teeth were black and rotten[715] and he often covered his mouth while speaking[716] and made a point not to laugh with his mouth wide open. Despite his size, he was agile and loved dancing. He also enjoyed singing and composed his own songs. He frequently choreographed the dances of his women and his warriors and would often join in the singing and dancing.

Trusted male attendants cooked Dingane's meat while his maids prepared vegetables and porridge for him and when the king dined, a maid of honour rapidly and continuously banged two iron hoe-heads together to signal that nobody nearby should cough, sneeze or spit. The water that was drunk in his household was collected by his women from the cool, clear waters of the Mkhumbane spring that originated from Mthonjaneni Heights.

When a person left Dingane's presence, he or she never turned his or her back on the king and had to walk backwards away from him. Similarly, Dingane demanded that anyone who wished to approach him had to do so crawling on his or her hands and knees and anyone who coughed, sneezed or laughed in his presence without his permission would be punished or executed.[717]

Despite being a total despot, his people considered him to be more liberal and compassionate than Shaka had been. For instance, one of the first changes he had introduced when he took the throne was to allow men of any age to court and marry a woman. In contrast, Shaka had insisted that young men finish their military service before courting and marrying.[718]

Dingane's rule was marked by daily executions at *kwaMatiwane* and his victims often had committed trivial offences. Their bodies were never buried.

Retief and his party arrived at Umgungundlovu at sunset on 5 November 1837. The unseasonal cold wind cut through their clothes like a knife. Dingane sent Owen to greet them and they then proceeded to the entrance of the village. There, they were met by one of Dingane's faithful captains, who escorted them into Umgungundlovu.[719]

When Retief requested a meeting with Dingane, the king sent a messenger to tell him that he would see them the next day. He demonstrated great hospitality toward the Boers and instructed his warriors to slaughter an ox for them to eat. However, he was extremely wary of these white men. Gardiner had previously written to Dingane to warn him that the Boers intended to take possession of the country inland of Durban and would establish their own government. Gardiner lied in the letter, claiming that the British settlers objected to Retief's plans and intended petitioning the colonial government for aid and to recognize the territory that Shaka had ceded to them as being under British control.[720] (This area had a radius of about hundred kilometres from the harbour mouth and they proposed calling it Victoria.)

When Retief's men were ushered before Dingane, they could not help but gape at the majestic figure. The king was sitting in a chair and was flanked by many courtiers and generals Umhlela and Tambuza. His favourite dog, Marquillana,[721] was lying next to him with his paws outstretched and tongue lolling out of his mouth. His beady eyes followed the Boers' every movement. Dingane wore a splendid robe with broad red, white and black stripes and a red veil covered his face, thereby allowing him to surreptitiously study the Boers.

Retief's men and Dingane's followers eyed each other silently as they approached. The Boers sat on the ground in front of the king to wait for him to greet them, as custom and courtesy demanded.

After a few minutes, Dingane broke the tense silence. "*Sakubona*," he said. (This traditional Zulu greeting means 'I see you'.)[722]

Dingane then asked which man was the Boers' chief and their interpreter, pointed to Retief. "You are too small to be a chief," he remarked. "You do not look like a chief at all."

Retief did not reply.

"You do not know me yet and I do not know you yet, therefore we must get better acquainted," Dingane added. Dingane then told Retief that they would discuss the matter that had brought him to Umgungundlovu but requested that he be patient, explaining that he wanted to entertain the Boers first.

On 6 November 1837, Retief lunched with Owen at his home, where the missionary warned him not to trust Dingane and expressed concern for the safety of his party.

For the next two days, Retief and his men were entertained by displays of military prowess, discipline and precision as well as dancing and mock battles by the Zulu warriors. Dingane ordered about 2,000 of his *amabutho* to parade in front of the Boers to demonstrate the manner in which they began a battle and used short stabbing spears to fight at close quarters. Then, the more experienced warriors were called upon to exhibit their skills. These warriors wore full battledress and staged a breathtaking display for the Boers. They started by assembling in their regiments of about 4,000 men and marched about. They then danced until their bodies were glistening with perspiration, despite the cold weather, and sang a song that the interpreter translated as meaning 'We are as hard as stones; nothing can hurt us'. Finally, the warriors split into two groups and staged a mock battle. The two groups charged each other and stopped 20 metres apart, paused and then continued the charge with screams and shouts before finally engaging in close combat.[723] The air vibrated with the sounds of *indukas* thudding against ox-hide shields and bloodcurdling screams. Dust swirled around the warriors' legs as they stamped their feet and the cattails on their kilts swung wildly from side to side as they pretended to crack the skulls of their opponents.

After the military display, the warriors danced and sang and Dingane joined in the singing.[724] In one of the dances, the warriors moved between 176 dehorned red oxen, each of which was adorned with a long strip of calf hide. For the next display, the oxen were divided into twos and threes and each company danced with its attendant oxen before approaching the king to salute him. Each group of warriors' oxen then walked back to the kraal, while the warriors withdrew from the king in a line. Afterward, 1,424 oxen with red and white patches on their backs were paraded past Retief and his men and Dingane modestly explained that this was his smallest herd of oxen.

Having been won over by the friendliness that Dingane had displayed toward him during the performance,[725] Retief assumed that when he and the king finally got down to business on 8 November 1837,[726] that their meeting would be amicable.

"What do you want here?" Dingane asked, getting straight to the point.

With Halstead's assistance, Retief communicated that he hoped Dingane would grant the Boers land on which they could settle and that he had left some of his people in their wagons on the other side of the Drakensberg Mountains to await his return.

"How can you ask me for land when a group of you stole cattle that belonged to me from one of my kraals last month?" Dingane snapped.

"That was not us," Retief exclaimed, shocked by Dingane's accusation.

"Yes it was," Dingane countered. "The men were dressed like you and rode horses as they drove my cattle away." He added venomously that onlookers had heard them shouting, "*Mabula, Mabula.*" (Boers, Boers.)

"That wasn't us," Retief stammered.

Realizing that Dingane must be referring to the Tlokwa that had been spotted crossing the mountains with many cattle, he hastily explained Dingane's error and pointed out that the tribesmen must have stolen clothes, guns and horses to masquerade as Boers. However, Dingane was sceptical about Retief's explanation and challenged him to retrieve the cattle that he alleged had been stolen by Sekonyela's people. He proposed that several Zulu and one of his captains accompany Retief's men to identify the missing cattle and to ensure their safe return. He stated that he would grant Retief and his people land if they returned with his stolen cattle and it was verified that Sekonyela had been behind the raid.

Retief accepted Dingane's challenge and went to see Owen. He asked the missionary to write him a note that recorded that Dingane had authorized him to recover the cattle from Sekonyela and that the king would reward Retief and his people with land to the north, south and west of Durban if they managed to retrieve his cattle from Sekonyela and returned them to Umgungundlovu. He planned to show this document to Sekonyela to prove that he was acting on Dingane's behalf.

Owen was extremely concerned about the mission Retief was embarking upon and tried to dissuade him from going after the cattle. However, Retief felt it was vital to prove his trustworthiness to Dingane so that the Boers and Zulu could

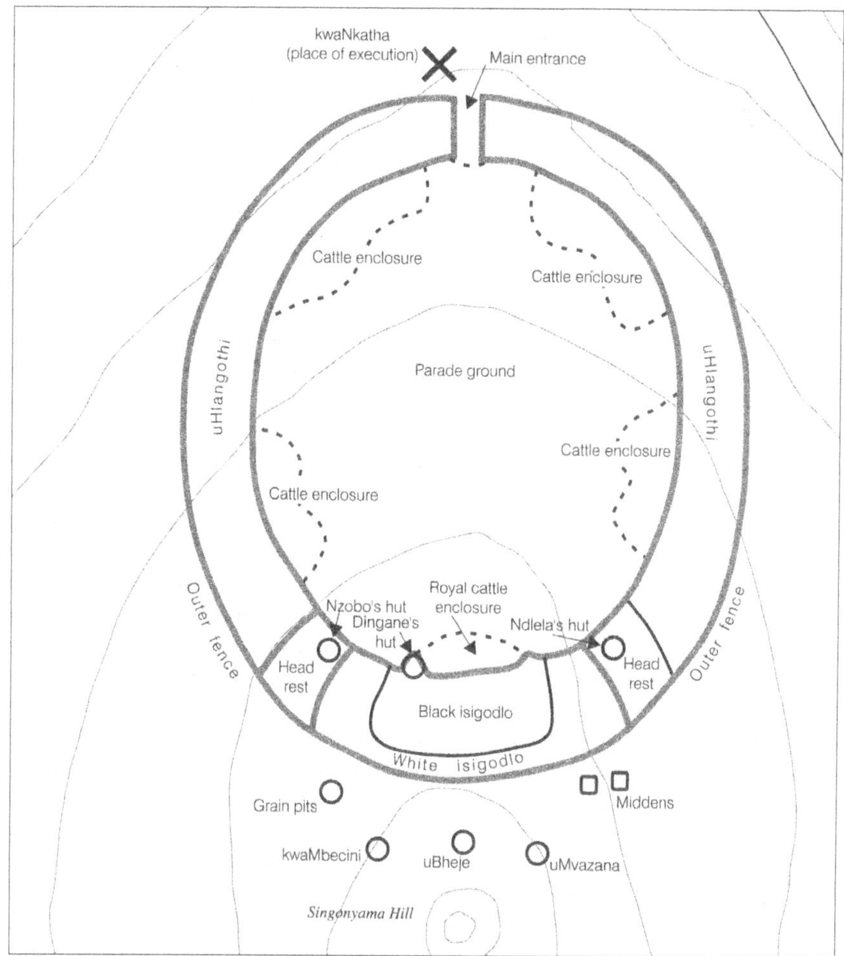

live in peace in future. The missionary reminded Retief that Dingane was not a man of his word, especially as the land that Retief had been promised had already been granted to Gardiner and, by extension, the British. Owen then asked Retief what he would do if the British settlers objected to the Boers' occupation of the lands near Durban and whether he and his men would agree to become British subjects again. Predictably, Retief rejected the idea and Owen asked him whether the Boers would occupy the land by force if the settlers resisted their occupation. Retief matter-of-factly told Owen that he would ask the king for land in the northern part of Zululand if the settlers objected to the Boers occupying the land that Dingane had granted them.

After this discussion, Owen translated the document into British so that Sekonyela could understand it and the two men went to Umgungundlovu to get

Dingane to sign it. When the king had signed the note, Owen brazenly asked Dingane whether he had granted Gardiner the same land that had been promised to Retief. Naturally, Dingane was flustered and he told Retief that they would discuss the matter further when he returned with the cattle.[727]

Unbeknown to Retief, the recovery of the cattle was a red herring: Dingane was fully aware that the Tlokwa had taken the cattle from his people, the Hlubi, and Sekonyela had already refused to return them when Dingane's messengers had requested that he do so. In fact, Sekonyela had sent an insulting message back to Dingane that referred to the fact that young Zulu men had stopped being circumcised since Shaka's rule. He reportedly told his messengers, "Tell that pubescent boy that if he wants to be circumcised let him come and I will circumcise him."[728]

Dingane planned to have Retief and his men killed after they left Umgungundlovu on 8 November 1837.

The following day, Dingane called for Owen and asked him to read a letter that he had received from Gardiner, who was evidently upset that Dingane intended sharing the land that he had granted him with the Boers. Dingane curtly told Owen that he had not specified to Retief which land he intended giving him. However, when Owen urged the king to inform Gardiner of this fact, Dingane refused to do so. (John Bird in his 1888 *The Annals of Natal: 1495 to 1845*, Vol. I records that Dingane sent a letter to Port Natal that described Retief's visit and requested that the English settlers enlighten him as to who Retief was. On receipt of the letter, three settlers consulted with Gardiner. Thereafter, they replied to Dingane and stated that neither Retief nor his party had any king or government and that they were deserters.)

Retief and his party had scarcely departed Umgungundlovu before Dingane asked Owen to lend him a bullet mould. However, Owen refused to assist the king as he had recently been admonished by Gardiner for giving him gunpowder. To Owen's intense humiliation, Gardiner had acerbically told him that this gunpowder would never have been sold to him if the store owner in Durban had known that it would be given to Dingane.

Retief sent Coenraad and Lucas Meyer ahead to the main body of trekkers camped at Kerkenberg, on the other side of the Drakensberg Mountains, to tell them about their plans and reassure them that nothing had happened to them. They reached the trekkers on 11 November 1837 and when they rode into the camp, they received a hearty welcome. The trekkers had heard a worrying rumour that Retief's party had been ambushed and murdered by the Zulu and that Dingane's warriors would soon attack them. Once the weary Meyer brothers had relayed Retief's plans, Reverend Smit called the excited Boers together and led them in prayer. "Praise and thanks be to the Lord for the great kindness He has shown us on our journey to Nieuw Holland," Smit concluded, to shouts of "Praise the Lord".

On 13 November 1837, some of the trekkers began to move southeast toward the coast, in defiance of Retief's instructions to wait for him to return to the camp.[729] The next day, they commenced their descent of the giant mountain and, by nightfall, were encamped by a stream at the bottom.[730] Encouraged by the news that Retief's meeting with Dingane had been successful, the trekkers started to traverse the Drakensberg Mountains *en masse*.

Over the next few weeks, close to 1,000 wagons crossed into Natal, including those from the parties of Maritz, Uys and Potgieter and, on some days, more than 100 wagons crossed over. Fortunately, not one of these wagons fell prey to any serious mishap, [731]in large part due to the clever manoeuvring of the Boer men. They took off the back wheels of the wagons and replaced these with heavy tree stumps that acted as brakes on the steep slope. In addition, the oxen tethered to the rear of the wagons enabled them to control the rate at which the cumbersome wagons were lowered.

While the men concentrated on getting the wagons down the mountain, the women walked alongside them with the children and babies and tended to the sick and elderly, who were carried by the men on makeshift stretchers.

Meanwhile, Retief was on his way back to the Tugela River. He stopped briefly at Ginani, where he was warmly welcomed by Champion and his wife as well as Joseph Kirkman, who worked at the mission as a translator. Retief told Champion how hospitable and friendly Dingane had been toward him and his men and that Dingane had agreed to grant the Boers land if they recovered his stolen cattle from Sekonyela. To that end, he was on his way to get reinforcements from Durban and would return with 60 armed men.

The missionary warned Retief that Dingane was well known for acts of treachery and pleaded with him not to return to Umgungundlovu, where he was sure the king would have Retief killed. He went so far as to admonish Retief for endangering his men, telling him that God would hold him responsible for the needless loss of their lives. However, Retief stubbornly refused to change the terms of his agreement with Dingane. Instead, he attempted to calm the anxious missionary by joking that Dutchmen could better understand the Zulu than the British. Champion quickly pointed out that he was American and Retief quipped, "The difference between an Englishman and American is so small it is negligible."

After Retief had left Dingane, Dingane instructed one of his chiefs, Silwebana, to intercept Retief and his party when they passed his kraal on the way to Durban. He ordered him to invite the men into his kraal, entertain them with dancing and ply them with milk and beer before killing them. Silwebana refused to carry out Dingane's order, even though he realized that Dingane would kill him and his people. He and his tribesmen hurriedly abandoned their kraal but were attacked by Dingane's warriors while attempting to cross the Tugela River. Over 600 of Silwebana's people were killed by Dingane's men and many drowned as they tried to escape. At Ginani, Champion and Kirkman watched helplessly as Dingane's warriors dragged their prisoners back toward Umgungundlovu. They were unmoved by the wailing of the women and children captives and jeered at Champion and Kirkman when they pleaded that they be merciful.

Unaware of Dingane's failed assassination attempt and the subsequent massacre of Silwebana's people,[732] Retief was confident that Dingane would uphold his end of the bargain when they returned to Umgungundlovu with the stolen cattle, particularly after his party overtook a group of Zulu herding sheep that had been retrieved from Mzilikazi that Dingane had promised to return to the Boers.

After Retief's party had joined up with the others by the Tugela River, they continued toward Durban. Their leader, however, decided to visit American missionary Reverend Lindley at his mission station near the Tugela River. (Reverend Lindley had been stationed at Mosega when Potgieter's men had attacked and defeated Mzilikazi and the Matabele earlier that year.)

Lindley was delighted to meet Retief and was impressed by his impeccable manners. As such, when Retief indicated that he wished to write to Dingane to appraise him of his progress, the missionary was only too happy to oblige with translating Retief's message into Zulu.

In the letter, Retief thanked Dingane for extending his friendship and assistance to the Boers with his offer to return the sheep that Mzilikazi had stolen from them and requested that Dingane keep the skins of these sheep. He implored Dingane not to pay any attention to those who maligned him and his people and, somewhat foolishly, wrote that "The great Book of God teaches us that Kings who conduct themselves as [Mzilikazi] does are severely punished, and that it is not granted to them to live or reign long; and if you desire to learn at greater length how God deals with bad kings, you may enquire concerning it from the missionaries who are in your country".[733] When the letter arrived at Umgungundlovu, Owen read it to Dingane.

When he reached the part that referred to approaching the missionaries to learn how God punished bad kings, Dingane told Owen that they would discuss this matter when he finished reading the letter. However, Dingane evidently opted not to take it up with Owen.[734] Dingane was greatly angered by Retief's letter because he believed that he was the supreme king and was not answerable to the Christian god. Moreover, he resented Retief's insinuation that he behaved as Mzilikazi did.

When Retief reached Durban, he wrote to Stockenström Jr about his dealings with Dingane and called a meeting with the settlers. Retief told the Durban residents that Dingane had granted him the land north, south and west of the town and informed them that it was his intention to give each Englishman 12,000 acres of this land. He stressed that he planned to establish a Boer government, as there would be far more Boers than British in the area.[735] (Naturally, many of the British were unhappy about the proposed government, especially as they had arrived in Natal before the Boers.)

Shortly after this meeting, Retief set off to rejoin the trekkers at the Drakensberg Mountains and sent a message ahead to ask Greyling to send him two teams of oxen and three fresh horses. When his party rode into the camp on 27 November 1837, the trekkers crowded the men in their eagerness to congratulate them on their successful negotiation for land in Natal.

CHAPTER 21

"Who can fight with you? No king is your equal"

Retief plans—Retief tricks Sekonyela—Dingane makes ready—expedition to Dingane—the commando leaves—clash of cultures—negotiations

No sooner had Retief returned to the main body of trekkers at Kerkenberg than he started planning the expedition to retrieve Dingane's cattle from Sekonyela. At a meeting on 5 December 1837, it was agreed that Retief would take 60 Boers and the 15 Zulu who had accompanied him from Umgungundlovu to recover the stolen cattle and Barend De Lange would assume overall command of the trekkers while he was away.

For the next few weeks, Retief called several planning meetings about the inevitable confrontation with Sekonyela. The celebratory mood at Kerkenberg was soon soured by the arrival of Pretorius and Uys on 15 December 1837 and it wasn't long before whispers of dissention were rampant, as Uys and his supporters did not approve of Retief's appointment as governor.

Fortunately, Retief's ally Gert Maritz arrived at the camp the following day. At a meeting on 19 December 1837, the trekkers agreed that a small group of Retief's men would attempt to negotiate the peaceful return of the cattle from Sekonyela. If they were unsuccessful, the main body of trekkers would join them and then attack Sekonyela. Before the meeting broke up, Barend Liebenberg handed Retief a petition to read out that stated that the trekkers wanted Uys to take the same oath of allegiance to Retief that they had all done and that any trekkers who joined them in future would be required to do the same. Uys announced that he intended returning to the main body of Voortrekkers in the near future to comply with their demands. The bickering had not been stilled.[736]

Uys stayed behind, but after a week, Pretorius proceeded to Durban where he bought the farm 'Summer Hill' from Thomas Carden, one of the English settlers. He then returned to Graaff-Reinet but fully intended, at some time in the future, settling on 'Summer Hill'.[737]

After a wet and windy Christmas Day, Retief and his party set out to journey the 250 kilometres over the Drakensberg Mountains and into the interior. The men stopped at the mission station of Reverend John Edwards (one of Reverend Archbell's missionaries), near the present-day town of Ficksburg, before embarking on the approximately 100 kilometre ride to Sekonyela's kraal.

On 4 January 1838, Sekonyela's scouts warned him of the approach of Retief's commando. On an earlier expedition, Retief had had discussions with Sekonyela about establishing a path through his lands for the Voortrekkers to use on their travels and had offered to pay him for this privilege.

After ordering the 15 Zulu in the commando to dress in western clothes, Retief sent Sekonyela a message that he was coming to see him to discuss the road he had proposed. When Sekonyela and Mr Allison (the Catechist of the mission station at Mparane) met with the Voortrekkers, Sekonyela informed Retief that his mother was still chief of the Tlokwa but that she would be willing to allow them to pass through their lands. During the ensuing discussion, Daniel Bezuidenhout pulled out a pair of handcuffs from his bag to show Sekonyela, who indicated that he wanted to try on the 'beautiful bracelets'. Accordingly, Bezuidenhout snapped the handcuffs around Sekonyela's wrists and shouted, "That is how we secure rogues in our country."[738]

Retief duly told Sekonyela that he had committed a crime by stealing from Dingane and ordered him to send for the cattle that he had taken from the Zulu. He warned the chief that he would remain a prisoner until all of the cattle had been handed over.

On the first day that Sekonyela was in the Voortrekkers' custody, the Tlokwa brought 150 head of cattle. However, the Zulu men in the party pointed out that only a small portion belonged to Dingane and that the Tlokwa needed to bring the remainder. The next day, Retief demanded that all of Sekonyela's cattle be rounded up and instructed the Zulu to take their cattle from Sekonyela's herd. He advised them that if they could not find all of their cattle, then they should take the difference out of the herd. However, he ordered them not to take any dairy cows that did not belong to them, as this would mean the Tlokwa could go hungry. He then took 53 of the Tlokwa's horses and confiscated 33 of their guns, to punish Sekonyela and the Tlokwa for the mischief they had caused with them. After the Zulu had picked out some 500 head of cattle, Retief set Chief Sekonyela free.

Before leaving with the men, Retief issued a harsh tongue lashing to the chastened Sekonyela. He stressed that Sekonyela should ask God for forgiveness for how he had behaved and suggested that he approach the missionaries for assistance with this. He also offered Sekonyela his friendship in future and promised that if any tribe attacked or harassed the Tlokwa, he would come to their aid when sent for.[739]

Delighted that the expedition had been successful and that no blood had been shed, Retief and his men began the journey back to their camp at the base of the

Drakensberg Mountains. Although it was summer, the weather was unseasonably cold and windy and there was even snow on the Drakensberg Mountains. The men huddled in their saddles as they wound their way through the Witteberge and crossed the escarpment. When they arrived back at the main camp on 11 January 1838,[740] the cheerful reception they received was underlined by a sense of unease among the Voortrekkers.

One week earlier, a trader from Durban called Mr Thomson had delivered some disquieting news to the trekkers. He told them that it was rumoured that Dingane intended to attack them. Consequently, some of the trekkers had fortified the defences at the camp by forming laagers with their wagons.[741]

At Umgungundlovu, Owen had received a message from Gardiner about how Dingane had ordered Chief Silwebana to kill Retief and his men and about Silwebana's subsequent defection after he defied the king. Gardiner stated that it was widely speculated that Dingane would send his army to attack the missionaries and Boers and offered Owen asylum at his mission station called Hambanati, which was halfway between Durban Bay and the Tugela River. Surprisingly, Owen did not heed Gardiner's warning and remained at Umgungundlovu.

It was only when Dingane asked Owen to translate a letter to Gardiner that he realized what a perilous position he was in: Dingane accused Gardiner of harbouring a deserter and of breaking his word to send all refugees to him. When Owen protested Gardiner's innocence, Dingane stubbornly refused to listen to him, but gave no indication that he had proof to support his claim. Dingane was evidently spoiling for a fight with Gardiner and Owen decided to leave Umgungundlovu as soon as he could.

Owen planned to trick the king into thinking that he was going to Durban with his family to get supplies and would leave his furniture behind to avert any potential suspicion that he was leaving Umgungundlovu for good. However, he had to abort this idea as Dingane had assigned warriors to guard all of the fords between Umgungundlovu and Durban in an attempt to capture and kill any survivors from Silwebana's kraal as they tried to escape from Zululand.

Over the next few days, Dingane's warriors poured into Umgungundlovu in full battle dress and armed with shields and assegais. They sang and danced, working themselves into a frenzy.[742] Owen was terrified by the sight of the army amassing in Umgungundlovu and his fear ratcheted up a notch when he heard one of the soldiers saluting Dingane: "Who can fight with you? No king is your equal; those that carry fire cannot match your power!" the soldier bellowed.

Dingane was on edge and his behaviour was unpredictable. For instance, he accused Owen of having had a hand in or knowledge about some black cloth that he alleged was missing. Dingane had provided the women at the mission with several rolls of black cloth and had asked them to sew jackets with the fabric.

He ordered three of his men to search Owen's quarters for black cloth and, in the process, these men threw clothing belonging to Owen's wife on the ground and manhandled Wood Jr. When the 'missing' fabric was not found in Owen's quarters, Dingane apologized and gave them an ox to slaughter in an attempt to make amends.

The residents of Durban had also heard that Dingane would kill the missionaries and Boers and knew that they would not be spared if he went ahead with his plan.[743] Later, the Voortrekkers learned that Mr Garnett and John Stubbs, two traders from Port Natal who represented the British faction opposed to the establishment of a Boer government, had visited Dingane while they had been on their expedition to recover cattle from Sekonyela. The traders had reportedly asked Dingane what punishment he doled out to unfaithful deserters and Dingane had replied that his laws dictated that deserters would be put to death. Garnett and Stubbs quickly pointed out that the Voortrekkers were deserters.[744]

Rivalry was rife among the Voortrekkers and even the trek minister, Reverend Smit, was not immune to its destructive influence. When Cilliers was asked to conduct the Sunday afternoon service in the camp, Smit took offence and objected vehemently to the suggestion, stating that no-one should be allowed to conduct a church service without the approval of the church council. He then summoned Cilliers to a church council meeting and read out the onerous set of rules that had been adopted by clergymen in the colony since 1824. (Naturally, Cilliers was intimidated by the church council members and, rather than submit to what would surely have been an arduous interview to determine his suitability as a layman preacher, he requested that Smit conduct the afternoon service.)

Smit did not endear himself to the trekkers with his jealous nature and sometimes spiteful actions. For instance, after the incident with Cilliers, one of the trekkers wrote him an anonymous letter in which he (or she) criticized Smit for having prevented Cilliers from preaching and urged him to pray for "patience and wisdom".[745]

Retief called a public meeting on 16 January 1838 to discuss the planned expedition to Umgungundlovu to finalize any issues around the land Dingane had promised the Boers. The other area of concern was how far into Natal the trekkers should move while Retief's party was away.[746]

There was much heated discussion at this meeting.

Many of the trekkers believed Dingane was treacherous and feared for the safety of Retief and his men. Cilliers even suggested that Retief should remain behind and the sickly Maritz volunteered to go with two men in Retief's place to conclude the contract with Dingane. However, the governor made it clear that this was out of the question.

He argued that Dingane would think badly of him if he sent a representative and that the king would likely question his motives for doing so. Moreover, he expressed the view that Dingane would be unimpressed (and possibly slighted) if the trekkers sent a small party of men to Umgungundlovu.[747]

The suggestion that 200 men accompany Retief was not well received by all.

Some contended that the departure of such a large force would leave the people in the main camp vulnerable to attack, especially as it would be difficult to form a laager with the wagons without these men. However, Maritz stoically pointed out that if anything happened to Retief, all of the trekkers would suffer. He then reiterated his offer to go in Retief's place, but the governor turned it down.[748]

Finally, the decision was made that Retief would take 200 men with him to Umgungundlovu, even though many felt that this was a bad idea. Subsequently, quite a few groups departed the main camp to settle elsewhere.[749]

Accounts at this time suggest that Retief seemed depressed after this meeting, possibly because he was having second thoughts about the wisdom of leaving the main camp in a weakened position.

Potgieter and some of his followers returned from a hunting expedition on 22 January 1838 with two wagons full of ivory[750] and intended to take their goods to Durban.

That same day, Retief auctioned off the eleven guns and the horses that he had taken from Sekonyela[751] and, in Umgungundlovu, Dingane received a letter Retief had sent several days earlier. As the evening shadows lengthened, Dingane sent for Owen as he wanted him to read the letter to him.

Owen nervously informed Dingane that the letter stated that Retief had taken Sekonyela prisoner and had seized cattle, guns and horses from the Tlokwa but that he had released the chief after he expressed remorse for his behaviour. Unsurprisingly, Dingane was not pleased that Retief had shown mercy toward his adversary and was vexed that he had only received the cattle and no share in the guns and horses.

Retief's letter also pointed out that the missionaries in the Tlokwa territory had been greatly relieved that the Voortrekkers had managed to retrieve Dingane's stolen cattle without any bloodshed and that they had been afraid that Dingane's army would have been unleashed on the Tlokwa to avenge the theft of the cattle.[752]

Early the following morning, Dingane summoned Owen again. After hastily pulling on some clothes, Owen made his way to the *isigodlo*, where he discovered that the king was evidently agitated. He curtly informed Owen that he wanted to respond to Retief's letter and told the missionary to write that Retief had lied to him and had not delivered on his promise to send Sekonyela to him when he captured the chief. Owen gently chided the king for making such a brash accusation and defended Retief's actions. Subsequently, Dingane told him to leave out that he believed Retief had lied to him but told him to write that his people believed that he had and that Retief should send the guns and horses he had taken as an act of good faith.

When Owen reminded him that Retief had already distributed the horses and cattle among the trekkers, Dingane replied that Retief must send the horses and guns if the Zulu people wished to have them.[753] Owen decided not to send this letter to Retief, as he believed that it would create enmity between Retief and Dingane and he hoped and expected that Retief would explain his actions when he met with Dingane.[754]

At a public meeting held on 22 January 1838 to discuss the planned expedition to visit Dingane, Retief announced that he would be taking 200 men with him. Much heated discussion flowed. There was a noticeable feeling of uncertainty and nervousness about Dingane's intentions. Cilliers again suggested that Retief stay behind and that the documents should be brought back to the camp to sign. So concerned were they for Retief's safety that Gert Maritz, who was unwell, volunteered to go in Retief's place. Maritz warned Retief that he was sure that he would not see Retief again if he went to the meeting with Dingane. Retief expressed the view that Dingane would think badly of him if he did not go as he had commenced the negotiations with the king.[755] When Retief finally called for volunteers to accompany him to see Dingane, only 66 men stepped forward.[756]

Potgieter was one of the most vocal critics of Retief's expedition and he cynically told a friend who had volunteered to go with Retief, "I bid you farewell, for I will never see you again."

When the rain finally let up on 25 January 1838, the trekkers gathered to bid farewell to Retief and his party and Smit led them in prayer.[757]

As the men were preparing to leave, Herklaas Malan called out a warning to Retief, "I fear treachery," he cried. "There is evil in the air. Dingane will betray us and I sense that the British will play a role in this."

"Come come, Malan," Retief admonished him. "You have let your French sentimentality get the better of you!"

"I pray that I am wrong, sir, with all my heart."

Retief and the 66 men under his command were accompanied by four young boys (Danie Liebenberg, Kosie Oosthuizen, Kootjie Opperman and Retief's son, Pieter Retief Jr) and 30 Zulu *agterryers* (after-riders), who herded the cattle they were taking back to Dingane.[758]

As they rode past Maritz's wagon, Retief shouted, "Farewell you old coward!"

"Piet, I warn you for the umpteenth time not to trust that kaffir!" Maritz yelled back.[759]

To mark the occasion, Retief's men fired several shots into the air with their *Sannas* and those who remained behind returned the salute. Some watched with tears running down their cheeks as they feared the worst.

At the Tugela River, 17 more trekkers joined the party, along with British translator Thomas Halstead,[760, 761] who had been instructed by Dingane to accompany Retief on the expedition to recover the cattle from Sekonyela.[762] Before leaving the Tugela River, Retief wrote to his wife and expressed his sadness at the dissension that had rippled through the camp prior to his departure. Nevertheless, he expressed optimism about the journey to Umgungundlovu and suggested that she not move their wagons from the camp until he returned. (Many Voortrekker families had left the main camp in search of better grazing for their livestock and, like grapeshot fired from a barrel, were scattered over a vast area between the Bloukrans and Bushman's rivers.[763])

Mrs Retief received her husband's letter on 28 January 1838 and wrote that all was well in the camp and that the trekkers planned to move their wagons closer to Durban in early February 1838.[764] However, the simmering anxiety among the trekkers soon escalated and it was not long before rumours that Retief and his party had been killed were whispered widely in the camp.

On 1 February 1838, Scheepers and Van Jaarsveld galloped into Retief's camp and shouted to Retief's son-in-law that two Zulu had told a herdsman on the other side of the Bushman's River that Retief and his party had been killed.[765] Evidently, a false alarm: Retief and his men were still on the way to Umgungundlovu. In the early morning of 2 February 1838, Dingane instructed Owen to write a letter to Retief in which he said that he was heartened that his cattle would soon be returned and requested that Retief bring all of his people to Umgungundlovu, without their horses. When Owen queried this, Dingane changed his mind: Retief should make sure to bring his horses so that they could be used in a parade and made to dance alongside his people. He promised Retief that there would be much dancing and feasting when the Boers arrived and emphasized that he would uphold his promise to give the Boers land.

Owen was highly suspicious of Dingane's intentions and was certain that the king was contemplating some form of treachery.[766] Dingane also sent a letter to Gardiner and Cane requesting that they attend the meeting with the Boers. When Hulley delivered this letter to Gardiner at Durban, Gardiner told him that he feared there would be a violent end to this meeting and ignored Dingane's invitation.[767]

That evening, hundreds of warriors poured into Umgungundlovu in anticipation of the Boers' arrival and two regiments, the *Isihlangu Mhlope* (white shields) and *Isihlangu Mnyama* (black shields), comprising over 3,000 warriors each were packed into the huts like sardines in a can, hidden from view.[768] (The warriors in the *Isihlangu Mhlope* regiment were experienced soldiers while the regiment of *Isihlangu Mnyama* was made up of younger, less experienced warriors.)

Later that evening, the *Wildebees* regiment entered Umgungundlovu and, after greeting and paying tribute to Dingane, marched to the hill of *Hlomo Amabutho*, where the men would spend the night.[769]

At around ten o'clock on the morning of 3 February 1838, Owen heard gunshots from the west while praying with his family. When the family went outside to investigate, they saw the Boers riding two by two down the hill toward the main gate of Umgungundlovu[770] and, behind them, the more than 500 cattle which had been retrieved from Sekonyela being herded by the 30 Zulu servants accompanying them, churning up great clouds of red dust. [771]

A great crowd of Zulu emerged from the huts to watch the men ride through the village and Dingane immediately called on Retief to display his horses in the central kraal. Shouts of laughter and appreciation issued from the Zulu onlookers as the Boers made their horses 'dance' by urging them to move sideways as they trotted.

Retief's men then divided into two groups, with one group lined up on the northern side of the kraal and the other on the southern side. On a shouted command from Retief, the men charged at each other at full gallop, repeatedly firing their *Sannas* into the air. Soon the scene was covered in dust from the horses and gunfire smoke hung like a voluminous white-grey cloud over the arena. Neither Dingane nor his warriors had ever seen a display like this before and were determined to impress the Boers with their demonstration.

The warriors swung into action and while they performed their traditional war dances, the ground trembled and thudded as they stamped their feet. They shouted and waved their sticks in the air in mock anger as they charged each other (and the Boers), always stopping short of engaging in close combat with their respective opponent. They swung their *indukas* with ferocity and skill in the heat of the morning and soon beads of sweat streamed down their shiny ebony-coloured muscular bodies as they glistened and shook, oxhide shields waved aloft as if in greeting. After the display by the warriors, the Boers retired to the shade of a euphorbia tree outside the main gate. Near the euphorbia tree stood a stump and two milkwood trees.

Little did they know that they would cause offence by resting near the decaying stump of a large tree. This stump was considered sacred as Dingane's father, Chief Senzangakhona, had died under this tree[772] and no one was allowed to touch the stump. This hallowed area was referred to as the burial-place of the kings (or *kwaNkosinkulu)* and any animal that was on this ground was not allowed to be harmed or scared off. Similarly, any person that was on this site would not be attacked—even if he or she had been sentenced to death by the king.[773]

When the sun was directly overhead, one of Dingane's captains (known as 'Dingane's mouth') approached Retief's party to determine the number of trekkers present and how many cattle they had brought with them. The Zulu men that had been sent with Retief on the expedition to Sekonyela's kraal confirmed that the Tlokwa had stolen the cattle, not the Boers.

After making his report to Dingane, the captain announced to the Boers that a cow would be slaughtered for them and that the king would see them the next day. He then directed them to set up their camp on the slope of a hill near that of *Hlomo Amabutho* and *kwaMatiwane.*

Their designated site was about 200 metres from Umgungundlovu, on the other side of a stream that ran past the village, and the stench of corpses left to rot on *kwaMatiwane* was an ever-present reminder of Dingane's power and cruelty.

When the captain asked Retief to hand over the Boers' horses and weapons, Retief pointed to his greying hair and asked, "Do I look like a child to you?" Nevertheless, he instructed his men to give their weapons to their servants to keep, as a compromise, and they walked about unarmed.[774]

That evening, Retief and two of his men paid a courtesy visit to Owen's hut and accepted an invitation to attend the Sunday service the next morning.[775] When none of the Boers attended the service, Owen assumed that they had not come because they did not wish to offend Dingane. However, unbeknown to Owen, Retief and Boer leaders Abraham Greyling, Marthinus Oosthuizen and Barend Liebenberg had actually been summoned by Dingane to attend a meeting, along with their interpreter, Thomas Halstead.[776] One of Dingane's *indunas* escorted the five men to Dingane's hut, where the king invited them to sit on the new mats on the floor. He sat in his armchair with his favourite dog stretched out in front of him and was flanked by his generals and councillors, including Tambuza, Umhlela, Maoro, Joelawoesa and Manondo.[777]

Dingane's usual translator, Hulley, was still away on his errand to deliver

Dingane's letter to Gardiner in Durban. As such, Halstead and Wood Jr acted as interpreters at this meeting.[778] After Retief described the events surrounding the recovery of Dingane's stolen cattle from the Tlokwa, Dingane declared that he was satisfied with the way in which Retief and his men had conducted the operation. He then asked Retief where his people had come from and why they had left. He also wanted to know how many cattle they had, why they had declared war on Mzilikazi, where Mzilikazi was now and why they had not asked him for land.[779]

Retief answered Dingane's questions as truthfully as he could. He explained that they did not wish to live in Mzilikazi's land as they had not exchanged anything for it and that they could not negotiate an exchange with Mzilikazi as he had fled after they retaliated against the Matabele. Clearly satisfied with Retief's logic, Dingane instructed that Owen be sent to him with paper and writing material as he wanted him to draw up a document ceding land to the Boers.[780]

Drafting the agreement was a laborious process: Dingane and Retief negotiated the terms via Wood Jr; Owen recorded these terms and then read them to Wood Jr, who in turn translated them for Dingane and Retief; the king and governor discussed the terms and ironed out any misunderstandings via Wood Jr and, finally, Wood Jr relayed the amended terms to Owen, who recorded them in British. (It would appear that Dingane no longer trusted Halstead, as he was only marginally involved in putting together the agreement.)

The agreement outlined that Dingane would permanently grant Retief and his people the land west of the Tugela River, up until the Umzimvubu River and including Port Natal, and northward from the sea to "as far as the land is useful" (presumably the Drakensberg Mountains). After Dingane and Retief signed the document, the members of Retief's party and Dingane's generals and councillors also added their signatures.[781]

At the Umhlatusi mission station on 5 February 1838, American missionary Henry Venables and translator James Brownlee were preparing to leave for Umgungundlovu to visit Dingane as Venables was concerned that the number of Zulu people attending the Sunday church service had dropped dramatically. He had heard that Chief Mungo, one of the *indunas* at Congella, had forbidden his people to attend the services and hoped to solicit Dingane's support in the matter.

While Venables and Brownlee were packing, four of Dingane's messengers arrived at the mission station to request that the men come to Umgungundlovu immediately as Dingane needed assistance with translation work.

When Venables asked the messengers where Dingane's usual interpreters were, namely Halstead and Hulley, he was simply told that they were not available. The messengers were most anxious that Venables and Brownlee get to Umgungundlovu speedily and urged them to ride through the night so that they would arrive by nightfall the next day. Consequently, Venables and Brownlee set off at ten o'clock that morning.[782]

Back at Umgungundlovu, the unarmed Voortrekkers explored the village, enjoyed the entertainment organized by Dingane and his generals and the hospitality of the Zulu.

CHAPTER 22

"Kill the wizards!"

Execution or murder?—Owen fears for his life—Venables and Brownlee—Hulley returns—Owen flees

Despite the festive atmosphere in Umgungundlovu, the Boers and Zulu were on edge. Dingane didn't know what to make of his sentries' reports that Retief's men had circled the royal homestead on horseback for the past two nights, fully armed,[783] but assumed that they intended to attacking the Zulu. Nevertheless, he invited the Boers into Umgungundlovu to watch a fearsome display of military precision by some of the regiments, some dancing and a cattle parade and then asked Retief to demonstrate his commando's prowess to the Zulu.

After sending for their horses, Retief and his men galloped in circles around the arena and fired a three-shot volley into the air before heading outside Umgungundlovu, where they staged horse races. To the onlookers' delight, some of the more athletic Zulu men tried to outrun the horses.

Shortly after the Boers finished eating lunch, they received an invitation from Dingane to attend a farewell meeting the next morning.[784]

Wood Jr, who wandered around Umgungundlovu at will and was accepted by the Zulu there overheard a few comments that made him suspect that foul play was afoot in the village.

"You will see that they will kill the Boers tomorrow," he confided to Jane Williams.[785]

"Don't be silly," she snapped. "You are always saying things like that. You told me a long time ago that the king said he would kill you because you talk too much."[786]

That night, under cover of darkness, Dingane's *Wildebees* regiment marched into Umgungundlovu[787] and, in the early hours of the morning, the Boers yet again circled the village on horseback. Those warriors and sentries who heard the patter of hooves and soft whinnying of the Boers' horses outside Umgungundlovu started to whisper among themselves that the Boers must be wizards. Disturbed by the latest reports about the Boers' strange nocturnal practices, Dingane was now certain that they would attack. Nevertheless, he wanted to see for himself whether the reports were true and early that morning accompanied his generals and witchdoctors to inspect the tracks made by the Boers' horses.[788]

On a beautiful bright sky-blue morning, over breakfast at the mission station on 6 February 1838, Owen cautiously asked his two Voortrekker guests what they thought of Dingane.

One of the men, after glancing at his colleague as if for confirmation responded, "We think he is good. He has granted us land and today it is being finalized."[789]

As the Boers strolled into Umgungundlovu, enjoying the warm sunshine, William watched them with apprehension. A small knot of Boers walked past him and after greeting them and wishing them good morning, he said, "I do not think that all is right. I really think you must be careful and be on your guard. I suspect Dingane is up to something and it could well be a plot to kill you."

The Boers glanced at each other in amusement, chuckling at the boy's nervousness. One shouted back as they continued to the meeting, "We are sure the king's heart is right with us. There is no cause for fear."[790]

At Dingane's hut, the *Isihlangu Mhlope* and *Isihlangu Mnyama* regiments formed up in a large circle in front of their king, who was flanked by general Umhlela of the *Isihlangu Mhlope* on his right and Tambuza of the *Isihlangu Mnyama* on his left. Dingane then dispatched a messenger to instruct Retief to come to him with his men as he wished to have a farewell drink with them and that they must not bring their weapons to the party.[791]

Retief told his men to leave their weapons with two of the Hottentot servants who would stay behind to see to their horses[792] and the whole party then made its way to Dingane's *isigodlo*. The Boers finally entered the circle of warriors in front of Dingane's hut, who parted to allow the men through, where their apprehension evaporated when Dingane greeted them.

"It saddens me that you are leaving," Dingane said. "Before you go, you must enjoy a drink of *tywala* [traditional brewed beer] with me and my warriors."

At this invitation, Retief told his men that they, with the servants, should sit on the ground a short distance away, but still within the circle of warriors. Retief, with his riding whip in hand, a water bottle by his side and the satchel with the signed concession granting him the land, nodded to his men and sat down with Halstead in front of Dingane.[793]

"Please give my greetings to your people and tell them that they must come here soon, as it is my desire that your people occupy the land I have granted you as soon as possible," he continued while attendants poured beer and sour milk (*amasi*) for the Boers. "I wish you a pleasant journey back to your people," the king concluded before ordering his warriors to entertain his guests with singing and dancing.

While Retief's men watched the performances, Dingane whispered instructions to a messenger, who sped of toward the mission station. Owen had been reading his Bible in the shade of his wagon on the hill opposite Umgungundlovu[794] and probably saw the entertainment beginning in the village as well as the messenger coming up the hill toward him. When the messenger arrived at Owen's side, he blurted out that Dingane was going to kill the Boers but that the king would spare Owen and his people as they were King George IV's children. He clarified that Dingane believed the Boers were runaways from the British king and therefore deserved to be killed[795] and added that Halstead would also be spared.[796]

Owen was thunderstruck by this news and did not believe the messenger's assertion that Dingane had uncovered a plot by the Boers to attack him. He was also aware that he had to keep his feelings to himself about Dingane's planned treachery lest he forfeit his life and those of his family.

Owen was determined to warn the Boers of the danger they were in.[797] However, before he could make his way down to Umgungundlovu, he heard the warriors singing one of Dingane's gruesome compositions, which translated as: 'Drink oh drink the beer! Your burning throats call for it! Drink as much as you can for tomorrow you drink no more.'[798]

In the kraal, the ground trembled and the dust swirled as the warriors stamped their feet in unison to the beat of many drums. The rhythm of the drumbeats began to increase and the *Isihlangu Mhlope* and *Isihlangu Mnyama* regiments gradually moved closer to the Boers, tightening the ring around them like a hangman's noose as they surged forward then moved back.

The dancers stamped and leaped high in the air. The ground trembled as their feet smacked down in unison like moving parts of a well-oiled machine. Clouds of dust rose as the feet stamped down. The rhythm of the drums began to quicken faster and faster. The dancers swirled and pranced as they waved their shields above their heads, and behind the dancers the *Isihlangu Mhlope* and *Isihlangu Mnyama* moved closer still. The Boers glanced at each other nervously as the dancing became more frenzied. They realized that this style of dancing was more menacing than that of earlier displays—even their dogs sensed the threatening attitude of the warriors and some began to growl softly, and bare their teeth while others howled and barked angrily.

Retief signalled to Dingane that he should order the dancers to move away from his men.[799] Instead, the king whistled to his men and shouted, "To me, my soldiers! *Bamba* [Seize them]; grab them tight; kill them! *Bulalani amatakati* [Kill the wizards]!"

"We are done for!" Halstead shouted to the Boers. "Listen to me. Let me speak to the king," he screamed at the hissing warriors manhandling Retief's men.

"Kill the wizards!" Dingane yelled, dismissing Halstead's request with a wave of his hand.

The Voortrekkers screamed as the Zulu smashed some of their comrades' skulls in with their *indukas* and shouts of "Treason! Treason! We are betrayed!" issued from some of the Boers as they struggled to break free from their captors, who were intent on dragging them to *kwaMatiwane* to kill them there instead of spilling blood by the *isigodlo*.[800]

"Help! Oh Lord."

"God help us!"[801]

Halstead managed to stab one of the attackers in the stomach with his hunting knife and then slashed the throat of another before he was overpowered. The remaining trekkers followed his example and killed as many as 20 warriors.[802]

One of the trekkers managed to wriggle out of the grasp of his assailants and sprinted for the gate, only to be overtaken by the Zulu, grabbed and dragged back to the seething mass of slaughter.

Owen and his family were terrified as they listened to the yells of anger, groans of anguish and screams of pain coming from the village below. They could hear the Boers' dogs attempting to defend their masters, the warriors thumping their shields with their *indukas* and Dingane's repeated command of "*Bulala! Bulala!*" They soon heard the warriors silencing the Boers' faithful dogs.

As the doomed Voortrekkers were pulled through the village, the bystanders cheered and egged the warriors on and Dingane shouted loudly, "Take the heart and liver of the king of the Boers and place them in the road."[803]

After being dragged out the gate, the sobbing Voortrekkers were forced to cross the spruit and then onto *Hlomo Amabutho* and finally, up *kwaMatiwane*.

Owen and his family trembled with fear and revulsion as they watched the massacre of the Boer men and boys—some younger than eleven—through a telescope and Owen eventually collapsed from shock and anguish.[804] The warriors crushed the Boers' heads with *indukas* and impaled some with sharpened wooden sticks up their anuses before bludgeoning them. Retief and his son were the last to die, after having witnessed the cruel and painful deaths of their friends and relatives.[805]

The vultures screeched and flapped their wings as they tore at the Boers' carcasses and, in similar fashion, one of the warriors dismembered Retief's stomach and chest. After removing Retief's heart and liver, he wrapped them in a cloth and carried the dripping organs back to Dingane, leaving behind Retief's leather satchel that contained the agreement granting land to the Boers on the ground next to him.[806]

Soon, six heavily-armed warriors arrived at the mission station and sat next to Owen's hut, allegedly to guard Owen and his family. Owen hastily ordered his traumatized family and several other residents at the mission station to get inside the hut and read Psalm 91[807] to them, as tears streamed down his face. Owen and Wood Jr took turns with the telescope to observe the happenings in Umgungundlovu and it was not long before Owen saw Umhlela and Tambuza deep in conversation with Dingane at his *isigodlo* and several divisions of the army forming up in front of the king to await his command.[808] He also saw Dingane dispatching a series of messengers to the mission station.

When Mrs Owen asked the first messenger that arrived where Halstead was, he ignored her. However, another messenger informed Owen that Halstead had been sent to Durban to deliver a message to Gardiner. Yet another messenger told them that Dingane did not want them to be frightened as he respected their king, King George VI, and would not harm them. After this message, they were informed that the king wanted them to pack up and leave for Port Natal. However, the next messenger told them that Dingane insisted that they stay at the mission station.[809] Unsurprisingly, Owen and the others were thoroughly confused by the many contradictory messages Dingane had sent them but sensed that they were in danger.

While Dingane was meeting with Umhlela and Tambuza, Venables and Brownlee arrived at Umgungundlovu. Immediately, the missionaries noticed a crowd of Zulu surrounding the Voortrekkers' baggage and weapons and that some of the braver souls were handling their guns.

"Where are the Boers under Retief?" Brownlee asked one of the nearby Zulu men.

"They have gone hunting," he replied evasively.

Venables and Brownlee realized that something dreadful had happened to the Boers and they promptly asked to see Dingane. They waited at the gate for over an hour before Dingane summoned them and were then escorted into Umgungundlovu, where Umhlela received them and told them that the Boers were dead.

When the general asked Venables why he was not grateful, and why Venables did not thank the King for killing Retief and his party,[810] the two men quickly masked their horror and Venables casually asked why Dingane had killed them. Umhlela duly explained that Dingane had discovered that the Boers had intended to attack him[811] and then asked why they had settled near Umgungundlovu.

"We have come to teach," Venables answered calmly.

"To teach what?" Umhlela asked.

"The Good Book and the Word of God," the missionary replied.

"Can you not rather teach us to ride and shoot?" Umhlela pleaded.

In an attempt to sidestep answering the general's question, Venables told Umhlela that he and Brownlee were ravenous after their long journey and requested that they be allowed to go to Owen's hut to get some food.

When the missionary and his interpreter approached the mission station, they saw no-one but the Zulu sentries outside Owen's hut and were thus hugely relieved when they discovered Owen and his distraught party praying inside.

Hulley's wife was particularly distressed as her husband had not yet returned from his errand to Durban and she sobbed uncontrollably. Little did she know that flooded rivers had caused the delay in his homecoming.

As Venables and Brownlee walked into the hut, they saw one of the Zulu messengers comforting her. "Shhhh! Shhhh! Quietly, quietly. Do not weep. Shhh! Shhh!" the Zulu man soothed her.

They took in the tear-stained faces of the people in Owen's hut and when they asked what was the matter, one of Owen's children pointed to *kwaMatiwane*, where the vultures were engaged in a feeding frenzy on the Voortrekkers' corpses.

The barbarism perpetrated by Dingane's men left the party of white people at the mission station in no doubt that Dingane was not to be trusted and that they were in danger, despite receiving a message from the king that the Boers had been killed because they were wizards.

When Owen instructed Wood Jr to tell the latest messenger that he should tell Dingane that he disapproved of the killings, Wood Jr used his initiative. "Tell the king that we [consider] that he has acted perfectly [rightly] in killing the farmers, as no doubt they would otherwise have killed us, as well as the king and his people,"[812] Wood Jr told the messenger instead.

Naturally, Dingane was pleased with Owen's response and went as far as to reward him with an ox. In the village, Dingane and his generals had reached agreement that the army would attack the Boers' wagons near the Bushman's River.

Dingane's soldiers were ready and each of the captains approached Dingane individually to mock attack him. They thrust their spears and shields close to his face, feinted with their assegais and pretended to stab the king, all the while shouting their praise for him (including descriptions of Dingane's bravery, leadership and power).

"We will go kill the white dogs; we will go kill the white dogs," the warriors chanted as the various divisions started running out of Umgungundlovu to track down the Boers.[813]

The army's intention to attack the Boers was soon reported to Owen at the mission station and he prayed that God would protect them from the Zulu onslaught. He also kept up a constant vigil on the frenzied activity in Umgungundlovu with his telescope. He watched as Dingane conducted several meetings and dispatched messengers with a cursory wave of his hand and was horrified to see warriors collecting their weapons and preparing to follow the army.

That afternoon, there was fresh cause for alarm: between 50 and 60 warriors arrived at the mission station. As they approached Owen's hut, one of the captains shouted that Dingane wished to see Owen but added that the king did not intend to hurt him or his people. Nevertheless, Owen and Wood Jr walked alongside the soldiers to the *isigodlo* with legs like jelly.

The king looked at Owen and Wood Jr silently for some time before asking, "Are you afraid?" When Owen nervously shook his head, Dingane laughed. "You behaved well," he said. "Do you wish to go to Durban?" he asked.

Owen again shook his head, scared that he might aggravate the king if he answered truthfully.

"Good," Dingane smiled. "Go back to your huts now then."

Venables and Brownlee stayed with the small frightened group at Owen's hut that evening and the next and must have talked with them about the future of the missionaries in the country and about the imminent danger in store for them all.

When Dingane again sent an *induna* to reassure Owen that his family was in no danger, the messenger added that Dingane had wanted him to tell Owen and his party that he did not intend killing any of the missionaries, as there were only a few in his lands and he could live in peace with them. The messenger also emphasized that the king liked all British people and considered them allies but did not like the Boers and would try to kill all Boers that entered his kingdom. He then offered several explanations as to why the king had killed the Boers, including that they had planned to kill the king and the Zulu people; had assembled an army for this purpose; and had disobeyed the king by not bringing Sekonyela back to him to be punished and had instead set him free.

Owen did not believe that the king had had a legitimate reason for killing the Voortrekkers other than that he had wanted to and he sensed that the killings had been premeditated. However, he merely remarked that he wished to teach the Bible in Dingane's country and was not a fighter. He added that he and the other missionaries would probably not be able to handle a weapon, as those who taught the Word of God in his country did not handle weapons.[814]

That evening, Dingane sent for Venables and Brownlee and ordered them to show him how to unsaddle and unhalter the horses that had belonged to Retief and his men.

Afterwards, he reiterated that he would not harm the missionaries and told them that he had ordered that Halstead not be killed along with the Boers. He claimed that his warriors had killed Halstead accidentally.

In light of the fact that Dingane appeared to have a soft spot for the missionaries, Venables took the opportunity to express his concern that Chief Mungo had ordered his people not to attend church services at Umhlatusi. To Venables's relief, Dingane assured him that he would command Mungo to rescind that instruction and emphasized that he would never chase the missionaries away from his lands. The king then went on to lament that the residents in Durban were afraid of him and that they had built a fort to protect themselves from him. He also informed Venables that he and Gardiner had fallen out.[815]

The next morning, Venables and Owen discussed what course of action they should take as both men were sure that Dingane would not let the missionaries alone. They determined that they should head for the safety of Durban as soon as possible and Venables and Brownlee left Umgungundlovu immediately to return to Umhlatusi to fetch those who had remained at the mission station.[816]

Soon after Venables and Brownlee departed the village, Hulley returned to the area. After seeing the pile of guns and horse saddles at the entrance to Umgungundlovu and the hundreds of hunched-over black forms of the vultures feeding on the reeking and rotting flesh of the Voortrekkers' at *kwaMatiwane*, he galloped to the mission station to search for his family. At his hut, he saw plates on the dining table covered in mouldy food and immediately ran toward Owen's hut, as he wanted to see whether it was also empty. He was overwhelmed with relief when his young son emerged from Owen's hut yelling, "Father's come! Father's come!"

He embraced his wife and children in the hut and, sipping a coffee, listened impassively as they told him what had happened to Retief and his men. He did not want to add to their already considerable fear about what the future held in store for them all. Soon after finishing his hot drink, a messenger arrived to take him to see Dingane.

No sooner had he arrived at the *isigodlo* than Dingane started justifying why he had killed the Boers and claimed that he had conclusive proof that the Boers would have attacked him and his people: his *indunas* had found that the late Boers' guns had been loaded and ready to fire.[817] He also said that Retief had gone against his wishes by releasing Sekonyela and that he saw every white person as an enemy.

"Don't you think I have done a good thing in getting rid of my enemies in one stroke?" the king demanded.

"I am not in a position to comment," Hulley replied softly.

"What did Gardiner and Cane hear that they refused to come to the meeting?" he pried.

"I cannot say," Hulley replied.

"I am sorry that they were not here," Dingane continued. "They deserved the same treatment that the Boers received."

Hulley was flabbergasted: Dingane's comment completely contradicted his reasoning for having had the Boers killed.

When Dingane asked Hulley what news he had heard in Port Natal, Hulley matter-of-factly answered, "I heard that the Boers' camps stretch all the way from the Bushman's River to the Orange River".

Dingane was astounded by this news.

"If what you say is true, my men have deceived me," he said, reflecting that his warriors would soon be approaching the Bushman's River. "They told me that there was only one camp and that there were only about 30 men and boys to defend it."[818]

After this meeting, Hulley told Owen that there was no doubt in his mind that a war between the Boers and the Zulu was inevitable.[819] As such, Owen decided to leave Umgungundlovu. Knowing that it would be too dangerous to remain at the mission station and that he and his family would be hunted down if they fled to Durban, he visited Dingane that afternoon in the hope that the king would give them permission to leave his territory.

Owen took a piece of bright red cloth to give to Dingane at their meeting and, fortunately, Dingane greeted Owen amicably and asked him to speak plainly about the reason for his visit. When Owen said that he wished to leave Umgungundlovu, Dingane asked him whether his desire to leave stemmed from the fact that he had had the Boers killed. Owen wisely replied that he felt that war would erupt between the Boers and the Zulu in future and that he needed to consider the safety of his family.

After the briefest pause, Dingane wished Owen a pleasant journey and beseeched him to visit him at least once more before he left. He implied that he wanted to tell him something but could not do so now. [820] Relieved that the discussion had gone so well, Owen promised to return to the *isigodlo* when summoned and added that he would leave all the cattle that Dingane had given him behind as well as any household items that would not fit into his wagon.

That night, in the oppressive heat, Owen tossed and turned in his bed as he dreamed about the massacre of the Voortrekkers. He woke several times in the night and could not help mulling over how calm the king had been when he announced his intention to leave the mission station. His gut instinct screamed that Dingane had something sinister in store for him and his family.

The following morning, a messenger summoned Owen to meet with Dingane, who apparently wanted to brief him on what he should say regarding the killing of the Boers to the people in Durban.

Owen and Hulley promptly walked to the *isigodlo* to see the king, who explained to his attendant *indunas* that Owen wanted to leave the mission station. He stated that he did not object to the missionary's departure and suspected that Owen's sudden desire to leave was due to what had happened to the Boers. When Dingane smiled at Owen and again wished him a pleasant journey, Owen felt cold shivers of apprehension running up and down his spine as he realized the insincerity of the king's words.

Unbeknown to Owen, his servants at the mission station had been spying on him and had reported every harsh word uttered about Dingane in his household. The friendly tone of the meeting soon evaporated and Dingane became aggressive and threatening, launching a venomous tirade.

He shouted that Gardiner had promised him a shipful of gifts on his second visit but had only sent him Owen."I never intended for the whites to build houses in my country. I had made it very clear and repeated myself time after time, but they would not take 'no' for an answer," the king mused before turning to Owen. "Who sent you? Who asked you to come here?" he yelled. "Did I ask you to come here?"

Owen respectfully reminded Dingane that he had come with Gardiner and that the king had welcomed him when he arrived.

Dingane sarcastically replied that it was only Gardiner's persistence that had led him to build a house for Owen. He then demanded that Owen reveal his real reason for coming to Umgungundlovu. "I have received reports that you believe I will kill you," Dingane said, pointing toward the mission station.

Owen's heart must have flipped at hearing this.

"My people work for you and have told me what you have said. They have told me that you speak evil of me. They say that when you praise your god, you do so with hatred for me in your hearts. You and all who live with you tell lies about me, except the translator, Hulley."

When the king sent for the woman who worked for Owen, the missionary began to think that he and his family would soon be dispatched into the next world.

Owen must have been on the point of collapse as the woman informed Dingane and the *indunas* that she had overheard Mrs Owen and her daughter referring to the king as a murderer and rogue and Owen praying that God would protect his family from Dingane and condemn the king for his behaviour. She also told them that she had seen Owen spying on the comings and goings of the Zulu in the village with his telescope.

"Did you hear what they said?" Dingane asked his *indunas*. He then jabbed his finger at Owen and accused him of treachery.

Owen pleaded with the king that the servant could not possibly have understood the conversations or prayers of his family as she did not speak British and Dingane appeared to be momentarily placated. Nevertheless, Owen realized that he and his family were not off the hook yet and that Dingane could still see to it that they were murdered on their way to Durban but pretend he had not ordered their executions.[821] As such, Owen cleverly pointed out that he was afraid that Dingane's captains might kill him and his family while they were travelling, despite not being ordered to do so.

The king shrugged off this suggestion and, to Owen's surprise, instructed him to write a letter to the governor of the colony on his behalf and requested that he deliver this letter when he left Umgungundlovu. Dingane ordered Owen to write that he had killed the Boers because they had kept the cattle they recovered from Mzilikazi and the Matabele when these had originally been stolen from him and because they had planned to kill him and his people. The king also commanded Owen to write that he would not allow white people to build houses on his land in future and that Owen had unsuccessfully attempted to deceive him. Naturally, Owen did not query what the king meant by this. When Dingane had finished dictating the letter, he allowed Owen and Hulley to leave the *isigodlo*. They were escorted to the main gate by a horde of Zulu warriors who, fortunately, then let them continue to the mission station while they headed off to join the army that would attack the Boers. Their wives sobbed with relief when they saw them walk up the hill to the mission station late that afternoon and their families started loading their wagons the minute they returned.

As it was nearly nightfall by the time they finished packing and many of their cattle were sick, Owen and Hulley decided that their families would only leave the mission station in the morning. After an uneasy night's rest, a messenger arrived early on the morning of 11 February 1838 to tell them that the king wanted them to leave all but the bare essentials behind but that he would give them fresh oxen.[822] Owen and Hulley's group duly unpacked many of their belongings and hastily left the mission station to start their journey for Durban.

When their wagons trundled past the entrance to Umgungundlovu, their hearts sank as an *induna* came out to inform them that Dingane wished to see Owen and Hulley. A crowd of Zulu warriors then marched the two men toward *kwaMatiwane* while Mrs Owen and her daughter, Wood Jr, Mrs Hulley and her three children as well as Jane Bird traipsed behind them.

"The rougher the road, the sweeter the glory!" Mrs Owen cried, throwing her arms around Jane Bird to comfort the young woman.

They all believed they would be executed shortly and were therefore surprised when the *induna* called out that they were to come back to the village. Owen and Hulley were then taken to Dingane at the *isigodlo*. However, they soon returned to their relieved families and set off again. The small group solemnly walked alongside their wagon as they passed the pile of guns and saddles that had belonged to the men and boys in Retief's party.[823]

CHAPTER 23

Blood stains at the place of weeping

Zulu attack—massacre—the aftermath—orphans—Maritz organizes

By February 1838, many more groups of Boers had left the colony and the Voortrekkers were now mainly spread out along the Bloukrans and Bushman's Rivers as well as near the confluence of the Little Tugela River and the Tugela River, in an area greater than 1,000 square kilometres. Uys had returned to Transoranje (the area between the Orange and Vaal *rivers)* to fetch his followers and Maritz had assumed control of the trekkers.

The main camp at Doornkop comprised about 78 wagons and included Retief's wagons and those of the Greylings, Scheepers, Viljoens, Van der Merwes and Hattinghs; Maritz's wagons and those of the Rudolph family were about six kilometres from the Bushman's River (near today's town of Escourt) while Cilliers had settled with about 50 families not far from them, close to the Bushman's River, and more than 100 wagons were at the camp under Commandant J. du Plessis near Spionkop (between the Little Tugela River and the Tugela River and between Doornkop and the Drakensberg Mountains), including those belonging to the De Klerks, De Beers, Mullers and De Winnaars.

A number of small treks were found near the Great Moordspruit River, including those under Barend Liebenberg, Wynand Bezuidenhout, A.J. Rossouw, Robberts Jacobus Hattingh and the De Beers, Bothas, Breslers, Smits, Engelbrechts, Greylings, Jouberts, Van der Merwes, Prinsloos, Bothmas, Steenkamps and Kloppers while the Malans, Swarts and Breedts were near the Mooi River.[824]

The Boers near Bushman's River were deeply concerned that Retief and his men had not yet returned and, by 15 February 1838, rumours were rampant that they had been killed.[825] Consequently, Maritz sent Greyling with a small patrol into Zululand to establish whether there was any substance to these rumours. The patrol pretended that they were on a hunting expedition and, after crossing the Tugela River, they encountered an old Zulu man as they approached a koppie.

"What are you looking for?" he asked them and Greyling answered that they were hunting buffalo.

"I saw herds of buffalo over there, only a short while ago," the man told them, directing them away from the koppie.

When Greyling's party continued toward the koppie, the old man trotted alongside them. He asked whether they were really hunting buffalo as they were ignoring his advice about where they could be found. It was clear that he was agitated and, not wanting to arouse his suspicions further, the Boers doubled back and headed toward their camp. Little did they know that the Zulu army was camped behind the koppie and they had been less than 200 metres away from Dingane's warriors.

When they arrived back at the laager near the Bushman's River that evening, they reported their strange meeting with the old Zulu man and that they were sure something sinister was afoot, despite not having any evidence to support this.[826]

At this time, several of the men were away on hunting trips while others had returned to the Drakensberg area to assist fellow trekkers to cross over into Natal. The few men as well as the many women and children at the camp took no heed of the unease felt by those who had been in Greyling's expedition that warm summer evening. While the trekkers' herds of cattle and sheep contentedly grazed near the wagons, the children played in the rivers, the women sewed, picked vegetables from their gardens and cooked the evening meal while the men folk repaired wagons and picket fences and made ammunition and biltong.

As the evening fires died down on 16 February 1838, and the laughter of the children became less and less as they were put to bed and went to sleep, quietness descended like a cloud under the black mantle of the darkness of a moonless night over the groups of two or three wagons huddled together for comfort and comradeship. Shortly after midnight, the Zulu regiments began to form up near the farthest outlying wagons which belonged to the Liebenbergs[827] that were next to the Bloukrans River, close to those of the Bezuidenhouts. (Barend and Daniel Liebenberg had gone with Retief to Umgungundlovu.[828]) Under cover of the dark night the warriors divided and stealthily took up their positions and formed a 40-kilometre front.[829] On this hot and humid night the soft reassuring sounds of frogs croaking hoarsely in the streams could be heard. Nightbirds called, crickets chirped, all was peaceful. The peace was shattered by the urgent and angry barking of some of the trekkers' dogs. The newly-married Petrus Liebenberg (he had been married for a month) and his three younger brothers rushed from their wagons in alarm with their *Sannas* to investigate.

The Zulu warriors charged out of the darkness, hurling their assegais at the Boers, who were astonished that the Zulu aggressors appeared to be accompanied by a coloured man. Unbeknown to the trekkers, this was trader Alexander Biggar's son, George, and he had been sent by his father to inform the trekkers of the tragedy that had befallen Retief and his men at Umgungundlovu.[830] He had arrived at their camp just before the Zulu warriors attacked and had managed to weave his way through the mass of warriors unharmed. (In a cruel twist of fate, Richard (Dick) King had been sent by the American missionaries at Durban to warn George Biggar and the Boers that the Zulu were planning an attack. However, King only arrived in the area after the Zulu assault on the Liebenbergs' camp had started and he therefore ran on to the next cluster of wagons, where he helped to defend the wagons and fought the Zulu with as much resolve as the Boers did.[831, 832]) Barend Liebenberg's son-in-law, Van Vuuren, promptly shot at the 'traitor'.

"You have shot off my arm!" George Biggar screamed.

"What are you doing among the Zulu?" Van Vuuren shouted and, not waiting for a reply, fired at him again. His second shot killed Biggar.[833]

The Liebenberg men realized that they were no match for the Zulu and abandoned their surrounded wagons to flee to the Bezuidenhout camp. If any of these wounded men had looked back, they might have seen the ruthless slaughter of Christina Susanna (who had married Petrus one month and three days earlier), Hester (who was married to Barend) and Susanna (Daniel Liebenberg's wife).[834] The second wave of warriors then engulfed the wagons of Adriaan Rossouw on the outskirts of the Bezuidenhout camp and slaughtered him, his wife and four children within minutes. Young Adrian was stabbed 32 times and Elizabeth Joanne sixteen.

The warriors then moved upriver, where they attacked the Bezuidenhouts in their five wagons and three skin tents[835] at about one o'clock in the morning. At first, 25-year-old Daniel Bezuidenhout thought that the snarling, yelping and growling of their dogs must be due to a lion or leopard in the vicinity. He climbed out of bed and, dressed only in his shirt and drawers, stumbled out of his wagon to quiet them. He jerked fully awake as he realized that the dogs were defending their masters from a much more deadly enemy about 275 metres away from the wagons. He saw the Zulu warriors stabbing the dogs and yelled a warning to the sleeping trekkers. "The Zulu are attacking! They are stabbing the dogs!" he screamed, running back toward the wagons to fetch his *Sanna*.

Daniel's young brother, 14-year-old Petrus Johannes, thought that Daniel had shouted that the sheep were running away and promptly jumped out of his father's wagon to chase after them. His speedy response saved his life: he made it out of the wagon just before the Zulu soldiers stormed into it. Although he was wounded in the back outside the wagon, he managed to escape to some nearby trees, where the horses were kept. There, he used his braces to harness the tamest horse and rode off, taking seven other horses with him, and arrived at Doornkop the next day.[836]

At the Bezuidenhout camp, the trekkers fired from their wagons and tents into the darkness as Daniel pushed his way forward through the mass of Zulu warriors. He managed to get close enough to the wagons to hear his father gurgle as he choked on his own blood, "Oh God!" before he died from an assegai wound to his throat and Roelof Botha shout, "Oh Lord!" before being fatally stabbed.[837]

Daniel realized that he was of no help to those in the wagons—he glimpsed his dead wife with her breast cut off and his 11-month-old baby lying on the blood-soaked breast dead; also lying dead in their own blood were his mother, mother-in-law, brother, four sisters and five-year-old niece[838]—and so retreated, charging directly at the Zulus and weaving his way through the throng of assegai-wielding Zulu.

He barely noticed the assegais penetrating his body: one struck him in the chest but glanced off his ribs; another was plunged into his thigh; a third struck him above the left knee and the fourth above the left ankle, where it severed his sinews.

Driven by desperation and adrenaline, he ran to the cattle kraal, where he hid among the agitated livestock and listened in terror to the triumphant shouts of the Zulu warriors as they smashed crockery, tipped the wagons over, spilling the contents onto the ground with the sounds of breaking wood, the ripping and shredding of tents, and the barks and yelps of terror and pain of the dogs and chickens as they too were killed.[839]

Eventually, when the camp was quiet, Daniel slipped out from his hiding place and made his way along the Bloukrans River to warn the other trekkers of the imminent danger they were in.

At the wagons belonging to the Malans, Swarts and Breedts near the Mooi River, the trekkers heard the shots from the Bezuidenhout camp and assumed that Retief and his men had returned and were firing a salute.

Later, however, Jacobus Malan sent his young nephew Dawid Malan on horseback toward the sounds of gunfire to establish what was happening. Dawid hurried back to the camp with a wounded servant loaded on his horse. The ashen-faced boy proceeded to tell his uncle and the others that the Zulu were slaughtering the Voortrekkers along the Bloukrans River. The Malans, Swarts and Breedts immediately abandoned their wagons and ran toward a small koppie, where they hid. Cilliers and those in his camp near the Bushman's River also imagined that the gunfire was a salute from Retief's party. However, he soon realized that they must be mistaken as round after round was fired. "Something is wrong! Saddle up your horses and be on your guard!" he shouted, before sending the women and children to hide in a bush-covered ravine and heading off with five men to see where they could be of most help.[840]

While the Bezuidenhout camp was under siege, another regiment of Zulu warriors attacked the De Beer camp. There, some of the children huddled in one wagon and were fatally stabbed while some of the smaller children suffocated in the pile of bodies in the wagon. Two of the De Beer men and four of the De Beer women were also murdered.[841]

The wounded wife of Johannes de Beer, Elizabeth, grabbed her nine-month-old baby and hid under the wagon. However, the Zulu warriors found her and repeatedly stabbed her through the spokes of the wagon wheels. She sheltered her baby with her body and pretended to be dead.

When the Zulu eventually moved on, Elizabeth crawled out from under the wagon, clasping the small, blood-stained bundle to her breast, and fled to the Bloukrans River, where she discovered that her baby was dead. She left the infant next to the river in its blankets and ran for her life. Emotionally and physically exhausted, she climbed high into a thorn tree and wedged herself into position. When two Zulu men stopped underneath the tree, droplets of her blood dripped onto one of them[842] and one of the warriors immediately looked up. He attempted to stab her with his assegai but she desperately scrambled to a higher branch and, in the process, was again scratched by the sharp thorns. He then began to climb the tree and tried to pull Elizabeth down. Fortunately, he jumped down when he heard shots nearby and left a sobbing but relieved Elizabeth behind.[843]

Most of the families who had been camped along the Bloukrans River and its tributaries, the Great Moordspruit and the Klein Moordspruit, were killed in the attack. When a servant ran into Gert Viljoen's camp shouting about the Zulu invasion, Viljoen did not believe the news. However, when a messenger from the nearby camp of his brother-in-law, Johannes Breytenbach, soon arrived with the same information, Viljoen pushed his wagons into laager formation and crammed thorn branches between the wheel spokes.

Early that morning, the Zulu army approached the Viljoen camp and Gert and Karel Viljoen, Gert Combrink, Izak Breytenbach, Mr Schutte and Mr Strijdom decided to ride out of the laager in the hope that they could protect the camp by acting as decoys. Gert Combrink and Izak headed toward the Bezuidenhout camp while the other four men rode toward the Engelbrecht and Bothma camp. They soon saw that the camp of the Van Dyk and Snymans families was under siege and before long, the Zulu warriors surged toward them. The two men fired at the Zulu pursuing them and then withdrew out of range of their assegais before firing again. They repeated this tactic several times and, in so doing, successfully led the warriors away from the wagons. Gert, Karel, Schutte and Strijdom headed for Doornkop and, on the way, joined up with De Lange and his party.[844]

Meanwhile, Daniel Bezuidenhout ran along the Bloukrans River to warn as many of the Voortrekkers as possible of the attack and eventually stumbled into the camp of Sybrand van Dyk at around two o'clock in the morning. "Wake up! Get out of the wagons. The Zulu are coming!" he shouted.

The women and children scrambled from the wagons and ran with Daniel to the Scheepers's camp, where he collected the women and children there. (The men from this camp had left with Retief.) Daniel picked up many more people from other camps along the Bloukrans River and led a crowd of bedraggled and terrified refugees away from the Zulu as they wreaked death and destruction over a vast area. Some of the Voortrekkers were slaughtered in their beds while others were cut down by assegais as they fled or attempted to hide. The screams of the victims floated through the dark night air as the flames from torched wagons punctured the blackness.

Just before sunrise, Daniel's group arrived at the laagers of Hans Roets, Petrus van Vuuren and Karl Geer to warn them and their families, who immediately joined the fleeing refugees as they stumbled through the veld toward Doornkop.[845] The sky began to lighten as the sun rose. The 196 bedraggled, hysterical group of refugees made a pathetic sight in the early morning light as they stumbled, many of them barefoot and in night attire, across the veld in the direction of the wagons of Retief and Greyling at Doornkop. At nine o'clock that morning, a panting Bushman girl ran into the De Klerk camp on the Little Tugela. She was in a state of shock and could not tell the trekkers what was wrong. However, minutes later, a blood-stained Daniel staggered out of the bushes and shouted, "All have been killed by the Zulu." He then breathlessly recounted his nightmare journey along the Bloukrans River warning as many camps as possible of the Zulu attack. Shortly after this, two horses galloped into the clearing, with Heila Robberts on the one horse and her two daughters and son on the other. Heila had heard gunfire and the shouts of the Zulu army and had ridden past Doornkop to warn those in the outlying camps of the attack and to rally the men to help.[846] At this stage, she did not know that her husband had been killed at Umgungundlovu along with the rest of Retief's party.

The refugees finally arrived at Doornkop at midday. After walking under a scorching sun for many hours, they were exhausted and in shock. Nevertheless, some of the women fell to their knees and thanked the Lord for their deliverance and prayed for the souls of those who had been killed.[847] The slaughter of the Voortrekkers continued throughout the day, as did the many acts of bravery and determination by those being attacked. Near the Great moorspruit stood three wagons which belonged to a small group of Italian traders. One of them, Thersea

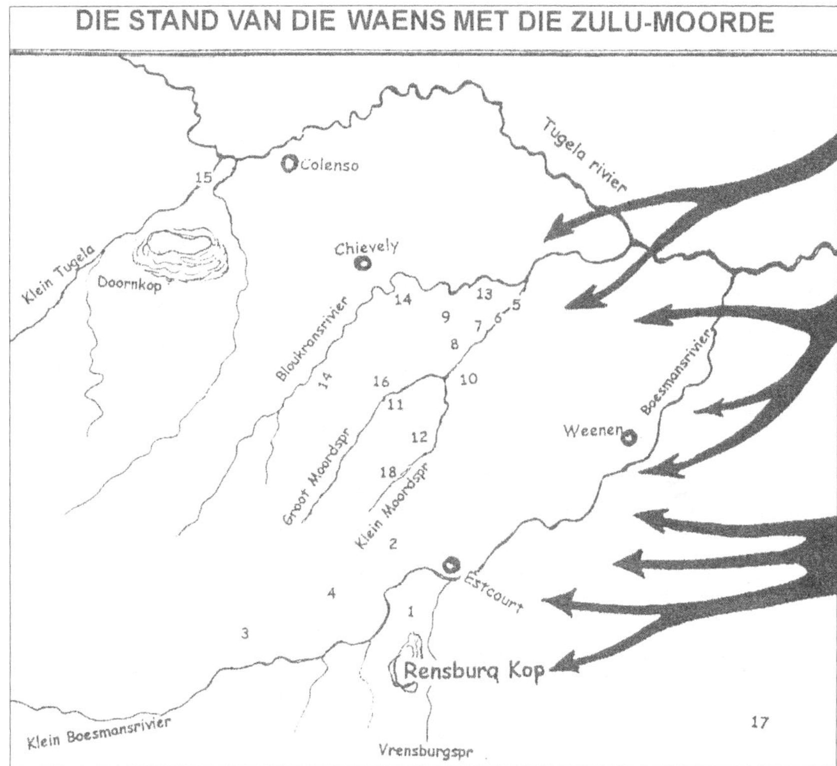

Position of wagons at the Bloukrans & Boesman Rivier Massacre 1) Willem Cornelis J. van Rensburg, Willem Sterrenberg Pretorius, Harmse & Loggerenberg 2) Gerrit Barends 3) Maritz, Rudolph & Jacobus Potgieter 4) Sarel Cilliers 5) Christiaan de Beer 6) Barend Liebenberg 7) Bezuidenhout, Roelof Botha & Adriaan Rossouw 8) Botha, Bresler, Smit & Gert Viljoen 9) Johan Hendrik Breytenbach 10) Engelbrecht & Greyling 11) J. Hattingh, Joubert & Van der Merwe 12) Kloppers & Steenkamp 13) Joseph van Dayk & son 14) Scheepers & Hans Roos (Roets), Petrus van Vuuren, Karel Geer, Willem Jacobs & Prinsloo 15) De Klerk 16) Abraham Bothma 17) Malan, Swart & Breedt 18) Wife of Izak Jacobus Robberts & children

Viglione, leaped on her horse and galloped from camp to camp shouting out warnings of the Zulu attack. Then, when the battle was over, she tirelessly tended to the wounded and dying and so earned a place of honour in Boer history.[848]

At Maritz's camp, the trekkers formed a laager with their wagons before the Zulu arrived and, when the attack came, young boys also took part in the battle. Even Maritz's ten-year-old son did. "I see no place to hide myself. Give me the pistol and let me shoot too!" he begged his mother, who was still dressed in her nightgown, while carrying ammunition to the men.[849] In light of such courage, one can understand how the Zulu were unable to penetrate this laager.[850]

Cilliers and the five men with him galloped past Maritz's laager to the Barend camp, which was already being attacked by the Zulu. "Have God before your eyes; let not a hair on your head show fear. Follow me," Cilliers shouted to his men as they charged the surprised Zulu from behind.

The warriors scattered, abandoning the wagons, and many drowned as they attempted to swim across the Bushman's River to escape the persistent gunfire from Cilliers's men.[851] By the time Cilliers and his men encountered the next regiment of Zulu warriors attacking wagons, 12 more Voortrekkers had joined the commando. The men rode into battle with guns blazing. Cilliers fired so many times that the barrel of his gun became hot to touch and he was scared that the gunpowder in his weapon would ignite and explode.[852] The Zulu fled over a nearby mountain, their path marked by dead and dying Zulu that had been shot by Cilliers and his men. Cilliers then spotted cattle that had been driven off by the Zulu on a nearby hill and set about recovering them. At the top of the hill, Cilliers and his men saw a group of trekkers fighting the Zulu and joined in the fray. They killed eleven warriors and drove off the others, then tried to herd the cattle back toward the Boer camps.

While doing so, they saw the Van Rensburgs and a group of Boer men protecting the women and children from eight or ten families. They were completely surrounded by the warriors and were low on ammunition.

Earlier, 18-year-old Marthinus Oosthuizen had ridden through the mass of about 1,500 Zulu soldiers to collect gunpowder from Willem Pretorius's wagon two kilometres away. The ammunition he brought back had enabled the besieged trekkers to hold the Zulu at bay[853] until Cilliers and his men arrived to help.

More and more Boers joined Cilliers's party. The Zulu warriors turned to face this new attack as Cilliers and his men charged at the Zulu. With shouts of "*Bulala! Bulala!*" the Zulus charged at the mounted Boers. The Boers fired, then retreated to reload, then charged and fired again. More and more Boers attracted by the sound of gunfire arrived. Gradually the Boers edged closer to the Zulu ranks. The Zulus turned and fled.

Cilliers and his men began to round up the cattle and in so doing came upon a place where many of the Boers had been murdered and lay dead. The sight that met their eyes filled them with horror and revulsion as they gazed on the scene of carnage. Babies lay dead still clasped to the bosoms of their blood-covered mothers. It was too much for Cilliers. He raised his face to the heavens and screamed in agony, "O, my God! Shall the blood of the sucklings be unavenged?"[854]

Near the Great Moordspruit on a small koppie, the Bothma family and their friends repeatedly fired into the massed ranks of warriors and killed a number of Zulu. However, they could not hold them off for long: the Zulu chased their cattle up the hill and used the livestock as shields. When they were close enough to the Boers, they leaped out from behind the cattle and engaged the

Voortrekkers in bloody hand-to-hand combat. One by one, the Bothmas and their friends were killed.

That afternoon, the Zulu army finally ceased their attack on the trekkers and retreated, taking thousands of cattle, sheep and goats with them. The surviving Voortrekkers transformed their wagons and tents into emergency hospitals to care for the wounded and many men, women and children staggered about aimlessly, in shock. A number had lost the power of speech and some would never regain it.

The Voortrekker camps had been demolished: many of the wagons were smouldering wood and steel husks or lay on their sides, their canopies torn and their floorboards dripping with blood. The grass around the wagons was blackened and slimy with the trekkers' blood and feathers from ripped cushions and pillows floated idly in the breeze. Among the piles of dead, the odd survivor was found. For instance, Johanna van der Merwe and Margaretha Prinsloo had more than 20 stab wounds apiece but lived. Sadly, Elizabeth Johanna Rossouw was found alive but died later in the day. She had been stabbed 18 times.[855]

Survivors of the attack wept as they stumbled over broken crockery and household items, looking for loved ones. They sought out friends, huddling together, drawing comfort from each other. They picked through the smashed and burned wagons to collect their stained bed linen, broken furniture and slashed cushions which spewed out trails of delicate white feathers from the slashes of the Zulu assegais among scattered items of clothing, broken dolls and babies' cribs in the bloodstained grass, like clues in a macabre treasure hunt.

One of the survivors, Mrs Steenkamp, described the scene in her diary: "Oh! Dreadful, dreadful night! Wherein so much martyred blood was shed … Oh! it was unbearable for flesh and blood to behold that the frightful spectacle the following morning. In one wagon were found fifty dead, and blood flowed from the seam of the tent-sail down to the lowest [part]. Ah! how awful it was to look upon all those dead and wounded. The following day we fled altogether to another encampment at Doornkop, between the Tugela and Bushman's River … The commandant had the dead buried and the wounded attended to. On all sides one saw tears flowing, and heard people weeping by the plundered wagons, painted with blood; tents and beds torn to shreds; pregnant women and little children had to walk for hours together, bearing the signs of their hasty flight. Oh! how weary and fatigued were those women and children, and how terrible it was to see unborn children rent asunder by the murderous kaffirs. When the women came up to us they fell upon their knees and thanked God for their deliverance out of the hands of the cruel tyrant."[856]

For the next few days, wagons from outlying sites trundled into the camps of Retief and Maritz carrying bloodied and wounded survivors and possessions they had managed to salvage. As the wagons drew to a halt, men and women surrounded them to help unload and comfort the wounded, who were tenderly carried or escorted to a central place to receive medical treatment. After the wounded came the corpses, many of them babies still wrapped in the blood-soaked blankets they had been lying in when stabbed in their cribs. Their lifeless bodies were solemnly passed through the coarse hands of the Voortrekker men. Cries to God, like thin useless reeds, and heartfelt curses and oaths at Dingane and the Zulus came from the mouths of the distraught men and women as they looked at the devastation wrought by the Zulus

The hundreds of bodies were then placed side by side on the ground and covered with thorn bushes to protect them from animals and vultures. There were only a few coffins and when these ran out, Maritz ordered that five to six bodies be bundled together and wrapped in blankets. Over the next ten days, these sad bundles were buried in two mass graves approximately seven square metres each. Amidst the sadness and tragedy the wife of Jacobus de Wet gave birth to a baby.

The Voortrekkers dragged over 500 bodies of the Zulu warriors in the vicinity of the camps away from the wagons using ropes and chains.[857]

The party of men who had been away hunting in the direction of the Drakensberg at the time of the attack were horrified to see from a distance the plumes of telltale black smoke rising. As they drew close they saw the sky speckled with vultures as they circled above. During the day the vultures and crows feasted on the grisly remains and at night hyenas and jackals fought each other over the scraps.

The Voortrekkers had lost over 600 of their people: 110 men (including the 60 slaughtered at Umgungundlovu with Retief and 50 in the attack), 56 women, 185 children and 250 faithful coloured servants had perished.[858] In total, the Boers had lost one in ten of their people and one in six of their men.[859] The Zulu had plundered over 2,500 cattle and large flocks of sheep and herds of goats.[860] However, the Voortrekkers still had over 1,000 wagons, 40,000 cattle, over 300,000 sheep and 3,000 horses after the attack. Many Voortrekkers who had been wealthy before the attack were now destitute. For example, one of the Bezuidenhouts had lost his whole stock of 7,000 sheep and all of his other belongings, retaining only the shirt and trousers he had been wearing during the Zulu assault.

Reverend Smit hardly slept in the aftermath of the massacre and moved from wagon to wagon and camp to camp administering comfort to the living and praying for the dead and dying. This took its toll on him and he cried in anguish, "Ach God! Ach Lord! How severe, how great are Thy judgements upon us. The groaning of the wounded, and the anxiety and fear of others cry to heaven."[861]

Many children had been orphaned in the attack and an orphanage board was set up. Maritz was appointed chairman of this board and worked tirelessly to encourage families and individuals to adopt the surviving children.[862] (Daniel Bezuidenhout took four orphans into his care.[863]) As most of those killed in the massacre had died without leaving a will behind and their direct descendents had also been killed, Maritz called all of the trekkers together and auctioned off the goods of the murdered trekkers to raise funds for the families and orphans of those killed.[864]

After scouts returned to Maritz to inform him that it was unlikely the Zulu would attack the Boers in the immediate future, Maritz, Cilliers and a commando set off to follow the tracks left by the warriors. Caution had given way to rage. Near the Tugela River, they came upon a large group of Zulu warriors herding cattle and sheep they had stolen from the Boers across the river. The Boers charged them in a surprise attack and many of the Zulu on the riverbank jumped into the river to avoid being shot and were swept away by the swiftly moving waters. Those Zulu who had already made their way to an island with a portion of the sheep dived for cover under the bushes as the Boers fired at them. However, darkness was rapidly approaching and Maritz, with tears of frustration trickling down his cheeks, had no choice but to call his men off and return to camp.

As the days passed and no official word came regarding the fate of Retief and his men, Retief's wife grieved for her husband as she was certain that she would never see him again. On 20 February 1838, the trekkers received a letter from an Englishman from Durban confirming their suspicion that Retief and his men had been killed.[865]

Today, the area where the massacre took place is marked by the town of Weenen, which means 'place of weeping'.

CHAPTER 24

A hero dies and a hero falls

Planned revenge—the locust army—Uys and Potgieter ride out—Uys trapped—Uys dies—Potgieter's men retreat—Modderlaager—Maritz the leader

All of the trekkers feared there would be further attacks as Zulu scouts were often seen in the vicinity. Consequently, the Voortrekkers moved their wagons into laagers at Doornkop or Maritz's camp and Maritz ordered that sentries keep vigil over the camps at night.

The trekkers' food supply was running out as the Zulu had burned their crops and food stores or stolen their food and their dire situation gave rise to many heated arguments as to what they should do. Many wished to return to the colony and the ailing Maritz furiously tried to boost the morale of the trekkers and to encourage them not to give up on their dream of establishing a land of their own.

Although a few families did return to the colony, the majority stayed put, in large part due to the women's stalwart belief that they should not allow the Zulu to drive them off and should avenge the deaths of their people.

Maritz sent several letters to the trekker camps on the eastern side of the Drakensberg Mountains telling them what had happened and appealed to Potgieter and Uys to come to their aid. Soon, Maritz received messages promising that trekkers from areas near the Modder, Riet and Caledon rivers would come to assist them. However, to Maritz's dismay, only eight volunteers arrived—bringing various excuses from their comrades and their very best wishes for the future.

The charismatic Uys set out to assist the beleaguered trekkers as soon as the news of the Zulu attack reached him at Winburg. Naturally, when he arrived at Maritz's camp on 1 March 1838, the trekkers were immensely relieved that a man with his military experience and success had come to help them.[866] Nevertheless, they were on edge and rumour after rumour swept the camps that the Zulu were poised to attack them again.

An expedition of over 100 men was mounted and crossed over the Tugela River in search of the Zulu army, which they believed was already assembled to attack them. On this and other occasions, the Boers did not find any Zulu regiments in the area.

Soon after Uys arrived at Doornkop, the trekkers received a disturbing message from Sekonyela, who had heard of the massacre of Retief and his men at Umgungundlovu and of the Zulu attack on the Voortrekker camps. Believing that the Voortrekkers' resistance was at a low ebb, he demanded the return of the cattle that Retief had taken from him. Naturally, the Voortrekkers worried that they could be attacked by Dingane as well as Sekonyela.[867]

After the initial poor show of assistance from the Voortrekkers east of the Drakensberg Mountains, it was a great comfort when Potgieter and some of his party arrived at Doornkop as well as 100 wagons under Karel Landman and Bernhard Rudolph.

On 18 March 1838, the patrol Maritz had sent to Durban to determine what had happened to Retief and his men returned to Doornkop. The patrol leaders, Jan Gerrit Bantjies and Jan Hammes, were accompanied by three Englishmen and relayed to Maritz that the British settlers in the colony would attack Dingane if he launched another assault on the trekkers. Moreover, the British settlers would be assisted by 1,200 Zulu men who had turned against Dingane.

Soon after receiving this report, Maritz moved all of the wagons to Doornkop and established two major laagers there that were named Veglaer (or Vechtlaager) and two more Englishmen, Stubbs and Mr Blanckenberg, from Port Natal arrived to offer their support to the Voortrekkers.

Maritz had by this stage taken over Retief's role as leader of the trekkers and appointed De Lange as *vegkommandant* and Rudolph, Greyling and Potgieter as lieutenants. The Voortrekkers decided to attack Dingane and to avenge the killings of Retief and his men and of their people.

On 17 March 1838, a force of 30 Europeans and 1,500 Zulu left Durban to attack Dingane at Umgungundlovu. This army was under the command of John Cane, who wore an old straw hat with an ostrich feather stuck into the band and carried an elephant gun covered in panther skin during their march to Dingane's stronghold. The men carried two banners—one bearing the name of the commando, namely *iziNkumbi* (locusts) and the other their motto, 'For justice we fight'.

On the way to Umgungundlovu, they attacked Zulu settlements and razed them to the ground. In the process, they slaughtered hundreds of men and captured over 500 women and children. When they arrived at a small village, the 7,000 Zulu inhabitants fled and Cane and his men quickly rounded up all of the cattle and began to divide up the booty. Soon, arguments broke out about how the booty should be shared and Cane's supporters engaged in a stick fight with Henry Ogle's supporters.[868] It was patently clear that the factions within the commando made continuing with the attack on Dingane pointless and the men thus returned to Durban. Fortunately, this band of bounty hunters had only lost two men: one had died of a snakebite and the other had been shot dead by Cane for pilfering from his comrades.[869] However, the men had been warned by a Zulu spy they had caught that they and the Boers would soon be crushed by Dingane.[870]

In Doornkop, rival Voortrekkers soon stirred up old resentments and disagreement arose as to who should lead the force that would attack Dingane. Maritz wished to be the commander-in-chief of the army, despite his failing health, and Potgieter and Uys refused to serve under him. They also would not serve under each other. Consequently, a vote was taken on 28 March 1838 to decide who would lead the Boer army against Dingane. At this meeting, Uys was appointed commander-in-chief.[871] However, he would have to consult with the other officers who had been appointed, including the prickly Potgieter.

Uys then appointed Lucas Meyer as his deputy, after Peter Erasmus declined the position[872] and it was decided that the trekkers would leave on 5 April 1838 to attack Dingane. Fortunately, De Lange had managed to persuade the British settlers in Durban to assist the Boer army when it attacked Dingane.

It was decided that the army would not travel with wagons, as Uys and Potgieter felt that the wagons would slow them down and, as they argued, they had not used wagons in the successful assault on Mzilikazi and the Matabele. Although Maritz argued that the laager formation had been hugely effective in defending the Voortrekkers against the Zulu, he was overruled as Uys and Potgieter rallied more support for leaving the wagons behind.

The force of 347 men left the camps in two divisions on 5 and 6 April 1838: Uys led 147 men, including his 12-year-old son Dirkie and Cilliers, while Potgieter commanded 200 men.[873] After the commando crossed the Buffalo River on the morning of 11 April 1838, the men saw the vanguard of the Zulu army ahead of them and hastened to follow them. Little did they know that the Zulu were deliberately luring them deeper and deeper into Zululand, where the main body of the Zulu army waited for the Boers at the Ital Berg or Italeni, not far from Umgungundlovu.

The Zulu army numbered several thousand and was divided into three sections by the experienced and respected commander, Nzobo, namely: the *umKhulutshane* and *iziGulutshane* regiments and a regiment comprising small bands of *amabutho*.[874]

After following a group of Zulu herding cattle through a ravine, the Boers found themselves in a wide valley bordered by low ridges on their left and a steep hill on the right. The floor of the valley was criss-crossed by dongas and ravines. On the sides of the valley were 7,000 Zulu warriors in full battle dress: on the Boers' left, in front of a low slope, were 3,000 *Isihlangu Mnyama* warriors and on their right, against a steep hill, were 4,000 *Isihlangu Mhlope* warriors. Unbeknown to the Boers, a further Zulu regiment was hidden in the numerous ravines and dongas and, as they moved into the valley, their escape route was closed off by even more Zulu warriors.

After the Boers threaded their way through the narrow defile, they saw one division of the Zulu army in front of them on the plain and one to their left, by the steep hill. Uys and Potgieter drew their horses together and hurriedly conferred as to how they should proceed. They could not reach consensus on what course of action would be best and eventually agreed that Uys's men would attack the Zulu on the steep slope and Potgieter's men would attack the Zulu on the plain but did not discuss any contingency plans. In effect, the Boer divisions would be back to back and would not be able to observe or aid the other group if difficulties arose.

On the slope, 3,000 Zulu sat on their haunches on their shields and watched Uys's men rapidly ascend the hill and Potgieter's men moving cautiously across the plain toward the main body of the Zulu army as they inspected every donga and gulley for concealed warriors. When Potgieter and his men were 180 metres from the Zulu, he waved a white cloth to signal that the Boers should open fire.

On the hill, Uys instructed his men to dismount 45 metres from the enemy frontline and to charge the Zulu on foot with guns blazing. The Zulu on the hill were momentarily taken aback when Uys's men dismounted and launched a lethal first volley of gunfire.

"Stay where you are and aim straight," Uys shouted to his men as the Zulu rallied and rushed at them. "Give them the slugs!" he yelled. (The slugs were bags containing 12 or 14 shots of lead that would explode in all directions when fired; the women at Doornkop had carefully sewn these bags in previous weeks.)

Nzobo was hit by a slug from Pieter Nel's gun when he turned to scream encouragement to his warriors and instantly died. Incensed by the death of their commander, the Zulu charged the Boers shouting "*Bulala ibhule!*" (kill the Boers). After the third volley felled numerous Zulu, the warriors fled uphill. The Boers immediately gave chase, firing as they ran, but found it difficult to navigate the rough terrain and several ravine crossings. Consequently, they began to break up into smaller groups and eventually lost sight of one another.

When Uys saw the Malan brothers chasing a group of Zulu into thick brush, he realized the perilous position they might find themselves in and followed them with 19 other Boers, including Dirkie. They stumbled through a narrow sluit at the foot of the hill at a snail's pace, watched by about 100 Zulu hidden in the long grass bordering the sluit. A shower of assegais suddenly whirred through the air at the Boers and they scrambled to fire at the nearby Zulu warriors. Uys was struck in the back by an assegai, which entered near his kidneys and exited his chest, and stoically pulled the assegai head out. The blood from the wound was so profuse that it poured down the sides of his horse, Welsier. Nevertheless, Uys managed to scoop up a comrade who had fallen off his horse and they rode in tandem away from the Zulu.

The Boers began to retreat when they saw how badly wounded Uys was and two of his men helped him to stay upright on Welsier. While being pursued by the Zulu, Pieter Nel's horse stepped into a rabbit hole and bucked him off before bolting away. His brother, Willem, chased after the runaway horse, grabbed its reins and pulled it alongside his horse. Pieter had not been hurt in the fall and urged Willem to bring his horse to him so that he could re-enter the battle.

"Look out, Piet! Behind you; he's going to throw at you," Koos Moolman cried. His warning was too late: an assegai fatally pierced Piet between the shoulder blades.

Willem urged his horse to gallop away from the approaching Zulu and was devastated to see a crowd of Zulu repeatedly plunging their assegais into his brother's body.

Uys was by now bleeding from the nose and mouth and encouraged the men to leave him behind. "Men, I am badly wounded. Save yourselves," he begged them. They ignored his request and instead gave him brandy and water to revive him.

Uys seemed to be faring better. However, the Boers had only ridden about 500 metres when Uys fainted and fell from his horse. Again, his men made him sip brandy and water and managed to bring him around. The two Malan men had been holding the Zulu at bay so that Uys could be taken to safety but were eventually killed by the Zulu warriors. When Uys slipped from his saddle for a third time, he again pleaded to be left behind and told Karel Landman that he should assume command.[875]

After the fleeing Boers crossed a spruit, some chose the path to the left of a koppie while those riding with Uys chose the path to the right. They soon realized that they had made a mistake: they would not be able to rejoin forces on the other side of the koppie as a ridge separated the two paths.

Those who had taken the left path soon encountered a regiment of Zulu and rode directly at the warriors, scattering them as they fired from the saddle. They then dismounted and engaged in hand-to-hand fighting as they attempted to break through the ring of Zulu surrounding them. During the ensuing battle, three Boers were killed.

The Boers who had taken the right path struggled to keep Uys in the saddle and when he slipped off Welsier for the fourth time, Moolman helped the Boer leader back on his horse.

"Here I must die," Uys gasped, looking back at the Zulu closing in on his men. "You cannot get me to go any farther; there is no use in trying to do so. Save yourselves, but fight like brave fellows to the last and hold God before your eyes," he added. "Please look after my family."

The men knew that Uys was slowing them down and that the Zulu were gaining on them. With great reluctance, they left Uys behind. Dirkie turned and looked back and saw the fair hair of his father as he lay on the ground, raising his head for a farewell look at his comrades. It was too much for the boy. He turned his horse to return to his father's side. Hands grabbed at him as the men tried to prevent him from certain death. He shook them off, shouting, "I want to be with my father." As he rode back to his father, he shot two Zulu dead. He jumped off his horse and knelt at his father's side, firing as the Zulu surged toward him before he and his father perished in a hail of assegais.[876, 877]

Meanwhile, Potgieter's men had begun to ascend the hill. However, when they were halfway up it, Potgieter ordered his men to return to the valley, where they became restless and agitated as they waited for Potgieter to fill them in on his plan of attack.

Soon, a lone horseman from Uys's division galloped toward them. "Help us, we are in trouble!" Gert Rudolf shouted.

Although some of the men wanted to go to the aid of the Uys commando, Potgieter would not allow them to do so. Nevertheless, 18 men decided to ignore Potgieter's instruction. They rode up the hill and each man fired between ten and 12 shots at the mass of Zulu on the summit. Instead of causing the ranks of Zulu to break, their small show of force instead spurred the Zulu to charge them and they wheeled their horses around and galloped back to the main body of Potgieter's men, which in turn galloped away from the encroaching Zulu.

While the Voortrekkers fled, Joseph Kruger rode up to the enemy alone. When he was a few metres away from the screaming Zulu warriors, he dismounted, knelt on one knee, took aim and calmly fired at one of the Zulu. He then leaped back onto his horse to make his retreat but was bucked off. He immediately started running from the advancing and furious Zulu. Hermanus Potgieter shouted that Kruger should grab his horse's tail but, as he did so, an assegai struck the rump of the horse and it kicked Kruger in the stomach. He collapsed and was stampeded by the Zulu within seconds. They also smashed his skull with their *indukas* and slashed his body with their assegais for good measure.[878]

The third division of Zulu soon joined those pursuing Potgieter's men, who were by now hopelessly outnumbered and outmanoeuvred. After Potgieter's commando fell back over the Umhlatuzi Spruit, they found that the Zulu were blocking their path and they urged their horses over the Ital Berg, stopping occasionally to fire at the approaching horde of warriors. Realizing that Potgieter and his men looked set to escape, one regiment of warriors gave up the chase and stormed off toward the beleaguered Uys commando.[879] Koos Potgieter and some of the men in Uys's commando blasted a path through the wall of Zulu warriors and rushed in the direction of their packhorses, which were loaded with reserve supplies of ammunition and food.

They had left several trekkers to tend to the approximately 60 horses in their absence but discovered that the men had fled and that the Zulu had seized the horses and supplies. Koos and his men realized that they would not be able to recover their animals and concentrated on saving their own skins.

Next to the Umhlatuzi Spruit, the Zulu surrounded the men in the Uys commando and tried to pull them off their horses, all the while thrusting their assegais at the Voortrekkers, who could not fire their *Sannas* without risking harm to themselves. (Uys's brother, who was known as 'Swart Dirk' Uys, blew off his thumb when his *Sanna* exploded in his hand.) Consequently, they used them as clubs to smash the heads and arms of the Zulu as they grabbed at their stirrups and bridles and only occasionally managed to get a successful shot off, when the Zulu momentarily stepped away from the horses.

The Boers in the Uys commando managed to reach the eastern slope of the Ital Berg, where the summit was covered with the corpses of Zulu warriors that Potgieter's men had shot earlier. The two commandos then united and crossed the Buffalo River. The main body of the Zulu army did not attempt to follow them. However, two hours later, the Boers saw that 12 Zulu were following them on horseback. The group slowed its pace and six trekkers doubled back and ambushed these Zulu, killing more than half of them. One of the deceased was an *induna* and was riding Piet Retief's horse.

The men rode through the night back to Doornkop and arrived at the camp in groups of three and four. They slumped in their saddles from exhaustion and grief.[880]

They had lost ten of their men, including their commander and leader as well as his son, Dirkie.[881] In contrast, the Zulu had lost between 500 and 1,000 men. Significantly, Potgieter lost his reputation as a great military leader and his commando became known as the '*Vlugkommando*' (flight commando).

Compounding the gloomy atmosphere at Doornkop was the incessant rain in subsequent weeks. The ground soon squelched underfoot and the Voortrekkers' clothes and blankets were permanently damp. Hail sometimes lashed their tents so fiercely that they were shredded and as there was no dry firewood, the Voortrekkers were forced to burn the yokes and other parts of their wagons to enable them to cook. Moreover, medicines were woefully short at Doornkop and measles and flu swept the laagers, killing many children. The laagers at Doornkop were aptly nicknamed Modderlaager (mud laager).

The losses from the latest battle with the Zulu caused many to despair and make plans to leave for the colony. However, many widows such as Mietjie Kruger demanded that their husbands' deaths be avenged and shamed many men at a meeting when she and other women stated that they would avenge the killing of their people and fight the Zulu if the men were too cowardly to do so.[882] Many were openly critical that Potgieter and his men had failed to go to the aid of Uys and those in his commando and questioned why Potgieter had not followed Uys's commando in the first place. When he responded that he had realized the Zulu had ambushed Uys and his men, he invited further criticism. Many could not forgive him for not at least attempting to aid the men in Uys's commando as they were attacked.[883] Potgieter vehemently argued that the trekkers could never defeat the Zulu, citing that there were so many of them that they could easily cover all the hills and the valleys in the vicinity and still have warriors to spare.[884] To Potgieter's fury and disgust, most of the trekkers became more and more hostile toward him as the days passed. As such, he encouraged those still loyal to him to return to Transoranje with him and told anyone who would listen that he and his followers should have stayed there instead of coming to assist the others after the massacre by the Zulu. Potgieter and 160 families soon left Doornkop[885, 886] to cross the Drakensberg Mountains and leave Natal. Maritz was now completely unopposed as the Voortrekker leader.[887]

CHAPTER 25

Port Natal burns

Grand army of Natal—Zulu crush the Grand Army—arrival of Trichardt in Delgoa Bay—Zulu attack on Durban—Comet

A few days after the crushed Voortrekkers returned to Doornkop, the Grand Army of Natal prepared to leave Durban to attack the Zulu. The army would be led by John Cane and Robert Biggar and, given the infighting with Ogle and his followers on the *iziNkumbi* commando's earlier expedition to attack Dingane, they were excluded from it. Fifteen Englishmen, 20 Hottentots and between 800 and 1,500 Zulu set off with Cane and Biggar from Durban. Four days after crossing the Umvoti River, the ragtag army ascended a hill and saw about 150 Zulu resting around their campfires in the distance. Cane and Biggar sent armed spies on a reconnaissance mission. However, the scouts took it upon themselves to fire at the Zulu who fled, leaving their belongings behind. The commando gave chase and when the men arrived at the Tugela River that evening, they set up camp there for the night.

The next morning, on 17 April 1838, after crossing the river, they spotted the Zulu and prepared to attack. While surrounding a kraal called Ndondakusuk, the *induna* in charge of it watched them from his hiding place and did nothing to stop them from burning it to the ground or from slaughtering his people. If the men had not been flushed with the success of their first victory, they might have heeded the words of one of their victims before he died. "You can kill me now, but the great elephant is coming and will trample you underfoot," he smirked.

The Grand Army of Natal soon had to contend with the superb tactical planning of the commander of the Zulu army, namely Dingane's half-brother Mphande, and generals Nongalaza kaNondela and Madlebe kaMgedeza. In addition, many of the warriors were hungry to prove themselves on the battlefield, in particular those from the *Njandune* regiment who were in disgrace because they had recently lost their 'colonel' in battle. Dingane had ordered the members of the regiment to be publicly thrashed by boys to humiliate them. Now they had the opportunity to redeem themselves. Like wild dogs straining at the leash, they were eager to prove their valour on the battlefield.

The Zulu army used the 'horns of the beast' tactic and moved south in two columns, effectively cutting Cane and Biggar's forces off from the Tugela River and surrounding the stranded men. The combined left and right horns comprised over 7,000 Zulu warriors. It is little wonder then that some of the Zulu that accompanied the army from Durban ran to the musket-bearing Englishmen for protection and tore off the white calico they were wearing to distinguish them from the enemy Zulu.

During the furious battle that ensued, the Zulu attacked in three waves. Each time, they were driven back by the Grand Army of Natal but with heavy losses on both sides. "Look to the north! There are more savages coming!" one of the men shouted.

Biggar's heart sank when he saw the bulk of the Zulu army approaching and he immediately ordered his forces to split into two divisions in the hope that they would be able to hold off the new arrivals. However, the Zulu warriors already on the scene moved between the two divisions, thereby isolating and weakening them.

When one of these divisions attempted to flee to the Tugela River, the men were hotly pursued by the Zulu and many were cut down as they ran. Tellingly, more of Cane and Biggar's men were killed while retreating than while fighting. The few that managed to escape the massacre hid in the bushes next to the Umhlali River. The other division was soon surrounded and, although the men in it fought bravely, they were killed one by one. Cane was stabbed through the chest and shoulders and when one of the Zulu fighting in his army tried to assist him from his horse, he shot the man, despite the monumental effort it took to raise his head, let alone his gun. He died shortly after this and slipped off his horse.

Nearby, Stubbs fell off his horse and, looking up at the young warrior who had stabbed him, he gasped with his last breath, "Am I to be killed by a boy like you?"

Biggar was also killed during the battle and, overall, the Grand Army of Natal lost 530 men, including 13 of the 17 Englishmen.[888] Richard 'Dick' King was one of the only four Englishmen to survive.

Although the bodies of Zulu men littered the battlefield, the Zulu army had only been marginally reduced in the battle with Cane and Biggar's army and swept south with a view to obliterating the settlement of Durban.

Some 500 kilometres northeast of this battlefield, the 57 members of the Trichardt trek finally arrived at Delagoa Bay in the afternoon of 13 April 1838.[889] During their five-month journey of 400 kilometres, their herds of cattle and sheep had been decimated by sickness, theft, crocodiles and lion. Moreover, many in the group had malaria and while some staggered along, others were carried on sickbeds toward the settlement. As they approached the fort of *José António da*

Silveira, the trekkers fired their *Sannas* in salute, which caused great alarm among the Portuguese there, who thought they were under attack. Unsurprisingly, the welcome received by the trekkers was somewhat cool.

Da Silveira, the acting governor of the fort, knew that Trichardt's party would come to the settlement but did not inform Antonio Gamitto, who relieved him. As such, the arrival of the trekkers was a surprise to Gamitto, who questioned their motives for coming to Delagoa Bay.[890] He interrogated Trichardt and asked why he and his followers had fled the colony. Trichardt's plausible explanation—that the colony was under permanent threat of attack by the Xhosa and Zulu; that the government had freed the slaves and the Boers were being forced to serve in the army[891]—did nothing to allay Gamitto's fear that the arrival of the first contingent of Boers threatened the Portuguese occupation of the East Coast and he demanded that they surrender their weapons to him.

Trichardt and his men were devastated by the manner in which they were being treated. While Trichardt felt that they should perhaps leave the fort, his son, Carolus, wept with rage and frustration. Nevertheless, Trichardt ordered his party to hand over their weapons.[892] Within a few days, the Portuguese settlers warmed to the Voortrekkers, particularly when they learned what they had endured before and during their journey to Delagoa Bay.

The Voortrekkers' trials were not over: on their fourth day in the settlement, five Voortrekkers succumbed to malaria and 20 of the group would die in subsequent weeks, including Trichardt's wife, Martha. Overwhelmed with grief, Trichardt sent Carolus north to see if he could find a suitable place for the trekkers to settle. Within ten weeks of Martha's death, Trichardt died, unaware of Carolus's travels 560 kilometres into the interior and up to present-day Harare, by land and sea. Carolus also visited Zanzibar, Abyssinia (Ethiopia) and Madagascar.[893]

On 17 April 1838, the little settlement of Durban was rocked by the news that the Grand Army of Natal had been annihilated by the Zulu. One of the Zulu allies had run 140 kilometres from the battlefield and breathlessly blurted out a description of the battle and killings, spurring mass hysteria among the Zulu women at the settlement.

One of them ran around like a headless chicken with her hands clasped behind her head, crying "*Buya bawa! Buya bawa!*" (Come back father! Come back father!) and the few Englishwomen at the settlement joined in the shrieking and sobbing, which could be heard two kilometres from the village.[894]

That night, Reverend Owen visited Captain Haddon, the skipper of a small trading vessel called the *Comet* to discuss the defeat of the Grand Army of Natal and the likelihood that Dingane would launch an attack on Durban. The men agreed that should the Zulu army be spotted heading toward the village, two cannon shots would be fired from the *Comet* to warn the residents of Durban of its approach and the people would be allowed to shelter onboard.

In mid-April 1838, Maritz sent several men on a four-day journey to Durban to request provisions for the beleaguered Voortrekkers. The deputation was led by De Lange, William Cowie, Gert Viljoen, Jacobus Uys and Jan Joubert[895] and they delivered the tragic news to the settlement of the Boers' recent defeat by the Zulu army and the loss of Piet Uys and many other men. Nevertheless, they assured the British that they would send 200 Boers to help defend Durban if the Zulu were to attack the settlement.[896]

On 23 April 1838, the night fires of the Zulu army were seen 12 kilometres away, on the banks of the Umgeni River, and the *Comet* fired its cannon to warn the British inhabitants (18 men, 14 women and several children[897]) of the imminent danger. Together with the visiting Boers,[898] they scurried down to the bay and rowed out to the *Comet*. The Zulu refugees hid in the nearby bushes.

On the morning of 24 April 1838, the small group of British, including missionaries Owen, Lindley, Grout, Champion and Gardiner as well as Wood Jr and his mother, huddled onboard the *Comet* as they watched the Zulu army amassing on the hill where the Berea mission station stood.

The following morning, a group rowed to shore as they wanted to see what the Zulu were doing in the settlement. However, they were observed by one of the Zulu captains while still in the bay. He yelled that he wanted to talk to Mr Ogle, who promptly stood up in the boat and, perhaps emboldened by the expanse of water between them, bellowed, "You want me?"

When the captain shouted, "Yes", Ogle retorted, "Then you shan't get me."

"Who are you?" the captain shouted, pointing at Wood Jr.

"Do you not know who I am? After I served the king for so long?" the boy shouted, standing up.

"Come here, I want to speak with you," the captain replied.

"I am not a fool," Wood Jr answered, before sitting down and assisting the group to row back to the *Comet*.

For nine days, those aboard the ship watched helplessly as the Zulu set fire to the buildings and stole or destroyed the settlers' belongings before returning to Umgungundlovu. When the refugees on the *Comet* finally came ashore, they discovered that Dingane's warriors had shot many of the Zulu men who had been friendly toward them. The Zulu women who had been caught had been placed in an enclosure, where they had been wrapped in grass mats with their hands tied behind them and then set on fire. The settlers' Zulu allies had attempted to resist the attackers. One of Dingane's warriors killed by the friendly Zulu was found lying on the ground, wearing Mrs Wood's dress and stockings. Containers of salt, sugar, tea, rice and flour had been emptied onto the floors and pianos, chairs, tables, beds, cupboards and crockery had been smashed. Even Ogle's treasured bottles of French brandy had been poured onto the ground[899] and all that remained of the settlers' homes were walls. In addition, their livestock and poultry had been slaughtered, as had their dogs and cats.

At Doornkop, the Voortrekkers anxiously awaited the return of the delegation that had been sent to Durban. Finally, De Lange and his companions rode into the camp on 3 May 1838 and relayed how they had sought refuge aboard the *Comet* during the Zulu rampage at Durban. He also described the defeat of the Grand Army of Natal by the Zulu and how Garnett had encouraged Dingane to kill Retief and his men by describing the Boers as runaways from the colony who deserved the same punishment as would be meted out to anyone who deserted the king, namely death.

There was a loud murmur of anger from the Voortrekkers when they heard about Garnett's role in the killing of Retief's party and when de Lange elaborated that Garnett, Stubbs and Blanckenberg had described the Boers as "bad people" to Dingane, they were incensed.[900] They surely must have reflected on Potgieter's parting words: "Behind Dingane there, sits the English!"[901]

Naturally, they were pleased to hear that the three Englishmen had abandoned their farms and possessions to sail to Delagoa Bay to escape the Zulu attack on Durban.

Reverend Smit's diary aptly records the bitterness felt toward Garnett, Stubbs and Blanckenberg: "The white English chiefs and Blanckenberg, the degenerate Cape colonist, who as tools have helped to bring about the death of His Excellency Piet Retief and his 60 men, have obtained their reward already in that they have been killed in this treacherous war against Dingane. Our God has caused them to fall into their own snares and nets, into the pit of death which they had dug for us."

After the *Comet* set sail for Delagoa Bay on 11 May 1838, only a handful of British settlers remained at Durban. While Ogle, Daniel Toohey, Adam King, Dunn and his wife and Alexander Biggar, who had lost his wife, two sons, daughter and son-in-law, stayed behind, the rest set off for what they hoped would be greener pastures, including Owen.[902]

CHAPTER 26

"We have seen the Promised Land but only one of us was chosen to live in it"

Natal population grows—Stockenström investigated—Landman annexes Durban—Napier wishes to occupy Durban—plans to avenge Retiefs death—attack on Gatsrand—attempts to curtail the Boers—death of Maritz

Once the Voortrekkers felt that the immediate threat of another attack by the Zulu was over, many left the two main laagers at Doornkop and established themselves elsewhere. Maritz and his followers began to farm near the Little Tugela River while Koos Potgieter took over the leadership of about 500 wagons, which settled near a branch of the Modder River. The Malans were based at Moordspruit, the Rensburgs were at 'Saai Laager' (which means sowing laager) on the Bushman's River (near modern-day Escourt) and other groups of trekker wagons were near Congella and the Umgeni and Umlaas rivers.

Toward the end of 1838, the Boer population in Natal would explode: it is estimated that there were over 1,000 wagons, 640 men and 3,000 women and children in the region.[903]

Morale was low among the trekkers in Natal: many had been killed or had lost everything in the Zulu attack, good grazing was in short supply, the laagers were unsanitary, ammunition was perilously low, only a few horses were fit enough to go out on commando, food was being rationed and appeals for assistance from fellow Voortrekkers not yet in Natal had met with a poor response.[904]

Maritz wrote many letters to friends and acquaintances in the colony about the misfortunes the Voortrekkers had endured and sent one of his people to Graaff-Reinet to invite Andries Pretorius to come to Natal to take over the leadership of the Voortrekkers and to lead another punitive commando against Dingane with a view to finally defeating him.[905]

In the colony, stories about the sorry plight of the Voortrekkers spread like wildfire and the colonists established a committee to raise funds and provide material aid to the Voortrekkers. Of course, it took the committee a long time to amass contributions, which came from all sectors of the community. D'Urban had lost the fight with Glenelg regarding compensation for the settlers and Boers on the frontier who had suffered losses at the hands of the Xhosa, largely due to the damning testimony about them given by Stockenström Jr and the missionaries to the Select Committee on Aborigines in London. While d'Urban viewed the Boers who had left the colony as brave, industrious and religious people who were important to the welfare and the economy of the colony, Glenelg considered them to be dishonest bullies who attacked the "feeble and defenceless".[906]

Glenelg had effectively fired d'Urban as the governor of the colony and had replaced him with Major General George Thomas Napier on 22 January 1838. Despite this, d'Urban remained in the Cape. (The British government would later appoint him a Knight Grand Cross of the Order of the Bath in 1840.[907]) Glenelg also saw to it that Stockenström Jr was removed as lieutenant governor of the Eastern Province. While visiting the frontier on 19 December 1837, Glenelg had headed a trial in which Stockenström Jr was investigated for killing a Xhosa man five years earlier. The court had declared that Stockenström Jr had killed the man in an act of war and had effectively let him off the hook on a charge of murder. However, Stockenström Jr felt that the charge had been maliciously instituted by Campbell and Van Ryneveld and recognized his unpopularity with the settlers and farmers. As such, he decided to return to England to resign and was succeeded by Colonel John Hare.

Although Andries Pretorius would ultimately succeed Maritz, the Voortrekker leader was so ill that he appointed Karel Landman as chief commandant. He attempted to assist Landman with some duties, but it was clear that he was becoming progressively sicker.

Shortly after this, Maritz, Landman and more than 150 men in 26 wagons squelched their way across waterlogged earth and crossed swollen rivers on their journey to Durban. They intended to bring back the few Boers who had not returned with De Lange and his companions and any British settlers who wished to join the Boers.[908]

When they returned on 21 May 1838, they brought three wagons of provisions with them and a ten-pound cannon. Maritz returned sicker than ever. The supplies, which were divided among the the Voortrekkers, included maize, vegetables, rice, gunpowder and alcohol. However, as Reverend Smit noted, only one Voortrekker disgraced himself by drinking to excess but did not cause problems in the camp as he had "fallen asleep".[909]

On 16 May 1838, Landman sent a letter to the few remaining residents of Durban in which he declared that he had taken possession of Durban and the surrounding areas "in the name of the United Camp".[910]

In May 1838, two visitors from the colony arrived at Maritz's camp: Gideon Joubert, a wealthy and successful farmer from the Colesberg district, and Jacobus

Nicolaas Boshoff, a government employee in Graaff-Reinet and the first clerk to the civil commissioner of Graaff-Reinet. The two men brought the good wishes of the people of Colesberg as well as a small amount of ammunition and 330 rix-dollars to assist the Voortrekkers.

Boshoff had come to see whether he and his family should join the Voortrekkers, while Joubert wanted to persuade the Boers to return to the colony. He was fighting a losing battle, however. The Boers' hearts had hardened against the British as a result of the role Blanckenberg, Garnett and Stubbs had played in colluding with Dingane to have them killed and they would not even contemplate submitting to British rule again.

Boshoff remained with the trekkers and rapidly earned their respect. He chaired a number of meetings at which the Voortrekkers discussed their future and, finally, on 12 June 1838, was unanimously elected as president of the Council of Representation of the People, which comprised 24 members and governed the Voortrekkers.[911]

After taking office, Napier wrote to Glenelg to request that compensation be paid to the farmers on the frontier due to the attacks by the Xhosa. He explained clearly why the Voortrekkers had been unhappy in the colony and highlighted some of the major causes for their departure, namely the severe losses experienced during the frontier wars and their opposition to the treaty system with the Xhosa chiefs; the need for better grazing due to the two-year drought in the area; their desire to maintain their cultural heritage; the lack of compensation received for freed slaves and the difficulty they had had in claiming the money and the fact that many still did not possess the legal title to their farms. Napier also pointed out that the farmers were not to blame for the frontier wars in which they had lost their properties and left their homes and described them as having behaved "gallantly".

Having beaten the drum for the Voortrekkers' cause, he then proposed taking occupation of Port Natal "in order to protect the natives [...] from extermination or slavery by the Boers who are already there and commencing a war with Dingane". He also recommended that the British living there who had attacked Dingane should be punished, as they had "thrown off allegiance to their [British] Sovereign", and warned Glenelg that unless steps were taken to improve the lives of the Boers on the frontier, the number of emigrants trekking beyond the borders of the colony would increase by "an alarming degree".[912]

Glenelg's response to Napier at the beginning of June 1838 was unsympathetic. He stated that Stockenström Jr had informed him of the massacre of the British from Durban and expressed his view that it was not a surprise that the Zulu had retaliated against people they saw as "invaders" and who committed acts of "plunder and aggression". While he would allow troops to be sent to Durban, he stressed that it was not the intention of the British government to occupy the adjacent territory and that the troops would merely protect and offer assistance to those who wished to return to the colony. He made no mention of paying compensation to the Boers.[913]

When Boshoff and Joubert returned to the colony, both expressed their sympathy for the Voortrekkers and all they had been through. Boshoff's letter about the plight of the Voortrekkers, how Dingane killed Retief and his men, the Voortrekkers' retaliatory attack on the Zulu and the subsequent massacre of the Voortrekkers was published in the *Grahamstown Journal* and resulted in Stockenström Jr firing him as a government employee. He then returned to Natal with his family to join the Voortrekkers.[914]

Joubert also attempted to rally support for the Voortrekkers and a report of his views appeared in *The Mediator* shortly after he returned to Colesberg. The article stated that there were at least 100 families in need of food and clothing and that some children were walking about naked as they had no clothes.[915]

On 25 May 1838, Maritz called a meeting with the trekkers, who agreed that they should avenge the deaths of those in Retief's party and of the Voortrekkers at Weenen. It was decided that a force of 350 men would attack the Zulu army at Umgungundlovu and would take three cannon and 50 wagons on the commando.

When it became clear that the Boers in the colony would not be able to join the trekkers in the attack on Dingane due to the shortage of available horses in the colony, the trekkers had no choice but to shelve the planned assault.[916]

Bad luck continued to dog the Voortrekkers. For instance, Nicolaas Vermaak's wagon was blown up after the gunpowder in it exploded while two children were playing with it. Sadly, the two children were severely injured and an 18-year-old boy was killed by the force of the explosion.

Two days later, the wagon belonging to the De Bruyn family overturned while they were moving to a new site and Mrs De Bruyn and two of her children were severely injured. A third child was fatally crushed by the wagon.[917]

On account of the rain and muddy conditions at the end of May, some leaders wanted to move their laagers. Families made their way across the raging rivers, sometimes with disastrous consequences. For example, the disselboom of Reverend Smit's wagon broke mid-river and many other wagons also became stuck in the mud and had to be towed out of the river by two spans of oxen. In addition, the wagon of Retief's family capsized and although the men quickly waded through the swirling brown waters and righted the wagon, all of the Retief family's possessions were soaked through.[918]

Jacobus Uys moved to the Bushman's River, as did Stephanus Erasmus, Koos Potgieter, De Lange and Jan du Plessis[919] and Maritz and his people moved to the west bank of the Little Tugela River, where there was plenty of grazing and firewood to be had and they successfully planted crops. Their laager was known as Sooi Laager (sods laager) and, later, as Sooilaer. The Rensburgs remained at Saai Laager, which became known as Saailaer,[920] while Karel Landman and his followers left the laagers to move to Durban.[921] The main laager of 290 wagons was situated on a ridge called Gatsrand and was under the commands of De Lange and Jacobus Potgieter. It boasted an iron cannon that was light enough to be moved if needed and the trekkers dug pits on its southeastern side in order to trap any enemy that crossed the river to attack them.[922]

The wagons in the laagers were all tied together with chains and riempies and any openings were packed with thorn bushes to prevent intruders from entering. The Voortrekkers had also obtained two cannon: the four-pounder, iron *Ou Grietjie* was 490 millimetres long, fired 2.3 kilogram shot[923] and was mounted on the mobile undercarriage of a wagon and *Stelletjie*, a three-pounder, copper, wheel-mounted cannon belonging to Gert Rudolph that was a two metres long and had a barrel with a diameter of 6.35 centimetres.[924]

While Boshoff presided over the Volksraad that administered the Voortrekkers' affairs, Stephanus Maritz was elected landdrost, Stephanus Lombard became commandant of Sooilaer and De Lange was appointed field commandant.[925] Although the provisions from Durban had provided some small relief to the trekkers, they soon ran out, to the point where there wasn't even wine for communion. Consequently, Frans Hattingh, Willem Jurgen Pretorius and Cilliers were sent to the colony at the beginning of August 1838 to try rally support for the Voortrekkers.

Cilliers travelled to the Nuwe Hantam district, Willem Jurgen Pretorius went to Beaufort West and Hattingh travelled to Graaff-Reinet, where he met with Andries Pretorius and received his assurance that he would join the Voortrekkers shortly, along with Pieter Daniel Jacobs, a field commandant from the Beaufort district. Much to their disappointment, the three men only managed to muster a small amount of ammunition and gunpowder from the Boers in the colony.[926]

Three days after Frans Hattingh, Willem Jurgen Pretorius and Cilliers left for the colony, Dingane's army struck again. Soon after night had fallen on 12 August 1838, a Boer sentry called Christoffel Snyman spotted a Zulu scout and fired at him. Subsequently, the trekkers hastily finished digging the ditch around the laager. (Upon completion, it was two metres wide and had a depth equal to that of a tall man.)[927]

At about nine o'clock the next morning, a *smous*, a trader named Butler galloped into Gatsrand shouting that a band of Zulu had robbed two men herding the Voortrekkers' livestock. De Lange and Johann Prinsloo immediately set off with 30 men to find the cattle rustlers.[928, 929]Instead, they found the Zulu army heading toward the laagers, with many warriors riding horses and carrying arms they had seized from the Voortrekkers in earlier battles.

The trekkers galloped back to the laagers and shouted the warning that the Zulu were coming. The women and children huddled together in a hastily constructed shelter made from boards and wagons in the centre of the laager and Reverend Smit comforted them as best he could. "May God give us His Almighty help against these our numerous enemies. May He give us, if we must fight, the victory so that we thank Him. Since we have received so many untrue reports, may God grant that this may also be untrue, and if it be true He has the power to strengthen our hearts and in dying to be merciful to our souls," the reverend prayed.[930]

The men quickly herded the horses into the laager, leaving the cattle and sheep in the veld, and loaded their guns as 10,000 Zulu under General Umhlela advanced on the wagons from the northeast. While 30 of Voortrekker men were near the Drakensberg Mountain tending the cattle, a number were visiting Durban, which meant that there were no more than 150 men at the laagers (and possibly as few as 75).[931]

The Zulu passed Sooilaer and headed toward Gatsrand, killing some of the Voortrekkers' servants tending livestock outside the laagers. Johannes Coenraad Froneman was with these servants and hid in the reeds on the riverbank when the Zulu army approached. However, he was soon spotted by the warriors and stabbed to death. (Those who discovered his body later on were horrified to see that his penis and testicles had been cut off and stuffed into his mouth.)

Some regiments of the Zulu army crossed the river below Gatsrand but the bulk of the army came from the east, then swept around to attack from the west, as this provided the warriors with good cover and lessened their chances of being killed by the Boers' *Sannas* as they crept toward the wagons.[932, 933]

The Boers changed tactics: they would face the Zulu charge from outside the wagons. After a final check on the stock of gunpowder and ammunition inside the laager, they waited for the Zulu to make the first move. A blast from a cow horn signalled the start of the attack as three regiments of Zulu charged, screaming "*Bulala! Bulala amaboele!*" and assembled into the customary 'horns of the beast' formation. Simultaneously, the Zulu launched a fusillade of bullets from their stolen guns from a nearby hill and hundreds of Zulu crept toward the laager on the western side. The Voortrekkers held their fire as the frenzied mass of warriors drew closer, until De Lange fired at the Zulu frontline 50 paces away. After this, the Voortrekkers' guns all belched smoke and flames as they repeatedly shot at the Zulu.

"Shoot at the points of the horns!" De Lange shouted to the men, who immediately followed his order, with great success.

Every time the Zulu attempted to gain entry into the laager, they were driven back and the assegais they hurled over the wagons like javelins failed to injure anyone inside. Seeing that the Zulu appeared to be stymied as to how to proceed and were beginning to retreat, 15 trekkers moved forward to pursue them. They fired and reloaded repeatedly as they chased after the Zulu and a thick, acrid cloud of smoke surrounded the laager. The rattle of the Boers' gunfire was augmented every few minutes by the roars from *Ou Grietjie* and *Stelletjie* as the cannon shots ploughed through the mass of Zulu warriors. The war cries and screams of injured Zulu filled the air and the Voortrekkers' dogs howled piteously whenever the cannon were fired. Every time *Stelletjie* fired, the cannon would recoil so violently that it flipped over and somersaulted backwards and would have to be heaved back into position.[934]

Before long, the Zulu army returned. This time they attacked in single lines. Whenever a warrior was shot, the next man in the line quickly replaced him. It was clear that the Zulu wanted the Voortrekkers to expend all their ammunition and that the cannon killed fewer warriors when this formation was adopted. Nevertheless, the Zulu army retreated again. When it did so, De Lange led 25 men out of the laager on horseback and attacked from the rear, forcing the Zulu farther and farther away from the wagons with their incessant gunfire.

That afternoon, the Voortrekkers went on the offensive, attacking the Zulu while they rounded up the Boers' livestock outside the laager. However, they were too far away to make much of an impact. In addition, the animals served as shields for the warriors ... until they were butchered by the Zulu, who cut out chunks of their flesh, cut off their tails and cut out their tongues while they were still alive. The Voortrekkers watched helplessly as the warriors tortured the livestock and held up the bloody pieces of meat before throwing them onto the fires they had lit. The sounds of the distressed animals and the jubilant shouting and laughing of the Zulu continued all night. The terrified Boers did not sleep that night and strapped lanterns onto whips that they attached to the outside of the wagons to illuminate the immediate surroundings.[935]

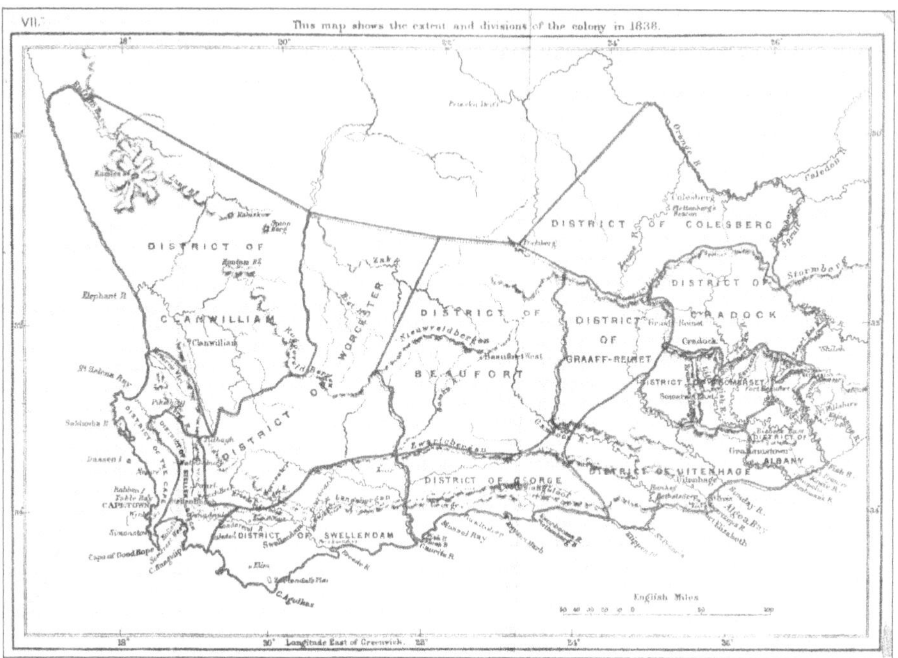

At first light the following day, De Lange led 60 men to attack the Zulu and managed to drive them back toward the wagons, where *Stelletjie* roared a fiery "good morning" to the warriors. Later, the Zulu changed tactics: while the frontline advanced on the wagons, a second row of warriors behind this threw assegais wrapped in burning grass into the laager. Many of these fiery javelins landed on the wagon canopies and thorn bushes between the wagons and, soon, the air was filled with smoke. The women and children screamed as they ran with buckets of water to douse the flames and ammunition and gunpowder were moved away from the danger area.

On the second day of the battle, 14 August 1838, one of the Zulu commanders was killed by shot from *Stelletjie*. His death appeared to affect the morale of the Zulu army. However, the warriors rallied after dark and set fire to the veld near the laager. As the flames closed in on the wagons, the Voortrekkers realized that the best means of defence would be to create a firebreak. Consequently, they burned the grass surrounding the wagons in phases and stamped out the flames. When the fire started by the Zulu reached the blackened earth around the wagons, it soon died.[936]

That night, while the Zulu were driving away the remaining Voortrekkers' livestock, those in the laager listened attentively as Reverend Smit read verses from Psalm 28:

Blessed be the Lord
Because he has heard the voice of my supplications!
The Lord is my strength and my shield;
My heart trusted in Him, and I am helped;
Therefore my heart greatly rejoices,
And with my song I will praise Him.[937]

When the Zulu saw the commando led by De Lange the next morning, they headed back to Umgungundlovu with the Boers' livestock. After two days of furious fighting and having lost many men, the Zulu were reluctant to deal with a fresh attack from the Boers. The Voortrekkers' horses were so thin and weak at this stage that the men were unable to pursue the army or to attempt to recover their stolen animals.

More than 3,000 Zulu had been killed during the battle[938] and the bodies were scattered on the burned ground surrounding the wagons for a distance of three kilometres. The sunny weather caused the corpses to rot quickly and the stench became unbearable to the Voortrekkers. Eventually, they used oxen to haul the decaying bodies away and dumped them in a sluit some distance from the laager,[939] which became known as Veglaeer from this time on.

Maritz was suffering from dropsy and had not taken part in the battle. Nevertheless, he assisted in the aftermath by sending oxen to help move the wagons to a new site near Sooilaer. (A new laager was also formed at this time and was to be commanded by Koos Potgieter.)

Lord Napier had received reports about the conflict between the Voortrekkers and the Zulu and issued a proclamation on 6 September 1838 prohibiting the private gunpowder magazines in the colony from issuing gunpowder, in the vain hope that this would restrict the supply of gunpowder to the Voortrekkers. However, he soon heard that money, goods and gunpowder were being donated to the Voortrekkers and that these had been loaded onto the *Mary*. Consequently, he issued another proclamation that prohibited the export of gunpowder, firearms and "munitions of war" from the colony to any other part of the country and instructed the harbourmaster at the Port Elizabeth harbour to seize gunpowder and weapons onboard the *Mary*.[940] (The harbourmaster only confiscated the excess gunpowder and munitions when the *Mary* returned to Port Elizabeth, after the Boers had purchased their requirements.)

When word arrived at the laager that the *Mary* had docked at Durban with provisions and ammunition for the Voortrekkers, Maritz and a commando of 50 men travelled to the settlement to collect the goods, which were taken ashore by

Alexander Biggar and J.P. Muller. Half of the gunpowder and provisions were given Maritz, while Landman and Greyling each received a quarter of the goods.

While in Durban, Maritz's body and face swelled painfully. Consequently, Alexander Biggar took him into his home and nursed him, in a futile attempt to return him to good health.[941] When Maritz brought the much-needed provisions back to his laager, the Voortrekkers were shocked to see that he was too ill to walk. He had to be carried from the wagon to his tent.

On the wet, cold morning of 23 September 1838, a messenger summoned Reverend Smit to Maritz's bedside, as Maritz was apparently sinking fast. Smit and the messenger immediately set off into the lashing rain. After piggybacking on the messenger's back across the river,[942] Smit entered the dark interior of Maritz's tent. Trickles of water ran down Smit's forehead. He took off his coat and shook off the drops of rain. In the dark of the interior of the tent he could see the shape of his friend in bed. He remained with Maritz the whole day, watching him slip in and out of consciousness. People came and went to pay their respects for the last time to the man who had played such a major role in their lives.

As the gloomy day gave way to the lonely dark of night, candles and lanterns were lit in the tent of Maritz. Gusts of wind stirred the flames of the lanterns, making giant grotesque shadows of the visitors on the sides of the tent as if dancing in a final farewell ritual. As the black-clad visitors bent over the bed one by one to bid farewell, the flickering candles and lanterns showed the white puffy face of Maritz which stood out like a ghost in the gloom. Finally, Maritz's family gathered around his bed to say their goodbyes and to whisper comforting prayers to him as the wind and rain lashed the tent. Smit prayed in a hushed voice. At times the sound of the wind and rain outside muffled his words.

"Are you afraid?" Smit asked.

"Yes," Maritz answered his brother-in-law softly.[943]

Smit prayed and through his words gave Maritz relief.

Maritz opened his eyes and looked at the people gathered, some already with tears trickling down their cheeks. "Like Moses of old, we have seen the Promised Land, but only one of us was chosen to live in it.[944] It is my time to go," he whispered.

In his wheezy voice Reverend Smit then began to sing Psalm 123 and Maritz joined him, his voice becoming weaker and weaker. He sang until his last breath left his body. Maritz died at eleven o'clock that night. He was 41 years old.[945]

CHAPTER 27

The river ran red

Pietermaritzburg—apprentices—Napier plans troops for Durban—news of Pretorius—The Vow—Battle of Blood River

On 23 October 1838, a month after Maritz passed away, the Volksraad gave Sooilaer the name of Pietermaritzburg, in honour of 'Pieter' Retief and Gert 'Maritz'.[946] By this time, the Voortrekkers in the Piet Greyling laager had begun to mark out plots on a plain by the Umsindusi River[947] and planned to settle there permanently.

Napier was desperate to stop the migration of Boers from the colony and so instructed all government officials to do everything in their power to dissuade the Boers from leaving. He also requested that the ministers of the church do the same. He then tried a different tactic: going after the Boers for taking slaves from the colony illegally. (Although the slaves in the colony had been freed in 1834, they were required to complete an apprenticeship until 1 December 1838.) Napier tasked Joubert with bringing back the apprentices from Natal, as he had already visited the Voortrekkers with Boshoff and was accepted by the Boers due to his service as a field cornet in the Colesberg district.

In a letter dated 16 October 1838, Joubert was instructed to explain to the apprentices that they would be considered free men or women from 1 December 1838 and that they should choose whether to remain with their employers or return to the colony. If any apprentices wanted to continue working for the Boers, they would have to sign a declaration to that effect and any Boers who resisted letting their apprentices go would be warned that they would "forfeit all further claim upon the favourable consideration of the British government".

Napier also ordered Joubert not to enter into any negotiations or discussions with the Voortrekkers about any form of future government they were planning and stressed that the British government would never support any government body that gave the Voortrekkers a separate or independent territory. He also wanted Joubert to warn the Voortrekkers that they were British subjects and could therefore still be punished by the British government. However, he emphasized that the British government would do everything it could to protect the Voortrekkers from attacks by local tribes. Moreover, he instructed him tell any Xhosa and Zulu that he met that the Voortrekkers had left the colony against the government's wishes and would be punished should they commit any violent acts against or attack them.

On the same day that Napier wrote to Joubert, he sent a letter to Glenelg in England informing him that he would send a small body of troops under Major Charters to Durban in three weeks to take possession of the settlement in the queen's name. The force would comprise one captain, two subalterns; 80 men of the 72nd Highlanders; one subaltern and one sergeant with ten men of the Royal Artillery and three guns; one sergeant who was a sapper; one assistant surgeon; one clerk and one translator, a man called Theophilus Shepstone.[948]

Joubert set off on his mission on 22 October 1838 in style, accompanied by 15 men, two wagons and 50 horses. He first visited the trekkers in the camps of Hendrik Potgieter and Jacob de Clercq between the Sand and Riet rivers and met with those Boers who had apprentices. Joubert was interested to note that many of the Boers there were preparing to join the Voortrekkers in Natal in their battle against the Zulu.

Joubert and his party then met up with Cilliers, who was returning to the laagers in Natal after his mission to the colony to rally support for the trekkers. The colonists had donated sufficient gunpowder, provisions, gifts and clothing to fill two wagons. However, Cilliers was disappointed that so few Boers in the colony had been willing to come join the commando that would attack the Zulu.

Cilliers and Joubert's parties arrived at Sooilaer on 2 November 1838[949] and Joubert immediately started visiting the nearby camps to inform the apprentices there of their rights. (While 46 of the apprentices he spoke to signed declarations stating that they wished to remain with their masters, 38 elected to return to the colony.)

The deaths of Retief, Uys and Maritz had been a heavy blow to the Voortrekkers, as had Potgieter's departure for Transorange after the commando he led at Italeni failed to aid Uys's men while they were besieged by the Zulu. In addition, sickness and disease were rife in the camps and many families were destitute. All of the Voortrekkers worried that the Zulu would attack them again and they were plagued by many misfortunes. For instance, a fire ravaged Reverend Smit's wagon during on 5 November 1838.

In light of this, there was great excitement among the Voortrekkers when they heard that Andries Pretorius and his followers were on their way to join them. Near the Caledon River at the end of October 1838, Pretorius decided that he and 13 of the men in his trek would travel ahead to the Voortrekkers in Natal. He sent a messenger to tell the Voortrekkers at Sooilaer to prepare for the attack on Dingane and cautioned them not to work the horses too hard nor to waste ammunition. He instructed them to harvest and store food, make *veghekke* (fighting gates, or hide-covered hurdles, used when there was a scarcity of thornbush) and to sew bags in which lead shot would be loaded.[950] The commando left Modder River at the beginning of November 1838 and on their journey, encouraged other Voortrekkers to join them.

On 15 November 1838, the former commandant of Beaufort, Pieter Daniel Jacobs, joined Pretorius with several men and as word of the commando's approach spread, men drifted into the main camp to join the growing army.[951] By the time Pretorius reached the camp of Jacobus Potgieter at the Klein Tugela on 22 November 1838, the commando comprised about 60 men and eight wagons.[952]

Pretorius's arrival was greeted with enthusiasm and excitement. He already enjoyed the admiration and respect of the majority of the trekkers, as demonstrated by Reverend Smit's description of him being "a worthy fellow emigrant".

Pretorius was duly appointed chief commandant on 25 November 1838, the day after Joubert left with the apprentices for the colony. He wasted no time in organizing the men and gave Smit a list with the names of all the men who would be in the commando that would attack Dingane.

Smit held a service for the 460 men,[953] which included Englishmen Alexander Biggar and Edward Parker. Pretorius arranged the men into five divisions, with C.P. Landman, P.D. Jacobs, J. Potgieter, J. de Lange and S. Erasmus as the respective field commandants, with all five reporting to him. Recognizing that the trekkers had fared better against the Zulu from a fortified position than when fighting them in open combat, Pretorius decided that the commando would take 57 wagons and three cannon, namely *Ou Grietjie*, *Stelletjie* and *Weeskind*. The latter was a 6.35-centimetre calibre, 1.21-metre-long copper cannon that belonged to Pretorius.[954] In addition, 60 servants would accompany the army as well as close to 1,000 oxen and horses.[955] On 27 November 1838, the first division under Pieter Daniel Jacobs left Sooilaer for the rendezvous next to the Tugela.

The next morning, Pretorius and his men rode out of the camp with the wagons and formed a laager on the north bank of the Tugela River. A further 123 men from Landman's commando would join them in a few days.[956] At the laager, Pretorius immediately showed his leadership skills by allocating the Voortrekkers into night watches and ensuring that the cattle into the laager were brought into the laager to prevent theft and that the *veghekke* were put in the spaces between the wagons to fortify the laager. He then called a meeting with his divisional commandants and field cornets to discuss the strategy of the attack on Dingane.

Being a God-fearing man, Pretorius spoke to Cilliers about making the men take an oath that they would forever honour God for helping them to defeat the

Zulu. "My brother, I think we must make the Lord a promise. That if he grants us victory we will honour that day of the victory as a day like the Sabbath and that we shall give credit to the Lord for the victory. We must also promise to build a place of worship in thanksgiving," he said.[957]

Although Cilliers thought that it would be a good idea to commit the men in this way, he had reservations about whether the men would meet their obligations to God if they were victorious[958] and Pretorius therefore discussed his idea with the divisional commanders after prayers that night. All were in favour of making some form of commitment to God[959] and it was decided that prayer meetings would be held twice a day for the duration of the expedition. Later that night, Pretorius ordered Commandant Erasmus to take a group of scouts to spy on the kraals of Jobi, a nearby Zulu chief.[960]

While Pretorius waited for Landman's force to join his, he drew up regulations and rules for his men. He then gave a copy of these to each of his divisional commanders. Landman's commando joined the main army on 2 December 1838, together with some Zulu deserters.

Pretorius allowed no dissension among the men and demanded total obedience from them. For instance, when Daniel Bothma refused to stand guard for the night and was verbally abusive toward Commandant Jacobs, he was hauled before Pretorius and was severely reprimanded. After Bothma apologized and promised to behave better in future, Pretorius pardoned him.[961] His slogan was *Eendragt maakt magt* (unity is strength) and he routinely spoke to the men about the importance of demonstrating valour, manliness, decency, discipline and, above all, Christian behaviour, as they were "God's warriors".[962]

On the morning of 3 December 1838, the commando set off in an easterly direction. Pretorius instructed the men to travel in rows of four wagons so that the cavalcade was compact and therefore easy to defend and move into laager formation in the event of an attack and, after crossing the Klip River, the convoy set up camp for the night awaited the return of scouts.

In Durban the following day, 80 men of the 72nd Highlanders that Napier had sent aboard the Helen docked in the bay. Major Charters immediately seized Maynard's Store, which belonged to Robert Dunn, and a wooden building that belonged to J. Owen Smith. He then set up his headquarters in the settlement, without any opposition. [963]

On 5 December 1838, Pretorius climbed onto *Ou Grietjie* to address the men. After reading them several letters of support for their crusade, he encouraged them to be brave in the upcoming battle and to behave in a Christian manner. They were not to kill innocent women and children as the Zulu had done. He ended his talk by shouting loudly, "*Eendragt maakt magt!*" and the men shouted the slogan back to him.

Landman, Pretorius's second-in-command, then climbed onto the cannon and called on the men to give thanks to God for having provided a leader of Pretorius's calibre and for their good health and spiritual wellbeing.[964]

Later, a Zulu messenger informed Parker that Englishman Robert Joyce wanted to join the commando but requested that Parker send him a horse, as he could not continue his journey to their camp on foot. After Parker sent the horse, Joyce rode to the camp and became the third Englishman to join the commando.[965]

Shortly after this, De Lange returned to the camp with three of the scouts and 14 cattle and eleven fat-tailed sheep. He reported that the men had been involved in a skirmish at one of Jobi's kraals and, after some discussion with Pretorius, it was decided that the army would move toward Jobi's kraal and that a commando would be sent to attack him.

On 6 December 1838, Pretorius instructed the men to form a laager next to a spruit and to prepare for an attack by the Zulu. He then rode off with 300 men.[966]

After hearing about Pretorius's commando, Charters wrote to Pretorius to instruct him not to attack the Zulu and warned him that any that attack on the Zulu would be in direct opposition to the wishes of the British government. In a second letter to Pretorius, Charters wrote that Parker had duped the Boers into thinking that he was a British agent and that he would be arrested by the British as soon as they caught him.[967] Charters was aware that these letters would not reach Pretorius before the clash with Dingane but nevertheless recruited two Zulu messengers to take the letters to him. The messengers would receive one cow each when they returned with a signed receipt from Pretorius stating that the letters had been delivered.[968]

When the two Zulu messengers arrived at the Boer camp on the Little Tugela River on 11 December 1838, although they carried a white flag, the Boers seized them and confiscated the two letters for Pretorius as well as copies of the proclamation issued by Napier that Durban and the surrounding territory had been seized in the name of the queen of England. After reading the documentation, J.S. Maritz, L.J. Meyer and P.H. Opperman responded to Charters's letters, signing their letter as "representatives of the people".

Their letter highlighted the daily dangers faced by the Voortrekkers and described their situation as "perilous". It requested that Charters rescind his decision to seize all arms and ammunition from the Boers and pointed out that if he did not, they would be unable to defend themselves against "blood-thirsty savages". It also requested that he return the gunpowder that had been sent to them and which he had seized upon his arrival in Durban.[969] When Pretorius and his men arrived at Jobi's kraal, they found it deserted and, after rounding up 27 goats and seven sheep, they returned to their camp on 7 December 1838. The full commando crossed the Sundays River on 8 December 1838 and then proceeded to Wasbank River, where they set up camp. Potgieter and Uys had named this river Blyderiver but it became known as Wasbank River as the Voortrekkers washed their clothes in it.[970]

After prayers in Pretorius's tent on 9 December 1838, Cilliers addressed the men from *Ou Grietjie*[971] and read out the promise they had committed to: "My brethren and fellow countrymen, at this moment we stand before the holy God of heaven and earth, to make a promise, if He will be with us and protect us, and deliver the enemy into our hands so that we may triumph over him, that we shall observe the day and the date as an anniversary in each year, and a day of thanksgiving like the Sabbath, in His honour; and that we shall enjoin our children that they must take part with us in this, for a remembrance even for our posterity; and that if any one sees a difficulty in this, let him retire from this place. For the honour of His name will be joyfully exalted, and to Him the fame and the honour of the victory must be given."[972]

The following day, the commando crossed the Wasbank River and soon found that the thick grass on the other side impeded the movement of the convoy. As such, Pretorius ordered the men to burn the grass ahead of the wagons. While the commando crossed the steep and rocky Heuningberg mountain range, Alexander Biggar's cart tumbled over. (Hence, it was renamed Biggarsberg). On the other side, the men saw smoke in the distance and Pretorius sent patrols to find out where the enemy was camped.

They returned with nothing to report.[973] However, the next day, the scout spotted the enemy and Pretorius had the wagons moved into laager formation by the Umzinyathi (Buffalo) River. He then sent more scouts to establish how large the enemy camp was and when they returned, they reported that they had only seen nine of Dingane's spies, whom they had killed.

That evening, the Voortrekkers saw a Zulu man walking along the flat land in the distance. When two of the men rode out to apprehend him, he hid in a bush and then leaped out and attempted to hurl an assegai at Parker as his horse approached. Fortunately, the Englishman reacted swiftly and blasted a hole in the Zulu's head with his *Sanna*.[974]

On 12 December 1838, rain again drenched the Voortrekkers' laager. Nevertheless, the patrols continued to explore the surroundings. When Parker and some of the Zulu men took their turn, they captured a Zulu spy and several women and children. While Parker's companions watched the women and children, he tied his prisoner to his horse and rode off toward the laager.

Suddenly, the Zulu reached up to grab Parker's gun. When he failed to pull it from Parker's grasp, he pulled Parker to the ground, where the Englishman wrestled the gun from under the Zulu man. Parker shot the spy in the arm and shoulder. He died shortly after Pretorius arrived on the scene, without revealing any information that could be useful to the Voortrekkers.

Pretorius allowed the Zulu women and children to go free but instructed one of the women to deliver a message to Dingane at Umgungundlovu. He gave her a white cloth with his name written on it and told the woman to hand it to Dingane and to inform him that the Voortrekkers were coming to do battle with him. She was to tell him that if he declared peace and gave them back the guns and horses from Retief's party, they would leave him in peace and that if he did not do so, they would wage war with him until he died, even if that took ten years.

The women were most appreciative of Pretorius's actions, telling him that their king would never have pardoned or freed defenceless women. In turn, Pretorius told them that if they or their husbands returned with a message for him, they should carry the white cloth with his name on it so that his men would know not to harm them.[975]

The morning of 13 December 1838 was grey, misty and wet. Consequently, Pretorius moved the wagons eastward to be closer to dry firewood. That afternoon, a patrol galloped into the laager to report that they had seen a large number of Zulu near a mountain herding many cattle and had attacked them. After killing three of the Zulu, one of their guns had jammed and they therefore withdrew.[976]

The increased Zulu activity in the area caused the tension in the Boer camp to skyrocket and the sentries were on high alert at the laager. Moreover, Pretorius decided that it would be prudent to attack the Zulu the next morning. The sound of the horses' hooves of the 120-man commando was muffled by the drizzling rain as they rode out of the camp early the next morning and, by the end of the day, they had only encountered one small group of Zulu and had killed eight of them. Nevertheless, they sensed that they would soon find the main Zulu army.

The following morning, 15 December, the main column crossed the Buffalo River.[977] Pretorius sent patrols to search for the Zulu army, which had by this time left Umgungundlovu. However, scouts were constantly relaying information about the Voortrekkers' whereabouts to generals Tambuza and Umhlela.

No sooner had the main body of Voortrekkers outspanned next to a tributary of the Buffalo River, the Ncome River, than scouts galloped up to Pretorius to report that they had seen a large body of Zulu. Subsequently, some men reported that they had clashed with a Zulu patrol earlier, but had only killed one of the Zulu as the others had escaped up the nearby banks or into ditches.[978]

Shortly after this, De Lange sent Johannes (Hans) Hattingh and Jan Robberts to Pretorius to report on the findings of his patrol: that the entire Zulu army was about 20 kilometres southeast of the Voortrekkers' current position, or about an hour's ride away, behind the Nqutu Hills.[979, 980]

Pretorius realized that he would have to exercise great care in selecting a suitable site to set up a laager and that it would need to withstand the inevitable Zulu attack. The land in front of him was flat but with hills in the distance and the site he selected for the laager was between a large donga and a hippo pool. The donga was about four and a half metres wide and as tall as it was wide. It ran from east to west, into the Ncome River, and had a giant hippo pool in front of it that ran north to south and stretched 1,300 metres into the Ncome River. The hippo pool made the river impassable, whether on foot or horseback.[981]

The natural barriers provided by the hippo pool and donga meant that the laager would be protected on two sides. Pretorius therefore had the men position the wagons about 275 metres from the bank of the Ncome River and 20 metres from the edge of the donga.[982]

He left 'Rooi Piet' Moolman in charge of setting up the laager in a half-moon or 'D' shape, with the straight edge running east to west along the nearby donga. He also instructed Moolman to get the men to position the *veghekke* between the wagons and to chain the wheels and disselbooms of the wagons together. He was also tasked with covering the *veghekke* with animal skins to prevent assegais being pushed through them.

Once the laager was set up, the straight edge of the 'D' was 90 metres long and the radius of the semi-circle was 45 metres. This ensured that the men were able to herd all of the 800 cattle and about 700 horses inside it.[983] The three cannon were positioned strategically, with *Ou Grietjie* on the northern side, the cannon of Gert Rudolf, *Stelletjie*, on the eastern side and the copper cannon of Pretorius, which later became known as *Weeskind* (orphan), on the western side.[984] This not only ensured a strong defence but also would disperse the sound of the cannon fire and therefore lessen the chance that the livestock inside the laager would stampede in fright.

In drizzling rain, Pretorius and 220 men then set off to the Nqutu hills to test the strength of the enemy, taking only a horse-drawn cannon with them.[985] When Pretorius's men came across the Zulu army late that afternoon, they saw row after row of warriors sitting on their shields, evidently waiting for them. The feathers in the headdresses of the men in the 36 regiments stirred in the breeze and looked like a forest of tree ferns. As the Boers rode closer to the Zulu, they saw that what they had first taken to be the whole Zulu army was, in fact, only part of it: two further regiments were hidden in folds of the mountains. All the crack Zulu regiments were there: the *Isihlangu Mhlope* (white shields), *Isihlangu Mnyama* (black shields), the *Izinyozi* (the bees), the *Udlambedlu* (the fearless), the *Imkulutyani* (the wild bucks), the *Ufazimba* (the body), the *Udlanggeswa* (the hard of hearing), the *Umkhutyana* (devious), the *Undlangubo* (the clothed) and the *Umbebeya* (those who come toward you).[986]

Pretorius arranged his men into units of 50, spacing each 50 metres apart, in an attempt to make the Zulu think that he had a far larger force than he did. The Zulu hoped to tempt the Boers into following their cattle into a ravine, where they would be ambushed.[987]

Cilliers tried to persuade Pretorius to let him approach the Zulu with a force of 50 men as he believed they could draw them out into the open. However, Pretorius argued that this would be a foolhardy move as it was already nearly dusk and that they should make no further moves until the next day.[988] He then led his men back to the laager and left De Lange and his scouts behind to keep a watchful eye on the Zulu.

The misty rain had stopped and as the setting sun bathed the landscape in blood red light, the Voortrekkers saw the Zulu settling on the ridges opposite the laager, on the other side of the Ncome River.[989] Consequently, Pretorius ordered the men to fire one of the cannon to signal that De Lange and his men should return to the laager. A heavy mist sank over the river and laager and the Voortrekkers could barely see in front of them it was so thick. As such, the men lit lanterns attached to whips and mounted these on the wagons and stuck them into the ground 45 metres from the laager.[990]

Although Pretorius hoped that the battle would not begin the next day, as this was a Sabbath, he did not get his wish: that evening, De Lange and his scouts returned to the laager with news that the Zulu army was moving toward the laager from their position near the Nqutu hills.

Pretorius and his commanders immediately set about preparing the men for the battle to come and positioned eight men between each wagon. Each man would fire in succession, thereby ensuring that the Zulu met with a constant wall of firepower, and was issued with a small leather pouch of buckshot (otherwise known as *lopers*) that would burst approximately 40 metres after being fired. These had been prepared in advance by the women. In addition, each man was equipped with two or three *Sannas*[991] and would have saucers filled with gunpowder and ammunition within easy reach.

The men also loaded the cannon with grapeshot and stacked small, hard projectiles such as metal pot legs, pieces of iron and even stones next to the cannon.[992] The cannon were between two wagons that were back-to-back and the space between these could be made bigger or smaller relatively easily. This would ensure that the Voortrekkers could exit the laager on horseback. Four wagons containing ammunition were positioned near the openings so that the men could easily equip themselves with fresh ammunition as they exited the laager.[993] The servants would load and prime each spent gun to ensure that the Boers' firepower did not let up and would also be in charge of the horses to be used in the battle. They organized the horses into groups of four and would hold the reins so that the Voortrekkers could easily mount them to pursue the enemy. (They also tethered the oxen together and pegged the riems securing the livestock into the ground, to prevent them from bolting and possibly damaging the wagons.) The Voortrekkers were concerned: if the mist persisted through the night, their gunpowder would become soggy and ineffective and it would be difficult to see[994] the Zulu approaching. Pretorius inspected the men and the security of the wagons and ensured that all the openings were covered with *veghekke*, which in turn were covered with ox-hides and that the wagons were securely chained together.

Under cover of darkness, the Zulu army moved closer to the wagons, led by their commander-in-chief, Umhlela and his second-in-command, Tambuza. Two of Dingane's half-brothers accompanied them.[995] General Umhlela and his high command had considered leading the Voortrekkers into an ambush but realized that they would have learned from the mistakes they made at Italeni. They then debated the merits of surrounding the laager until the Voortrekkers could be starved into submission. However, this would mean that the livestock within the laager could die and they would not be able to seize the animals after the battle. In addition, they concluded that this option was not appropriate and not the customary style of Zulu fighting. Finally, they decided to immediately launch an aggressive assault.

Perhaps foolishly, Umhlela lost the element of surprise. He did not take into account that the more than 15,000 warriors[996] would be slower than usual due to their long march from Umgungundlovu and that the poor visibility on this misty night would further slow the army down.[997] He stationed the main body of the massive army on a hill known as Zongonka and several divisions to the east, in front of the Khalatu, Nceceni and Teleza hills.[998] Late that night,

Cilliers led the Voortrekkers in prayer and the men repeated their promise to God and pleaded for dry weather. The sound of the Boers singing hymns and psalms drifted to the Zulu by the Ncome River[999] and the warriors there were unnerved by it. Further, they considered the ghostly glow of the laager in the mist to be a bad omen. "We cannot attack at night," one of the warriors cried. "The *mahlozis* [protective spirits] of the white people will take care of them and protect them!"[1000] Although the Zulu army refrained from attacking that night, they readied themselves to attack the following day. Through the mist they heard the Voortrekkers, led by Sarel Cilliers, singing a few stanzas from Psalm 38:

Pray forsake me not forever;
Be though never
Far removed from me, O God.
Hasten Lord of my salvation,
In compassion
To uphold me with thy rod.
Amen.

Unfamiliar with the strange singing, a warrior shouted across the river in derision, "Keep on weeping! The sun of tomorrow you will never see set!"[1001]

After prayers, Pretorius instructed the men to get into position two hours before sunrise. It is unlikely that sleep came easily to any of the men that night as they worried that the mist would not lift and many of the men spent the night praying to God for protection from the Zulu. Pretorius checked the laager defences and quietly whispered words of encouragement to the men as he shook their hands or patted their backs as he walked past. He oozed confidence.

Later that night, it was the Boers' turn to listen to the Zulu singing melodies in beautiful baritone voices and chanting words of praise for Dingane. They then sang a war song, which one of the Boers translated in a hushed voice:

We journey to war
Over the hills yonder,
Over the hills where the sun sets,
To a country we do not know.
We journey for you, king and father,
Lion! Elephant! Liberator!
King of kings! King of the Zulu! Dingane!
We greet you![1002]

Umhlela split his men into two groups. He instructed 5,000 of the warriors in the *Isihlangu Mhlope* regiment (which made up one third of the army) to wait with him on the eastern bank of the hippo pool and instructed Tambuza to lead the main army of *Isihlangu Mnyama* to attack the Boers. When their enemy ran out of ammunition, the *Isihlangu Mhlope* would cross the river and move in for the kill.

Late that night, the Boer scouts heard a whispering noise. At first it sounded like running water which became stronger as they listened, ears straining in the dark and mist. The noise built in volume until it sounded like thousands of stones being rolled under water on the riverbed. It was the sound of the Zulu crossing the Ncome River, some distance from the hippo hole.[1003] At three o'clock in the morning,[1004] the few Voortrekkers who had managed to sleep awoke to the sound of the army closing in on the laager.

In the pre-dawn light the Boers discovered the source of the noise. As the mist began to thin and soften the thickness of night, etching the flat-topped mimosas against the sky, they saw thousands of Zulu warriors resting on their shields, very close to the wagons. They had surrounded the laager and sat, row upon row in their respective regiments, in the shape of a giant fan. The front row was only 40 metres from the laager, with the last 1,500 metres from the curve of the 'D' of the wagons. Other warriors had packed the donga and stood shoulder to shoulder like sardines in a can. One third had been left in reserve under Umhlela, while Tambuza commanded the seated black shields that awaited his order to attack. It was an awesome sight.[1005]

As the sun peeped over the horizon and infused the veld in pink light, Cilliers declared that God had taken away the mist and rain so that the Boers could see and shoot the enemy. The men immediately took aim and awaited the signal from Pretorius to open fire. Pretorius's first shot was followed by a tremendous roar from more than 400 of the Voortrekkers' *Sannas*, as they spat fire and *lopers* at the Zulus, causing a cloud of grey-blue smoke, like a magician's trick to appear in front of the wagons. The first volley of lead smashed into the closely packed bodies of the seated *amabutho*[1006] and killed hundreds of members of the *Mabuto*, *Impholo*, *Udhlambedla*, *Umkulutwane* and *Izinyozi* regiments. As the smoke cleared slightly it could be seen that hundreds of Zulu lay dead and wounded.[1007]

The rest of the Zulu leaped to their feet to wait for Tambuza to signal them to advance and within seconds, the long, mournful blast of the *icilongo* (war trumpet)[1008] had been sounded, like that of a flat, wavering trumpet note which rent the morning air and drowned the bird sounds from the wakening bushes. The Zulu warriors turned their life-size war shields (*isihlangu*)[1009] to face forward.

This immediately gave the impression of double the numbers of warriors attacking as they began to run toward the laager while beating their shields with their *indukas* and assegais. The noise made by the approaching army sounded like rumbling thunder, punctuated by the ululation and shouts of the warriors.

Each regiment's commander, identified by his headband with lourie feathers, led the men in their battle cry of "*Bulala aMaboela!*", rousing their enthusiasm for battle by jumping, prancing in front of them, whistling and stamping his feet.[1010] In addition, *sangomas* (witchdoctors) dressed in skins and feathers and wearing necklaces of yellowed animal teeth pranced and leaped in front of the warriors as they dispensed *muthi*, magical medicine of animal blood, to the warriors as they believed it would protect the warriors from the Boers' bullets.

Each warrior wore an *umqele*, a headband of animal skin. In the soft morning light the plumes of feathers on the top of their heads swayed like a forest of leaves rustling in the wind. Each man held his black shield in one hand while the other clasped his stabbing spear and *nduku*. As they charged the noise was ear-splitting as they whistled and screamed, "*Usutu! Usutu! Usutu!*"

"*Djie! Djie Djie*" came the answering war cry as they beat their shields with a noise like rain on a tin roof.

A black tidal wave charged at the wagons shouting, "*Ulululululu!*"

Before the army reached the wagons, the Boers had fired three volleys. Every shot found its mark in the mass of warriors and as the injured Zulu slumped to the ground, they were overrun by their comrades. Wave after wave of Zulu like pounding surf headed toward the wagons. Pretorius ordered the men to fire the two cannon facing the army. The loud booms startled the horses and cattle inside the laager, some of which managed to break the riems used to tether them together and galloped about wildly as they tried to escape the noise and find a safe haven.

Soon, smoke cloaked the laager and the area around.

"Cease fire!" Pretorius shouted, determined that the men would not waste ammunition firing at an enemy they could not see.

When the smoke lifted, the Boers saw that the veld was strewn with wounded, dying and dead Zulu and that some of the wounded were crawling back to the main army, which had retreated and was now 500 metres from the laager.

"Clean your weapons," Pretorius yelled to his men. "They will come again. Its not over yet."

The Zulu had a few guns with them and fired at the Voortrekkers. However, the laager was out of range and they caused no damage. Having cleaned their guns, the Boers watched Tambuza call his commanders together for an *indaba*

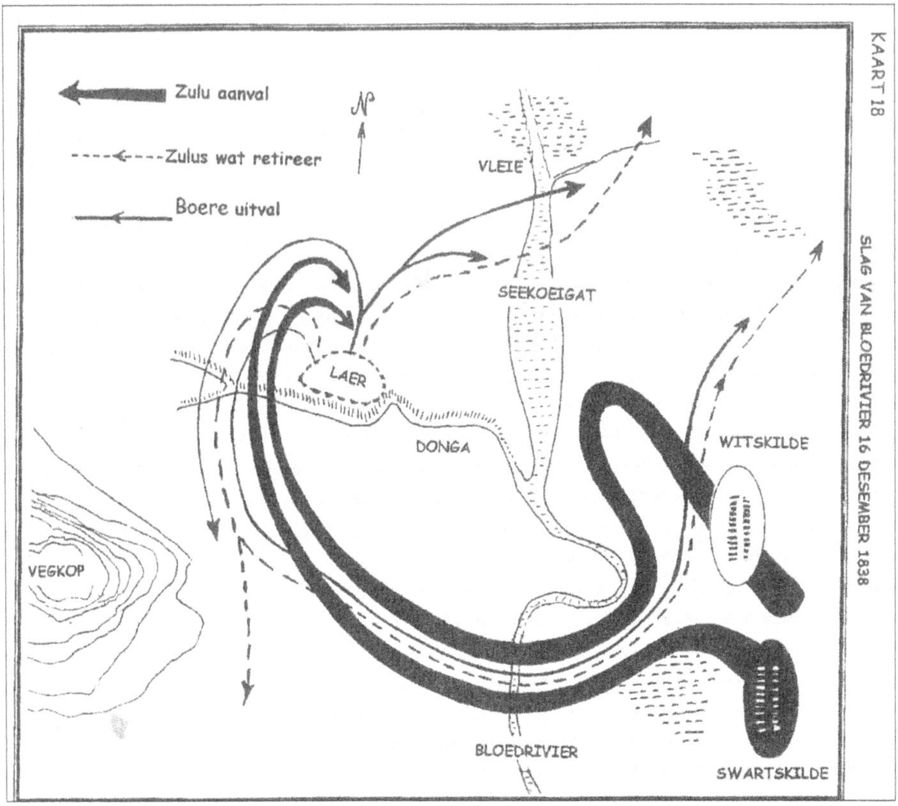

KAART 18
SLAG VAN BLOEDRIVIER 16 DESEMBER 1838
Zulu aanval
Zulus wat retireer
Boere uitval
N
VLEIE
SEEKOEIGAT
LAER
DONGA
WITSKILDE
VEGKOP
BLOEDRIVIER
SWARTSKILDE

4.
N
Zulus
(To Vryheid)
(To Dundee)
Final Boer Attack
Final Boer Attack
Zulu Attack
W
ZONGONKA
Zulus
Zulu Attack
Laager
Boer Horses and Cattle
Boer Wagon
Long Reach (Zekoe Gat)
Blood River
Zulus
E
Zulus
VEG KOP
Zulus
Zulu Attack
Donga (occupied by Zulus)
S
BATTLE OF BLOOD RIVER (Dec. 16, 1838).
Sketch Plan.

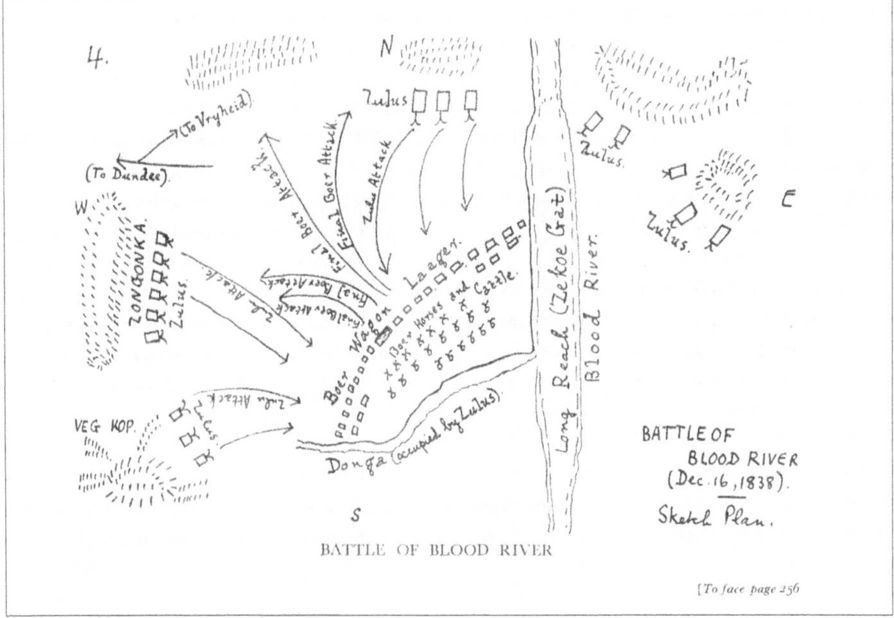

BATTLE OF BLOOD RIVER

[To face page 256

(council meeting) and saw several messengers running back and forth across the river.[1011] It wasn't long before the eerie sound of the *icilongo*, like a bad bugler, echoed across the veld again and the Zulu charged the laager with the determination of lions chasing their prey. This time, the Zulu who surged into the donga were so tightly packed together that their assegais were ineffective. Consequently, Cilliers directed about 50 Voortrekkers to fire on these Zulu.[1012] Like rats in a sinking ship, they tried desperately to scramble to safety. However, escaping up the steep walls of the donga was impossible and the Voortrekkers shot over 400 of the Zulu trapped in the gully.[1013]

The others charged again at the wagons. The Voortrekkers shot and shot. Gun barrels became scorching hot and there was an ever-present danger that the barrels of the Sanna*s* would explode when more gunpowder was poured in.

Thus far, only Philip Fourie had been injured by the Zulu. However, when he was pierced in the thigh by an assegai, he re-entered the fray as soon as his wound had been attended to.

The trumpeting *icilongo,* battle cries and screams of pain and fury from the Zulu mingled with the Boers' shouts of terror and rage as they fought for their lives.[1014] Added to this was the crack of gunfire, the booming cannon and the bellowing and whinnying of the Boers' panic-stricken livestock.

As the Zulus moved forward, so the firing of the Boers punched holes in their attack. Gaps began to appear in their ranks. As the cannon roared, so the projectiles pounded holes in the ranks of the Zulu as easily as a man punching a paper bag. The noise was intense. Screams of pain and fury from the Zulu mixed with shouts of terror and rage from the Boers, the battle cries of "*Usuthu! Usuthu!*" and the trumpeting of *icilongos* from the Zulus. The Zulus charged like lions and fell poleaxed in pools of blood. The wounded cried in agony for help. Sobs of fear came from the Boers as they fought for their lives. The crackling from *Sannas* and the boom of the cannon accompanied the bellows of panic and fear of the cattle, with horses whinnying and bucking pounding the eardrums. Eyes watered from cordite and gunpowder. As the sun climbed in the sky and warmed the earth, the smell of blood and stench of death assailed the nostrils.

Some of the men left the firing line to assist the servants with capturing and securing the livestock and they stumbled around like drunkards as they felt their way around the smoky laager.

The Zulu commanders ordered the *amabutho* to again charge the Boers but some of the warriors realized that they were to be the sacrificial lambs in this battle and ignored the instructions of their superior officers and retreated out of range of the gunfire.[1015] Pretorius called another ceasefire, two hours into the battle, to allow the smoke to clear and also to conserve the men's ammunition. The sudden silence was eerie and made the ringing of the men's eardrums seem deafening. Gradually, the thick smoke cleared and the Boers were able to assess the carnage on the battlefield: thousands of corpses were piled in front of the wagons. They also saw that the Zulu had again withdrawn; this time, they had regrouped 450 metres from the laager. Heartened that none of the Zulu had penetrated their defences, the Voortrekkers cleaned their weapons and prepared for the next attack.

When the Zulu did nothing further, other than send messengers across the river, Pretorius decided to take action: he wanted to draw the army into attacking the laager from close range so that his men could again fire upon the warriors. Consequently, he instructed Phillip Coetzer to goad the Zulu. Coetzer was fluent in Xhosa, which the Zulu could understand. Coetzer promptly climbed onto one of the wagons, cupped his hands around his mouth and shouted to catch the attention of the warriors, bellowing "Hey!" as loudly as he could. The hush that fell over the army indicated that the Zulu were intrigued by this development.

"Hear me! What is now your idea, men of Dingane? Coetzer yelled. "We have come here to fight ... not against defenceless women and children like you did before but against strong men. Are you afraid to face us?"

The Zulu reacted to Coetzer's taunt with an angry rumble and a hissing "Sssssshhhhhh!"

One of the commanders walked toward the wagons and shouted, "Who are you to talk to me? You can't tell us what to do. I know my time. Today, we will crush your houses on wheels into ash!"

When Coetzer shot the brazen Zulu captain in the thigh, two warriors immediately rushed forward to drag their leader out of harm's way.[1016]

There was no movement from the Zulu while the Boers waited for the next attack. Half an hour into the stalemate, Pretorius ordered his brother Bart to ride out to provoke the Zulu to attack the laager as he was anxious to capitalize on the Voortrekkers' earlier success. As Bart Pretorius and his seven companions neared the army, they fired at the warriors[1017] from the saddle and then beat a hasty retreat.

The ploy worked. There was a noise like that of an attacking swarm of bees: "*Djieeeee! Djieeee!*" as the warriors leaped to their feet, yelling "*Bulala amaboela! Bulala amabula!*", and the plaintive bellow of the *icilongo* sounded. This time, the Zulu spread out as much as they could while sprinting in lines toward the wagons. The Voortrekkers' guns and cannon were not as effective as they had been when the Zulu army had charged in rows.[1018]

Pretorius recognized that the Zulu would be able to keep up this new style of attack indefinitely and that reinforcements would be sent across the river when these warriors tired. In addition, the Boers' bullets were not killing the enemy as they had done before. As such, Pretorius ordered cannoniers Gerhardus Pretorius (his brother) and Piet Rudolph to move two of the cannon and directed them to aim one at the rear ranks of the attacking *Isihlangu Mnyama* and the other at the seated *Isihlangu Mhlope* who had as yet only watched the battle from the far bank of the Ncome River.

The two cannon roared and with each shot recoiled backwards. The shell fired at the Isihlangu Mnyama exploded among the charging Zulu, leaving many dead and causing those warriors nearby to stop in their tracks. They gazed in horror as the projectile aimed at the Isihlangu Mhlope across the river whistled through the air and like a giant fist thrust by the devil himself from deep in the bowels of the earth, the ground erupted. As the missile fell among the Isihlangu Mhlope showers of soil, grass, blood and bones erupted skyward. When the smoke cleared 69 warriors lay dead and dying in a rough circle around the crater. Among those killed were two Zulu princes, Dingane's half-brothers. Shouts of outrage drifted across the river to the watching Boers as the veteran warriors of the Isihlangu Mhlope leaped to their feet and stampeded into the Ncomo River. In their eagerness to join the attack some tried to swim across, but red patches on the water marked where the Boers bullets had struck their targets. Others ran down the banks and crossed beyond the hippo hole in shallower water.[1019]

"You've stirred up a hornet's nest; now we will have to face the whole Zulu army," Commandant Jacobs admonished Pretorius as he looked out at the combined force of Umhlela and Tambuza's men.

"We must get the enemy to move into a dense group. That way, we can kill with every shot and the battle will be over sooner. We must bring this to an end; otherwise, our ammunition and gunpowder will run out and they will besiege us," Pretorius replied.[1020]

Fortunately for the Boers, the ranks of the Zulu army surged forward in tight formation and Pretorius's men shot so many of the attackers that the warriors had to climb over the piled corpses of their comrades to reach the wagons.

Soon after this, many of the *Isihlangu Mnyama* began to retreat. They had had enough. Subsequently, the more experienced warriors in the *Isihlangu Mhlope* regiment took up the charge, disgusted by the cowardice shown by those in the *Isihlangu Mnyama*.

Pretorius decided to take the initiative and ordered Bart Pretorius with 100 men to mount their horses. While the Voortrekkers kept up covering fire, Bart and his men, hunched low in their saddles, charged the Zulu. When Bart saw that the Zulu were trying to come between his group and the wagons and cut him off, he wheeled his horse and led his man back into the laager. An hour later he tried again but again failed and had to return to the laager. On his next foray he took about 150 men This time, the men exited the western gate and rode straight at the enemy. They gained sufficient momentum to trample any Zulu in their path and shot any who tried to stop them from carving a path through the mass of warriors. They then cut back behind the Zulu and charged at the *Isihlangu Mhlope.* The warriors were now being fired at from two directions: Bart and his men from the rear and the Voortrekkers in the laager keeping up a barrage of gun- and cannon fire. The *Isihlangu Mnyama* who had continued with the attack suffered terrible casualties in the front ranks and attempted to retire to escape the guns of the Boers. However, the panicked warriors met with a wall of advancing *Isihlangu Mhlope.* During the ensuing chaos, another 150 Voortrekkers rode out onto the battlefield with guns blazing. The army was now being attacked from three sides and had no choice but to flee. Initially, the warriors ran from the battlefield in two groups: the majority of the *Isihlangu Mnyama* ran in the direction of the donga and the *Isihlangu Mhlope* raced toward the Ncome River. However, the relentless pursuit of the Voortrekkers soon drove the Zulu ranks to split up and the warriors raced pell-mell in all directions.[1021]

With the laager no longer under threat, Pretorius decided to enter the battle and ordered a further 100 Voortrekkers to accompany him. His own horse was already being used by one of the men in an earlier commando and he therefore commandeered a horse that had yet to be broken in and led the men in chasing a large group of Zulu.

One of those being pursued by Pretorius's men realized the futility of trying to outrun the horses and turned to confront Pretorius. When Pretorius fired at the warrior, his terrified horse bucked, causing his shot to go wide. He immediately attempted to fire the second barrel. However, the stopper of the lock was closed and he could not cock the gun. After dismounting, he used the butt of his gun to parry two thrusts aimed at his chest. However, the Zulu's assegai plunged into his hand on the third thrust when Pretorius attempted to parry the blow with his left hand. Pretorius pushed the warrior to the ground, despite his painful injury, and tried to pin the struggling Zulu down with his body. The two rolled over and over each other but it was clear that the warrior was stronger than Pretorius: when Pretorius was astride the Zulu, the man clamped his hands around Pretorius's throat and started strangling him. Pretorius's face soon reddened and his eyes began to bulge. While desperately scrambling to pull his hunting knife from its sheath, Piet Rudolph arrived to help him. He pulled out the assegai lodged in Pretorius's hand and stabbed the Zulu with it. A grateful Pretorius then returned to the camp to have the wound attended to.[1022]

Meanwhile, the *Isihlangu Mnyama* trying to get across the deep donga were being mercilessly gunned down by about 50 Voortrekkers lining the gully. Their shields could not protect them from the unrelenting gunfire of the Boers.[1023] The Zulu hid wherever they could but the Boers searched them out and shot them down. As one of the surviving warriors, Lunguza kaMpukane later recalled, the battle became a massacre: "After we had been repulsed, we ran in all directions. The Boers split up and charged at us. Four came in our direction riding red horses, five in another direction and six in another. They fired at us with their guns. We hid in antbear holes, under antheaps, stuffing our heads into holes even though otherwise exposed. Others hid themselves under the heaps of corpses that were everywhere. Even warriors who were dead were shot again. We stood no chance of escaping."[1024]

Many of the *Isihlangu Mhlope* hid in the reeds by the Ncome River and some submerged themselves when the Boers approached. The Boers soon flushed them out and shot them. They also fired on those in the water when they broke the surface to take a breath. Soon, over 1,000 bodies floated in the Ncome or by the reeds; the water had taken on a bloody hue. From that day on, the Ncome became known as Blood River and the Zulu would swear never to drink from the river again.[1025]

The Voortrekkers pursued the Zulu north and south for over three hours before heading back to the laager and only when their ammunition started to run low. As they arrived back at the laager in twos and threes, there was much back-slapping and jubilation. They whooped joyfully as they rode into the camp, overwhelmed by the enormity of what they had achieved and exhausted beyond measure. Smiles and laughter replaced the grim tension of the morning. Nevertheless, Pretorius soon ordered the men to clean their weapons and to start making bullets and posted sentries, on the off chance that the Zulu would regroup and attack them again.

Little did they know that while they had been fighting the Zulu that morning, Charters had hoisted the red, white and blue Union Jack flag in Durban as Britain formally took control of the territory and that martial law had been declared.[1026]

Not one Voortrekkers had been killed and only four of the men had been injured. In contrast, the Zulu had lost more than 3,000 on the battlefield and hundreds more had been severely wounded.[1027] It is certain that many wounded warriors died as the defeated army limped back to Umgungundlovu.

As Cilliers surveyed the bodies around the wagons and in the river, he commented, "It looked like a field of pumpkins after a rich harvest."[1028] He was also scornful of the men's behaviour at the laager as they celebrated their victory and the bravery of their comrades and criticized some of the men for not crediting God for their triumph over the Zulu.[1029]

The victory of the Voortrekkers was a remarkable feat. Just how remarkable is illustrated by the following: 41 years later, on 22 January 1879, the Zulu army defeated the British army and killed 1,357 men during the Battle of Isandlwana, even though the British were equipped with machine guns, Martini-Henry repeater rifles, rockets and cannon.[1030] During the Battle of Blood River, the 464 Voortrekkers had taken on the Zulu army of up to 20,000 warriors with front-end loaders and three cannon and had not lost a single man.

After the men had prayed and eaten a meal, Pretorius sent a strong commando under Landman to wipe out the remnants of the Zulu army and ordered other men to kill any living Zulu found among the corpses on the battlefield. That afternoon, the Boers shot many Zulu warriors who were either badly wounded or feigning death. There were several incidents in which the Zulu put up a fight. For instance, Marthinus Scheepers and Nicholas van Rensburg were both attacked. Consequently, the Boers also started shooting the 'dead' bodies. Landman's commando only returned at eight o'clock that night and reported that they had not encountered any Zulu on their 23-kilometre ride.[1031]

After a thanksgiving service at which the men promised that they would always honour God on 16 December, Pretorius wrote his name on a piece of white cloth and gave this to two Zulu prisoners. He instructed them to take the cloth to Dingane and to tell the Zulu king that the Voortrekkers were willing to make peace with his people, on condition that Dingane accepted his terms to return all stolen cattle and to pay compensation for the massacres at Weenen.

That night, the Voortrekkers slept soundly, undisturbed by the chorusing jackals, wild dogs and hyenas feasting on the Zulu corpses nearby.

CHAPTER 28

Final closure

After the battle—Umgungundhlovu revisited—Boers tricked—the trap—Battle of Umfolozi—the British size up the Boers—Pretorius seeks help—Church of the Vow—Dingane turns to the British—Jervis—Pretorius appointed Chief Commandant—Dingane repulsed by the Swazis—Volksraad—Stockenström returns

On 17 December 1838, Pretorius ordered the Voortrekkers to count the corpses around the laager and to prepare to depart the camp. Realizing that the battle with the Zulu would inevitably recur unless Dingane was dead, Pretorius set off in a southeasterly direction for Umgungundlovu with the commando of 464 men, who were now referred to as the *Wenkommando* (winning commando).

The hot December sun had hastened the decomposition of the corpses and the bloated bodies in the river had already polluted the water to such an extent that the Voortrekkers were unable to draw fresh water before leaving on their 80 kilometre journey to Umgungundlovu.[1032] Nevertheless, the convoy of wagons and men made good progress.

As Pretorius's men approached Umgungundlovu, they spotted several Zulu men spying on them and immediately shot them. Having received no word from Dingane about the peace offering, Pretorius sent another one of the Zulu warriors the men had captured to Dingane to repeat the offer.

On 20 December 1838, the convoy outspanned a quarter of an hour's ride from Umgungundlovu[1033] and Pretorius sent out a small patrol under Jacobus Uys to scout out the land surrounding Umgungundlovu and, if possible, the village.

The commando remained undetected by the Zulu and drew close to the impressive capital. Then, Uys foolishly fired at a crow circling overhead.[1034] This gunshot served to warn Dingane of the Boers' proximity to the deserted Umgungundlovu and set in motion Dingane's instruction to those still in the village to set it alight. Soon, smoke billowed into the summer sky and Umgungundlovu was ablaze. Dingane and the remnants of his army had fled.

When the flames died down, Pretorius ordered the men to start searching the smouldering town for any valuable items, in particular for goods made of iron or copper. The few Zulu stragglers that were discovered were shot.

The next day, the convoy set up camp next to the hill of *kwaMatiwane* and

Pretorius dispatched some of the men to ride to Italeni to bury the remains of the fallen Voortrekkers there. When the party found Piet Uys's body, which was easily identifiable due to the characteristic silver buttons on his tattered waistcoat, they took it back with them. He was later buried at Uysdoorns, a farm near Pietermaritzburg. Sadly, they did not find the body of brave Dirkie Uys and assumed that it had been washed away by a river in flood during the last nine months.

By 21 December 1838, the trekkers had found copper and iron farm and cooking implements, ivory, 48 guns as well as two small cannon in Umgungundlovu. These cannon had belonged to Louis and Gert Nel, who had died with Uys at Italeni.[1035]

When the men eventually made their way to *kwaMatiwane*, they were shocked to discover hundreds of skeletons and the remains of the enemies (and friends) that Dingane had had executed. As they walked among the stinking corpses, the vultures snapped at them insolently before flapping off to nearby tree branches. There, they kept a beady eye on the men as they stumbled upon the skeletons of Retief's men. They stared in horror and wept openly when they gazed upon their smashed skulls and at the assegais that still protruded from some of their ribcages.

While gathering their fallen comrades' personal effects to give to their families, someone shouted that he had found Retief's skeleton. The scraps of a distinctive satin waistcoat that Retief had worn still cased the skeleton and Retief's water bottle with the mark of the Freemasons on its leather covering as well as his damaged leather satchel were near the skeleton.

There were many documents inside the satchel and although those near the satchel flap had been damaged by rain, the papers at the bottom of the satchel appeared to be in perfect condition.[1036] When Pretorius examined the satchel, he found the agreement that Dingane had signed granting the Boers the lands between the Tugela and Umzimvubu rivers. (Later, copies of the original were made and were certified by Andries Pretorius, Karel Landman, Bart Pretorius, P. du Preez and Evert Potgieter, all of whom had been present when the contract was found in Retief's satchel. The original found its way into the hands of the British agent Henry Cloete and was stored in the archives of the Transvaal. During the South African War in June 1900, the document was to be sent to Dr Leyds in the Netherlands. However, during a battle between the Boers and British troops near Machadodorp, four boxes containing papers, including the contract, were taken from the train and buried next to the railway line, to prevent them from falling into the hands of the English. After the war, the boxes were dug up but the contents had been damaged beyond recognition by ants) Subsequently, Pretorius used some of the blank paper from Retief's satchel to write to Boshoff about their victory over the Zulu.[1037] One of the Zulu prisoners with the Boers at *kwaMatiwane* described what he had seen on the day that Retief and his men were murdered but claimed that he had only been a spectator to the proceedings.

Afterwards, the Voortrekkers carefully gathered the bones of their comrades and one of the men etched onto a giant rock that Pretorius and his men had taken occupation of the Zulu capital on 21 December 1838.[1038]

The next day, the Voortrekkers gathered at the foot of *kwaMatiwane* to bury Retief and his 60 men in a mass grave they had dug. While the mourners placed the hats and pipes of the deceased in the grave, Cilliers conducted a funeral service that moved many of the Voortrekkers to tears. Pretorius then sent a full report of the Battle of Blood River to Napier and attached a copy of the agreement in which Dingane had granted land to the Boers.[1039]

Pretorius wanted to reward those in the *Wenkommando* and decided to auction all of the items recovered from Umgungundlovu and to distribute the money from the auction among these men. On 24 December 1838, ivory, crockery, pots and pans, coffee grinders, guns and silver cups were auctioned off[1040] and 6,050 rix-dollars (or £450) was raised.[1041] Pretorius purchased the most items, including a silver cup for 300 rix-dollars. However, it was several months before the men received their share of the proceeds, namely 12 rix-dollars and 6 shillings,[1042] as all of the men purchased goods on credit.

On Christmas Day, Biggar and a small group of Boers captured several Zulu spies, including a captain called Bongoza. He told Pretorius that the Zulu were hiding in a kloof with their cattle a short distance from Umgungundlovu.

After an intense interrogation, Pretorius decided that Bongoza was telling the truth and, the next day, the prisoner guided the Voortrekkers eastward. As a precaution, Pretorius insisted that Bongoza's hands be bound at all times, even when riding.

From their laager at Intonjaneni Heights, near the White Umfolozi River,[1043] Pretorius and his men used telescopes and binoculars to spy out the 2,000 head of cattle[1044] far below them in the valley on the other side of the river.

Early on 27 December 1838 Pretorius ordered a commando to recover the cattle and finish off the remnants of the Zulu army. The 300 Boers under Commandant Landman as well as Biggar and about 50 of his 'friendly' Zulu departed the camp on this dull, wet morning with a horse-drawn cannon. When they reached the top of the ridge, they saw the cattle grazing among the thorn trees across the river and about 30 Zulu on the same side of the river that they were on. According to Bongoza, these men were herding the cattle and would pose little threat to them.

Pretorius's arm was in a makeshift sling and he did not join the 350 men on their dangerous ride down the steep and rugged cliff into the canyon. Instead, he remained on top of the cliffs with De Lange and would guard the cannon.

Soon after the men began their descent, Pretorius instructed De Lange to assist Landman in leading the commando and then returned to the laager at Intonjaneni Heights with the cannon and a guard of ten men. His wound had become unbearably painful and he rationalized that the men would not be able to transport the cannon down the cliff.[1045]

While making the descent, the men pondered the way in which the cattle were grouped: the black oxen were together, as were the white and red oxen. Suddenly, between 500 and 600 Zulu ran out of the scrub below toward the river.

"That is all that is left of Dingane's army," Bongoza assured the worried men. "The others have all deserted."

"Be careful; there is treachery in the air," Landman shouted to his men. "Keep your eyes open."

When the Voortrekkers reached the bottom of the valley, they chased after these Zulu, firing from the saddle as the Zulu ran from them and crossed the river.[1046] They rode after the Zulu along the riverbank but eventually had to cross the river when it made a sharp turn.

No sooner had they reached the other side than a chilling shout echoed from the cliff next to them:

"*Izi pagati; izi pagati!* (They are inside; they are inside!) *Bulala amaboele!*"

Suddenly the 2,000 'cattle' stood up on two legs: the Zulu had been hiding under their shields and when viewed from above, looked like cattle.

The Boers were surrounded. "Shoot the Zulu traitor!" Landman shouted to Commandant Erasmus. However, his instruction came too late: Bongoza kicked his heels into his horse's flanks and it galloped off with him into the ranks of the approaching Zulu.

Realizing that the Boers would have to shoot an escape route through the mass of the Zulu in front of them, Landman ordered the men to make their shots count. "Do not waste your ammunition," he cried as he charged toward the warriors. His men followed suit and the Zulu scattered before the Boers' furious gunfire and galloping horses.

The commando split in two: De Lange led one group up the spruit while Stephanus Erasmus and Landman led their men in the opposite direction. Soon, Landman's party arrived at a cliff that was effectively a dead-end. "Off your horses," he shouted. "Form a laager with the horses and fight for your lives!"

The men quickly starting tying the horses together to form a defensive wall and would fire from behind this barrier when the Zulu caught up to them.

De Lange and his men had also come to a dead-end and had been forced to turn around and retreat. When they reached Landman's group and their makeshift laager, De Lange shouted, "Fools! There are too many Zulu to remain here. You will run out of ammunition and be killed. The only chance we have is to break through their ranks. Those that love me, follow me!"

Landman's men immediately cut the horses loose, jumped into their saddles and galloped after the others while shooting the Zulu running toward them. The Zulu in turn hurled a shower of assegais at the men on horseback, some of whom rode into the river to escape the Zulu.

While Gert van Rooyen was crossing the river, an assegai penetrated the flank of his horse. Fortunately, Commandant Koos Uys swept him onto his steed and they continued across the White Umfolozi River with their comrades. The Boers then headed north, surrounded by an angry mob of Zulu hell-bent on avenging the recent defeat of their army at Blood River. They knew that their survival depended upon escaping the confines of the valley and reaching the open plains of Ulundi, where their horses would be able to outpace the Zulu.

The Voortrekkers' progress was slow as they could only move forward by blasting a path through the mass of Zulu warriors, which they did with great difficulty. In addition, the rocky terrain and thorn bushes made their retreat even more treacherous.

About 25 Voortrekkers defended those at the back of the group from a line of Zulu warriors behind them[1047] who had realized that spreading out made it more difficult for the Boers to shoot them.

Back in the laager, Pretorius heard the sound of shooting and ordered his secretary, Jan Bantjies, to take a telescope to the edge of the valley and to report what he saw.

Pretorius was furious to learn of the ambush by the Zulu, as he had warned Landman and De Lange to be careful and felt that they had not taken heed of his advice.[1048]

The besieged Voortrekkers started riding, in four columns of 50 men, and took turns defending the rear from the pursuing Zulu. Each rearguard would shoot at the Zulu from behind the bushes and rocks, thereby enabling the front riders to ride out of range of the Zulu attackers, then gallop off to join the main body. Another 50 men would then remain behind and allow the others to advance. Eventually, they arrived at the plain and headed west, with a view to taking a circuitous route back to the laager. They soon outpaced the Zulu and, after riding hard for two hours, turned south toward the laager. They then slowed their pace so that their horses could recover. However, the Zulu had worked out the Boers' escape strategy and their commanders ordered 5,000 *Isihlangu Mnyama* to intercept them. While some sprinted into position to attack the Boers on their left flank, others ran to the river so that the Boers would not be able to cross it.[1049] The Voortrekkers fired at the Zulu attacking their commando's flanks and spurred their exhausted horses on toward the river, desperate to reach it before the enemy did.

Suddenly, a new threat appeared: more than 30 mounted Zulu armed with muskets galloped toward the Boers from the direction of the White Umfolozi River, on horses that had belonged to Retief's and Uys's men. Their shots sailed above the Boers' heads.[1050] Nor could they rein in the horses which recognized the horses belonging to the Boers and so raced to join them. As such, many of the panicked Zulu riders leaped off to avoid being carried straight into the Voortrekkers. The few Zulu that remained on their steeds soon reached the Voortrekkers.

There was turmoil as the Zulu's horses galloped into the Voortrekkers' ranks and, during the chaos that ensued, one of the warriors stabbed Jan Oosthuizen in the loin and caused him to fall from his horse in pain. Fortunately, he was able to remount his steed and he quickly joined his comrades in shooting the Zulu on horseback and capturing any riderless horses.

When the Boers finally neared the river, they saw hundreds upon hundreds of warriors on both banks rapidly advancing from the east to where the Boers were planning to cross. The Boers tried desperately to urge their fatigued horses to get to the crossing point before the Zulu.[1051]

When about 60 Boers under Field Cornet Stephanus Lombard and Commandant '*Grootvoet*' (Bigfoot) Potgieter broke away westward to start on a roundabout route back to the wagons,[1052] Landman implored them not to split from the main group. However, they continued riding west.

At the point where the Umkhumbane tributary entered the White Umfolozi River, Landman's men encountered the waiting warriors. Landman ordered the men to form into a long line and they then charged the Zulu. They dismounted their horses 50 metres from the front ranks of the Zulu and continued the charge on foot.

"The first men to cross the river must take up positions and cover the rest of us with heavy fire," Landman yelled to his men over the loud screaming of the warriors. The Boers immediately leaped back on their horses and galloped toward the river, over the corpses of the Zulu. The Boers saw that escaping to the right was impossible due to the steep krantzes rising from the riverbanks on that side[1053] and the pursuing Zulu were closing in on them[1054] from behind and on their left flank. In front of them was an embankment over three metres high. They had several choices: they could take a stand and fight the Zulu approaching them; tackle the difficult descent of the embankment and then ride across the river; or abandon the horses, swim across the river and then fight their way through the Zulu on the other side of it.[1055] Ultimately, they decided to cross the river with their horses.

The Zulu on the opposite bank swarmed toward the river, ululating and shouting with delight as the Voortrekkers' horses struggled through the swiftly flowing river. They then waded into the river and surrounded the Boers. During the fierce close-combat fighting in the water, the horses snorted wildly as the Voortrekkers fired their guns at the Zulu trying to stab their horses or haul them off them. Until attacked, the Voortrekkers found it difficult to differentiate between the enemy Zulu and those serving under Biggar.[1056]

When De Lange and about 15 men reached the far bank, they immediately began to fire at the Zulu surrounding the men in the river. Some of the panicky horses' hooves became stuck in the river sand and their riders jumped off them to continue fighting in the water. Biggar was the first Voortrekker fatality, followed by Nicholaas le Roux. Then, Jan Oosthuizen lost consciousness due to a great loss of blood from his earlier injury. He slipped off his horse and died in the river. Field Cornet van Staden was also fatally stabbed, in the loin. Although Barend Bester managed to cross the river without incident, he was soon stabbed by a group of Zulu when he exited the water. Jacob Gouws and Du Plessis met the same fate as Bester.[1057] In addition, more than 30 of Biggar's Zulu were killed in the river by Boers who mistakenly thought they were part of the enemy army.[1058] When Bart Pretorius's horse was killed, he leaped off it into the swirling water and was immediately surrounded by four Zulu. As they were too close to him to shoot at, he used his *Sanna* to block the thrusts of the Zulu assegais and fatally smashed three of his attackers in the head. He then punched the last Zulu in the face with such force that the man lost consciousness. Seeing a riderless horse nearby, he quickly mounted it and made for the riverbank.

The Voortrekkers fought valiantly as they inched their way across the river and soon, many had reached the other side. There, they were able to shoot more effectively at the Zulu in the river.

Theunis Nel and Koos Uys had unfortunately been intercepted by the Zulu before entering the river and, realizing they had no hope of crossing to the main party on the other side, rode westward. They then crossed the river at a point where there were no Zulu in the vicinity and would join the commando later.

Sixty Voortrekkers guarded the rear of the Voortrekker commando while the majority of the men galloped over a ridge toward the laager, with four badly wounded men in tow. Fortunately, reinforcements arrived then to assist Landman's men and the Zulu started to retreat.

The bedraggled and exhausted Boers under Landman had been in the saddle for ten hours without food or water before they finally reached the safety of the laager.

That night, the Voortrekkers in the laager tensely awaited an attack by the Zulu and hoped that more men would return.

Happily, Stephanus Lombard, Koos Potgieter and several other men rode into the laager at around 11 o'clock that night. (It later transpired that some of the men in this party had fled to Sooilaer.[1059])

More than a thousand Zulu had died[1060, 1061] during this battle and although the Voortrekkers' losses were on a significantly smaller scale, they felt them keenly.

Pretorius was furious with Lombard and Koos Potgieter for leading 60 men away from the main body of Boers and believed their actions had contributed to the deaths of their comrades.

His goal of destroying Dingane's power had been thwarted by the cunning of the Zulu and he hoped that Dingane's warriors would attack the laager so that his men could finally defeat them. The exhausted horses made it impossible for the commando to pursue the Zulu.

On 29 December 1838, the Voortrekkers broke camp and moved back toward Umgungundlovu, in the hope of enticing the Zulu to attack them there. However, it soon became clear that the Zulu were not coming and Pretorius ordered his men to pack up the wagons and make for the laager at the Little Tugela River.

After departing Umgungundlovu on 31 December 1838, the Voortrekkers travelled south at a leisurely pace, to encourage the Zulu to attack again. All of the men were desperate to finish the war Dingane had started.[1062]

During their journey and perhaps in an attempt to provoke Dingane, De Lange led an attack on a Zulu village. In the ensuing battle, the Boers killed more than 50 Zulu warriors and recovered 5,000 cattle, sheep and goats that had been taken from them.[1063, 1064] When the *Wenkommando* rode into the Boer camp on 8 January 1839, Pretorius shared the spoils among the people and allocated every family five head of cattle.[1065] The initial joy felt by those who had stayed behind was soon replaced by grief when they learned that the men in the commando had found (and buried) the corpses of Retief's party at *kwaMatiwane*.

Meanwhile, Charters had been assessing the strength of the Boers in and around Durban and near the Tugela River. He reported to Napier on how many families made up the respective Boer camps and, according to his estimation, the Boers would be able to put together a force of about 800 men. He emphasized that although the Boers were impoverished, he believed that they were determined to remain in Natal.[1066] Charters had been consolidating the British occupation of Durban and had turned Maynard's stone warehouse and O.J. Smith's store into barracks for his troops. In addition, he had ordered his men to cut down mangrove poles, make bricks, dig wells, build sheds in which to store provisions and to erect a wooden palisade around the barracks of the camp, which he named Fort Victoria.[1067]

He also wrote a full report to Napier in which he reported that Dingane's army had attacked the Boers' laager and that the Boers had killed 3,000 Zulu on the battlefield. He added that he had attempted to warn Pretorius not to take action against the Zulu but that some of the Boers had intercepted his letter to Pretorius and had replied to him, in the name of the Volksraad. Charters also informed Napier that he had learned that Mr Parker was serving with the Boers and had killed two Zulu and that he believed Parker should be brought to justice for these murders.[1068]

Pretorius was incensed by the British occupation of Durban and sent Landman to meet with Charters to negotiate the return of the nearly 1,400 kilograms of gunpowder that the Boers had purchased from John Dunn and which British troops had seized.[1069] When Charters told Landman that he would hand over the gunpowder if the Boers undertook not to cross the Tugela River again, Landman stated that the Boers were "free and independent people" and that they the gunpowder rightfully belonged to them. Consequently, Charters would not release the gunpowder.

Early in January 1839, Charters handed over command of the garrison at Fort Victoria to Captain Jervis of the 72nd Highlanders and, on 20 January 1839, set off into the interior with interpreter Theophilus Shepstone to explain to Chief Faku of the Pondo that the British intended occupying Durban and surrounding areas and to reassure him that the British would support the Pondo.

In a report sent to Glenelg in England, Napier emphasized that he did not plan to colonize Natal and requested that Glenelg instruct him on how to proceed in future. He also informed Glenelg that he had instructed Charters's replacement, Captain Jervis, to view the British occupation of Durban merely as a means to prevent the Boers in Natal from receiving supplies by sea.[1070]

The Boers began to move to a more permanent site near the Stinkhoutberg

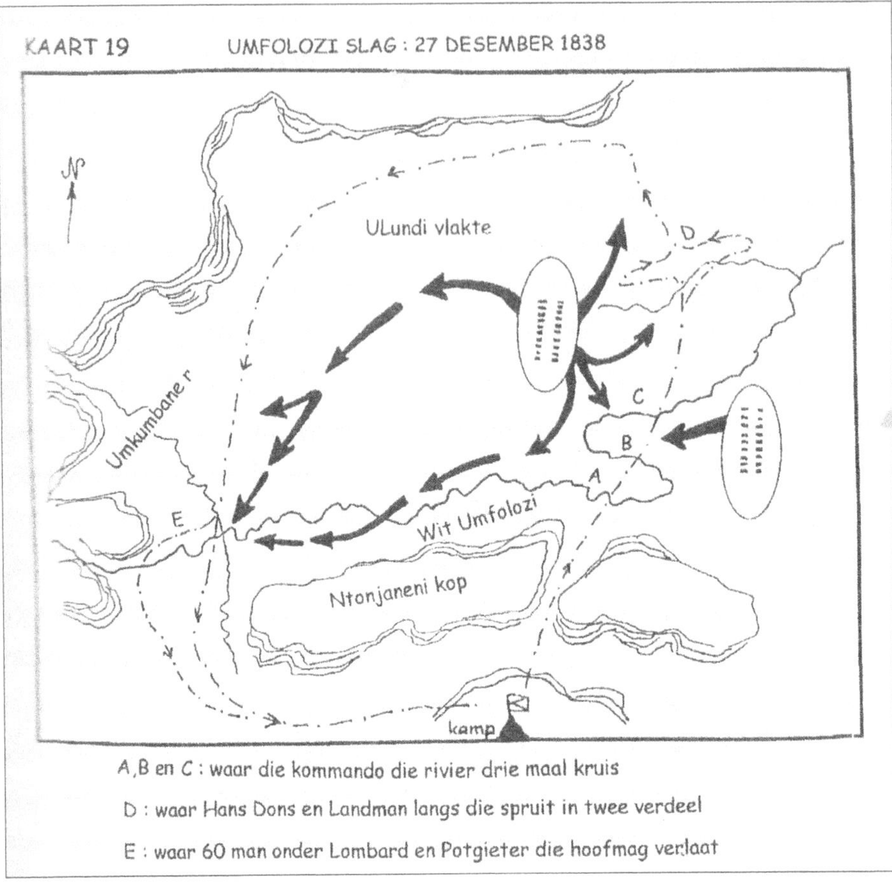

KAART 19 UMFOLOZI SLAG : 27 DESEMBER 1838

A,B en C : waar die kommando die rivier drie maal kruis

D : waar Hans Dons en Landman langs die spruit in twee verdeel

E : waar 60 man onder Lombard en Potgieter die hoofmag verlaat

mountain range close to Pietermaritzburg and hoped that peace with the Zulu was in the offing. Nevertheless, they were determined to recover all of the cattle that Dingane had taken from them.

On 11 January 1839, Pretorius and his brother left the Voortrekkers to return to the Modder River to collect their families and then set off to request help from the Boers in the colony for the struggling trekkers in Natal.

In the colony, they received donations of 185 sheep, ten goats, one ox, soap and 124 rix-dollars to take to the Voortrekkers in Natal. Significantly, Chief Sekonyela and Chief Moroka II made contact with them to congratulate Pretorius for leading the Boers to victory against Dingane.

At the Sand River, Pretorius left his family behind and travelled north to the meet with Potgieter, as he wanted to reconcile with him. After being criticized for heading up the *Vlugkommando* that had not come to the aid of Uys's men at Italeni, Potgieter and his followers had left the Voortrekkers in Natal to establish themselves in the Transvaal–Transoranje district. There, the two leaders attempted to mend the relationship between the Voortrekkers in Natal and those under Potgieter in the area across the Vaal River.

Cilliers had also left the Voortrekkers in Natal to return to the colony, mainly because he wanted his young son, Dirk Petrus, to be christened by an ordained minister in the colony rather than by Reverend Smit. After Dirk Petrus was christened in Colesberg on 17 March 1839, Cilliers and his family headed to the Riet River, where his wife gave birth to their eighth child, a second daughter. He was eager to travel to Pietermaritzburg as he had heard that the Voortrekkers were well on their way to building the church they had promised to erect if God granted them a victory against the Zulu. (More than 4,000 rix-dollars and donations of wood and materials had been collected for the construction of the church.) Nevertheless, Cilliers and his family only arrived in Pietermaritzburg at the beginning of 1840.[1071]

While visiting Potgieter, Pretorius received a letter from J.J. Burger that urged him to hurry back to Pietermaritzburg due to the activities of the Zulu in the area and of the British in Durban. He and his family hastily left the Transvaal-Transoranje district and arrived in Pietermaritzburg on 19 March 1839.[1072] The settlement of Pietermaritzburg had grown substantially by the time Pretorius and his family arrived: about 2,000 men were capable of bearing arms.

When Pretorius learned that Charters had not returned the confiscated gunpowder to the Voortrekkers, he immediately wrote to Jervis to demand that he hand it over. He stressed that the Boers were the legal owners of this gunpowder and that the Boers wanted to live in peace with the British. He added that if the gunpowder was not returned soon, then he would come in person to fetch it.

Jervis had attempted to stamp his and the British authority on the Boers at Durban. To this end, he had summoned a local Boer, Mr Kemp, to appear before him for assaulting a Zulu, under the Cape of Good Hope Punishment Act. Subsequently, Kemp's father had written to Jervis to object and his letter stated that the Boers had elected their own magistrate, which alone had authority over the Boers. Unsure how to respond, Jervis referred the matter to Napier, who replied that it would be inexpedient to take any further action. Consequently, Jervis desisted from following through with this and other attempts to exert British control over the Boers in Natal.[1073]

Jervis then turned his attention to facilitating peace between the Boers and the Zulu, as he recognized that the Boers wanted to make peace with Dingane. He asked Ogle to send one of his servants to the king, who had fled to the Nongoma district and built a new royal village near the iVane River (a tributary of the Black Umfolozi River), to test the waters on whether he would consider making peace with the Boers.

"I am on the brink of ruin," Dingane claimed in his message to Jervis. "I will come to terms with the Boers in any way that you propose. It was never my intention to fight with either the English or the Boers. However, I have never acknowledged the Boers and never will. I have always acknowledged the English. I ask for the English government's assistance in sending the Boers out of my country."[1074]

Jervis proposed to facilitate a meeting to be held between Dingane's *indunas* and the Boers.[1075] The meeting was set for 25 March 1839 and would take place at a site between Berea and the sea. At the meeting, captains Gikwana and Gungwana and several *indunas*, including Gambutshi, made up the Zulu delegation and brought 316 stolen Boer horses as a peace offering.[1076, 1077] The Boer contingent included Pretorius, members of the Volksraad, secretary J.J. Burger and Lourens Badenhorst. The British were represented by Jervis and several officers, all of whom were in full ceremonial uniform to add solemnity to the occasion. Despite the return of the stolen horses, Pretorius remained suspicious of the Zulu and he also did not trust the British present.

After interpreters Joseph Kirkman and Andries Verwey were sworn in, Pretorius asked the Zulu whether they were making peace with the British or Boers.

"Understand me well," Pretorius said. "The Boers are not the same people as the English. We do not welcome the mediation or interference of outsiders," he added, looking pointedly at Jervis. "If you want to make peace with the Boers, then you talk to me."

Pretorius then questioned them about the killings of Retief and his men and asked, "Did Dingane instruct you to give us the land that he ceded to Retief?"

The Zulu spokesperson hesitated and glanced at Jervis before answering, "Yes. Jervis will determine the boundaries."

Pretorius nearly exploded. "Let me repeat: we do not welcome the interference of outsiders," he shouted.

Jervis quickly interjected, "I have nothing to do with the land. The English have not come here to acquire land." He looked at the Zulu before continuing. "I have been sent by my queen to help to make peace between Dingane and the Boers. The chief of the Boers with whom you went to war is in front of you. Make peace with him, not me. My queen is not at war with your king."

Pretorius and the Zulu eventually agreed that the boundary between the Boers and the Zulu would be the Tugela River and that any Zulu messengers crossing the Tugela would have to carry a pass that identified him or her as a messenger. Pretorius stipulated that any Zulu found in the Boer territory without a pass would be assumed to be a spy and be shot. In addition, he demanded that the Zulu return all firearms, saddles and equipment that had been stolen from the Boers and pay to them 19,300 head of cattle as compensation for their losses.

Pretorius instructed the *indunas* that Dingane should send a messenger to him at Pietermaritzburg when they were ready to hand over the cattle and other stolen goods. He also warned them that this would be the Boers' last effort at making peace with Dingane and that if the king did not comply with the agreed terms, Pretorius would deal with him swiftly. To emphasize the gravity of his words, he showed the *indunas* the scar on his hand he had received during the Battle of Blood River. They nodded without comment and soon set off to convey the terms of the peace agreement they had concluded to Dingane.[1078]

At this time, Dingane was attempting to gain a foothold in the southern part of the land of the Swazi people and had moved some of his people across the Pongola River. By doing this, he would ensure that his kingdom was safe from the encroachment of the Boers into Zululand.[1079] (It also indicated that he intended to go to war with the Swazis.)

When Jervis wrote to Pretorius on 3 April 1839 to inform him that he could not return the confiscated gunpowder without Napier's consent and that any attempt to seize it would be met with aggression from the British, Pretorius immediately replied that the British were endangering the Boers' lives by not returning it and informed him that he would soon complain to European governments about the situation. Jervis buckled and agreed to return the gunpowder but maintained that the Volksraad had to sign an undertaking that it would not be used against the Zulu.[1080]

On 13 April 1839, Gambutshi arrived at Durban and informed Jervis that the Zulu were ready to deliver the cattle and goods to the Boers and that Pretorius should select the site for the handover. He also informed Jervis that Dingane requested that the Boers come to assist with the cattle and that he and Ogle be present to witness the handover. Subsequently, Jervis took Gambutshi to the trekkers camped at Congella, where Dingane's messenger delivered the message to Frans Roos and three members of the Volksraad, Cornelis Uys, Jan Visagie and Gert Kemp.

The Voortrekkers admonished the messenger for not obeying Pretorius's instructions: firstly, he had gone to the British at Durban instead of directly to Pretorius at Pietermaritzburg and, secondly, he had not come bearing a peace sign. They duly instructed him to return to Dingane, fetch a white flag and return to Pietermaritzburg eight days after the full moon.[1081]

Pretorius put together a small commando to accompany Gambutshi, even though he questioned Dingane's motives for requesting that the Boers come to retrieve the cattle.[1082] However, when an outbreak of measles ravaged the laager, the commando was disbanded.

On 13 May 1839, Gambutshi and five other Zulu arrived in Pietermaritzburg carrying a white flag. As Pretorius was not there and the site for the handover had not yet been identified, Gambutshi was sent back to Zululand to await instructions from Pretorius.[1083]

The Volksraad met in May 1839 to confirm the terms of the peace agreement with Dingane, which would be in effect once Dingane returned the cattle and possessions promised to the Boers. In addition, a proviso was added that the northern boundary of the Boers' land would be three kilometres north of the river that ran into St Lucia Bay and that Dingane would leave the land and port of Durban clean and uninhabited, no doubt a reference to the British occupation.

On 22 May 1839, the Volksraad reappointed Pretorius as chief commandant. Previously, he had been appointed only as chief commandant of the *Wenkommando* and his role ended when their mission did. This time, his appointment was for an indefinite period.

Pretorius sent a delegation comprising William Cowie, Izak Abraham van Niekerk, Philip Johannes Roscher and translator Klaas Pommer to inform Dingane that he was ready to receive the cattle. His written instructions to Dingane included a request that he personally attend the handover and specified that if he was unable to attend, then he should send two of his senior chiefs in his stead. He also insisted that the Zulu at the handover be kept to a minimum.

On 7 June 1839, 112 Zulu arrived at Pretorius's laager at Doornkop with only 1,300 head of cattle, 400 sheep, 52 guns and 43 saddles. It soon emerged that Dingane had sent two junior captains to negotiate with Pretorius.

When Pretorius opened the discussions by reminding the captains that the Boers would forever remember how Dingane had betrayed Retief and his men and that the Zulu had slaughtered women and children near the Bloukrans and Bushman's rivers, the captains nervously told him that they had not been sent to discuss the wars of the past but rather peace in the future but conceded that Dingane would compensate the Boers with cattle and ivory for the damage inflicted on them by the Zulu.

At this point, Pretorius reminded them that Dingane still owed the Boers 18,000 head of cattle,[1084] as per their agreement, and that if the king wanted to give them ivory, he would deduct the value of the ivory from the value of the cattle owed. He also warned the captains that if Dingane broke the peace agreement, he would lead a commando against Dingane to punish him. To reinforce his intent, he ordered his men to fire two of the cannon a few times. As Pretorius had hoped, the Zulu were terrified to see the cannon spitting flames and belching smoke and promptly signed the peace agreement[1085] after this demonstration.

While Pretorius waited for the balance of the cattle to be delivered,[1086] great excitement swept Natal when the *Mazeppa* put into Durban on 20 July 1839. She had departed Lourenço Marques with the 25 survivors of the Trichardt trek as well as three of their servants.

No sooner had the bedraggled, malaria-riddled group stepped ashore than Jervis rather insensitively demanded that they hand over their weapons, which happened to be their only possessions. (He did return them later but the Boers would never forgive or forget the lack of compassion he had shown toward the group.[1087])

Pretorius finally decided to divide the 1,300 cattle he had received from the Zulu among the 334 men in the laager.

One of the Boers, William Cowie, only received two head of cattle. Furious to receive such a paltry number of cattle, he challenged Pretorius's decision to only allocate him two animals, on the grounds that he had carried out a dangerous mission by visiting Dingane and that the two head of cattle was not sufficient recognition for the dangers he had faced. However, Pretorius wouldn't budge and Cowie resorted to threatening Pretorius that he would tell everyone how unfairly Pretorius had treated him. He also gave his two head of cattle back to show his unhappiness at the token payment.[1088]

Meanwhile, Dingane dispatched four regiments (the *Mbelebele*, the *uNomdayana*, *umKhulutshane* and *imVokwe*) to clear the bush and establish a military base at Nguthumeni Ridge, north of the source of the Ngwavuma River. He called this *Mbelebele*.

To Dingane's surprise, the Swazis did not retreat when the Zulu advanced. In fact, General Mngayi Fakudze led the Swazis in an attack on the Zulu. In the ensuing battle at Lubuye, the Zulu were taken by surprise by the Swazis, who killed two whole regiments of Zulu warriors. When Dingane sent a further two regiments to drive the Swazis back, his warriors encountered staunch resistance and were forced to withdraw. Consequently, Dingane abandoned his plan to occupy the land of the Swazis. The loss of face Dingane had suffered in conceding land to the Boers and his failure to defeat the Swazis led to a severe decline in his popularity among the Zulu. In addition, he had been unable to secure a northern bolthole, which would have come in useful if he experienced further trouble with the Boers.[1089]

The Voortrekkers in Natal were becoming more organized: the governing body of the Volksraad, which had 24 members aged between 25 and 60, was soon emulated in Winburg when Potgieter established a similar body to oversee the trekkers in the Potchefstroom area.[1090]

The members of the Volksraad were certainly industrious and on 29 July 1839, announced that any male older than 15 who enrolled in the militia would be entitled to claim a piece of land in Pietermaritzburg. They also decreed that no Zulu should be allowed to "sojourn" with the Bushmen and that any Bushmen found to be harbouring Zulu would be put to death.[1091] Then, on 31 July 1839, they sent a letter to Jervis in Durban to inform him that that they would not sign any document stating that they would not use the gunpowder against the Zulu if he returned it to them, as they considered the gunpowder theirs by law. They also pointed out that they expected him to return it immediately, with no conditions attached, as the British troops under Jervis had been sent to Durban to keep the peace and they had already concluded a peace agreement with the Zulu. Further, they stressed that the British had no legitimate reason for occupying the port and should therefore leave.

The letter also expressed their anger that he had confiscated the weapons belonging to the trekkers who had disembarked from the *Mazeppa* and stated that they had heard that a certain Mr Bannister had aired his views in several Cape newspapers that a British colony should be established in Natal. They made it very clear that if any British remained in Durban, they would be deemed to be under the jurisdiction and government of the Volksraad and Boers.[1092]

Despite the exchange of rattling letters between the Volksraad and Jervis, the relationship between most Boers and British in Natal was good. In fact, a number of soldiers under Jervis deserted and married young Boer women.[1093]

Back in Britain, the Marquess of Normanby had replaced Lord Glenelg as secretary of state. Although he approved the occupation of the Durban port, he had no intention of expanding the British Empire by colonizing Natal.[1094] Glenelg had resigned suddenly, largely due to being undermined by the British prime minister.

After Stockenström Jr was acquitted on a charge of murdering a young Xhosa boy and it was conceded that the evidence against him had been delivered by "overzealous" colonists from the eastern frontier who could not stand him, he had returned to England. There, he handed his resignation to Glenelg, who accepted it but expressed his full support for Stockenström Jr. Subsequently,

Stockenström Jr withdrew his resignation and Glenelg arranged that he would return to the frontier as lieutenant governor of the eastern districts and with an increased salary.

Shortly after this, the prime minister informed Glenelg that certain changes were to be made in the administration and government of the Cape colony and Glenelg resigned in a fit of rage, as he had not been consulted about these changes.

When word reached Lord Normanby about the intense distrust and dislike felt by the people of the eastern frontier toward Stockenström Jr, he informed Stockenström Jr that he would not be posted to the eastern frontier and offered him a knighthood and post as governor of one of the West Indian Islands. Stockenström Jr refused to accept Normanby's proposal but managed to convince the secretary of state to pay him a pension of £700 per annum and a baronetcy. He then returned to the colony as Sir Andries Stockenström on 31 May 1840.[1095]

On 6 September 1839, Dingane's messengers arrived at Pietermaritzburg carrying a giant elephant tusk and informed the Voortrekkers that there were vast amounts of ivory at Dingane's new village and that they should send two wagons to collect it. They also told Pretorius that Dingane had a further 5,000 head of cattle for the Boers to collect. William Cowie, Izak Abraham van Niekerk and Van Rooyen duly set off from Pietermaritzburg with the wagons. However, on 14 September 1839, just 30 kilometres into their journey, a messenger instructed them to turn back as the Zulu had been spotted massing south of the Tugela River.

Fearing a Zulu attack, they hastily returned to Pietermaritzburg, where Pretorius ordered a commando to ride out and head off the approaching Zulu. Fortunately, De Lange arrived at the settlement before the men left and announced that the Zulu had not crossed the Tugela River with a view to attacking the Voortrekkers but because civil war had broken out among the Zulu. Half of the Zulu nation had rebelled against Dingane and were camped between the Tugela and the Umvoti rivers. Despite the relief the Boers felt at hearing this news, they nevertheless prepared for an attack.[1096]

CHAPTER 29

Betrayal and murder

Mphande meets Volksraad—Mphande istalled as king of emigrant Zulus—Dingane reneges on cattle debt—Natal Association—British depart—Beeskommando—execution of Tambuza—death of Umhlela—death of Dingane

Dingane's half-brother Mphande had deserted with some 17,000 of his followers and 25,000 head of cattle and sought protection from the Boers. Forces loyal to Dingane had pursued them to the Umvoti River, intent on bringing them back. However, they gave up the chase when they neared the Boer settlement as they wanted to avoid being attacked by a Boers.

Mphande was about 44 years old. He was born to Senzangakhona and Songiya but was raised by Chief Dibandlela, who ruled over the coastal plain between the Tugela and Umdloti rivers. As a young man, he had served in the Zulu army and had become a member of the *unGumanqa ibutho* regiment in 1819. Due to his record of good service to King Shaka, the king had rewarded him with two wives.

When Dingane murdered Shaka (his other half-brother), he had spared Mphande. However, he viewed Mphande as a threat to the throne as he had sired many sons while Dingane had no acknowledged heirs. Despite Mphande's frequent attempts to persuade Dingane of his loyalty to him and assurance that he did not aspire to be king, Dingane did not trust him.

During Dingane's military campaign against the Swazis, Dingane sent word to Mphande to send reinforcements from Mphande's regiments to replace those he had lost. He also instructed his half-brother to prepare to move his people across the Pongola River into the Swazi territory he aimed to conquer.

Realizing that this would weaken his powerbase and scatter his followers over a large area, Mphande stalled. He also stopped paying visits of respect to Dingane and claimed that he was ill. Dingane soon started to believe that Mphande was conspiring against him to seize the throne and decided to bring matters to a head by sending Mphande a gift of hundred heifers. Etiquette demanded that Mphande visit the king to thank him for his gift and Dingane planned to murder his half-brother when he visited him. However, the *indunas* tasked with taking the cattle to Mphande, namely Nxagwana kaZivalele and Mathunjana kaSibaca, warned Mphande of Dingane's plan. Subsequently, Mphande rallied his people together as well as those who wanted to escape Dingane and they fled to seek protection from the Boers. Mphande and 40 of his *indunas* and commanders arrived in Durban, where Mphande confirmed that he was leading the uprising against Dingane. He then asked the Boers at Congella for protection against Dingane and for permission to remain south of the Tugela River with his people.[1097]

In a wattle and daub hut in a kraal on the southern side of the Umlazi River, Mphande and his delegation first met with the main Boer negotiator, Wessel Wessels and several others. Wessels informed him that he would need to meet with the Volksraad in Pietermaritzburg. Consequently, Mphande, his young son Cetshwayo and his entourage walked the roughly 100 kilometres to Pietermaritzburg.

On 15 October 1839, Mphande met with the Volksraad and requested that he and his people be allowed to settle between the Umvoti and Umhlali rivers and be treated as Boer subjects. He also asked whether it would be possible for his heir, Cetshwayo, to be educated by the missionaries.[1098]

The members of the Volkraad were naturally suspicious that Mphande was acting on Dingane's behalf and that some form of treachery was afoot. As such, they peppered him with questions before considering his requests. For instance, they asked why he had crossed the border agreed with Dingane and why he had he rebelled in the first place. They also wanted to know details about Dingane's attack on the Swazis and what his relationship had been like with King Shaka and what he had done for the Zulu king.

Finally, they pointed out to Mphande that Dingane's tactic of killing innocent women and children was intolerable and that, as he was aware, they could do battle with him in the near future.

Mphande's frankness and willingness to answer the Volksraad's questions was somewhat reassuring and they agreed that he and his people could live south of the Tugela River while settling their score with Dingane and undertook to protect them if Dingane attacked them, provided that Mphande demonstrated his friendship and alliance to the Boers.[1099]

After Mphande left to return to his people, the members of the Volksraad debated whether they had made a mistake by supporting Mphande. While the majority felt that they should drive Mphande and his people back over the Tugela border as they had broken the treaty with the Zulu, they eventually rationalized that they had insufficient ammunition to shoot them.[1100] In addition, the large amount of cattle Mphande's people had with them did not go unnoticed by the Boers and they decided to send a deputation to negotiate further terms with Mphande.[1101]

A few days after this meeting, Dingane sent a message to remind the Boers to come and collect the ivory from him and promised that he would hand over a large herd of cattle within 20 days.

On 24 October 1839, a Boer delegation of 28 men under Frans Roos left Durban in 13 wagons, having adorned the leading wagon with the Boers' new flag, which comprised red, white and blue vertical stripes. (Included in the group were French naturalist Adolphe Delegorgue, American missionary Edmund Morewood, a Prussian Archaeologist called Dr Ferdinand von Krause and the Englishman, Parker.)

Of course, Jervis viewed their departure with great suspicion and was agitated that they would instigate a breakdown in the newly established relations with Dingane.[1102] When they arrived at Mphande's temporary residence, they planned to announce the terms of the alliance and to install Mphande as reigning prince of the emigrant Zulu, with a view to declaring him king of the Zulu nation when Dingane was dethroned.[1103]

Roos's delegation arrived at *kwaMahambehlala* (which means 'the place where I intend to stay') two days after leaving Durban. As the wagons approached the village, thousands of excited Zulu streamed toward them and crowded around the wagons, to the extent that some of the *indunas* had to wave sticks and whips at them so they would move out of the way.

Mphande evidently viewed the Boers' arrival as an occasion worth celebrating and before meeting them, he donned a magnificent cloak that emphasized his large stature. Known to be an ostentatious dresser, [1104]he had a stout body, high forehead with jutting brows, a generous mouth and strong, square jaw. His most noticeable facial feature was his large eyes, which sparkled like "black diamonds", and he always spoke clearly and in a calm manner, even when he was excited or angry. As Delegorgue later remarked, "He had such precise gestures and charm that a Parisian might well have believed that Mphande in his youth had frequented the palaces of kings." The Frenchman also observed that Mphande's grace and sophisticated bearing made the Boers appear awkward and unrefined in comparison.[1105]

When the Boers explained that their visit was not a social one, Mphande appeared to be crestfallen. However, when they told him that it was their intention to install him as prince of the emigrant Zulu and requested that he make the necessary preparations for the ceremony, he reiterated his commitment to the new friendship and alliance with the Boers. He then instructed his captains to convey what he had said to the Boers to the approximately 6,000 onlookers, who roared their approval, and requested that the Boers fire a volley of shots after the formal proceedings to salute and honour him in front of his people.

The next morning, the Boers presented Mphande with several gifts: their tricolour flag, a hunting dagger and a blue cloak, which Mphande wrapped around himself like a toga.[1106] They then erected a large tent in which to host the discussions with Mphande and joined in the feast held in their honour that evening.

Despite having enjoyed the hospitality of the Zulu, sleep did not come easily to the Boers, who could not help but remember how Retief and his men had initially been heartily welcomed by Dingane at Umgungundlovu. Accordingly, they kept their loaded weapons close at hand and draped the reigns of the horses over their arms while they slept.

The next day, more than 6,000 Zulu surrounded the tent to watch the proceedings. Roos clarified that Mphande and his people would be allowed to remain where they were until Dingane was defeated, whereafter Mphande would be declared king of the Zulu nation and he and his people would have to return to the area north of the Tugela River.[1107] Subsequently, the two men agreed to join forces in attacking Dingane and that Mphande would cede the land around St Lucia Bay to the Boers once he was king. In addition, Mphande agreed to give the Boers the 18,000 head of cattle that Dingane owed them and that his people would not practise witchcraft, go to war with anyone without receiving permission from the Volksraad or kill or injure women and children in the forthcoming battle against Dingane.[1108]

Although Mphande readily agreed to the terms laid out by Roos, it was clear that he felt dejected.[1109] After Roos drew up the agreement, he 'crowned' Mphande as the "ruling prince of the emigrant Zulu" and asked him to select three generals to protect him. These men would be held liable if Mphande were injured or killed and if any act of aggression was perpetrated against the Boers. Mphande duly selected Mpangazitha ka Mncumbatha, Nongalaza and Mleni to be his generals.

Shortly after Mphande had left the meeting, a crowd of about 300 warriors gathered near the tent. Their shouts and screams prompted Roos to send a young Zulu interpreter to find out the cause of the disturbance[1110] and the Boers soon saw a horrifying scene: one of the newly elected generals, Mpangazitha ka Mncumbatha, was being beaten by the angry mob. He vainly tried to protect himself as the warriors bludgeoned him with their *indukas* and finally collapsed into a crumpled heap. It was clear that he was dead.

By the time the Boers grabbed their guns, the violent episode was over and Roos immediately sent for Mphande, who told him that Mpangazitha had been killed because he was a *sangoma* and had been responsible for the murder of

Retief and his men. Later, it transpired that Mpangazitha's death had actually been prompted by the people's intense dislike of his overbearing and arrogant behaviour.

He played the matter down in front of the Boers and gave no indication that he was concerned that some of his people had defied him by killing his appointed general.[1111] However, he summoned one of his captains, Mkhonto, and gave him a tongue-lashing. "Why have you allowed them to commit such an act in front of the white people?" he demanded angrily. "What will they think of me when, just a few moments ago, I promised that my people wound not commit acts of this nature? We will need their friendship in future."

The Boers urged Mphande to start the celebrations as they hoped the festivities would diffuse the tension among the Zulu.[1112] Soon, a few thousand Zulu had surrounded Mphande and his guests and the Boers watched them anxiously. At first, they did not comprehend that the whistling and ululating mob was in fact celebrating the announcement that Mphande was now recognized as their prince. However, they were quick to join in the revelry and hoisted their flag and fired several shots to salute Mphande. Subsequently, the Zulu started dancing jubilantly.

Morewood warmed himself by a fire while watching the merriment and the gunpowder in his powder horn eventually overheated. His powder horn exploded with a mighty bang. Subsequently, the celebratory mood among the Zulu soured abruptly and Mphande returned to his residence, looking more depressed than ever. [1113] (Fortunately, Morewood sustained only superficial injuries, despite his singed clothes.)

The next day, Mphande gave the Boers the first instalment of 378 cattle[1114] before they left. Having settled matters with the Zulu, the Volksraad wished to stabilize affairs with the Pondo. Consequently, Roos was sent to visit Faku, the chief of the Pondo people, to inform him that the Umzimvubu River would form the southern border of the Boer Republic and to negotiate a peace treaty with him.

Pretorius realized that the ongoing conflict between the Boers and Dingane would only be concluded with a decisive battle. As such, he started putting together a commando that would attack Dingane and his followers, with the support of Mphande's army. He sent Field Cornet Jan du Plessis across the Drakensberg Mountains and into the colony to recruit Boer volunteers to fight in the *Beeskommando* (Cattle commando), so named as they would attempt to recover the cattle that Dingane still owed the Boers.[1115]

Dingane was greatly concerned by Mphande's defection and berated General

Umhlela for advising him not to kill his half-brother. Realizing that Mphande was allied to the Boers, he tried to turn them against Mphande by sending an envoy to the Volksraad to tell them that Mphande was "not a man. He has turned away his face: he is a woman. He was useless to Dingane his master, and he will be [of] no use to you. Do not trust him, for his face may turn again".[1116] He also tried to curry favour with the Boers by sending cattle to them at Pietermaritzburg in dribs and drabs. However, the Boers' patience with him had already been exhausted.

In the Boers' camps, it was rumoured that the colonial government had sold Natal to a number of British emigrants. This rumour was fuelled by a report in the *Grahamstown Journal* in October 1839 regarding a company, namely the Natal Association, that had been founded in England with the purpose of colonizing Natal. In addition, they had read that the Earl of Ripon presented a petition to the House of Lords from several merchants from Liverpool motivating the colonization of Natal.

The Boers were infuriated by the reports and, on 11 November 1839, the Volksraad issued a declaration of protest warning that any new emigrants who arrived in Natal would be treated as enemies of the state.[1117]

The declaration set out at length the reasons for the Boers' departure from the colony and the daily dangers, difficulties and sacrifices they lived with. It also pointed out that their faith had helped them to survive and bitterly described how Dingane had murdered Retief and other fellow trekkers and slaughtered women and children by the Bushman's and Bloukrans rivers. Further, it detailed the good relations between the Boers and the "existing inhabitants" (British settlers) in Durban and highlighted that Charters had assured the Boers that the British occupation of Durban was merely to prevent bloodshed between the Boers and the Zulu.

According to the document, the anticipated arrival of thousands of British citizens in Durban with the intention of driving the Boers from their "dearly purchased and lawfully acquired country" would not be tolerated. It concluded that the Boers would view future emigrants as enemies and that if they were accompanied by any military force, the Boers would take up arms against them.

Unbeknown to the Boers, on the same day that the Volksraad issued their declaration, the governor of the Cape colony sent a letter to the secretary of state in England to inform him that Jervis and the 72nd Regiment were to be withdrawn from Durban and sent back to England. [1118]

Much to the delight of the Boers, the British troops in Durban boarded the *Vectis* on Christmas Eve. Before the ship set sail for England, Jervis wished the Boers well and told them that he hoped they would behave as Christians and "enlighten ignorance, dispel superstition, and cause crime, bloodshed and oppression to cease".

The jubilant Boers unleashed a volley of gunfire to see the troops off and then quickly replaced the red, white and blue flag of Great Britain at Durban with their own and took back their confiscated gunpowder.[1119] They were finally free from British interference. Or so they thought.

The following day, Pretorius ordered all Boer men able to bear arms to rally at Kommando Drift, where they were joined by a large force under Commandant M.A. Oberholzer. He instructed them to organize themselves into groups of six or eight and each group was assigned one wagon and two *veghekke*.

On 4 January 1840, the Volksraad met and issued instructions to Pretorius to proceed with the commando to recover the cattle promised. They now demanded 40,000 head of cattle, slightly less than double what had been agreed with Dingane.

Although Pretorius was itching for the *Beeskommando* to launch their attack on Dingane, he heard reports that there were 120 wagons camped between the Elands and Tugela rivers and that the burghers manning them were on their way over the mountains to join their commando. Consequently, he postponed the departure of the expedition until 15 January 1840.[1120]

Dingane was not oblivious to the Boers' plans and sent Umhlela to deliver over 60 elephant tusks to Pretorius in an attempt to stave off an attack and, in early January 1840, sent Tambuza and Kombazana, one of his lieutenants, to plead for peace.

Dingane trusted Tambuza implicitly and he made quite an impression when he arrived at the small settlement of Pietermaritzburg with 200 extremely thin oxen. The high ranking general and commander of Dingane's forces was a giant of a man and had led the *Isihlangu Mnyama* regiment at the Battle of Blood River and been an integral tactician in the Zulu's surprise attacks at the Bloukrans and Bushman's rivers.[1121]

Mphande was in the settlement at the time as he was preparing his warriors to accompany Pretorius's commando. He was shocked to see his arch enemy's commander and warned Pretorius that Tambuza was as dangerous as Dingane and had played a major role in the massacre of Retief's party and of the Boers at the Bloukrans and Bushman's rivers.

Taking Mphande's warning to heart, Pretorius had Tambuza and Kombazana arrested and hauled before the Volksraad. Although Tambuza tried his best to persuade thc Boers that Dingane wanted peace, Pretorius scoffed at the 200 scrawny beasts that Tambuza had brought as a peace offering and demanded that he tell Dingane to immediately provide the Boers with the 40,000 head of cattle he had promised them.

When Tambuza replied that these cattle had not yet been rounded up, a furious Pretorius had the two Zulu stripped naked and put in chains. He also proposed to the Volksraad that Tambuza be brought to trial for his involvement in the murders of the Boers at Umgungundlovu and at the Bloukrans and Bushman's rivers.[1122]

Before departing, he was provided with a 22-point document outlining his priorities and instructions. This document contained several obvious instructions, such as the need to organize the wagons scattered around Pietermaritzburg into laagers before the commando departed the settlement, and was clearly intended to show him that he was answerable to the Volksraad and, ultimately, not the boss. The enemies Pretorius had made of some members of the Volksraad due to his popularity and power among the Boers used this opportunity to cut him down to size.

Mphande's army would be under the command of Nongalaza, who had been a general in the Zulu army when it defeated Cane and Biggar's Grand Army of Natal, and he would lead the 4,500 warriors[1123] to Dingane's new village along the Lower Tugela River and then coastal route. Simultaneously, the Boers would take a route that led over the Umzinyathi and Ncome rivers.

When the commando left Pietermaritzburg on 14 January 1840, Pretorius shared a wagon with Mphande, who was ostensibly his guest.

Although the prince had brought 24 bodyguards with him, Pretorius was determined to kill him if it turned out that he had double-crossed the Boers and therefore wanted him within his sights at all times. Mphande must have been simultaneously alarmed and amused by the fact that the infamous Tambuza was naked and in chains, as was Kombazana. When the commando reached the Tugela River four days later, they found Andries Spies camped there with 70 Boers from the colony. They made a welcome addition to the commando, which now comprised 335 armed men, 60 Hottentot servants and 400 Zulu servants. With the small army were 600 horses and 50 wagons drawn by 700 oxen.

Pretorius was still worried that there were too few men in his commando and therefore sent field cornet P.M. Bester back to Pietermaritzburg to try to recruit more soldiers. In light of this and no doubt influenced by the fact that other reinforcements were dribbling over the Drakensberg Mountains, Pretorius again decided to halt the march of the commando for several days.

Dingane had moved with his army to the Magudu Mountains, where Umhlela divided the warriors army into two sections: one would guard the king while he hid in a cave[1124] about 13 kilometres south of the Pongola River while the other would attack the combined forces of Pretorius's commando and Nongalaza's men. Finally, Pretorius and his cumbersome convoy was ready to move on and progressed slowly over the rain-sodden grass.

By now, the commando included Delegorgue as well as Englishmen Parker, Hamilton and Howard and other Boers soon joined the slow-moving caravan of wagons, as did many Zulu warriors led by minor chiefs in the areas they passed through. These minor chiefs had turned against Dingane and relished the opportunity to fight against him.

Most of the Boers on commando viewed the expedition in a positive light, as an opportunity to enrich themselves. The agitation and fear displayed that had been evident among the men in the *Wenkommando* at Blood River was absent. In fact, the journey was characterized by a festive and relaxed atmosphere among the Boers and it appeared as though they had lost their fear of and respect for the Zulu. The men played games and wrestled one another good-naturedly and many enjoyed the wine provided by trader F. Lingenfelder, who had over 3,000 litres in his wagon. Much to Pretorius's dismay, the men were often drunk. However, there was little he could do to curtail the drunkenness of his men.

It was whispered that Pretorius seemed to have dropped his guard and was no longer the brilliant leader he had been during the Battle of Blood River.[1125] As Delegorgue cynically commented later, "Pretorius had his own tactics, and that was not to have any tactics at all."[1126]

On 21 January 1840, the 60 wagons of the commando snaked across the wet veld in a six-kilometre train, despite that this formation made the over 300 Boers extremely vulnerable to an attack. Pretorius had appointed a 12-man war council, of which he was the chairman. Interestingly, of all the senior commanders who had been with Pretorius in the *Wenkommando*, only Jacobus Potgieter was chosen to be a senior commander in the *Beeskommando* and in the council. Moreover, while De Lange had been given permission by the Volksraad to accompany the *Beeskommando*, despite having been demoted from commandant for having illegally retained cattle confiscated from the Zulu, he elected not to join the commando on this mission.[1127]

There was confusion and concern in the Boer camp on 22 January 1840 when 254 Zulu warriors in full battle dress approached the wagons. However, it quickly emerged that they were being led by Zikhali, the son of Matiwane of the Ngwane tribe, and they made it abundantly clear that they were no friends of Dingane and wanted to join Pretorius to assist in crushing their common enemy.

In fact, they arrived singing praise songs about Pretorius and how he had freed them from Dingane and then put on a magnificent dance performance for the Boers.

Afterwards, Pretorius dragged the naked Tambuza before the Ngwane warriors and they pleaded with Pretorius to kill him. "He must die; he must die!" they chorused before accusing Tambuza of having encouraged Dingane to kill Retief and his men and of feeling no compunction toward spilling innocent blood. They shouted that Pretorius must never forget that Tambuza had led the Zulu army to massacre the Boers at the Bloukrans and Bushman's rivers.

The continuous rain and the arrival of further Boer reinforcements prompted Pretorius to eventually halt the convoy for two days. After 50 Boers who were soaked to the bone joined the commando on 25 January 1840, Pretorius's Boer force comprised 400 men.

After a church service on Sunday 26 January 1840, the convoy finally moved on. The men travelled the 25 kilometres to the Sundays River through the thick mud.[1128] There, Pretorius received a message the following day informing him that Nongalaza and his army had reached the Maqongqo Hills near the Magudu Mountains and that the battle was imminent.

At this time, the convoy still had 200 kilometres to go before it would reach the Maqongqo Hills and Pretorius immediately dispatched a messenger to order Nongalaza not to engage Dingane's army until the commando arrived, which he hoped would be in four days' time. He then sent four 100-man patrols to make a path for the wagons over the rugged terrain of the Biggarsberg mountain range. Although the wagon belonging to the Wessels family tipped over at one point, all 60 of the wagons successfully traversed the mountain and then outspanned by the Sand River. (Here, French naturalist Delegorgue discovered a seam of coal and later sent samples to London to be analyzed.[1129])

The next day, they crossed the fast-flowing Buffalo River and, during the perilous river crossing, the wagons were submerged to the level of their floorboards in the foaming water. After two wagons overturned while crossing the steep walls of Kommando Drift, the convoy continued to Blood River, where many silently observed the bleached skulls and bones of the thousands of Zulu who had been killed two years earlier in the Battle of Blood River.

From Blood River, the commando moved east toward Dingane's new headquarters and by late afternoon, had reached the Vanyana River. There, Pretorius received word from two of Nongalaza's messengers that Dingane was planning to flee in a northwesterly direction to join forces with Mzilikazi of the Matabele and that he was hiding near his headquarters.[1130]

Pretorius assembled his war council next to the Vanyana River on 31 January 1840 to determine what should be done with Tambuza and Kombazana. During their trial, Mphande acted as the chief prosecutor and chief accuser, while Pretorius served as judge and the members of the war council made up the jury. Once the two naked and manacled prisoners had been brought before the court and many onlookers jostling to get a good view of proceedings, Mphande furiously accused Tambuza of having instigated the atrocities committed by Dingane. In particular, he blamed Tambuza for the murders of Retief and his followers and subsequent attacks on the Boers. In addition, he charged Tambuza with having attempted to murder him, citing that Tambuza had ordered Dingane's warriors to drag him to *kwaMatiwane*. He added that if it had not been for the intervention of his mother, he would certainly have been killed.

Tambuza listened to Mphande's accusations impassively and it seemed as though he accepted that his death was inevitable. When Pretorius asked Tambuza if he wanted to say anything in his defence, Tambuza matter-of-factly answered that Mphande had told the truth and that he was prepared to die for his crimes. However, he asked that he be shot by grown men and not boys.[1131] Surprisingly, he pleaded that Pretorius spare Kombazana's life and explained that he had had nothing to do with these crimes. Nevertheless, Pretorius sentenced both prisoners to death and instructed Commandant Spies to oversee their execution.

"You are about to appear before the highest Judge, the Master on High, so I urge you to confess your crimes before God and seek His forgiveness and, by doing so, avoid eternal punishment," Pretorius urged Tambuza and Kombazana.

"I have but one master, and I must remain faithful to that master until the end. If I do that, I am sure that the Master on High, if there is one, will approve of my conduct," Tambuza replied calmly.

Spies ordered H. van Coller and Hans Terblanche to march the prisoners to the river and to shoot them there. While Kombazana crumpled to the ground and died almost instantly, Tambuza did not. The wounded former general struggled to his feet, despite still being chained to Kombazana, and faced the Boers' guns again. Mercifully, he died after the second volley of gunfire.[1132]

Pretorius had acted out of character by executing Tambuza and Kombazana: irrespective of Tambuza's role in the killings of Retief and the Voortrekkers, he had presented himself to Pretorius as Dingane's envoy who had been entrusted to negotiate peace with the Boers on behalf of his king.

After the two prisoners had been executed, a young Boer called Van Deventer was called before the court and charged with having assaulted Englishman John Howard's son. After reprimanding Van Deveneter sternly, Pretorius warned him that if he was caught committing any similar misdemeanour again, he would be manacled to a wagon and would continue the journey on foot.[1133]

Soon after the court adjourned, a messenger arrived with the news that Nongalaza and his forces had almost reached Dingane's hideout. Consequently, Pretorius ordered the convoy to speed up so that the men could join Nongalaza's army as soon as possible.

On 1 February 1840, Pretorius sent patrols to seek a suitable route for the wagons across the mountainous region of Ntabankulu. Shortly after they had left the Boer camp, a messenger arrived to tell Pretorius that the battle was already over. Nongalaza's forces had clashed with and beaten the Zulu army on 30 January 1840.

Pretorius immediately dispatched Izak Abraham van Niekerk and Christiaan Muller to verify the report, with two bottles of brandy.[1134] Pretorius later learned that Nongalaza had led Mphande's forces against Dingane's army near the Maqongqo hills in a fierce battle.

Although both sides had a similar number of warriors, namely about 5,000 men, the morale of the warriors under Nongalaza had proven to be higher than that of the warriors under Umhlela.

The confidence of Nongalaza's forces was perhaps bolstered by the knowledge that the Boers would reinforce their efforts with their firepower. In addition, the premier Zulu *sangoma*, Mahlungwana kaTshoba, had abandoned Dingane and was lending his skills to Nongalaza's warriors. In particular, he had dispensed *muthi* to them before the battle and used it on a large patch of grass that he had burned, which would allegedly result in the defeat of Dingane's men the moment any of them touched it.

Initially, it had looked as though Umhlela's men would overpower the warriors in Nongalaza's army, especially when the *Udlambedlu* regiment had surged forward. However, Nongalaza's men, led by the *iziBawuibutho,* rallied and drove Umhlela's men back.

There were many casualties in Umhlela's three regiments and many of his men started to defect to Nongalaza's side when they heard shouts that the Boers were coming. Seeing so many comrades defecting, Umhlela's men began to retreat. An exception was Nozitshada kaMagoboza, the *induna* of the *Udlambedlu*: he furiously stabbed at Nongalaza's warriors, until he had no strength left in his arms to use his assegai and was overwhelmed by his enemy. Even while prostrate on the ground, he demonstrated what a brave individual he was. "Stab me! The king is dead. Come, stab me!" he shouted to those crowded around him, which they did.

Nongalaza's warriors killed all of the men in two of Umhlela's regiments and those who had not already defected from the third regiment turned tail and fled.

While Nongalaza's men pursued them, they finished off any of Umhlela's wounded men that lay on the grassy plain. Moreover, they flushed Bhibhi, Umhlela's sister and Senzangakhona's widow, from her hiding place and killed her, despite her distinguished royal status.[1135]

Umhlela had been injured in his right thigh with a stabbing spear but managed to limp off the battlefield. He and the remainder of the army then joined his fugitive king and the remnants of the royal household that were hiding at the kraal of Lwana ka Ngqengelele across the Pongola River, in Swaziland.[1136]

When Dingane saw his defeated warriors, he shouted, "Where is Ndhlela? He too must die. It is he who used to say that Mphande was less than nothing. I see that it is he who has ruined my army as well!"[1137] He then spotted his wounded commander-in-chief and unleashed his wrath upon him. "You are a coward and useless," he screamed, before ordering that Umhlela be arrested.

Warriors seized Umhlela, bound him and dragged him before Dingane, who strangled Umhlela with an ox-hide thong, in front of his warriors and *indunas*. There was a rumble of disquiet from the many onlookers while Umhlela's body jerked spasmodically before finally becoming still and when Dingane shouted that Umhlela was not worthy of a proper burial and ordered that his corpse be left out for the hyenas and jackals, many of the Zulu seethed with discontent.

The *indunas* in particular were shocked by Dingane's savage treatment of a man who had given his king his all and many of them began to plot to have Dingane assassinated. Others realized that his brutal behaviour indicated that his powerbase was weakening and fled to Mphande to pledge their allegiance to him.[1138]

Although Pretorius had received reports that Nongalaza and his forces were chasing Dingane and his followers, he instructed his men to prepare for an expedition in which they would deal with the remnants of Dingane's army. By this stage, a steady stream of deserters from Dingane's army was pouring into the Boer camp with cattle for the Boers.

Van Niekerk and Muller soon returned and confirmed the victory by Nongalaza. However, they reported the it had been a bloody battle in which at least 1,200 of Nongalaza's warriors were wounded and thousands of warriors from both sides had died. They also informed Pretorius that Nongalaza was attempting to drive Dingane and his severely diminished army of between 3,000 and 4,000 warriors south so that the Boers could assist them to finish the Zulu army off.[1139]

On 3 February 1840, Pretorius ordered 220 men to ride out in the hope that they would encounter the Zulu army and then engage them in battle. However, under cover of thick mist, Dingane's warriors managed to escape into the mountains, where they hid in kloofs and caves before splitting into small groups and eluding their Boer pursuers.

When Pretorius returned to the laager that night, he was shocked to find that some of the Boers who had remained at the camp had been drinking heavily. Enraged by the unruly behaviour of his men, he summoned Lingenfelder to appear before the *krygsraad* (war council) the next day.

At the meeting, Pretorius reprimanded Lingenfelder for having sold liquor to the men and for causing the rampant drunkenness in the camp during his absence. The *krygsraad* then banned any further sale of alcohol to the men and ordered that all of the taps on the wine vats be locked.[1140] Afterwards, Pretorius ordered 250 men to prepare to proceed to the Pongola River and to pursue Dingane.

They left early on the morning of 5 February 1840 and rode northeast as they had heard that some of the Zulu stragglers were hiding in a cave in the hills in that direction. Upon reaching the cave and reuniting with Nongalaza and his men, Pretorius ordered the Boers to surround the cave. Then, he instructed interpreters to shout to the Zulu in the cave that they should surrender and come outside.

When there was no response, Pretorius ordered Commandant Lombard to take 25 men into the cave and to shoot every man they found. He insisted that they take care not to shoot any women and children.

At the entrance to the cave, the men encountered three warriors and promptly shot them. Almost immediately, they heard shouts from farther inside the cave. "Stop, stop, we shall all come out!" someone yelled.

Two Zulu men and a 'knobnose' of the Magwamba tribe, who was evidently being held prisoner, emerged from the darkness, followed by 50 Zulu women and children.

Half an hour later, the two Zulu men attempted to flee and were shot down by the Boers. Nongalaza had watched the Boers closely during this operation and was deeply impressed by the way in which they had conducted themselves. "You really are people who fear nothing," he said, placing his hand on Pretorius's shoulder.

Shortly after this incident, Pretorius's men and Nongalaza's warriors continued pursuing Dingane. However, heavy rain forced them to shelter in a deserted kraal until the rain subsided.

The following day, Nongalaza approached Pretorius on behalf of Kowana and Maphita, two of the enemy Zulu captains, to beg him to show mercy toward them. They claimed that they had been unhappy under Dingane and had been waiting the right opportunity to make their escape. They hoped that they and their followers would be allowed to join Mphande.

Pretorius informed Kowana and Maphita that he would be prepared to view them as Mphande's subjects but that they and their people should present themselves to him by twelve o'clock the next day. He warned them that if they did not come as summoned, the Boers would kill all of the Zulu found who had until recently been loyal to Dingane. Subsequently, the two men scurried off to tell their lieutenants and people about their discussion with Pretorius.

The Boers reached the Pongola River the next day and learned that Dingane and about 100 warriors had crossed it five days earlier. As they travelled, they encountered hundreds of Zulu who had fled from Dingane and discovered that most of these refugees felt bitter toward Dingane. Some even claimed that they were so enraged by how he had behaved that they would willingly tear him to pieces with their bare teeth.

Soon, ten of the Boers' horses had died from horse sickness and the loss of these horses, combined with relentless rain, prompted Pretorius's men to return to their camp next to the Umfolozi River with the 10,000 head of cattle they had rounded up.

Pretorius left Nongalaza in charge of continuing to hunt down Dingane and his few remaining warriors.[1141]

On 10 February 1840, Pretorius sent for Mphande and his captains and informed them that they had proved their loyalty and trustworthiness in the past few days. He then declared that he would appoint Mphande as king of the Zulu nation on behalf of the Volksraad, as it was clear that Dingane had been ousted.

Naturally, Mphande was delighted with this news and he made an impassioned speech in which he promised to remain faithful to Pretorius and the Boer government and thanked the Boers for delivering him and his people from Dingane's evil. "Should any nation or people ever attempt to do you any injury, you have only to appraise me thereof, and depend upon it that I shall immediately order my whole force to assist you, and for your sake sacrifice my whole army to a man; For I was dead and you have restored me to life; I was cast away, and you have lifted me up again. All my happiness and prosperity I owe to you," he declared.

When word reached Pretorius that chiefs Kowana and Maphita were nervous to bring their people to the Boer camp as they feared they would incur some form of retribution from the Boers, despite Pretorius's promise to the contrary, Pretorius sent word that they would not be harmed.

Nongalaza and his forces had been unable to locate Dingane and requested that they be allowed to return to the Boer camp with the cattle they had confiscated from Dingane. Pretorius agreed to their request and decided to abandon the search for Dingane and return to Pietermaritzburg.

Meanwhile, Lingenfelder had been up to his old tricks. In direct disobedience to the orders issued by Pretorius and the *krygsraad*, he had been selling liquor to the Boers, as indicated by the several incidents of drunken (and sometimes reprehensible) behaviour in the Boer camp. For instance, Botha and Gideon van der Schyff got into an altercation after Botha held Van der Schyff's head underwater in the river. The inebriated Van der Schyff lost his temper and the two men came to blows. Then, Van der Schyff returned to the camp to fetch his gun and proceeded back to the river to shoot Botha. When he discovered that Botha had left, he shot dead a young Hottentot boy.

As soon as Pretorius learned what had happened, he had Van der Schyff arrested and brought before the *krygsraad*, who found him guilty of murder. However, the men in the war council felt that they could not sentence him as they "did not have any jurisdiction over civil and criminal matters", despite having sentenced Tambuza and Kombazana to death without any hesitation or compunction. Instead, they resolved to take Van der Schyff to Pietermaritzburg as a prisoner.[1142]

That same day, Lingenfelder was brought before the *krygsraad* and the members decided to confiscate all of his liquor and to transport it to Pietermaritzburg in a sealed wagon. Of course, Lingenfelder was most unhappy with this form of punishment and he threatened to blacken Pretorius's name in the colony, as he felt that he had been unjustly treated by him. [1143]

Once in Pietermaritzburg, the Volksraad released Van der Schyff and dispensed with a murder trial and Lingenfelder was set free as he had "had sold liquor outside the territory over which the Voortrekkers had any jurisdiction".[1144]

On 14 February 1840, Pretorius called a meeting in front of the wagons with all of the Boers and Mphande and his *indunas*. After the Boers' flag had been raised, Pretorius solemnly read out a proclamation to the crowd in which he claimed from Dingane 122,600 rix-dollars for expenses incurred during the war against his army.

He also announced that he had seized all of the land from the Tugela River to the Black Umfolozi River in the name of the Volksraad and that the boundary was the Umzimvubu River to the south, the Black Umfolozi River to the north (including St Lucia) and the sea to the east.

When Pretorius finished reading the declaration, he ordered a 21-gun salute and the Boers cheered wildly as they threw their hats into the air. The enormous noise generated by Boers' cannon terrified the Zulu and Mphande told Pretorius that he wanted to leave the proceedings. Subsequently, he and his captains ran across the muddy veld toward their camp, diving for cover every time the cannon was fired.

The *Beeskommando* then set off for Pietermaritzburg with 31,000 head of cattle. Unfortunately, the torrential rain slowed their progress and they decided to outspan by the White Umfolozi River. They were so eager to get home that they travelled on the Sabbath and broke camp immediately after the church service on 16 February 1840.[1145]

During the day, Jobi Jr, Zikhali and Nongalaza arrived at the Boer camp and were requested to appear before the *krygsraad* the following day. At this meeting, Nongalaza relayed to the Boers that he had discovered Dingane's mother about 50 kilometres from the Pongola River and that Dingane had abandoned her when she became too tired to continue walking. When Nongalaza questioned her as to her son's whereabouts, she told him that Dingane had fled east toward the Lebombo Mountains with a small group of followers and their cattle. He added that although he had sent scouts to look for Dingane, they had been unsuccessful, and he decided to give up the chase because malaria was prevalent in the area. However, he had brought Dingane's mother with him.

The *krygsraad* was well pleased with what Nongalaza reported and commended him for his bravery and honourable conduct. Conversely, they were less than happy with Jobi Jr and Zikhali, as they had heard tell that these two had siphoned off 1,000 head of cattle seized from Dingane's people and hidden in the mountains. In addition, they had murdered many Tlokwa and had in some instances cut off some of their lips.

Pretorius ordered that they be arrested and told them that they would be tried by the *krygsraad* in Pietermaritzburg. One can only assume that Jobi Jr was attempting to lessen the severity of his imminent punishment when he sent a message to his followers to return the cattle he had stolen to Pretorius.[1146] When the commando reached the Buffalo River on 18 February 1840, they found that the riverbanks were submerged. The prospect of crossing the swollen river was certainly daunting and when the Voortrekkers started across it, some of the wagons sunk so deep into the water that only a metre of so of canvas could be seen. By the time they reached the other side, they had lost as many as 60 oxen as well as their ammunition and provisions to the raging waters of the Buffalo River.[1147]

On 20 February 1840, Pretorius sent a messenger ahead to report to the Volksraad in Pietermaritzburg on the outcome of the battle and to request that men be sent to assist with herding the livestock, which now numbered 36,000 head of cattle.

The following day, the rain finally relented and the victorious commando made its way to Pietermaritzburg, relishing the first sunshine in eight days.

At the settlement, the *krygsraad* listened to the evidence against Zikhali regarding the cattle he had stolen and the murders of some of the Tlokwa people and decided to postpone the case. However, during the same hearing, other Zulu were dragged before the court to face charges for a variety of crimes and misdemeanours. Each of those found guilty was bound, made to lie on the ground and then flogged 12 times with two metre-long horse whips.[1148]

On 24 February 1840, Pretorius allocated 14,000 head of cattle to those who had suffered under the hands of Dingane. He handed the remaining 27,000 cattle to the Volksraad to distribute among the Boers and dissolved the *Beeskommando.*

It was only in April 1840 that the Boers heard any significant news about Dingane: two of Mphande's messengers arrived in Pietermaritzburg to tell them that the Swazis had murdered the deposed king. Then, five Swazis arrived a few days later to confirm the news and to claim the 25 head of cattle and five blankets that Pretorius had offered as a reward to the person or people responsible for killing Dingane.[1149]

Dingane's death was later verified by Carolus Trichardt upon his arrival in Durban. When it was rumoured in Lourenço Marques that Dingane would attack the settlement, Carolus had sailed up the Maputo River to investigate the rumour and learned of Dingane's demise.[1150] Dingane and his followers had fled through the lands of the Nyawo people in Swaziland and Dingane made a fatal mistake by taking possession of a hill called *Hlathikhulu* (Great Forest). When he began to build his new headquarters there, he earned the wrath of the Nyawo people, who considered this hill to be a sacred hunting ground.

The regent of the Nyawo, Silevana, worried that Dingane could become a threat to his people and that the Boers might perceive him to be harbouring their enemy. Consequently, decreed that Dingane and his followers should be driven from the land at the first opportunity. However, when he consulted with Sambane, the heir apparent, and Sambane's councillors, he was advised not to attack Dingane until he had consulted with the queen regent of Swaziland.

Unbeknown to Dingane, his *indunas* were plotting to betray him. Many of Dingane's followers were tired of living in exile, the constant scarcity of food and the threat of being attacked by Nyawo's army of Swazis and when they learned that Pretorius would pardon all Zulu who returned to Zululand to serve under Mphande, the *indunas* decided that they would lead the fugitive Zulu back to their homeland … after they had killed Dingane.

One of the *indunas* visited Silevana at the end of February 1840 to inform him of their unhappiness under Dingane and requested that the regent arrange for Dingane's murder, as none of the *indunas* were prepared to take responsibility for killing him.

Silevana feigned shock and surprise upon hearing the request and expressed his indignation that the *indunas* would even consider spilling royal blood. Naturally, he made no mention that he and his people were already planning to drive the Zulu from *Hlathikhulu* and that they planned to capture and kill Dingane.

The *induna* doggedly informed Silevana that the bulk of Dingane's warriors were away: some of his subjects were foraging for food and cattle, while others had travelled to the district of Ngotshe to collect cattle or were guarding a great herd of cattle in the valley of the Pongola River. To his dismay, it appeared as though Silevana was baffled that he was providing this information to him and he did not hold out much hope that the regent would have Dingane assassinated, even though Silevana told him that he would consider his request.

Early in March 1840, Silevana set out for *Hlathikhulu* with Sambane, his *indunas* (Nywayo and Mdluli) and a contingent of warriors that the queen regent of Swaziland had sent as well as his own army. It was still dark when Silevana's forces silently surrounded Dingane's settlement and then crept into the fenced area around his hut and took up positions on either side of its entrance. When a couple of bleary-eyed warriors staggered out of the hut to urinate outside, the Nyawo fell upon them. Their screams woke all of those in the settlement and men came tumbling out of their huts toward the central cattle kraal.

Although a few of the Zulu were prepared to fight, most attempted to flee their attackers and were immediately cut down by the Nyawo's spears. "Lay down your arms," one of the Nyawo cried. "If you do, your lives will be spared. We have not come to butcher innocent people but to kill Dingane, who has killed many of our people in the past."

Dingane heard the shouts and the barking of his dog, Marquillana, and crawled out of his hut into the bright sunlight. Outside, Silevana, Sambane and the two Nyawo *indunas* were waiting for him and Silevana hurled an assegai at Dingane. It passed through his thigh and penetrated his lower intestines and, before he could leap to his feet, he was assaulted with another blow to his thigh.

Dingane bellowed in rage and pain and rolled onto his side. He begged the four men to be merciful but they paid no heed to him as he grovelled on the ground before them. Then, Zulu Nywayi stabbed him. When he tried to speak, one of his followers brought him a gourd of water and two of his *indunas*, Ndikili and Ndlebeyemkhonto, knelt beside him and attempted to wash his gaping wounds. However, they soon realized that the king could not survive with such severe injuries for long and hastened his end by enlarging the wounds with an assegai.[1151] (The actions of Dingane's *indunas* prior to his death have led to many urban legends in which Dingane was alleged to have been tortured. For instance, some believe that Dingane was pricked from head to toe with sharp spears, bitten by dogs and/or blinded and starved before he died.) Some of the onlookers thought, but could not be sure they had heard correctly, that Dingane whispered, "I am now dead. Go and return to Mphande and pay homage to him." No sooner had Dingane taken his last breath than Silevana ordered Dingane's followers to dig a hole for his corpse and to cover it with branches and three large rocks after he had been lowered into it. Many of Dingane's subjects wailed as they watched their king being buried and, over the next few days, they trickled back into Natal to start life afresh under their new ruler, Mphande.[1152, 1153]

CHAPTER 30

Dark clouds of war

Boer Republic—Potgieter seeks seaport—Potchefstroom—Volksraad clips Pretorius's wings—the Bhaca—more trouble from the missionaries—British camp at Umngazi River—Russell instructs Napier—Boers "not British" —Pretorius resigns—Pretorius re-instated—troops march from Umngazi—arrival of the Brazilia—Smellekamp

The might of Dingane had been broken, King Mphande was an ally to the Boers and the British had left Durban. For the first time, the future appeared bright for the Voortrekkers in Natal. In addition, the Boers in Natal and those to the north under Potgieter entered a period where there was mutual cooperation between the groups.

The settlement of Pietermaritzburg was expanding and the Boers had already experienced several hardships there. The first disaster to befall the Boers in Pietermaritzburg occurred in 1839 when a lit candle fell over in one of the houses. In the ensuing inferno, 13 houses were burned down, in large part due to the gunpowder kept in them, and a number of Boers were killed. In addition, some of the nearby wagons caught alight and were incinerated. A measles epidemic then swept the village and, in some cases, whole families comprising 20 or 30 members became ill.[1154]

However, the Boers in Pietermaritzburg had also made great strides in expanding the settlement. For instance, the church they had promised to build if God gave them victory against the Zulu, known as Gelofte Kerk (the Church of the Vow) had been built in the centre of the town, opposite the market square. Within its walls of slate and yellowwood timber, American Reverend Daniel Lindley conducted the services "admirably" in Dutch.[1155] (Lindley also conducted occasional services in Durban and the district of Weenen and crossed the Drakensberg Mountains once a year in order to conduct services for the trekkers under Potgieter at Winburg and at their settlement on the Mooi River.[1156])

The Volksraad decreed that every Voortrekker over the age of 17 could be allocated two farms. Each of these farms was five and a half square kilometres, or 3,705 morgen.[1157] Some of the Boer leaders had many farms scattered over a wide area extending from the Drakensberg to Durban. For instance, Pretorius eventually owned 12 farms while Gert Rudolph had 40.[1158] There were three districts in the new Boer Republic: Durban (or Port Natal), Pietermaritzburg and Weenen, the site of the Bloukrans Massacre. While Pietermaritzburg and Durban were developing rapidly, Weenen grew at a slow pace and, by 1843, had only 16 homes.[1159] In contrast, the first sale of 120 sites in Durban occurred in June 1840.

The prime sites, which overlooked the bay and had a sea view, were sold for £18 and 15 shillings, while the less attractive and smaller pieces of land sold for £3 and 15 shillings.[1160]

The Volksraad introduced port regulations in Durban and appointed a harbourmaster, even though not many vessels called at the port at this time.[1161]

After the *Beeskommando* was disbanded, Pretorius had reverted to being an ordinary citizen. His role as chief commandant was effectively redundant as it conveyed only military powers, not civil powers. Like other Boers in Natal, he was governed by the Volksraad and had no recognizable leader. Consequently, Natal was like a ship without a rudder and chaos eventually resulted.[1162]

The district of Natal was divided into 12 wards and two representatives from each ward made up the 24 members of the Volksraad. At this time, there was a landdrost in Durban and Weenen respectively and Pietermaritzburg's three-member committee was responsible for managing the day-to-day affairs of the settlement.

The Volksraad met on the first Monday of January, April, July and October each year and at each session, a chairman was elected to act as president of the Volksraad. For the next three months, the president and a few selected members formed the Commissie Raad and conducted the affairs of the government.

Members of the Commissie Raad were frequently subjected to verbal abuse from the general public when they made decisions that were contrary to the wishes and preferences of the people and as the public was invited to attend meetings related to important issues and could vote to accept or reject resolutions, decisions made on one day were frequently reversed the next. Naturally, these meetings often became heated and violent.

Essentially, a state of mob rule with a veneer of democracy existed in Pietermaritzburg and Durban and although the respective landdrosts were deemed to have power over the general population, anarchy reigned. When the landdrosts made decisions that the general population disagreed with or disliked, they were totally ignored.[1163] Consequently, the landdrosts were often unable to enforce decisions or even to compel any Boer to attend court if he or she did not want to do so.[1164]

Potgieter had established a similar form of government and a 12-member Volksraad assisted him in administering the affairs of the trekkers north of the

Vaal River. Despite the fact that Potgieter's Volksraad functioned independently of that in Natal, the Boers in Natal probably considered the land north of the Vaal River to be part of their republic. The land between the Orange River and Vaal River was deemed to form part of Natal. The Volksraad in Natal had appointed Jacob de Klerk as landdrost of the land west of the Drakensberg Mountains and he administered the area between the Vet and Vaal Rivers on their behalf.[1165]

The trekkers in the north had entered into treaties of friendship with many of the local chiefs such as Danzer, Moroka II, Sekonyela, Davids and Makwana and made it clear that although they had no desire to be British subjects, they wished to live in peace with the British.

Their only known enemy was Mzilikazi and his Matabele people, who attacked them and stole their cattle time and again. Consequently, the trekkers under Potgieter embarked on punitive expeditions to recover their stolen cattle.

Potgieter was determined that the Boers should have access to the sea and, in 1840, he set off with a large party of friends and family for Delagoa Bay to cement relations between the Boers and the Portuguese. Soon after arriving in Delagoa Bay, Potgieter met with Antonio Gamitto, the governor of Mozambique. As luck would have it, both men were keen to establish trade links. However, Gamitto highlighted that it would be a great deal easier to establish formal trade relations if Potgieter settled closer to Lourenço Marques.

Potgieter returned to Witstinkhoutboom, his farm near the town of Vryburg or Mooiriviersdorp, happy in the knowledge that he and his people now had access to two ports, namely Durban and Lourenço Marques, and that they were no longer dependent upon the favour of the British.[1166]

When the Natal Volksraad sent J.J. Burger to deliver a letter to Potgieter in Potchefstroom in early 1840 inviting him and his people to join forces politically with the Boers in Natal, Potgieter respectfully declined the invitation. Not all of Potgieter's followers shared his view that they should maintain their independence though and many believed that they should align themselves with the Natal Boers. For instance, Casper Kruger, the chairman of the council in Potchefstroom wrote to the Natal Volksraad to indicate that some of the Boers north of the Vaal River were more than willing to participate in a joint venture.

In October 1840, the Natal Volksraad sent Pretorius and G.R. van Rooyen to visit Potgieter to discuss matters further. The two elected delegates left Pietermaritzburg with eight wagons and after their 12-day journey, they finally arrived in Potchefstroom. (At this time, Potchefstroom comprised about 30 to 40 houses and was situated ten kilometres north of the present-day town of Potchefstroom, on the right bank of the Modder River.)

On 16 October 1840, more than 300 Boers from outlying farms trundled into Potchefstroom to hear an address from Potgieter and Pretorius and to discuss the merits of unifying the two Boer republics.

After much discussion, it was eventually decided that an alliance between the two groups would be beneficial to all and it was agreed that Pietermaritzburg would be the capital of the united republics and that one Volksraad would rule the two entities. It was also agreed that a Volksraad with 12 members would be elected for the area west of the Drakensberg Mountains and that at least three of those members would attend the meetings of the Natal Volksraad.

Pretorius was then elected as commandant-general of the Republic of Natalia and Potgieter as chief commandant of the district of Potchefstroom. Both men would report to the Volksraad of Natalia and the Act of Unification was duly signed.

Shouts of joy and flashes from the Boers' guns lit the night sky when Pretorius and Van Rooyen arrived back in Pietermaritzburg on 2 November 1840 with the news that Potgieter had agreed that his people would join the Republic of Natalia.[1167]

Pretorius had shown great diplomacy in dealing with Potgieter and had managed to cement his relationship with the usually stubborn and pugnacious Potgieter and that of the Natal Boers with those to the north.

While Potgieter had certainly not forgotten that he had been branded a coward during the battle at Italeni by those who now wanted to strike up a friendship with him and his followers, he appeared to be willing to overlook this. In fact, Pretorius and Potgieter seemed as though they were close friends, to the extent that Pretorius remarked, "Whoever insults Hendrik Potgieter, insults me! I will give my life for Hendrik Potgieter."[1168]

In February 1841, Potgieter and Kruger attended a meeting of the Volksraad of Natalia. At this meeting, it was agreed that an *adjunk-raad* (sub-council) would be established in Potchefstroom and that it would handle local affairs. However, the decisions of the sub-council would have to be ratified by the Volksraad of Natalia from time to time.

One contentious issue debated at this meeting and which was not resolved at this time was about what action the Boers west of the Drakensberg would take if the British or any other foreign power attempted to take control of Durban and Natal from the Boers.[1169]

Pretorius was an executive official of the Volksraad of Natalia at this time,[1170] in recognition of the valuable contribution he had made to improving the lives of the Boers, and had had been invited to attend sessions of the Volksraad since October 1839. He was not allowed to vote on matters but was allowed to participate in discussions and therefore had a measure of influence in the debates that occurred.

Some members, including the chairman, Stephanus Maritz, aimed to undermine his popularity and power among the general population. Perhaps unsurprisingly, the Volksraad of Natalia received a petition signed by 52 Voortrekkers expressing their "concern" that Pretorius was influencing its decisions. The petition did not go into any specifics.

Gert Maritz's brother, Stephanus, was no friend of Pretorius. In fact, it is almost certain that he envied the popularity Pretorius enjoyed among the Boers.

After the Battle of Blood River, the charismatic Pretorius enjoyed almost superstar status among the Boers and, as Stephanus Maritz was an ambitious and vain man, he must surely have resented Pretorius. In addition, the Maritz family had had come to Natal well before Pretorius had and therefore had borne the brunt of all of the hardships suffered by the first Voortrekkers as well as later hardships. In short, Maritz did not like Pretorius.[1171]

He had raised concerns with the Volksraad of Natalia that there would be a conflict if Pretorius was allowed to be chief commandant and a member of the Volksraad at the same time. Consequently, the Volksraad had only appointed Pretorius as chief commandant of the *Beeskommando*, under the proviso that he would no longer hold this position when the military operations of the *Beeskommando* ceased.

After the *Beeskommando* broke up in February 1840, Pretorius managed to delay stepping down as chief commandant and being sworn in as a member of the Volksraad until 4 March 1840. Two days later, 127 of Pretorius's followers signed and presented a petition to the Volksraad requesting that Pretorius be reinstated as chief commandant while simultaneously being a member of the Volksraad of Natalia. The request was denied. Concerned by Pretorius's growing powerbase, the Volksraad determined that no chief commandant would be appointed unless there was a specific task that called for such an appointment and that the role of chief commandant would expire as soon as the task did. This essentially left the Boers without any effective leadership other than that provided by their local landdrosts.

Pretorius recognized the role that Stephanus Maritz had played in persuading the Volksraad to reach this decision and, consequently, the animosity between the two men worsened. Then, on 18 May 1840, all of the field cornets signed a document requesting that Pretorius to be reinstated as chief commandant. It was becoming clear to the Volksraad of Natalia just how big Pretorius's support base was and, on 3 June 1840, they resolved that a member of the Volksraad could simultaneously hold another official position (with the exception of harbourmaster).

There was great jubilation in the Boer camps when they learned of the ruling, which effectively meant that although Pretorius accepted a position in the Volksraad of Natalia, he could still be chief commandant.

Of course, Stephanus Maritz and his supporters did not share their enthusiasm. In fact, when Pretorius and Stephanus Maritz were both re-elected to the Volksraad of Natalia later that year, Stephanus Maritz excused himself from all subsequent meetings that year at which he would have to serve alongside his rival.[1172]

In England, many believed that the British should annex Natal and the governor of the Cape colony shared this desire. In June 1840, Napier approached Glenelg's successor as secretary of state, Lord John Russell, in this regard.[1173] He pointed out that the British had been slow to clarify what the relationship between the British government and Boers would entail in future and that this silence had led the Boers to believe that the British government supported their occupancy of Natal.

On 4 September 1840, the Volksraad of Natalia met to discuss the relationship between the Boer and British governments. In a resolution signed by Lourens Badenhorst and J.J. Burger and which was sent to Napier, they outlined how the Boers had, against all odds, achieved peace in Natal and that they hoped to realize permanent prosperity there. The document expressed regret that the British did not appear to empathize that the Boers had gone to great lengths to achieve this peace and formally requested that the British government acknowledge the Boers as a free and independent people who had earned such freedom after much bloodshed. The Volksraad of Natal also requested that the British government extend the same privileges to the Boers as it did to British citizens in the colony. In addition, the document proposed that two representatives be sent from Natal to the Cape colony to conclude formal arrangements with Napier but added that the Volksraad of Natalia would readily conclude arrangements by letter, should Napier so desire.

In England, Russell had heard some alarming rumours about the state of affairs in Natal. Not only had he learned of the war between the Boers and the Zulu and the death of Dingane, he had also read reports from the *Grahamstown Journal* that described Natal as being in a state of anarchy and as a place in which slavery still thrived and injustice was perpetuated with impunity.[1174]

He wrote to Napier to confirm that he was in favour of the British resuming military occupation of Durban and that a president and council should be appointed by the Boers to liaise with (and answer to) the commander of the British troops that would occupy Durban.[1175]

Napier replied to the Boers' letter on 2 November 1840 and asked the Boers to clarify their proposed terms. He also requested that they not send any representatives to the colony at this time.

Toward the end of 1840, the Voortrekkers in the southern part of Natal were raided by Bushmen and Bhaca tribespeople under Chief Ncapayi.

The Bhaca lived west of Chief Faku's Pondo, along the northern banks in the valley of the Umzimvubu River. (Both the Pondo and the Bhaca used to live in northern Natal but had been driven out by Shaka.) The Bhaca constantly attacked and robbed the Pondo and after Dingane was killed, the Pondo thought it would be safe to move to the land across the Umzimvubu River to escape the thieving Bhaca. Faku and the Pondo had always enjoyed good relationships with the Boers, to the extent that Faku had sent messengers to the Boers in Pietermaritzburg asking the Boers to attack the Bhaca. When over 700 head of cattle and 50 horses were stolen from the Boers near Weenen, Gert Rudolf was sent to Faku and to find out who the guilty party was. Faku did not hesitate in telling Rudolf that it was Ncapayi. The Boers decided to retaliate, even though some members of the Volksraad thought that the Cape government would resent any attack on the people living on the frontiers of the colony. In addition, some thought that it would be imprudent to cause friction, particularly as the Boers were attempting to solidify a peaceable future with the British.[1176]

A commando of 260 men led by Commandant Hendrik Stephanus Lombard joined forces with men from Chief Fodo's Nlangwini people, who had also suffered losses at the hands of the Bhaca, and set out[1177] from Pietermaritzburg on 26 November 1840 with 50 wagons.[1178]

Early on 19 December,[1179] the commando crept up to Ncapayi's kraal. In the ensuing attack, 26 men, ten women and four children were killed. Recovered were 3,000 head of cattle and 2,000 sheep, some of which had been stolen from the Boers. There were no casualties among the Boers. When Pretorius heard that the Nlangwini had taken the sheep and goats and captured a number of Bhaca women and children, he demanded that the sheep be returned to him and the Bhaca be released immediately. However, it emerged that 17 Bhaca children had been orphaned in the attack and were kept as apprentices by the Boers. One child was exchanged for a horse and later sold for 100 rix-dollars.[1180]

The next day, Faku brought the sheep to Pretorius's camp. Pretorius was furious when he realized that 36 sheep were missing and learned that the Nlangwini

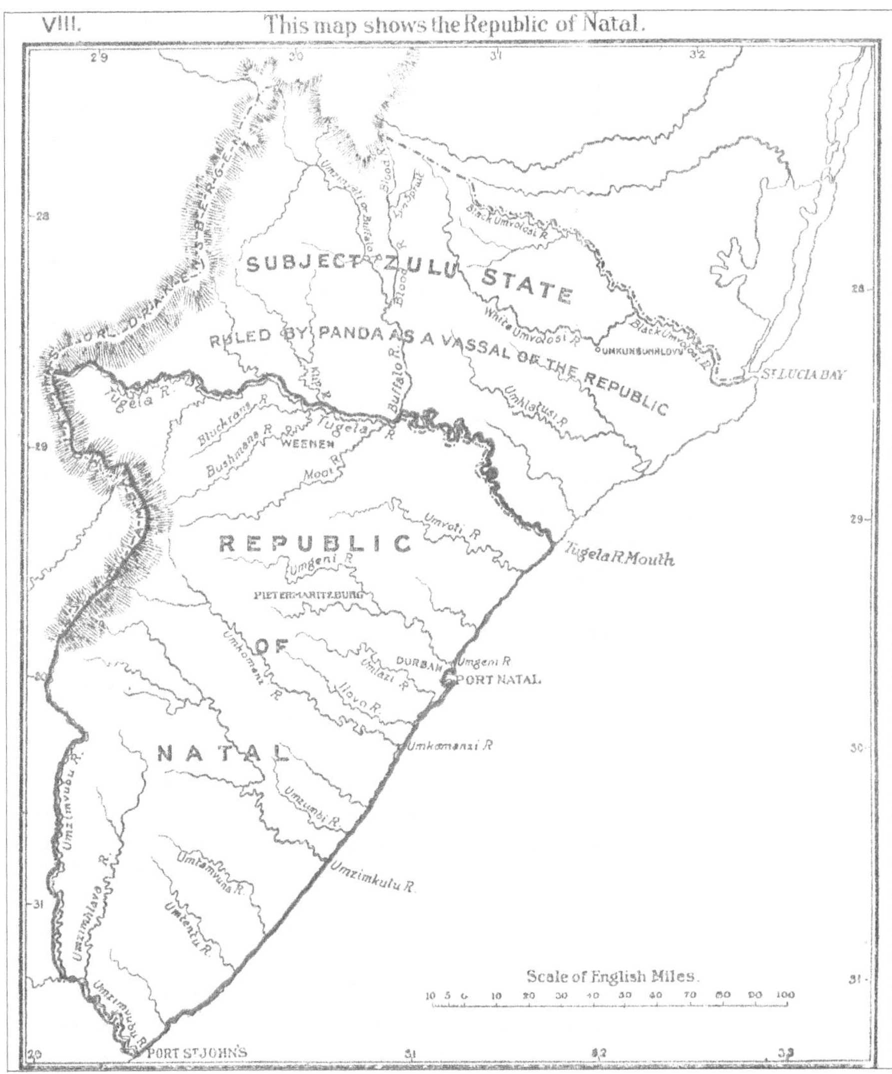

VIII. This map shows the Republic of Natal.

had slaughtered them. Fodo explained that the sheep had become tired along the journey to the camp and that he and his men had decided to slaughter them rather than abandon them, so that they could keep their fleeces. Pretorius rejected Fodo's explanation and had him chained to one of the wagons. (He would be taken back to Pietermaritzburg, where he would serve one year in jail.) After Fodo was safely secured, Pretorius instructed his men to grab his accomplices. The Nlangwini prisoners were then tied with riems, held above the ground by Pretorius's men and stretched.

When they were released, some were so badly injured that they could not move.[1181] Although Faku was delighted that Ncapayi had been defeated by the Boers, he began to realize just what a formidable force the Boers were and recognized that if he and his people did not toe the line, they could suffer the same fate as Ncapayi and his people had. His concern about the potential threat the Boers presented to his people prompted him to send messengers to the mission station at Buntingville to request that the missionaries there visit him.

At the beginning of 1841, the three Wesleyan missionaries, William Hinde Garner, Reverend Jenkins and S. Palmer, met with Faku at his residence at the Umgazi River. Over the next few days, Faku must have convinced the missionaries that the Boers would attack him and his people[1182] and they then travelled into Ncapayi's territory. There, they heard about how the Boers had attacked his kraals and Ncapayi asked them to write to the governor to request protection from the British against the Boers. (Faku also wrote to Napier and expressed his fear of being attacked by the Boers in his territory between the Umtamvuna and Umzimvubu rivers.)

The three missionaries reported to Shaw, the superintendent of the Wesleyan missions, who immediately wrote to Napier. In Shaw's letter, he described the Boer attack on the Bhaca as having been "unprovoked" and "wanton".

Shaw was based at Peddie, hundreds of kilometres from the scene of the attack on the Bhaca, and based his comments solely on the remarks of the missionaries who had met with Faku and Ncapayi and who had evidently believed that there were no mitigating factors to the two chiefs' stories.

These letters, as well as the rumour circulating in Grahamstown that the Natal Boers were making slaves and prisoners of Zulu children, played into the hands of those ready to condemn them.

Napier wrote to the Volksraad of Natalia on 5 January 1841 and expressed his anger toward the Voortrekkers for attacking Ncapayi and his people. He went so far as to accuse them of being wicked and stated that it was inconceivable to him that the Boers could call themselves Christians and yet behave in such a deplorable way. He wrote that he hoped that the reports he had heard were incorrect and warned the Boers that they would be punished most severely and as British subjects should the reports turn out to be true.[1183]

He then ordered that a British military post be established on the Umgazi River to protect Faku and Ncapayi from any further attacks by the Boers. On 28 January 1841, Captain Thomas Charlton Smith of the 27th Regiment marched from Fort Peddie with two companies from his regiment and 50 men from the Cape Mounted Rifles (under Captain H.D. Warden), eight Royal Artillery and four Royal Engineers to the Umgazi River.[1184]

Unaware that they had inadvertently stirred up a hornet's nest, the Boers wrote to Napier on 14 January 1841 to outline the details of their future relationship with the British. In the letter, they requested that the British recognize that they had established a free and independent state under the name of the "Republic of Port Natal and adjoining countries" and specified that they would never initiate hostilities against the "native or inland tribes" without first informing the governor of their intention to do so. They also promised their allegiance to Britain and undertook never to enter into the slave trade.[1185]

During the following months, there was a flurry of correspondence between the Volksraad of Natalia and Napier and between Napier and Russell. Finally, on 21 August 1841, Russell instructed Napier to make suitable arrangements to occupy Durban.

At around this time, an American trading brig called *Levant* arrived at Durban. The Americans were disappointed that trading prospects were dismal and had to content themselves with trading their cargo for skins and ivory rather than money. Nevertheless, the incident demonstrated that Durban was a viable commercial port through which trade could pass into the interior and so threatened the traders in the colony.[1186]

When Pretorius wrote to Potgieter to ask him what his attitude was toward the British, Potgieter replied on 28 August 1841: "I cannot speak for the burghers but only for myself. I do not wish to be the subject of the British or of any other nation in the world. I am not British and trust never to become British. I pray God this not only for my sake but for our whole united burgher society—rather would I take ten steps forward than one backward. In connection with our country which we bought with human blood, I hope and trust that not only I but all our members of a united community will be prepared to defend not only land but people. I place myself in the hands of the Hon. Volksraad and that of Your Honour, but we may as well bear in mind that there is no true unity either here or below the mountain."

After receiving instructions from Russell, Napier wrote to the Boers on 3 September 1841 to reject their request to form an independent republic. He pointed out that they were still British subjects. However, he assured them that the occupation of their lands would be viewed with "justice and expediency" and informed them that when a British military force arrived in Durban, their trade would be placed on the same footing as that of a British possession. (In other words, they would trade with the colony without incurring taxes or special levies.) The letter asked the Volksraad of Natalia to confirm that they accepted the commands of Queen Victoria.[1187]

Shortly after this, Captain Smith wrote to Napier to inform him that all of the Boers except one had relocated to Pietermaritzburg when they heard that Smith and his troops would soon arrive at the Umgazi River and he believed that the British would therefore have no problem seizing Durban.

The Volksraad of Natalia held a meeting on 10 October 1841 to discuss the rapidly unfolding events and, the following day, they replied to Napier's letter.

In no uncertain terms, they informed Napier that they were not British, but in fact Dutch South Africans by birth; had declared their independence and had acted as independent people; had governed themselves and had therefore ceased to be British subjects; had acquired the land they now occupied according to legally acceptable practices and that this land had never been a British province; had not asked for the assistance of a British military force and had no need of it as they were at peace with their neighbours and therefore could not consent to the arrival of this military force; and they found the proposal that the Boers enter into a treaty with the British while under duress due to the presence of a British military force ludicrous. They stated that they were "unable to comprehend the full meaning of it".[1188]

Pretorius was becoming increasingly irritated by the attempts of his fellow Boers in the Volksraad of Natalia to clip his wings and, in October 1841, asked the members to give him the title deed to a plot of land outside Pietermaritzburg that had been promised to him in 1839. He also requested that the members allocate Hendrik Stephanus Pretorius, his son-in-law, a farm as he had not yet been allotted one.

The Volksraad of Natalia turned down both of these requests. They informed him that he would be given his title deed when all of the title deeds for land in that area were allocated and that his son-in-law had not accompanied him to Natal but had arrived there later and was therefore not classified as a Voortrekker.

Not in the habit of being rejected, Pretorius resigned as commandant general on 12 October 1841, while the black storm clouds of war with the British were growing heavier. The Volksraad had no choice but to accept his resignation, which would be in effect from January 1842. After tendering his resignation, Pretorius continued with his duties as commandant general, which included travelling across the Drakensberg Mountains in November 1841 to lay out boundaries for the residents' farms, hear charges by the residents there and to appoint officials on behalf of the Volksraad of Natalia.

In Pretorius's opinion, he had once again proved his worth to the Volksraad of Natalia and therefore felt that the time was ripe to again raise the matter of being issued the title deeds for his plot of land.

To placate him, the Volksraad of Natalia suggested that he select one of the plots within the laager, as he could take ownership immediately rather than waiting until the title deeds for the outlying areas had been allocated. However, they maintained that if he had his heart set on taking the plot he had originally been promised, then they would, in the interim, acknowledge his ownership. Pretorius was dissatisfied with the proposal: he wanted the plot and the title deeds immediately,[1189] but was told that he would only be given title when all the surrounding land had been sold off.

The arrival of the British and the Voortrekkers had ruptured boundaries and damaged tribal and traditional values among the Zulu. In addition, the conflict between the Boers and the Zulu and among the Zulu themselves had led to many of the Zulu people being displaced.

After the defeat of Dingane and the relative calm which prevailed in Natal, many thousands of Zulu drifted back into the territory and erected kraals or squatted near the Boers' farms. Understandably, the Boers were extremely nervous about the proximity of the Zulu to them and gave the Volksraad of Natalia endless headaches about the issue.

Consequently, it was decided that these displaced people should be relocated to an area between the Umtamvuna and Umzimvubu rivers in eastern Pondoland, which was, paradoxically, the land that Dingane had ceded to Retief and his doomed Boers.

Although the Volksraad of Natalia had resolved what to do about the issue of the Zulu settling on the Boers' doorstep, it made no moves at this stage to implement any form of relocation.[1190] Unbeknown to the Boers, this was the land that Chief Faku had claimed belonged to the Pondo in his letter to Napier in early 1841.

Napier did not reply to the letter from the Boers dated 11 October 1841 but issued a proclamation on 2 December 1841 in which he sternly admonished the Boers for wishing to relocate the Zulu to land that belonged to the Pondo. It also stated that the Boers had no right to declare an independent state for themselves and that they remained British subjects.

In addition, the letter stated that Napier intended to send troops to reoccupy Durban and that any resistance to the British occupation would be met with force, as would be the possession of firearms that were being kept for the purpose of attacking the local people.[1191]

Four days later, Napier wrote to Russell to tell him that he had informed the Boers that he intended to send troops to occupy Durban and that the men under Captain Smith were already at the Umgazi river. He stated that he was confident that there would be no bloodshed as a large and growing number of Boers were "weary of anarchy and confusion among their government", sought order through law and authority and were opposed to the formation of a Boer Republic. In addition, he recommended to Russell that Natal not be declared a settlement of the Cape colony but rather that they merely retain a military presence there until such time that full colonization could occur. He also quashed the recurring rumour that the Dutch intended to occupy Natal and dismissed the possibility that another foreign power would try to take steps to occupy Natal.[1192]

Napier's proclamation had infuriated the Boers and the Volksraad of Natalia called a special meeting on 10 January 1842 to discuss it. Pretorius was still piqued that the Volksraad of Natalia had turned down his request for the title deed to his land and therefore did not attend this meeting. Instead, he wrote to them to reiterate that his resignation as commandant general was now effective and tendered his resignation from the Volksraad of Natalia. He also reminded them of all of the things that he had done for them and the people and expressed his anger at the opposition he had experienced from Jacobus Boshoff, the landdrost of Pietermaritzburg, and his old foe, Stephanus Maritz, now the landdrost of Durban. He added that the Volksraad of Natalia had been extremely tardy in paying him his salary, that claiming his money had always been difficult and asked them to donate all his outstanding salary to the church. He concluded that the Volksraad of Natalia could deduct 50 rix-dollars from his salary as a fine for having resigned with immediate effect. His timing was perfect: with the imminent British occupation of Durban and rumbles of war growing louder, he knew that the Boers would be lost without his leadership.

On 19 January 1842, the Volksraad instructed Commandant Jan Meyer to protest the arrival of any British troops in Durban by sea. If the British did not heed the Boer protest, he was to report to the Volksraad of Natalia as soon as possible so that they could decide on a course of action.

The news of Pretorius's resignation and the rumours of a British attack created anxiety among the Boers in Natal. Consequently, a public meeting was called in Pietermaritzburg on 14 January 1842 to discuss the issue of "public safety".

After the meeting, the residents of Pietermaritzburg wrote to Pretorius to request that he remain and take on the mantle of commandant general again. However, Pretorius made it clear that he would not and, three days later, the Volksraad of Natalia appointed H.S. Lombard as acting commandant for the district of Pietermaritzburg.[1193]

The Volksraad of Natalia was totally undecided as to what should be done when the British occupied Durban and issued a notice to the public requesting their opinions on the matter. The Boers were adamant that Pretorius should be reinstated as commandant general and petitions to this effect were sent to the Volksraad of Natalia from as far afield as Winburg. One petition even posed the question: "What is heaviest? The small piece of land or the services of Pretorius?"[1194] The Volksraad could no longer ignore Pretorius"s growing support base and reappointed him as commandant general under the proviso that he would assume this position until the danger from British was over.

Despite Pretorius's reinstatement, nervousness swept Natal. The landdrosts called several public meetings to discuss ideas on how to prevent the British occupation of Durban. Most wished to retain their independence at all costs, particularly from the British, and some even signed declarations stating their willingness to fight. However a large number of Boers, tired of the lawlessness and dissension among their leaders, were prepared to sacrifice their independence for the stability and good governance that they felt would come with British control. This faction were prepared to sacrifice their independence for the stability and good governance they felt the British could affect in Natal. These conflicting opinions caused heated arguments and fiery speeches. Nevertheless, it was eventually decided that the Boers would oppose the British. On 28 January 1842, Captain Lonsdale led a force of two captains, four lieutenants, two ensigns and 237 soldiers from Grahamstown to march to the Umgazi River, where they would reinforce Captain Smith's troops. (Lonsdale's retinue also included three drummers, a staff surgeon, ten horses and three field guns.) Between 21 February and 26 February 1842, the Volksraad of Natalia prepared a letter of protest to Napier that Commandant Meyer would deliver to the British when they arrived in Durban.

The letter rebuked Napier for promoting a course of action that would lead to war and bloodshed and expressed that the Boers had faith that God would be on their side, as they were in the right in this context. It also stated that the Boers had left the colony due to the injustices perpetrated against them by the British and likened the Boer nation to the Canadians who had been forced to take up arms against the British. "No; we gave the coat also to him who had taken the coat from us; we got rid of our immovable property at ridiculous prices," it stated. The letter then reiterated that the Boers had received no sympathy or help from the British during their struggles to establish themselves in Natal and that they were hurt by the malicious and unfounded reports about their actions that had circulated in the colony. Moreover, the letter made it clear that should the Boers have to retreat due to the British, they would not remain in Natal but trek into the interior. However, it concluded with the warning that the Boers would take no responsibility for the inevitable bloodshed that would follow if the British occupied Natal.[1195]

The Volksraad of Natalia was concerned that there might be an exodus of Boers from Natal when the British troops arrived and so issued instructions that no Boer was allowed to leave Natal and cross over the Drakensberg Mountains without first receiving permission to do so. They also ordered that all burghers must be ready to take up arms against the British when called upon to do so. In addition, they issued Pretorius with secret instructions to take a commando of armed men to Durban as soon as he received word that the British were coming. There, he would meet with the British and protest their arrival, verbally and in writing. If they refused to leave, he was to try to intimidate them by moving his men into a defensive position or by seizing the trek oxen of the British. If that did not achieve the desired result, then he should attack the British troops and send for reinforcements, if needed.

Pouring rains delayed the departure of Captain Smith and Lonsdale's combined forces and the men only marched out of their camp at the Umgazi River on 1 April 1842.[1196] They sang *We Fight to Conquer* as they marched[1197] and were accompanied by Wesleyan missionary Reverend James Archbell and his family. Archbell intended to found a mission station in Natal.[1198]

On 21 March 1842, the *Brazilia* was seen anchored near Durban harbour. The arrival of this ship signalled the opening chapter of one of the strangest events in the history of Natal.

In the Netherlands, the news that thousands of people of Dutch decent were leaving the Cape colony and their subsequent hardships caused much interest and concern. Moreover, many Dutch people saw the establishment of a Boer republic in South Africa as opening up excellent business prospects for them. George Gerhard Ohrig, a partner in the firm Klyn & Co., wanted to establish an association and to raise money for a business venture that would commence trading with the Natal Boers.

He published a leaflet titled *The Emigrants at Natal* that extolled the former greatness of the Netherlands and praised the Voortrekkers, who were referred to as "worthy descendents of the men who had fought for their freedom from Spain and then had established trade links around the world". The pamphlet also pointed out the advantages of trading with the Boers in Natal and of securing the Cape as a strategic position for Dutch ships to utilize in times of war.

Ohrig began to distribute the pamphlet privately in the Netherlands and took every precaution to ensure that copies did not fall into the hands of the British. The British consular agents serving in the Netherlands were unable to lay their hands on a single copy. Although Ohrig failed to raise the capital required to form his own company, Klyn & Co. were so enthusiastic about his scheme that they funded the construction of the *Brazilia*, with a view to shipping an assortment of goods to Natal and commencing trade with the Voortrekkers.[1199] (The town of Ohrigstad was later named after Ohrig in his honour.) When the *Brazilia* was first sighted near Durban, the Boers believed that the ship was carrying British troops. To their intense relief, however, the Dutch flag was soon seen fluttering from the masthead. A longboat carrying men armed with pistols and cutlasses and the captain of the ship, Cornelius Reus, soon pulled up to the jetty.

"Are the English yet in possession of this place?" Reus shouted to the men watching them from the shore.

"You have come just in time because the English are about to come and take it!" the landdrost of Durban replied.

One of the men to come ashore with Reus was Johan Arnold Smellekamp and no sooner had their feet hit dry land than they started handing out *The Emigrants at Natal* pamphlets to the Boers, who read them eagerly. They tacitly indicated to the Boers that they were on a political errand and the Dutch would assist the Boers to escape British rule.[1200] Excitement swept the port when the Boers realized that the Dutch would protect them from the British and take Natal under the Netherlands' paternal arm. Messages were sent urgently to Andries Pretorius, J.J. Burger (the president of the Volksraad of Natalia) and Jacobus Boshoff (the landdrost of Pietermaritzburg) to inform them of the arrival of the Dutch. The three men were ecstatic to hear this news and promptly invited Smellekamp and Reus to meet with the Volksraad of Natalia in Pietermaritzburg.[1201]

When Smellekamp and Reus approached Pietermaritzburg, a great crowd of Boers welcomed them heartily at the Umsindusi River, including Pretorius, Boshoff and Burger. The cheering people surrounded their wagon, waving their hats excitedly, and dozens of the men fired their guns into the air, unharnessed the Dutchmen's oxen and pulled the wagon to the town themselves to demonstrate just how pleased they were to see Smellekamp and Reus. The villagers had gone out of their way to make the men feel welcome and had used every available piece of red, white and blue calico and ribbon to decorate the houses and buildings in the colours of the Netherlands flag. Pietermaritzburg was in a state of celebration for eight days and the arrival of the Dutch was lauded at public meetings, debates, feasts and church services.[1202]

Many of the Boers wept with relief and emotion as Smellekamp and Reus distributed Bibles and prayer books that Jacob Swart, a lecturer and examiner at the naval college in Amsterdam, had sent to the Boers, as well as *The Emigrants at Natal*. The latter were pored over by men and women who had seldom read anything other than their Bibles and they immediately assumed that it contained official words of support from the Dutch government.

Finally, the Boers were ready to get down to business: a special open meeting of the Volksraad of Natalia was convened and between 50 and 60 members of the public were invited to hear what Smellekamp and Reus had to say.[1203] There was a hush as the Boers listened to Smellekamp read a letter from Ohrig in support of their struggle for freedom from the British.

Afterwards, the public was asked to leave the room and the chairman of the Volksraad of Natalia pressed Smellekamp as to whether the king of the Netherlands had any message for the Boers. When Smellekamp informed them that his king had not sent any word, the chairman told him that they were anxious to have Natal placed under the official protection of the Netherlands, as the British would not leave them in peace, and asked him whether he could provide them with some small piece of evidence to this effect that they could show to the British troops when they arrived.

In a bid not to lose his newfound celebrity, super salesman Smellekamp told the Boers that he would enter into a formal treaty with the Volksraad of Natalia in the name of the king of the Netherlands. In this document, he referred to Natal as "a province of colonial occupation of the Netherlands" and signed the treaty as having been "accepted in the name of the King of the Netherlands, subject to His Majesty's approval".[1204] [1205]

The Volksraad of Natalia hoped that presenting this document to the British would delay the British occupation of Natal, until such time that Smellekamp had received a promise of protection from the king of the Netherlands.

"What should we do if the British arrive to occupy Port Natal?" Pretorius asked Smellekamp.

"What would you have done if we had not come to Natal?" he retorted.

"We were going to do what we had told Napier we would do: defend ourselves against any British attack," Pretorius replied.

"I suggest you go ahead with your plan," Smellekamp said.[1206]

Shortly after this meeting, Smellekamp and Reus returned to the *Brazilia* and, on 16 April 1842, auctioned the goods that had been sent by merchants from Amsterdam. The cargo consisted of shaving soap, gin, Eau de Cologne, cigars, pipes, wine, linseed oil, law books, cheese, shoes, silks, ribbons, tin, glass- and copperware and white, green and black paint.

CHAPTER 31

Boer vs Brit in Durban

*Smellekamp arrested—Smith's troops arrive—negotiations fail—
Volksraad instructs Pretorius, "Drive out the British!"—Battle of Congella—
Dick King's ride—the Conch—plight of the British troops—truce signed*

The British residents of Durban had watched the arrival of the *Brazilia* and subsequent celebrations by the Boers with some misgiving. Two of the British settlers, George Cato and J. Douglas, removed a flagpole that belonged to Cato and which had been requisitioned for the flying of the Dutch flag when the *Brazilia* left harbour. When Reus learned what they had done, he and several of his sailors beat Douglas within an inch of his life for this "affront" against the Dutch nation. (Cato had fled when he saw the Dutch delegation approaching.) He then wrote to the Volksraad of Natalia to tell them what had happened before setting sail for Holland on 24 April 1842, without Smellekamp.

Pretorius travelled to Durban with ten men to investigate the incident and Douglas and Cato were made to attend a preliminary enquiry headed by Pretorius on 29 April 1842. Pretorius fined Douglas 500 rix-dollars and set him free but took Cato back to Pietermaritzburg as a prisoner. During the hearing, Pretorius received a report that one of the Englishmen had joked, "We will go to fetch the British soldiers in our wagons." He then read a letter from Potgieter that stated that all of the Boers, including those in Potchefstroom, Bloemspruit and Doornkop, were prepared to fight to the death if the land was attacked and would also defend the territory west of the Drakensberg Mountains.[1207]

Smellekamp then set off on an overland journey to Cape Town with Boshoff. After passing through Graaff-Reinet, Smellekamp was arrested by the authorities in Swellendam for travelling from one part of the country to another without a pass. Subsequently, he was taken to Cape Town and imprisoned for two days. He was only released after the attorney general had interviewed him and was satisfied that Smellekamp had not been involved in any armed resistance by the Boers. Smellekamp returned to Holland[1208] with the funds he had been given by the Volksraad of Natalia and had promised to negotiate a treaty with the king of the Netherlands and to recruit teachers and clergyman to come to Natal.[1209]

When Pretorius arrived back in Pietermaritzburg on 30 April 1842, he was unaware that the British army under Captain Smith was only 50 kilometres from Durban. The British troops were already in a sorry state: many were badly sunburned and had blisters on their feet because their boots had become wet during their 122 river crossings or had filled with sand while they marched along the beach. Moreover, the river crossings had been perilous as most of the rivers were in flood and some were between 600 and 700 metres wide. One of the men, James Devitt, had died of exhaustion.[1210]

When Captain Smith's troops were a few days away from Durban, Henry Ogle and a group of Englishmen rode out to greet them, armed with their swords, pistols and double-barrelled guns. They wanted to inform Captain Smith about the visit by Smellekamp and Reus and had left Durban because they were worried that they might be conscripted by the Boers. When they finally met with Smith, they complained bitterly about their "ill treatment" at the hands of the "Dutch barbarians" and "Boer ruffians".[1211]

On 3 May 1842, Jan Meyer and three other Boers approached Smith and his troops and Meyer attempted to present the letter of protest that the Volksraad of Natalia had entrusted him to deliver to the British.

"I cannot accept a letter of protest against the entrance of the queen's troops into territory that belongs to the queen of England," Smith told him matter-of-factly.

Meyer duly returned to Durban and sent one of his men, Paul Bester, to Pietermaritzburg to report to the Volksraad of Natalia what had transpired.

The next day, Pretorius learned that Smith's troops had arrived at the Umbilo River and had set up camp near the house of James Dunn, only six kilometres from Durban.[1212] Dunn spoke with Smith, cynically unconvinced that Smith's small force could defeat 1,500 armed Boers. When the British troops arrived in Durban, they could not help but notice the Dutch flag fluttering above the new flag of the Republic of Natalia; some of the men pulled the flags down and hoisted the Union Flag in their place. They then spiked the small six-pounder cannon next to the flagpole.[1213]

Smith's scouts found a suitable place at which to set up camp one kilometre north of Durban, in an area referred to as *Kommetjiesvlakte* by the trekkers and *Itafa Amalinde* by the Zulu, and the troops marched there with their fixed bayonets at the ready and swords drawn.

Soon after, a four-man Boer delegation galloped up to Smith to present him another protest note from the Volksraad of Natalia. Smith refused to accept the note as it had not been drawn up by British subjects. Disregarding Smith's petulance, the Boers then informed Smith that the Volksraad of Natalia had entered into an agreement with the king of the Netherlands and that Durban now fell under Dutch sovereignty. Smith scoffed at this statement and promptly dismissed them.

The next day, Captain Smith relocated his men to the site now known as the Old Fort, four kilometres from the Boers' camp at Congella, where he instructed the men to set up their tents and positioned the wagons in laager formation.

Realizing the gravity of the situation, Pretorius sent a messenger over the Drakensberg Mountains to call upon Potgieter to send help. To Pretorius's surprise, Potgieter refused to come his aid. However, Commandant Johan Godfried Mocke called out his burghers from between the Modder and Vet rivers and prepared to go to Natal.

In Natal, the burghers from Pietermaritzburg and Weenen were preparing to drive the British out and many Boers began to make their way to Congella to join their countrymen for the looming confrontation.[1214] The day after Pretorius had posted a notice on the door of the landdrost's offices in Durban that stated that no burghers could leave their district without the permission of the field cornet and that all field cornets should ready their men for battle, Captain Smith tore it down and replaced it with the governor's proclamation regarding the occupation of Durban. Pretorius's small force amounted to 62 men at Congella.

The next morning, Pretorius and two burghers rode out from Congella to confront Captain Smith about the presence of the British troops in the vicinity. Half a kilometre from the British camp, they saw a column of 100 British soldiers heading toward their camp with a cannon and Pretorius dispatched his companions to warn the British to halt. However, when the two Boers relayed the message to Captain Smith, he haughtily informed them that nobody could stop him and shouted to his troops to continue to Congella. Pretorius then sent Karel Landman and Lodewyk de Jager to ask Smith to order his men to stop marching toward their camp as there were women and children at Congella and to inform him that he wanted to meet with him.[1215]

When Smith saw Pretorius approaching, he ordered his men to halt and told them to stand down. Pretorius could not help but overhear one of the British soldiers whisper "He has a belly on him like a bass drum!' but shrugged off this insult. In fact, he courteously took off his hat and bowed deeply before greeting Captain Smith and his escorts, whose guns were trained on him. He then asked Captain Smith to instruct his men to lower the half-cocked hammers of their muskets so that he was not "shot accidentally"[1216] and told him that he had come to talk. He proposed that he and Smith return to the British camp or go to Congella to discuss matters privately. However, Smith told Pretorius that they would talk where they were.

Having no option but to proceed, Pretorius explained to Captain Smith that the arrival of the British troops had caused much anxiety among the Boers and that as he had refused to accept the written protests they had sent to him, Pretorius was forced to deliver the protest in person. Smith contemptuously told Pretorius that he would not receive any address of protest from someone who was not a British subject.

Pretorius proceeded to explain that the Boers would not welcome the British to Natal. He spoke of a newspaper report where the governor had stated that the Boers in Natal would welcome the occupation of Durban by the British and pointed out that this report was totally incorrect. As Smith seemed to be of the opinion that many Boers desired that the British take control of Natal, Pretorius suggested that a public meeting be held so that Smith could see for himself how the Boers felt. Smith spurned the suggestion. After 45 minutes of discussion, it seemed as though the two men had achieved some common ground. However, it later emerged that there had been a misunderstanding: Smith believed that Pretorius had agreed that the Boers would disperse and return to their farms, when Pretorius had actually said that the Boers would wait at Congella until the Volksraad issued them with new instructions. Smith ordered his men to return to camp and Pretorius returned to his now 264-man force at Congella.[1217]

The new secretary of state, Lord Stanley, wrote to Napier on 10 May 1842 to clarify that the British government did not wish to establish a colony in Natal and explained why the government had taken this decision. The dispatch also maligned the Boers for having perpetrated "slaughter and oppressions, to which, in the pursuit of their enterprises they have subjected the native tribes". In addition, Stanley expressed his wish that the Boers would return to the Cape colony and that if they did not, the British government would do all in its power to make life difficult for them and would stop any trade between the Boers in Natal and the colony. Stanley added that the Boers would not enjoy any protection or rights afforded to British subjects as long as they remained outside of the Cape colony and he promised to aid and protect local tribes if the Boers attacked them. He concluded by instructing Napier to withdraw the troops from Durban upon receipt of the dispatch.[1218]

Pretorius ordered his men at Congella to break up into small groups of ten or 12 and posted them in thickets to keep an eye on the activities of the British. Some of the groups were instructed to ride around the British camp, deliberately provoking the British soldiers by making rude hand gestures.

Irritated by the Boers' taunting, on 11 May, Smith decided to meet with Pretorius to establish why he and his men had not withdrawn as he believed

Pretorius had promised. Smith and 100 of his men marched toward the Boers' camp with two six-pounder cannon that afternoon and Pretorius and 50 armed men rode out to confront them, a kilometre from the British camp. Upon seeing the Boers approach, Smith ordered his men to form a line between the two cannon preparatory to forming a battle square. The Redcoats made an impressive sight. In contrast, the Boers appeared a bedraggled group without any order.[1219]

Pretorius sent two messengers to tell Smith that they were merely on their way to Durban to visit Jan Meyer. Captain Smith was all but frothing at the mouth when he heard this and ranted and raved at the two messengers, alleging that Pretorius had been duplicitous and had breached their agreement. He told the messengers to warn Pretorius that if the Boers approached the British camp again, the British troops would attack Congella and burn the settlement to the ground. He concluded by ordering the messengers to inform the Boers to disperse and to tell Pretorius that if he sent any more messengers to him, he would have them taken prisoner and tried by court martial.[1220]

This incident persuaded Captain Smith that the Boers' resistance would soon crumble. Simultaneously, Pretorius realized that Smith was not going to back down and that no amount of discussion would persuade him to leave the area with his troops. Consequently, he sent for reinforcements from Pietermaritzburg.[1221]

The Boers had removed all of the food from Durban before the British arrived and the British troops were forced to subsist on only one handful of rice a day. However, on 13 May 1842, a small brig called the *Pilot* sailed into the harbour with precious cargo: salted beef and pork, biscuits and plenty of rum as well as two 18-pounder cannon for Captain Smith.[1222]

On the night of 15 May 1842, the reinforcements Pretorius had called for arrived.

The next day, Pretorius addressed his men. When asked whether they wanted to become British subjects, the 500 armed and angry Boers unanimously shouted "no". Voices chorused, "We do not wish to be British subjects", "This is our land", "Tell the British to get out", "We don't need the British here", "We are ready to ", "We will drive the British away if they won't leave peacefully", "The British must pay for what they have done", "Send Captain Smith and his men back to the Cape" and "We will take their flag and their guns".

After Pretorius informed the Volksraad of Natalia later that day that the Boers wanted to fight the British invasion tooth and nail, he was instructed to order Captain Smith to leave Durban with his troops by midday on 18 May 1842. Subsequently, he sent a letter to Captain Smith throwing down the gauntlet.

Smith's reply was addressed to "Mr Pretorius" and his signature was appended with "Commandant of Natal". In his letter, he matter-of-factly pointed out that he would obey his order to remain in Durban and requested that the Boers return to their farms. He promised that if they did so, he would not interfere in their affairs or attempt to stop supplies from reaching them.

When Pretorius noted that the letter was addressed to "Mr Pretorius" and, against customary practices, did not include his military title, he decided not to open it. He sent it back to Captain Smith with the message, "I am not sure which Pretorius the letter is meant for".[1223]

The Volksraad of Natalia acknowledged that the hostilities between the Boers and the British could not drag on indefinitely but were reluctant to initiate a battle and so, early on 18 May 1842, they softened their ultimatum to Captain Smith by asking him to sign a declaration that the British would not attack the Voortrekkers unless instructed to do so by the governor. They added that if Smith and his men left the Voortrekkers alone, the Boers would leave them in peace while they were in Durban.

Smith once again refused to receive a message from the Boers. This was the final straw for the Volksraad of Natalia: the following day, they instructed Pretorius to drive the British out of the Republic of Natalia. Pretorius was hesitant to attack the British without a carefully considered battle plan and still hoped that some form of diplomatic solution was possible. To this end, Pretorius sent two messengers to see Captain Smith in a last-ditch attempt at peace.

When the messengers relayed the contents of the letter that Smith had refused to accept from the Volksraad of Natalia, Smith informed the messengers to tell Pretorius that he had no intention of leaving the land. Nevertheless, Pretorius did not want to appear to be the aggressor and so decided to provoke the British into firing the first shots. His plan was simple: the Boers would steal the 600 cattle belonging to the British[1224] that were grazing between the two camps, a kilometre from the British troops' base. Captain Smith would not be able to ignore such a blatant act of provocation.

On the morning of 23 May 1842, Pretorius instructed 150 Boers to hide in the bushes near the cattle. He then sent Stephanus Maritz to ask Captain Smith to order his men back to the colony and to warn him that if any violence broke out between the British and Boers that it would be on his head. As usual, Smith treated the messenger with contempt and would not engage in diplomatic discussions. Consequently, Pretorius's plan was put into action.

Shortly after Stephanus Maritz arrived back at Congella, the armed burghers emerged from the bushes and began to drive the cattle toward their camp. When the alarm was sounded in the British camp, Captain Smith ordered the large

18-pounder cannon to open fire at the Boers. Ten shells fell among the oxen and killed two of them, but the Boers were unscathed.

Captain Smith then sent Lonsdale and 100 men to recover the cattle but by the time they reached the area where the cattle had been grazing, the cattle and the Boers had disappeared. However, a few shots were fired at the British soldiers from the bushes and Smith immediately ordered the bugler to sound the retreat as he was nervous that the men would be ambushed.

At Congella, Pretorius divided the 234 men into groups of ten or 20 and ordered them to take up positions in the bushes between the two camps to await the approach of the British. He also sent one group of Boers to the home of Adolphe Delegorgue, which was between the two camps, while he and 20 men remained at Congella. If necessary, he would call for assistance from the Boers under Pieter Joubert in Durban.[1225]

At 11 o'clock that night, Smith marched out of his camp with 109 men of the 27th regiment, 18 men of the Royal Artillery, eight engineers and two Cape Mounted Rifles to attack the Boers at their camp. He directed the men to march along the beach, which they could only do as it was low tide. They took two field guns with them. In addition, a howitzer was onboard a longboat of the *Mazeppa* and Captain Smith hoped that it would be possible to row it to shore at high tide, a full seven hours away, and set it up before the troops arrived at Congella. While the British marched silently past the mangrove thicket above the beach, they were being watched by 25 of the best Boer marksmen hiding in the dense bush.

As soon as Pretorius received word that the British were marching toward the camp, he evacuated the women and children and had them taken to the thicket some distance from Congella. They were to hide there until it was deemed safe for them to return. When the unsuspecting detachment was 100 metres from the Boers marksmen, a flash of fire and a single shot rang out. Four more shots followed in quick succession. One ox at each of the gun carriages fell dying. Lieutenant Wyatt and another soldier were shot in the head. Chaos broke out. The other oxen panicked. The guns were immobilized as the wounded oxen lay bellowing on the ground. The fully loaded cannon were useless anyway, their barrels pointing the wrong way. The Redcoats dived for cover and fired back at the unseen Boers. The British were trapped like moths in a flame, clearly illuminated by the moon shining onto the beach. Every Boer shot counted..

The howitzer on the boat was of no assistance to the British on the beach as it had been caught in a strong current and forced to move out of range. The one shot fired from the howitzer presented no threat to the Boers but fell alarmingly close to the Redcoats and caused even greater confusion among their already broken ranks. Just three minutes into the attack, Captain Smith ordered the buglers to sound the retreat.

The British were still under fire a half hour later. Smith led the retreat from the safety of his horse while his men panicked. Redcoats ran through the mud and water, splashing frantically in the waves as they were caught by the rising tide. Hell bent on escape, some threw away their muskets and nearly all threw away their ammunition pouch-belts to lighten their loads. Under the relentless fire from the Boers, some moved deeper into the sea and were swept off their feet and drowned.

It was a rout.

After the retreat, the Boers found the bodies of 17 dead and a number of wounded Redcoats as well as the two abandoned cannon, discarded muskets, pouch-belts and ammunition littering the beach.

The next day more bodies were washed up, making the final count 22 dead, 31 wounded and six missing in action.

Not one Boer had been killed.[1226]

Smith and his bedraggled and defeated troops arrived at their camp at two o'clock in the morning. To their horror, they saw that the camp was surrounded by Boers, who had made sure that the Redcoats inside the camp had been unable to send reinforcements to Captain Smith and his men on the beach.

Pretorius had returned to Congella well satisfied with the Boers' victory against a force four times bigger than his own. The Voortrekkers, though, thought that the time was ripe to finish the British off and their attitude persuaded Pretorius to set off for the British camp with his men at three o'clock in the morning.

Half an hour later, the Boers crept toward the British camp and Pretorius ordered his men to open fire at three sides of the camp. Suddenly, the Boers found themselves being attacked from the rear by George Cato and fellow British settlers. They were effectively sandwiched between two British forces.

A 15-year-old boy and three Boers were wounded in the return fire from the Redcoats before Pretorius ordered his men to retreat, an hour before sunrise. The Boers had only managed to wound three British soldiers during the attack on their camp and Pretorius realized that if they were to defeat the British, he would need to send off for reinforcements and more gunpowder and ammunition.

That morning, he requested that the minister in Pietermaritzburg pray for the burghers in Durban[1227] and sent Edmund Morewood to tell Captain Smith that he was willing to return the dead and wounded British soldiers to him.

Smith accepted Pretorius's offer and, the next day, Pretorius sent several wagons to Captain Smith's camp with the dead and wounded British soldiers.

When Smith requested that Pretorius give him permission to fire a volley of salute during the soldiers' funeral, Pretorius assented, on condition that the volley was fired from muskets and not cannon.

A shocked and humiliated Smith then wrote to Lieutenant-Colonel Hare, the lieutenant governor of the colony, to describe the losses that he had incurred in the battle and to request that Hare send reinforcements, as he was sure that the Boers would persist in demanding that the British leave the Republic of Natalia.

That same day, Smith contacted Cato to ask him to recommend someone that could be sent to Grahamstown to request reinforcements. Although Cato offered to take the message himself, Smith pointed out that he needed him in Durban and that he was too valuable a man to spare.

Richard King, a farmer from Isipingo who could speak some Zulu, readily accepted Smith's assignment, despite having helped the Boers during the Zulu attacks at the Bloukrans and Bushman's rivers. On 24 May 1842, King stationed himself onboard the *Mazeppa*. He was woken by Cato at midnight and, under cover of darkness, King and his servant Ndongeni mounted their horses and were towed across the bay, past Salisbury Island, by George and Christopher Cato. They then got out of the water below the Bluff and, unseen by the Boer lookouts, spurred their horses away. So began an epic ten-day ride in which the men covered nearly 1,000 kilometres and crossed many rivers, swamps and unfamiliar territories before reaching Grahamstown, where King delivered Smith's plea for assistance to Shepstone, the resident agent.[1228]

As Pretorius was keen to keep up the pressure on the British, he sent 100 of his men to attack the Redcoats stationed in a store at the Point early on the morning of 26 May 1842. After the Boers opened fire, the Redcoats returned fire with four or five shots from their 18-pounder cannon before retreating into the stone building. Subsequently, they fired only a few desultory shots at the Boers through the rifle slots of the stone building and the Boers shouted at them to surrender.

Finally, 19 Redcoats and three civilians emerged from the store with their hands raised in surrender. Civilian Charles Adams had died and two Redcoats had been wounded.

The Boers took the 19 Redcoats as prisoners and seized the 18-pounder cannon as well as two six-pounders, gunpowder, ammunition and food. Having taken possession of the Point meant that the Boers had assumed total control of the bay and could easily keep an eye on the two ships in the harbour, the *Mazeppa* and the *Pilot*, which were housing nine British settlers and Reverend Archbell and his family.

Pretorius ordered the British settlers, including George Cato, to come ashore and then had them arrested as traitors the minute they set foot on dry land. Although Burger and some of his men insisted that the men should be shot, Pretorius ordered that they be taken to Congella, where they were held for eight days before being transported to Pietermaritzburg and put in gaol there.[1229]

The next day, Pretorius ordered the captains of the *Mazeppa* and *Pilot* to inform Captain Smith that they were prepared to transport his troops back to the Cape colony. Smith asked that Pretorius allow him until 31 May 1842 to consider the request, as he hoped that the reinforcements requested by King would reach Natal by then.

Unaware that King and Ndongeni had managed to get through the Boer blockade undetected, Pretorius agreed to Captain Smith's request and ordered a ceasefire. He also informed Captain Smith that when the British troops left Natal, he would require the British to pay the Boers £10,000, in damages and leave behind all of their possessions, including oxen, wagons, tents, guns and ammunition.

By 31 May 1842, Pretorius had started to feel uneasy that he had not yet heard from Captain Smith regarding the withdrawal of his troops and he ordered an end to the ceasefire. At six o'clock that morning, some of the Boers took up position in the trenches they had dug near the British camp. (These trenches were over a metre deep, half a metre wide and extended nearly a kilometre. The sandbags piled at the edge of the trench facing the camp provided ample cover for the Boers.[1230])

Others trained their cannon, including the captured 18-pounder and two six-pounders, on the British camp and unleashed a fusillade of cannon fire that would only cease late that afternoon. Snipers kept up continuous harassing fire.

On the first day of what would turn into a 26-day siege, Pretorius sent Reverend Archbell to deliver a message to Captain Smith that the Boers would allow the women and children in the British camp to be evacuated to the *Mazeppa*. The Englishwomen who had been evacuated to the *Mazeppa* included George Cato's wife and Mrs Benningfield, whose husbands were both prisoners in Pietermaritzburg.

Five days into the attack, the Boers began to run out of cannonballs. Consequently, Servaas van Breda was sent to the *Mazeppa* to retrieve the ship's anchor chain, which the Boers then chopped up and melted with molten lead in brick moulds. The result was a lead cannonball with an iron centre.[1231]

On the afternoon of 10 June 1842, the 80 Boers at the Point were astonished to see that the *Mazeppa* was sailing out of the harbour and it soon emerged that

Joseph Cato had ordered that the anchors of the *Mazeppa* be raised and the strong south-westerly breeze was pushing the *Mazeppa* out to sea.

However, just before the *Mazeppa* reached the sandbar near the Point, the breeze lightened and she slowed to a stop. The Boers at the Point opened fire on the ship, only 30 metres from them, and the ammunition from their muskets and four-pound cannon soon ripped through the sails and rigging. Some of the shots struck and severely damaged the longboat being towed behind the Mazeppe and it began to sink.[1232]

One of the passengers on the ship quickly cut the longboat adrift and, shortly afterwards, the wind picked up and drove the *Mazeppa* over the sandbar and out of the range of the Boers. Within minutes, the *Mazeppa* was making her way up the coast to Lourenço Marques and safety.

On the night of 18 June, a patrol of Redcoats under the command of Lieutenant Molesworth crept up to the trench and opened fire on the 12 Boers sleeping there. In a fierce skirmish, two Boers were killed, namely 15-year-old Hendrik Hattingh and Jan Strydom. Three Redcoats were killed and four were badly wounded. Soon, food began to run out in the British camp and the troops resorted to killing the 20 oxen to make biltong. Each soldier was issued with less than 250 grams of biltong daily and when the meat ran out, the men killed their horses to make biltong. By 24 June, the Redcoats were in a perilous state: they were subsisting on the crumbs of biscuits and a handful of rice a day and hoped that the horsemeat biltong and eleven bags of corn feed could be made to last for a month. The bombardment continued unabated, the Boers firing a total of 651 cannon shots. By the end of the siege, the Redcoats had lost eight dead and eight wounded, and the Boers four dead and ten wounded.

At Congella, Pretorius's army now numbered over 400 men, mainly from Natal and the areas near the Modder, Riet and Orange rivers. To Pretorius's chagrin, Potgieter had not sent a single man to assist him, even though he had asked him to help on two occasions. When reports surfaced that Potgieter was ill, the Volksraad of Natalia bypassed Potgieter by writing to the landdrost of Potchefstroom on 22 June, requesting that he ask the burghers in that area to come to Natal to assist Pretorius. Before the letter arrived, developments took a new twist.[1233] At midday on 24 June, the Boers anxiously shouted, "Ship ahoy!" as the *Conch* schooner neared Durban harbour. They did not let their guard down until she was identified as a trading vessel. However, unbeknown to the Boers, she carried 100 grenadiers of the 27th Regiment under the command of Captain Durnford and most of the soldiers were hidden below deck. Those who were manning the ship were wearing civilian clothes.

King had successfully summoned reinforcements and was a passenger on the *Conch*, which the British had chartered from Captain Bell for £390 to bring the British troops to Natal from Algoa Bay, however, the crew were less than enthusiastic and were on the point of mutiny. The port captain, Edmund Morewood, and the Boers' military secretary promptly rowed out to the *Conch* to inspect the cargo. After clambering up the rope ladder and stepping onto the deck, they were greeted by a horrific sight: a sea of Redcoats.

"I am a friend of the British!" Morewood blurted out, while the military secretary steadied himself with a thick rope. He had almost fainted when he saw the Redcoats and requested a glass of water when he could finally speak.[1234]

Captain Durnford then instructed Morewood that he was to deliver a note to Pretorius that requested that he be permitted to send a doctor from the ship to Captain Smith's camp. Fearing some sort of treachery was afoot, Pretorius refused this request. Consequently, Durnford fired a rocket into the sky that night to signal to Captain Smith that the reinforcements had arrived.

The next evening, a British warship, the *Southampton*, under the command of Captain Ogle, anchored outside the harbour. She had 50 cannon onboard as well as 300 soldiers under the command of Lieutenant-Colonel Josias Cloete.

Abraham Josias Cloete had been born in the Cape colony but educated in Holland, as his parents had mistakenly assumed that the Cape would remain under Dutch control. (His father, Pieter Cloete, had been a government official in the Cape colony.) In 1814, he had been aide-de-camp to Governor Charles Somerset in the Cape and had then served in India before returning to the Cape, where he had assisted with the logistics involved in the landing of the 1820 settlers at Algoa Bay and served in the Sixth Frontier War in the Eastern Cape. Now, the 48-year-old lieutenant-colonel was in command of the British forces relieving Captain Smith's troops.[1235]

When the *Conch* was first sighted, Pretorius had stationed a number of burghers at the Point and the Bluff as well as a four-pounder cannon at each area, facing seawards. The arrival of the *Southampton* did not bode well for the Boers and Pretorius desperately scrambled to prepare his men and defences for the imminent hostilities.

On the morning of 26 June, the British made their move. While a favourable southeaster blew, the *Southampton* was moved closer to shore, to the sandbar. from where, she opened fire with a broadside. The Boers then returned fired with their two four-pounders, a total mismatch. The *Conch*, the smaller of the two ships, then started to cross the sandbar into the harbour. Onboard the *Conch* were 135 men under Cloete and a further 85 men commanded by Royal Navy officer Commander Hill were in boats being towed behind the *Conch*. The Boers fired at the *Conch* with their cannon as she sailed across the sandbar, but were unable to affect sufficient damage to stop her from entering the harbour. They then directed a hail of lead at the *Conch* and the boats trailing behind her.

Although the boats were riddled were holes, the soldiers managed to row them to shore.[1236] The Boers realized they were powerless to stop the troops from landing so hastily retreated to Congella, where they and the other Boers gathered their belongings before abandoning the settlement and moving away from the coast. During the 20-minute battle at the harbour, the British had lost three soldiers with only three soldiers and three sailors wounded. When all the soldiers were ashore, they formed up in three divisions, under Major W.J. d'Urban (son of Sir Benjamin), Cloete and Durnford, respectively, and marched toward Smith's camp, without opposition,[1237] to be met by Smith at 4 o'clock that afternoon.

The Boers' defence of Durban had left a lot to be desired and many felt that Pretorius had failed as a leader by not providing stiffer resistance to the arrival of the British, particularly as the terrain surrounding the harbour could have provided excellent cover for the Boers and Pretorius had had a large force at his disposal. Many Boers (and British) felt that even a handful of burghers should have been able to successfully defend Durban from the British invasion and as W.J. d'Urban later commented, "When I went over the ground a few days after the landing, I felt that my life had been given me."

In fact, public sentiment among the Boers was so strongly against Pretorius in this regard that 20 burghers wrote to the Volksraad of Natalia to request that Gert Rudolph replace Pretorius as commandant general. Their letter stated that one of the reasons that they had lost faith in Pretorius was due to the lack of leadership he had demonstrated in the defence of Durban against the British reinforcements.[1238]

When the new British troops marched into Captain Smith's camp, they were shocked to see dead horses and rubbish on the ground and were overwhelmed by the stink of rotting meat, offal and hides from the oxen and horses the Redcoats had killed as well as of old garbage.[1239] Strips of rotten, blackened horsemeat hung from the wagons, which were riddled with bullets, and the only horse that had not yet been killed for meat was in a sorry state: it could not stand it was so weak. Even worse, 26 wounded men lay in shallow trenches, covered with horse hides, and dysentery had struck down many of the men, some of whom had lost limbs and were pestered by flies that crawled over their bloodied stumps.

During the almost month-long siege, the British had lost more than 30 men and the Boers five. As far as Captain Smith was concerned, the British

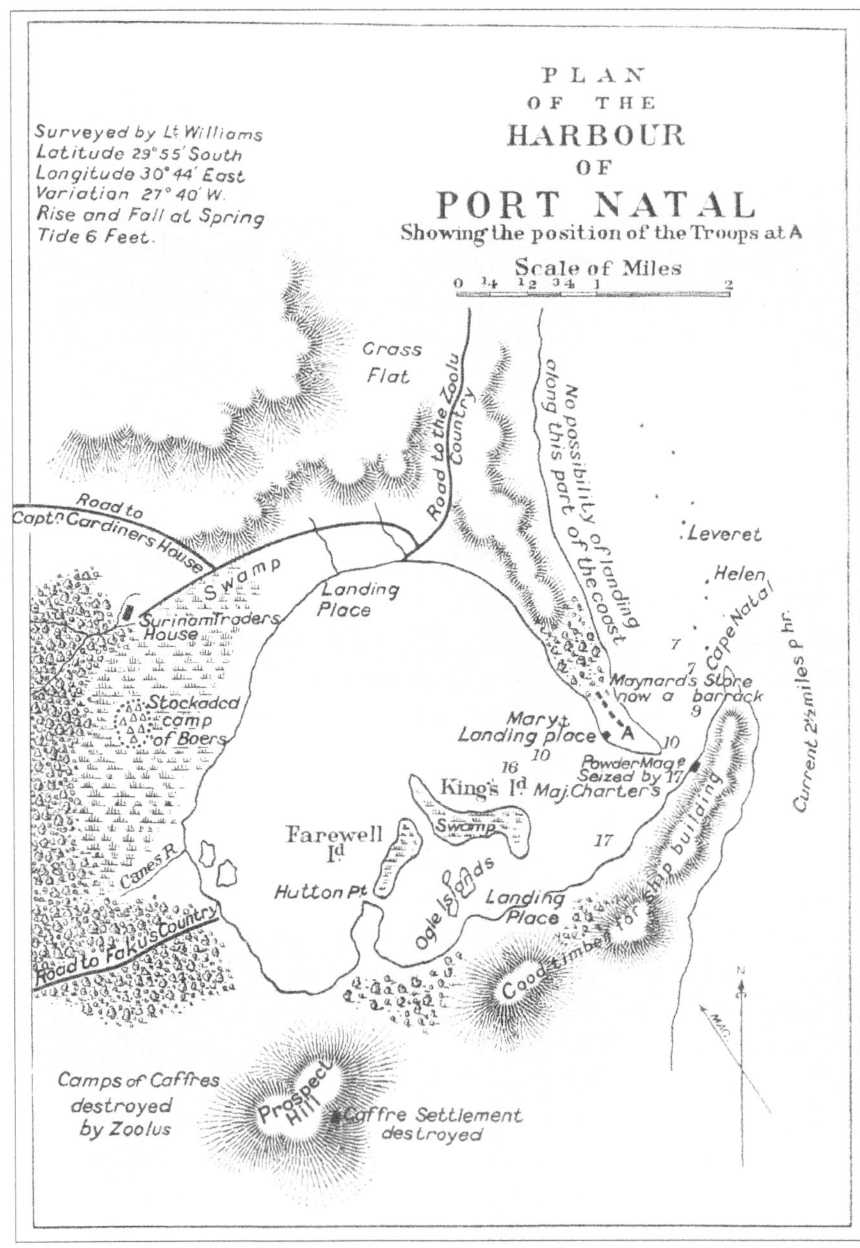
PLAN
OF THE
HARBOUR
OF
PORT NATAL
Showing the position of the Troops at A
Scale of Miles
0 ¼ ½ ¾ 1 2
Surveyed by Lt Williams
Latitude 29°55' South
Longitude 30°44' East
Variation 27°40' W.
Rise and Fall at Spring
Tide 6 Feet.
Grass
Flat
Road to the Zoolu Country
No possibility of landing along this part of the coast
Road to Captn Cardiners House
Swamp
Landing Place
Surinam Traders House
Stockaded camp of Boers
Leveret
Helen
Cape Natal
Current 2½ miles p hr.
Maynard's Store now a barrack
Mary
Landing place
A
Powder Mage Seized by Maj. Charters
King's Id
Swamp
Farewell Id
Hutton Pt
Ogle Islands
Landing Place
Canes R.
Road to Faku's Country
Ship building
Good timber for
Camps of Caffres destroyed by Zoolus
Prospect Hill
Caffre Settlement destroyed
MAG.
N

reinforcements could not have arrived a minute too soon. The mood in the British camp improved rapidly, especially when the *Mazeppa* returned to the harbour the next day and many of the soldiers were able to be reunited with their families.

Meanwhile, Pretorius and the 400 Boers under him had made their way to Steilhoogte (Cowies Hill), where they set up camp.

Totally disillusioned by the unexpected turn of events, Commandant Mocke and many of the burghers under him continued further into the interior and returned to their homes west of the Drakensberg Mountains. Even some of Pretorius's men had had enough of the fight and drifted back to Pietermaritzburg and Weenen. Pretorius, however, stayed at Steilhoogte to await further developments, which weren't long in unfolding.[1240]

On 28 June 1842, Cloete's troops marched to the deserted settlement of Congella—all but Dr Wilhelm Schultz, two Boers and a German man called W. Gueinzuis had fled—and instructed his men to collect whatever provisions they could find. [1241] Cloete noticed that there were several Zulu onlookers and told his translator to shout to them that they could keep the Boers' livestock. He then sent a messenger to Pretorius to tell him that he would grant amnesty to all Boer deserters who submitted to British rule.

When Pretorius sent the messenger back to inform Cloete that he was prepared to discuss peace but not prepared to submit to British rule, Cloete's answer was unambiguous: there would be no negotiations until the Boers accepted British rule.[1242]

Realizing that a shortage of food presented a major problem for the troops, Cloete noticed several Zulu onlookers. Through his translator he shouted to them, "Go and fetch the cattle and horses of the Boers and bring them to me." He also assured them that doing the British this service would mean that the British would protect them from the Boers and warned them that they should not attack the Boers unless "the Boers attempt to use firearms to recover their property".[1243]

Up until this point, the Zulu had observed the two factions of white people slogging it out impartially. However, Cloete's offer of a reward and protection for seizing the Boers' animals turned the Zulu into allies of the British. Little could Cloete know that the Zulu would stop at nothing in their quest to seize the Boers' animals for him and that he had sparked the growing animosity of the Zulu toward the Boers.

Soon, Dirk van Rooyen and Theunis Gerhardus Oosthuizen had been killed by the Zulu. After their cattle were stolen from their farms between the Umlaas and Illovo Rivers, the two men banded together and followed the tracks left by the Zulu. Shortly after making a campfire, they were attacked by the Zulu, who stabbed them to death and then returned to the men's homes and cut and beat the women there. They stripped the women naked and chased them into the veld, where they were only found three days later by a Boer patrol under Bart Pretorius. The terrified women had had no food since they were attacked and had endured the relentless rain with no clothing. Ironically, Van Rooyen and Oosthuizen had refused to join Pretorius's commando against the British.

Then, the Zulu killed farmer Cornelius Van Schalkwyk when he tried to prevent them from taking his cattle.[1244] When Pretorius heard about these violent incidents, he wrote to Cloete on 3 July 1842 to rebuke Cloete for having encouraged the Zulu to kill and rob the Boers. He also warned Cloete that the Republic of Natalia was under the protection of the king of the Netherlands.[1245]

In Cloete's reply to Pretorius, he admitted that he had encouraged the Zulu to take the Boers' cattle but stated that the Boers had "caused the horrors of this state of things; and you must bear the consequences to yourselves, your properties, your wives, and your children". He condemned Pretorius and his men for having stolen cattle from Captain Smith and informed Pretorius that Smellekamp had duped him into believing that the Dutch would protect the Boers from the British. He concluded that while the Boers took up arms against the British government, any harm done to the Boers would please the British government.[1246]

Although Cloete had written to Napier to inform him that he had heard rumours that Mphande had risen up against the Boers and would march to attack them, he was nevertheless surprised when a messenger from Mphande arrived in Durban on 8 July 1842 to tell him that Mphande was eager to assist the British and that his warriors were assembled and ready to attack the Boers in Pietermaritzburg. Cloete immediately sent the messenger back to Mphande to instruct the king not to attack the Boers, under any circumstances, and to order his army to stand down.

That same day, two messengers from the Volksraad of Natalia (Mr Van Aardt and S. Maritz) arrived in Durban to negotiate an end to the hostilities between the Boers and the British. After meeting with Cloete, Van Aardt and S. Maritz were dispatched with a letter for Pretorius in which Cloete set out his terms and warned Pretorius that if the Boers refused to accept these terms, they would "suffer the consequences of the evils which they had brought on themselves".

Cloete's terms called on the Boers to submit to the authority of the British government, release all prisoners and return all cannon and property they had taken from the British. In return, Cloete promised that the British would return all property that had been confiscated from the Boers, allow them to return to their farms with their guns and horses and protect them from any attack by the Zulu. The terms also specified that the Boers would be granted amnesty. However, certain Boer leaders, namely Pretorius, Prinsloo, Burger and Servaas and Michiel Breda, were to be exempted from this and their cases would be considered separately.[1247]

Cloete also undertook not to interfere with the Boer administration other than in the district bounded in the east by the Umgeni River and in the west by the Umlazi River. The northern border would be the crest of the hills of Berea, which would be under the control of the commander of the British troops. In addition, all revenue was to remain in the Boers' hands except for port and custom dues.[1248]

On 10 July 1842, the Volksraad of Natalia held a public meeting to discuss whether to accept or reject the terms of the treaty. Tempers and temperatures ran high at this meeting as the people appeared to be split equally on the issue. Pretorius and his supporters were in favour of accepting the terms, particularly as Pretorius did not believe that the peace treaty with the British would be in effect for long. He and many other Boers held that the Dutch would soon free them from British oppression, as soon as Smellekamp presented their case to the king of the Netherlands.

Eventually, Pretorius managed to persuade the Boers that accepting the terms was in their interests. Subsequently, the Volksraad of Natalia sent a delegation to meet with Cloete at Cowies Hill and, on 11 July 1842, the truce was concluded between the British and Boers.[1249]

The terms of the truce were ratified on 15 July 1842, even though many of the Boers, particularly those under Mocke who had not returned with him to their homes west of the Drakensberg Mountains, still believed that they should not accept the terms Cloete had laid out.[1250]

The next day, Boshoff handed Cloete a memorandum in which he proposed several ideas that he felt would ensure the establishment of an effective and accepted form of administration in Natal. He suggested that a commissioner be appointed to regulate a civil government and that there be minimal military involvement in the day-to-day affairs of the Boers; that a representative council be elected; that the commissioner should determine boundaries and control land sales; that the sale of weapons and ammunition to the Zulu should be banned; and that the Boers be allowed to remain in the towns and on the farms that the Volksraad of Natalia had already granted them. Finally, he proposed that Cloete's brother, Henry Cloete, be appointed as commissioner. Cloete departed Durban on the *Isis* on 21 July 1842 with four companies of the troops that had been sent to assist Captain Smith. Soon after this, the *Joseph Nourse* was sent from the Cape with a strong-armed crew. She was anchored in the inner harbour, where she served the purpose of a floating fort until June 1844. Upon her arrival at Durban, the remaining company of the 25th were withdrawn.[1251]

Captain Smith was left with 275 men from the 27th Regiment, 12 Cape Mounted Rifles, 24 artillerymen and 20 engineers. After the departure of the British troops, the Volksraad of Natalia continued to function much as it had done before the truce and Pretorius resigned as commandant general and returned to his farm, *Welverdiend*.[1252] His successor was Gerrit Rudolph.

Life continued as before, as if the British troops had never come to Natal—even after Napier offered a reward of £250 for the apprehension of Prinsloo, Burger and S. and M. van Breda on 11 August 1842. While these men had not been granted amnesty by the British, Cloete had persuaded the government to grant Pretorius amnesty. Nevertheless, the four Boers continued to live as publicly as they had before and it appeared that no-one was tempted to turn them in to British authorities.[1253]

CHAPTER 32

"Barefoot over the mountains to die in freedom"

Boer defiance—faction fighting—Potgieter scorns Pretorius—Henry Cloete—return of Smellekamp—Zulu refugees—Suzanne Smit—Mocke's planned annexation—troops return—patriots—Volksraad buckles—Boer marriages—Natal incorporated into the Cape Colony

Although the British troops were based at Durban under Captain Smith, the Voortrekkers had lost little of their independence. For instance, Gert Rudolph had carried out a raid to recover stolen cattle from the Zulu without getting permission from Captain Smith or even notifying Captain Smith of his intentions. In the ensuing skirmish, six Zulu were killed.

The Boers considered themselves to be independent and intended to do their own thing.[1254] In the period following Cloete's departure, both Boers and British settlers lived in a state of confusion and unhappiness. Many Boers were angry and disillusioned and felt that the Volksraad of Natalia had been weak to accede to the demands of the British. The British military presence in Natal was largely ignored by the Boers and they did not view Captain Smith in the same way that he viewed himself, namely as governor of the region. As a result, there were often administrative clashes between the Boer government and Captain Smith. In fact, most Boers believed that Captain Smith's jurisdiction was limited to Durban and that they controlled the Republic of Natalia.

Captain Smith was thwarted by the Boers at every turn. When he sent two wagons to Pietermaritzburg to recover the property that the Boers had seized from the British at the start of the siege, they were returned with only a handful of damaged muskets and the message that "this is all we have". Moreover, the Boers commenced laying out plots and erecting buildings in Durban, without Captain Smith's consent.[1255]

Napier wallowed in a sea of indecision while he awaited word from Lord Stanley and the colonial office in England as to what should be done with the settlers in Natal and whether Natal would be incorporated into the Cape colony or be annexed as a separate colony and whether the troops would be withdrawn.

Meanwhile, a pamphlet had been distributed among the Boers that repudiated the claims made by Smellekamp and Reus that the Dutch government intended to free the Boers in the Republic of Natalia from British rule. (Although many believed that it had been generated by Napier in an attempt to shepherd them back to the Cape colony, it later emerged that the pamphlet had actually been put together by the Dutch minister of foreign affairs, Baron Kattendycke.)

With great bitterness, the Natal Boers finally had to concede that Smellekamp and Reus had had no authority to make any assurances of protection on behalf of the king of the Netherlands. Although the majority of Boers reluctantly accepted that they had been suckered, there were many who clung to the dream that the Dutch would assist. They also worried that the Zulu were increasing in the area and that they had lost face among the Boers west of the Drakensberg Mountains.

The Boer nation split into factions: those who called themselves "patriots" and wanted to attack the British; those in the "peace party" who wanted to submit to British rule; and those who wanted to return to the Cape Colony.

By this time, Potgieter and the Boers in the Republic of Winburg-Potchefstroom had begun to believe that Pretorius had possibly had a lucky fluke with his victory at Blood River and openly condemned him as a coward for having persuaded the Volksraad of Natalia to meekly accept the terms of the British. Their view was also shared by many of the firebrands in Natal. Mr Schoemann proposed raising a volunteer corps to attack the British in Durban and the Van Bredas, Prinsloo and Burger plotted the downfall of the British in Weenen.[1256]

In January 1843, Mocke vainly tried to persuade the Volksraad of Natalia to allow him to return to Natal with more men than Captain Smith had at his disposal, namely an army of 500 men from the interior, and, with the help of the Pietermaritzburg Boers, then "chase the British into the sea".[1257]

The British at Durban were perhaps as unhappy as the Boers there. Consequently, British soldiers deserted and were sometimes assisted by the Boers, who provided them with clothing, food and even ammunition. In addition, the British questioned Captain Smith's credibility as a leader. Napier finally received word from Stanley on 23 April 1843 announcing that Her Majesty intended to recognize and adopt Natal as a British colony.[1258]

Stanley instructed Napier to appoint a commissioner and that this person was to travel to the Republic of Natalia to meet with the Boer leaders and to listen to their problems and opinions. He further expressed his view that Natal should not be incorporated into the Cape Colony but rather have its own government under British protection; that all revenues from the sale of land, rent, duties and customs should be used for the maintenance of its civil government; that title deeds should be issued to those who had occupied farms for 12 or more months; that there should be no discrimination on the grounds of colour, creed or language; that no attacks on the Zulu were to be permitted unless authorized by the British government; and that the ownership of slaves would not be permitted.

Napier included all of these regulations in a proclamation that also announced that he had chosen the Honourable Henry Cloete to be commissioner of the Republic of Natalia. Napier's choice of commissioner was well received by the Boers, particularly as he spoke Dutch and he was known to be sympathetic toward the Boers.[1259]

On 8 May 1843, the *Brazilia* pulled into the harbour carrying Smellekamp and Reus, who had skippered the ship, and when the news of their arrival reached Pietermaritzburg, shouts of "We are free; we are free!" emanated from the jubilant Boers.[1260]

After Smellekamp had returned to Holland, the government of the Netherlands had made it very clear that they would not act in any way that encouraged the Boers to resist British authority. In fact, the minister of foreign affairs in the Netherlands had reassured the British representative at the Hague of this fact and a copy of that reassurance had been printed as a pamphlet, which had then been circulated among the Boers. However, the Dutch people greatly sympathized with the trekkers and so had formed a society called the Commission for Supplying the Religious Wants of the Inhabitants of Natalia, which was directed by Mr Swart.

Swart, together with Ohrig (who had engineered the previous visit of the *Brazilia* to Durban), then established a trading company in Holland that had chartered the ship, which set sail for Durban with Reverend Ham and his wife, a teacher called Mr Martineau and Smellekamp, who was appointed as chief director of the group. They had been instructed to place themselves at the disposal of the Volksraad of Natalia.

Shortly after the *Brazilia* anchored at Durban, Smellekamp and Reus went ashore, where Major Smith (who had recently been promoted from captain) refused to allow the two men to meet or communicate with any of the Boers. Consequently, they returned to the ship. Major Smith suspected that the *Brazilia* was carrying weapons destined for the Boers in Pietermaritzburg and so sent Lieutenant Nourse to search the ship. Although no contraband was found, Major Smith still would not allow the crewmen to offload any cargo. As no trade would be possible in Durban, the *Brazilia* travelled to Delagoa Bay, where the frustrated party went ashore. In Delagoa Bay, Mrs Ham died in childbirth, Mr Martineau also died and the *Brazilia* continued to Java to look for a market for her cargo.[1261]

The fact that Major Smith had banned Smellekamp from contacting the Boers sparked a rumour among the Boers that the leaflet had in fact been a ploy to entice them back to the colony and that Smellekamp had been trying to deliver a message from the government of the Netherlands promising them assistance.

At this time, many more Zulu began to appear in Natalia and soon, at least 50,000 Zulu fled to the region in a bid to seek the protection of the British. Mphande, their king, had executed his brother, Xoxo, and then murdered Xoxo's wives and children. Many of the Zulu had been appalled by Mphande's barbaric behaviour and willingly followed Chieftainess Mawa across the Tugela River into Natal. Mphande sent messengers to Major Smith to request that he compel the refugees to return to him, with the cattle that they had taken with them. However, Major Smith refused to accede to Mphande's request and, subsequently, sent a message to Mawa ordering her and the refugees to remain near the Umvoti River.[1262]

However, the 50,000 Zulu wandered up and down Natal and settled wherever they wanted to, including on the Boers' farms. Consequently, many Boers hastily abandoned their farms and made for Pietermaritzburg, taking only essential items with them in their wagons.

In Pietermaritzburg, the displaced Boers grumbled that a commando should be sent to chase the Zulu back over the Tugela River and insisted that they should be made to remain in a designated area.

Very soon, the refugee Zulu had spread out over the whole of the Republic of Natalia and were fighting with the Zulu who had been living in areas near Boer settlements and stealing their cattle, as well as the livestock belonging to the Boers. In short, the Republic of Natalia was simmering with tension. The antagonism felt by the Boers toward the British and toward Major Smith in particular increased when Major Smith refused to accept a letter dated 15 May 1843 from the Volksraad of Natalia enquiring why he had not allowed Smellekamp to communicate with the Boers. Major Smith's refusal to accept the letter fuelled the belief held by many Boers that Smellekamp had been bringing the Boers good news from the Netherlands.[1263] Consequently, many residents of Durban wrote to the Boers west and north of the Drakensberg Mountains to ask them to spread the word about the arrival of the *Brazilia* and that they anticipated that the Dutch government would send other ships from the Netherlands.[1264] These letters even prompted some of the Boers in the interior to come to the Natalia, as they wanted to be on hand when the Dutch finally sent help.

The new commissioner arrived in Durban on 5 June 1843 and, upon being informed of the incursions by the refugee Zulu and that many of the Boers were leaving or planning to leave the Republic of Natalia to join Potgieter, Henry Cloete acted decisively. He immediately sent a message to inform the residents of Pietermaritzburg that there would be a public meeting on 9 June 1843 and set off for the settlement. When he arrived at Pietermaritzburg on the morning of 8 June 1843, a delegation of five solemn Boers accompanied him into the town, which Henry Cloete could not fail to note was decorated with Dutch flags, the Dutch colours and the tricolour flag of the Republic of Natalia. Unsurprisingly, the Boers encountered by the British representative that day appeared cool and uncommunicative.

The next morning, the town buzzed with anticipation as practically every Boer man, woman and child crowded into the *raadsaal* (council chamber). Over 500 people had come to listen to Henry Cloete and many were intent on speaking their piece about their discontent under the British. At ten o'clock, Advocate Cloete entered the *raadsaal* in a robe that bore the insignia of his office. He was accompanied by several members of the Volksraad of Natalia and as he took his seat, the Boers craned their necks and jostled their neighbours to get a better view of him. Advocate Cloete read his commission and the proclamation Napier had issued in early May amidst much shouting, heckling and interruption. When Henry Cloete had finished reading, Anton Fick stood up and informed him that the Boers had made several decisions a few days earlier and that he would read these to him. Subsequently, Henry Cloete made it clear that this was not the time or place for Fick to speak to him about these matters. In addition to the catcalls and abuse hurled at Cloete, there was, once again, arguing among the Boers, as not all were in favour of rejecting British authority.

Fick then announced that the Boers would not negotiate with Henry Cloete or the British until they had heard from Smellekamp or the king of the Netherlands. Egged on by the shouting crowd and particularly the women, Fick then started to read a petition that had been signed by over 100 women. However, Henry Cloete became so agitated by the hostility expressed toward the British in the petition that he waved a hand dismissively at Fick and turned away from him, thereby indicating that he would not listen to him any longer. The women screamed at him that he should pay attention to Fick as he was describing the suffering and hardships the Boer women had had to endure and when Henry Cloete stood up to leave, the angry women blocked his path.

Susanna Smit, the very large and domineering wife of the Reverend Smit, yelled at Henry Cloete in rage and her husband attempted to calm her, saying "Be quiet, my wife. Please, my child, restrain yourself".

To the astonishment of those watching, she turned on her mild-mannered husband and shrieked "You wretch! Shall I be still while you stand there silent? I will wear the breeches now!"[1265]

Cloete finally managed to shoulder his way through the livid mob of women and exited into the street with a sigh of relief. In the *raadsaal*, Stephanus Maritz and J.P. Zietsman informed the Boers that a meeting would be held on the first Monday of August 1843 where all matters would be decided upon.

Fick and other Boers who were patriots were happy with the way in which Henry Cloete had been ousted from this meeting, as they were hell bent on war with the British. (The patriots tended to be the lowest order of the community and were led by people such as Fick who had the "worst description of character within the Cape of Good Hope". In fact, Fick had fled the Cape colony after having been found guilty of fraud.)

Those in the peace party were naturally disappointed that the meeting had degenerated to such an extent, as they were prepared to make things work with the commissioner and the British. Members of this school of thought included opinion leaders and educated, wealthier people such as Pretorius, Landman, Boshoff, the Zietsman brothers, Stephanus Maritz, Otto and Joachim Prinsloo.[1266]

After returning to Durban, Cloete was so concerned that he wrote a report for the governor. He described Natalia as "close to anarchy" and stated that ordered government of the Volksraad did not exist. To this end, he issued a notice that all claims, including those for building ervens in Pietermaritzburg, were to be brought to him by the last day of June 1843. The Boers were so incensed that he had given them so little time to comply with his order that three members of the Volksraad of Natalia asked him to withdraw this instruction. Cloete refused and the Boers then tore down all of the notices he had had posted and adopted a policy of passive resistance: by the end of the month, no claims to farms had been submitted by the Boers and only 120 of the 450 ervens in Pietermaritzburg had been registered, mainly by British, German and other non-Boer nationalities.

The Boers in the Republic of Natalia were on the verge of revolt—German settlers in Pietermaritzburg wrote to Henry Cloete to express that they were afraid the Boers would attack them and other minority groups loyal to the British—and Boers under the militant Mocke were getting ready to come to the aid of the Natal Boers. Boer dissent soon spread over the mountain.

When the commandant at Riet River, M.A. Oberholzer, refused to attend a meeting at Winburg, he was warned that any attempt by the residents of his area to discuss their affairs independently of the Volksraad of Natalia would result in them being attacked by armed forces of Boers. Oberholzer duly resigned as commandant and secretly wrote to the commissioner to inform him of the threats made by his fellow Boers and to ask for protection from the British.[1267]

Oberholzer also informed the commissioner that Mocke intended proclaiming the whole country north of the Orange River as a republic.

A few days later, the British official Justice Menzies arrived at Colesberg for a sitting of the circuit court. When he heard the news of Mocke's plans, he proceeded to Allemans Drift, crossed the river there and then hoisted the Union Jack, while watched by several British officials and military men and Boers, including field cornets Joubert, Visser and du Plessis as well as Adam Kok and about 50 of his Griqua.

In a loud voice, he then proclaimed that the whole country, from the 22nd degree of longitude eastward to the sea and from the Orange River northward to the 25th parallel of latitude, was British territory, exception for the areas already under Portuguese control.[1268]

Back in the Republic of Natalia, Henry Cloete requested that Major Smith occupy Pietermaritzburg. However, Major Smith protested that it would not be possible to do so without receiving reinforcements. After Major Cloete requested additional troops from Napier, 200 Redcoats of the 45th Regiment, with artillery, were sent from Simon's Town on board the *Thunderbolt*.

The men and weapons arrived at Durban on 21 July.

Meanwhile, reports had reached Henry Cloete and Major Smith that many Boers commandos were assembling at Weenen. In fact, more than 800 men and 1,500 good horses were camped there and would soon set off to Pietermaritzburg. The Boers were preparing for war. Again.

Reluctant to enter into another fight with the Boers, Major Smith refused to move his men from Durban to Pietermaritzburg when Henry Cloete requested that he do so. The commissioner had his heart set on having British troops in the settlement before the Boers' meeting scheduled for early August 1843 and before any more Boers from the interior arrive. He argued that while his men journeyed the 100 kilometres to Pietermaritzburg, the Boers might seize Durban.

The captain of the *Thunderbolt* overheard the discussion between Captain Smith and Henry Cloete and set sail for the Cape the following day to request that the government send more troops to the Republic of Natalia to tackle the Boers.

When Henry Cloete received a letter from Pretorius and another from Mocke, Rudolph, Kok and 19 others that both requested that he come to Pietermaritzburg without any soldiers and which guaranteed his safety, Cloete acceded.

On 4 August 1843, 80 unarmed Boers met Henry Cloete at Uysdoorns, about eight kilometres from Pietermaritzburg, and escorted him into the village and to his accommodation.

He was shocked to see that between 800 and 1,000 Boers from the interior had set up their 20 wagons in the market square and that they were all armed and looked eager to fight. Despite the alarm he felt at seeing this display of military might, he declined the offer of armed guards.

Henry Cloete remained at his lodging with Mr Behrens while the Volksraad of Natalia met on 5 August 1843. At this meeting, only 18 of the 24 members of the Volksraad of Natalia attended and it appeared that Mocke was calling the shots. By the end of it, Mocke had managed to expand the number of members of the Volksraad of Natalia to 36 and ensured that representatives from across the Drakensberg were included.[1269] (During five lectures delivered by the Honourable Henry Cloete to the Natal Society at Pietermaritzburg, he stated that the number of seats in the Volksraad of Natalia was increased to sixty.)

That night, the patriots held a secret meeting to discuss whether they should be armed when they attended the meeting scheduled for the next day and resolved to provoke a scuffle or incite the crowd to violence. In the ensuring chaos, they would then assassinate peace-makers Pretorius and Boshoff. Little did they know that Pretorius's informants learned of their plan and that his followers would also be armed at the meeting.

Early the next morning, an unruly crowd of armed Boers assembled outside the *raadsaal*. It was clear to Henry Cloete and others that these Boers had no intention of submitting to the British and were willing to fight their fellow Boers in an attempt to persuade them to adopt their way of thinking.

When Pretorius finally entered the hall with his loyal supporters, a large mob of Boers, the majority of which hailed from beyond the Drakensberg Mountains, muttered and shouted abuse at him.[1270] Pretorius then addressed the crowd and made it clear that he knew of the plot to assassinate him. He stared pointedly at the clique of plotters as he spoke and evidently shamed them into inaction.

After Henry Cloete informed the crowd that the British had no intention of expanding their sphere of influence to incorporate the Boers in Transoranje, Winburg or Potchefstroom, the Volksraad of Natalie passed a resolution that members not affected by the British occupation had no right to vote. Consequently, the Boers from across the Drakensberg lost interest in the whole affair and departed the meeting under the firebrand Mocke.

Before hastily leaving Pietermaritzburg to return home, they swore that they would never return to the Republic of Natalia to render any form of assistance to the Boers there.[1271] The 25 remaining members of the Volksraad of Natalia resumed the meeting and one of the men read a letter that Dr Poortman had received from a friend in Holland that clarified that the Boers should expect no aid from Holland and that Smellekamp had duped them.

While the Volksraad deliberated the implications of the letter, a deputation of

Boer women approached Henry Cloete. Susanna Smit was spokesperson for the group and she declared that their husbands had agreed that Boer women should be allowed a say in how the country was run. She took the opportunity to express the view that the women were determined never to yield to British rule but were fully aware that resisting would be futile. She added that they intended to seek their freedom from the British by leaving the Republic of Natalia.

"You have invaded our country and taken it from us," widow Mieta Kruger shouted at Henry Cloete. "You have taken our harbour and have allowed the kaffirs to commit murder. You have unleashed the kaffirs upon us after promising to protect us from them. You also have taken down our flag."

Egged on by Susanna Smit and the other women, she continued, "We have wandered for years and our feet are worn through. We have been broken by our roaming and suffering. However, we are prepared to go on. We are prepared to cross the Drakensberg Mountains on our bare feet, to meet either liberty or death, rather than to bow to a government that has treated us as the British government has done."

"Yes!" Susanna Smit yelled. "We are ready to cross the Drakensberg Mountains on our bare feet and die in liberty, as death is dearer to us than the loss of our freedom!"

After great deliberations, the Volksraad of Natalia signed their acceptance of Napier's proclamation on 8 August 1843.[1272] In effect, the Boers who remained in the Republic of Natalia were now answerable to the British. Nevertheless, many were bitter that the Volksraad or Natalia had accepted the terms of the British and verbally assaulted them and their supporters for days.

It appeared as though the Natalia Boers were on the verge of civil war: at night, small groups of unhappy residents threw stones through the windows of the homes of the peace party followers, emptied rubbish onto their gardens and hurled abuse at them. The situation became so tense that Major Smith set up camp outside Pietermaritzburg and stationed 200 Redcoats and two cannon there on 31 August 1843. Fort Napier would later be built here.[1273]

Soon, many dejected Voortrekkers packed up their wagons and deserted the Republic of Natalia to continue their trek north to the Transvaal, where they would join Potgieter. By the end of 1843, the population in the Republic of Natalia had dwindled and there were no more than 500 families there and possibly as few as 350.[1274] The exodus of Boers that started with the acceptance of Napier's terms would continue for the next five years. Potgieter had been right when he said, "Where you have the sea you have the British."

The British had declared that they would take into consideration the wishes of the people when setting up a new administration for Natalia. Consequently, the Volksraad met in September 1843 to draw up a long list of suggestions. These included that the four Boers who had not been granted amnesty by the British should be pardoned; that Natal should be considered completely separate to the Cape colony; that the burghers select a legislative council of 12 members; that every town or village should have its own municipality if the residents requested one; that the Boers be allowed to continue to practise their religion as they saw fit; that paper money should not be forced into circulation; that there would be no compulsory military service and that all lands that the Volksraad of Natalia had already granted to Boers not be taken away.

The British authorities at the Cape and in England did not pay much attention to these suggestions but allowed the Volksraad of Natalia to continue with their administrative duties while they pondered how to establish an effective government in the region.

By this stage, the influx of Zulu into the Republic of Natalia had increased to between 80,000 to 100,000 and the Volksraad of Natalia eventually approached Henry Cloete to request that the British drive the Zulu north over the Tugela River and south over the Umzimvubu River.

Henry Cloete refused to release troops for this task and warned the Boers not to take action against the Zulu as Her Majesty's government was still considering the issue of land ownership in the Republic of Natalia. However, Henry Cloete met with Mphande in early October 1843 and, after a few days of talks and the customary military and dancing displays put on by the Zulu for important guests, they signed an agreement on 5 October 1843 that determined the boundaries between Zululand and the Republic of Natal. Ultimately, the boundary was to be the Tugela River in the north—from the mouth of the Tugela River to the confluence with the Umzinyathi River (Buffalo) and north along the Umzinyathi River to the Drakensberg Mountains. Cloete managed to persuade Mphande to grant the British (and not the Boers) a concession on being in the lands surrounding St Lucia Bay, as he wanted the British to have access to the sea. In return, he undertook to provide military assistance to Mphande when his cattle were stolen.

It was not long before Mphande took him up on his offer: on his return to Durban, he was approached by Mphande's messengers, who informed him that a renegade petty chief who lived at by Umgeni River was harbouring large herds of Mphande's cattle. Cloete instructed them to ask Major Smith to mobilize troops to assist with the recovery of the cattle. This resulted in a series of acrimonious letters between Smith and Cloete which deteriorated to such a low that the letters were eventually sent to Napier for arbitration, Napier expressed his belief that the commissioner had exceeded his authority by telling Mphande that British troops would assist in dealing with cattle rustlers.

Reverend Smit had finally become too old and infirm to continue with his duties at the Dutch Reformed Church in Pietermaritzburg, which created major problems for the Boers. No ordained ministers had accompanied the Boers on their trek due to the Cape colony's instigation that the ministers in the colony turn their backs on Boers leaving the colony.

The dearth of Boer spiritual leaders and officials meant that couples wanting to get married or christen their children had to wait, sometimes for several months, until a minister became available and the ceremonies would then be en masse. In addition, marriages were frequently conducted by Boers who had not been ordained or appointed by any civil body, which necessitated obtaining a marriage certificate by an ordained minister, in some instances as many as 20 years after the marriage ceremony.[1275] As late as 1839, marriage certificates in the Dutch Reformed Church in Graaff-Reinet were signed in English, which indicated that English-speaking ministers had officiated.[1276]

It was not uncommon for Voortrekker girls to marry by the age of 12. For instance, Trichardt's wife had married at 15, Gerrit Maritz's wife at 15 and the fearsome Susanna Smit at age 12.

The practice continued long after the Voortrekkers settled down in places like Weenen and Pietermaritzburg and, even in the established town of Graaff-Reinet, more than half of the 94 marriages conducted in the Dutch Reformed Church in 1840 and 1841 involved women defined as minors (under 21). Similarly, of the 160 marriages conducted in Swellendam in 1840, 72 involved women under the age of 18, two of twelve-year-olds and two of thirteen-year-olds.[1277]

In Pietermaritzburg, the Boers were lucky enough to be sent American Reverend Daniel Lindley, who conducted services and dispensed spiritual healing not only in Pietermaritzburg but also in Weenen and the far-off communities of Winburg and Potchefstroom. The Boers petitioned that Henry Cloete allow them to appoint Reverend Lindley as the permanent minister of the Dutch Reformed Church and finally, in November 1843, the commissioner granted their request and even agreed to pay him a stipend. Many of the Boers hoped that Reverend Ham, the minister who had accompanied Smellekamp on the *Brazilia* and was still with him in Delagoa Bay, would come to the Republic of Natalia to administer to the Boers in Dutch.

Despite having been told repeatedly not to expect any aid from the Netherlands, many Boers still clung desperately to the belief that if Smellekamp had been allowed to communicate with them at Durban, they would be free of the British or at least working their way toward independence. Wanting to hear the truth from the horse's mouth, Joachim Prinsloo, Gert Rudolph, Cornelis Coetsee and one of the Bezuidenhout men left Weenen on horseback for the long and tough journey to Delagoa Bay, where they intended to see Smellekamp and Reverend Ham and to finally resolve whether the government of the Netherlands had truly abandoned them to British rule. At Delagoa Bay, the meeting with Smellekamp was short and to the point: he explained that although the commercial community in the Netherlands sympathized with the Natalia Boers, they could not expect recognition or help from the government of the Netherlands.

Ever alert to a business deal, Smellekamp then advised the four men to encourage the burghers in the Republic of Natalia to move north, above the 25th parallel of latitude, where they would be beyond British control and able to trade with the company that he represented.

The disappointed Boers soon set off on a hellish journey back to Weenen. Along the way, the horses died from malaria, as did Coetsee and, two weeks after arriving in Weenen, Prinsloo also died from the mosquito-borne illness. Fortunately, Bezuidenhout and the hardy Rudolph survived without any ill effects. The news this party brought back to Weenen and the Republic of Natalia finally persuaded the Boers that their hardships were theirs alone to bear.

Shortly after this, an expedition of 50 Boers set out from Winburg to see Reverend Ham in Algoa Bay as they hoped to persuade him to become their minister. However, when they rode through an area infested with the tsetse fly, their cattle and horses began to die and they were forced to give up the expedition and return to Winburg.

Reverend Ham eventually departed Lourenço Marques for Cape Town on a visiting vessel and spent the remainder of his life there in the capacity of a clergyman. Meanwhile, Henry Cloete was attempting to address the issue of land ownership by the Boers. Upon embarking upon a tour of the Republic of Natalia, he soon discovered that the Volksraad of Natalia had granted farms to the Voortrekkers fairly indiscriminately and that many of the Boers' farms exceeded the 6,000 acres that they had been allowed. He wrote a lengthy and comprehensive report on the status of land ownership in the Republic of Natalia to Stanley, who recommended that the size of the Boers' farms should be halved, to 3,000 acres, and that the quite rent should be increased from 18 shillings per annum to £2 ten shillings. He did concede that Henry Cloete should not implement his recommendations if he "should be deliberately of the opinion that this would be likely to produce a renewed immigration by the Boers".

Once the Boers had registered their land with Henry Cloete, they waited anxiously to hear whether the British would take their land.

During 1844, the Natalia Boers continued to worry about their future under the British, particularly as the Volksraad of Natalia appeared to have no say when it came to decisions about important matters. Major Smith vetoed any decision of the Volksraad of Natalia that he did not approve of and the British government had given no indication as to when a new government structure would replace or supplement the Boer government. As a result, the hamstrung Volksraad on Natalia conducted little business when it met and it was widely rumoured among the Boers that the British might be intending to leave the region and that Captain Smith's troops would be ordered out of Pietermaritzburg. It was even rumoured that the Boers planned to enlist Mphande's help to attack the refugee Zulu in Durban. These rumours were encouraged to flourish due to the lack of communication between British decision-makers and the Boers.[1278]

On 31 May 1844, Royal Letters were sent to the new governor of the Cape colony, Sir Peregrine Maitland, to proclaim the formal annexation of Natal as a British possession and that the region would form part of the Cape Colony. In essence, no court at the Cape would have jurisdiction over Natal and no laws passed in the Cape would extend to the district of Natal. However, the Cape legislature was to draw up laws for Natal, govern the district of Natal and appoint a lieutenant governor to represent Queen Victoria in Natal. On 13 November, Martin West was provisionally appointed as the first lieutenant governor of the district.

The first horse races were staged in Pietermaritzburg on 8 July 1844, after the Maritzburg Turf Club was established, and proved so popular that races in Durban were organized for later that month.[1279] However, no matter how much the Boers enjoyed this form of entertainment, it could not prevent a steady exodus of Boers from Natal.

In August 1844, new members were elected to the Volksraad of Natalia. As many of the newly elected members refused to take the oath of allegiance to Queen Victoria, Major Smith reinstated the new members with the those who had stepped down. However, they proved to be as intractable as the new members and passed a resolution that all Zulu should leave Natal. Without the support of Major Smith's troops, however, the Boers were unable to act upon the resolution.

Across the Drakensberg Mountains and north of the Vaal River, the Voortrekkers formed small, independent communities and, within no time, jealousy, rivalry and antagonism existed between the various groups. Typically, once a number of emigrants settled at one spot, the most domineering character in the group appointed himself leader of that community. Subsequently, his word became law and, in most cases, the people under his sphere of influence elected ancillary leaders that were usually skilled in warfare.

Although there was a loose confederacy between one community and the next, arguments and disagreements frequently occurred between communities and, sometimes, the fighting was so bitter that members would break away to form new, smaller groups. The cycle would then be repeated every time tensions escalated between the communities.[1280]

Whereas Pretorius was not anti-British, Potgieter was. On 10 April 1844, Potgieter sent a declaration to Henry Cloete informing the commissioner that he and his *burgherraad* (council) did not see themselves as having agreed to the treaty concurred between the British and the Natal Boers, as the Natal Boers had not consulted with them before accepting the terms of the agreement. In addition, Potgieter stated that he and his people were not willing to negotiate with the British and that they considered themselves to be free and independent in their lands, which extended to the Great (Orange) River.[1281]

Potgieter sent this declaration to Henry Cloete after learning of a petition signed by 265 burghers from the Winburg district in which they requested that they be deemed to be under British control. At the time, Adam Kok's Griqua were harassing them and they craved the protection of the British.

Although there were many Boers north of the Vaal River who considered themselves British subjects, Potgieter ignored the loyalists in his midst and drafted a constitution of 33 articles which was referred to as the 'Potgieter Constitution for his Boer Republic', as it made no provision for the appointment of an executive leader and the Boers assumed that this role would be taken by Potgieter. But he was not without his detractors and enemies.

After Reverend Ham left Lourenço Marques, Smellekamp stayed on until the *Brazilia* called at the port on her return journey from Java. Before boarding her and returning to the Netherlands, he met with Potgieter.

Although Smellekamp explained that the Boers could expect no assistance from the government of the Netherlands, he advised Potgieter that trade opportunities would abound if his followers moved beyond the 25th parallel of latitude. "Potchefstroom is too far away," he stated matter-of-factly. "I assure you that Mr Ohrig, my employer, has your interests at heart. Now that the port of Durban is closed to you, Delagoa Bay offers a good alternative."

After meeting with Smellekamp, Potgieter then met with the Portuguese governor in Lourenço Marques and concluded an agreement with him that allowed the Boers to settle west of the Lebombo Mountains, behind the

Portuguese harbour, in order to facilitate easier trade with Mozambique.[1282]

On the way back to Potchefstroom, Potgieter selected a beautiful site in the mountains for the future Boer town and named it Andries Ohrigstad before continuing to his farm, Buffelshoek, in the Magaliesberg. By this time, he had been married four times and had 17 children.[1283] Potgieter appeared to demonstrate a paternalistic attitude toward the indigenous people in his 'kingdom' and made a point of cementing his relationship with the local leaders. For instance, he granted the Barolong chiefs land in the western part of his territory if they would agree not to buy arms and ammunition from anyone.

Nevertheless, the missionaries in the area wrote to Lord Stanley in England as early as 1843 to inform him that the Boers had "commenced their aggression upon the unoffending tribes".

CHAPTER 33

Enter the Griqua and Basotho

Moshoeshoe—Union Flag at the Orange—Adam Kok—Griqua prepare for war—British troops move again—dividing up the land—meeting of the chiefs

While the events in Natal were unfolding, the power of Basotho chief Moshoeshoe was increasing in Basotholand due to the broken tribes and small groups of refugees streaming into Thaba Bosiu (mountain of the night) seeking protection, mainly from Mzilikazi and the Matabele, and an alliance with the Basotho chief. Moshoeshoe's people included the Bataung clan under Moletsane. Along the Orange River, the refugee Baputhi under Chief Morosi were becoming more and more powerful, as refugees, including Thembus from the Eastern Cape as well as Bushmen, joined them.

Some of the Barolong minor chiefs, namely Gontse, Tawane and Matlabe, had moved across the Vaal River in 1841 and had approached Potgieter to request that they be granted land. As Potgieter had never forgotten that Chief Moroka II had come to his aid after the Battle of Vegkop, he granted these three chiefs land in the district of Potchefstroom.

In 1842, French missionaries in Basotholand estimated that Moshoeshoe's Basotho people numbered between 30,000 and 40,000 and, upon the advice of the missionaries, the astute Moshoeshoe recognized that he would be better served by throwing his lot in with the British rather than the Boers.

On 30 May 1842, he approved a letter to be written by Reverend Casalis to Lieutenant Governor Hare of the Cape colony asking for a treaty and protection from the British government. Subsequently, Napier issued a proclamation that announced that certain tribes would be protected by the British against any aggression or encroachment on their lands. Essentially, the proclamation granted protection to the Basotho of Moshoeshoe, the Barolong of Chief Moroka II, the Batlapin of Lepui, the coloureds of Carolus Baatje and the Griqua of Barend Barends and Adam Kok and subtly identified the Boers as the aggressors.

When Justice Menzies raised the Union Flag on the land north of the Orange River on 22 October 1842, he ordered that a willowtree be cut down. On the stump, which was placed in a cairn of stones, he nailed a board marked with the words 'Baken van Koningen van England' (land of the queen of England).

Two days late, Mocke and 300 armed and angry Boers arrived in the area to dispute the legality of what Justice Menzies had done and to inform him that the Boers in the territory would reject his claim that the land was British. Moreover, Mocke told him that the Boers had established a republic in the land north of the Orange River and down to the military boundary of Port Natal. However, he did not lower the Union Jack nor remove the sign. As soon as Napier heard of Justice Menzie's annexation, he issued a notice repudiating Menzie's actions and stated that he had acted without the authority of the colonial government. Nevertheless, he added that the Boers in the area were British subjects.

In early 1843, Potgieter visited Thaba 'Nchu and called an indaba with all of the chiefs south of the Caledon River, including Moshoeshoe. When Moshoeshoe arrived at Chief Moroka II's village, Potgieter shouted to him, "Are you my friend?"

"Yes," Moshoeshoe answered, "but I am also the friend of the British."[1284]

Despite Potgieter's anti-British stance, he entered into an agreement with Moshoeshoe (and the chiefs) promising that the Boers and indigenous peoples would to live in harmony.

On 26 August 1843, Adam Kok sent a letter to Napier to request that a treaty of alliance be entered into between his people, the Griqua, and the British. Kok and his 2,000 half-caste people were known as the Griqua and claimed to own some 20,000 square kilometres of land between the Orange and the Modder rivers, including that occupied by the Barolong and Batlapin. He explained to the governor that their land had become home to more Boer settlers than Griqua.

Shortly after receiving Kok's letter, Napier signed a treaty with Moshoeshoe and the Basotho people and with Kok and the Griqua on 5 October 1843. Although Napier clearly defined the limits of Moshoeshoe's territory, he only specified the southern border of the Griqua's territory, namely from the area of Ramah on the Orange River to Bethulie. The treaties also promised Moshoeshoe and Kok money, arms and ammunition in exchange for their commitment to non-violence.

The Boers were highly irritated by and bitter about the two treaties and felt, rightly so, that they had been 'handled' by the British. Moshoeshoe was also annoyed: he demanded that Napier grant him more territory in the north and that Thaba 'Nchu should be included as his. Moreover, some of the Griqua leaders such as Carolus Baatje and Pieter Davids and Korana leader Gert Taaibosch challenged the validity of their agreement, as they did not accept Moshoeshoe as their chief.

The Boers warned the British that the treaties would lead to bloodshed and that Napier had planted the seeds of war. They blamed the Wesleyan ministers for having misled Napier into believing that they were to blame for the conflict.[1285] There were more than a thousand Boer settlers along the Riet River at this time and they entrusted Willem Oberholzer and Lukas van den Heever to deliver a petition signed by 258 heads of families to Henry Cloete in Natal. It stated that the signatories and their families would be willing to accept the same terms that the commissioner had proposed to the Natal Boers.

Some of Mocke's armed supporters stopped the two men in Winburg and, after searching them, confiscated a copy of the petition. However, Oberholzer and van den Heever had concealed another copy and delivered this to Henry Cloete, who took no heed of it.[1286]

When Hermanus van Staden killed George Mills during a fight near Philippolis in January 1844, Kok ordered that Van Staden be arrested and taken to Colesberg for trial. Thereafter, he took possession of Mills's property, claiming that he was keeping it for Mills's heirs. Upon learning of the incident, Mocke's secretary immediately wrote to Kok demanding that Van Staden be handed over to the Boers so that they could try him in their courts and stated that the Boers were responsible for maintaining order in the area.

Kok's taunting reply, "Your requests have been complied with for us all emigrants from the Colony are looked upon as British subjects," spurred Mocke to threaten Kok that the Boers would go to war with the Griqua. Subsequently, Kok obtained 90 kilos of gunpowder and 180 kilos of lead from the British military garrison at Colesberg.

Fortunately, the tension between Mocke and Kok subsided after Van Staden was released and, in June 1844, the Boers and the Griqua attended a meeting at Philippolis in an attempt to resolve their differences. At this meeting, Michiel Oberholtser repudiated that the Boers had to submit to the Griqua just because the British wished it so and he and Kok concurred that anybody who rejected allegiance to the British government would not be permitted to live in the territory.

Chaos erupted, however, when the popular and charismatic Boer, Commandant Jan Kock, stood up to announce that he would resist this resolution by force and that his many supporters would be on hand to defend their right to live in the territory, as free Boers. The meeting collapsed and, from that time on, the friction between Oberholtser's supporters and Kock's supporters intensified.

Kock was well read, educated and outspoken and, as such, commanded the respect and admiration of his fellow Boers, many recognizing him as an able leader. He longed to bring all of the Boers and other white emigrants north of the Orange River under the rule of Potgieter's government in Potchefstroom.

When Kok and the Griqua pressured Oberholtser and his party to return to the Cape colony or accept that they would live under Griqua control, Oberholtser wrote to Sir Peregrine Maitland, Napier's successor as governor to complain about their behaviour.

Having only recently taken office, Maitland realized that he did not possess the military force to police the implementation of the treaties that Napier had signed with Kok and Moshoeshoe. In addition, he had received two letters asking for the British to provide protection: one was from Kok and the other was from Oberholtser and Jacobus Snyman, a farmer from the Caledon Valley. Moreover, the letter from Oberholtser and Snyman concluded by stating that if the British did not protect them, they would have no alternative but to place themselves under the control and protection of Potgieter and his Potchefstroom government.

When Jan Kock held out the peace pipe to Adam Kok by inviting him to meet with Commandant Potgieter so that the Boers and the Griqua would try to establish a peaceful relationship, Kok replied via missionary Reverend W.Y. Thompson that he did not wish to meet anyone who assumed he had authority over subjects of the queen of England.

However, in the latter half of December 1844, Potgieter came to Philippolis and met with Kok. Potgieter proposed that the Boers and the Griqua should live side by side in peace, as both groups were emigrants. However, Kok argued that he regarded all emigrants as British subjects and stated that he would abide by Napier's treaty, which had granted him the land between the Orange and the Modder rivers. Potgieter must have had great difficulty in controlling his temper when he heard this and the meeting ended abruptly, with no agreement having been reached.

Kock and his people were getting ready to fight and most of them were permanently armed. Consequently, Kok wrote to the governor to request that a fort be established and manned by Redcoats and warned that the Boers needed to be watched closely. Maitland duly informed Kok that should the Boers intend to attack Kok and the Griqua, then he would dispatch an armed force from the colony to assist him. The festering sore between the Griqua and the Boers soon began to ooze.

When two Moroleng brothers by the names of September and April quarrelled with and threatened a Boer with their assegais on the farm at which they were employed, the owner, Jan Krynauw, arrested them and held them prisoner. After tying them up, he took them to Jan Kock in Winburg for punishment. As Kock refused to punish them, Krynauw took the law into his own hands and had the two men tied to a wagon wheel and given 29 lashes with a leather stirrup.[1287]

Upon hearing of this, Kok asked Mr Rawstorne, the civil commissioner in Colesberg whether he would receive Krynauw for a trial.

Recognizing that taking such action might be tantamount to sticking his hand into a hornet's nest, Rawstorne advised Kok to proceed with caution. Nevertheless, Kok ignored the magistrate's advice and sent 100 armed Griqua to arrest Krynauw.

When the Griqua commando arrived at Krynauw's home, they entered the house and one of the men shouted, "Come out, Krynauw! This is the day when your blood will flow."[1288]

Krynauw had fled and the angry Griqua subsequently hurled abuse at his wife, smashed the furniture in the house and stole three guns and a quantity of ammunition. This incident fuelled the Boers' already simmering frustration with the Griqua and they prepared for war: they set up a laager at Touwfontein, Adriaan van Wyk's farm, which was about 50 kilometres from Philippolis and soon, farmers from between the Orange and Caledon rivers assembled there under Commandant Jacobus du Plooy.

Shortly after this, several skirmishes broke out between the Boers and the Griqua in which shots were fired by both parties and they began stealing each other's cattle. Mr Rawstorne called on the Boers to keep the peace but supplied Kok with 100 muskets and ammunition and requested that Major Campbell move his Redcoats from Colesberg to Allemans Drift on the Orange River in order to protect Griqua fugitives and to stop the Boers from receiving reinforcements.[1289]

In a letter from Colonel Hare to Kok, the lieutenant governor blamed Kok for aggravating the Boers and urged him to come to reach some form of settlement with Krynauw and the Boers. Then, on 22 March 1845, Mr Rawstorne sent a message to Jan Kock and suggested that they meet. He hoped to persuade Kock to influence the Boers to disperse and return to their homes.

In Kock's reply, he addressed Rawstorne as "Chief of the colonists on the other side of the Groot [Orange] River" and stated that he would not attend a meeting with him unless he was instructed to do so by his burgher senate. He did, however, agree to send Rawstorne's letter to them.

More and more armed Boers arrived at Touwfontein in early April 1844. Realizing that war with the Boers was imminent, Kok attempted to defuse the tension between the Boers and the Griqua by finally accepting an invitation to Touwfontein to discuss a settlement. The Boers had made it clear to Kok that they would guarantee his safe passage to the farm. Nevertheless, he approached Touwfontein with a commando in full battle array. Naturally, the Boers believed that they were about to be attacked and scurried off to prepare their defences.

When Kok sent a message ahead to tell the Boers that he was ready to talk, they responded that they were ready to give him what he so evidently desired: war. The Griqua hastily withdrew to a nearby waterhole to consider their next move. Suddenly, shots rang out—there is some question as to whether the Boers who had followed the Griqua launched a surprise attack by firing five shots, as claimed by the Griqua, or whether the Griqua had seen that they were being pursued and fired nine shots at the unsuspecting pursuers, as claimed by the Boers—and the Griqua dived for cover. The war had started.

During the two major battles between the Boers and the Griqua, the Boers came off worst. While only one Griqua was killed and six taken prisoner, the Boers lost ten men.

While the conflict between the Boers and the Griqua escalated, 200 Redcoats under Major Campbell moved to Allemans Drift and set up camp there. They were to be on hand to assist Kok and were strategically positioned to stop any Boers from the colony from crossing the Orange River to come to the aid of their fellow Boers. Maitland also instructed Colonel Hare in Grahamstown to hold the 7th Dragoon Guards in readiness to proceed to the Orange River should matters deteriorate further. Rawstorne sent a final warning to the Boers before sending the troops over the river: "I hereby solemnly warn all such emigrants against further pursuit of this wicked and atrocious design. It will not alone be the Griqua territory from which you will be driven, but there will be no rest for the soles of your feet in any part of South Africa, until the demands of justice have been fully satisfied."

Mocke and his colleagues, Commandant Kock, H. Steyn and Jan du Plooy, rejected Rawstorne's warning and informed him on 18 April 1844 that as Kok had started the fire, he should be the one asking for peace. Kok realized that he had gone too far in provoking the Boers and fled to Allemans Drift to beg that the British sent a message to the Boers informing them that he was ready to stop fighting. However, when the Boers received his message, they responded that they had wanted peace all along but that the Griqua had commenced hostilities and therefore had to be prepared to suffer the consequences.

Rawstorne recognized that the Griqua would be annihilated if the Boers made good on their threat of war and added fuel to the fire by issuing Kok with 60 muskets and 102 kilograms of gunpowder and lead. He also called upon Colonel Hare to immediately depart Grahamstown with the 7th Dragoon Guards.

Accompanied by Rawstorne, Major Campbell crossed the Orange River with his troops and marched to Philippolis, which he and the troops only reached on the night of 23 April 1845.

Rawstorne again sent a message to the Boers warning them that he would not allow them to declare war against the Griqua, an ally of the British, and that if they did not disperse, they would have to contend with the British army.

The Boers addressed their response to "the representative of Adam Kok" and requested a meeting, which took place two kilometres from the British camp. At the meeting, the Boers argued that they were not British subjects and therefore only owed their allegiance to the councils of Winburg and Potchefstroom. They requested that a line be drawn demarcating the land that they occupied and that of Kok and the Griqua and also asked that the British declare them a free people and place them on the same footing as the Griqua. They pointed out that they couldn't return to their farms because many of them lived in the territory where the Griqua resided and faced constant attacks and robberies by them. Finally, they offered to halt hostilities with the Griqua, provided that the Griqua would agree to peace with them, but refused to return any cattle that had been taken from the Griqua. Nothing was agreed at this meeting.

In the meantime, British reinforcements were on their way from Fort Beaufort. After an 11-day march over 390 kilometres, 94 men of the 7th Dragoon Guards under the command of Colonel Richardson and 24 members of the Cape Mounted Rifles under the command of Captain H.D. Warden arrived at Colesberg. They then crossed the Orange River and joined the 160-strong army of the 91st Regiment under Major Campbell at Philippolis on 27 April 1845.

Richardson issued the following proclamation to the Boers: "The emigrant British subjects unlawfully assembled in arms are hereby summoned to surrender themselves unconditionally to Her Majesty's troops, or they will be proceeded against as Rebels."

At midnight on 1 May 1845, Richardson marched out of Philippolis with the infantry of the 91st Regiment and the majority of Kok's Griqua soldiers toward the Boers' camp at Touwfontein, where they hoped to catch the Boers by surprise.[1290]

The small army passed Driekuil, where only 12 Boers remained out of 400. The others had abandoned the camp, which was directly in the path of the British advance, and relocated to Zwartkoppies, about eight kilometres away.[1291] As the Redcoats neared Zwartkoppies, they heard the sound of gunfire ahead of them as the Boers and Griqua clashed.Richardson immediately ordered his cavalry to speed up. However, the thundering of the galloping horses' hooves warned the Boers of their approach and they hid in crags and behind large rocks and watched the infantry advance in an open line in skirmishing order. A volley of fire from the approaching Redcoats killed the Boers' cannonier stationed by their three-pounder cannon and Lieutenant Gray of the Dragoon Guards hastily captured their gun when the Redcoats swarmed the area. The Boers fled in panic and those who were not swift enough to outrun the Redcoats (a Redcoat deserter who had been assisting the Boers as well as 14 others) were captured.

One Griqua had been killed in action, as had two Boers. However, the biggest damage was to the Boers' self-confidence. That evening, a number of Boers approached the British camp with white flags and offered to accept any terms that the British made. As soon as the captives and new arrivals took the oath of allegiance to Queen Victoria, they were set free.

At midnight on 1 May 1845, Richardson led 118 cavalry and 160 infantry Redcoats as well as the Griqua toward the Boers' main camp at Zwartkoppies. The Griqua were sent ahead as a decoy and were instructed to take up position on a hill where they were clearly visible to the Boers. Simultaneously, the Redcoats took up position behind another hill, out of sight of the Boers' camp. The Boers fell for Richardson's trap and exited the camp to attack the Griqua. After Richardson ordered the men to charge, the 7th Dragoon Guards attacked the Boers from the rear while the infantry swarmed into the Boers' camp and seized control of it. The Boers fled in all directions.

Mocke, Kock, Du Plooy and their followers managed to ride to Winburg, where they joined forces with Potgieter, who was formally acknowledged as the commandant general and supreme commander of the Boers north of the Vaal River on 5 May 1845 at a public meeting,[1292] while the followers of Michiel Oberholtser and Hermanus Steyn remained near Zwartkoppies, as they intended to surrender to the British.

After Rawstorne established his base at Zwartkoppies, where he would preside as special magistrate, the British troops attacked the main Boer camp at Touwfontein. There, they met with no resistance from the 100 or so men that had remained at the camp and seized the Boers' guns and ammunition.

Over the next few days, parties of Boers made their way to the British camp, laid down their weapons and took the oath of allegiance to the queen of England and, by 17 May 1845, 316 Boers had taken the oath. Not too far from Zwartkoppies was a large party of Boers under the leadership of Snyman. This farming community along the Lower Caledon River had decided to stay out of the fighting, as they claimed that their lands had been granted to them by Moshoeshoe and they therefore had no complaints against the Griqua.

Shortly after the Boers had been defeated by the British, the governor set off for Touwfontein, where he hoped to finally resolve the conflict between the Boers and the Griqua. However, Maitland fell off his horse and was forced to convalesce at Colesberg. As such, he sent several messages to the chiefs north of the Orange River requesting that they attend a conference at Touwfontein. He also sent a letter to Mocke and the Boers at Winburg which was threatening and imperious in tone and which served to further alienate the Boers from the British and augment their perception that the British discriminated against them.

On 24 June 1845, Kok and Maitland met and reached agreement that the British would recognize the sovereignty of each of the chiefs over the territory in which his people lived; that those Boers who had farms in those territories would be allowed to retain their lands; that certain territories would be established as 'reserves' and that only approved traders and missionaries would be allowed to settle there; that a British agent would be appointed, would reside among the people in the proposed reserves, would settle disputes and punish wrongdoers as well as act as an intermediary with the colonial government; that a quit rent would be levied on every farm and that half of this income would be allocated to pay the costs of the 'resident agent' while the other half would go to the chief of the territory in question; that the chiefs would guarantee to provide men to police the territory; that the country controlled by Kok would be divided into two parts and that no leases would be granted to any British subject in one part while the chiefs could give permission to grant leases in the other part.

Although the boundaries on the 'open' area were not clearly defined, it was specified that Bloemfontein was included in it and that the resident British agent would be based there. Maitland defined the boundaries of the land he had granted to Kok and the Griqua: from Ramah on the Orange River, a line was drawn which crossed to a point on the Riet River, about eight kilometres east of the present-day Modder River Station. This line was about 56 kilometres long and ended at Krom Elleboog. The boundary then ran along the Riet River, to its confluence with the Krom Elleboog Spruit. Then, it followed the Krom Elleboog Spruit south, to a spot 15 kilometres beyond its source. It then turned sharp right to the east and after 48 kilometres, started following the course of the Orange River, from a point 20 kilometres east of the present-day Bethulie Bridge, back to Ramah.

All the above comprised Kok's territory and included the larger portions of Jacobsdal, Fauresmith, Philippolis and Bethulie and, within this area, there were approximately 80 farms occupied by Boers. As some of these farms had been purchased from individual Griqua but had not been sanctioned by the Griqua government, Maitland declared that they would be regarded as leased for a 40-year period.

On 30 June 1845, the great meeting between Maitland and the chiefs took place. Moshoeshoe of the Basotho; Moroka II of the Barolong from Thaba 'Nchu; Gert

Taaibosch of the Korana; Pieter Davids and Carolus Baatje, leaders of breakaway groups of Griqua; Adam Kok and Andries Waterboer plus Moletsane of the Bataung as well as the local missionaries attended. The only notable leader to be absent from this meeting was Sekonyela of the Tlokwa. The most powerful of the leaders, Moshoeshoe, claimed all of Kok's territory and the land north of the Orange River, while the other chiefs claimed that the land which they occupied was now theirs. He was happy to abide by the terms agreed between Maitland and Kok and indicated that although he was unhappy that the Boers had moved into his country, he would be prepared to sacrifice a small portion of his land to them if they would move out of the remainder of the area under his control. He then proposed that they live in a triangular section of land bounded by the Orange and Caledon rivers.

After the meeting, the governor issued instructions to Commandant Gideon Joubert to tour all of the areas that would be affected by any decisions he had made and to identify the chiefs in the respective areas, the number of followers they had and the number of Boers that had settled in each of the areas.

Before returning to the Cape colony, Maitland appointed Rawstorne to act as magistrate at Philippolis and left a small contingent of men from the Cape Mounted Rifles under Captain Warden there to maintain a British presence.

Joubert set off to conduct his 'census' without delay and during his two-month assignment, he established that there were 50,000 Basotho under Moshoeshoe; 10,000 Barolong under Moroka II at Thaba 'Nchu; 1,000 Bataung under Moletsane; 300 Korana under Taaibosch at Merumetsu; 200 Griqua under Baatje and 200 Griqua under Davids. He estimated that in the areas that he had covered, there were 1,154 Boer families and up to 6,000 Boers.

After the executive council at the Cape appointed Captain Sutton as the British resident north of the Orange River on 18 August 1845, he set up his base on the farm of a Boer named Brits Bloemfontein, in the middle of the territory that had been granted to Kok. However, in January 1846, he was replaced as resident by Warden,[1293] who moved to the farm with a company of men from the Cape Mounted Rifles and built a fort there which was named Fort Drury.[1294]

CHAPTER 34

North of the Vaal

Andries Ohrigstad—Sekwati—Potgieter and Volksraad clash—meeting in Lydenburg—departure of Cloete; Location siting for Zulus—Pretorius meets with Stockenström—Pretorius snubbed by authorities

Potgieter had decided to take Smellekamp's advice to move farther away from the sphere of colonial influence and also to widen his own territory. At the end of 1844, a few families had moved from Potchefstroom to Andries Ohrigstad and put down roots there and, in 1845, Potgieter moved to the settlement and established a separate Volksraad there. Eventually, this would become the supreme Volksraad and the legislatures of Winburg and Potchefstroom would assume a subordinate role to the Volksraad of Andries Ohrigstad. The area around the new capital of Andries Ohrigstad was rife with malaria and it was not long before the Voortrekkers began to die like flies from the deadly mosquito-borne disease. Consequently, many families packed up their wagons and trekked to higher ground some 50 kilometres south. They named the area Lydenburg and soon established another Boer republic, namely the Republic of Lydenburg.

The Boers were now centred around Winburg, Potchefstroom, Andries Ohrigstad and Lydenburg. However, Potgieter and some of his followers soon moved farther into the interior and settled at Zoutpansberg, near where Trichardt had established base a few years before. The capital of Lydenburg was in the land occupied by Chief Sekwati and the Bapedi.[1295] Consequently, Potgieter set out to obtain a title deed for the area of Lydenburg from Sekwati and to establish the boundaries for this land on behalf of the Boers.

Some years earlier, the Bapedi had lived east of the Olifants River but had been forced to flee across the Limpopo River when they were attacked by Mzilikazi and his Matabele army. Sekwati, the son of the great chief of the country, Tulare, had finally returned to his land when Mzilikazi withdrew from the area. Subsequently, he began to assimilate the surviving Bapedi with the numerous refugees from other tribes that had drifted into the area. These refugees adopted the identity of the Bapedi and swelled the number of Bapedi under Sekwati.

By the time Potgieter encountered the Bapedi, they had become a formidable group. As such, it was imperative that the Boers get Sekwati's permission to stay at Lydenburg.[1296] Sekwati had met the trekkers from Van Rensburg and Trichardt's parties and had been friendly toward them. However, when the Boers began to settle in the Bapedi neighbourhood, the Bapedi could not resist stealing their cattle and soon, the cattle raids escalated into attacks. Evidently, Sekwati's attitude toward the Boers had changed: he encouraged his people to steal from the Boers.

The Bapedi attacked a Boer laager at Strydpoort. It was mainly occupied by women at the time and Sannie Visser led them in a fierce defence of the laager. The women eventually managed to drive off their attackers, despite the fact that when they fired their men's guns, many of them were knocked flat onto their backs or were bruised and battered due to the strong kick of the guns. It is believed that Potgieter called the flintlock gun that the Boers liked to use a *Sanna*, in honour of Sannie Visser.[1297]

Potgieter was furious when he learned of the Bapedi attack at Strydpoort and raised a commando of 150 trekkers, over 100 of Chief Matlabe's Barolong warriors as well as a small party of between 20 and 30 black warriors under Doors Buys (the coloured son of Coenraad de Buys). When they attacked the Bapedi, Sekwati's people fled. Subsequently, Potgieter instructed the men to round up 8,000 of their cattle and 6,000 of their goats and he then divided the spoils equally among the men in the commando.

Sekwati had learned his lesson and humbly asked Potgieter to recognize him as "the dog of the Boers" and to allow him and his people to live in the area in peace. He also requested that the Boers protect the Bapedi in the event of an attack by the Swazis.

Potgieter and the Volksraad of Andries Ohrigstad clashed on the issue of land ownership[1298] in that Potgieter felt that the land surrounding Lydenburg belonged to the Voortrekkers as they had won it in battle, whereas the Volksraad insisted that Potgieter obtain a title to the land and believed that this title or permission to settle should come from Mswazi II of the Swazis.

On 25 July 1846, Potgieter concluded a contract of sale with the Swazis. In return for 100 head of cattle, the chief of the Swazi ceded to "the Dutch South African Nation" all of the territory that had been conquered by Sobhuza, which extended north from Andries Ohrigstad to the Olifants River, along that river to the boundary of Mozambique; westward to Elands River as far as the 26th parallel of latitude; eastward to the junction of the Komati and the Crocodile rivers and southward to the Crocodile River. The Swazis also offered to "cleanse the land of the dogs" (Sekwati and the Bapedi) before the Boers moved into the territory. However, the Boers declined Mswazi II's offer.

The clash between Potgieter and the Volksraad of Andries Ohrigstad led to a split in the legislative body: one group supported Potgieter while the other supported the Volksraad of Andries Ohrigstad and preferred democratic rule rather than the autocratic style displayed by Potgieter.

The majority of Boers north of the Vaal River supported Potgieter and viewed him as the "father of the trek". As such, he could do no wrong. However, although he commanded the lion's share of support from the Boers, who saw him as the ultimate commander of the republics and as ruling over the Volksraad of Andries Ohrigstad, a growing number of Boers believed that the Volksraad of Andries Ohrigstad was the supreme authority. This opposition to Potgieter was fuelled by J.J. Burger, the former president of the Volksraad of Natalia, who respected Potgieter for his achievements but felt that he was answerable to the Volksraad and not that the Volksraad was answerable to him.[1299]

Without the consent of the Volksraad, Potgieter led a large commando on an expedition to attack Mzilikazi on the other side of the Limpopo River. On the journey, Potgieter met with two chiefs, Melitsi and Maraba, and demanded that they acknowledge the overlordship of the Boers. Maraba accepted his order but Melitsi did not. Subsequently, Potgieter and his men attacked Melitsi, defeated him and claimed his territory as belonging to the Boers before continuing their march north. When Potgieter failed to find the Matabele, he and the commando returned to Lydenburg. On the return journey, Potgieter proclaimed the new district of Zoutpansberg and decided to settle and live in the area, at Schoemansdal.

When the Volksraad next met, they declined to ratify Potgieter's agreement with Melitsi. Furious, Potgieter announced that, as commandant general and supreme commander of the Boers north of the Vaal River, he would take no notice of resolutions passed by the Volksraad. At this point, even some of Potgieter's staunchest supporters started to question the wisdom of their devotion to him and only a handful of Boers followed him to Schoemansdal. Others, such as his closest adherents, Erasmus, Wolmarans, Minnaar and Bronkhorst, trekked to a new district in what they considered a better territory. This area later became known as Pretoria.

Matters were brought to a head when Potgieter had J.J. Burger, his outspoken opponent and secretary of the Volksraad of Lydenburg, arrested and imprisoned. Unsurprisingly, there was a public outcry and it appeared as though civil war would break out between Potgieter and Burger's supporters. Finally, Potgieter agreed to submit to arbitration by the people.

All of the burghers from Potchefstroom and Lydenburg were summoned to a meeting in Lydenburg to discuss their future. This was to be the first Boer *folkmote* (assembly of people from a town, district or region) to decide critical issues and, later, the people of the Transvaal reserved the right to decide any matter of importance directly, in which case the executive government as well as the Volksraad took a back seat, and matters would be settled by a show of hands. Thereafter, the Volksraad would take control of the meeting but be bound to implement whatever the people had decided.

At the fiery meeting, the people eventually resolved that all burghers must either join Potgieter's party or that of the Volksraad; that nobody should be intimidated for their choice of party; that the existing governmental structures would remain in effect until such time as Smellekamp could arbitrate the disagreement between Potgieter and the Volksraad of Andries Ohrigstad and that the people would accept whatever Smellekamp decided. At this time, Smellekamp was in Holland but was expected to return to South Africa shortly.

Meanwhile, Pretorius's farms in Natal, Welverdiend and Rietvallei, were being besieged by Bushmen and Zulu and they frequently stole Pretorius's cattle and sheep. Nevertheless, Major Smith saw Pretorius as having instigated the trouble and described him in a letter to the Cape government as having "been unceasing in his endeavours to cause excitement on this subject [cattle stealing by the Bushmen], and he is, I believe, one of the most evil-disposed persons in the community".[1300]

By the time that Henry Cloete had left Natal for Cape Town in April 1844, no final decision had been made or communicated to the Natal Boers regarding what was to become of them now that they were deemed British subjects.

On 6 January 1845, the Volksraad in Natal wrote to Maitland to complain that it had been two and a half years since the Boers had signed the agreement with Cloete and that they had yet to hear when they would be issued with title deeds for their farms, whether the refugee Zulu would be relocated to specific territories or locations and what form the future government in Natal would have. They also pointed out that the uncertainty caused by the lack of communication by the Cape government had stunted what should have been a period of expansion and development. Instead, they stated, people had left Natal and flocked across the Drakensberg Mountains to join Potgieter and the Boers in the north.[1301]

Finally, on 31 May 1844, the British government in London signed a document that annexed Natal to the settlement of the Cape of Good Hope. However, it would be another 14 months before Maitland promulgated the annexation by public proclamation on 21 August 1845.[1302]

The Durban bay echoed with gunfire when Lieutenant Governor West arrived at Durban on 4 December 1845 onboard the *Rosebud*. He was greeted by a salute from 13 guns onshore, which was immediately answered with a salute from 13 guns onboard the ship.[1303]

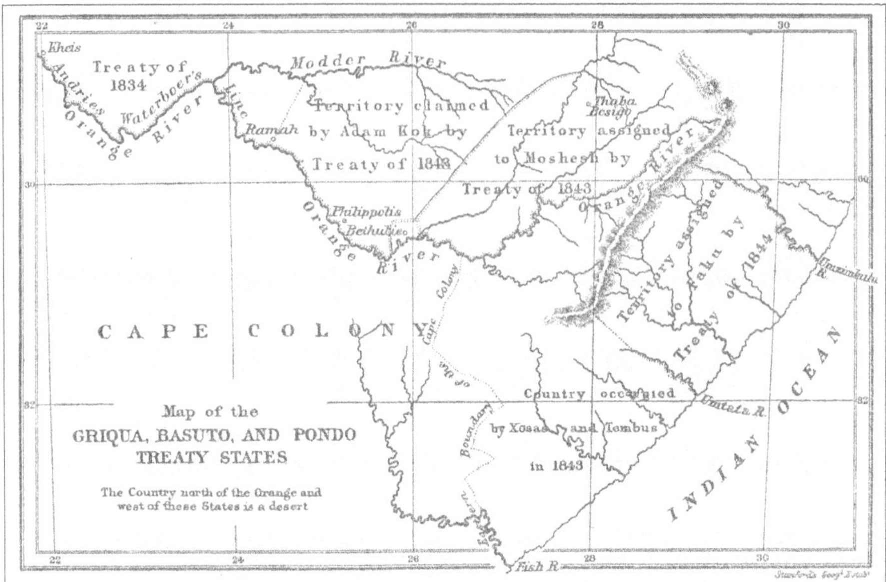

Eight days later, West travelled to Pietermaritzburg and was welcomed by Colonel Boyce (Major Smith's successor) and 60 Boers. Over the next few days, West held discussions with the Boers, including Pretorius, and listened to some of their complaints. He soon realized that many of the Boers had left Natal and that many more were preparing to leave due to the uncertainty on the issue of land rights. Consequently, he increased the size of the farms to 6,000 acres. As much as this pleased the Boers, the delays they experienced in receiving the title deeds to their farms caused much unhappiness and discontent, which was exacerbated by several issues: their fear of the growing number of Zulu in the region; the frequent stock theft at the hands of the Bushmen; and, of course, that they had conceded to live under British control and as British subjects.

Pretorius wrote to West to complain about the stock thefts experienced by the Boers and that the Zulu were squatting on his farm but refused to work for him. In subsequent letters, he complained that firewood was being stolen from his farms. West soon established the Location Commission and one of its members' primary tasks was to deliberate the problem of where to locate the thousands of refugee Zulu in Natal.

At a meeting on 28 May 1846, the members of the Location Commission proposed three locations (Welverdiend, Swartkops and Rietvallei) that they deemed appropriate sites to which to move the Zulu.

The ball had bounced badly for Pretorius as one of the locations proposed, Swartkops, was between his two farms. Consequently, Pretorius submitted a list of 13 suggestions to West as to what should be done with the Zulu and proposed five locations that he felt would be more appropriate than the three suggested by the Location Commission. West rejected his proposal and proceeded with his original plan, which meant that one of the Zulu location zones would border both of Pretorius's farms.[1304]

The next year, on 24 August 1847, Pretorius set off from Pietermaritzburg on the over 700 kilometre ride to Grahamstown, where he wanted to meet with the new governor, Sir Henry Pottinger, and to explain to him what problems the Boers faced in Natal. On his way, Pretorius stopped at Winburg, where he found that a meeting was in session to discuss whether the appointment of a landdrost had to be endorsed by the British. A huge crowd had assembled and there was much discussion and argument on the matter.

The chairman of the meeting, Willem Jacobsz, finally shouted over the crowd that the Boers were on free land and that the governor of the colony should have no say in what they did.

Pretorius took the opportunity to address the Boers of Winburg and expressed his hope that they and the Boers from Potchefstroom would come to the aid of the Natal Boers if the relationship between the British and the Boers in Natal deteriorated any further. Jacobsz was certainly not one of Pretorius's admirers and scoffed that it couldn't be very dangerous in Natal seeing that Pretorius had left his family behind at the mercy of the Zulu, Bushmen and British. Pretorius calmly replied that the fact that Piet Otto was in Winburg buying horses for the British soldiers indicated clearly how dangerous the situation was in Natal.

The Winburgers decided that someone from their community should accompany Pretorius to Grahamstown to see the governor and elected C.J.F du Plooy for the task. The two men passed through Maasstrom (Bedford) and visited Stockenström Jr there. Pretorius had got to know Stockenström Jr while he was the landdrost of Graaff-Reinet and respected his opinions.

As he and his companion were forced to remain on Stockenström Jr's farm for three days due to heavy rain, Pretorius spoke at length to Stockenström Jr and poured his heart out about how bitter he felt about the situation in Natal and that he longed for the Boers to throw off the British yoke of oppression. After listening to Pretorius's views, Stockenström Jr made it clear that he did not agree with him on a number of issues and advised him to accept that the British had the right to be in Natal and to accept British sovereignty.[1305]

By the time that Pretorius and Du Plooy were ready to continue their journey, Stockenström Jr believed that Pretorius had had a change of heart and he later commented that Pretorius had left "with the thorough conviction that independence of Great Britain could ultimately lead only to anarchy and ruin of himself and his followers".

Stockenström was wrong, however. Pretorius still believed that he and his people should be free of British rule. When Pretorius and Du Plooy arrived in Grahamstown on 15 October 1847, Pretorius immediately requested an interview with Pottinger.

The following day, Pretorius still had not received word on whether the governor would meet with him and so addressed a letter to Pottinger outlining his complaints and those of the Boers. These primarily focused on the fact that title deeds had not been issued to the Boers; the frequent theft of the Boers' cattle and property by the Bushmen; the influx of and lack of control over the Zulu in Natal; the aggressive actions of the British under Major Warden against the Boers across the Orange River; and that so many Boers had left Natal that only 22 or 23 farms were still occupied in the whole of the Pietermaritzburg district.

Two days later, Pretorius approached Pottinger's secretary, Mr Woosnam, to ask whether the governor had granted him an interview. He was told that Pottinger would not be able see him but that he should submit all of his points in writing.

Extremely frustrated that he had been fobbed off by the governor, Pretorius resubmitted his correspondence and documentation to Woosnam on 20 October. He then asked Pottinger's secretary (for the third time) to be allowed to speak to the governor and was again refused an audience with Pottinger.

By now, Pretorius had been in Grahamstown for five days. Pretorius then approached his friend, Henri Meurant, the editor of the *Het Kaapsche Grenblad* newspaper, for help with writing a letter to Pottinger. In it, Pretorius requested that the governor state in writing why he was refusing to see him and explained that he would like some form of documentation to take back to the Boers in Natal regarding why he had failed to get an audience with the governor.

On 21 October 1847, Pretorius received a memorandum from Pottinger that stated, "I have read Mr Pretorius' letter, and its accompaniments, with attention. The perusal of these has only strengthened the resolution I had previously formed of not attempting to investigate the matters to which they relate."[1306]

Pottinger then listed his reasons for not seeing Pretorius: he was too busy to see him, West was not able to tell his side of the story and, in any event, he would be leaving the Cape colony for another posting in the near future.

Pretorius was still remembered fondly as the hero of the Battle of Blood River by the Voortrekkers and Pottinger's high-handed attitude toward him caused great anger among the Boers in Natal and beyond the Orange River. In fact, many Boers viewed the way in which Pottinger had disrespected Pretorius as the last straw and hundreds of families decided to turn their backs on the British by heading north to join Potgieter's republics.

By the middle of the 1840s, an estimated 14,000 Boers had trekked across the Orange River. Significantly, this constituted one fifth of the white population of South Africa at the time.[1307]

News travelled quickly that the governor had refused to meet with Pretorius and, after he crossed the Orange River on his return journey, he met many Boers who were anti-British and only too eager to lend him a sympathetic ear. Pretorius made no secret of the fact that he was furious about the way in which he had been treated in Grahamstown and evidently told this to many people … the chief of the Barolong, Moroka II, sent word to Warden in Bloemfontein that Pretorius was agitating the Boers and talking of rebellion against the British.[1308] When Pretorius reached Winburg, he received a message from his wife that the Boers in Natal were fleeing as they had been warned that an attack by the Zulu was imminent.[1309]

CHAPTER 35

Arrogance and humiliation

Klipriver Boers—West—return of Sir Harry Smith—insult of Maqoma—British Kaffraria—Smith and Moshoeshoe—Smith meets with Pretorius—Smith shocked—Smith breaks his word

While Pretorius was away, the whole area of Natal had become even more unstable and a number of Boers had moved to an area known as the Kliprivier, as there was better grazing for their cattle there than around Pietermaritzburg or Weenen and they wanted to be as far from the British in Port Natal as possible. Mphande had declared to the leader of the Kliprivier Boers, Andries Spies, that the Buffalo River was not the border of Natal and that the Kliprivier settlers were not in Natal but in Zululand. Although the Cape government secretary, Donald Moodie, informed the Boers this was not the case, the Boers readily accepted what Mphande had told them, as it meant that the British had no jurisdiction over them. The Kliprivier Boers then decided to purchase the land they were occupying from Mphande.

At meeting on 7 January 1847 between Mphande and Hans de Lange, the Boer offered Mphande 1,000 rix-dollars for the land between the Drakensberg Mountains, the Tugela River and the Buffalo River. Mphande accepted his offer and the men signed an agreement, which nobody bothered to inform the British of.

Then, in May 1847, the Kliprivier Boers selected their own management committee and elected Andries Spies as their commandant, Lodewyk de Jager as field cornet and Abraham Spies as the official responsible for handling land claims.

In the middle of May 1847, Philip Ferreira, the auctioneer from Pietermaritzburg, was instructed by the Cape government to auction off all of the assets of P.J.C. Scheepers, to defray his debts.

When Andries heard about the imminent auction, he vehemently protested that the authorities had no right to order the auctioning of Scheepers's assets because his farm Rhenosterfontein was on the northern bank of the Tugela River and was situated on land belonging to Mphande and the Zulu. The auction was stopped and Ferreira returned to Pietermaritzburg, where he immediately reported what had transpired and described the "belligerence" shown toward him by the Boers.

West soon wrote to Spies and asked him to describe the boundaries between Zululand and Natal that Mphande had stipulated. He also requested that Spies appoint a field cornet for the Kliprivier community and enclosed copies of Maitland's proclamation from 18 months earlier that defined the borders of Natal. Unfortunately, Spies was not at home when the messengers arrived with the letters and, on 10 June 1847, while West waited for a response from Spies, he sent two messengers to Mphande to ask for details of the negotiations with Spies.

Eleven days later, Spies replied to West's letter and informed him that he was unable to accept the proclamation about the boundaries as the document had arrived after he had concluded the arrangement with Mphande.

West then sent Dutch-speaking J.W. Archbell, the son of Wesleyan missionary Reverend James Archbell, to the Kliprivier Boers to read them the proclamation that Spies had refused to accept.

While J.W. Archbell was on his mission, the messenger West had sent to Mphande returned and informed him that Mphande had denied giving the Boers any land or that he had sold land to them. Mphande alleged that he had signed a document but was unaware of the contents. Mphande had made it perfectly clear that he felt that his bread was more thickly buttered by the British than by the Boers.

When J.W. Archbell read the proclamation to the Kliprivier Boers, there was an uproar. The Boers shouted angrily, "Go to hell!", "If you bring British troops here, we will shoot the officers in the head!", "We hope the kaffirs cut the throats of the English!", "That pretty girl Victoria that is liked so much by everybody must not think we are afraid of her. We would attack her just as we would attack the others!", "We wish that the kaffirs would attack the Government and drive all the members thereof into the sea" and "We wish that the Governor were dead!"[1310]

Spies then showed J.W. Archbell a *knobkerrie* that Mphande had given to him as his sign that he was a captain of the district and warned him that he recognized Mphande as his king and was therefore answerable to him and not to the British. He added that any attempt by the British to meddle in the affairs of the Kliprivier community would be met with force.

When J.W. Archbell later met with West, he confirmed that Mphande had sold the land west of the Buffalo River to the Boers for 1,000 rix-dollars and that he had appointed Spies as the captain of the district and had in fact given Spies a wooden staff to denote his badge of office. West realized that he had a major problem with the Kliprivier Boers in that he could not use military might to intimidate them, as he had limited troops at his disposal at that time. Moreover, he questioned which side Mphande would back if the tension between the Boers and the British evolved into a confrontation. He resolved to find out where Mphande's loyalties lay and sent two messengers, John Shepstone and Captain H.D. Kyle, to meet with the Zulu king. Simultaneously, he set off for the Kliprivier territory to assess for himself what the prevailing mood was among the Boers there. The cool reception West received from the Boer community in Kliprivier sent him scurrying back to Pietermaritzburg. He acknowledged that the Boers there must have been granted land by Mphande but was convinced that the Boers must have pressures Mphande to give it to them.

Soon after West returned to Pietermaritzburg, the Cape government sent John Bird, a land surveyor, to measure out the farms in the Kliprivier territory. However, the Boers sent him packing back to Pietermaritzburg with a flea in his ear. There was no way that they would agree to have their farms measured or surveyed by a British official on behalf of the British government. As far as they were concerned, they had bought the land and therefore fell under Mphande's authority and not that of the British.

West was furious about the way in which the Boers from the Kliprivier territory had treated the land surveyor and issued a proclamation stating that if they did not come to Pietermaritzburg by the end of the next month to make claims for their farms, their applications for land would be rejected.

Realizing that the situation was becoming more and more confrontational, Spies sent his stepson, Jacobus Uys, to Pietermaritzburg on 2 September 1847 to request that West send an official to Kliprivier to investigate the complaints of the Boers there and to visit Mphande and finally establish the truth of the land deal.

On 20 September 1847, West sent the highly respected state prosecutor, Walter Harding, with John Shepstone and Field Cornet Dewald Pretorius to meet with Spies at Platberg, his farm on the Sundays River. At this meeting, Spies explained that the Kliprivier Boers would feel safer if the Zulu were moved to secure areas (locations) and asked that every farmer in the area be allowed to own one farm. In addition, he pleaded that the British not punish them for the stance they had taken on the land ownership issue up until this point.

When Harding returned to Pietermaritzburg, he reported to West that it seemed as though Mphande had misled the Boers regarding the border of Zululand. Nevertheless, West issued a proclamation on 25 October 1847 that declared that the Kliprivier Boers were to swear an oath of allegiance to Queen Victoria within a two-week period and that those who refused to do so would be prosecuted.

West then appointed Jacobus Boshoff as acting magistrate of Kliprivier and gave him the task of administering the oath.

While Boshoff read West's latest proclamation at a meeting at Lodewyk de Jager's farm near the Kliprivier on 16 November 1847, the crowd jeered at him and shouted angrily that they would rather trek over the Drakensberg Mountains than sign an oath of allegiance to Queen Victoria. In addition, they were willing to fight British occupation of Kliprivier. They made it clear to Boshoff that they resented that the British government had not responded to their request that each Boer be granted a farm; that they were certain that the Zulu would stream into Kliprivier if it came under British control and that the British would not be able or willing to protect the Boers from the Zulu. Shortly after this, Spies sent his son-in-law, Gert van Niekerk, to see Mphande and to inform him that West was demanding that the Boers in Kliprivier submit to the British.

When Van Niekerk returned, he relayed to Spies that Mphande had agreed to send his army to Kliprivier to assist the Boers there and that if the British government wanted to make war against the Boers, Mphande would be a Boers ally and that he would would "clean out all the land of Natal from the Umzimvubu River to the Kliprivier".

Some Boers decided to leave Kliprivier to ensure that they were not caught in the impending confrontation between Mphande's army and the British. After packing their wagons, they made for Doornkop or Emmadale, a farm belonging to John van der Plank. At these sites, their wagons were moved into laager formation. By 28 November 1847, 16 wagons were clustered at Doornkop and the Boers in the laager there nervously awaited the arrival of the Zulu army.

Spies sent messengers to warn the Natal Boers that they should leave the region as he was sure that the whole country would soon be "soaked in blood". The whole of Natal was in a state of panic due to the many rumours and false sightings of the advance of Mphande's army that were circulating.

Spies rode to Winburg in a desperate attempt to rally some assistance for the Natal Boers against the British. However, he met with a cool reception from the Winburgers and the landdrost refused to order a commando to return with him to Natal. Finally, Jacobsz conceded to allow volunteers to accompany Spies. However, none of the Winburgers would assist and Spies then sent two messengers to Commandant Kock and Landdrost H.S. Lombard at Potchefstroom to ask for help. The messengers asked that they send as many men as possible and informed them that Spies believed the time was ripe to "take Natal back" and that the war would probably begin by the beginning of March 1848 or "as soon as you arrive with the men to help us". In addition, the messengers requested that Kock and Lombard relay Spies's plea for help to the Boers at Andries Ohrigstad. Spies next travelled to Platberg, where he met with Pretorius in mid-December 1847. As Pretorius was still smarting from the humiliating treatment he had received from Pottinger, he did not need much encouragement from Spies to take up arms against the British.

While Pretorius was making his way to Doornkop to collect his wife and family, the fiery Commandant Kock readied his commando and finally departed Potchefstroom for Natal on 31 December 1847.

Pretorius encountered several minor Zulu chiefs on the way to Doornkop and warned them about the imminent war between the Boers and the British. He made it perfectly clear that they would be required to pick a side: when the time came, they would either have to back the Boers or the British.

When Pretorius eventually reached Doornkop, he discovered that his wife was ill and his daughter had been seriously injured while leading a team of oxen. In addition, the Zulu had stolen all his cows.

Pretorius soon continued to Welverdiend, one of his farms near Pietermaritzburg. As he approached Welverdiend, he saw West addressing a crowd of 1,200 Zulu from the bordering Zwartkop location.

When Pretorius realized that West was attempting to rally support for the British from the local Zulu in the event of a confrontation between the Boers and the British, he became even more determined to join the Boers' armed struggle and hastily crossed the Drakensberg Mountains, followed by the wagons of his two brothers, Piet and Bart, and wife and children.

On 4 January 1848, Pretorius wrote to the Volksraad of Andries Ohrigstad from Spies's laager at Platberg and requested that the Boers in Potgieter's republic raise an army from the lands beyond the Orange River and come to the aid of the Boers already assembling to fight the British. He also requested arms and ammunition and cannon from Delagoa Bay.

During the next few weeks, the tension among the Boers was high, particularly as some Boer families that did not wish to fight the British were streaming out of Natal. In fact, by the end of January 1848, about 100 wagons were lumbering toward the Drakensberg Mountains with a view to departing Natal.

After leaving his family by the Tugela River on 29 January 1849, Pretorius headed west of the Drakensberg Mountains to organize the Boers there for the forthcoming war.

On 1 December 1847, Sir Harry Smith had returned to South Africa as Pottinger's successor as governor of the Cape of Good Hope. He set off for Port Elizabeth without delay to confront the Xhosa chief, Maqoma, as he had heard that Maqoma had returned to the colony from Algoa Bay. Pottinger had sent him to Algoa Bay to ensure that he could not render aid to any of the other chiefs in the ongoing wars on the frontier of the colony.

After Sir Harry Smith walked up from the beach to a local hotel, he spotted Maqoma in the crowd that had gathered to welcome him. He gazed fixedly at Maqoma and started to draw his sword. However, he eventually thrust it back into the scabbard "with an expressive gesture of anger and scorn" and when Maqoma came toward him and held out his hand in greeting,[1311] Sir Harry Smith ordered the chief to kneel before him and to bow his head.

When Maqoma begrudgingly complied with Sir Harry Smith's command, the governor placed his foot on Maqoma's neck and said, "This is to teach you that I come hither to teach Kaffirland that I am chief and master here and this is the way I shall treat the enemies of the Queen of England."

As Maqoma rose, he hissed at Smith, "I always thought you were a great man, until this day".[1312]

Smith left for Grahamstown shortly after this where crowds lined the streets to welcome him. He ordered the release of Chief Sandile from prison and appointed him a magistrate. He then annexed the province between the Fish and Keiskamma rivers to the Cape colony and named the region Victoria. All land north of this territory up to the Orange River was proclaimed as the district of Albert and the area between the Kei and Keiskamma rivers became British Kaffraria. In addition, all of the land up to the Orange River was incorporated into the Cape colony.

After Smith rode to King Williamstown, like a whirlwind, he ordered a parade on 23 December. The Rifle Brigade and 7th Dragoon Guards were resplendent in their red coats and blue serge trousers as they lined up on the parade ground in front of thousands of Xhosa and all of the frontier chiefs, including Sandile, Phato and Mhalla. Once the men were assembled, Sir Harry Smith had two long objects brought to him: a brass doorknob on the end of a wooden tent pole and an ornamental pike. He explained to the Xhosa that these were the staves of peace and war, respectively, and then ordered each of the chiefs come forward to touch the stave that represented their intentions.

After all of the chiefs had laid hands on the stave of peace, Sir Harry Smith read a proclamation reinstating the province of Queen Adelaide under the name of British Kaffraria and explained that this was to be administered directly from England and would not be dependent on the Cape colony. Moreover, this was to be occupied by the Xhosa and Sir Harry Smith would be their Great Chief.

The chiefs listened in amazement while Sir Harry Smith lectured them, while still astride his horse, on what would happen to them if they "misbehaved". To their shock, he concluded his speech by commanding them to kiss his foot. When all of the chiefs had reluctantly completed their gesture of submission to Smith, he threw the stave of war to the ground, shouting, "This is the end of war!" and called for three cheers from the soldiers, Xhosa and spectators alike.[1313]

At a further meeting on 7 January 1848 in King Williamstown, Sir Harry Smith addressed a vast crowd of Xhosa chiefs, councillors and more than 2000 of their attendants. He informed them in his strident voice that they had lost their right to independence, that they would in future be British subjects and live in "locations" in the lands between the Keiskamma and Kei rivers, which would be known as British Kaffraria. Moreover, they would all have to learn English at the schools Sir Harry Smith proposed establishing and would no longer be permitted to be "wicked barbarians". They would be taught to plough and how to earn money and sheep farming would eventually replace cattle farming as, according to Sir Harry Smith, cattle ownership caused friction between people. Further, he warned them that if he heard of any arguments about cattle, he would "shoot the lot across the land".

The governor informed them that the practice of *lobola* (the payment of cattle for a woman's hand in marriage) would be abolished, as would witchcraft. Additionally, murderers would be "hung like dogs" and the chiefs were to ensure that they and their people showed respect toward all missionaries and converted to Christianity.

He would be the high commissioner of British Kaffraria and known as *Inkosi Inkhulu* (great chief). Effectively, he would replace the present paramount chief of the Xhosa, Sarili, who would be allowed to remain in the trans-Kei lands but had to concede a two kilometre strip of land to be used as a route for traffic to Natal and by the missionaries.

After the chiefs were made to swear allegiance to Queen Victoria and acknowledged their acceptance of the terms Sir Harry Smith had described, the governor announced that he would demonstrate what he would do to them if they broke their word.

"You dare to make war? You dare to attack our wagons! See what I will do to you if …"[1314] he shouted before ordering that a nearby wagon be blown up. (Earlier, he had ordered that a wagon be positioned on high ground that was clearly visible from the parade area and that gunpowder be placed under it.)

In the ensuing explosion, the thousands of fragments of wagon shot skywards and as the smoke billowed upwards, Sir Harry Smith turned to address the shocked crowd. "That is what I shall do to you if you do not behave yourselves," he said, shaking his cane at the Xhosa while he spoke. "Do you see this?" he shouted, waving a piece of paper above his head before tearing it to shreds. "There go the treaties!" he yelled. "No more treaties! Do you hear? No more treaties!"[1315]

After visiting the Eastern Cape and still ojn the move, Smith sent a letter to Major Warden to invite Moshoeshoe to meet him in Winburg and then travelled north across the Orange River with his retinue.

When he reached Philippolis on 24 January 1838, he met with Kok and yet again unleashed a series of theatrical antics. When Kok objected to Smith's insistence that he pay him £200 per annum in lieu of quit rents, Smith shouted, "I will see you hanged by the neck in public, sir!" and stripped him of his authority over the Boers.

At Bloemfontein, Sir Harry Smith was given a rousing welcome as many of the Boers there knew him from the Eastern Cape and some had served with him in the Sixth Frontier War. After making several enthusiastic speeches about the bright future of the country, Sir Harry Smith was on his way again.

Outside Winburg, a party of Boers rode out to meet Sir Harry Smith and his escort, as did Moshoeshoe and his Basotho party. After riding along the single dusty road into Winburg, Sir Harry Smith addressed the large crowd that had gathered and explained that he had come to clarify several issues to the Boers north of the Orange River and that he was determined to establish a lasting peace "between the natives, the colony and all British subjects, which included the emigrant Boers". He added that he had decided that the Boers should be left unhindered in the lands they occupied but that there should be no further encroachment into Basotho lands. "I will at once proclaim sovereignty of the queen of England over all lands held by the Boers … I see no other way of coming out of the dilemma in which I find the country. Trust me," Sir Harry Smith said, turning to Moshoeshoe. "No one will dare raise a hand against the great chief of the Basotho."

After lunch, Sir Harry Smith leaped onto a table and addressed the surprised Boers and Basotho watching him. He vowed to punish the Boers if they encroached on the lands of Moshoeshoe, "even though it were to the gates of the infernal regions!" and, in a voice that cracked with emotion, he implored the Boers to help him create a haven of peace and prosperity in the region. "We must get to work at once," he shouted, "and build a church." He then dramatically extracted £25 from his purse to donate to the building of this church, knelt on the table and called on the French reverend, Eugene Casalis, to lead the gathering in prayer. To the astonishment of those watching, tears poured down his cheeks during the prayers and he eventually buried his face in a handkerchief before leaving with Casalis and Moshoeshoe. He later explained that presenting the Boers with money for a church had been his happiest experience.[1316]

Like a whirling dust devil, Smith set off for Natal to meet with Pretorius, as he was alarmed at the numerous reports that the Boers were leaving the colony. He sent Richard Southey, his secretary to inform Pretorius that he had already left Winburg and was on his way to meet with him, as he hoped to ascertain what was causing the unhappiness of the Boers in Natal.

In turn, Pretorius sent a message to Sir Harry Smith regarding the best route that he and his 60 men should take over the Drakensberg Mountains and then travelled to Rhenosterfontein, a farm that belonged to his friend, Piet Scheepers, to await their arrival.

On 1 or 2 February, Pretorius received word that Sir Harry Smith was approaching and he rode out to meet him and escort his party to Rhenosterfontein, where between 300 and 400 men were waiting to voice their grievances to the governor. Among them was Commandant Kock, who had been asked to come to Natal from north of the Orange River to help with the liberation of Natal. However, Spies was notably absent.[1317]

Smith invited Pretorius to ride with him in his horse-drawn wagon and while sitting together, the governor was shocked to see so many wagons and people trudging up the Drakensberg Mountains and leaving Natal.

Smith listened attentively as Pretorius explained why the Boers were unhappy and convinced Pretorius and his fellow Boers that he was sympathetic to their cause and appeared to understand their problems. On the way to the scheduled meeting place at Rhenosterfontein, Pretorius ordered the wagon to take a detour past his own camp, as he wanted to show Sir Harry Smith the conditions in which the Boers lived.

One of Sir Harry's secretaries wrote after the event: "His Excellency witnessed what I am sure made his heart bleed–sickly women and children of all ages crammed together in tents, wagons, etc., not more than half sheltered from the wet, and all hurrying away from their valuable farms and other property, fearing that a longer continuance in the district would cost them their lives."[1318]

Similarly, Sir Harry Smith wrote a dispatch after the meeting that summarized his shock at what he had seen: "On my arrival at the foot of the Drackenberg Mountains I was almost paralysed to witness the whole of the population, with few exceptions "trekking"! Rains on this side of the mountain are tropical … and these families were exposed to a state of misery which I never before saw equalled, except in Massena's invasion in Portugal, when the whole of the population of that part of the seat of war, abandoned their homes and fled. The scene here was truly heart-rendering. I assembled all the men near me through the means of a Mr Pretorius … Who had recently been into the Colony to lay the subject of dissatisfaction of his countrymen before the Governor (Sir Henry Pottinger) where he was unfortunately refused an audience, and returned after so long a journey, expressing himself as the feelings of a proud and injured man would naturally prompt. At this meeting I was received as if among my own family … The scene exhibited by about three or four hundred fathers of large families assembled and shedding tears when representing their position was more, I admit, than I could observe unmoved."

The Boers had elected Pretorius to put their case to Smith and he did so with eloquence and passion. Many in the crowd wept as he described the loss, pain and suffering the Boers had endured and how people were yet again being forced to abandon their farms and lands to flee.

Smith shouted to the Boers that he would address their complaints. However, they did not at first believe him, as many authorities had made and broken promises to them before this.

After much discussion, Sir Harry Smith offered compensation to the Boers whose farms were in the newly declared reserves and promised that the long-awaited title deeds would be issued immediately, provided that the trekkers returned to their farms and gave up the idea of leaving Natal. He also tried to persuade Pretorius to become a member of the Land Commission and offered Pretorius a seat on it. Pretorius didn't fall into the trap of being a lackey for the British, however.[1319]

While Sir Harry Smith had every intention of addressing the Boers' problems, he was only prepared to do so if the Boers would accept that they were British subjects and were to be ruled by the British in Natal.

When Pretorius clarified to Sir Harry Smith that the Boers wanted to be independent, the governor announced that he had received information that the majority of Boers were willing to remain under British rule. There was an uproar as the Boers shouted their denial of this fact.[1320]

In a private conversation with Pretorius earlier, Sir Harry Smith had promised Pretorius that if he could obtain the signatures of two thirds of the Boers expressing their desire to be independent of the government, he would leave the Boers to govern themselves.[1321]

Smith tried desperately to persuade Pretorius to return to Natal and went as far as to offer him financial encouragement to make the journey. Pretorius was unwavering in his decision not to accompany the governor.[1322]

Smith had brought a proclamation with him that announced that all of the lands occupied by the Boers, including the lands beyond the Orange River and the Vaal River, would be declared British territories.

When he showed this to Pretorius in a private meeting, Pretorius was aghast at the idea and was rendered speechless for a few moments. "That would be a ghastly mistake," Pretorius finally stated matter-of-factly. "We will either have to fight for freedom or retire far into the interior. We will not and in fact could not live under British rule."

"My dear fellow," Smith said smugly, "I can assure you that the majority of the farmers want the queen's sovereignty. When I was at Winburg, where anti-British sentiment is supposed to be strong, I was presented with an address in which 27 heads of families and 22 others asked me to extend British jurisdiction over the country."

Pretorius urged Smith not to publish the proclamation and argued that the Boer signatures appended to it represented the wishes of only a few Boers and not of the majority, which were totally opposed to British rule. Although Sir Harry Smith was not convinced that this was the case, he nevertheless recognized that Pretorius's opposition to the proclamation was sincere.

When Pretorius informed Sir Harry Smith that he intended riding to Winburg to work for peace between the Boers and the British, Sir Harry Smith encouraged him in this endeavour. "Let us then arrange that you proceed over the mountains and attend public meetings at every centre of population and ascertain the views of the people. I will withhold the proclamation until you give me your report," he said.[1323]

After this meeting, Pretorius and Sir Harry Smith parted on good terms at the Tugela River, where the governor was escorted across it by Pretorius's brothers, who had been designated as Sir Harry Smith's guides. Sir Harry felt that he had won Pretorius over and Pretorius felt that the Boers had found a sympathetic champion. However, both men were wrong in their assumptions.

The next day, on 3 February 1848, Sir Harry Smith issued the proclamation declaring the whole territory between the Orange and Vaal rivers to be subject to Queen Victoria and called it the Orange River Sovereignty.[1324] In it, Sir Harry Smith stated, "I hereby proclaim, declare and make known, the Sovereignty of Her Majesty the Queen of England over the territories north of the Great Orange River, including the countries of Moshoeshoe, Moroka, Moletsane, Sekonyela, Adam Kok, Gert Taaibosch and other minor chiefs as far north as the Vaal River, and east to the Drakensberg or Quathlamba Mountains."[1325]

Later, Sir Harry Smith would deny that Pretorius had voiced any objections to him publishing the proclamation and the jury is still out (and is likely to remain out forever) as to what exactly transpired between the two men during their meeting. In addition, he claimed that his agreement with Pretorius had related only to the land north of the Vaal River.

Whether arrogance or foolishness prompted the governor to send Pretorius a copy of the proclamation on 12 February 1848, one cannot be sure. Nevertheless, adding a note that his actions had been motivated by his affection and concern for Pretorius and the Boers could only have fuelled their fury. The kindest interpretation of Sir Harry's Smith's actions would be that there had been a misunderstanding between him and Pretorius. However, most Boers believed that he had deliberately betrayed Pretorius and would not forget his treachery.

CHAPTER 36

Orange River Colony

Pretorius lobbies support—Orange River Sovereignty—Warden—Pretorius in Potchefstroom—death of Christina Pretorius

At Joseph du Plessis's farm near Winburg, 240 burghers gathered to hear Pretorius speak. He opened the meeting with a prayer and followed it with a fiery summary of what the Voortrekkers had endured under British control. He then stated that no Christian and God-fearing person could possibly submit to British authority and that he had sworn a solemn oath in front of his wife and children that he would never again submit, or make his family submit, to British rule. In an attempt to stir the largely non-responsive crowd into action, Pretorius stated that the British troops were being recalled to the Cape and would soon be called up to fight in European wars and it was therefore the perfect time to stand together to throw off the yoke of British oppression. However, many in the crowd believed that living under British rule was an attractive option as it warranted that they would be able to farm without interference or cattle raids and their safety would be assured.

Even so, the Boers present agreed that the land between the Orange River and Andries Ohrigstad would be declared an independent Boer state and that they would take up arms if the British refused to acknowledge this. In addition, all British families in the Boer state would appear before Landdrost Willem Jacobsz and be required to renounce their loyalty to Queen Victoria. If they opted not to do so, then they would be executed. Moreover, it was decided that any Boers who refused to fight against the British would be considered traitors and executed. Pretorius was chosen to lead the Boers and given the rank of commandant general while Jan Kock was selected as his second-in-command. Then, the Boers elected other commandants and field cornets.

Soon after this meeting, Pretorius set off to rally further support for the Boers. He first called at Moshoeshoe's residence on 14 February 1848. As the chief was not there at the time, Pretorius explained to two of Moshoeshoe's sons, Letsea and Nehemiah, that he was seeking the support of Moshoeshoe and the Basotho. He added that he could not understand why Moshoeshoe had entered into agreements with the British and when Letsea and Nehemiah informed him that their father had already given his allegiance to the British, Pretorius hastily readied his horse to depart and shouted, "Then Moshoeshoe is no longer a friend of mine! I will get the great chief Mphande to be our ally."

Over the next few days, Pretorius addressed crowds near the Vals River and, on 18 February 1848, wrote to Sir Harry Smith from Potchefstroom, Potgieter's territory. He demanded that the governor grant the same rights to the Boers outside the borders of the Cape colony that he had granted to Moshoeshoe and Kok: the right to govern themselves.

Then, on 21 February 1848, Pretorius addressed a crowd of 60 Boers at Potchefstroom. He began the meeting by reading the proclamation Sir Harry Smith had recently issued but soon launched into a tirade against the British.

"The proclamation of the governor makes no provision for us," he said. "We are left to fend for ourselves and, more than that, to protect ourselves from those who steal from us and attack us. We have to become soldiers."

The crowd murmured unhappily at this.

"Will you become soldiers?" he shouted.

"No! No!" the Boers responded.

"What do you intend doing then?" he continued. "I have travelled far and have held many meetings to determine the mood of the people—at the Drakensberg Mountains, Winburg, the Vals River, Mooi River and now here. I wish us all to be united and to prevent the government from taking possession of this country. I have not given up hope that Natal will once again belong to us and I want to know whether I can rely on your assistance if I wish to retake Natal."

There was silence from the crowd.

"Well, what is it to be?" Pretorius shouted again. "I want to know … Will you support me or not?"

Again, the response was far from enthusiastic.

After much pleading and cajoling, Pretorius managed to persuade the Boers at Potchefstroom to agree to support him and to elect him as their commandant. He unsuccessfully tried to convince them to appoint him as commandant general and when they would not, he informed them that they should discuss the issue at length at another time.

Major Warden, the British resident in Bloemfontein, was extremely anxious that Sir Harry Smith's latest proclamation would incite a Boer uprising and wrote to Sir Harry Smith to plead that he not be made to send his troops to the Cape. In fact, he requested that additional troops be sent from the colony.

However, the governor replied, "My dear fellow, pray bear in mind that the Boers are my children, and I will have none other here for my soldiers; your detachment will march for the colony immediately."

Subsequently, Warden's troops marched off for the Cape and left a garrison of 50 to 60 Cape Mounted Rifles to defend a territory larger than 80,000 square kilometres.[1326] The Voortrekkers in Winburg immediately began to plot revolution.[1327]

On 8 March 1848, Sir Harry Smith proclaimed a form of government for the Orange River Sovereignty. The chief authority was to be the British resident and Bloemfontein was to be the seat of government. A civil commissioner and resident magistrate, Thomas Jervis Biddulph, was to be positioned at Winburg and James O'Reilly would be in the Lower Caledon Valley. However, when someone was charged with a crime, he or she would be sent back to the colony, to Colesberg, to be tried. In addition, Sir Harry Smith declared that a land commission would be established to determine the boundaries for three districts in the sovereignty, namely Bloemfontein, the Caledon River and Winburg. This commission would inspect farms, issue title deeds and collect the quit rent for each farm. The governor conceded that the people could elect commandants and field cornets but stipulated that every able-bodied man in the territory was required to come to the defence of the British when called to do so.[1328]

As the control of the British extended only as far as the Vaal River, many Boers in the Orange River Sovereignty headed north ... to escape British authority once again.

On 22 March 1848, Pretorius addressed a crowd of burghers at Andries Ohrigstad and asked them to back him when he made his move to drive the British out of Natal. However, the reception he received there was even cooler than it had been at Potchefstroom.

When he shouted, "Who is with me and prepared to fight?", only one burghers stepped forward. Pretorius was devastated.

While Pretorius was attempting to round up support north of the Vaal River, his lieutenants met with some of the minor chiefs and attempted them to join them in fighting the British. They managed to sow the seeds of dissention among the chiefs and it was not long before the opposition movement against British occupation had gathered momentum.

Finally, Warden wrote to the governor to express his concern about the rapidly growing anti-British sentiment among the people. He wrote, "I regret to have to inform Your Excellency the fact that the country continues in a state of ferment. Nine tenths of the Boers beyond the Modder River having enrolled themselves to support Mr Pretorius, and his agents in other parts of the country have been most active. On both banks of the Caledon this rebel Emigrant's authority is acknowledged by the greater portion of the inhabitants ... Your Excellency can hardly conceive what a string of falsehood and misrepresentations this Mr Pretorius has had recourse to in order to gain over and mislead his countrymen, having succeeded thus far, being as he boasts at the head of sixteen hundred Emigrants, he will no doubt attempt to carry out his designs."[1329]

Potgieter was not pleased by Pretorius's arrival in his republic and feared that Pretorius was beginning to exert his influence over a far wider area than just Natal.[1330] Meanwhile, Smith realized that the Boers were preparing for war and, on 29 March 1848, he wrote a manifesto that included several approaches to deter the Boers from this course of action, and covered every ambit of emotion including pleading, cajoling, threatening and attacking. The manifesto began with an explanation that "some evil-minded persons, prone to wickedness, to mischief and evil ways" had been misrepresenting the facts of the proclamation that he had issued the previous month proclaiming the land between the Orange and the Vaal Rivers as British territory. Then, it rationalized why the area had been annexed and gave reasons for the annexation, which included that the residents of the area had begged the governor to annex the region and that Pretorius had encouraged Smith to proceed with the annexation. Essentially, the governor had merely obliged with granting what he believed the people wanted.

"You have indeed had no government for years," he wrote. "Are you happier? Are you richer? Are you better Christians? You are miserable. You are paupers, the half of you ruined."

Subsequently, the manifesto set out the advantages of the annexation and stated that it would not be rescinded, irrespective of what the Boers thought. It also warned that any uprising by the Boers stood little chance of being successful. "Do you talk of resistance and assemblages—you whom two years ago a few Dragoons rode over like sheep? Do you presume to imagine that you are able to do what no mass of demagogues has ever yet done. The undisciplined to resist, and successfully maintain a protracted resistance against the disciplined force of a regular Government?" Moreover, Smith warned the Boers that if they continued to resist annexation, he would have no choice but to respond with force and see to it that their farms and cattle were seized and their homes destroyed. He then followed these threats with, "Let us together thus pray," and a rambling prayer.

The governor then had the manifesto translated into Dutch and had thousands of leaflets printed and distributed among the Boers.[1331] It is uncertain whether Sir Harry Smith's manifesto persuaded the Boers that resistance against the British would be futile or whether they arrived at this conclusion under their own steam. Nevertheless, the passion for a fight gradually diminished, despite Pretorius's continued attempts to rally the burghers for war.

On 8 April 1848, Pretorius addressed the burghers in Potchefstroom and again pleaded for their support to drive the British out of Natal and the Transoranje. He urged his fellow Boers to trust that God would give them victory over the British and not to abandon their principles. He also warned those that did not assist in the fighting for freedom would be severely punished and called on the commandants and field cornets to build up their stocks of provisions and ammunition. Finally, he informed the Potchefstroom crowd that the Boers from Andries Ohrigstad would be rallying at Liebenbergsvlei on 15 May 1848 and reminded them that "unity is strength".

Since taking leave of Sir Harry Smith in February 1848, Pretorius had travelled over 1,000 kilometres and addressed 15 meetings with the message that the Boers needed to stand together to free Natal and Transoranje from the British.

At the Asrivier, in Bethlehem, Pretorius joined his family and friends who were camped there to await the rally of the Boers on 15 May 1848. He had by this time declared that he would never return to Natal while it was under British control and had purchased a farm called Rhenosterdoorns in the foothills of the Magaliesberg in the Transvaal, in case the Boers were unable to drive the British from Natal and the Orange River Sovereignty.

At the meeting, Pretorius presented a letter he had drafted and which he hoped would be supported by all of the commandants and field cornets there before sending it Sir Harry Potgieter. However, Kock and Potgieter argued that the letter was far too aggressive and openly challenged Pretorius on his desire to make war with the British. Subsequently, it emerged that the majority of Boers there were against Pretorius's plans for war and, after the meeting concluded, two letters were sent to Sir Harry Smith, one from Potgieter and the other from the commandants and field cornets.

Potgieter's letter was conciliatory and he described himself as being "a man of peace". He also pointed out to Sir Harry Smith that he had purchased the land between the Vet and the Vaal rivers from Chief Makwana of the Bataung and he requested that the governor not place a magistrate in the area.

The letter from the commandants and field cornets requested that Sir Harry Smith not implement the threats made in his manifesto and, after outlining the Boers' requirements, stated that any disputes could be settled with "the pen rather than a sword". The signatories included A.H. Potgieter (chief commandant), G. Kruger (commandant) and A.W.J. Pretorius.

Pretorius had received a political hiding in that it had become clear that he did not enjoy the support of the Boers and had been undermined by Potgieter's letter.[1332]

Sir Harry Smith's reply was addressed to "my friend Potgieter" and the governor was at pains to emphasize that he desired the happiness and prosperity of the Boers. Moreover, Sir Harry Smith referred to Potgieter as "an old friend" and "a man far superior to the other man who I trusted and looked on as my brother" and who had "greatly deceived" him.

It didn't take much imagination for Potgieter to work out that the governor was alluding to Pretorius and he must have been flattered by Sir Harry Smith's praise and veiled criticism of his adversary.

Pretorius was politically broken and disillusioned by his defeat at the hands of his 'friends' and the unravelling of his plans for an armed uprising at the meeting at Asrivier. Consequently, he decided to retire from public life and returned to his farm in the Magaliesberg.

Nevertheless, he attracted a large number of followers and, before long, the 'Pretorius party' was formed. This meant that there were three contenders making a play for the authority of the lands north of the Vaal River: the Pretorius party, Potgieter party and the Volksraad of Andries Ohrigstad.

It didn't take long for the Voortrekkers to realize that Pretorius had been right.

On 22 May 1848, Biddulph arrived at Winburg to be installed as civil commissioner and magistrate and the Boers there suddenly faced the reality of the British annexation.

Up until this point, they had enjoyed relative 'independence' and, as such, resented Biddulph's intrusion into their way of life. Consequently, the republican party called a meeting on a farm outside Winburg and the senior members of the community, including the displaced landdrost Willem Jacobsz, field cornets and commandants resolved to notify Warden that the Boers would not accept or acknowledge Biddulph as magistrate. Additionally, they decided that Jacobsz would go to Pretorius to tell him that the Winburgers were prepared to take up arms against the British and regain their independence. They again appointed him as commandant general in his absence and Jan Kock as his second-in-command.

When Jacobsz arrived at Pretorius's farm to ask him to lead the Boers, he encountered a sad scene: Pretorius's wife Christina Petronella was wasting away from dysentery after having contracted malaria. It was clear that she would not recover. Although Jacobsz pleaded with Pretorius to return with him to Winburg, he refused to leave his wife's side. However, a wan-looking Christina turned to Pretorius and said, "By staying here, you cannot save my life; your countrymen need your services. Go and help them." He complied with her request and never saw her again, as she died shortly after this.

The newly appointed magistrate, Biddulph, was duly informed that if he remained in Winburg, he would be arrested. Terrified, he fled to Bloemfontein, where Warden immediately sent him back to Winburg. However, on 11 July 1848, Biddulph reported to Warden that the Land Commission could not continue to survey the Boers' farms because of the unrest among the Boers and the aggressive attitude they were demonstrating toward the surveyors.

When he received a warning scribbled in pencil on the back of a free pardon note that had been given to British army deserter Michael Quigley that a commando of Boers under Pretorius was on its way to Winburg and was camped on the False River,[1333] he fled the town and made for Bloemfontein as fast as his horse could carry him.

Warden was handing out land certificates at the time and Biddulph galloped up to him and the 12 Cape Mounted Rifles accompanying the British resident when he was about nine kilometres from Bloemfontein. He immediately blurted that Pretorius was on his way to Winburg. The two men and their escorts raced toward Bloemfontein, where they intended to alert the governor of the unfolding events in Winburg and to commence building earthworks for the defence of Bloemfontein. Warden only had 100 men at his disposal in Bloemfontein. Before they reached Bloemfontein, they encountered a burgher patrol of 25 men and one of the Boers informed Warden that they were going to take him prisoner and escort him to Pretorius's camp so that he could see how strong the Boers' opposition was to the British.

Warden promised to send Mr Frederick Rex to see the camp and report to him, then urged his horse to gallop toward Bloemfontein. Biddulph and the others galloped closely behind him and fired at the Boers pursuing them.[1334]

When Pretorius arrived in Winburg on 12 July 1848, the Boers rallied around him, offering to fight for their independence. Soon, Pretorius had raised a commando of 750 men and they shouted their praise for Pretorius and begged him to expel the British officials. "I will do so," Pretorius answered, "but I do not want to be bothered with so-called neutral or loyal men. Those that are not for me are against me, and they must get out."[1335]

When the commando seized Winburg, the Boers arrested a clerk, some of Biddulph's relatives and two constables and seized their properties. However, the Boers finally relented and when they set the frightened British prisoners free, they hastened toward Bloemfontein.[1336]

Shortly after this, Pretorius published a notice stating that no Boer would be allowed to remain neutral in the imminent "war of freedom" and that any who would not join or support Boers' cause would have to cross the Orange River into the colony by 20 July 1848. Several groups of Boers who considered the British annexation to be in their interests set up laagers and readied their defences to signal their defiance of Pretorius's order. The dissenters included Gerrit Hendrik Meyer, Johannes I.J. Fick, the Wessels family, Snyman and Oberholzer.[1337]

On 17 July 1848, Pretorius and his Boer army marched to Bloemfontein and camped three kilometres from the village. Then, Pretorius rode to the outskirts of the village with 400 men to deliver a letter to Warden that called on him to surrender Bloemfontein within the hour. If he would not accede to Pretorius's demand, the Boers would attempt to take the Orange River Sovereignty from the British by force.

Warden who had only two cannon, a force of 45 Hottentot soldiers from the Cape Mounted Rifles, 12 raw recruits plus 42 civilians capable of carrying arms. Consequently, he had little option but to surrender and requested an interview with Pretorius. Pretorius met Warden halfway between the Boer camp and Bloemfontein and, at this meeting, Pretorius agreed that all the British troops and inhabitants would be permitted to return to the colony with their movable property and even provided them with wagons to do so.

The Boer commando took possession of Bloemfontein on 20 July 1848 and, thereafter, Pretorius drew up a manifesto that was signed by the commandants, field cornets and some 900 others and stressed the Boers' anger that the British appeared to favour the black tribes at their expense, which had threatened their lifestyles and livelihoods while they were under British rule. Moreover, the manifesto emphasized that they were bitter that the British had allowed the black tribes to continue with their traditional form of governance, but had denied this right to the Boers. Lastly, the manifesto highlighted that Sir Harry Smith had stated that he would not declare the Orange River Sovereignty if the majority of Boers living in the area were against the occupation by the British.

To demonstrate that the majority was against the British occupation, the Boers marched to Middelvlei, which was on the north bank of the Orange River and close to Colesberg. There, they would wait to see what the next move from the colonists would be.

Sir Harry Smith received the Boers' manifesto on 22 July 1848 and was incensed by it. He immediately ordered that all available troops in the colony march to Colesberg and, that afternoon, published a proclamation that offered a reward of £1,000 to the person or people who captured Pretorius. Further, he issued a proclamation offering a reward of £500 for the capture of Jacobsz, the former landdrost of Winburg. Sir Harry Smith then left Cape Town for Colesberg to take command of his troops.

Pretorius anticipated that the British would retaliate when the governor received the Boers' manifesto and, while waiting for the British to mobilize their forces, he sent a letter across the river to Warden's camp. Warden had chosen to rather camp next to the river than stay in the village of Colesberg. The letter stated that as it was evident that the emigrants were united against the British, Sir Harry Smith ought not to trouble them any further and requested a meeting with the governor when he arrived at Colesberg.

Although Sir Harry Smith's reply referred to the emigrants as rebels, he still agreed to meet with the two Boers who had been nominated as emissaries, namely Gerrit Kruger and Paul Bester, and promised them safe passage across the river to the British camp. However, Pretorius wrote to the governor to inform him that there would be no meeting between the Boers and the British, as the governor had referred to his people as rebels. Two days later, he wrote to the governor requesting that he renounce his proclamation of occupation of the Orange River Sovereignty. Smith did not reply.

CHAPTER 37

Battle of Boomplaats

Troops cross the Orange—the battle—rebel execution—rebellion—Hendrik Buurman—Potgieter and Pretorius vie for power—Volksraad of Ohrigstad

A rumour had reached the Boers that further British troops would be coming to Colesberg from Natal and, together with the British forces across the river, would catch the Boers in a pincer-like movement. In addition, they had heard that Sir Harry Smith's army comprised 800 men.

There was much discord among the Boers as to what action they should take and now that a fight seemed imminent, many of the Boers declared that they had had no intention of actually fighting and had merely joined the commando to demonstrate that the majority was opposed to British rule. The Boers then retired to Bloemfontein and a small group set up camp near the road leading to the town so that they would be in position to attack the British when they came.

On 22 August 1848, Sir Harry Smith and his troops crossed the Orange River, which was in flood, on two rubber rafts. Once across the river, the governor's forces were strengthened by the arrival of a group of Boers under commandants Pieter Erasmus and J.T. Snyman as well as some 200 armed Griqua under Waterboer and Kok. Sir Harry Smith believed that the Boer uprising had only occurred because Pretorius had incited the Boers to violence and tried to divide them by sending letters to the various commandants in an attempt to turn them against Pretorius. Mr Halse took the letters to the Pretorius's camp outside Bloemfontein, where he was cordially received. However, Pretorius was no fool and quickly called a meeting with all of the burghers and, when he asked them whether he should give individuals letters from the governor, they agreed that it would not be prudent to do so. Subsequently, Halse was sent back to the governor with the unopened letters.

On 27 August 1848, the British troops marched from the Orange River to Philippolis and then on to Vissershoek. Scouts were sent out that evening but returned with no news of having sighted the Boers.

Early the next wintry morning, the crisp earth crackled under the boots of 800 of Sir Harry Smith's men as they marched. The men of the Cape Corps rode at the front of the procession in their green uniforms and were followed by the European officers and Hottentot soldiers, who carried carbines. Behind them were the men of the Rifle Brigade and then the Sappers and artillerymen, who would handle the army's three guns. At the rear of the procession were the men of the 45th and 91st regiments. Sir Harry Smith's army travelled with 117 wagons that were loaded with the men's baggage, provisions and ammunition and were guarded by the rebel Boers and Griqua.

Close to the Krom Elleboog River, the open plains the British troops had been marching across fell away and the landscape changed dramatically. The many hills in the area were dotted with boulders and the riverbanks were covered with reeds. Ultimately, this terrain offered plenty of cover for the Boers, who had hidden at the nearby farmhouse of Boomplaats the night before. A coloured shepherd informed Sir Harry Smith about the Boers' hiding place and Sir Harry Smith ordered Lieutenant Warren of the Cape Corps to move ahead to reconnoitre the farm. Warren soon came galloping back to the governor to inform him that a force of about 100 Boers was beyond the nearest range of hills.

Pretorius had sent Kock and these men to scout out the position of the British troops while he and the Boer army had returned to the laager at Velkraal on the Riet River. By this time, the number of men under Pretorius's command had declined, as many of the Boers had returned to their homes, under the pretext that they had only participated to demonstrate against the British. The remaining force (excluding those under Kock) comprised only 300 men.[1338]

Sir Harry Smith joined the advance troop of the Cape Corps under Lieutenant Salis and confidently rode back to the Boers under Kock. He was certain that they would not resist his troops as they were hopelessly outnumbered and was anxious for this to be the case. After all, the approval he had received from the government in England to annex the Orange River Sovereignty had been strictly on the understanding that the annexation was accepted and endorsed by the majority of the Boers. Consequently, he wanted to meet with Pretorius and his commandants to ensure the avoidance of bloodshed and ordered his men to take the caps from the nipples of their carbines so that they could not be the first to fire.

At eleven o'clock that morning, the men of the Cape Corps spotted the Boers, who had crept up the hill on their left after having left their horses at the base of the hill. Adriaan Stander was *vegkommander* of this group and ordered his men to hold their fire until he fired the first shot, which he would aim at Sir Harry Smith. As the British troops drew close, one of the Boers' nerves cracked and he squeezed off a shot. His comrades immediately followed suit, thinking that this was the signal from Stander.

The startled soldiers in the Cape Corps galloped back to the other troops behind them. A rifle ball had grazed the head of Sir Harry Smith's horse and one of his stirrup leathers had been cut in half by another. When he looked back, he cursed loudly: Salis's horse had been killed and the lieutenant was on the ground near the bodies of three Hottentot soldiers and was nursing his badly wounded arm. The injured lieutenant watched two Boers apprehensively as they approached him.

"Shoot him!" one of the Boers shouted in Dutch, which Salis understood.

"No, you must not. I have a wife and children," Salis pleaded.

"Are you wounded?" one of the Boers asked.

"Yes," he replied.

The Boers gestured that he could go and he crawled back to the troops. By this time, Pretorius and the remaining Boers had joined Stander's commando and Sir Harry Smith ordered his men to lug the cannon up the hill and Lieutenant Dyneley to open fire on the Boers with them when they were in position. As the shells crashed around the Boers, blasting earth and rocks into the sky, they rushed to crouch behind the large rocks nearby.

When Smith ordered the Rifle Brigade and the 45th Regiment to charge the Boers, they were assaulted by a hail of bullets and Captain Murray, who was leading the charge, was hit three times. He collapsed and was quickly stretchered back to the rear, but died in the next few hours.

Colonel Buller, the second-in-command, was wounded in the thigh and many of the soldiers were killed as they made their way up toward the crest of the hill. Before the British troops reached the summit, the Boers retreated to the next ridge of hills, where Pretorius positioned *Ou Grietjie* and fired off a few rounds that in turn drew the attention of the six-pounder cannon of the British.

While this battle raged, Commandant Kock and his men emerged from behind a ridge on the left of the British front and dashed onto the plain to attack the rebel Boers and Griqua protecting the 117 wagons[1339] and the provisions and ammunition in them. Seeing what was happening, Sir Harry Smith ordered the Cape Corps to arrange the wagons into laager formation and redirected two of the six-pounders to be trained on Kock's men. After sustaining heavy fire from the Cape Corps at the wagons, Kock and his men withdrew … only to be fired at by the British artillerymen.[1340]

The barrage of cannon fire that the British directed at the hills and the advancing infantry caused the Boers to retreat to Boomplaats, where they took up defensive positions in the cattle kraals along the spruit there. During the retreat, a shell whistled so close to Stander's ear, that he fell off his horse. While he lay on the ground, John Jack (one of the Boers who had sided with the British) splashed water on his face to revive him. Pretorius and his men left a small contingent near the farmyard and took up position away from the Boers' laager, as Pretorius hoped to draw the British away from their wagons when they came.

When the British arrived at Boomplaats, Sir Harry Smith sent his Griqua and Hottentot troops forward to attack Pretorius's group. However, the Boers' accurate gunfire caused them heavy losses and they had to fall back. The governor then ordered the infantry to advance with the six-pounder cannon. It would appear that the British had superior firepower to the Boers and Pretorius and his men were forced to withdraw from their position when the veld near them burst into flames.

Three hours into the battle, the smoke from the burning dry grass and the men's guns hung above them thickly, like a vast grey sponge, and by 2 o'clock that afternoon, the Boers dispersed. During the battle, the British had lost 22 men, including one officer, and 38 had been severely wounded, while the Boers had lost seven men, namely N. du Buisson, Diederik Laffnie, P. Erasmus, two of the De Beers men, D. Steyn and Fourie as well as had five severely wounded.[1341]

Surveying the battlefield, Sir Harry commented, "A more rapid, fierce and well-directed fire than that kept up by the rebels, I have never seen maintained nor have I seen a sharper skirmish."

After the battle, two of Sir Harry Smith's Griqua soldiers captured Michael Quigley, an English deserter from Natal who had joined the Boers but provided information to the British about their movements, and Thomas Dreyer, a young Boer man from the Magaliesberg whose horse had bolted during the combat.

Spurred on by some of the dissident Boers, in particular Pieter Erasmus who wanted to "make an example of the Boers", Sir Harry Smith ordered that the two men be taken to Bloemfontein, where they would appear before a military court chaired by the wounded Colonel Buller.

Quigley was charged with being a deserter and Dreyer as a rebel and both men were sentenced to death. On 3 September 1848, they were executed by a firing squad and as Pretorius commented, "The poor boy was tied and bound so tightly it would have taken him the rest of his life to untie himself. A wounded British officer then sentenced him to death in a military court. In Natal many troops fell into our hands, but never were they treated in such a monstrous manner."[1342]

The victorious Sir Harry Smith and his troops arrived at Bloemfontein on 2 September 1848 and, the next day, the governor issued a proclamation declaring that all those who had supported Pretorius were guilty of rebellion and would lose their properties. In addition, anyone who had assisted the rebels was to be fined. He also raised the reward for Pretorius's capture to £2,000 and pronounced his property confiscated, offering a reward of £500 for the capture of several other Boer leaders, including Andries Spies, Jan Krynauw and Louw Pretorius, and confiscated the properties of others.

Sir Harry Smith and his troops then moved on to Winburg. When they arrived on 7 September 1848, the governor was surprised that the burghers there did not resist the British in any way, particularly when he reissued his proclamation proclaiming the queen's sovereignty over the land between the Orange and Vaal rivers.

Sir Harry hoped to recover the costs of the military campaign from the fines imposed on the citizens in the district of Winburg, as most of the Boer support had come from there, and confiscated the properties of all those who had participated in the uprising. He also had these men banned from the district. The sale of these confiscated properties coupled with the fines came to over £10,000.

Those Boers who had not left for the Transvaal to escape British authority before the battle did so now. There were more than 1,500 families north of the Vaal River at this time and probably over 7,500 people.[1343]

Sir Harry Smith then issued another proclamation on 7 September 1848 stating that a fort would be built at Bloemfontein and that a large garrison of British troops would be stationed there. Recognizing the old rivalry between Potgieter and Pretorius, Sir Harry Smith created a fourth district in the Orange River Sovereignty, between the Vaal and Sand rivers and the Drakensberg Mountains, and offered Potgieter the position of magistrate of the Vaal River territory.

Due to the powerful and forceful personalities of Potgieter and Pretorius, the Transvaal had three district communities: Potgieter was followed with almost religious zeal in the Zoutpansberg; the anti-Potgieter and Volksraad supporters congregated at Lydenburg; and Pretorius still enjoyed a large following in Potchefstroom and the Magaliesberg-Marico.

When Sir Harry Smith invited Potgieter to Winburg to meet with him, Pretorius watched the dance of the scorpions unfold with wry amusement, from his farm in the Magaliesberg. Potgieter was wary of what his people might think if he appeared to be too amicable toward the governor and anxious not to do anything that might turn them against him. Consequently, he planned a mass meeting for 13 November 1848 to gauge public feeling on how much support there was for Pretorius and conflict with the British.

On the day of the meeting with the governor, Potgieter wrote to Sir Harry and claimed that he was too ill to attend it. He requested that he be allowed to instead meet a representative at the Vaal River and went on to address the issue of Sir Harry Smith's proclamation on 7 September 1848 in which the governor had annexed the territory of the Vaal River, which Potgieter considered to be his.

Although the governor had informed Potgieter that he could keep the land, he had stipulated that this would only be "under the queen's sovereignty".

Unsure quite what Sir Harry Smith meant but sure that he did not mean for the Boers to be independent in the Transvaal, Potgieter wrote, "I am extremely grateful to Your Excellency, but as for myself and in the name of all emigrants, I cannot accept it under such conditions. Your Excellency and everybody else know what we sacrificed to be free. That is why I say we would rather waive our rights to this territory, grievous loss though it may be, and surrender it to H.M. Government rather than to accept it on such terms."

Potgieter finished his letter by maligning Pretorius. He stated that it had never been his intention nor that of the majority of Boers north of the Vaal River to take the territory by force. Moreover, he explained that he had been "pained" by the militant actions of some of the Boers and had therefore arranged a mass meeting in Potchefstroom to discuss how to deal with those of his followers who had been involved and had fled the Orange River Sovereignty. He concluded by asserting that he wanted the Boers to live in peace with the British.[1344]

A new player soon entered the political stage in the Transvaal: a 26-year-old schoolmaster called Hendrik Buhrmann. He had come out from Holland with Smellekamp, who had eventually fallen out with Ohrig but was still intent on establishing trade links between the Dutch and the Boers and had promised to send them teachers and clergymen from the Netherlands. The members of the Volksraad of Andries Ohrigstad had little education and some were only able to read passages of the Bible by memory. As such, they were extremely impressed by Buhrmann and allowed him to express his views and opinions on important matters. Buhrmann gave his full support to Potgieter and expounded the view that there should be an entirely new and centralized Volksraad in the Transvaal, with Potgieter as its chief commandant.

As Potgieter was answerable to the Volksraad of Andries Ohrigstad and Pretorius was out of the equation, Buhrmann had the perfect opportunity to establish himself among the Boers and ensconce himself with the Volksraad of Andries Ohrigstad.[1345]

Excitement mounted among the Boers in Potchefstroom on 13 November 1848 as they would be attending the biggest meeting that had ever been held in the town. At the meeting, Pretorius and Potgieter pointedly ignored each other and were both surrounded by their loyal followers. Nevertheless, both used the opportunity to badmouth the other.

Since Boomplaats, Pretorius's image had suffered a severe blow and he had lost ground in the leadership stakes. As such, Potgieter presented himself as a peaceable man and criticized Pretorius and his followers for declaring war against the British and the disastrous defeat of the Boers at Boomplaats. Pretorius was not a man to accept criticism lightly and responded by denigrating Potgieter whenever he could.

Early on in the meeting, Buhrmann aimed to stir the emotion of those in the crowd by shouting out, "Should the war against the British be continued?"

The Boers unanimously cried "no" and, after more discussion, Buhrmann called on the crowd to vote for either Potgieter or Pretorius to represent them in discussions with the British. After the votes were tallied, Potgieter emerged the winner and it was decided that Commandant Kruger and Buhrmann would assist him in negotiations with the British.[1346] Potgieter then guided the meeting and made a commitment not to become involved in affairs of the Orange River Sovereignty. He promised the Boers that he would work toward achieving peace with the British but stressed that this would necessitate that no unauthorized person should negotiate or have any dealings with them.

Potgieter had clearly been referring to Pretorius and possibly to some of his followers and it looked as though Pretorius had been snookered. As an outlaw with a price on his head, he could not attend any meetings with the British, even if he were requested to do so.[1347] Finally, Buhrmann proposed his four points of government to the meeting, which were accepted by all except Pretorius and his followers.

The meeting with Sir Harry Smith's representative, Richard Southey, took place at the end of 1848 on Stephanus Jansen van Vuuren's farm between Potchefstroom and the Vaal River. At the meeting, Potgieter made an impassioned speech in which he stressed that most of the Boers north of the Vaal River wanted to be a free and independent nation. Southey was so impressed by Potgieter's eloquent oratory that he undertook to recommend to Sir Harry Smith that the Transvaal be granted full and total independence from the British. He also asked Potgieter to petition the governor for the independence of the Transvaal.

Potgieter recognized that if he did so, he would possibly be viewed by the British as a troublemaker. He also didn't want his people to see him as being too closely tied to them. Consequently, he declined the position of magistrate in the new district and stated that he did so reluctantly, upon the advice of his friends and supporters. Finally, he took another stab at Pretorius by telling Southey that the "evil activities" of Pretorius and his followers would only stop if the Transvaal was declared as independent.[1348]

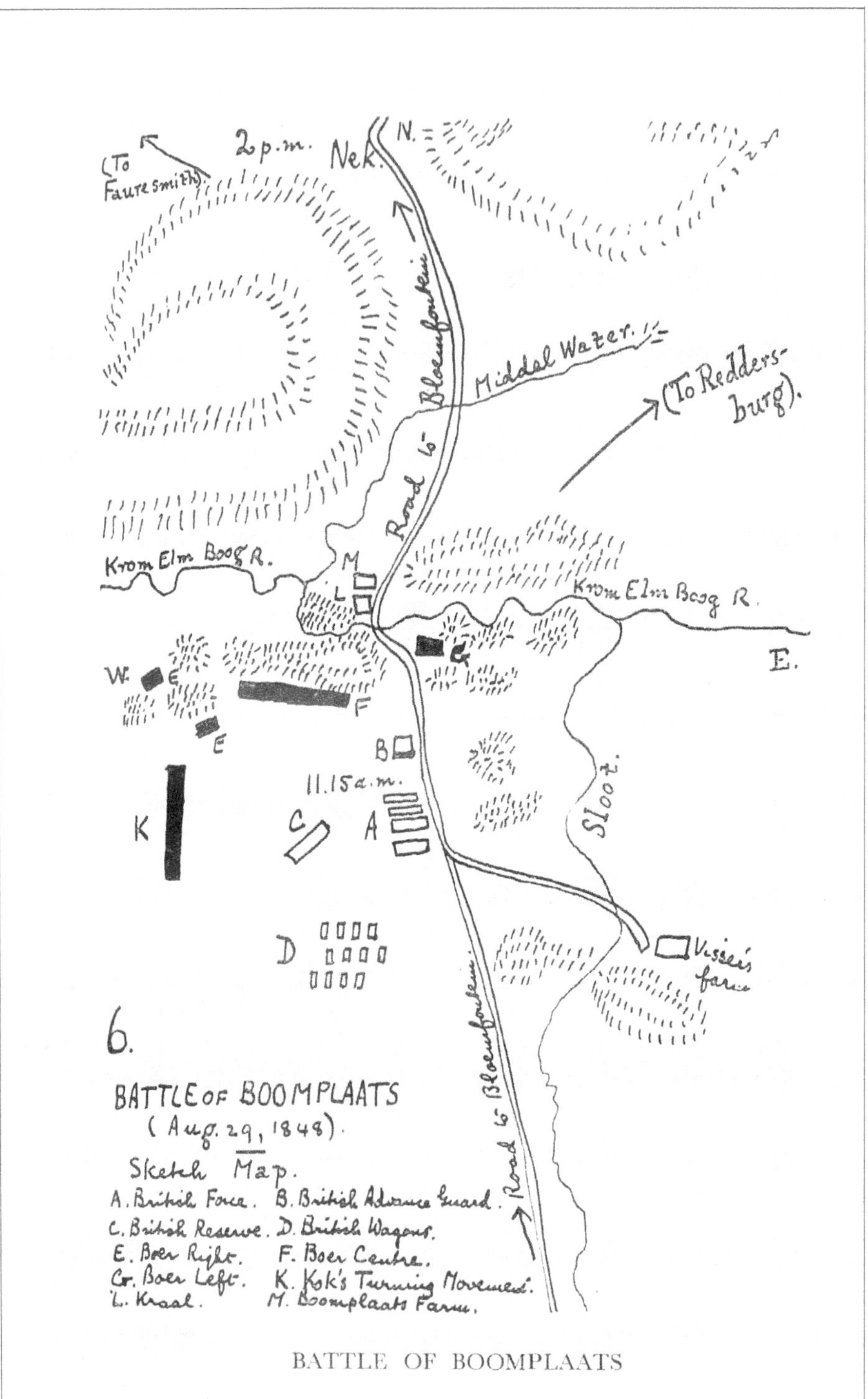

BATTLE OF BOOMPLAATS

Sir Harry Smith was most impressed by Potgieter's shrewdness and recognized that he had played a very clever political game by positioning Pretorius as the rabble-rouser and himself as the diplomat.

It wasn't long before Smith instructed Southey to acknowledge the independence of the Boers across the Vaal River but stipulated that this was on condition that he would have the final say in approving the names of officials elected by the people.

At a mass meeting of the burghers in Potchefstroom on 9 February 1849, Southey's proposal was rejected by the Boers, who had decided "never to recognize British authority north of the Vaal River", and when Buhrmann asked Pretorius how he felt about this, he replied that he had no intention of waging war with the Boers across the Vaal River.[1349]

The burghers agreed that the Volksraad of Andries Ohrigstad would be recognized as the highest authority north of the Vaal River and that all would be answerable to this body, including Potgieter, who apparently supported the decision. They also resolved that a meeting would be held at Olifantsrivier on 23 March 1849 to ratify this decision.

Afterwards, Buhrmann addressed a letter to the Volksraad of Andries Ohrigstad to invite the members to the upcoming meeting in Olifantsrivier. However, the president declined the invitation on the basis that the Volksraad of Andries Ohrigstad wanted to discuss their strategy and views with Smellekamp when he returned to South Africa before communicating these to the general public.

Buhrmann then set off for Andries Ohrigstad, where he failed to convince the burghers and the Volksraad there that they should attend the proposed meeting on 23 March 1849.

Buhrmann's tapestry of political intrigue had begun to unravel.

On 23 March 1849, a mere 200 burghers arrived for the meeting and one can only assume that they had begun to tire of their leaders' inability to reach accord and of being asked to attend meeting after meeting to rehash the same subjects.

Potgieter opened the meeting and announced that he did not approve of Buhrmann's plan for one Volksraad for the whole territory. He then spoke of the opposition of the Volksraad of Andries Ohrigstad to this idea and proposed that everything should remain as it was. (This would mean that he would continue as supreme commander and would not be answerable to the Volksraad of Andries Ohrigstad.) Buhrmann spoke next and launched an attack on Potgieter and the Volksraad of Andries Ohrigstad and even accused the government body of having used him for his ideas for their own gain.

"Enough!" Potgieter exploded. "You have said enough and have thrown enough stones at my head! I stand by my decision."

With that, Potgieter turned to the crowd and called out, "Those who love me, follow me!"

He stormed out of the meeting followed by about 18 of his staunch supporters. Those who remained at the meeting rumbled in discontent about Potgieter's dramatic exit but did resolve several issues. One of the decisions the people made that day was that the Volksraad of Andries Ohrigstad would be recognized as the highest authority in the land and that, after Potgieter's death or resignation, no other commander-in-chief would ever be appointed. In addition, a new Volksraad would be elected and would be sworn in at Derdepoort on 22 May 1849.

A deputation that included Buhrmann, the two Spies brothers, Lodewyk de Jager Sr, Hermanus Fourie, Jacob Mare and Stephanus Schoeman then set off in two ox wagons for Andries Ohrigstad to persuade the Volksraad there to accept the decisions made at the meeting.

At a meeting of the Volksraad of Andries Ohrigstad on 3 April 1849, those members present adopted the decisions taken at Olifantsrivier but stipulated that there would be two sittings of the Volksraad of Andries Ohrigstad to every one meeting of the new Volksraad of Derdepoort and that Andries Ohrigstad would be the capital of the new consolidated territory and would have 50 percent of the representatives on the new Volksraad.[1350]

Pretorius watched the political manoeuvrings of the Boers closely and found it hard to believe that the Voortrekkers were so taken in by Buhrmann when they had been at such pains to fiercely defend their independence before. However, he did not get involved, possibly because he had recently married the daughter of De Lange's brother, Petronella Aletta de Lange.

At Derdepoort on 22 May 1849, the new Volksraad was elected. It included six members of the Volksraad of Andries Ohrigstad and 13 others, including Pretorius, who was named chairman of the new political entity, namely "the united confederation of the whole community on this side of the Vaal River".

Potgieter was not present at this meeting and one can only hazard a guess that this was because he had begun to tire of his constant battle to remain in power. Nevertheless, the 33 articles that Potgieter had devised and which had been passed at Potchefstroom in 1844 would serve as a general guide for the new Volksraad. In addition, the existing laws passed at the various republican centres were confirmed at this meeting.[1351]

On 3 September 1849, the new Volksraad met at Krugerspost (Lydenburg). Although Pretorius had written to Potgieter to invite him to the meeting so that they could "put an end to all outstanding differences", he did not attend and when he learned that the position of chief commandant had been abolished, he continued acting as commander-in-chief in the Zoutpansberg area.[1352]

A further meeting of the new Volksraad was held on 19 September 1849 at Krugerspost in the hope that Potgieter would attend and finally submit to its authority. When Potgieter did not come to the meeting, the new Volksraad announced an embargo on all trade and communication with the Zoutpansberg district and ordered the landdrost of Potchefstroom to issue a summons to Potgieter that demanded that he and six of his strongest supporters appear in front of the landdrost on the third Monday of January 1849 to explain why they were not honouring the agreement that they had signed on 23 March 1848. The summons also warned that military force would be used to ensure that the decisions that had been taken were implemented.

Potgieter had, however, withdrawn his signature of support from the decisions taken at Olifantsrivier, which meant that the summons could not be issued.[1353] Pretorius was slowly consolidating his position as the overall commander of the Boers and when Potgieter wrote to him to express his desire to work with him, Pretorius set out to visit his old rival. However, along the way, he had an accident in his cart and badly injured his leg, to the extent that he had to cancel his plans to visit Potgieter. Thus, the two men exchanged letters and soon realized that they had a common enemy—Buhrmann—and that they both believed the Dutchman was not working for the best interests of the Boers but of himself. Pretorius resigned as a member of the Volksraad at a meeting in Potchefstroom on 22 January 1850, after a petition had been received with the signatures of 168 Boers requesting that he be reappointed as commandant general.

Buhrmann led a campaign to oppose Pretorius's reappointment as commandant general and the Volksraad finally decided on 15 January 1851 to pass the decision on to a council of war, which was made up of Commandant General Pretorius, commandants J.A. Enslin and W.F. Joubert, 17 field cornets as well as two magistrates, namely Lombard and De Clerque.

Finally, it was decided that four commandant generals would be appointed and each would be responsible for his own area. Joubert was assigned Lydenburg; Potgieter Zoutpansberg; Pretorius Magaliesberg, Mooi River and Marico and Enslin was allocated part of Marico.

At the Volksraad meeting in May 1851, these appointments were confirmed and Stephanus Schoeman was appointed as commandant of Potchefstroom. Meanwhile, Pretorius had been writing to Warden in Bloemfontein and to Moshoeshoe and had suggested to them that an independent commission examine the various parties' views regarding the boundaries of the Orange River Sovereignty and the southern boundaries of the Transvaal.

If Sir Harry Smith had thought that the Boers had been a thorn in the side of the British, he was in for an unpleasant surprise: Moshoeshoe and the Basotho would soon begin to cause trouble in the newly established Orange River Sovereignty.

CHAPTER 38

Dividing the cake

The Basotho and Tlokwe fight—meeting of Warden and the chiefs—border proposals—Boers fight for the British

Since February of 1848, skirmishes and cattle raids had been taking place between the Basotho and the Tlokwa tribes. However, when the Bataung boldly stole over 500 head of cattle from Sekonyela, Moshoeshoe intervened and had the cattle returned to the chief of the Tlokwa.

Then, in September 1848, one of Sekonyela's sons chased away the people from two Basotho kraals and set fire to their huts. Moshoeshoe's son, Molapo, retaliated by attacking the kraals of the Tlokwa. He also set their huts on fire, drove off their cattle and killed two Tlokwa men. Unsurprisingly, the Tlokwa hit back at Molapo and Moshoeshoe was again forced to intervene. This time, however, he sent a small army of Basotho warriors to assist with fighting off the Tlokwa and, in the ensuing battle, 17 Tlokwa were killed, including the wife of Sekonyela's brother, Mota.

The Basotho then encountered hundreds of cattle, goats and sheep as they approached the Tlokwa capital kraal of Joalaboholo ('great beer')[1354] and, instead of proceeding to the village and carrying out their intended attack, they captured the livestock and returned to Thaba Bosiu.[1355]

In Bloemfontein, Warden had heard about the ongoing battles between the Tlokwa and the Basotho and finally summoned Sekonyela and Moshoeshoe, as he hoped to mediate a truce between the two chiefs.

Things did not look promising when Moshoeshoe arrived in Bloemfontein with an army of 1,600 warriors ... and Sekonyela brought a thousand. However, Warden finally persuaded the chiefs to agree to settle any disputes with discussion and not on the battlefield.

A few weeks later, Southey sent a letter to Moshoeshoe inviting him to attend a meeting at which Sir Harry Smith would define the boundary line of Transoranje and define the lands of the Basotho and the Boers. Moshoeshoe refused to attend the meeting but promised to send Sekonyela in his place. Sir Harry Smith's intention was to create a boundary that separated the whites and the Basotho and that the British would govern the Basotho and the high commissioner would govern the Boers. He proposed that domestic affairs would then be handled by Moshoeshoe.[1356] When Sekonyela reported to Moshoeshoe that the governor had fixed the boundary as being from the Modder River, along the Langeberg Range and up to the junction of the Caledon and Orange rivers, Moshoeshoe was astonished and distraught. "If the British attempt to mark the line with beacons, I will call my army to arms and Sir Harry Smith's skull will be used to adorn the first beacon erected. The blood of our warriors, both black and white, will run as wide as the Caledon River," he said.

The peace Warden had introduced between Sekonyela and Moshoeshoe was short-lived. Soon, Moshoeshoe heard the rumours of an impending invasion of Basotholand by the Tlokwa and it wasn't long before Sekonyela sent a message to Moshoeshoe demanding that he send him his daughter, Nthe, as compensation for the 17 Tlokwa who had been killed in the earlier conflict. He warned the Basotho chief that he would declare war if he didn't comply with his demand. Moshoeshoe responded by sending a large army under Molapo and Chief Moletsane to attack the Tlokwa. Kraal after kraal was attacked by the Basotho, who rounded up cattle, sheep and horses and chased the Tlokwa women and children into the hills. Sekonyela then led of his 500 horsemen into the Thlotse district to engage Molapo's people in battle. As the violence between the Basotho and Tlokwa escalated, other parties were drawn into the conflict. For instance, bands of renegade Korana under Taaibosch, Griqua under Jan Bloem and Sotho-speaking warriors began to attack the defenceless settlements in Sekonyela's country.

Then, as they moved northwest, they started to attack the isolated Boer farms, where they sacked homes, sheds and outhouses and destroyed crops. Consequently, the Boers started to abandon their farms and formed a chain of laagers in the Caledon River district.

One of the brigand bands surprised some members of the high commissioner's Land Commission committee as they were erecting boundary beacons and, after handcuffing and whipping the men, they forced them at musket point into the hills.

Although Moletsane sent appeals for reinforcements to Warden in Bloemfontein, Warden's hands were tied: his garrison was far too small and ill-equipped to deal with the tribal uprising. However,

Moshoeshoe did not understand the passivity shown by the British resident. "You bound our hands behind our backs and strangers cut our throats," he wrote to Warden.

When rumours started to circulate that Moshoeshoe was about to launch a full-scale invasion into the Tlowka's land, Warden wrote to Sir Harry Smith and begged that he send more troops to Bloemfontein. However, when Smith replied three weeks later, he instructed Warden to remonstrate with Moshoeshoe and to assemble a force of Boers, Barolong and Griqua to invade Basotholand and Moshoeshoe's lands if diplomacy failed. "If Moshoeshoe should shut himself up on his mountain, Thaba Bosiu, I believe a few howitzer shells may be thrown upon him," Smith advised.[1357]

In an effort to bring about peace, Warden summoned all of the local chiefs to a meeting on 27 August 1849. Moshoeshoe declined Warden's invitation but sent two of his most trusted councillors in his stead. Sekonyela and the troublesome Taaibosch simply did not bother to send their excuses.

At this meeting, the chiefs blamed the absent Moshoeshoe for the conflict, stating that he would not withdraw his people from Sekonyela's lands, and formed a coalition that would be prepared to act against Moshoeshoe if the need arose.

While the chiefs were meeting with Warden, Sekonyela and Taaibosch used the opportunity to attack, burn and plunder several Basotho and Bataung kraals. When Moshoeshoe and Moletsane appealed to Warden for assistance, Warden admonished the chiefs in his reply for having engaged the Tlokwa and then invited Moshoeshoe to meet with him so that they could determine the boundary between the Caledon River district and Basotholand. He informed Moshoeshoe that if he cooperated, he would be considered a faithful friend of the British and that the Tlokwa and the Korana would be stopped from committing future aggressive acts. However, Warden warned him that if he did not meet with him and agree to the proposed boundary line, then all the petty chiefs would join the British and view him and his people as enemies.

Moshoeshoe sent his son Letsie and a counsellor to the meeting and when Warden described the proposed boundary line to Letsie and asked him to consent that he accepted it on behalf of his father, he answered, "My consent will be like that of a dog dragged by a riem around his neck."

Faced with no alternative, Moshoeshoe agreed to the boundary proposed by Warden and signed his acceptance to the limits of Basotholand on 1 October 1849. This came into effect on 18 December 1849 and, although Sir Harry Smith believed that the boundary heralded a new era of peace, he was mistaken.

In January 1850, Chief Moletsane's people attacked Barolong kraals near Thaba Bosiu and threatened to kill the local missionaries if they dared to interfere. Taaibosch and the Korana also attacked the Barolong, burned their crops and stole whatever they could from them. Simultaneously, Sekonyela and his allies slaughtered bands of Bushmen that they found living in caves on hilly slopes and continued to raid the Boers' farms. As such, the Boers appealed to Warden to provide them with protection from the Tlokwa and to drive them back to their own lands. However, Warden simply did not have the resources to help them.[1358]

Chaos and violence reigned, as did opportunistic crime. A party of Bushmen arrived at Mr Van Hansen's farm and demanded that he give them tobacco. When he refused to do so, the Bushmen attacked and killed him, along with his wife, four children and two servants, before setting fire to the house.

Shortly after this incident, Warden ordered a commando to sweep the area and to clear the Caledon River district of all Bushmen. Warden believed that the Bushmen had been encouraged in their violent pursuits by Poshuli, one of Moshoeshoe's brothers, and fined him 50 head of cattle for having sheltered renegade Bushmen. Poshuli refused to pay these to Warden, who then sent a Boer commando to seize the cattle, which they did with little resistance from the Basotho. However, some of the confiscated cattle belonged to Moshoeshoe's father and Moshoeshoe was, unsurprisingly, furious. He called the seizure of his father's cattle by Warden's men "an unjust and unfriendly act"[1359] and, this event sparked the disintegration of cordial relations between Warden and Moshoeshoe.

The situation was deteriorating daily—the Basotho were raiding the Barolong; the Bushmen were raiding the Boers; the Boers were attacking the Tlokwa; the Basotho were attacking the Boers; and the Griqua were stealing whenever they could and from whomever they could.

None of the inhabitants of the region were satisfied with the boundaries that the British had established or paid any attention to them.

Warden again summoned all of the chiefs to a meeting in Bloemfontein but called up a commando of 350 Boers and an allied force of 2,600 blacks who were opponents of the Basotho before the chiefs were due to arrive. Only Moroka II and Taaibosch arrived for the conference on 4 June 1851.

Warden then proposed to Sir Harry Smith that the British lead an attack on Moshoeshoe and install Moroka II as the paramount chief over Moshoeshoe and the others chiefs.

Sir Harry Smith agreed to Warden's proposal and the British resident quickly set about assembling his troops. He could only muster 120 Boers willing to go to battle for the British, partly because Moshoeshoe had already campaigned that the Boers to not aid the British if they were to take action against the Basotho.

Two Boers, Commandant Snyman and Josias P. Hoffman, met with Warden in Bloemfontein and tried to persuade him to stop meddling in the affairs of the tribes in the territory. They failed. Warden's ragtag army of 162 British soldiers, 120 Boers and an allied force comprising a mix of between 1,000 and 1,500

Fingoes, coloureds under Baatje, Moroka II's Barolong, Griqua under Kok and Korana under Taaibosch set up camp at Platberg on 20 June 1852, under the command of Major Donovan of the Cape Mounted Rifles.

Donovan and his force then moved against Moletsane, whose cattle kraals occupied a hill called Viervoet. However, Moletsane's warriors spotted Donovan's troops as they approached and abandoned the kraals. The Barolong then plundered their huts and rapidly consumed large quantities of freshly brewed *umqombothi* (beer made from maize) that they found.

While the Barolong were partying, three forces of Basotho under Letsie, Molapo and Moperi, respectively, crept up to the kraals and were joined by Moletsane's Bataung warriors who had fled the site a few hours earlier. Now, they attacked Donovan's allied force and surrounded the many drunken Barolong serving under him.

The Basotho killed many of Donovan's men with their battle-axes and assegais. Those that managed to escape death by steel were thrown, kicking and screaming, off the nearby cliffs. A party of Boers under the command of Commandant Erasmus soon arrived and engaged the Basotho in battle and, by so doing, managed to prevent a total massacre of the Barolong.[1360] Nevertheless, Donovan's troops had suffered a decisive defeat at Viervoet: more than 152 of Donovan's men had been killed and hundreds had been wounded. Most of the casualties from Donovan's side had been Barolong and Chief Moroka II's two brothers had been killed in the battle. In contrast, the Basotho had lost only 16 men. Donovan's allied commando hastily retreated to Thaba 'Nchu and then returned to Bloemfontein, which was being flooded by many of the minor chiefs' people.

Even the Barolong moved from Thaba 'Nchu to Bloemfontein. There were so many refugees in Bloemfontein that Warden had to issue them with rations to prevent them from starving. In addition, all of the allies clamoured for compensation from Warden for their losses at Viervoet.

Meanwhile, the Basotho moved into the lands that had been occupied by the Barolong, the Korana and the coloureds and destroyed their kraals and seized their cattle. When Warden could not get men to volunteer for a commando, he applied to the government of Natal for assistance and the lieutenant governor there, Mr Pine, sent two companies of infantry of the 45th Regiment, comprising 172 soldiers, 17 Cape Mounted Rifles and 520 Zulu. Warden stationed the troops at Winburg but sent the Zulu to Moroka II to help protect the Barolong.

Moshoeshoe kept stating that he was not an enemy of the Queen of England but farms in the districts of Harrismith, Winburg, Caledon River and Bloemfontein that belonged to Boers who had assisted the British were being singled out for raids by the Basotho.[1361]

Meanwhile, Sir Harry Smith was being kept busy on all fronts. Another war between the colonists and the Xhosa had broken out in the Eastern Cape and the colony was rife with bitterness and resistance to the plans of the British Government to turn the Cape colony into a penal colony.[1362]

CHAPTER 39

Peace at last

In search of allies—Pretorius expresses desire for peace—outlawing of Pretorius annulled—Pretorius the peace negotiator—meeting planned for Sand River—Sand River Convention—Pretorius and Potgieter reconciled

Throughout this period of conflict in the Orange River Sovereignty, Pretorius had been in touch with Warden and with Moshoeshoe. On more than one occasion, emissaries from Moshoeshoe had visited Pretorius to request that he and the Boers join the Basotho in an uprising against the British. The chief even offered to take 20,000 warriors to attack the British in Natal if Pretorius gave him the word to proceed. Moreover, even the Boers' old foe, Mzilikazi, offered to join the battle with his Matabele warriors if Pretorius so wished. However, Pretorius was horrified at the thought of forming an alliance with either the Zulu or the Basotho against the British.

On 25 August 1851, 137 Boers requested that Pretorius take up the position of administrator general and restore peace and tranquillity to the ravaged area of the Orange River Sovereignty. The petition rapidly gathered support from Boers around the territory and was supported by Moshoeshoe.

Toward the end of the year, on 8 September 1851, it was decided at a sitting of the Boers' war cabinet that Pretorius should travel to the Orange River Sovereignty to see whether he could affect peace there. The following day, Pretorius wrote to Warden to explain that Boers from Wittebergen and the Sand River had requested that he negotiate a settlement on behalf of all of the people in the Orange River Sovereignty and informed the British resident that Moshoeshoe had appealed to him to use his influence to bring about peace and to act as a mediator between the Basotho and the British government. Pretorius recognized that this would also give him the opportunity to ensure that the relationship between the Boers over the Vaal River and the British remained on a good footing.[1363]

Warden was extremely wary of Pretorius, largely because he had heard rumours that Pretorius planned to attack Bloemfontein with a large force of Boers, and so asked Reverend Andrew Murray to keep him out of the Orange River Sovereignty. He also sent two men to keep a lookout at the Vaal River, in case the Boer leader crossed it with a commando.[1364]

The rumour about an imminent attack by the Boers had also reached Donovan and he ordered Captain Parish to abandon Winburg and to escort all of the loyalist families as well as their livestock to shelter in the Queen's Fort.

A group of Boers proceeded to Thaba Bosiu and concluded their own peace deal with Moshoeshoe, independently of Pretorius. They undertook not to get involved in any conflicts between the Basotho and the other tribes and only to take up arms against tribesmen if the boundaries between the land of the whites were transgressed.

Then, on 3 September 1851, an agreement was drawn up and signed by Moshoeshoe and his sons, Molapo, Masupha and Nehemiah, and by Boer representatives G.F. Linde and Jan Vermaak.[1365] Both sides honoured the agreement and the Basotho made a point of only raiding Boers who were sympathetic to the British government and its laws.

Pretorius was aware that certain Boers were intent on endangering the peace negotiations he had initiated and that they were trying to embroil him in a conflict. Consequently, he wrote to Warden and expressed his commitment to a lasting peace with the British on 4 September 1851.[1366]

The same day, Reverend Murray arrived at Mooi River to meet with Pretorius and later sent Warden a report that expressed his view that the majority of Boers longed for peace. He also recommended that Sir Harry Smith should remove the price on Pretorius's head. After the meeting, Pretorius wrote to the Boers at Wittebergen and the Sand River to explain that his appointment as administrator general was under consideration and that any "premature movement would be extremely risky".

He also wrote to the chiefs to explain that the poor condition of his horses prevented him from coming to meet with them immediately but that he was sending his son to explain matters and that they could bank that "all of the emigrants desire peace and friendship with the chiefs".

Shortly after this, Moshoeshoe wrote to Warden to defend the actions of his people at Viervoet. He claimed that the Basotho had killed Donovan's men in self-defence and that he was totally opposed to the stock theft and plundering that was taking place in the region. In fact, he blamed much of the stock losses on the presence of the Zulu warriors stationed at Thaba 'Nchu and stated that, "The rumours prevailing at Bloemfontein about intentions on my part to combine with other parties in a war against you, are altogether groundless".

On 10 October 1851, there was much excitement and speculation when Marthinus Pretorius and D. Botha arrived in Bloemfontein to meet with Warden, who offered to forward their proposals on how to establish peace in the Orange River Sovereignty to Sir Harry Smith. He still considered Pretorius to be dangerous and a rebel and was therefore reluctant to take any action that might jeopardize his career and good standing with the governor. By this time, the loyalist Boers who had fled to Queen's Fort began to drift back to Winburg, as they realized that Pretorius and the Boers over the Vaal River had few, if any, evil intentions.

Things were not going well for Sir Harry Smith. Reports had filtered back to Lord Grey, secretary of state for the colonies, in England that were critical of the governor's lack of knowledge on and understanding of the political situation north of the Orange River Sovereignty that had caused Moshoeshoe to lose all of the land there that he claimed was his. In essence, Sir Harry Smith was being blamed for the unrest in the area.

Grey acted swiftly and appointed two officials to the Orange River Sovereignty. Assistant Commissioners Captain William Hogge and Charles Mostyn Owen[1367] were tasked with putting matters right in the territory and were to begin making arrangements to annul the outlawing of Pretorius, which would enable the British government to negotiate with him without embarrassment.[1368]

Soon after Hogge and Owen arrived in Bloemfontein on 27 November 1851, 17 Wittebergen Boers under the leadership of M. Cauvin met with them to request that they not act aggressively toward the Transvaal Boers. They finally decided to comply with the Boers' request as they realized that it would be advantageous to have the support of the Transvaal Boers in the event that the Orange River Sovereignty needed military aid.[1369]

In the Orange River Sovereignty, Hogge and Owen soon discovered that the Boers that ignored the British resident's authority lived in peace while all other sectors of the community were involved in one form of strife or another. They also learned that Warden had been supplying arms and ammunition to bands of Griqua and coloureds and put a stop to this.

The Boers in the Winburg district were constantly being attacked and robbed. Consequently, Warden moved the Zulu stationed at Thaba 'Nchu to the area to help restore order there and Moroka II was left to fend for himself.

Grey wrote to Sir Harry Smith and accused him of acting rashly in his dealings with Moshoeshoe and of misleading the British government into believing that there was a need for the establishment of the Orange River Sovereignty.[1370]

The chaos continued to unfold in the region and many people used this time of instability to further their own political ambitions. Boer renegade, criminal and escaped convict Adriaan van der Kolff encouraged Moshoeshoe and the Basotho to rise up against the British.

He arrogantly depicted himself as "general" and "ruler" of the Basotho people and, recognizing the strength of Pretorius's name and reputation, he forged Pretorius's signature and sent a letter to Sekonyela that threatened him and his people with death and destruction if they dared to assist the British in any action against Moshoeshoe. In addition, he informed the Boers in the Orange River Sovereignty that he would lead them if Pretorius did not come to assist them with challenging the British.

Although the war council had asked Pretorius to negotiate a peace settlement, the Volksraad of Andries Ohrigstad had not approved this, which led Warden to suspect that Pretorius's intentions were not honourable. He commented, "What might be done in good faith one day would be condemned the next."

Pretorius hoped that the Volksraad would give him the go-ahead to conclude the peace negotiations during a meeting in Rustenburg on 10 December 1851. However, Potgieter and his Lydenburg and Zoutpansberg constituencies were not represented at this meeting. Potgeiter later wrote to Field Commandant Minnaar in the Magaliesberg to express his opposition to Pretorius being chosen to communicate with the British and Moshoeshoe on behalf of the Boers. He added that Pretorius would lead the Boers to ruin, as he had done in Natal, and pointed out that he had already concluded a truce with the British on behalf of the Boers north of the Vaal River and that there was no need for new agreements.[1371]

When Pretorius wrote to Potgieter to inform him that he intended to take as many people with him as possible to assist with the negotiations, he sniped that it was likely that the British would have occupied the Transvaal if they were not engaged in frontier wars with the Xhosa and emphasized that he was determined to conclude a peaceful solution with the British rather than to initiate another conflict with them.

On 10 January 1852, five of the six members of the Lydenburg Volksraad met. They approved the decision of the war council to appoint Pretorius as peace negotiator but stipulated that any agreement would have to acknowledge the Volksraad as the highest authority in the Orange River Sovereignty and that Pretorius would have to report to the Volksraad. They also specified that Pretorius must reach agreement on that the Vaal River would replace the boundary of the 25th parallel of latitude.

Soon after this, Pretorius dispatched two men to Bloemfontein with a letter for Warden that requested that a meeting be arranged between Hogge and Owen. As a result, Pretorius finally received approval from the Volksraad on 10 January 1852 that he and his 15 delegates could begin negotiations with the British. However, it was stressed that any terms would need to be ratified at a full meeting of the Volksraad. Pretorius immediately wrote to Moshoeshoe to invite him to attend the meeting with the assistant commissioners at Sand River on 16 January 1852.[1372] Hogge and Owen then released a proclamation from Smith, rescinding those of July and September 1848 in which Pretorius and others had been declared outlaws. The meeting would be held at Piet Venter's farm, which was about ten kilometres from the confluence of the Sand River and Coal Spruit, or halfway between Winburg and the present-day town of Kroonstad. As word of the meeting spread, so the interest in it grew and many Boers set off for the venue from far-flung places. As it was certain that there would be a good turnout from the public, some traders in the Sand River area even converted their wagons into *winkels* (shops). At the farm, the Boer delegation created a laager with their 50 wagons while the two assistant commissioners and their armed escort pitched several tents. Pretorius soon arrived with 300 supporters from across the Vaal River and, on 15 January 1842, a large crowd of Boers from the Sand River and Wittebergen districts was seen approaching the farm. While Pretorius's supporters had been excited about the meeting, the new arrivals were solemn. They had good reason to be glum: unlike the Transvaal Boers, they were still hankering to be recognized by the British as free people.

Hogge soon heard that this group was being led by Van der Kolff, the man who had forged Pretorius's name, and instructed Pretorius to arrest him. However, Pretorius said that he had no jurisdiction in the Orange River Sovereignty. "I will give you the necessary authority and provide you with men to arrest him," Hogge told him.

Pretorius was reluctant to offend any of the Boers but had no choice but to do as Hogge had instructed. As such, he returned to the Boer camp with Mr Owen and two British lancers to arrest Van der Kolff. When they rode into the camp, some Boers protested the presence of the soldiers and Owen quickly dismissed the men, as he realized that their presence was aggravating a potentially volatile situation. Before Pretorius could formally arrest Van der Kolff, some of his followers gave him a horse and urged him to flee. A few hundred metres from the wagons, Van der Kolff turned and pointed his musket at Pretorius, who shouted that he needed to come closer to make good on his shot.

Van der Kolff decided to rather make his getaway and the lancers set off after him, followed by a crowd of excitable Boers. His pursuers gave up the chase as he had too great a lead on them. The Boers in the camp made it clear that they did not welcome the British there and Pretorius intervened, shouting that if any Boer was rude or unpleasant to the British, he would be asked to leave camp.

Owen and Hogge had both been apprehensive that Pretorius would orchestrate an alliance between the Transvaalers, the Boers in the Orange River Sovereignty and Moshoeshoe and the incident with Van der Kolff allayed their fears. It was patently clear to the Orange River Sovereignty Boers that Pretorius was not prepared to fight the British on their behalf and that his interests were north of the Vaal River. He confirmed their suspicions when he said, "I cannot do anything for you, unless you cross the Vaal River." [1373]Many did exactly that after the meeting.

A great number of the Boers from the Orange River Sovereignty made their way to the assistant commissioners' tents when they realized that no help would be forthcoming from Pretorius and apologized for opposing the British.

Although they had hoped that they would not be considered rebels by the British, Hogge and Owen would not guarantee them immunity from prosecution or fines.[1374]

Van der Kolff's undignified departure worried Moshoeshoe's representative and councillor, Joshua, particularly as Van der Kolff was a Basotho agent acting on behalf of Moshoeshoe. The fact that his Boer 'supporters' had not put up any form of resistance to protect him prompted Joshua to leave the farm with his attendants. Realizing that Joshua may have believed that the Transvaal Boers would form an alliance with the British against Moshoeshoe and the Basotho, Pretorius sent two messengers to Moshoeshoe to appraise him of the true situation among the Boers.

While Pretorius's scouts and guards around the Boer camp perimeter kept an eye out for Van der Kolff, Hogge and Owen sent for reinforcements, in case the troublemaker returned with an army of brigand Korana.

On the morning of 16 January, the Boer delegation met with Hogge and Owen. Reverend Andrew Murray, trusted by the Boers and the British, acted as translator[1375] After opening prayers, Pretorius argued that the Winburg district should be included in the negotiations but Hogge and Owen disagreed and overruled him. As a compromise, Pretorius then proposed that all of the Boers who had taken up arms against the British in the Orange River Sovereignty be granted a general amnesty. This request was refused and, as a result, many Boers came to look upon Pretorius as "a traitor and deserter of their cause".

Hogge and Owen also declined his suggestion that he should act as an arbitrator between the British and Moshoeshoe, as they did not want to allow him the chance to increase his standing among the Boers or Basotho people, lest he "appropriate the credit of bringing about a pacification and enhance his own consequence thereby".[1376] Much debate ensued but, finally, the agreement known as the Sand River Convention was signed on 17 January 1852 by Hogge, Owen, Pretorius and his 15 delegates.

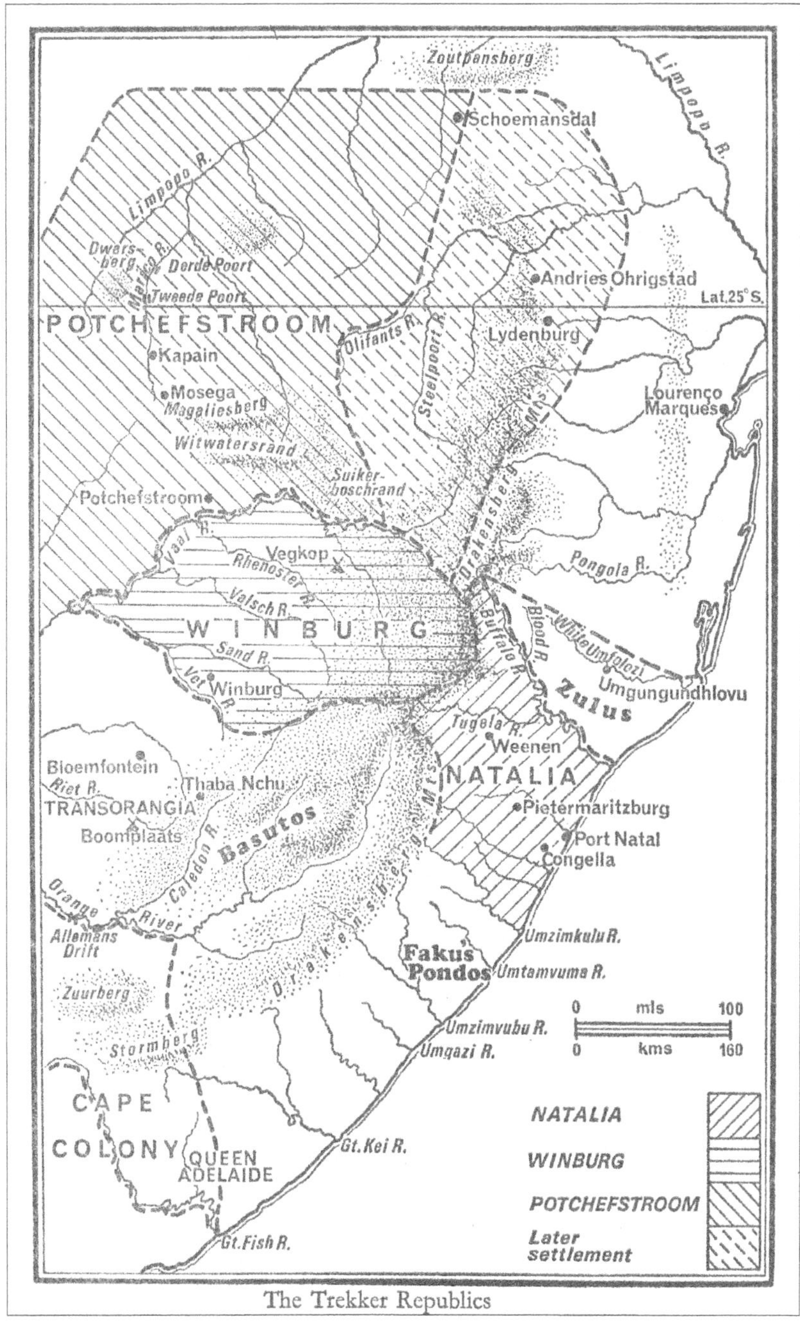

The Trekker Republics

It effectively put an end to Pretorius's influence south of the Vaal River, which was a big blow to the Boers in the Orange River Sovereignty, who had seen Pretorius as "a martyr to his patriotism". Compromises had been made on both sides. For instance, the British and Boers agreed that a system of "non-interference" and mutual benefits for travellers and traders who weren't providing arms and ammunition to local tribes would be allowed on both sides of the Vaal River. In addition, Hogge and Owen approved a clause disclaiming all alliances with the coloured people north of the Vaal River, while the Boers agreed not to tolerate slavery in their country. Both parties also agreed that, "as far as possible", there would be reciprocal recognition and enforcement of criminal and civil processes.[1377]

The Sand River Convention "guaranteed in the fullest manner, on the part of the British Government, to the emigrant farmers beyond the Vaal River, the right to manage their own affairs, and to govern themselves, according to their own laws, without any interference from the British Government, and that no encroachment shall be made by the said Government on the territory beyond to the north of the Vaal River".[1378]

Many of the Boers wept at the end of proceedings with the realization that they had finally achieved the goal for which so many miles, marked by the graves of many of their children, had been walked; for which so much pain had been suffered and so much blood spilled. They finally had their freedom ... and peace. Weather-beaten faces cracked into smiles as tears of relief and joy trickled down leathery cheeks.

It was not long before the assistant commissioners started chairing hearings in the Orange River Sovereignty and imposing fines and punishment on the Boers there for a range of 'crimes'. Most readily signed confessions of guilt and paid their fines. The heaviest fine, imposed on J.D. Cilliers, was for £150 but was later reduced to £100 when he pleaded that he had only participated in the rebellion against the British because he had been afraid of Pretorius and that he "was the father of ten motherless beings". These hearings led to an increase in the number of Boers crossing the Vaal River into the newly independent lands of the Transvaal. The terms of the Sand River Convention still had to be approved by the Volksraad and the people and Pretorius scheduled a mass meeting in Rustenburg for 16 March 1852. From the beginning of March 1852, the Boers' wagons and horses began to arrive in Rustenburg and, on 11 March 1852, Potgieter's arrival was heralded by a gun salute. Pretorius only arrived the day before the meeting. While Pretorius had many detractors—many of whom were led by Potgieter—he also had strong support in the form of Commandant Kruger. Significantly,

Kruger had once been a Potgieter supporter and had written to Potgieter to urge him to attend the meeting so that he could establish for himself what had been achieved with the Sand River Convention.[1379]

Men arrived at the *raadsaal* carrying weapons. The air was heavy with anticipation. It appeared as though a clash between the two forceful personalities was likely: there was a very good chance of a burgher war. Consultations had been taking place between the leaders and their respective advisers, with darkness providing a thick cloak of anonymity to the elders who had visited Potgieter offering their advice.

In the early hours of the morning, the last of the elders left Pretorius's tent. Despite the early hour, a large crowd of anxious Boers had assembled. In the soft morning light, Pretorius emerged from his tent. He strode to Potgieter's tent watched by the tense crowd of Boers. He entered the tent. The crowd stood quietly by, whispering and waiting.

As the sun rose higher and basked the land in its gentle warmth, the tent flaps of Potgieter's tent were flung open. The two leaders, Potgieter and Pretorius, stood behind a table on which lay a large family Bible.

The watching crowd cheered and shouts of joy erupted, as they saw the two men standing together, smiling. Calloused hands clasped together in friendship. The two leaders had made peace.

They had finally all come home.

Notes

1. Theal, George McCall. *History and Ethnography of South Africa Before 1795*, Swan Sonnenschein & Co., Lim, Bloomsbury, 1907 p. 12
2. Ibid p. 36.
3. Ibid pp. 29-33. *See also* Mostert, Noël. *Frontiers*, Jonathan Cape. Pimlico edition, London. 1993 pp. 62-69; Theal, George McCall. 1919. *Ethnography and Condition of South Africa Before A.D. 1505*. G. Allen & Unwin Ltd 1919, London pp. 143-162; Holden, William Clifford. *The Past and Future of the Kaffir Races*, *Africana Collectanea Vol III*, C. Struik, Cape Town, 1963 pp. 1-6
4. Theal pp. 19-23
5. Ibid p. 12
6. Elphick, Richard. *Kraal and Castle: Khoikhoi and the Founding of White South Africa*, Yale University Press, New Haven and London, 1977 p. 34
7. Raven-Hart, Rowland. *The Diary of Johann Jakob Merklein, 1653*. Cape Good Hope, p. 8
8. Gardiner, Allen Francis. 1836, *Narrative of a Journey to the Zoolu Country: In South Africa*, Struik. Cape Town, 1966 p. 106
9. Wright, John Kirtland. 2011, *The Geographical Lore of the Time of the Crusades: A Study in the History of Medieval Science and Tradition in Western Europe*, American Geographical Society, Research Series No. 15 Literary Licensing, LLC, 2011, p. 119
10. Theal p. 201
11. Ibid p. 202
12. Ibid p. 201
13. Ibid p. 202
14. Ibid p. 312
15. Welch, Sidney R. 1949, *South Africa under John III, 1521-1557*, Juta, Cape Town, 1948 p. 311
16. Theal p. 203
17. Ibid p. 202
18. Ibid p. 204
19. Ibid p. 204
20. Ibid p. 204
21. Ibid p. 204
22. Ibid p. 204
23. Ibid p. 204
24. Mostert, Noël. *Frontiers*, Jonathan Cape. Pimlico edition, London. 1993 p. 22
25. Ibid p. 22
26. Ibid p. 22
27. Theal p 206
28. Mostert p. 36
29. Ibid p. 206
30. Raven-Hart p. 2
31. Ibid p.2
32. Theal p. 210
33. Ibid p. 211
34. Ibid p. 211
35. Ibid p. 212
36. Ibid p. 213
37. Ibid p. 212
38. Welch p. 63
39. Theal p. 213
40. Ibid p. 213
41. Raven-Hart p. 3
42. Theal p. 213
43. Ibid p. 214
44. Ibid p. 214
45. Ibid p. 214
46. Raven-Hart p. 3
47. Theal p. 215
48. Ibid p. 214
49. Ibid p. 215
50. Ibid p. 216
51. Ibid p. 216
52. Ibid p. 216
53. Ibid p. 217
54. Ibid p. 218
55. Ibid p. 218
56. Ibid p. 219
57. Ibid p. 219
58. Ibid p. 219
59. Mostert p. 38
60. Ibid p. 219
61. Ibid p. 219
62. Ibid p. 219
63. Ibid p. 219,
64. Mostert p. 39
65. Theal p. 219
66. Ibid p. 220
67. Ibid p. 220
68. Ibid p. 220
69. Ibid p. 220
70. Ibid p. 227
71. Mostert p. 83
72. Elphick p. 74
73. Theal p. 240.
74. Mostert p. 83
75. Ibid p. 85
76. Theal p. 255
77. Ibid p. 256
78. Ibid p. 256
79. Ibid p. 257
80. Ibid p. 257
81. Mostert, Noël, *Frontiers* p. 86
82. Theal p. 257
83. Ibid p. 258
84. Mostert p. 87
85. Turner, Malcolm. *Shipwrecks & Salvage In South Africa: 1505 To The Present*, C. Struik. Cape Town, 1988 p. 121

86. Mostert p. 87
87. Ibid p. 90
88. Ibid p. 90
89. Elphick p. 74
90. Ibid p. 77
91. Ibid p. 79
92. Ibid p. 79
93. Ibid p. 79
94. Mostert p. 92.
95. Raven-Hart, Major R. *Before van Riebeeck*. Martin Pring p. 69
96. Mostert p. 93
97. Ibid p. 93
98. Elphick p. 80
99. Theal p. 426
100. Mostert p. 93
101. Theal p. 426
102. Ibid p. 427
103. Theal pp. 428-429
104. Raven-Hart. p. 137
105. Elphick pp. 84-85.
106. Raven-Hart p. 166
107. Ibid p. 169
108. Ibid p. 170
109. Ibid p. 172
110. Mostert p. 97
111. Ibid p. 103
112. Ibid p. 103
113. Ibid p. 103
114. Mostert p. 99
115. Raven-Hart p. 43
116. *Illustrated History of South Africa: The Real Story*, Reader's Digest, Cape Town, 1988 p. 36
117. SA History on line
118. Giliomee, Hermann & Mbenga, Bernard. *New History of South Africa*, Tafelberg, Cape Town, 2007 p. 46
119. Elphick p. 104
120. Ibid p. 46
121. Mostert p. 122
122. Raven-Hart. R. *Cape Good Hope*, A.A. Balkema, Cape Town, 1971, p. 3
123. Worden, Nigel; van Heyningen, Elizabeth & Bickford-Smith, Vivian. *The Making of a City*, David Philip, Cape Town, 1998 p. 32
124. Mostert p. 124
125. Ibid p. 127
126. De Kock, Victor. *Those In Bondage*, George Allen & Unwin, Ltd. London, 1950 p. 16
127. Boeseken, A.J. *Slaves and Free Blacks at the Cape 1658-1700* p. 8
128. Ibid p. 9
129. Heese, H.F. *Groep Sonder Grense: Huwelike en Ander Verbintenisse Tussen Europeers en Gekleurdes* p. 5
130. Ibid p. 16
131. Giliomee, Herman & Mbengu, Bernard. *New History of South Africa*. p. 46
132. Mostert p. 126
133. Ibid p. 130
134. Ibid p. 128
135. Elphick p. 105
136. Mostert, *Frontiers*. p 128
137. Elphick p. 102
138. Giliomee & Mbenga p. 20
139. Worden, van Heyningen & Bickford-Smith p 20
140. Elphick p. 110
141. Ibid p. 115
142. Mostert p. 131
143. Elphick p. 103
144. Ibid p. 106
145. Mostert p. 131
146. Ibid p. 107
147. Ibid p. 109
148. Mostert p. 132
149. Elphick p. 112
150. Ibid p. 112
151. Mostert p. 134
152. Ibid p. 134
153. Mostert p. 132; *see also* Elphick p. 112
154. Mostert p. 134
155. Elphick p. 113
156. Mostert p. 134
157. Theal, *Vol II* p. 122
158. Elphick p. 221
159. Worden, van Heyningen & Bickford-Smith p. 30
160. Elphick p. 201
161. Mostert p. 143
162. SA History on line. Van Riebeeck, left 7 May 1662
163. Elphick p. 202
164. Ibid p. 202
165. Ibid p. 202
166. Ibid p. 202
167. Worden, van Heyningen & Bickford-Smith p. 28
168. Theal, *Vol II* p. 125
169. Ibid p. 127
170. Ibid p. 127
171. Elphick p. 221
172. Ibid p. 223
173. Worden, van Heyningen & Bickford-Smith p. 32
174. Elphick p. 223
175. Ibid p. 224
176. Theale, *Vol II* p. 143
177. Worden, van Heyningen & Bickford-Smith p 38
178. Theal, *Vol II*. p. 143
179. Ibid p. 165
180. Ibid p. 169
181. Ibid p. 169
182. Ibid p. 169.

183. Ransford, Oliver, *The Great Trek*. John Murray, London, 1972 p. 4
184. Theal, *Vol II* p. 183
185. Ibid p. 191
186. Ibid p. 195
187. Ibid p. 203
188. Ibid pp. 203-205
189. Ibid p. 206
190. Theal, *Vol II* p. 204
191. Ibid p. 204
192. Ibid p 212
193. Ibid p. 214
194. Ibid p. 214
195. Elphick p. 130
196. Theal, *Vol II* p. 215
197. Ibid p. 225
198. Ibid p. 245
199. Ibid p. 245
200. Ibid p. 245
201. Ibid p. 246
202. Ibid p. 247
203. Ibid p. 248
204. Ibid p. 248.
205. Internet reference. Marco Ramerini: 'The Dutch in South Africa 1652–1795; 1802–1806'.
206. Theal, *Vol II* p. 249
207. Ibid p. 249
208. Ibid p. 270
209. Ibid p. 273
210. Ibid p. 273
211. Ibid p. 279
212. Elphick p. 137
213. Theal, *Vol II* p. 291
214. Ibid p. 291
215. Ibid p. 291
216. Ibid p. 292
217. Ibid p. 293.
218. Ibid p. 294
219. Ibid p. 294
220. Ibid p. 295
221. Ibid p. 295
222. Ibid p. 296
223. Ibid p. 302
224. Mostert p. 150
225. Davenport, Rodney & Saunders, Christopher. *South Africa: A Modern History* p. 11
226. Theal, *Vol I* p. 55
227. Soga, J.P. *The Ama-Xhosa: Life and Customs*, Lovedale Press p. 9
228. Morris, Donald R. *Washing of the Spears*, Pimlico, London, 1965 p. 25
229. Ibid p. 26
230. Ibid p. 26
231. Soga p. 10
232. Ibid p. 17
233. Ibid pp. 18-21
234. Milton, John. *Edges of War: A History of Frontier Wars 1702–1878,* Juta & Co, Ltd, Cape Town p. 11
235. Ibid p 13
236. Ibid p. 14
237. Soga p. 6
238. Internet site, www.tutufoundation.uk: "A person is only a person through other people. It is about the essence of being human, it is part of the gift that Africa will give to the world. It embraces hospitality, caring about others, being able to go the extra mile for the sake of others. We believe that a person is a person through another person, that my humanity is caught up, bound up, inextricably, with yours. When I dehumanise you, I inexorably dehumanize myself."
239. Theal *Vol II* p. 337
240. Ibid p. 341. 'They embarked in the ships *Wapen van Altemeyer* and *Zion'*. *See* list pp. 242-243.
241. Ibid p. 346
242. Mentzel, O.F. *Life at the Cape in the Mid-eighteenth Century: The Biography of Rudolph Siegfried Alleman*. Van Riebeeck Society, Cape Town, 1919 p. 92
243. Theal, *Vol II* p. 371
244. Ibid p. 377
245. Mostert p. 160. *See also* Theal, *Vol III* p. 396
246. Theal, *Vol III* p. 401
247. Ibid p. 403
248. Ibid p. 404
249. Ibid p. 405
250. Ibid p. 406
251. Ibid p. 406
252. Ibid p. 407
253. Ibid p. 409
254. Ibid p. 410
255. Ibid p. 431
256. Ibid p. 432
257. Ibid p. 433
258. Ibid p. 448
259. Ibid p. 452
260. Ibid p. 486
261. Mentzel p. 85
262. Ibid p. 87
263. Ibid p. 87
264. Theal, *Vol III* p. 493
265. Ibid p. 494
266. Ibid p. 496
267. Ibid p. 497
268. Ibid p. 497
269. Ibid p. 504
270. Ibid p. 506
271. Ibid p. 507
272. Ibid p. 507
273. Ibid p. 507
274. Mostert, p. 162

275. Mentzel p. 130
276. Theal, *Vol III* p. 508
277. Theal, *Vol III* p. 20
278. Ibid pp. 32-33
279. Ibid p. 39
280. Ibid pp. 57-58
281. Ibid pp. 101-102
282. Mostert p. 168
283. Ibid p. 174
284. Ibid p. 174
285. Ibid p. 174
286. Ibid p. 178
287. Ibid pp. 177-179. *See also* Raper, Peter E. & Boucher, Maurice. *Robert Jacob Gordon Cape Travels 1777–1786* p. 294
288. Mostert p. 179,
289. Gardiner, A.F. *Narrative of a Journey to The Zoolu Country in South Africa*, C. Struik, Cape Town, 1966 p. 106
290. Mostert p. 218
291. Ibid p. 219
292. Ibid p. 219
293. Ibid p. 221
294. Ibid p. 223
295. Mostert p. 230
296. Penn, Nigel, *The Forgotten Frontier*, Double Storey Books, Cape Town, 2005 pp. 136-137
297. Theal, *Vol III* p. 174
298. Cape Archives. GR 1/9. Letter from inhabitants of Zuurveld, 11August 1788.
299. Mostert p. 224
300. Theal, *Vol III* p 178
301. Ibid p. 213
302. Ibid p. 213
303. Ibid p. 213
304. Mostert p. 238
305. Ibid p. 244
306. Ibid p. 245
307. Ibid p. 249
308. Ibid p. 250
309. Theal, *Vol III*. p. 239
310. Ibid p. 239
311. Mostert p. 265
312. Ibid p. 252
313. Theal, *Vol III* pp. 240-241
314. Mostert p. 257
315. Raper & Boucher p. 27.
316. Theal, *Vol III* p. 270
317. Worden, van Heyningen & Bickford-Smith p. 86
318. Theal, *Vol III* p. 277
319. Raper & Boucher p. 25
320. Theal, *Vol I* p. 10
321. Theal, *Vol I* p. 10
322. Ibid p. 16
323. Ibid p. 18
324. Mostert p. 261
325. Milton, *The Edges of War* p. 38
326. Ibid p. 39
327. Raper & Boucher. Reference farmers found on travels
328. Theal, *Vol I* p. 39
329. Mostert p. 278
330. Ibid p. 289
331. Ibid p. 289
332. Ibid p. 290
333. Theal, *Vol I* pp. 58-59.
334. Mostert p. 291
335. Theal, *Vol I* p. 58,
336. Lenta, Margaret & le Cordeur, Basil. *The Cape Diaries of Lady Anne Barnard, 1799–1800, Vol I*, Van Riebeeck Society, Cape Town, 1999 p. 149
337. Elphick, Richard & Gilomee, Herman, *The Shaping Of South Africa*, Maskew Miller Longman, 1990 p. 111
338. Ibid p. 114
339. Ibid p. 119
340. Ibid p. 122
341. Ibid p. 216
342. Ibid p. 126
343. Ibid p. 195
344. De Kock, Victor, *Those in Bondage*, George Allen & Unwin Ltd, London, 1950 p. 119
345. Ibid p. 122
346. Ibid p. 124
347. Ibid p. 115
348. Ibid p. 118
349. Elphick & Giliomee p. 197
350. Heese p. 41.
351. De Kock p. 42-43.
352. Ibid p. 43
353. Elphick & Giliomee pp. 197 & 216
354. De Kock p.146.
355. Elphick & Giliomee pp. 120-122; Penn p. 215
356. Penn p. 215
357. Penn pp. 210-213
358. Mostert p. 288
359. Ibid p. 288
360. Skotness, Pippa, *Claim To The Country: The Archive of Wilhelm Bleek and Lucy Lloyd* pp. 98, 103
361. Ibid p. 99
362. Ibid p. 99
363. Mostert p. 294
364. Peires, J.B. *The House of Phalo* p. 52
365. Lenta & Le Cordeur p. 149
366. Mostert p. 307
367. Peires p. 77
368. Mostert p. 309
369. Mostert p. 307
370. Ibid p. 323
371. Mostert pp. 324-325

372. Worden, van Heyningen & Bickford-Smith p. 86
373. Mostert p. 326
374. Ibid p. 328
375. Ibid p. 330
376. Legassick, Martin. *The Struggle For The Eastern Cape, 1800-1854* p. 7
377. Mostert p. 337
378. Ibid p. 341
379. Theal, *Vol I* pp. 197-199
380. Worden, van Heyningen & Bickford-Smith p. 89
381. Mostert p 361
382. Ibid pp. 369-375
383. Ibid p. 375
384. Human Sciences Research Council. *Dictionary of of South African Biography. Vol I* p. 510
385. Mostert p. 381
386. Ibid p. 384
387. Theal, *Vol I* p. 256
388. Dracopoli, J.L. *Sir Andries Stockenström: The Origins of Racial Conflict In Southern Africa, 1792–1864*, A.A. Balkema, Cape Town, 1969 p. 27
389. Ibid p. 290
390. Ibid p. 292
391. Ibid p. 299
392. Peires p. 63
393. Mostert pp. 465-466
394. Peires p. 63
395. Mostert p. 467
396. Theal, *Vol I* p. 381
397. Mostert p. 472
398. Ibid p. 474
399. Theal, *Vol I* p. 319
400. Sheffield. T. *The Story of the Settlement* p. 121
401. Mitford-Barberton, Ivan. *Commandant Holden Bowker* p. 20
402. Theal, *Vol I* p. 356
403. Mostert p. 533
404. Pringle. Thomas, *Narrative of a Residence in South Africa*
405. Hockly, Harold Edward. *Story of the 1820 Settlers*, Juta, Cape Town, 1957 p. 57
406. Mostert p. 554
407. Cory, G.E. *The Rise of South Africa, Vol II* p. 69
408. Hockly p. 81
409. Gledhill, Eily & Jack. *In the Steps of Piet Retief*, Human & Rousseau, Cape Town, 1980 p. 15
410. Preller, Gustav S. *Piet Retief*, Nasionale Pers, Kaapstad, 1920 p. 2
411. Nathan, Manfred. *The Voortrekkers of South Africa*, CNA/Gordon & Gotch Ltd, Johannesburg, 1933, p. 40
412. Preller p. 2 & Ransford p. 43
413. Preller p. 9
414. Gledhill p. 68
415. Theal. *Vol I* p. 389
416. Ibid p. 390
417. Cory, *Vol II* p. 182
418. Pringle p. 189
419. Hockly p. 81
420. Mostert p. 565
421. Ibid p. 576
422. Dracopoli p. 62.
423. Ibid p. 64,
424. Ibid p. 68
425. Theal, *Vol I* p. 426
426. Mostert p. 896
427. Mostert p. 589
428. Ibid p. 591
429. Macmillan, W.M. *Bantu, Boer and Briton: The Making of the South African Native Problem*, Faber & Gwyer, London p. 76
430. Mostert p. 615
431. Mostert p. 618
432. Mostert p. 620
433. Ibid p. 622
434. HSRC, *Vol I* p. 802
435. Le Roux. T.H. *Die Dagboek van Louis Trichardt*, J.L. Van Schaik, Pretoria, 1966, pp. xiv-xv
436. Mostert p. 630
437. Muller, C.F.J. *Die Britse Owerheid en die Groot Trek* p. 55
438. Muller, C.F.J., *Die Oorsprong van die Groot Trek* p. 337
439. HSRC, *Vol III* p. 123
440. Gledhill p. 108
441. Ibid p. 110
442. Mostert p. 636
443. Norval, E.J.G., *Bloed Sweet en Trane*, Bienedell Uitgewers, Pretoria, 2002 p. 64
444. HSRC, *Vol IV* p. 670
445. HSRC *Vol I* p. 634
446. Ransford p. 30
447. HSRC, *Vol IV* p. 670
448. Preller p. 276
449. Norval p. 65
450. Ibid p. 66
451. HSRC, *Vol IV* p. 670
452. Le Roux p. xv
453. Preller p. 6
454. Theal, George Mc Call. *History of the Boers in South Africa* p. 71
455. Raper & Boucher p. 126.
456. Cory, *Vol II* p. 463
457. Ibid p. 461
458. Mostert p. 646
459. Theal, *Vol II* p. 75
460. Cory, *Vol III* p. 56
461. Ibid p. 57
462. Theal, *Vol II* p. 89
463. Gledhill p. 116

464. Hockly pp. 87, 120
465. Liebenberg p. 12
466. Gledhill p. 17
467. Ibid p. 117
468. Mitford-Barberton p. 80
469. Ibid p. 89
470. Mostert p. 667
471. Gledhill p 118
472. Ibid p. 119
473. Ibid p. 121
474. Mitford-Barbeton p, 89.
475. Rivett-Carnac, D.E. *Hawk's Eye* p. 96
476. Mostert p. 896; Cory, *Vol III* p. 94; Rivett-Carnac p. 132
477. Cory, *Vol III* p. 93
478. Rivett-Carnac p. 96,
479. Mostert p. 677
480. Dracopoli p. 96
481. Cory, *Vol III* p. 96
482. Theal, *Vol II* p. 95
483. Cory, *Vol III* p. 103
484. Mostert p. 685
485. Ibid p. 686
486. Ibid p. 691
487. Cory, *Vol III* p. 123
488. Mitford-Barbeton p. 117
489. Ibid p. 119
490. Ibid p. 117
491. Mostert p. 712
492. Mitford-Barberton p. 128
493. Ibid p. 131
494. Ibid p. 129
495. Ibid p. 130
496. Cory, *Vol III* p. 142
497. Ibid p. 142
498. Mitford-Barberton p. 130
499. Mostert p. 722
500. Cory, *Vol III* p. 15
501. Mostert p. 725
502. Cory, *Vol III* p. 154
503. Mostert p. 725
504. Ibid p. 726
505. Cory, *Vol III* p. 156
506. Ibid p. 173
507. Theal, *Vol II* p. 122
508. Mostert p. 733
509. Ibid p. 738
510. Ibid p. 740
511. Theal, *Vol II* p. 123
512. Mostert p. 746
513. Franken, J.L.M., *Piet Retief: Sy Lewe in die Kolonie* p. 325
514. Cory, *Vol III* p. 220
515. Mostert p. 755
516. Gledhill p. 122
517. Cory, *Vol III* p. 42
518. Theal, *Vol II.* p. 143
519. Dracopoli p. 110
520. Mostert p. 782.
521. Muller p. 354
522. Ransford p. 34
523. Meintjies, Johannes. *The Voortrekkers* p. 29
524. Muller p. 355
525. Ibid p. 357
526. Muller p. 361
527. Ibid p. 362
528. Meintjies p. 46
529. Ransford p. 35
530. Muller p. 357
531. Ransford p. 37
532. Ibid p. 40
533. Ibid p. 42
534. Ibid p. 42
535. Nathan p. 95
536. Ibid p. 96
537. Ransford p. 46
538. HSRC, *Vol IV* p. 83
539. Meintjies p. 45
540. Gledhill p. 125
541. Cory, *Vol III* p. 263
542. Ibid p. 265
543. Ibid p. 268
544. Nathan p. 140
545. Mostert p. 807
546. Preller p. 122
547. Meintjies, p. 46
548. Ibid p. 47
549. Preller p. 122
550. Ibid p. 123
551. Ransford p. 64
552. Nathan p. 141
553. Ibid p 142
554. Norval p. 82
555. Gerdener p. 28
556. Meinties p. 209
557. Ibid p. 32
558. Cory, *Vol III* p. 271
559. Ibid p. 327
560. Ibid p. 328
561. Norval p. 83
562. Cory, *Vol III* p. 334
563. Mostert p. 790
564. Cory, *Vol III* p. 342
565. Norval p. 90
566. Ibid pp. 85-88; Theal, *Vol III* pp. 289-290
567. HSRC *Vol I* p. 511
568. Norval p. 90
569. Ibid p. 91
570. Gerdener p. 30
571. Meintjies p. 54

572. Cape Archives. Gov. Stockenström dispatches received, 8/1
573. Gerdener p. 33
574. Ransford p. 70
575. Nathan p. 147
576. HSRC, *Vol II* p. 403
577. Meintjies p. 54.
578. Ransford p. 72
579. Preller p. 126
580. Meintjies p. 57
581. Ibid p. 57
582. Norval p. 96
583. Ibid p. 96
584. Gerdener p. 37
585. Ibid p. 37
586. Nathan p. 148
587. Gerdener p. 38
588. Norval p. 101
589. Meintjies p. 59
590. Ransford p. 76
591. Holy Bible, Psalm 118
592. Preller p. 32
593. Ransford p. 77
594. Preller p. 32
595. Norval p. 108
596. Ibid p. 105
597. HSRC, *Vol I* p. 509
598. HSRC, *Vol I* pp. 510-511; Meintjies p. 61
599. HSRC, *Vol I* p. 728
600. Ibid pp. 510-511
601. Meintjies p. 63
602. HSRC, *Vol I* pp. 802-803
603. Le Roux p. 13
604. Norval p. 109
605. Schoon, H.F. *The Diary of Erasmus Smit*, C. Struik, Cape Town, 1972 p. 2
606. Ibid p. 4
607. Gledhill pp. 133-135
608. Cape Town Archives. Stockenström Memorials, 8/1 p. 224
609. Gledhill pp. 136-139
610. Ibid p. 142
611. Ibid p. 143
612. Ibid p. 150
613. Cape Town Archives. Stockenström Memorial
614. Ibid. Letter, 3 November 1837
615. Gledhill p. 140
616. Ibid p. 141.
617. Schoon p. 6
618. Cory, *Vol III* p. 364
619. HSRC, *Vol I* p. 511
620. Schoon p. 6
621. Norval p. 109
622. Schoon p. 9
623. Ibid pp. 10-11
624. Norval p. 121
625. Nathan p. 155.
626. Norval p. 122
627. Ransford p. 80
628. Kotze. D.J. *Letters of the American Missionaries,1835–1838* p. 154
629. Meintjies p. 67
630. Norval p. 125
631. Ransford p. 80
632. Schoon p. 20
633. Ibid p. 24
634. Meintjies p. 72
635. Schoon p. 25
636. Ibid p. 18
637. Ibid p. 28
638. Meintjies p. 75
639. Schoon p. 31
640. Ibid p. 32
641. Norval p. 128
642. HSRC, *Vol I* p 803
643. Nathan p. 102
644. Ibid p. 105
645. Ibid p. 110
646. Le Roux p. 150
647. Ibid p. 170
648. Gledhill p. 160
649. Cory, *Vol III* p. 403
650. Meintjies, p.76
651. Cory p. 401
652. Gledhill p. 166
653. Schoon p. 41
654. Ibid p. 41
655. Preller p. 119
656. Schoon p. 42
657. Ibid p. 42
658. Preller p. 113
659. Gledhill p. 169
660. Schoon pp. 45-47
661. Meintjies p. 76
662. Preller p. 121
663. Schoon p. 49
664. Meintjies p. 79
665. Schoon p. 48
666. Gledhill p. 171
667. Schoon p. 52
668. Walker, Eric. *The Great Trek* p. 146
669. Schoon p. 52
670. Norval p. 130
671. Meintjies p. 79
672. Pretorius, C. Celastine. *Op Trek* p. 24
673. Meintjies p. 82
674. Norval p. 133
675. Meintjies p. 83
676. Meintjies pp. 84-86
677. Norval p. 131

678. Meintjies pp. 84-86
679. Norval p. 164
680. Schoon p. 57
681. Norval p. 167
682. Walker p. 148
683. Bird, John. *Annals of Natal, Vol I*, P. Davis & Sons, Pietermaritzburg, 1888 p. 368
684. Gardiner p. 4
685. Ibid p. 35
686. Ibid p. 68
687. Ibid p. 77
688. Ibid p. 82
689. Ibid p. 82
690. Ibid p. 108.
691. Ibid p. 127.
692. Ibid p. 173
693. Ibid p. 192
694. Ibid p. 219
695. Ibid p. 212
696. Ibid p. 392
697. Ibid p. 394
698. HSRC, *Vol II* p. 527
699. Ibid, *Vol V* p. 897
700. Stuart, James & McK.Malcolm, D. *The Diary of Henry Francis Fynn*, Shuter & Shooter, Pietermaritzburg, 1969 p. 263
701. Cory, G.E.O. *Owen's Diary*, Van Riebeeck Society, Cape Town, 1926 p. 40
702. Morris, Donald R. *The Washing Of The Spears*, pp. 131-138
703. Bird, *Vol I*, p. 320
704. Preller p. 152
705. Ibid p. 154
706. Gledhill p. 181
707. Preller p. 162
708. Cory, *Vol IV* p. 36
709. HSRC, *Vol II* p. 194
710. Laband, John. *Rope of Sand*, Jonathan Ball Publishers, Johannesburg, 1995 p. 65
711. Meintjies p. 94
712. Laband p. 61
713. Becker p. 28; Ndlovu, Sifiso Mxolisi. 'The Changing African Perceptions of King Dingane in Historical Literature', unpublished thesis, Wits University p. 38
714. Laband p. 68
715. Ransford p. 112
716. Laband p. 57
717. Ibid p. 68
718. Ndlovu p. 19
719. Preller p. 184
720. Gledhill p. 182
721. Gardiner p. 43
722. Gledhill p. 186
723. Cory p. 62
724. Ibid p. 62
725. Gledhill p. 185
726. Cory, *Vol IV* p. 37
727. Preller pp. 170-173
728. Laband p. 83
729. Walker p. 155
730. Schoon p. 64
731. Walker p. 156
732. Cory, *Vol IV* p. 40,
733. Bird, *Vol I* pp. 362-364
734. Gledhill p. 190
735. Walker p. 154
736. Schoon p. 74
737. Gledhill p. 193.
738. Bird, *Vol I* pp 367-369
739. Gledhill p. 196; Cory, *Vol IV* p. 40
740. Ibid p. 197
741. Schoon p. 78
742. Cory p. 89
743. Ibid p. 95
744. Bird, *Vol I* p. 369
745. Schoon p. 80.
746. Ibid p. 82
747. Preller p. 222
748. Ibid p. 222
749. Schoon p. 82
750. Ibid p. 82
751. Ibid p. 82
752. Cory p. 100
753. Ibid p. 100
754. Bird, *Vol I* p. 403
755. Preller p. 222
756. Gledhill p. 199
757. Schoon p. 83
758. Gledhill p. 204
759. Meintjies p. 104
760. Norval p. 185
761. Bird, *Vol I* p. 402
762. HSRC, *Vol III* p. 367
763. Schoon p. 82
764. Nathan p. 197
765. Preller p. 228
766. Cory, *Owen's Diary* p. 104
767. Norval p. 186
768. Laband p. 85,
769. Preller p. 258
770. Nathan p. 198
771. Gledhill p. 204
772. Bird, *Vol I* p. 379
773. Ndlovu p. 45
774. Nathan p. 198
775. Norval p. 187
776. Gledhill p. 206
777. Ibid p. 206
778. Norval p. 187

779. Nathan p. 200
780. Gledhill p. 206
781. Ibid p. 205
782. Bird, *Vol I* p. 216
783. Ndlovu p. 45
784. Norval p. 190
785. Cory, *Vol IV* p. 45
786. Becker p. 223
787. Norval p. 190
788. Becker p. 222
789. Cory, *Owen's Diary* p. 108
790. Bird, *Vol I* p. 380
791. Ibid p. 380
792. Norval p. 190
793. Bird, *Vol I* p. 380
794. Cory, *Owen's Diary* p. 106
795. Nathan p. 215
796. Ibid p. 107
797. Cory, *Owen's Diary* p. 107
798. Preller p. 274
799. Norval p. 192
800. Ibid p. 275
801. Ibid p. 275
802. Norval p. 192
803. Preller p. 275
804. Cory, *Owen's Diary* p. 116
805. Nathan p. 212
806. Meintjies p. 109
807. Cory, *Owen's Diary* p. 109
808. Ibid p. 108
809. Gledhill p. 211
810. Cory, *Owen's Diary* p. 110,
811. Becker p. 226
812. Bird, *Vol I* p. 382
813. Gledhill p. 211
814. Cory, *Owen's Diary* p. 110
815. Preller p. 28
816. Cory, *Owen's Diary* p. 111
817. Ibid p. 112
818. Gledhill p. 213
819. Preller p. 286
820. Cory, *Owen's Diary* p. 112
821. Becker p. 229
822. Cory, *Owen's Diary* pp. 112-120
823. Gledhill p. 215
824. Preller pp. 290-293
825. Cory, *Vol IV* p. 47
826. Schoon p. 88
827. Norval p. 221
828. Ibid p. 221
829. Ibid p. 221
830. Becker p. 231
831. Mackeurten, Graham. *Cradle Days of Natal* p. 227
832. Ibid p. 227
833. Bird, *Vol I* p. 370
834. Norval p. 248
835. Bird, *Vol I* p. 371
836. Ibid p. 372
837. Ibid p. 372
838. Ibid p. 372
839. Ibid p. 372
840. Gerdener p. 56
841. Norval p. 222
842. Nathan p. 223
843. Norval p. 222
844. Ibid p. 226
845. Bird, *Vol I* p. 373
846. Preller p. 296
847. Bird, *Vol I* p. 373
848. Nathan p. 223
849. Mackeurton p. 235
850. Meintjies p. 115
851. Bird, *Vol I* p. 241
852. Ibid p. 242
853. Nathan p. 224
854. Bird, *Vol I* p. 242
855. Meintjies p. 115
856. Nathan p. 226
857. Norval p. 240
858. Laband p. 91
859. Walker p. 168
860. Norval p. 239
861. Schoon p. 89
862. Meintjies p. 117
863. Laband p. 91
864. Schoon p. 93
865. Ibid p. 89
866. Ibid p. 92
867. Nathan p. 229
868. Walker p. 173
869. Becker p. 231
870. Cory, *Vol IV* p. 62
871. Schoon p. 98
872. Ibid p. 100
873. Laband p. 92
874. Ibid p. 92
875. Norval p. 258
876. Bird, *Vol I* pp. 410-411
877. Norval p. 261
878. Ibid p. 264
879. Ibid p. 265
880. Ibid p. 266
881. Ibid p. 267
882. Norval p. 268
883. Meintjies p. 120
884. Bird, *Vol I* p. 412
885. Nathan p. 236
886. Norval p. 270
887. Meintjies p. 120
888. Mackeurtan p. 226

889. Le Roux p. 181
890. Meintjies p. 123
891. Le Roux p. 176
892. Ibid p. 177
893. Meintjies p. 124,
894. Cory, *Owen's Diary* p. 13.
895. Schoon p. 107
896. Norval p. 271
897. Cory, *Vol IV* p. 63
898. Norval p. 271
899. Mackeurton p. 228
900. Schoon p. 108
901. Ibid p. 108
902. Norval p. 272
903. Cory, *Vol IV* p. 65
904. Ransford p. 142
905. Nathan p. 239
906. Theal, *Vol II* p. 170.
907. Ibid p. 172
908. Schoon p. 109
909. Norval p. 275
910. Cory, *Vol IV* p. 66
911. Schoon p. 116
912. Bird, *Vol I* p. 394
913. Ibid p. 398
914. Ibid p. 399
915. De Jongh, P.S. *Sarel Cilliers*, p. 146
916. Norval p. 277
917. Schoon p. 119
918. Ibid p. 113
919. Norval p. 276
920. Nathan p. 248
921. De Jongh p. 147
922. Laband p. 95
923. Voortrekker Monument, *Reeks 1, Die Kanon 'Grietjie'*
924. Norval p. 281
925. Nathan p. 246
926. De Jongh p. 149
927. Schoon p. 126
928. Nathan p. 241
929. Norval p. 283
930. The Diary Of Erasmus Smit p. 126
931. Norval p. 284
932. Ibid p. 284
933. Nathan p. 242
934. Norval p. 284
935. Nathan p. 243
936. Norval p. 288
937. Schoon p. 128
938. Norval p. 289
939. Ibid p. 288
940. Ibid p. 291
941. Ibid p. 291
942. Schoon p. 138
943. Ibid p. 138
944. Norval p. 138
945. Schoon p. 139
946. Ibid p. 143
947. Nathan p. 246
948. Bird, *Vol I* p. 415
949. De Jongh p. 150
950. Nathan p. 247
951. Ibid p. 17
952. Ibid p. 17
953. Schoon p. 148
954. Voortrekker Monument *Reeks 1, Die Kanon 'Grietjie'* pp. 9, 11
955. De Jongh p. 154
956. Liebenberg p. 23
957. Gerdener p. 66
958. De Jongh p. 156,
959. Ibid p. 157
960. Bird, *Vol I* p. 439
961. Meintjies p. 440
962. Ibid p. 132
963. Mackeurtan p. 239
964. Bird, *Vol I* p. 442
965. Ibid p. 443
966. Liebenberg p. 31
967. Bird, *Vol I* p. 435
968. Ibid p. 433
969. Cory p. 80
970. Liebenberg p. 31
971. Gerdener p 67
972. Nathan p. 252
973. Liebenberg p. 33
974. Bird, *Vol I* p. 446
975. Ibid p. 446
976. Ibid p. 447
977. Norval p. 307
978. Bird, *Vol I* p. 447
979. Ibid p. 448
980. Norval p. 307
981. De Jongh p. 165
982. Norval p. 308
983. Laband p. 99
984. Norval p. 308; Nathan p. 255
985. Ibid p. 308
986. d'Assonville, V.E. *Bloed Rivier*, Marnix p. 28
987. Norval p. 310
988. De Jongh p. 166
989. Nathan p. 255
990. Preller p. 187
991. Meintjies p. 138
992. Laband p. 99
993. Norval p. 309
994. Preller p. 187
995. d'Assonville p. 29,
996. Numbers vary in different accounts by different

historians. However, if as stated there were 36 regiments, it is unlikely that there were less than 18,000 warriors
997. d'Assonville p. 29
998. Nathan p. 256
999. d'Assonville p. 32
1000. Ibid p. 29
1001. Norval p. 311; d'Assonville p. 32
1002. d'Assonville p. 32
1003. Ibid p. 31
1004. Ibid p. 35
1005. Preller p. 188,
1006. d'Assonville p. 39
1007. Norval p. 313
1008. d'Assonville p. 39
1009. Knight, Ian. *The Anatomy of the Zulu Army from Shaka to Cetshwayo, 1818–1879*, image Zulu warrior
1010. Ibid p. 120
1011. d'Assonville p. 41; Norval p. 316; Bird, *Vol I* p. 448
1012. Norval p. 316
1013. d'Assonville p. 42
1014. Mackeurtan p. 243
1015. Laband p. 100
1016. Norval p. 317
1017. Preller p. 189
1018. d'Assonville p. 44
1019. Norval p. 319
1020. d'Assenville p. 44
1021. Norval p. 320
1022. Ibid p. 321; Bird, *Vol I* p. 449
1023. Preller p. 190
1024. Knight p. 246
1025. Preller p. 194
1026. Nathan p. 267
1027. Bird, *Vol I* p. 449
1028. Gerdner, G.B.A., *Sarel Cilliers: Die Vader van Digaansdag*, p. 71
1029. Ibid 71
1030. Knight, Ian. *The Sun Turned Black* p. 150
1031. Norval p. 323
1032. Ibid p. 325
1033. Bird, *Vol I* p. 450
1034. orval p. 325
1035. Ibid p. 326
1036. Bird, *Vol I* p. 450
1037. Liebenberg p. 41
1038. Norval p. 328
1039. Bird, *Vol I* p. 453
1040. Ibid p. 451
1041. Norval p. 360
1042. Liebenberg p. 42
1043. Norval p. 360
1044. Preller p. 201
1045. Bird, *Vol I* p. 451
1046. Norval p. 362
1047. Ibid p. 364
1048. Bird, *Vol I* p. 452
1049. Norval p. 365
1050. Preller p. 203
1051. Norval p. 366
1052. Liebenberg p. 43
1053. Ibid p. 43
1054. Ibid p. 44
1055. Norval p. 367
1056. Liebenberg p. 44
1057. Nathan p. 265
1058. Norval p. 368
1059. Ibid p. 370
1060. De Jongh p. 173
1061. Bird, *Vol I*, Letter from Pretorius to British Government, 9 January 1839 p. 457
1062. Ibid
1063. Ibid
1064. Norval p. 371
1065. Ibid p. 371
1066. Ibid p. 375
1067. Cory, *Vol IV* p. 86
1068. Bird, *Vol I* p. 492
1069. Meintjies p. 148
1070. Bird, *Vol I* p. 502
1071. De Jongh pp. 176-180
1072. Liebenberg p. 49
1073. Nathan p. 272
1074. Bird, *Vol I* p. 517
1075. Meintjies p. 148
1076. Liebenberg p. 57
1077. Bird, *Vol I* p. 517
1078. Meintjies p. 150
1079. Laband p. 110
1080. Norval p. 382
1081. Liebenberg p. 59; Norval p. 382
1082. Liebenberg p. 59
1083. Norval p. 382
1084. Liebenberg p. 61
1085. Ibid p. 61
1086. Ibid p. 62
1087. Meintjies p. 152
1088. Liebenberg p. 62
1089. Laband p. 110
1090. Bird, *Vol I*. Rules and Regulations, Board of Representatives of the people (*Raad na Representanten van het volk*) at Port Natal and Surrounding country
1091. Eybers. *Select Constitutional Documents Illustrating South African History, 1795–1910* p. 152
1092. Bird, *Vol I* p. 533
1093. Ibid p. 94
1094. Meintjies p. 152
1095. Theal, *Vol II* p.182

1096. Liebenberg p. 62
1097. Ibid p. 63
1098. Laband p. 112
1099. Meintjies p. 156
1100. Norval p. 387
1101. Laband p. 114
1102. Meintjies p. 156
1103. Ibid p. 156
1104. Laband p. 114
1105. Cory, *Vol IV* p. 99
1106. Bird, *Vol I* p. 541
1107. Norval p. 389
1108. Laband p. 114; Norval p. 389
1109. Cory, *Vol IV* p. 99
1110. Bird, *Vol I* p. 542
1111. Laband p. 115
1112. Bird, *Vol I* p. 542
1113. Ibid p. 542
1114. Norval p. 390
1115. Liebenberg p. 66
1116. Laband p. 115
1117. Cory, *Vol IV* p. 101
1118. Bird, *Vol I* pp. 544, 547
1119. Mackeurten p. 255
1120. Liebenberg p. 66
1121. Ibid p. 67
1122. Becker p. 249
1123. Norval p. 394
1124. Becker p. 250
1125. Liebenberg p. 70
1126. Ibid p. 71
1127. Ibid p. 70
1128. Nathan p. 289
1129. Mackeurten p. 257
1130. Liebenberg p. 78; Laband p. 115
1131. Mackeurten p. 257
1132. Cory, *Vol IV* p. 108
1133. Liebenberg p. 80
1134. Ibid p. 82
1135. Laband p. 116
1136. Laband p. 117; Theal, *Vol II* p. 395
1137. Laband p. 117
1138. Becker p. 254
1139. Bird, *Vol I* p. 571
1140. Ibid p. 588
1141. Ibid p. 590
1142. Ibid p. 594
1143. Liebenberg p. 86
1144. Ibid p. 86
1145. Ibid p. 87
1146. Ibid p. 88
1147. Ibid p. 89
1148. Ibid p. 90
1149. De Jongh p. 90
1150. Meintjies p. 162
1151. Laband p. 121
1152. Becker p. 254
1153. There are a number of different versions of Dingane's death, e.g. Norval p. 405: '*Daar bestaan verskeie weergawes met betrekking … Volgens oorlewering het die Swazi's ook Dingane se hart of kop saamgestuur*' & Mackeurten p. 259: 'He was finally dispatched by the Swazis under their chief Masusa Mswazi, the successor of Sopusa … according to one account he was tortured to death. On the first day he was pricked skin deep with assegais from head to foot. On the second he was bitten by dogs. On the third he was told to look for the last time at the sunrise and his eyes were bored out. At sunset he was dead.'
1154. Mackeurten p. 261
1155. Meintjies p. 167
1156. Theal, *Vol II* p. 400
1157. Liebenberg p. 93
1158. Ibid p. 93
1159. Mackeurten p. 261
1160. Ibid p. 260
1161. Meintjies p. 166
1162. Liebenberg p. 109
1163. Five Lectures on the Emigration of the Dutch Farmers, delivered to the Natal Society at Pietermaritzburg by the Hon. Henry Cloete LLD, Recorder of the District, p. 112
1164. Theal, *Vol II* p. 401
1165. Liebenberg p. 110
1166. Meintjies p. 166
1167. Liebenberg pp. 111
1168. Meintjies p. 167
1169. Liebenberg p. 114
1170. Ibid p. 130
1171. Ibid p. 131
1172. Ibid pp. 132, 134
1173. Cory, *Vol IV* p. 117
1174. Norval p. 407
1175. Bird, *Vol I* pp. 611-613
1176. Nathan p. 301
1177. Meintjies p. 170
1178. De Jongh p. 188
1179. Meintjies p. 171
1180. Theal, *Vol II* p. 311
1181. Liebenberg p. 147
1182. Theal, *Vol IV.* p. 411
1183. Bird, *Vol I* p. 624
1184. Cory, *Vol IV* p. 123
1185. Bird, *Vol I* p. 627
1186. Theal, *Vol IV* p. 414
1187. Bird, *Vol I* p. 650
1188. Ibid p. 657
1189. Liebenberg p. 137
1190. Cory, *Vol V.* p. 126

1191. Bird, *Vol I* pp. 658-660
1192. Ibid pp. 660-666
1193. Liebenberg p. 137
1194. Ibid p. 139
1195. Bird, *Vol I* pp. 691-699
1196. Cory, *Vol IV* p. 136
1197. Holden, William C. *History of the Colony of Natal* p. 105
1198. Mackeurten p. 270
1199. Theal, *Vol II* p. 419
1200. Cory, *Vol IV* p. 132
1201. Liebenberg p. 157
1202. Cory, *Vol IV* p. 132
1203. Liebenberg p. 157
1204. Cory, *Vol IV* p. 133
1205. Ibid p.133
1206. Liebenberg p. 158
1207. Ibid p. 159
1208. Cory, *Vol IV* p. 134
1209. Theal, *Vol II* p. 420
1210. Holden p. 105
1211. Mackeurten p. 271
1212. Cory, *Vol IV* p. 137
1213. Holden p. 109
1214. Theal, *Vol II* p. 421
1215. Holden p. 114
1216. Ibid p. 114,
1217. Cory, *Vol IV* p. 138
1218. Bird, *Vol I* pp. 700-704
1219. Ibid p. 718
1220. Holden p. 114
1221. Liebenberg p. 163
1222. Holden p. 112
1223. Liebenberg p. 164
1224. Bird, *Vol I* p. 718
1225. Liebenberg p. 164
1226. Cory, *Vol IV* p. 142
1227. Liebenberg p. 68
1228. Nathan p. 309
1229. Ibid p. 310
1230. Liebenberg p. 174
1231. Ibid p. 173
1232. Cory, *Vol IV* p. 149
1233. Liebenberg p. 175
1234. Cory, *Vol IV* p. 151
1235. HSRC, *Vol I* p. 170
1236. Mackeurten p 281.
1237. Liebenberg p. 177; Nathan p. 312
1238. Liebenberg p. 177
1239. Preller p. 257
1240. Theal, *Vol II* p. 436
1241. Meintjies p. 188
1242. Liebenberg p. 179
1243. Nathanp. 313
1244. Preller p. 260
1245. Holden p 142
1246. Ibid p. 142
1247. Cory, *Vol IV* p 162
1248. Theal, *Vol II* p. 439
1249. Liebenberg p. 181
1250. Cory, *Vol IV* p. 162
1251. Theal, *Vol II* p. 440
1252. Liebenberg p. 224
1253. Theal, *Vol II* p. 440.
1254. Cory, *Vol IV* p. 166
1255. Ibid p. 167
1256. Preller p. 274
1257. Meintjies p. 192
1258. Mackeurten, p. 284
1259. Cory, *Vol IV* p. 169
1260. Liebenberg p. 187,
1261. Mackeurten p. 287; Cory, *Vol IV* p. 171
1262. Cory, *Vol IV* p. 176
1263. Ibid p. 171
1264. Liebenberg p. 187
1265. Cory, *Vol IV* p. 173
1266. Liebenberg p. 188
1267. Bird, *Vol I* pp. 182-183
1268. Theal, *Vol II* p. 479
1269. Cory, *Vol IV* p 180
1270. Five Lectures on the Emigration of the Dutch Farmers p. 154
1271. Ibid p. 155
1272. Cory, *Vol IV* p. 183
1273. Theal, *Vol II* p. 452
1274. Meintjies p. 199
1275. Genealogical Instituut van SA Dutch Reformed Church Records. Marriage certificate of Gerrit de Lange and Susanna van der Merwe. Married in Somerset East in 1836 and issued in 1856. Signed in English by Minister Pears[on?]
1276. Ibid. Marriages Graaff Reinet 1839
1277. Ibid. Kerkregisters in Swellendam 1840
1278. Cory, *Vol IV* p. 194
1279. Mackeurten p. 293
1280. Nathan p. 319.
1281. Cory, *Vol IV* p. 198
1282. HSRC, *Vol I* p. 638
1283. Meintjies p. 204
1284. Becker p. 133
1285. Ibid p. 136
1286. Theal, *Vol II* p. 481
1287. Cory, *Vol IV*, p. 305
1288. Ibid p. 305
1289. Theal, *Vol II* p. 485
1290. Ibid p. 490
1291. Cory, *Vol IV* pp. 309-310
1292. Meintjies p. 208
1293. Cory, *Vol IV* pp. 315-319
1294. Ibid p. 320

1295. Theal, *Vol II* p. 504
1296. Ibid p. 505
1297. Meintjies p. 209
1298. Nathan p. 326
1299. Ibid pp. 327-328
1300. Liebenberg p. 214
1301. Cory, *Vol IV* p 202
1302. Ibid p. 205
1303. Mackeureten p. 299
1304. Liebenberg p. 227
1305. Dracopoli p. 165
1306. Liebenberg p. 247
1307. Mostert p. 810
1308. Liebenberg pp. 243-250
1309. Ibid p. 249
1310. Ibid p. 254
1311. Mostert p. 931
1312. Ibid p. 930
1313. Ibid p. 933
1314. Ibid p. 936
1315. Dracopoli p. 164
1316. Becker p. 154
1317. Liebenberg pp. 251-267
1318. Ibid p. 268
1319. Dracopoli p. 166
1320. Nathan p. 332
1321. Liebenberg p. 269
1322. Ibid p. 269
1323. Meintjies p. 225
1324. Nathan p. 333
1325. Cory, *Vol IV* p. 324
1326. Theal, *Vol III* p. 277
1327. Meintjies p. 229
1328. Theal, *Vol III* p 278
1329. Liebenberg p. 286
1330. Ibid pp. 283-286
1331. Ibid p. 287
1332. Ibid pp. 293-295
1333. Theal, *Vol III* p. 280
1334. Ibid p. 281
1335. Meintjies pp. 231-233
1336. Theal, *Vol III* p. 282
1337. Ibid p. 281
1338. Preller p. 359
1339. Ibid p. 358
1340. Theal, *Vol III* p. 288
1341. Preller pp. 359-363
1342. Ibid p. 362
1343. Ibid p. 387
1344. Meintjies p. 241
1345. Ibid p. 242
1346. Preller p. 390
1347. Meintjies p. 241
1348. Ibid p. 243
1349. Preller p. 392
1350. Ibid p. 394-397
1351. Nathan p. 335
1352. Meintjies pp. 245-246; Preller p. 396
1353. Preller p. 404
1354. Becker p. 162.
1355. Theal, *Vol III* p. 299; Becker p. 160
1356. Theal, *Vol III* p. 301
1357. Becker p. 162
1358. Ibid p. 164
1359. Theal, *Vol III* p. 313
1360. Becker p. 174
1361. Theal, *Vol III* p. 317
1362. Cory, *Vol V* p. 197
1363. Preller p. 421; Theal, *Vol V* p. 322
1364. Archives Year Book for South African History, 1949, *Vol II* p. 380,
1365. Theal, *Vol III* p. 322
1366. Preller p. 425
1367. Ibid p. 426
1368. Meintjies p. 252.
1369. Archives Year Book for South African History, 1949, *Vol II* p. 389
1370. Becker p. 178
1371. Preller p. 430
1372. Ibid p. 431
1373. Meintjies p. 254
1374. Archives Year Book for South African History, 1949, *Vol II* p. 392
1375. Preller p. 434
1376. Archives Year Book for South African History, 1949, *Vol II* p. 394
1377. Ibid p. 393
1378. Meintjies p. 254
1379. Preller p. 439

Bibliography

Archives Year Book for South African History Vol II, 1949

Becker, Peter, *Hill Of Destiny*, Longmans, 1965

Becker, Peter, *Rule of Fear*, Longmans, London, 1964

Bird, John, *Annals of Natal* Vol I, P. Davis & Sons, Pietermaritzburg

Boeseken, A.J., *Slaves and Free Blacks at the Cape, 1658–1700*, Tafelberg, Cape Town, 1977

Cape Archives, GR 1/9, letter from inhabitants of Zuurveld, 11 August 1788

Cory, George, *Owen's Diary*, Van Riebeeck Sociey, Cape Town, 1926

Cory, George, *Rise of South Africa* Vols I–V, Longmans, 1919

d'Assonville, V.E., *Bloed Rivier*, Marnix, 2000

Davenport, Rodney & Saunders, Christopher, *South Africa: A Modern History*, Palgrave Macmillan, 2000

De Jongh, P.S., *Sarel Cilliers*, Perskor, 1987

De Kock, Victor, *Those in Bondage*, George Allen & Unwin Ltd., London, 1950

Diary of Erasmus Smit

Dracopoli, J.L., *Sir Andries Stockenström*, A.A. Balkema, Cape Town, 1969

Elphick, Richard & Gilomee, Herman, *The Shaping of South Africa*, Maskew Miller Longman, 1990

Elphick, Richard, *Kraal and Castle: Khoikhoi and the Founding of White South Africa*, Yale University Press, New Haven & London, 1977

Five Lectures, Delivered to the Natal Society at Pietermaritzburg by the Hon. Henry Cloete L.L.D., Recorder of the District

Franken, J.L.M., *Piet Retief: Sy Lewe in die Kolonie*, 1949

Gardiner, Allen Francis, *Narrative of a Journey to the Zoolu Country: In South Africa*, Struik, Cape Town, 1966

Genealogical Instituut van SA. Dutch Reformed Church Records

Gerdener, G.B.A., *Sarel Cilliers: Die Vader van Dingaansdag*. J.L. van Schaik, Pretoria, 1925.

Giliomee, Hermann & Mbenga, Bernard, *New History of South Africa*, Tafelberg, Cape Town, 2007

Gledhill, Eily & Jack, *In the Steps of Piet Retief*, Human & Rousseau, Cape Town, 1980

Heese, H.F., *Groep Sonder Grense, C-Reeks*, Navorsingpublikasies, 1984

Hockly, Harold Edward, *The Story of the 1820 Settlers*, Juta, Cape Town, 1957

Holden, William Clifford, 'The Past and Future of the Kaffir Races', *Africana Collectanea* Vol III, C. Struik, Cape Town, 1963

Holden, William Clifford, *History of the Colony of Natal*, A. Heylin, London, 1855

Human Sciences Research Council. *Dictionary of South African* Biography, Vols I–V *Illustrated History of South Africa: The Real Story*, Reader's Digest, Cape Town, 1988

Internet reference: Marco Ramerini, 'The Dutch in South Africa, 1652–1795'

Internet site: www.tutufoundation.uk

Knight, Ian, *The Anatomy of the Zulu Army: From Shaka to Cetshwayo, 1818–1879*, Greenhill Books, London, 2006

Knight, Ian, *The Sun Turned Black*, 2nd ed., William Waterman, South Africa, 1995

Kotze, D.J., *Letters of the American Missionaries, 1835–1838*, Van Riebeeck Society, Cape Town, 1950

Laband, John, *Rope of Sand*, Jonathan Ball Publishers, Johannesburg, 1995

Le Roux, T.H., *Die Dagboek van Louis Trichardt*, J.L. van Schaik, Pretoria, 1966

Legassick, Martin, *The Struggle for the Eastern Cape, 1800–1854: Subjugation and the Roots of South African Democracy*, KMW Review Publishing Co., 2011

Lenta, Margaret & Le Cordeur, Basil, *The Cape Diaries of Lady Anne Barnard, 1799–1800* Vol I, Van Riebeeck Society, Cape Town, 1999

Liebenberg, B.J., *Andries Pretorius in Natal*, Academica, Pretoria, 1977

Mackeurten, Graham, *Cradle Days of Natal*, Shuter & Shooter, Pietermaritzburg, 1931

Macmillan, W.M., *Bantu, Boer and Briton: The Making of the South African Native Problem*, Faber & Gwyer, London

Meintjies, Johannes, *The Voortrekkers*, Cassel, London, 1973

Mentzel, O.F., *Life at the Cape in the Mid-Eighteenth Century: The Biography of Rudolph Siegfried Alleman*, Van Riebeeck Society, Cape Town, 1919

Milton, John, *Edges of War: A History of Frontier Wars (1702–1878)*, Juta & Co., Ltd, Cape Town, 1983
Mitford-Barberton, Ivan, *Commandant Holden Bowker*, Human & Rosseau, Cape Town, 1970
Morris, Donald R., *Washing of the Spears*, Pimlico ed., London, 1965 & 1994
Mostert, Noël, *Frontiers*, Jonathan Cape, Pimlico ed., London, 1993
Muller, C.F.J., *Die Britse Owerheid en die Groot Trek*, Academika, 1948
Muller, C.F.J., *Die Oorsprong van die Groot Trek*, Unisa Press, 1988
Nathan, Manfred, *The Voortrekkers of South Africa*, Central News Agency Ltd. & Gordon & Gotch, Johannesburg,1937
Ndlovu, Sifiso Mxolisi, 'The Changing African Perceptions of King Dingane in Historical Literature', unpublished thesis, University of the Witwatersrand
Norval, E.J.G., *Bloed Sweet En Trane*, Bienedell Uitgewers, Pretoria, 2002
Peires, J.B., *The House of Phalo*, University of California Press, Los Angeles, 1982
Penn, Nigel, *The Forgotten Frontier*, Double Storey Books, Cape Town, 2005
Preller, Gustav, *Die Dagboek van Louis Trichardt*, 1918
Preller, Gustav, *Voortrekkermense* Parts I & IV, Nasionale Pers, Cape Town, 1920 & 1938
Preller, Gustav. S., *Piet Retief*, Nasionale Pers, Cape Town, 1920
Pretorius, C. Celestine, *Op Trek*, Protea Boekhuis, Pretoria, 2008
Pringle, Thomas, *Narrative of a Residence in South Africa*, Edward Moxon, London, 1834 & Struik, Cape Town, 1966
Ransford, Oliver, *The Great Trek*, John Murray, London, 1972 & Cardinal Books, London (Birr), 1974
Raper, Peter E, & Boucher Maurice, *Robert Jacob Gordon: Cape Travels, 1777–1786*, Brenthurst Press, Johannesburg, 1988
Raven-Hart, R., *Cape Good Hope*, A.A. Balkema, Cape Town, 1971
Raven-Hart, R., *The Diary of Johann Jakob Merklein, 1653*, A.A. Balkema, Cape Town, 1971
Raven-Hart, Rowland. *Before Van Riebeeck: Callers at South Africa from 1488 to 1652*, C. Struik, Cape Town, 1967
Rivett-Carnac, D.E., *Hawk's Eye*, Howard Timmins, Cape Town, 1966
Schoon, H.F., *The Diary of Erasmus Smit*, C. Struik, Cape Town, 1972
Sheffield. T., *The Story of the Settlement*, T.G. Sheffield, Grahamstown, 1882
Skotness, Pippa, *Claim to the Country: The Archive of Wilhelm Bleek and Lucy Lloyd*, Ohio University Press, Athens OH, 2007
Soga, John Henderson, *The Ama-Xosa: Life and Customs*, Lovedale Press, Alice
South African History On Line
Stuart, James & McK.Malcolm, D., *The Diary of Henry Francis Fynn*, Shuter & Shooter, Pietermaritzburg, 1969
Theal, George McCall, *Ethnography and Condition of South Africa before A.D. 1505*, G. Allen & Unwin Ltd., London, 1919
Theal, George McCall, *History and Ethnography of South Africa before 1795* Vols I–III, Swan Sonnenschein & Co., Bloomsbury, 1907
Theal, George McCall, *History of South Africa since 1795* Vols I–V, Swan Sonnenschein & Co., Lim, Bloomsbury, 1907
Theal, George McCall, *History of South Africa since 1795*, Vol II, Cambridge University Press, 2010
Theal, George McCall, *History of the Boers in South Africa*, Swan Sonnenschein & Co., London, 1888
Turner, Malcolm, *Shipwrecks and Salvage in South Africa, 1505 to the Present*, C. Struik, Cape Town, 1988
Voortrekker Monument *Reeks* 1
Walker, Eric, *The Great Trek*, A.& C. Black Ltd., 1934
Welch, Sidney R., *South Africa under John III, 1521–1557*, Juta, Cape Town, 1948
Worden, Nigel; van Heyningen, Elizabeth & Bickford-Smith, Vivian, *The Making of a City*, David Philip, Cape Town, 1998
Wright, John Kirtland., *The Geographical Lore of the Time of the Crusades: A Study in the History of Medieval Science and Tradition in Western Europe*, American Geographical Society, Research Series No. 15, Literary Licensing, LLC, 2011

Index

Robin Binckes was born in Kokstad, Eastern Cape in 1941 and educated in Umtata in the Transkei. His career spanned Public Relations, sport promotion, management, owning a fishing company and food retailing. He volunteered as a Peace Monitor in the townships in the turbulent pre-democracy period before being inspired by the late David Rattray, who introduced him to the art of storytelling, Robin has his own business, Spear of the Nation, which specializes in historical tours; he also conducts experiential tours and talks for many South African and international companies and learning institutions, focusing on diversity and transformation. His interest in history motivated the move from oral storytelling to writing his first novel, *Canvas under the Sky* (2011). Robin – married, with two children, two stepsons, a grandson and two Scottie dogs – lives in Johannesburg and holidays at his spiritual home, Haga Haga, on the Eastern Cape coast.